Making Math Meaningful
to Canadian Students, K–8

Marian Small

University of New Brunswick

NELSON / EDUCATION

NELSON / EDUCATION

Making Math Meaningful to Canadian Students, K–8
by Marian Small

Associate Vice President, Editorial Director:
Evelyn Veitch

Editor-in-Chief:
Anne Williams

Executive Editor:
Cara Yarzab

Marketing Manager:
Heather Leach

Developmental Editor:
Sandy Matos

Photo Researcher and Permissions Coordinator:
Melody Tolson

Senior Content Production Manager:
Natalia Denesiuk Harris

Production Service:
Newgen–Austin

Copy Editor:
Linda Szostak

Proofreader:
Christine Gever

Indexer:
David Luljak

Manufacturing Coordinator:
Loretta Lee

Design Director:
Ken Phipps

Managing Designer:
Katherine Strain

Interior Design:
Greg Devitt

Cover Design:
Dianna Little

Cover Images:
Top, L to R: Stockbyte/Getty Images; © JUPITERIMAGES/ BananaStock/Alamy; © Janine Wiedel Photolibrary/Alamy; © Masterfile Main image: © toy Alan King/ Alamy

Compositor:
Newgen

Printer:
RR Donnelley

Library and Archives Canada Cataloguing in Publication Data

Small, Marian

Making math meaningful to Canadian students, K–8 / Marian Small.

Includes bibliographical references and index.
ISBN 978-0-17-610427-6

1. Mathematics—Study and teaching (Elementary)—Canada. I. Title.

QA135.6.S53 2008   372.7'044
C2008-900472-8

ISBN-10: 0-17-610427-5
ISBN-13: 978-0-17-610427-6

Brief Table of Contents

Contents

Chapter 5: Mathematics for the Younger Learner 83

Chapter 6: Developing Early Operation Concepts 103

Chapter 8: Computation with Whole Numbers 159

Chapter 9: Fractions 195

Contents

Chapter 14: Location and Movement 337

Chapter 23: Developing a Teaching Style. 653

Preface

To the prospective or practising K–8 teacher using this book:

Many teachers who teach at the K–8 level have not had the luxury of specialist training in mathematics, yet they are expected to teach an increasingly more sophisticated curriculum to an increasingly diverse student population in a climate where there are heightened public expectations. They deserve help.

This text is designed to start you on your way to a successful career in teaching mathematics by providing you with insight into how to make mathematics make sense to students and to capture their interest. Many of my students have told me that there were so many ideas in math that they never understood; they just did what they were told. This text provides you with those missing explanations. As a result, you are more likely to gain the confidence to teach mathematics with a student-centred, problem-solving approach. You will be better able to let students explore because you will have a deeper understanding of the mathematics, which will make it easier for you to deal with students' varied ideas.

You will be better able to focus discussion in your classroom because you will be more aware of possible misconceptions and of what aspects of the mathematics are worthy of development. You will also be better able to critically evaluate other people's ideas about how to approach mathematics instruction because you will be starting with a well-founded base of knowledge.

More than that, this text can serve as a resource to which you will return again and again when you are ready to focus on particular content or particular strategies.

Features you will notice in the text include

- chapters dealing with many different aspects of mathematics instruction
  - background chapters dealing with the fundamentals of the kind of mathematics students should and can learn, research on how students learn mathematics, and an indication of how mathematics can be organized using key ideas and key processes
  - chapters dealing with mathematical processes like problem solving and communication
  - chapters dealing with the teaching process, including assessment, planning instruction, and developing a teaching style
  - chapters making the content clearer and more meaningful to you
- chapter problems to engage you mathematically and that you can later use with students
- the "In a Nutshell" feature to help you focus on the main ideas of each chapter
- highlighted sections that clearly articulate the main principles associated with the content of many chapters
- activities you can use with students
- student sample responses to show you how students typically respond to certain mathematical tasks
- samples from Canadian student texts and attention to Canadian curricula
- an indication of valuable manipulatives for each content area, with clear descriptions of how to use them

- an indication of some appropriate technology for each content topic
- charts with common errors and misconceptions and strategies to deal with them for each content topic
- some important assessment considerations for each content topic, to supplement an entire chapter on assessment
- children's literature suggestions to support the various content topics
- opportunities to apply what you have learned in the chapter through self-reflection, by talking with your classmates, and by interacting with students and teachers in schools
- references to allow you to delve more deeply into topics of interest

To the university instructor:

There are many texts already available for courses for teacher education in mathematics, so why another one?

I think you will find that this text is particularly accessible to students, while, at the same time, being thorough. Many teachers who have perused the text have commented on how readable it is, with many ideas presented visually as well as with text.

I think you will appreciate the Canadian focus. It was written by a Canadian for a Canadian audience. Sample text pages are from Canadian resources and the decisions made about what curriculum should be addressed are based on the various regional curricula in Canada.

I also think you will appreciate the recognition that most of our teacher education programs in Canada do not allow us the instructional hours to introduce our students to as much as we would like to. This resource provides a way to supplement the instruction you offer with the material you would like students to meet, but do not have time to introduce during class hours.

Acknowledgments

It has been a privilege to be able to take my many years of working in and thinking about mathematics education and translate it into this text. So many people have played a part—my wonderful university colleagues; the thousands of university students with whom I have worked over the years; the many teachers whose classrooms I have been invited to work in; and my many other professional colleagues across the country and internationally, in school board offices, ministries of education, and other universities.

I wish to acknowledge the work of the many editors who have shaped my thoughts into text and graphics that make those ideas so much easier to access. Although many editors have contributed, I must single out the enormous contribution of Jackie Williams, an editor, who, over the 20 years we have worked together, constantly challenges and impresses me.

For this particular text, I received excellent advice from

- Thomas Falkenberg, University of Manitoba
- Daniel Jarvis, Nipissing University
- Heather Kelleher, University of British Columbia
- Beverley Kula, University of Alberta
- Ann LeSage, Nipissing University
- Pat Margerm, York University
- Douglas McDougall, University of Toronto

• Joan McDuff, Queen's University
• David Watson, The University of Western Ontario

I must also thank Nelson Education Ltd., both the Higher Education Division and the School Division, for their faith in me and for their support.

Last, but certainly not least, I would like to thank my family. Ultimately, no one matters more to any of us than our families.

About the Author

Marian Small is the former Dean of Education at the University of New Brunswick. She has been a professor of mathematics education for over 30 years and is a regular speaker on K–12 mathematics throughout Canada and the United States.

The focus of Dr. Small's professional work has been the development of curriculum and text materials for students of mathematics. She has been an author on seven text series at both elementary and secondary levels in Canada, the United States, Australia, and the country of Bhutan, and a senior author on five of those series. She has served on the author team for the National Council of Teachers of Mathematics Navigation series, PreK–2 and, for four years, as the NCTM representative on the Mathcounts question writing committee, and on the editorial panel of the 2011 yearbook on motivation and disposition.

Most recently, Dr. Small has led the research resulting in the creation of maps describing student mathematical development in each of the five mathematical strands for the K–8 level, and has created the associated professional development program, PRIME. She has also written three professional books focusing on differentiated instruction, big ideas in math, and teacher questioning, *Big Ideas from Dr Small K-3, Big Ideas from Dr Small, 4-8*, published by Nelson Education, and *Good Questions Great Ways to Differentiate Instruction,* co-published by Teachers College Press, the National Council of Teachers of Mathematics, and Nelson Education.

Chapter 1

How Students Learn Mathematics and What Mathematics We Want Them to Learn

IN A NUTSHELL

The main ideas in this chapter are listed below:

1. There is a strongly held belief in the mathematics education community that mathematics is best learned when students are actively engaged in constructing their own understandings. This is only likely to happen in classrooms that emphasize rich problem solving and the exchange of many approaches to mathematical situations, and that give attention to and value students' mathematical reasoning. Research is increasingly supportive of this approach.

2. There are different perspectives on the discipline of mathematics in terms of what aspects of the content and which processes are valuable and, even when the perspectives are similar, on when

(continued)

CHAPTER PROBLEM

A bike is travelling at 35 km/h.

A car is travelling at 80 km/h and begins 180 km behind the bike.

How long will it take the car to catch up to the bike?

> **IN A NUTSHELL** (*continued*)
>
> various pieces of content and processes should be encountered. These differences result in varying curricula across the country and affect public responses to mathematics teaching.
>
> 3. One of the most influential organizations in mathematics education in North America is the National Council of Teachers of Mathematics (NCTM), in which many Canadian educators take an active role. Many of the central documents produced by this organization have had a profound effect on the mathematics directions taken in Canada and the United States.
>
> 4. There continues to be a strong belief that the teacher is key to many students' ability to learn mathematics. Research supports the importance of teachers' development of pedagogical content knowledge, built upon a deep understanding of how students think and develop mathematically.

Research on Mathematical Learning

One of the valuable tools that teachers of mathematics have in the twenty-first century is an increasingly more solid base of research on student learning and mathematics teaching that they can draw upon to inform their instructional strategies. Although research in psychology informed mathematics education in the past—particularly research around optimal ways to teach procedures—research is now much more broadly based, dealing with the acquisition of conceptual understanding as well as skills.

Two particularly valuable and accessible research compendiums are *A Research Companion to Principles and Standards for School Mathematics* (Kilpatrick, Martin, and Schifter, Eds., 2003), and *Adding It Up: Helping Children Learn Mathematics* (National Research Council, 2001), which address some of the research cited below, in addition to many other studies.

The Importance of Conceptual Understanding

We all have our own mental pictures of what mathematical understanding looks like. Basically, we all think it means that the student really "gets it." However, that is not a very helpful definition for professionals to use to help them assess whether a student does or does not understand a mathematical concept of interest.

Carpenter and Lehrer (1999) help us to clarify what we might mean by mathematical understanding. They speak to the development of understanding not only as the linking of new ideas to existing ones, but as the development of richer and more integrative knowledge structures. These structures allow students to use the new ideas they learn, rather than being in the position of only being able to repeat what they have learned.

For example, a student who fully understands what 3×5 means not only realizes that it equals 15, but, at some point, understands all of the following as well:

- It represents the amount in 3 equal groups of 5, no matter what is in the groups.
- It represents the sum of $5 + 5 + 5$.
- It represents the area of a rectangle with dimensions 3 and 5.
- It represents the number of combinations of any 3 of one type of item matched with any 5 of another type of item (e.g., 3 shirts and 5 pairs of pants $=$ 15 outfits).
- It represents the result when a rate of 5 is applied 3 times (e.g., going 5 km/h for 3 hours).
- It is half of 6×5, 5 more than 2×5, and 5 less than 4×5.

Because the student realizes what 3×5 means, he or she can use it to figure out 6×5, 4×5, 3×6, etc., as well as multiply multi-digit numbers like 3×555 and solve a variety of problems involving multiplication of 3 by 5.

Carpenter and Lehrer suggest that understanding is achieved as students engage in these processes:

- constructing relationships
- extending and applying mathematical knowledge
- reflecting about their mathematical experiences
- articulating what they know mathematically
- personalizing mathematical knowledge

They speak to the fact that understanding is most likely to develop in classrooms that focus on problems to be solved, rather than exercises to be completed; classrooms where alternative strategies are discussed and valued; and classrooms where student autonomy is valued.

There have been a number of studies that have examined how students learn mathematics with a deeper understanding. Most of these studies focus on the instructional methods teachers use to facilitate understanding. For example, Ross et al. (2002) report on a variety of studies that show the success of methods based on math reform, that is, classrooms with rich tasks embedded in the real-life experiences of children, and with rich discourse about mathematical ideas. Success was measured on both traditional math tasks as well as on problem-solving tasks.

A Constructivist Approach

The classrooms advocated by Carpenter and Lehrer inevitably value a constructivist approach. Unlike a more traditional approach where teachers focus on the transmission of mathematical content, in a constructivist classroom students are recognized as the ones who are actively creating their own knowledge.

For example, in a constructivist classroom, rather than showing students how to add 47 + 38 by grouping the ones, trading, and then grouping the tens, the teacher might provide students with a variety of counting materials and pose a problem such as, "One bus has 47 students in it; another has 38. How many students are on both buses?" and allow students to use their own strategies to solve the problem. There would normally be a follow-up discussion where various approaches are shared and additional ideas become available to students to augment their own.

Cobb (1988) explains that the two goals of a constructivist approach to mathematics are students' opportunity to develop richer and deeper cognitive structures related to mathematical ideas, and students' development of a level of mathematical autonomy. In a constructivist classroom, it is through interactions with other students as well as with the teacher, and with the opportunity to articulate their own thoughts, that students are able to construct new mathematical knowledge. These classrooms, as described above, are ones where varied approaches are expected, shared, and valued.

"Active" Learning

The type of constructivist classroom described above is an active learning environment, a place where students are sharing mathematical ideas and working through mathematical problems. The activity is not necessarily physical, but mental.

The National Center for Research on Teacher Learning in Michigan (1994) has produced a document to share information about the value of active learning. The paper points out that much of the broader public, particularly the business community, has advocated the need for graduates who can use math to solve problems, develop their own ideas, and build upon the ideas of others. It is believed that these skills cannot be cultivated in a classroom based on memorization of the facts and procedures modelled by the teacher, but can only happen in a more active classroom.

The focus in the active math classroom is not just a lot of walking and talking, although this may occur, but, rather, on problem solving, reasoning, and the evaluation of evidence in mathematical situations.

Using Manipulatives

Since the mid-1960s, there has been a belief that the use of manipulative materials—concrete representations of mathematical ideas—is essential to develop mathematical understanding. Throughout this text, you will see many examples of how manipulatives can be used to make math make sense. For example, the model below is an embodiment of place value concepts by showing how the three different digits of 2 in the number 222 represent three different amounts.

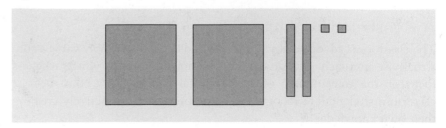

It is believed that manipulatives will help students in each of the following ways:

- to provide visual models the student can refer to even when the manipulatives are no longer present
- to provide a reason for students to work together cooperatively to solve mathematical problems
- to provide a reason for students to discuss mathematical ideas and verbalize their thinking
- to provide a level of autonomy since students could work with the materials without teacher guidance

Research was conducted in the 1960s, 1970s, and 1980s on the value of the use of manipulatives. Examples are articles by Suydam (1984) and Ball (1988). For example, Ball found that Grade 4 students in the United States using manipulatives scored significantly higher on conceptual understanding of fractions than students using no manipulatives.

There is less current research on manipulatives because their value is rarely questioned anymore. However, there are a few more recent studies, for example, Nute (1997), and some newer discussions on the use of virtual (computer) manipulatives (Moyer, Bolyard, and Spikell, 2002). Virtual manipulatives are valued for a number of reasons, but particularly because they are freely available to all students, even at home.

What Mathematics We Want Students to Learn

We have talked about how we teach mathematics, but there is also a question about what mathematics we should teach.

The mathematics that teachers teach is based primarily on the outcomes/expectations that their province has decided warrant focus at a particular grade level. Sometimes, teachers supplement this material with other material that they value. But what determines what is valued, either by the provincial government or by the individual teacher? And what determines the teacher's approach to teaching the mandated curriculum? Often, it is a perspective on what mathematics really is (Mewborn and Cross, 2007).

Differing Perspectives on What Mathematics Is

Some people might wonder how there could be a debate about what mathematics is. For them, it is arithmetic, or perhaps arithmetic and algebra and some high school topics relatively few people worry about. But there really are different perspectives on what mathematics is all about.

Mathematics as a Set of Procedures

For many, and certainly for most people in earlier generations, mathematics is viewed as a set of procedures that people memorize, whether arithmetic procedures like adding, subtracting, multiplying, and dividing, or procedures in high school like factoring or solving trigonometric equations.

For many of these people, there is only one "optimal" procedure for each of these purposes. For example, there is an appropriate way to do "long division," an appropriate way to add a negative integer to a positive one, or an appropriate way to factor quadratics.

Mathematics as a Hierarchy of Concepts and Skills

Some people have a broader view of mathematics. They believe that the learning of mathematics should focus as much, or more, on mathematical concepts and ideas as on the skills. For them, it is not just how to add numbers, but it is also what addition is all about, including when it is used. This view of mathematics involves students in recognizing the real-world situations in which mathematics is applied, although it may also encompass concepts, such as divisibility tests, which may have less applicability outside of the mathematical realm.

Many view mathematics as a very hierarchical subject. They believe there is a well-defined sequence for teaching various concepts and skills. For example, most would suggest that you cannot teach about area until you have taught about length. But even though there are numerous points on which many educators agree, there is no single definitive sequence for the teaching of mathematical concepts and skills.

The lack of agreement becomes apparent simply by examining how different provinces teach the same topic at different grade levels. Researchers, too, do not always agree. For example, although some argue that you cannot teach division before multiplication, others say that a child could solve the problem, *How many cookies do each of the 2 children get if they are sharing 8 cookies?*, at the same time or even before he or she could solve, *How many cookies are on two plates if there are 4 cookies on each plate?* Notice that the first problem is essentially a division one, and the second problem is a multiplication one.

Mathematics as a Study of Pattern

Some suggest that what distinguishes mathematics from other subjects is the central role that pattern plays in its development. Keith Devlin (1996) argues that numbers are based on recognizing patterns in the world; there is no such object as the number 2, but we see a pattern of *twoness* to help us understand what 2 represents. If we see enough things that look like

we get the idea of what 2 is supposed to mean.

There is a strand of mathematics often called patterns and algebra. In this strand, students explicitly study repeating, growing, shrinking, and recursive patterns (see Chapter 20). But patterns underlie number, geometry, and measurement as well. For example, not only do we use pattern to define number, as described above, but we use it to understand number. Patterns help us learn to multiply by powers of 10, for example, why $3 \times 10 = 30$, $3 \times 100 = 300$, and $3 \times 1000 = 3000$; they also help us to understand how our counting system works, for example, counting in a pattern where we say twenty, twenty-**one**, twenty-**two**, etc., to twenty-**nine**, going to thirty, and then starting all over again with thirty-**one**, thirty-**two**, etc.

Patterns in the place value system help us recognize why the first digit to the right of the decimal point must be tenths and the second digit must be hundredths. Patterns even allow us to relate a number we have never used before to ones we know, like 478, as a number between 400 and 500.

Patterns help us understand our measurement system, for example, why a distance of 2 m can be written as 2000 mm, much as a capacity of 2 L can be written as 2000 mL. They also help us interpret geometric situations, for example, the tessellation (or tiling) shown below as a pattern of hexagons positioned based on geometric transformations.

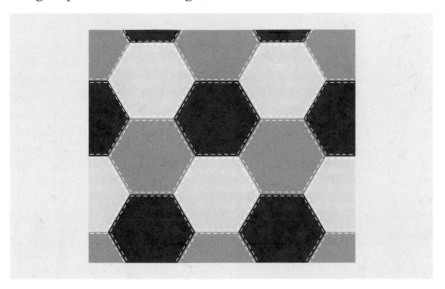

Mathematics as a Way of Thinking

Still others look at mathematics in terms of the processes we use to interpret a situation. Devlin (2000) spoke about mathematics as a way of looking at the world. People who think mathematically look at a phenomenon and see the mathematics in it. For example, on a road trip, people who think mathematically often think about what fraction of the trip they have completed at a certain point, and what their speed would have to be to arrive in a certain amount of time. They may even notice the numerical patterns in license plates of cars that they pass. As you learn about the various Canadian provincial and regional curriculum documents, you will see that all of them focus on mathematical processes that should be cultivated to provide the opportunity for students to develop their abilities to think mathematically.

Consider the four views of mathematics described above. Depending on the perspective taken by the teacher or curriculum writer on what mathematics fundamentally is, you can see that different topics might be emphasized or taught in a different way.

Differing Perspectives on What Mathematics Is Valued and at What Grade Levels

Provincial Mathematics Curricula

In Canada, each province or territory has jurisdiction over its curriculum. Each has its own program of studies. However, there are regional agreements wherein provinces and/or territories have agreed to share curriculum frameworks for particular topics, including mathematics.

There are currently four major curriculum frameworks in mathematics in Canada. These are the Western and Northern Canadian Protocol (WNCP), applying to Manitoba, Saskatchewan, Alberta, British Columbia, and the three territories; the Ontario curriculum; the Québec curriculum; and the APEF (also called CAMET) curriculum, applying to the four Atlantic provinces. The WNCP and APEF documents are then particularized by the various jurisdictions that form a part of each consortium.

Content Issues

The various curriculum documents differ in the level of detail, the specific topics in each grade level, and the processes that are emphasized. For example, if you examined the 2007 curriculum documents with regards to teaching number in Grade 1, you would notice many commonalities, but also some noticeable differences, for example, whether it is expected that facts be memorized, whether students encounter fractions, whether there is use of ordinal numbers, and whether the emphasis is on numbers to 20, 50, or 100.

It is unlikely that children in the various parts of the country are that different from one another developmentally, so the curriculum differences are clearly an expression of beliefs and/or values.

Processes

Each curriculum document identifies what are perceived, in that jurisdiction, as the critical mathematical processes to be developed. There are similarities, but, again, there are also differences in the various documents.

The WNCP (Alberta Education, 2006) document identifies seven mathematical processes of importance. These are

- communication
- connections (to real-world phenomena as well as between mathematical ideas)
- mental mathematics and estimation (also listed under content)
- problem solving
- reasoning
- technology
- visualization

The Ontario (Ministry of Education, Province of Ontario, 2005) document identifies seven processes. These are

- problem solving
- reasoning and proving
- reflecting
- selecting tools and computational strategies
- connecting
- representing
- communicating

The Québec curriculum (Ministère de l'Éducation, Gouvernement du Québec, 2001) is actually built around three competencies that feature much more prominently in the document than do the content goals. These are

- communicating (using mathematical language)
- reasoning (using mathematical concepts and processes [instruments, technology])
- problem solving (situational problems)

The Atlantic curriculum (Atlantic Provinces Education Foundation, 1996) is built around four processes, called unifying ideas. These are

- problem solving
- communication
- reasoning
- connections

Once again, there are similarities among the lists, but there are clear differences as well. Not only can different mathematical content be valued, but also different mathematical processes.

Moving from one part of the country to another, you may need to alter the content you teach or perhaps even the language you use to emphasize processes, but you will be teaching content that is focused on students gaining and applying a deep understanding of mathematical ideas and processes wherever you teach in Canada.

National and International Documents/Activities Related to Math Curriculum

Although there is no national curriculum in mathematics, there is certainly discussion of mathematics directions among provinces under the jurisdiction of the Council of Ministers of Education, Canada. This organization supervises national testing, called the Pan-Canadian Assessment Program (previously called SAIP, the School Achievement Indicators Program), which, on a cyclical basis, looks at the mathematics performance of students at ages 13 and 15 (previously 16).

There has also been some attention given to the approaches taken to the teaching of mathematics in other countries, particularly in Japan and Singapore, where students tend to perform well on international tests. Opinion is mixed on emulating these international approaches. Some educators point out that the cultural differences in those countries make it impossible for Canadians to simply adopt their approaches; students' responses would be quite different to the same stimuli here. Others believe that the Asian focus on problem solving and their decision to deal more deeply with less content in each grade are worth copying.

The Netherlands is another country whose approaches are making their way into Canada. Many of the Freudenthal Institute's approaches to teaching mathematics, often described under the name Realistic Mathematics Education, have been adopted informally by Canadian jurisdictions. These include a focus on visualization, which includes use of a number of organizational tools, such as an empty number line or a ratio table (discussed in subsequent chapters), and the setting of rich problems for guiding classroom mathematics exploration.

By far, however, the most powerful influence on Canadian curriculum remains the United States and, in particular, the *Principles and Standards for School Mathematics* document (National Council of Teachers of Mathematics, 2000), produced by the National Council of Teachers of Mathematics, an organization to which many Canadian teachers belong.

National Council of Teachers of Mathematics (NCTM) Principles and Standards

The NCTM is a long-standing organization with a very large membership. Math teachers, consultants, and researchers in both the United States and Canada belong to and contribute to the organization.

NCTM produced the *Principles and Standards for School Mathematics* (2000) document to articulate a vision for mathematics. The organization indicated which content and which processes should receive focus, and listed a set of six key principles:

> *Equity.* Excellence in mathematics education requires equity—high expectations and strong support for all students.
> *Curriculum.* A curriculum is more than a collection of activities: it must be coherent, focused on important mathematics, and well articulated across the grades.
> *Teaching.* Effective mathematics teaching requires understanding what students know and need to learn, and then challenging and supporting them to learn it well.
> *Learning.* Students must learn mathematics with understanding, actively building new knowledge from experience and prior knowledge.
> *Assessment.* Assessment should support the learning of important mathematics and furnish useful information to both teachers and students.
> *Technology.* Technology is essential in teaching and learning mathematics; it influences the mathematics that is taught and enhances students' learning.

Important content is identified in each of five mathematical strands (number and operation, algebra, geometry, measurement, and data analysis and probability), and five processes are singled out for consideration: problem solving, reasoning and proof, communication, connections, and representation. At different grade bands, different strands receive more emphasis, but the processes are critical throughout the grades.

More recently, NCTM (2006) released a document called *Curriculum Focal Points*. In response to the call for a deeper curriculum, this document shapes the standards espoused in the *Principles and Standards* document into a list of foci for each grade level from K to 8.

The organization produces journals for teachers and researchers in mathematics at all levels, including *Teaching Children Mathematics*, *Mathematics Teaching in the Middle School*, *The Mathematics Teacher*, and the *Journal for Research in Mathematics Education*, as well as other electronic resources. These are among the most cited references in mathematics education work.

Public Involvement and Expectations for a Mathematics Curriculum

Increasingly, the public is expressing its opinion about how mathematics should be taught. Many educators find this unsettling; they point out, for example, that the public does not express its opinion in the same way about how medicine or the law should be practised. Yet, because almost every citizen has gone to school, it appears that citizens believe their opinions about educational practice are informed; the notion that there is a body of educational research that is part of the specialized knowledge of educators is not universally accepted.

Similar to the many citizens who expressed concern about a change in philosophy from teaching reading phonetically to what was called a whole language approach (learning to read by reading), many citizens have questioned the advisability of teaching mathematics in a way that does not emphasize standard and uniform approaches to calculations. There has also been concern about less emphasis on memorizing the facts and allowing calculator use. Some have even given the name *fuzzy math* to what they perceive as this change in approach. The term *Math Wars* has been used to describe the very loud and impassioned debate on these matters. The debate rages hotter in the United States than in Canada, but it sometimes finds its way into Canadian media as well.

It is important for teachers to know how non-teachers feel about these topics, and it is equally important to have answers to questions that are raised. For example, although it is true that fact memorization is now seen as something that should follow an understanding of what the facts mean, most curricula still speak explicitly to the recall of facts. In other words, we still expect students to recall their facts.

Similarly, although it is true that students are sometimes allowed to use their calculators when they are not really needed, there is research that shows that appropriate calculator use does not adversely affect computational performance and does enhance problem-solving performance. For example, Smith's (1997) analysis of research showed that the calculator had a positive effect on increasing conceptual knowledge. This effect was evident through all grades and statistically significant for students in Grade 3. Smith also reported that calculator usage had a positive effect on students in both problem solving and computation, and did not hinder the development of pencil-and-paper skills. In this day and age, a calculator is a tool much like a pencil, which we certainly expect to be available to students.

The belief that there is only one way to perform an algorithm is a mistaken one. Although members of the community may feel that there is a best way to divide, for example, and are not happy that a variety of algorithms are taught to students, in another country a completely different algorithm may be the norm. Neither is better—they are different. In fact, the more tools and approaches that we have, the more likely we are to be successful at a task.

Some believe that there is simply not enough time for students to "discover" math themselves. However, since we know that many adults who grew up with a more traditional mathematics curriculum continue to be math anxious, there is ample evidence that something other than the previous rote approaches to instruction are needed.

Teaching Developmentally

Subsequent chapters speak to other research on how students develop mathematically. However, in this chapter—your initial look at what we know about how students learn mathematics—it is essential to also point out the importance of teachers having a firm understanding of student development in mathematics in order to teach effectively.

Starting with early counting research by Gelman and Gallistel (1978), and later the highly influential Carpenter and Moser (1984) study on children's learning of addition and subtraction, there has been an increasing body of research looking at the sequence with which students make sense of mathematical ideas. As teachers become more familiar with which ideas are more complex for students and why, they are better able to ensure that their instruction is at the appropriate developmental level for students, and that it challenges students' mathematical conceptions in appropriate ways. This minimizes the likelihood of students developing mathematical misconceptions.

This examination of developmental research has led to the creation of important professional development programs, such as Cognitively Guided Instruction (Fennema, Carpenter et al., 1996), mentioned in the section below. More recently, work on developmental learning has led to the Early Numeracy Project in Australia (Communication Division for the Office of School Education et al., 2001), and PRIME in Canada (Small, 2005), among others.

Research on Mathematics Teaching

Much of the literature in mathematics education focuses on student achievement, but some of it also looks at the instructional approaches of math teachers. Our intuition and experience tell us of the important role of the teacher in a student's mathematical development. It has been difficult for research to pinpoint which characteristics of a teacher make a difference, given the complexity of the teaching situation. However, we do know a few things about the difference a teacher can make.

There has always been a feeling that teachers need math content background. Most education programs require teachers to have some content courses in mathematics and some methodology. Over the last decade, though, the focus has shifted not so much to how much content, but to what content.

Importance of a Teacher's Pedagogical Content Knowledge

Since the mid-1980s, there has been a significant push to make sure that teachers understand the mathematics they are teaching from the perspective of the student. Questions teachers would address might include the following:

- What might the student be thinking when I present this problem and why?
- How might this subtraction problem look different to a student than that one?

Growing out of a major research study (Carpenter and Moser, 1984) in the mid-1980s was a movement called Cognitively Guided Instruction (CGI). The premise is that if teachers truly understand children's thinking in solving problems related to the topic being addressed, they will be better able to make the mathematics make sense to their students.

In 1996, a long-term, longitudinal study (Fennema, Carpenter et al., 1996) validated that, indeed, student achievement improved significantly in concept knowledge and problem solving in the classrooms of CGI teachers. The researchers witnessed changes in the teachers' behaviour in those classrooms. Teachers were more likely to

- provide time for students to work for significant periods of time with richer problems,
- provide opportunities for students to talk to each other about the mathematical ideas with which they were dealing, and
- adapt instruction to the problem-solving level of the students.

Another study in California (Gearhart et al., 1999) looked at changes in performance after a significant curricular change. It showed that children seemed to learn more in classrooms with a teacher focus on students' ways of thinking, richer problem-solving opportunities, and the provision of many chances to make connections between the concrete and the symbolic using manipulative materials.

A very significant research thread has developed in Michigan, where Deborah Ball and her colleagues (Ball, Hill, and Bass, 2005) have been studying what they call pedagogical content knowledge, that is, at teachers' knowledge of the mathematics they are teaching in light of how students might think about the mathematics. This research adds to the work of Liping Ma (1999), who contrasted the deep content knowledge that many Chinese teachers bring to their teaching of mathematics as compared to American teachers.

Educators with whom Ball, Hill, and Bass work focus on why a student might get something wrong, how to represent a mathematical idea in alternate effective ways, or how to respond when a student performs a task correctly, but in an unexpected way. Ball has spoken widely on how the mathematics that teachers need to know is quite specific and that many teachers do not have the relevant knowledge. Her group has been developing instruments that other researchers and education officials are using to assess math teachers' pedagogical content knowledge, so that teachers become aware of their limitations and can work on them. A paper (Hill, Rowan, Ball, 2005) speaks to the effectiveness of looking at teachers' pedagogical content knowledge as a tool to improve student performance.

The next few chapters delve more deeply into some of the issues raised in this chapter. They look at how to focus instruction on key ideas and mathematical processes, and how problem solving and communication are essential processes to develop at any grade level to ensure that students really do learn mathematics with understanding.

Applying What You've Learned

1. The chapter problem was designed to be a problem that could be solved in a variety of different ways. Show that there are both algebraic and non-algebraic ways to solve the problem.

2. Do a bit of research on the topic of "a constructivist classroom." Describe a list of things that you might see that would convince you that a classroom is constructivist in nature.

3. Describe a mathematics topic that you really understand and one that you are uncomfortable with.

   a) What evidence do you have that you do understand the topic you selected?

   b) What evidence do you have that you do not understand the other topic?

4. Which of the perspectives on mathematics described in this chapter is closest to what you believe? Why?

5. Select a grade level of interest to you in a province of interest to you. Explore the outcomes/expectations that you will be expected to teach.

   a) How is what is on the list different from what you might have expected?

   b) How much support do you feel that you, as a teacher, would be given from the curriculum document for that grade?

6. View the NCTM website (www.nctm.org). Report on some ways that this resource might be useful to you as a teacher of mathematics.

7. Find out about the difference between approaches to teaching math in Japan and North America. What lessons might we learn from the Japanese? What lessons might they learn from us?

8. Investigate the media to locate an argument against a constructivist approach to teaching mathematics. If you, as a teacher, were faced with this argument from a parent, how do you feel you might respond?

9. Find out more about pedagogical content knowledge. If possible, have a look at some of the released items that are deemed to measure this knowledge. What surprised you about these items?

Interact with a K–8 Student:

10. Ask a student about a mathematical topic he or she has recently explored. Ask the student how he or she knows that he or she really did or did not understand the math learned. Observe whether students focus on their ability to use procedures or their ability to solve problems.

Discuss with a K–8 Teacher:

11. Ask a teacher how the changes in approach to mathematics in the last 10 to 15 years have made it easier (or harder) than expected for him or her to effectively teach mathematics.

WebConnect

www.makingmathmeaningful.nelson.com

Visit Nelson's Making Math Meaningful website to find links to problems you might use with your students.

Selected References

Alberta Education. (2006). *The common curriculum framework for K–9 mathematics.* Edmonton, AB: Western and Northern Canadian Protocol.

Atlantic Canada Education Foundations. (1996). *Foundation for the Atlantic Canada mathematics curriculum.* Halifax, NS: Atlantic Canada Education Foundation.

Ball, D.L., Hill, H.C., and Bass, H. (2005, Fall). Knowing mathematics for teaching: Who knows mathematics well enough to teach third grade, and how can we decide? *American Educator,* 14–17, 20–22, 43–46.

Ball, S. (1988). Computers, concrete materials and teaching fractions. *School, Science, and Mathematics,* 88, 470–475.

Bishop, A.J., Clements, M.A., Keitel, C., Kilpatrick, J., Leung, F.K.S. (Eds.). (2003). *Second international handbook of mathematics education.* Berlin, Germany: Springer International Books of Education.

Carpenter, T.P., and Lehrer, R. (1999). Teaching and learning mathematics with understanding. In Fennema, E., and Romberg, T.A. (Eds.). *Mathematics classrooms that promote understanding.* Mahwah, NJ: Lawrence Erlbaum Associates, 19–32.

Carpenter, T.P., and Moser, J.M. (1984). The acquisition of addition and subtraction concepts in grades one through three. *Journal for Research in Mathematics Education,* 15, 179–202.

Cobb, P. (1988). The tension between theories of learning and instruction in mathematics education. *Educational Psychologist, 23*, 87–103.

Communication Division for the Office of School Education, Department of Education, Employment and Training. (2001). *Early numeracy in the classroom.* Melbourne, AU: State of Victoria. [Videocassette].

Devlin, K. (1996). *Mathematics: The science of patterns.* Gordonsville, VA: W.H. Freeman and Company.

Devlin, K. (1998). *The language of mathematics: Making the invisible visible.* New York: W.H. Freeman and Company.

Devlin, K. (2000). *The language of mathematics: Making the invisible visible.* Gordonsville, VA: W.H. Freeman and Company.

English, L.D. (2003). *Handbook of international research in mathematics education.* Mahwah, NJ: Lawrence Erlbaum Associates.

Fennema, E., Carpenter, T.P., Franke, M.L., Levi, L., Jacobs, V.R., and Empson, S.B. (1996). A longitudinal study of learning to use children's thinking in mathematics instruction. *Journal for Research in Mathematics Education, 27*, 403–434.

Gearhart, M., Saxe, G.N., Seltzer, M., Schlackman, J., Ching, C.C., Nasir, N., et al. (1999). Opportunities to learn fractions in elementary mathematics classrooms. *Journal for Research in Mathematics Education, 30*, 286–315.

Gelman, R., and Gallistel, C.R. (1978). *The child's understanding of number.* Cambridge, MA: Harvard University Press.

Hill, H.C., Rowan, B., and Ball, D. (2005). Effects of teachers' mathematical knowledge for teaching on student achievement. *American Educational Research Journal, 42*, 371–406.

Kilpatrick, J., Martin, W.G., and Schifter, D. (Eds.). (2003). *A research companion to principles and standards for school mathematics.* Reston, VA: National Council of Teachers of Mathematics.

Lester, F. (2007). *Handbook of research on mathematics education.* Charlotte, NC: Information Age Publishers, Inc.

Ma, L. (1999). *Knowing and teaching elementary mathematics.* Mahwah, NJ: Lawrence Erlbaum Associates.

Mewborn, D.S., and Cross, D.I. (2007). Mathematics teachers' beliefs about mathematics and links to students' learning. In Martin, W.G., Strutchens, M.E., and Elliott, P.C. (Eds). *The learning of mathematics.* Reston, VA: National Council of Teachers of Mathematics, 259–270.

Ministère de l'Éducation, Gouvernement du Québec. (2001). *Québec education program.* Québec: Ministère de l'Éducation, Province of Québec.

Ministry of Education, Province of Ontario. (2005). *The Ontario curriculum grades 1–8: Mathematics, 2005*, revised. Toronto: Ministry of Education, Province of Ontario.

Moyer, P.S., Bolyard, J.J., and Spikell, M.A. (2002). What are virtual manipulatives? *Teaching Children Mathematics, 8*, 372–377.

National Center for Research on Teacher Learning. (1994). How teachers learn to engage students in active learning [Online]. Available: http://ncrtl.msu.edu/http/teachers.pdf.

National Council of Teachers of Mathematics. (1969 ff.). *Journal for Research in Mathematics Education.* Reston, VA: National Council of Teachers of Mathematics.

National Council of Teachers of Mathematics. (1993 ff.). *Teaching children mathematics.* Reston, VA: National Council of Teachers of Mathematics.

National Council of Teachers of Mathematics. (1994 ff.). *Mathematics teaching in the middle school.* Reston, VA: National Council of Teachers of Mathematics.

National Council of Teachers of Mathematics. (1996 ff.). *The mathematics teacher.* Reston, VA: National Council of Teachers of Mathematics.

National Council of Teachers of Mathematics. (2000). *Principles and standards for school mathematics.* Reston, VA: National Council of Teachers of Mathematics.

National Council of Teachers of Mathematics. (2006). *Curriculum focal points.* Reston, VA: National Council of Teachers of Mathematics.

National Research Council. (2001). *Adding it up: Helping children learn mathematics.* Kilpatrick, J., Swafford, J., and Findell, B. (Eds.). Mathematics Learning Study Committee, Center for Education, Division of Behavioral and Social Science and Education. Washington, DC: National Academy Press.

Nute, N. (1997). *The impact of engagement activity and manipulatives presentation on intermediate mathematics achievement, time-on-task, learning efficiency, and attitude.* (Doctoral dissertation, University of Memphis, 1997). *Dissertation Abstracts International* 58(08), 2988.

Ross, J.A., Hogaboam-Gray, A., and McDougall, D. (2002). Research on reform in mathematics education, 1993–2000. *Alberta Journal of Educational Research, 48*, 122–138.

Small, M. (2005). *PRIME: Number and operations strand kit.* Toronto: Thomson Nelson.

Smith, B.A. (1997). *A meta-analysis of outcomes from the use of calculators in mathematics education.* (Doctoral dissertation, Texas A&M University, 1996). *Dissertation Abstracts International, 58*, 787A.

Suydam, M. (1984). Research report: Manipulative materials. *The Arithmetic Teacher, 31*, 27.

Chapter 2

Focusing Instruction on Key Ideas and Key Processes

IN A NUTSHELL

The main ideas in this chapter are listed below:

1. By organizing content around key ideas, teachers can teach more efficiently, but, most importantly, students can make connections between seemingly disparate topics that help them learn new mathematical ideas.

2. There are a number of mathematical processes that can and should be developed no matter what content is being taught. Although the list of identified processes differ in different jurisdictions, these processes almost always include problem solving, communication, and reasoning. Other processes that are mentioned in Canadian curricula are connections, representation, using technology, visualization, mental math and estimation, reflecting, and selecting tools and computational strategies.

CHAPTER PROBLEM

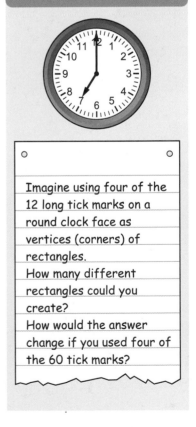

Imagine using four of the 12 long tick marks on a round clock face as vertices (corners) of rectangles.

How many different rectangles could you create?

How would the answer change if you used four of the 60 tick marks?

Organizing Content around Key Ideas

A significant body of educational research has established the effectiveness of using organizers to present new knowledge to students (Borko and Putnam, 1995; Schifter, Bastable, and Russell, 1997; Kennedy, 1997). These organizers are sometimes called "big ideas," "enduring understandings," "key concepts," or "key ideas." The thinking behind this approach is that, if we can connect a new idea being taught to related ideas that have been previously learned, it is more likely that the new knowledge will be assimilated.

By focusing the learning of each strand in mathematics around a few key ideas, it will be easier for students to relate new knowledge to previously learned ideas. In addition, it simplifies the teacher's job of prioritizing and organizing what is usually a fairly lengthy list of specific curriculum expectations/outcomes by organizing them around a relatively small number of key ideas. Despite increasing abstraction as students go up the grades, and shifts in focus from grade to grade, key ideas remain fundamentally simple.

What is important, though, is that the key ideas not be implicit, but explicit. Whether it is through questioning, ensuring that a student has the opportunity to bring up a key idea, or through teacher talk, it is important that key ideas be said out loud. The more students hear an idea, the more likely it is that they will internalize it and be able to use it to support further learning.

It is helpful to consider what the key ideas are in the different mathematics strands around which curricula are organized. Described below is a list of key concepts in each strand.

Key Concepts in Number

Number instruction, not involving number operations, can be organized around five key concepts (Small, 2005a).

Concept 1: Numbers tell how many or how much.
Concept 2: Classifying numbers provides information about the characteristics of the numbers.
Concept 3: There are different, but equivalent, representations for a number.
Concept 4: We use a number system based on patterns.
Concept 5: Benchmark numbers are useful for relating and estimating numbers.

- Realizing that the fraction $\frac{1}{2}$ tells how much of the pizza has been eaten is an example of *Concept 1* because it tells how many or how much.
- Noting that the sum of any even number and the number 2 is another even number is an example of *Concept 2* because it is about classifying numbers as even.
- Relating fractions to decimals is an example of *Concept 3* because the same number is represented differently.
- Extending place value to decimals is an example of *Concept 4*, focusing on the power of our number system.
- How numbers are rounded is an example of *Concept 5*, which is about the value of using benchmark numbers.

Most key concepts are represented at every grade level, from K to 8. Occasionally, however, the nature of the concept is such that it would not be associated with the early grades. For example, younger children who are still dealing with small whole numbers would not consider the place value system. As a result, *Concept 4* would not be a key concept for the earlier grades.

As well, the focus of a key concept will change over the grades. For example, most whole number calculations are familiar to students well before they deal with the more sophisticated topics associated with the later grades. As a result, the focus of *Concept 5* in the later grades is more on decimals and fractions than on whole numbers.

As was mentioned, structuring around key ideas helps students see how new topics relate to ideas they have already learned. For example, understanding that rounding whole numbers to the nearest ten or hundred is the same idea as looking at a fraction and deciding if it is closer to 0, $\frac{1}{2}$, or 1, helps students see the connections between fraction and whole number work.

Key Concepts in Operations

Three key concepts can be used to organize instruction in number operations across the K to 8 grades (Small, 2005a).

Concept 1: Addition leads to a total and subtraction indicates what is missing. Addition and subtraction are intrinsically related.

Concept 2: Multiplication and division are extensions of addition and subtraction. Multiplication and division are intrinsically related.

Concept 3: There are many algorithms for performing a given operation.

The first two concepts are represented in every grade, from K to 8, although the focus and level of abstraction changes. In the early grades, the focus is on operations with whole numbers, whereas later, decimals and fractions become the focus. Since complex algorithms are not appropriate for young children, *Concept 3* is not represented in the early grades.

Key Concepts in Geometry

Four key concepts can be used to describe geometry instruction (Small, 2007).

Concept 1: Shapes of different dimensions and their properties can be described mathematically.

Concept 2: There are many representations of 2-D and 3-D shapes.

Concept 3: Any 2-D or 3-D shape can be created by either combining or dissecting other shapes.

Concept 4: 2-D and 3-D shapes can be located in space. They can be relocated and reoriented using mathematical procedures.

Concept 1 is about developing concepts and vocabulary for identifying and relating shapes and solving problems about shapes. The focus is on what attributes we use to describe shapes and how much information is necessary to identify the shape we mean. The topic of patterning, which falls within *Concept 1*, is an excellent medium for helping students focus on shape attributes.

Younger students create very simple shape patterns and describe them by naming the shapes: ball, box, ball, box, ball, box, ... or by describing geometric properties: rolls, stacks, rolls, stacks, rolls, stacks, ... Older students create and describe more complex shape patterns with multiple attributes.

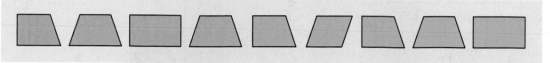

The shape pattern repeats: trapezoid, trapezoid, parallelogram. The angle measure pattern also repeats: right angles, no right angles. Shape follows an AAB pattern, and angle measure follows an AB pattern. The attributes in the pattern are independent.

Whenever students are exploring representations of shapes, they are working with *Concept 2*. For example, younger students are expected to recognize a 3-D shape from its picture. Older students might judge whether one pictorial representation of a 3-D shape is better than another representation of the 3-D shape for a particular purpose.

The following diagrams show some of the ways to represent a triangle-based prism pictorially.

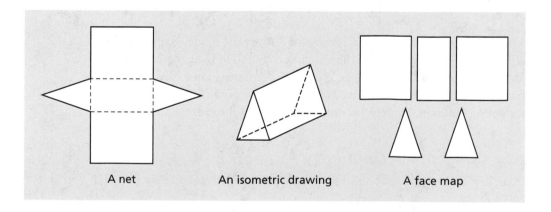

A net   An isometric drawing   A face map

When students put together four linking cubes to build a tower, they are working with *Concept 3*. Sometimes they create new shapes by combining smaller shapes. Other times, they do the opposite—they dissect a large shape into smaller component shapes. For example, using a hexagon to tile a floor involves combining shapes to create a larger shape, but it may also be viewed as dissecting a larger shape to create smaller component shapes. Students' experience with jigsaw puzzles can help them see how shapes can be made up of other shapes.

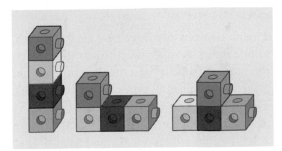

Three 3-D shapes that can be made by combining four congruent cubes.

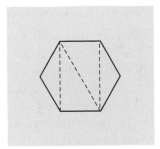

Four 2-D shapes (in this case, all triangles) that can result from dissecting a hexagon.

Young students learning to use the words *above* and *below* are exploring *Concept 4*, as are older students examining the effects of transformations on shapes. In both situations, students are thinking about spatial and positional relationships.

"The cloud is above the girl."

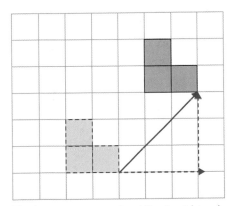

The hexagon was translated 3 units right and 3 units up.

Again, focusing on key concepts provides valuable connections. For example, recognizing that any shape can be created by combining or dissecting other shapes (*Concept 3*) allows students not only to understand why doubling the side lengths of a shape produces a shape with four times the area, but also to see why a regular polygon can be subdivided into congruent triangles.

Knowing that any shape can be divided into smaller shapes ...

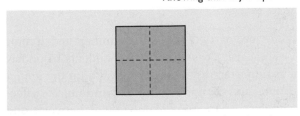

... helps students understand why doubling the side lengths of the green square results in a new square with four times the area.

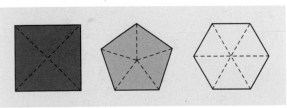

... helps students understand why any regular polygon can be divided into congruent triangles that meet at a central point.

Key Concepts in Measurement

Although work with measurement is often organized by type—length, area, volume, and so on—it is important to emphasize the commonalities. For example, the notion that the numerical value of a measurement varies with the size of the unit being used is valid for all types of measurements. Once a student grasps this concept for linear measurement, for example, he or she will be able to carry the same concept over into other types of measurement.

Four key concepts can describe measurement instruction across types of measurements (Small, 2009).

Concept 1: Some attributes of objects can be described using measurements.

Concept 2: The numerical value attached to a measurement is relative to the measurement unit.

Concept 3: Standard units, estimates, and measurement formulas are used to simplify communication about and calculation of measurements.

Concept 4: Tools, units of measure, and degree of precision must be appropriate to the purpose and context.

Whether primary students are measuring to see how many small cubes they can fit inside a box, or determining which of two boxes has a greater mass, they are working with two important aspects of *Concept 1*:

• Objects often have many attributes, and some of these can be measured.
• Measurements give us information about the attributes of objects that we can use to solve problems.

Some Attributes We Can Measure

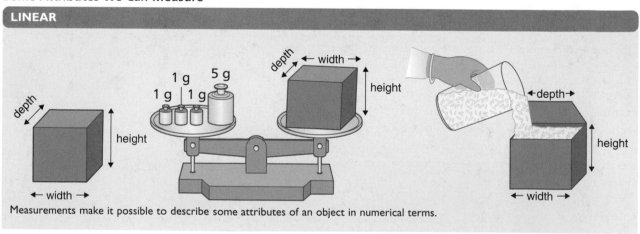

Measurements make it possible to describe some attributes of an object in numerical terms.

A measurement is made up of two parts—a number and a unit (whether non-standard or standard). It is essential for students to understand that the unit is just as important as the number. Without the unit, a measurement has no meaning, and cannot be used to communicate effectively about a particular object or to make comparisons between one object and another. As students explore *Concept 2*, they also come to realize that the number of units required to describe a particular measurement increases as the unit size decreases (and vice versa).

> Teacher: What did you use to measure your desk?
>
> Student: I used pens first, and then I used paper clips.
>
> Teacher: Did you need more pens or more paper clips?
>
> Student: I needed more paper clips. Pens are bigger, so you don't need as many to go all the way across.

One student suggests that everyone in the class should report their height in centimetres, since non-standard units such as pencils and paper clips are not always uniform. Another student estimates that an object weighs about 10 kg, aware that the estimate provides enough information to give others a good feel for the mass, without the need to be more precise. Still another student uses a formula to calculate the area of a square, rather than taking the time to fill the space with tiles. All of these students are using *Concept 3*, and recognizing the value of using conventions and estimates to streamline the measurement process or to communicate more efficiently about the results.

The student in the early years who chooses a centimetre ruler over a metre stick as an appropriate tool for measuring a short distance is applying *Concept 4*, as is the older student who has chosen to measure a similar distance in millimetres instead of centimetres because a more precise measurement is required. Each student recognizes that the selection of a measurement unit and tool both depend on the purpose and context for measuring.

You are making a model airplane. You must measure and cut out small pieces of wood that have to fit together perfectly.

a) Which ruler would you use? Circle one:

Ruler 1: A ruler marked only in **decimetres**

Ruler 2: A ruler marked only in **centimetres**

(Ruler 3:) A ruler marked in **millimetres**

b) Explain your choice of ruler.

With ruler 3, you can be precise because it has the smallest markings.

Student Response

This student recognizes that there are choices to be made in the selection of tools and units, and that these choices depend on what is being measured and why.

Key Concepts in Data Management

Three key concepts encompass data instruction (Small, 2006).

Concept 1: To collect data, you must create appropriate questions and think about how to best gather the data.

Concept 2: A set of data can be collected, organized, and then displayed in a variety of ways, depending on the type of data and the purpose for its collection.

Concept 3: Once a set of data is displayed, it can be analyzed to look for patterns, make comparisons, draw inferences, predict, and make decisions.

Students should be focused on the overall process for data collection, regardless of whether they are designing a simple survey question in Kindergarten or, in higher grades, evaluating the appropriateness of a survey sample or deciding whether to use first-hand or second-hand data.

Concept 1 can be characterized as "asking the right people the right question in the right way in the right circumstances." Young students use provided recording systems for collecting and organizing data. As they get older, they are able to create their own tables/charts. Older students are also able to evaluate different organization schemes. Young students organize or sort objects using a single attribute. As they get older, they are able to sort the same set of objects in multiple ways, and eventually sort the same set of objects using multiple attributes.

Young students use concrete objects and then pictures to organize and display their data. Older students use more sophisticated graphs, such as pictographs with and without scales, then bar graphs with scales and/or intervals, and then broken-line graphs, stem-and-leaf plots, circle graphs, histograms, and box plots.

As students discover more ways to display data, they are able to recognize and create equivalent displays of data and make choices about which format to use in different situations. It is important for students to realize that the format should suit the type of data and their purpose for collecting and displaying the information. This is what *Concept 2* is all about.

For example, the two displays on page 25 show the results of the same spinner experiment. The difference between the two displays is that, while the bar graph only shows how many results were in each interval, the stem-and-leaf plot shows each individual result. For example, the bar graph tells us that four students spun red between 0 and 9 times in the experiment. The stem-and-leaf plot shows that those students actually spun red 3 times, 6 times, 7 times, and 8 times.

Whether they are analyzing tables/charts, concrete graphs, or stem-and-leaf plots, or determining measures of central tendency to summarize data, students are working with *Concept 3*.

Even the youngest students are able to see that factual information can be extracted from a graph. As they gain experience, they begin to draw increasingly sophisticated conclusions from those facts. A young student might simply conclude from the circle graph shown in the margin that "a lot of children take the bus." More experienced students might conclude that "more students take the bus than walk or get a ride." Even more advanced students make inferences, draw conclusions, and use the information to make decisions; for example, "Because so many students take the bus, we should have our homework help time at lunch instead of after school."

In the later grades, students determine measures of central tendency and data distribution (e.g., range). This requires analyzing and calculating with the data.

How We Get to School

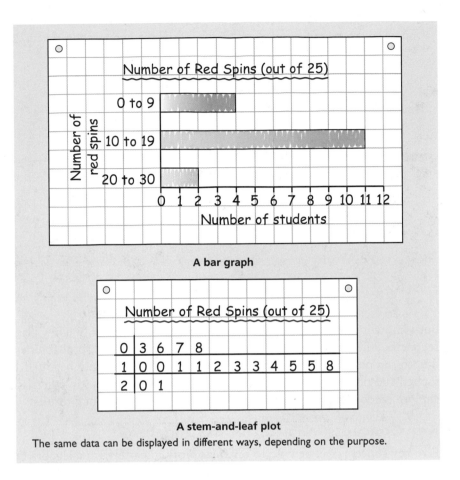

A bar graph

A stem-and-leaf plot

The same data can be displayed in different ways, depending on the purpose.

Key Concepts in Probability

Two key concepts can be used to describe probability instruction (Small, 2006).

> Concept 1: Probability involves the use of mathematics to describe the level of certainty that an event will occur.
>
> Concept 2: Probabilities, both theoretical and experimental, can be determined in different ways.

Initially, students explore *Concept 1* by conducting very simple probability experiments and by thinking of very simple everyday events that sometimes, always, or never happen. Later on, students consider possible outcomes, conduct more complex experiments, and use fractions to describe experimental or theoretical probabilities.

Concept 2 involves conducting experiments to determine experimental probabilities. Young children conduct very simple experiments with assistance. Older students design and conduct probability experiments.

Young students are able to use everyday probability language to make predictions for very simple situations and experiments ("I *always* go home right after school," and "The coin will *sometimes* flip heads."), while older students make numerical predictions ("I flipped 50 tacks and 23 landed head down, so, in 100 flips, about 50 will land head down.").

For older students, *Concept 2* also involves the notion of how theoretical probability relates to experimental probability ("I predict 5 heads in 10 flips

Student Response

This student has identified all the possible sums that are outcomes of rolling two dice (Concept 1).

Suppose you rolled two dice and found the sum of the two numbers rolled. What are all the possible sums?

2 - 12

Name a sum that is not possible.

1

Tell why it is not possible.

There are two dice and the lowest number is one on each die.

---

but I know it's possible to get anywhere from 0 to 10 heads."). They also reconcile differences between theoretical and experimental probabilities due to sample size ("I flipped a coin 10 times and got mostly heads. If I flipped 100 times, it would be closer to half heads."). These students also explore randomness in explaining discrepancies in experimental results.

Key Concepts in Patterns and Algebra

Five key concepts can be used to organize work in patterns and algebra in Grades K to 8 (Small, 2005b).

Concept 1: Patterns represent identified regularities based on rules describing the patterns' elements.

Concept 2: Any pattern can be represented in a variety of ways.

Concept 3: Patterns underlie mathematical concepts and can also be found in the real world.

Concept 4: Data can be arranged to highlight patterns and relationships.

Concept 5: Relationships between quantities can be described using rules involving variables.

- Recognizing that 100 000 comes after 10, 100, 1000, 10 000, ... is an example of *Concept 1*. The rule that describes the pattern's elements is "multiply by 10."
- Understanding that another way of describing the square numbers 1, 4, 9, ... is through the set of square shapes (as shown in the margin) is an example of *Concept 2*. The same pattern is represented both numerically and geometrically.
- Realizing that multiplying a whole number by 10 is accomplished by annexing 1 zero, and multiplying by 100 by annexing 2 zeros, and so on, is an example of patterns underlying mathematical concepts, which is one of the notions central to *Concept 3*.
- Arranging the numbers from 1 to 100 in different ways to highlight different patterns is an example of *Concept 4*. Displaying the numbers in 10 columns highlights the fact that adding 10 only changes one digit in a numeral (22, 32, 42, 52, ...). On the other hand, displaying

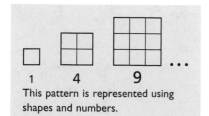

1   4   9   ...

This pattern is represented using shapes and numbers.

the numbers in 6 columns, rather than 10 (as shown in the margin), highlights the fact that all prime numbers greater than 3 are 1 more or 1 less than a multiple of 6.

- Using variables, formulas, and rules in number, geometry, and measurement situations is an example of *Concept 5*. For example:
  - The solution to an equation such as $3 \times \blacksquare = 12$ can be generalized using an algebraic equation that uses variables: $a \times \blacksquare = b$ so $\blacksquare = a \div b$.
  - The rule or formula for the number of edges for a pyramid with a base of $\blacksquare$ sides is always $e = 2 \times \blacksquare$.
  - The rule or formula for the perimeter of a square is always $P = 4 \times \blacksquare$, where $\blacksquare$ is the side length.

1	(2)	(3)	4	(5)	6
(7)	8	9	10	(11)	12
(13)	14	15	16	(17)	18
(19)	20	21	22	(23)	24
25	26	27	28	(29)	30
(31)	32	33	34	35	36
(37)	38	39	40	(41)	42
(43)	44	45	46	(47)	48
49	50	51	52	(53)	54

Prime number patterns

Most key concepts are represented at every grade level, from Kindergarten to Grade 8. However, the use of a variable (*Concept 5*) is inappropriate for the youngest students. When the concept of a variable is eventually introduced, it is first presented in the form of an open frame in a number sentence (for example, $5 + \blacksquare = 7$), and not as a literal variable.

The formula for the area of a rectangle is: $A = L \times W$

a) What is the formula for the perimeter of a rectangle?

$$P = L + W \times 2$$

b) Why does your formula make sense?

It make sense because there are four sides and ^each 2 sides are same.

Student Response

Eventually, students use variables to describe relationships (*Concept 5*). This student has used variables to write a formula that relates the side lengths and perimeter of a rectangle. What makes this a concept (rather than just a skill) is that the student is able to justify the formula and not simply apply it. Observe that the student has not internalized symbol conventions to notice that $P = L + W \times 2$ means that only the W is multiplied by 2. Clearly he or she meant $(L + W) \times 2$.

The focus of a key concept will change over the grades. For example, with respect to *Concept 1*, students in earlier grades will be quite comfortable with simple repeating patterns, but will not be able to predict or extend patterns like 1, 1, 2, 3, 5, ... (the Fibonacci sequence), in which terms result from adding the two previous terms. These more complex patterns are introduced in later grades.

As with the other strands, teaching around key ideas supports better instruction. For example, understanding that pattern rules can be used to predict the colour for subsequent shapes in very simple patterns like red, blue, red, blue, red, blue, ... motivates students to look for a rule to predict values in more complex patterns like 3, 9, 27, ...

Focusing Instruction on Math Processes

Thinking about what the key concepts are is certainly one essential element of good mathematics teaching. Another is focusing on the mathematical processes.

The NCTM Process Standards

The National Council of Teachers of Mathematics identified five mathematical processes in their *Principles and Standards* document (NCTM, 2000). These are problem solving, communication, representation, reasoning and proving, and connections. These five processes underlie mathematical content through all grades, from early childhood to higher-level mathematics. Just as it is important to develop students' understanding of various mathematical concepts, it is equally and perhaps more important to develop their process skills; these are the tools students use to learn new mathematics.

A detailed discussion of problem solving and communication is found in the next two chapters. This chapter mentions some of the other processes.

Representation

Because mathematics is the study of abstract concepts like numbers and shapes, the way that these ideas are represented is critical to students' understanding. The more flexible students are in recognizing alternate ways to represent mathematical ideas, the more likely they are to be successful in mathematics.

For example, suppose a child realizes that the number 9 can be represented as $10 - 1$. The child is more likely to be able to calculate $35 + 9$ mentally (as $35 + 10 = 45$, and then $45 - 1 = 44$). If he or she also recognizes that 9 is 3×3, it becomes easier to divide 333 by 9 (as $333 \div 3 \div 3$). The more representations students are comfortable with, the more flexible their calculation skills will be.

Different representations of numbers help clarify ideas. For example, calling 16 a square number makes more sense when students see it as a square array of dots.

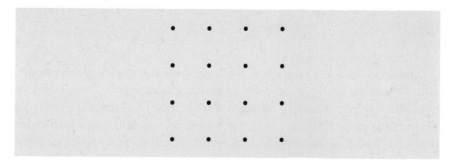

Realizing that $\frac{5}{5} = 1$ helps students see why $\frac{3}{4} \times \frac{5}{5}$ is another name for $\frac{3}{4}$.

Representing the sum of $(-4) + (+6)$ with counters helps a student see why $(-4) + (+6)$ is the same as $6 - 4$ since every $+1 + (-1)$ combination is 0.

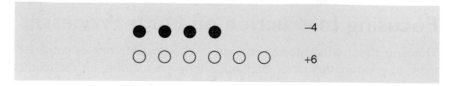

Representing the difference of $(+5) - (-3)$ as the distance from -3 to $+5$ on a number line helps a student understand why $(+5) - (-3)$ is the same as $5 + 3$.

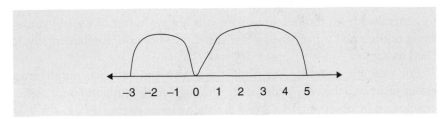

One way to encourage students to use multiple representations is to explicitly ask for them. Ask questions such as

– How many ways can you show 10?
– Can you write the number five using only fours?
– Can you represent a square as a combination of other shapes?
– Can you represent this pictograph as a bar graph?

Some of these representations for 10 are symbolic, but not all of them.

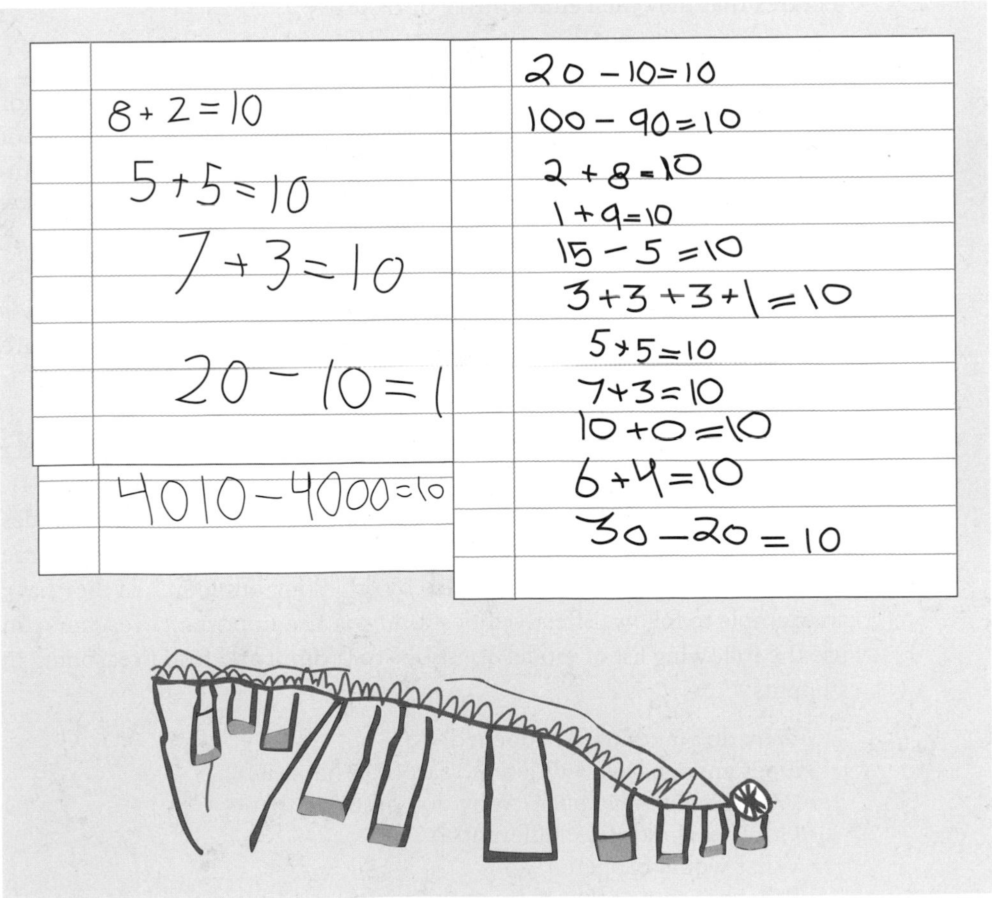

$8 + 2 = 10$

$5 + 5 = 10$

$7 + 3 = 10$

$20 - 10 = 1$

$4010 - 4000 = 10$

$20 - 10 = 10$
$100 - 90 = 10$
$2 + 8 = 10$
$1 + 9 = 10$
$15 - 5 = 10$
$3 + 3 + 3 + 1 = 10$
$5 + 5 = 10$
$7 + 3 = 10$
$10 + 0 = 10$
$6 + 4 = 10$
$30 - 20 = 10$

Reasoning and Proof

Many regard mathematics as being all about logic and reasoning. Indeed, there is a great deal of reasoning that students use to learn new mathematical ideas. Reasoning is about making inferences, generalizing, and verifying. Students infer by deriving implicit information from explicitly stated information. They sometimes attempt to generalize their conclusions through the creation of mathematical conjectures, which they verify (prove) using logical reasoning. These skills develop as students mature intellectually. One of the important ideas they learn is that it is dangerous to generalize from too few examples. It is always better to explain something not because it happened a few times, but because, fundamentally, it "had to happen."

For example, consider the notion that you can add two numbers in either order and the sum is the same. Although some students come to this conclusion by observing that 2 + 3 has the same answer as 3 + 2, 4 + 5 as 5 + 4, and 2 + 6 as 6 + 2, others recognize that if you put together two items, the sum has to be the same. If you held some items in one hand and some in the other and laid them down, it would not matter which items you let fall first; the total number of items is the same since they are the same items. This sort of generalization is based on proving, a very powerful form of reasoning.

One of the ways students develop their reasoning skills is to make conjectures that they then either prove or disprove.

Making and Testing Conjectures

A *conjecture* is a statement that has not yet been proven to be true nor shown to be false. Students use their observations and reasoning about relationships and patterns to develop these conjectures. For example, students might conjecture that when you add two odd numbers, the result is even. Then they need to develop strategies for testing their ideas.

Conjecture-testing strategies take time to develop. For many students, three or four examples are enough to convince them that something is always true. It is important to note that, although multiple examples are not enough to prove a conjecture is true, only one counterexample is required to prove it false.

What might some of these conjectures look like and how can we expect students to prove or disprove them? Two examples are shown on page 31.

Activities to encourage reasoning can begin at the very earliest grades and should be continued through to higher-level mathematics. For some students, reasoning must be modelled by "thinking out loud," so they have an example to follow. Effective questioning is also important. Teachers can use the following list of model questions to prompt and foster reasoning in students:

- Why do you think it happened?
- Does anyone have a different reason? What is it?
- Will this always happen? Why do you think that?
- How are these alike? different?
- What would happen if ...?
- What are some other ways to do this?
- What patterns do you notice?

Connections

The notion of connection is fundamental to all new learning, whether in mathematics or other areas. It may be connections between some mathematical ideas and other ones; it may be connections between mathematical concepts and everyday life experiences; it may be connections between

Conjecture and Test (Counterexample)

CONJECTURE

If you combine any group of congruent shapes, you will always be able to make the same type of shape.

Example

These four congruent triangles combine to make a larger triangle.

DISPROVING THE CONJECTURE BY COUNTEREXAMPLE

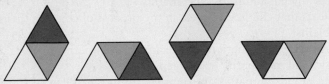

These three congruent triangles cannot be combined to make a triangle of any kind. The only possible shape is a trapezoid.

Sometimes a certain number of congruent shapes cannot be combined to make the same type of shape. The conjecture is false.

DISCUSSION

Another conjecture about adding 3-digit numbers

The previous conjecture about sums of 3-digit addends having 3-digit sums has been proven to be false by counterexample, but it leads to another conjecture about the sums of 3-digit addends: The sum of two 3-digit numbers has 3 or 4 digits. Students will be able to find multiple examples to support the conjecture and will be unable to find a counterexample to disprove it. But this is not enough to prove the conjecture true; reasoning must be used to prove the conjecture.

CONJECTURE AND TEST

Conjecture

The sum of two 3-digit numbers has 3 digits or 4 digits.

Test

It works for the five examples I tried, but I am not sure it always works.

Proof

Teacher: What is the least possible answer?
Student: You'd have to add 100 and 100. That's 200 and it has 3 digits.
T: What is the greatest possible answer?
S: It's what you get if you add 999 + 999. That's 1998, which has 4 digits. So, if the least sum has 3 digits and the greatest has 4 digits, all the sums must have 3 or 4 digits.

what is learned in math and what is learned in a different subject in school. Any and all connections are helpful for students to make sense of new ideas they encounter. In fact, it is almost impossible for students to solve a set of problems or even complete a set of exercises without making connections. We rarely give students exactly the same numbers to work with twice, so when solving a new question, students must see how it is like a question they have already encountered. Connections to real life contexts and to literature are particularly important for young learners.

Some possibilities for contexts to help students make connections are

- children's literature that is enjoyable and that also has mathematical value. Note that not only do children like to hear stories, they also like to create them. This is a wonderful way to link math and language arts.
- contexts in the child's world, such as collections, the classroom, friends, and family; for example, How many outfits can you make with 3 T-shirts and 2 pairs of pants?
- cross-cultural contexts; for example, contexts related to students' cultural backgrounds
- contexts that are whimsical, fanciful, and even silly, such as superheroes and space monster characters
- contexts in the world of grownups; for example, how much things cost and what adults do with math
- contexts that children suggest in the process of creating their own problems
- cross-curricular situations; for example, symmetry in art, fractions in music, and measurement in science
- other strands of math; for example, number patterns or measurement situations that involve addition or subtraction

One caution is to be careful not to overuse money contexts. Many adults see this as very practical, and indeed it is. Nonetheless, it is important that teachers cultivate interests that are not always tied to the consumer aspect of our society.

Other Processes

Particular educational jurisdictions in Canada have identified other processes that they want to stress for students as well. These include visualization and mental imagery as well as mental math and estimation in the Western provinces, and selecting tools and computational strategies and reflecting in Ontario.

Visualization

Visualization or *mental imagery* "involves thinking in pictures and images and the ability to perceive, transform, and re-create different aspects of the visual spatial world" (Armstrong, 1999). Visualization, as applied in mathematics, is a process of representing abstract concepts as mental images. These images allow the visualizer to remember and "manipulate" the concepts and to make the concepts meaningful.

There are obvious visualization opportunities for mathematics in geometry, measurement, and data management. Visualization is also important, however, in developing number sense. Although many teachers tend to concentrate on verbalization in their teaching, it is just as important to bring attention to the visual representation of concepts. Students visualize in their minds. At the youngest grades, students become familiar with what 3 (or 4 or 5 ...) looks like. When concrete materials, such as blocks used to represent an addition problem, are no longer present, it is the many previous concrete experiences with such physical aids that enable students to solve the problem, because they have internalized the relevant images. It is essential, therefore, that students receive frequent and varied exposure to manipulatives and other visual representations of mathematical objects and concepts.

Some tools to foster visualization skills are described throughout the chapters of this text.

Mental Math and Estimation

Subsequent chapters in this text present many mental math and estimation processes. One of the reasons these are highlighted is that solving questions mentally helps to force a student to focus on the relationships between numbers and the effect of number operations, as opposed to simply memorizing rules for performing particular types of computations.

For example, students might solve $49 + 99$ mentally by adding 100 to 49 and subtracting 1, but they might solve $123 + 34$ mentally by adding 30 to 123 and then another 4. Each time they are decomposing one of the addends in a different way.

Mental math and estimation strategies are also useful in everyday life. Sometimes we need to do a quick calculation without benefit of pencil or a calculator, and often an estimate is sufficient.

Selecting Tools and Computational Strategies

Many secondary school teachers complain that students reach for their calculators for even simple calculations like 20×30. Their concern is real. Calculators are useful tools, but students should be considering when a tool is appropriate to use. The same is true of other technology or physical models like manipulatives. We want students to make reasonable and considered decisions about what tool to use and when.

For example, it is useful to use base ten blocks to model 23×14 (see Chapter 8), but perhaps not to model 236×48. It is useful to use Cuisenaire rods to model $14 + 8$ (see Chapter 6), but not $139 + 52$. It is useful to use a calculator to calculate 389×420, but mental calculation is more appropriate for 30×2. It is useful to use a spreadsheet to perform a large number of calculations, particularly if the values might change, but not to perform a single addition of two numbers. Students learn how to make good choices by being exposed to options. They need to become familiar with possible tools, and then learn which are most efficient and when.

It is also important for students to learn that, for a particular computation, there are many possible approaches. Here, again, students need to know that there are choices and have experience in making those choices. For example, to multiply 50×84, it is reasonable to use the equivalent computation 100×42. This strategy of doubling and halving would be less useful for multiplying, for example 39×67. By exposing students to alternate algorithms, particularly mental math algorithms, students will have choices open to them.

Reflecting

Reflecting involves students looking back at their work or thinking to consider why the steps they took were useful ones, which steps were not useful, how the work they did relates to the concept they are trying to explore or the problem they are trying to solve, thinking about what made the work easy or difficult, or thinking about other situations to which the procedures or strategies they used might apply.

Reflecting can also involve listening to what others think and reflecting on how these alternate ideas relate or do not relate to students' own thinking about a situation.

Students should be encouraged to reflect regularly. This can be accomplished by asking questions such as

- Why was that a useful step?
- What would you have done differently if the number had been ...?
- Why was it important to include that example?
- Do you agree with ...? Why?

Although many adults think of learning mathematics as the learning of numerous individual topics, students who have developed process skills and who have a sense of what the important content concepts are have a definite edge in being successful in mathematics.

Assessing Student Understanding

- Make sure that you include items involving a variety of processes when assessing student understanding of a particular topic. For example, after a unit on multiplication, rather than giving a test that only involves computation, make sure to include items that require problem solving, communicating, reasoning, and representation, as well as other processes. For example, you might ask students in Grade 5 to explain why the model below is a good model to show 23 × 34.

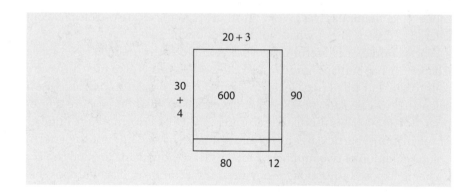

- Help students focus on key concepts by asking about them. For example, you may want to find out if students recognize that any shape can be decomposed into other shapes. You could ask a Grade 7 student this question:

    Show that you can combine two triangles to make any of these shapes:
    – another triangle, a parallelogram, a rectangle, a hexagon
    Would the same be possible with three triangles?

Applying What You've Learned

1. What key ideas in geometry did you call upon to solve the chapter problem at the start of the chapter?

2. How could knowing the key concepts in measurement help teachers organize their teaching of a Grade X measurement unit? (You can choose the grade.)

3. Provide two examples of topics taught in early grades (K–3), and two examples of topics taught in later grades (5–8) for each of the key concepts in number.

4. Select either the data strand or the geometry strand. Provide an example of an activity to elicit connections to other mathematical concepts, other subjects, or everyday experiences. Indicate why you think the activity elicits connections. Indicate if any of the activities you select are also likely to elicit other processes, which processes, and why.

5. Consider and discuss ways that multiple representations or visualization play a role in the teaching of fractions.

6. Give three or four examples of how students might use reasoning in working with patterns or algebra.

Interact with a K–8 Student:

7. Use one of the activities you created for question 4. Use that activity with a student and describe evidence you observed to show that the process you expected was elicited.

Discuss with a K–8 Teacher:

8. Ask a teacher what he or she knows about key concepts or big ideas, and how, or whether, he or she uses them in planning instruction.

9. Discuss with a teacher how he or she focuses on multiple representations or reasoning.

Selected References

Armstrong, T. (1999). *Seven kinds of smart: Identifying and developing your many intelligences.* New York: Plume.

Borko, H., and Putnam, R. (1995). Expanding a teacher's knowledge base: Cognitive psychological perspective on professional development. In Guskey, T., and Huberman, M. (Eds). *Professional development in education: New paradigms and practices.* New York: Teacher's College Press, 35–65.

Charles, R. (2004). Big ideas and understandings as the foundation for elementary and middle school mathematics. *Journal of Mathematics Education Leadership*, 7, 9–24.

Kennedy, M. (1997). *Defining optimal knowledge for teaching science and mathematics (Research Monograph 10).* Madison: National Institute for Science Education, University of Wisconsin.

National Council of Teachers of Mathematics. (2000). *Principles and standards for school mathematics.* Reston, VA: National Council of Teachers of Mathematics.

Schifter, D., Bastable, V., and Russell, S.I. (1997). Attention to mathematical thinking: Teaching to the big ideas. In Friel, S., and Bright, G. (Eds.). *Reflecting on our work: NSF teacher enhancement in mathematics K–6.* Washington, DC: University Press of America, 255–261.

Small, M. (2005a). *PRIME: Number and operations: Background and strategies.* Toronto: Thomson Nelson.

Small, M. (2005b). *PRIME: Patterns and algebra: Background and strategies.* Toronto: Thomson Nelson.

Small, M. (2006). *PRIME: Data management and probability: Background and strategies.* Toronto: Thomson Nelson.

Small, M. (2007). *PRIME: Geometry: Background and strategies.* Toronto: Thomson Nelson.

Small, M. (2009). *Professional resources and instruction for mathematics educators: Measurement.* Toronto: Thomson Nelson.

Chapter 3
Focus on Problem Solving

IN A NUTSHELL

The main ideas in the chapter are listed below:

1. Teaching through problem solving is the natural approach to teaching for those who believe that students learn best by confronting ideas that require them to establish new connections for themselves.

2. There is a set of problem-solving strategies, or approaches, that are often developed independently by children; it can be valuable to introduce these strategies explicitly.

3. Some problem-solving strategies are more natural to younger students than others, but those strategies continue to be valuable throughout those students' mathematical growth.

CHAPTER PROBLEM

Ian has 75¢ in quarters, dimes, and nickels.
He has at least one of each type of coin.
How many coins could he have?

Teaching through Problem Solving

To teach through problem solving, the teacher provides a context or reason for the learning by beginning the lesson with a problem to be solved and later drawing out any necessary procedures. This approach contrasts with the more traditional approach of presenting a new procedure and only then offering a few problems for students to solve.

Resnick (1987) points out that teaching in this way helps students become adaptable to new situations, for example, new work environments, in their later life. This is likely because students get much more opportunity to *mathematize* real-life situations.

Some of the ways teaching through problem solving differs from a traditional approach include

- an increased level of mathematical dialogue between students
- the teacher's role as a guide or coach more than as a presenter
- the teacher's more judicious use of intervention

A compelling discussion of the importance and efficacy of teaching through problem solving describes Lampert's year-long journey teaching Grade 5 mathematics through problem solving (Lampert, 2001).

Why Teach through Problem Solving?

There are many other reasons for teaching through problem solving:

1. *The math makes more sense.*
   When the problem is a "real life" one, students have the chance to build essential connections between what the math is, why it is needed, and how it is applied.
2. *A problem-solving approach provides the teacher with better insight into students' mathematical thinking.*
   A problem-solving approach provides the teacher with useful information to improve his or her mathematical interactions with students. The teacher is able to see how effectively students can reach into their "mathematical tool box" to choose the right tools, as well as see how effectively they can use those tools.
3. *Problems are more motivating when they are more of a challenge.*
   Although some students are comfortable with being told how to do something and then doing it over and over, many do not enjoy this approach. Most students prefer a manageable challenge.
4. *Problem solving builds perseverance.*
   Many students think that if they cannot answer a math question instantly, it is too hard. Through problem-solving experience, they build up a willingness to persevere at solving a problem.
5. *Problem solving builds confidence, maximizes the potential for understanding, and allows for differences in style and approach.*
   Problem solving allows each individual the opportunity to create his or her own path through the mathematics.
6. *Problems can provide practice, both with concepts and with skills.*
   Many good problems have the potential to ensure that students learn concepts and also have the opportunity to practise valuable skills.
7. *A problem-solving approach provides students with better insight into what mathematics is all about.*
   Math requires the same kind of struggle as does creating a new piece of writing or a new work of art. Most rich problems invite many

possible solution strategies, and some are even designed to encourage many possible answers. This notion of creativity or choice in mathematics will not make sense to someone who has not struggled on his or her own to try to solve a mathematical problem.

8. *Students need to practise problem solving.*

   If the goal of mathematics education is to enable students to confront new situations involving mathematics, then they must practise doing this. Students need many opportunities to practise problem solving to be able to do so independently.

The Inquiry Process

In many jurisdictions, it is expected that a significant part of the science and math curriculums be taught using an inquiry process to solve problems.

Stages of the Inquiry Process

A well-known inquiry model, developed by George Polya (1957), includes the following four stages:

> Stage 1: Understand the problem
> Stage 2: Make a plan
> Stage 3: Carry out the plan
> Stage 4: Look back

The understand-the-problem stage is often a stumbling block for students, as it involves discerning whether all the necessary information is provided and if extraneous information is included. It is important to provide sufficient support to ensure that students understand the problem.

The look-back stage involves checking to see if an answer is reasonable and, where applicable, determining another answer for the problem.

Each stage of the inquiry process involves a certain level of communication or reflection about the mathematics that is being used. Students should be sharing their thinking at all stages with their peers.

What the Inquiry Process Looks Like

The following section provides an example of what each of these stages of the process might look like using the problem-solving strategy of drawing a picture. The example on the next page demonstrates how students can increase their understanding of a problem as they work through the solution.

Providing Experiences in the Inquiry Process

By seeing a teacher and fellow students model these approaches, students become more comfortable with the problem-solving process. Students also learn to be good problem solvers by

- having many opportunities to solve many kinds of appropriate and rich problems
- having a good sense of what is involved in the inquiry process
- being exposed to and learning to use a variety of problem-solving strategies that have proven to be fruitful when working through new situations
- being encouraged to think about and talk about how they solve problems (meta-cognitive activity)
- working with others as they solve problems
- creating their own problems

A Problem and Possible Solution

STAGE 1: UNDERSTAND THE PROBLEM	STAGE 2: MAKE A PLAN

A group of children wore boots to school. Some of them wore mittens. The teacher counted 12 boots and 8 mittens. How many children did not wear mittens?

> There are 12 boots and 8 mittens. Every child is wearing 2 boots. Every child wearing mittens has 2 mittens.

> If we figure out how many more boots there are than mittens, we can figure out how many children that would be.

> Let's draw a picture to see how many extra boots there are. Then we can figure out how many children that would be.

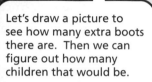

STAGE 3: CARRY OUT THE PLAN	STAGE 4: LOOK BACK

> There are 4 extra boots, but it's only 2 extra children.

> The answer makes sense because if there were 6 children with boots, that's 6 + 6 = 12 boots altogether. If there were 2 children without mittens, that's 4 + 4 = 8 mittens altogether.

Characteristics of Good Problems

A significant part of a teacher's role is creating good problems. A good problem always requires a student to think about mathematics in a slightly different way, but, in addition, it could have any of the following characteristics. The problem

- requires a student to connect new ideas to previously learned ones
- can be solved many ways, often using different problem-solving strategies
- has many possible answers
- piques curiosity
- has personal meaning or relevance to a student
- has a creative element to it

The problem may have a real-life context, or it may be an interesting mathematical situation.

Techniques for Creating Good Problems

TECHNIQUE	EXAMPLES
The "use-blanks" technique, for which you create a question with some of the numbers missing	• Put the digits 1, 2, 3, 4, and 5 in the boxes ▢▢▢ − ▢▢. What are the least and greatest possible answers? [531, 69] • How would you place the digits 6, 7, and 8 in the boxes ▢.▢ × 0.▢ so that the product is as close to 5 as possible? [8.7 × 0.6 = 5.22] • How many pairs of digits can be put in the blanks so that the answer to 6▢ ÷ ▢ is a whole number? [29]
The "what if ..." technique, for which you create a situation that is based on a particular set of assumptions, and then challenge one of the premises by posing a new question	• 35 + 5 × 8 = 75 because of the order-of-operation rules. What if the rule were to add and subtract before you multiply and divide? What would the expression be worth? [320]
The "turn-it-around" technique, in which you give students the answer and ask them to work backward	• Describe three different pairs of numbers with a common factor of 6. [e.g., 12, 18; 60, 24; 600, 300] • The answer is 45. What's the question? [e.g., 9 × 5 or 135 ÷ 3] • Write three additions with the same sum as 45 + 38. [e.g., 46 + 37, 35 + 48, 25 + 58]

Problem-Solving Strategies

Mathematics educators have identified a list of problem-solving strategies that have proven to be useful in approaching a wide variety of problems. The strategies are described over the next several pages.

It is important to understand that the strategy should be explicitly discussed with students, preferably after it comes up naturally because a student has chosen to use it. There is value in naming the strategies and keeping a strategy list posted, so students can discuss the strategies and use them again and again. The list becomes a menu for students to select from when they face a new problem and are not sure how to proceed.

PROBLEM STRATEGY

<u>Problem-Solving
Strategy Menu</u>

- Act it out.
- Use a model.
- Draw a picture.
- Guess and test.
- Look for a pattern.
- Use an open sentence.
- Make a chart/table or graph.
- Solve a simpler problem.
- Consider all possibilities.
- Consider extreme cases.
- Make an organized list.
- Work backward.
- Use logical reasoning.
- Change your point of view.

Students should also be encouraged to combine strategies that suit particular problems when necessary. For example, a student might use a chart or table to look for a number pattern.

Students also need to recognize that different strategies can be used at different stages of the inquiry process. For example, a student might draw a picture to understand a problem, and then use another strategy to carry out the solution.

Simpler Problem-Solving Strategies

Everyone benefits from learning through their senses, and this is particularly important for students at a young age. Thus, the act-it-out, use-a-model, and draw-a-picture strategies are particularly suited to young students. Students at this level are often more open than older students to taking risks; for this reason, the guess-and-test strategy is also suitable. These simple strategies continue to be useful to older students and adults as well.

STRATEGY

Act it out
Students literally "act out" the story of the problem. Sometimes the story is very straightforward, and other times more complex.

SAMPLE PROBLEM

There are 4 students on each of 2 teams. At the end of the tournament, students shake hands with members of the other team. How many handshakes will there be?

POSSIBLE SOLUTION

Students might act out the problem in a systematic fashion:

Two teams of 4 students line up across from each other. Each student shakes hands with each student on the other team, beginning with the first student on the other team and shaking everyone's hand on the other team in order from left to right. Someone keeps track of the number of handshakes. There are 16 handshakes.

STRATEGY

Use a model
This strategy can be very much like the act-it-out strategy, but students model the problem by representing its elements with simple, available materials.

SAMPLE PROBLEM

A company that makes bread sticks has hired you to design their new logo. They want the logo to show 8 bread sticks arranged to make the outline of a polygon. What different polygons can you make with 8 bread sticks?

POSSIBLE SOLUTION

A student might use toothpicks to represent the breadsticks to model the problem. Notice that this student has also approached the problem in a systematic way.

"I used 8 toothpicks. I know I can make an octagon because it has 8 sides."

"I need at least 3 sides to make a polygon. This is the only triangle I can make."

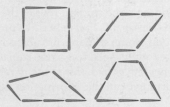

"Here are some quadrilaterals."

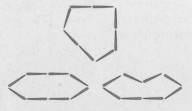

"Here are some with 5, 6, and 7 sides. I already made one with 8 sides and I know 9 sides is impossible."

"I know I can make a triangle, lots of quadrilaterals, a 5-sided shape, a hexagon, a 7-sided shape, and an octagon."

STRATEGY

Draw a picture
This strategy is much like the use-a-model strategy, but students use a pictorial model, rather than a concrete model. Students can draw the actual object or a simple symbol to represent the object.

SAMPLE PROBLEM	POSSIBLE SOLUTION
It was getting close to the school raffle. Ann's mother knitted 2 mittens on Monday and 2 more than the day before each day after. On what day did she knit 16 mittens?	A student might use a calendar as a graphic organizer:

Sunday	Monday	Tuesday	Wednesday	Thursday	Friday	Saturday

On Monday there were 16 mittens.

STRATEGY

Guess and test
For this strategy, a student guesses an answer and then tests it to see if the guess works. If it doesn't, the student revises the "guess" based on what was learned and tries again. This repetitive process continues until the answer is found. Some students are able to think through several guesses at once; others need to go one step at a time. Although we often talk about guessing as bad, this strategy reinforces the value of taking risks and learning from the information that is garnered.

SAMPLE PROBLEM	POSSIBLE SOLUTION
There are 8 more girls than boys in a room. Altogether, there are 24 people. How many are boys?	A student might guess and test several times, each time basing the guess on the results of the previous guess:

5 boys and 13 girls is 18 people   not enough people
10 boys and 18 girls is 28 people   too many people
7 boys and 15 girls is 22 people   not enough people
8 boys and 16 girls is 24 people
There are 8 boys.

Emergent Strategies

As they mature mathematically, students use a broader range of patterns as a tool for learning. Therefore, it is appropriate to introduce a pattern strategy to these students. This strategy continues to be useful to students as they move up the grades.

Look for a pattern
Because mathematics is so full of patterns, students soon learn
that using patterns is an effective way to solve problems.

SAMPLE PROBLEM	POSSIBLE SOLUTION

How many cans do you need to make the sixth stack in this shape pattern?

A student could draw a picture (or use a counter model) to figure out the number of cans in the fourth stack in order to be sure about the pattern and then use the pattern to figure out the number in the sixth stack.

1st   2nd   3rd   4th

There's 1 in the 1st stack, 1+2 in the 2nd stack, 1+2+3 in the 3rd stack, and 1+2+3+4 in the 4th stack. That means that there would be 1+2+3+4+5+6 in the 6th stack.

1+2+3+4+5+6=21   There are 21 in the 6th stack.

1st   2nd   3rd

As students become more familiar with the formal symbolism of mathematics, they are more likely to solve problems using open sentences. They are also more ready to deal with strategies requiring organized thinking, such as using charts/tables and graphs.

STRATEGY

Use an open sentence
As students become more comfortable with the symbolic forms of mathematical expressions, they can begin to model a problem with an open sentence. Some mathematics educators might argue that this is simply another form of the use-a-model strategy, but this time the model is mathematical rather than pictorial or concrete.

SAMPLE PROBLEM	POSSIBLE SOLUTION

An egg has a mass of about 50 g and an empty 12-egg carton has a mass of about 25 g. Jaden is carrying some cartons of eggs. The total mass is 5 kg. How many cartons is he carrying?

A student might determine which operation is needed to solve the problem by writing an open sentence that describes the problem situation.

(continued)

The eggs in one carton have a mass of
12 × 50g = 600g. The carton is 25g.
So, a full carton is 625g.

I have to find out how many groups of 625g are in 5kg or 5000g. I can write a multiplication sentence to find out

$$\square \times 625 = 5000$$

If $\square$ × 625 = 5000, then I can divide 5000 by 625 to figure out what $\square$ is. I'll use a calculator.

$$5000 \div 625 = \square$$

5000 ÷ 625 = 8, so 8 × 625 = 5000

Jaden is carrying 8 cartons of eggs.

STRATEGY

Make a chart/table or graph
Sometimes it is useful to organize data in a chart/table or a graph.
This helps students keep track of disparate pieces of information and
helps them ensure that they consider many possibilities.

SAMPLE PROBLEM

Suppose you spin each spinner
below and add the two numbers
you spin. Which is more likely?

• The sum will be less than 9.
• The sum will be greater than 9.

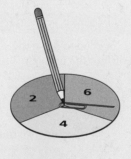

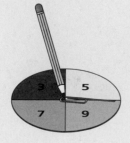

POSSIBLE SOLUTION

A student might conduct a spinner experiment and shade a bar graph on
grid paper to keep track of and show the results.

I started a graph with the two outcomes.
I spun the two spinners 10 times and shaded a
square each time for the sum. Sometimes the
sum was exactly 9 but I didn't need to keep
track of those sums.
A sum >9 is more likely than a sum <9.

<9
>9

STRATEGY

Solve a simpler problem
Sometimes the path through a problem is easier if the numbers are more accessible, or simpler.

SAMPLE PROBLEM	POSSIBLE SOLUTION
Norah has 3 dimes and 9 nickels. How much money does she have?	A student might begin with a simpler problem: If it were 3 dimes and 3 nickels, it would be $30¢ + 15¢ = 45¢$. But there are 6 more nickels, which is 3 dimes, or $30¢$. The money is worth $45¢ + 30¢ = 75¢$.

More Complex Problem-Solving Strategies

As students develop even more analytic skills, they are able to use organizational strategies more formally to ensure that no case is omitted. These students are also more ready to use logical reasoning and to work either forward or backward.

STRATEGY

Make an organized list
To use this strategy, a student must realize that there are many "cases," or possible answers. By being systematic in listing the cases, this student is less likely to leave something out and may, in fact, be able to "shortcut" the work. Students must learn to look through the list and eliminate any redundancy.

SAMPLE PROBLEM	POSSIBLE SOLUTION
How many different products are possible when you multiply the numbers on two dice?	A student might use an organized list to approach the problem systematically: Make a list, starting with $\times 1$, then $\times 2$ and $\times 3$, and so on. Check to make sure nothing was missed. Cross off any products that are the same. Count the products that are left.

$$
\begin{array}{cccccc}
1 \times 1 = 1 & \cancel{2 \times 1 = 2} & \cancel{3 \times 1 = 3} & \cancel{4 \times 1 = 4} & \cancel{5 \times 1 = 5} & \cancel{6 \times 1 = 6} \\
1 \times 2 = 2 & \cancel{2 \times 2 = 4} & \cancel{3 \times 2 = 6} & \cancel{4 \times 2 = 8} & \cancel{5 \times 2 = 10} & \cancel{6 \times 2 = 12} \\
1 \times 3 = 3 & \cancel{2 \times 3 = 6} & 3 \times 3 = 9 & \cancel{4 \times 3 = 12} & \cancel{5 \times 3 = 15} & \cancel{6 \times 3 = 18} \\
1 \times 4 = 4 & 2 \times 4 = 8 & \cancel{2 \times 4 = 12} & 4 \times 4 = 16 & \cancel{5 \times 4 = 20} & \cancel{6 \times 4 = 24} \\
1 \times 5 = 5 & 2 \times 5 = 10 & 3 \times 5 = 15 & 4 \times 5 = 20 & 5 \times 5 = 25 & \cancel{6 \times 5 = 30} \\
1 \times 6 = 6 & 2 \times 6 = 12 & 3 \times 6 = 18 & 4 \times 6 = 24 & 5 \times 6 = 30 & 6 \times 6 = 36 \\
6 & 3 & 3 & 3 & 2 & 1
\end{array}
$$

There are 18 different products.

STRATEGY

Consider all possibilities

In many mathematical situations, students must consider a number of different possibilities to ensure that all aspects of the problem are dealt with.

SAMPLE PROBLEM

A set of five data values, all whole numbers up to 10, has a mode of 8, a median of 8, and a mean of 8. There are more than two 8s in the set. What could the data values be? Find as many answers as you can.

POSSIBLE SOLUTION

A student could create and test all the possibilities to see if they follow the clues provided in the problem:

• There are five values.

• There are three, four, or five 8s.

• The mean is 8, so the sum of the values is 40 (5 × 8).

• The mode and median are both 8.

• The greatest value is 10 or less.

Five 8s: 8, 8, 8, 8, 8. This works.

Four 8s: 8, 8, 8, 8, ___   or   ___ 8, 8, 8, 8.
The missing number has to be 8 for the sum of 40.
Four 8s doesn't work.

Three 8s: 8, 8, 8, ___, ___ there's an 8 in the middle
for the median to be 8.) The last 2 numbers have to add
to 16 for a mean of 8. You can't make 16 with 9s and 10s.

Three 8s another way ___, ___, 8, 8, 8.
You can't make 16 with 2 numbers less than 8.

Three 8s another way: ___, 8, 8, 8 ___.
Two ways work: 6, 8, 8, 8, 10 and 7, 8, 8, 8, 9.

There has to be more than two 8s, so there are no
more answers.

The numbers are: 8, 8, 8, 8, 8. or 6, 8, 8, 8, 10.
or 7, 8, 8, 8, 10.

STRATEGY

Consider extreme cases

Sometimes students can solve problems related to a range of values.
This is a special case of considering all possibilities.

SAMPLE PROBLEM	POSSIBLE SOLUTION

You divide a 3-digit number by a 1-digit number and get a whole number quotient. How many digits can the quotient have?

A student might consider the greatest and least possible answers:

Divide the greatest 3-digit dividend by the least 1-digit divisor for the greatest quotient.

Divide the least 3-digit dividend by the greatest 1-digit divisor for the least quotient.

$$999 \div 1 = 999$$
$$100 \div 9 = 11 + R1$$

The quotient can have 2 or 3 digits.

STRATEGY

Use logical reasoning

Some people think of logical reasoning not so much as a problem-solving strategy, but as an aspect of mathematics that permeates all mathematical endeavours. However, others think of it as a strategy that is worthwhile to explicitly consider when faced with a mathematical problem.

SAMPLE PROBLEM	POSSIBLE SOLUTION

Jonathan writes his name, one letter per box, in a square 4-by-4 grid.

J	O	N	A
T	H	A	N
J	O	N	A
T	H	A	N

What size square grid is needed for the J to be in the bottom right corner?

To solve the problem, a student might reason:

The name Jonathan has 8 letters. 16 squares were needed to put the last N in the bottom right corner because 16 is a multiple of 8 and a square number (16 squares can form a square grid).

The number of squares must be a square number. To put the letter J in the bottom right corner, it must also be a multiple of 8 plus 1 more.

A square number that is 1 more than a multiple of 8 is 25 (5 x 5 is 3 x 8 + 1), so the grid could be 5 by 5.

There are other answers too.

49 (7 x 7 is 6 x 8 + 1), so the grid could be 7 by 7
81 (9 x 9 is 10 x 8 + 1), so the grid could be 9 by 9

STRATEGY

Work backward
Sometimes, by starting with the result, a student can work backward to determine information about the original situation.

SAMPLE PROBLEM	POSSIBLE SOLUTION

Aaron cut 0.5 m from a length of wire. Then he cut what was left into four equal pieces. If each of the four pieces was 1.25 m long, what was the length of the wire before Aaron cut it?

A student could work backward by determining the sum of the four equal lengths cut from the original piece of wire and then adding the 0.5 m length back on.

These are 4 pieces that are 1.25m long.
4 × 1.25 = 5

Aaron also has the 0.5m piece he cut first.
5 + 0.5 = 5.5

Before Aaron cut it, the wire was 5.5m long.

STRATEGY

Change your point of view
Sometimes, students are asked to calculate how many of something there are. In some cases, however, a better approach might be to calculate how many there are not.

SAMPLE PROBLEM	POSSIBLE SOLUTION

What is the probability that, when you roll two dice, you will get a sum that is the result of adding two different numbers?

A student might determine the theoretical probability of getting a sum that is the result of doubles, and then use this to determine the probability of getting a sum that is the result of non-doubles (that is, two different numbers).

There are a lot more ways to get sums from different numbers than from doubles.
I made an addition table to find the total number of sums and the number of sums from doubles.

Possible Sums for 2 Dice

+	1	2	3	4	5	6
1	(2)	3	4	5	6	7
2	3	(4)	5	6	7	8
3	4	5	(6)	7	8	9
4	5	6	7	(8)	9	10
5	6	7	8	9	(10)	11
6	7	8	9	10	11	(12)

There is a total of 36 sums. The 6 circled ones are from doubles. So 30 are not from doubles.

The probability of a sum from 2 different numbers is $\frac{30}{36}$.

Suitable Problems

Below you will find an assortment of problems selected so that the content is appropriate for students at a particular developmental level, using strategies suitable for that level. Recall that a problem is meant to "stretch" students, so these examples might be just beyond where the students are developmentally.

Many problems can be adjusted to make them more suitable for another developmental level by changing a few specific features. For example, a problem which requires students to put together two concrete triangles to make another shape can evolve, for more advanced students, into a problem where they must list all possible shapes that can be created, or where they are asked to determine how many congruent triangles can be combined to make a similar triangle.

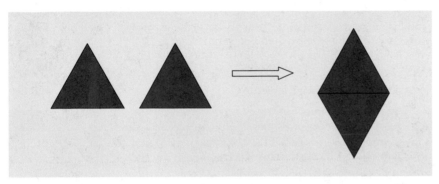

Problems for Early Elementary Students

EATING COOKIES

Three children eat 12 cookies.

Mei eats more cookies than Han.

Han eats more than Kiri.

The three of them eat all of the cookies. How many cookies did Kiri eat?

[**Possible Strategy:** Draw a picture;
Hint: Students could start by drawing 12 cookies, and then share them among the 3 children according to the clues given in the problem.]   [3]

PENNY SALE

You have 10¢ to buy school supplies.

An eraser costs 2¢; a pencil costs 3¢; and a paper clip costs 1¢.

a) What items can you buy?

b) Can you buy exactly 6 items and use all of your money?

[**Possible Strategy:** Act it out;
Hint: Students can use 10 play pennies to act out the problem. For b), students could start with 6 paper clips and trade up for more expensive items until 10 pennies have been spent.]   [e.g., a) 5 erasers;
3 erasers, a pencil, and a paper clip;
8 paper clips and an eraser;
b) yes, 4 paper clips and 2 pencils]

DRAWING TRIANGLES

The pattern below continues until there are 10 triangles altogether. How many shapes are there in the pattern?

[**Possible Strategy:** Draw a picture.]

[14]

MAKING SNOWMEN

You are making snowmen. Each snowman is made with 2 circles and 4 buttons.

You have 15 circles and 25 buttons. What is the greatest number of complete snowmen you can make?

[**Possible Strategy:** Draw a picture.]

[6]

DO YOU LIKE SPAGHETTI?

I asked students in my class if they like spaghetti. 5 said "no" and 10 more than that said "yes." How many students are in my class?

[**Possible Strategy:** Act it out or Use a model;
Hint: Students line up 5 red counters to represent the people who said "no," and then add 10 more.]

[20 students]

SHAPE HUNT

A block has some triangle faces and some faces that are not triangles. Find the block in the pile.

[**Possible Strategy:** Guess and test]

[triangle-based prism]

FILL IT IN

Show three different ways to cover this shape with pattern blocks.

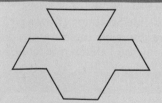

[**Possible Strategy:** Guess and test and Act it out.]

[e.g., ]

Problems for Mid-Level Elementary Students

PACKAGES OF PENS

Pens come in packages of 3, 5, and 8.

Mrs. O'Regan bought 26 pens for her class.

How many packages of each type might she have bought?

[**Possible Strategy:** Act it out;
Hint: Students can use 26 pens, or counters, to represent the
pens and try different groupings of 3, 5, and 8.]   [e.g., 2 packages of 5 and
2 packages of 8]

DART ADDITION

Leah must throw at least 4 darts to get a
score of 100.

a) What is the least score she can get with
   4 darts?

b) How could she get a score of 90 with
   4 darts?

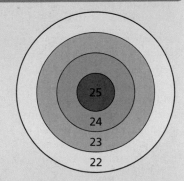

[**Possible Strategy:** Make a chart/table;
Hint: Students can make a chart to show the totals if all of the darts land in
the same ring. They notice that a score of 90 occurs between the scores for
four darts in the 22 ring and four darts in the 23 ring.]   [a) 88; b) e.g., 22,
22, 23, and 23]

WHAT'S THE DATE?

What is the date of the 100th day of a non–leap year?

[**Possible Strategy:** Make a chart;
Hint: Use a chart to show the number of days in each month in one
column, and a running total in a second column. Count the number
of days in the first 3 months: 31 + 28 + 31 = 90. You need 10 more
days into the 4th month.]   [April 10]

ADDING NUMBERS

Add the first 100 numbers (starting with 1). What digit is in the ones
place of the sum?

[**Possible Strategy:** Solve a simpler problem and Look for a pattern;
Hint: Try some simpler problems like 1 + 2 + 3 + 4 and 1 + 2 + 3 + 4
+ 5 + 6 to note the pattern. Then, look for the same pattern in 1 + 2 + 3
+ 4 + ··· + 97 + 98 + 99 + 100. Match up addends at either end: 100 + 1,
then 99 + 2, then 98 + 3, and so on. A pattern emerges of 50 pairs, each
with a sum of 101. 50 × 101 = 5050.]   [0]

FRUITS AND VEGETABLES

The pictograph shows the number of students who eat different numbers of servings of fruits and vegetables each day. 108 students were surveyed. How many students does each symbol represent?

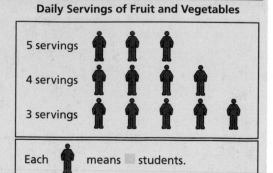

Daily Servings of Fruit and Vegetables

[**Possible Strategy:** Use an open sentence;
Hint: 12 × ■ = 108]

[9]

BALANCING ACT

Jenny had some loaves of bread, some cans of soup, and some boxes of cereal. She put one can of soup into the bag, and then added more items. When she was done, the total mass was between 900 g and 1 kg. What could be in the bag? Find as many different answers as you can.

[**Possible Strategy:** Use an open sentence;
Hint: To find the least and greatest possible combined mass of the other items, students might use open sentences: 105 g + ■ = 900 g and 105 g + ■ = 1000 g.

Once they determine that the other items are between 795 g and 895 g, they can look for combinations with this mass.]

[e.g., 9 soups;
1 loaf of bread and 4 soups;
2 cereals and 1 soup;
1 cereal and 5 soups]

MISSING MEASURES

How long is the red side of this shape? the green side?

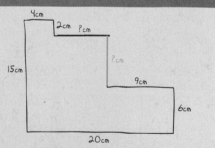

[**Possible Strategies:** Draw a picture (e.g., on grid paper) or Use an open sentence; **Hint:** To solve the problem with an open sentence, students need to recognize that the vertical sides on the right must have a total length of 15 cm, because they cover the same vertical distance as the 15-cm side on the left. The horizontal sides across the top must have a total length of 20 cm to match the bottom side.]

[Both are 7 cm.]

SQUARE CORNER DOTS

These two points are the corners of a square.

Draw two squares with these corners.

[**Possible Strategy:** Draw a picture;
Hint: Turn the paper and look at the dots from other perspectives.]

[e.g., 2 of these

]

Problems for Upper Elementary and Middle School Students

MULTIPLYING DOUBLES

A 2-digit number is multiplied by its double. The product is 5618. What is the number?

[**Possible Strategy:** Guess and test;
Hint: Students try a number, and increase or decrease as appropriate.] [53]

SWITCHING DIGITS

The digits of a 2-digit number are switched around to form a different 2-digit number. The new number is 27 less than the original number. What is the least the original number could be?

[**Possible Strategy:** Use logical reasoning;
Hint: Students reason that if the digits are switched and the difference is 27, the digits are probably 3 apart.]   [e.g., 41]

PERIMETER PAIRS

Two rectangles have the same perimeter, but the area of one is 6 cm^2 greater than the area of the other. What could their side lengths be, if the side lengths are whole number values?

[**Possible Strategy:** Guess and test or Work backward;
Hint: Students can look for two basic-fact products that are 6 apart, such as $5 \times 6 = 30$ and $6 \times 6 = 36$, for the possible areas of the two rectangles, and then use the perimeter formula to see if their perimeters are the same.]   [e.g., 2×9 and 3×8; 5×6 and 3×8; 6×7 and 9×4]

CLOSED DOORS

A set of doors marked from 1 to 100 are all open. 100 students walk by the doors, one at a time, and open and close the doors as described below:

The 1st student closes all the doors. The 2nd student opens every 2nd door.

The 3rd student changes every 3rd door by closing opened ones and opening closed ones.

The 4th student changes every 4th door.

This continues until all 100 students are done. How many doors are closed at the end?

[**Possible Strategies:** Solve a simpler problem, Draw a picture, and Look for a pattern;
Hint: Try 20 doors. Use O to represent an open door and C to represent a closed one. Show each step until a pattern emerges:

Start: OOOOOOOOOOOOOOOOOOOO. ...

After 1st: CCCCCCCCCCCCCCCCCCCC. ...

After 2nd: COCOCOCOCOCOCOCOCOCO. ...

After 3rd: COOOCCCOOOCCCOOOCCCO. ...

The pattern emerges after the 11th student that the closed doors occur at 1, 4, 9, 16, ... , the square numbers.]   [10]

WHAT'S THE FIRST NUMBER?

In a certain pattern, you add two numbers to get the next number. If the 9th number is 212 and the 10th number is 343, what is the first number?

[**Possible Strategy:** Use an open sentence and Work backward;
Hint: 10th term = 9th term + 8th term, so 343 = 212 + ▢ and the 8th term is 131; 9th term = 8th term + 7th term, so 212 = 131 + ▢ and the 7th term is 81; repeat over and over.]   [5]

ROLLING PRODUCTS

Two players each roll a die. Player A wins if the product of the numbers is even. Player B wins if the product is odd. If they roll 20 times, how often is Player A likely to win?

[**Possible Strategy:** Conduct an experiment or Make a chart/table or graph;
Hint: Students make a multiplication table to determine that there are 36 possible products, and that 27 are even. They use the theoretical probability $\frac{27}{36} = \frac{3}{4}$ to calculate the number of even products for 20 rolls.]   [15 times]

NO SQUARES ALLOWED

You can draw lots of different squares by using the dots in this design as vertices. What is the least number of dots you would have to get rid of so that no squares can be made?

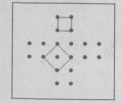

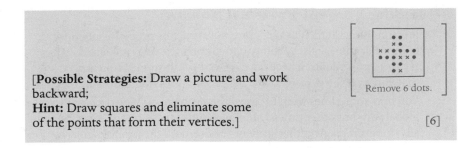

[**Possible Strategies:** Draw a picture and work backward;
Hint: Draw squares and eliminate some
of the points that form their vertices.]

Remove 6 dots.

[6]

Helpful Hints for Problem Solving

Aside from the strategies already discussed, which are mathematically focused, there are some generic helpful hints, or strategies, that students should consider when working on mathematical problems. These can be posted on a classroom wall.

<u>Helpful Hints for Problem Solving</u>

If you're stuck ...
- Take a deep breath and relax.
- Brainstorm: Write down everything you can think of about the problem.
- Highlight important parts of the question.
- Draw a picture of the problem, if possible.
- Model the problem using any materials you have, if possible.
- Talk yourself through the problem.
- Think about other problems you've solved that are like this one.
- Look at the strategy list. Decide which one to try first.
- Talk about the problem with another student.
- Convince yourself you can do it!

Sources for Other Problems

A wealth of mathematics problems is available from other sources:

The Internet provides a number of possibilities. One particularly valuable site is the Math Forum's Problems of the Week. Another is a site set up at St. Francis Xavier University in Nova Scotia for Grades 5 to 8 math problems.

Many textbooks designed for elementary-school-aged children are a source of good problems. Many of these problems can be modified to suit different developmental phases and to create other problems.

In addition, a number of print resources offer excellent math problems. Some of these are listed below:

Math League Contest Books
101 Brain-Boosting Math Problems
Awesome Math Problems for Creative Thinking series
Mathcounts handbooks

Assessing Student Problem Solving

- It is sometimes difficult to separate out students' problem-solving and communication skills. When you focus on assessing problem solving, try to assist students, if necessary, with the communication aspect, so that you gain better insight into the problem-solving processes they use.

- You may sometimes want to assess the problem-solving process in a global way, but other times you may want to focus on the steps individually; for example, whether students understand the problem may be considered apart from their development of a plan or the plan's execution.

- It is helpful to share in advance with students the assessment tools you will use. This helps students know what to focus on. Most of the time, a rubric with a set of four categories is used for measuring problem-solving performance.

(More on assessing student problem solving is discussed in Chapter 21.)

Applying What You've Learned

1. Which of the problem-solving strategies presented in this chapter would have helped you solve the chapter problem? Explain why these strategies would be useful.

2. Many people argue that problem solving should be a focus for high-ability students, but not for students who are struggling. Make an argument for why problem solving might be even more important for a struggling student.

3. Some teachers are uncomfortable with the guess-and-test strategy. They are concerned that students should not be encouraged to guess. Make an argument for why this is a valid and helpful strategy for solving math problems.

4. Locate and read a journal article that focuses on the notion of teaching through problem solving. List one or two of the most important points made in that article.

5. One of the elements of the inquiry process is the look-back step. Many students skip that step. How might you convince a student of the importance of this aspect of the problem-solving process?

6. Visit an Internet site that includes math contest problems or problems of the week. Create a small resource file of 20 rich problems that you might use with students at a grade level of your choice.

7. Explore several issues of one of the National Council of Teachers of Mathematics journals. What proportion of the journal seems to be devoted to problem solving in the mathematics classroom? Does this proportion seem reasonable to you?

Interact with a K–8 Student:

8. Choose one of your problems from Question 6. Observe how a student of an appropriate grade level for that problem solves it. What do you notice about the approach the student uses?

Discuss with a K–8 Teacher:

9. Ask a teacher how or whether she or he explicitly discusses the common problem-solving strategies with students and why she or he uses the approach they do.

10. Ask the teacher how often she or he assigns problems for student exploration, for example, problems of the day or problems of the week.

WebConnect

www.makingmathmeaningful
.nelson.com

Visit Nelson's Making Math Meaningful Website to find links to problems you might use with your students.

Selected References

Buschmann, L. (2003). Children who enjoy problem solving. *Teaching Children Mathematics, 9*, 539–544.

Buschmann, L. (2004). Teaching problem solving in mathematics. *Teaching Children Mathematics, 10*, 302–309.

Chandler, K. (Ed.). (2004). *2004–2005 Mathcounts school handbook*. Alexandria, VA: Mathcounts Foundation.

Conrad, S.R., and Fleger, D. (1996). *Math contests (grades 4, 5, and 6)*. (Vols. 1–4). Tenafly, NJ: Mathematics Leagues.

Egan, L.H. (1999). *101 brain-boosting math problems (grades 4 8)*. New York: Scholastic.

Findell, C., Gavin, K., Greenes, C., and Sheffield, L. (2000). *Awesome math problems for creative thinking, grades 3–8*. Chicago: Creative Publications.

Kalman, R. (2004). The value of multiple solutions. *Mathematics Teaching in the Middle School, 10*, 174–179.

Lampert, M. (2001). *Teaching problems and the problems of teaching*. New Haven, CT: Yale University Press.

Lester, F. (2003). *Teaching mathematics through problem solving: Prekindergarten–grade 6*. Reston, VA: National Council of Teachers of Mathematics.

O'Connell, S. (2000). *Introduction to problem solving: Strategies for the elementary math classroom*. Portsmouth, NH: Heinemann.

Polya, G. (1957). *How to solve it: A new aspect of mathematical method* (2nd ed.). Princeton, NJ: Princeton University Press.

Resnick, L. (1987). Learning in school and out. *Educational Researcher, 16*, 13–20.

Small, M. (2005a). *PRIME: Number and operations: Background and strategies*. Toronto: Thomson Nelson.

Small, M. (2005b). *PRIME: Patterns and algebra: Background and strategies*. Toronto: Thomson Nelson.

Small, M. (2006). *PRIME: Data and probability: Background and strategies*. Toronto: Thomson Nelson.

Small, M. (2007). *PRIME: Geometry: Background and strategies*. Toronto: Thomson Nelson.

Walter, M.I., and Brown, S.I. (1993). *Problem posing: Reflections and applications*. Hillsdale, NJ: Lawrence Erlbaum Associates.

Chapter 4
Focus on Communication

IN A NUTSHELL

The main ideas in the chapter are listed below:

1. Communication in mathematics, whether silent self-talk or communication with peers or a teacher, is essential to students as they learn; it is also a critical assessment tool for teachers.

2. There are many forms of mathematical communication, including oral, written, physical, and symbolic communication. A variety of types of communication should be encouraged.

CHAPTER PROBLEM

10 more families shop at Store E than Store C. How many families shop at Store A?

Where We Shop

Store A

Store B

Store C

Store D

Store E

Number of families

The Importance of Mathematical Communication

The National Council of Teachers of Mathematics (NCTM) has recognized the importance of mathematical communication in their document *Principles and Standards for School Mathematics* (2000) by creating a communication standard to help shape mathematics programs.

Facilitating effective communication requires time, changes teachers' expectations of students, and changes the nature and variety of assessments used. Therefore, the emphasis on communication in mathematics determines, to some extent, the nature of instructional activities.

THE NCTM COMMUNICATION STANDARD

Instructional programs from Pre-Kindergarten through Grade 12 should enable all students to

- organize and consolidate their mathematical thinking through communication
- communicate their mathematical thinking coherently and clearly to peers, teachers, and others
- analyze and evaluate the mathematical thinking and strategies of others
- use the language of mathematics to express mathematical ideas precisely

(NCTM, 2000)

Forms of Communication

Communication can take various forms in the mathematics classroom:

- oral communication (speaking and listening)
- written communication (reading and writing)
- symbolic, graphical, or pictorial communication
- physical communication through active involvement with manipulative materials

Oral versus Written Communication

Many people use different language to talk about math than they use to write about it. When you talk, you are much more likely to say, "2 and 3 are 5"; when you write, you are much more likely to record, "$2 + 3 = 5$." Written communication has elements of formality and symbolism that are not present in oral communication, and this causes difficulty for some students.

Oral Communication

There are four main types of oral communication in mathematics classrooms:

- teacher with student (or with small group)
- teacher with whole class
- peer talk
- self-talk

Self-talk is a metacognitive activity. Whether they speak silently or out loud, many people talk to themselves to clarify their thinking as they work through difficult problems or situations. This explicit self-talk is then accessible for use in future situations. The National Council of Teachers of Mathematics' *Principles and Standards* document (2000) points out that problem-solving failure is often tied to students' inability to call on what they already know.

Metacognitive behaviour is often learned through teacher modelling and questioning. A teacher should show how she or he thinks through a problem using self-talk. A teacher can also ask questions that promote metacognition, such as, "Do you have a plan?" and "Why do you think this?"

Purposeful oral communication allows for genuine student contribution; short responses to very narrow questions are much less valuable for developing communication skills. With younger students, communication is primarily oral with some written recording. With older elementary students, communication is more mixed, and usually includes more symbolic communication as well.

Why Peer Discussion Is Important

Abundant evidence points to the benefits of student discussion about mathematical ideas. We know that students can use "talking time" with peers to help one another

- understand a mathematical situation: "I don't get it. Do you, Megan?"
- work through a problem: "No, I think you should do this next."
- clarify their thinking: "Okay. Let me show you what I mean."
- reflect on their own learning: "Why did I think it was hard? I'll show you what I was thinking."

Fostering Oral Communication

In order to promote student or peer talk, teachers need to learn to listen. To encourage more elaborate responses from students, teachers should encourage group discussion of mathematical concepts, allow more wait

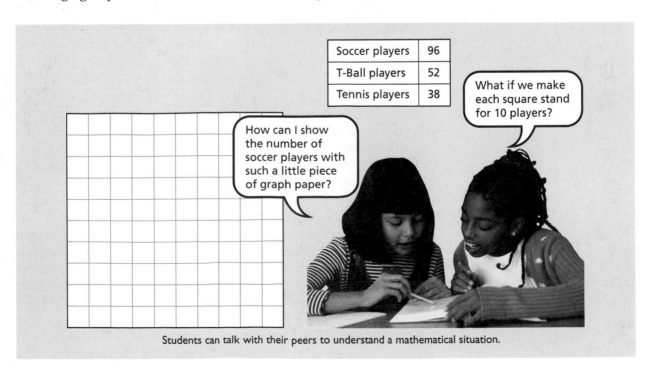

Students can talk with their peers to understand a mathematical situation.

time after a question is asked, and delay reaction to or evaluation of a student response, allowing students to be the authorities on what is right or wrong more often.

Grouping Students

Ensuring that students have peers with whom to talk can foster communication. Many teachers regularly seat students in groups, while others form groups for particular purposes. For students whose first language is not English, it may be appropriate to form groups that allow students to communicate about the mathematics in their first language; this makes it easier for them to deal with the mathematical content. On the other hand, to foster the development of their second language, there should also be times when these students work with others in English. See Chapter 23 for a more detailed discussion of alternative grouping strategies.

Wait Time

Without time to think about and respond to a question fully, students rarely have the opportunity to show what they really understand. Wait time may be particularly important for ESL students who need additional time to process the question and reformulate it. It is often suggested that teachers wait at least five seconds before saying anything else after asking a question, even though that silence may, at first, feel awkward to both teacher and students.

Teachers must also learn to wait for many volunteers and not to call on the first hand raised every time. There are a number of ways to encourage participation by a broader range of students, including tossing a ball and having whoever catches it respond; choosing names from a hat; or, for students who like to be prepared, using a visible roster for calling on students.

Evaluating and Responding to Student Responses

It is critical for teachers, who are supposed to be the authorities in the classroom, not only to retain the confidence of students, but also to encourage students to become independent. For example, a student asks the teacher if his or her response is correct. Rather than directly answering, the teacher can turn the opportunity around with a response such as, "Do you think it is? Tell me why."

There will, of course, be times when a student is stymied, and at this point, another question that might help the student carry the conversation forward is preferable to a simple yes or no reply. Occasionally, a yes or no reply to a response to a factual question may be appropriate. For example, a teacher asks, "What is $9 + 5$?" The student responds, "14," and it may be appropriate to say, "Correct." However, the teacher could still ask someone else if she or he agrees, or could follow up by asking, "How do you know that?"

Suppose a teacher poses the question, "How might you add $427 + 78$ in your head?" A student might reply, "I would add the 27 and 78 and then 400." Rather than indicating that this response is acceptable or, perhaps, that it is incomplete, the teacher should ask for more information, one question at a time—for example, *Why did you say that? What would you do next? Do you agree?* (to another student).

How a teacher handles an incorrect response can have an important effect on a student's willingness to continue to describe his or her mathematical thinking. Consider the following response and how the teacher refocuses the student.

Teacher: How many times are you likely to spin green if you spin this spinner 50 times?

Student: I think it will be 4.

Teacher: Why do you say that?

Student: Because $\frac{1}{4}$ of the spinner is green.

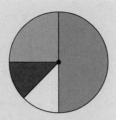

REFOCUSING QUESTIONS

What fraction of the spinner is blue $\left(\frac{1}{2}\right)$ Do you think you will spin blue 2 times?

What fraction of th e spinner is red? $\left(\frac{1}{8}\right)$ Do you think you will spin red 8 times?

Try spinning 10 times and see what happens.

A teacher should take time to consider the student's response before indicating he or she is wrong. Asking the student to explain himself or herself provides that extra time to think about the student's response, and also allows the teacher to gain a better understanding of what the student is thinking.

It is always important when responding to students to be prepared to re-evaluate the question asked. Sometimes, questions can be ambiguous.

Often younger students have greater difficulty communicating, and more prompting is required. However, it is easy to fall into the trap of asking questions that are too narrow and do not allow students to learn to choose the words they are going to use. Finding the right balance is essential, and the balance may be different for different groups of students.

Encouraging Listening

Listening is a very important aspect of oral communication. Many students are happy to talk but less interested in listening. To foster a real mathematics community, students need to learn from one another, and this involves listening and learning to analyze and reflect on what others say. This skill must be modelled and cultivated. For example, teachers can provide opportunities for students to explain a concept or how they solved a problem (perhaps by providing a "mathematician's chair"), and then have the listeners describe what they learned from the explanation.

Prompting Students

In an oral setting, teachers can prompt students with probing questions to elicit more mathematical thinking. Questions such as the following are useful in many situations:

- Why do you think that?
- Would it also be true if ...?
- Could there be a different answer?
- How did you figure that out?
- What was the hardest part of ...?

- What strategies did you use to ...?
- Why did you decide to ...?

Anticipation Guides

One particularly valuable way to prompt students, as well as to draw student attention to the important aspects of a lesson, is to use an anticipation guide at the start of the lesson. An anticipation guide is a set of statements, focused on the main idea(s) of the lesson, with which students can agree or disagree. Students normally complete the guide independently at the very start of the lesson, although the teacher may read the statements to the class. When finished, students share their responses and reasons with a partner or small group, or perhaps with the whole class. Later, after completing the lesson, students respond again to the same questions to see if any viewpoints have been changed.

For example, for a lesson on measuring in centimetres, a student might complete an anticipation guide such as the one shown below. The student has an opportunity to think about these ideas as the lesson proceeds and becomes invested in finding out the answers. Responding again to the same questions after the lesson allows the student to focus on what was learned and provides assessment information to the teacher.

Before the Lesson		After the Lesson
Agree Disagree	1. More things in the classroom are shorter than 10 cm than are longer than 10 cm.	Agree Disagree
Agree Disagree	2. You have to use a ruler to measure in centimetres.	Agree Disagree
Agree Disagree	3. A measurement is better if it's in centimetres rather than paper clips.	Agree Disagree

Opposite Sides

Another way to prompt discussion is to use the opposite sides strategy. Using this approach, the teacher makes a statement with which students can agree or disagree. Students who choose each option go to the side of the room assigned to that position. Students on each side work at justifying their position, which is then shared with the rest of the class. Students are allowed to change their minds after the justifications are heard. For example, the teacher might say, "It makes more sense to measure the length of my desk in metres than centimetres. Do you agree or disagree?"

Opportunities for Oral Communication

There are many things students can effectively talk about in the mathematics classroom. These include the following:

- **recalling past, but relevant, experiences:** Students are asked to recall situations where they had previously seen a graph.
- **determining how they will share a task:** Students can discuss in groups how to solve a particular problem, how they will know when they are satisfied with the solution, and how to share the work.
- **explaining:** Students can test out their explanations on one another before offering one to the whole group.

When 27 people were surveyed about their reading, 4 people said they never read for fun. Estimate the number of people who said they read sometimes or every day. Explain your thinking.

There were 4 out of 27 people who said "never," so 23 said "sometimes" or "every day." The "sometimes" section is bigger, so I estimate that 10 read for fun every day, and 13 do it sometimes. That works because 4 + 10 + 13 = 27.

Do you read for fun?

Students can test out their explanations on their classmates.

- **predicting:** Students are asked to predict whether more of the numbers between 10 and 50 have a 3 as one of the digits, or a 6 as one of the digits, and why. Students can predict and then discuss their prediction.
- **comparing approaches or ideas:** Three students in a group offer their ideas about how to find as many ways as they can to continue a pattern beginning with 3, 5, ... They can discuss their ideas, making judgments about which ones to include in the group's final presentation.
- **using manipulatives:** Manipulatives can act like "conversation pieces" in a classroom. They give students something to talk about and, in many cases, suggest appropriate language and vocabulary. For example, if students were asked to tell everything they know about a pyramid, having the pyramid in front of them would help initiate and extend the discussion.
- **discussing relationships they perceive:** Students are asked to comment on how squares are like circles and how they are different. Different students in the group can be asked to suggest possibilities.
- **justifying:** Students can describe how this number trick works. Think of a number. Double it. Double the answer. Subtract 8. Divide by 4. Add 2. The answer is always the number you start with.

Cultural Considerations

Teachers need to be sensitive about cultural issues related to communication. Some of the critical issues include being

- aware and respectful of cultures in which students are shy about responding or criticizing
- aware of cultures in which interrupting is considered acceptable, and setting up classroom practices that allow for children to speak without interruption
- aware of cultures in which people are reluctant to disagree openly, and ensuring that students feel comfortable about disagreeing with a classmate

- aware that, in many cultures, students are not encouraged to talk or ask questions in class, and that an openness to this may take time to develop

Integrating Language Arts and Oral Communication

Incorporating a significant amount of oral communication in the math classroom allows for the integration of the literacy goals for listening and speaking. Some purposes of communication in math class that would support general oral communication goals include the following:

- **sharing experiences with teacher and peers:** A student can describe how he or she solved a particular problem.
- **participating as listeners and speakers in group activities:** Students working in cooperative groups can be asked to come to a consensus before sharing their solution with the whole class.
- **using a variety of responses:** Students can include drama and role play, to explore mathematical concepts.

Pretend you are inside a cube. You cannot speak but use your hands, like a mime, to show what the cube looks like.

- **responding appropriately to simple oral instructions:** A student can be asked to hold up a rectangle (from a pile of shapes).
- **assessing the effectiveness of someone else's explanation**
- **listening or viewing critically and selectively:** A student can respond to a question such as, "What do you think of the explanation? Did you understand it? Do you agree?"

Written Communication

Written communication becomes an increasingly significant part of communication between teachers and students or among students, as students get older.

Why Written Communication Is Important

Written, as opposed to oral, communication has many advantages and is used for many purposes including the following:

- It allows for the creation of a more permanent record to enable a student or teacher to look back and see the progress of thought.
- It is slow enough to allow for considered reflection and organization. A student can look at his or her own work and actually "debate" with himself or herself about the ideas being recorded.
- It is deliberate enough that a student can focus on details.
- It provides sensory feedback as the hand is engaged in the writing, fostering better memory of the material.

A student is shown the following incomplete pattern.

_____, _____, _____, _____, 26, _____, _____,
110, _____, _____

The pattern rule is described as "add 42 each time." The student reasons
that the pattern rule is not correct, as shown below.

> If the pattern rule is "add 42 each time" and the
> 5th term is 26, then
> • the 6th term would be 26 + 42 = 68
> • the 7th term would be 68 + 42 = 110
> • the 8th term would be 110 + 42 = 152
> But the 8th term is 110.
> The pattern rule must be wrong.

- It is efficient since everyone in the class can be engaged simultaneously.
- It allows students to feel that they are making progress even if a problem is not completely solved.
- It is a "safer" venue for shy students.
- It can be a vehicle for learning. In the process of completing a written assignment, students might have to ask questions of their peers and teacher to find more information.
- It provides the teacher with a different sort of insight into student thinking than oral communication does, because the student is forced to stop and think. As well, students are not influenced by, or dependent on, the teacher's visual cues to decide what to say next.

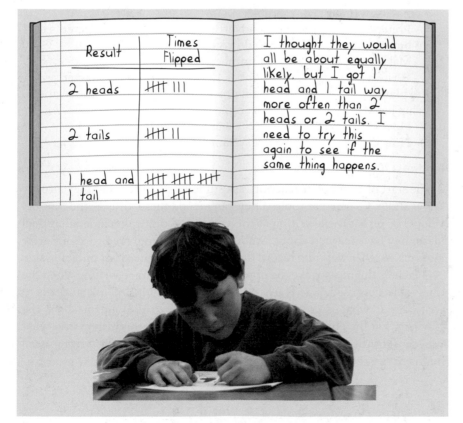

Written communication creates a permanent record of one's thoughts and allows for reflection and organization.

Types of Written Communication

There should be opportunities for students to inform, persuade, describe, and evaluate in their writing. Some of the kinds of writing students can use include the following:

- **personal writing**. For example:
  - What do you think we should ask about in our survey?
  - If you could measure any one of your toys and games, which one would you measure?
  - Why that one? What parts of it would you measure?
- **descriptive writing**. For example:
  - What is a geoboard and how can you use it?
  - What does the equation $2n + 5 = 19$ mean?
  - Tell where you have seen patterns around your home.
- **process writing**. For example:
  - What steps did you use to solve that problem?
- **creation of word problems**. For example:

Student Response

This student has created a word problem for two given conditions.

> Make up a word problem where multiplication is involved and the answer is 20.
>
> I have 4 Friends. We each have 4 tickets to sell for the raffle. How many tickets do we all have to sell?

- **creative writing**. For example:
  - Pretend you are writing an advertisement to encourage parents to buy tangram kits. What would you say?
  - Make up a poem about the number 100.
  - Write a story where the number 12 is an important character.
- **explanatory writing** to explain procedures, concepts, or the relationship between concepts. For example:
  - How would you calculate $72 \div 9$ in your head?
  - How do you find the line of symmetry for this triangle?

Finding Opportunities to Write

At the start of a unit of instruction, ask students to write what they already know about a particular topic. They can extend these ideas as the unit develops, or revisit their writing at the end of the unit to include additional ideas they have learned about. Students can be encouraged to summarize ideas discussed in class and record these in a "math journal" or on a blog site.

Teachers might also take the opportunity to encourage writing when the class looks confused. The teacher can stop everything and ask students to write about what is going on. When students read aloud or show the teacher what they have written, the teacher gets a better insight into what was causing the confusion. For many students, the task of writing itself might clarify their thinking.

Integrating Language Arts and Written Communication

Many of the language arts goals related to writing can be supported in math class. These include

- writing every day
- participating in a variety of experiences that nurture communication for a real purpose
- participating in and reacting to visual stimuli and topic selection
- using pictures and symbols to communicate meaning
- organizing and presenting subject matter in coherently linked sentences within paragraphs
- displaying and sharing selected pieces of work
- writing from a different perspective
- writing in a certain genre

Criteria for Written Communication

The ability to communicate mathematically is something that needs formal and focused attention. Students might find the following checklist of criteria helpful when writing (of course, not all criteria are relevant to all writing):

- Did you show all the steps?
- Did you include reasons for the steps?
- Did you show the right amount of detail?
- Did you explain your thinking?
- Did you use diagrams to help explain?
- Did you use math language and symbols?

The following samples show a selection of the communication criteria that can be explicitly discussed with students, according to the type of writing.

PROBLEM SOLVING

How could you arrange these three shapes to make a square?

When writing about solving a problem, students could focus on these criteria.

Did you
- show that you understood the problem?
- show all the steps in order?
- include reasons for each step?

I knew I had to use all three shapes to make one square.

I guessed that the shapes that had the square corners were the corners of the square so I tried these arrangements:

My third way worked because the missing space was the right size for the blue triangle.

This is how the shapes go together.

This student showed that she or he understood the problem and showed the steps in order. She or he also gave reasons for each step.

Student Response

This student explained each step in the procedure, including reasons for the steps. He or she also used an appropriate amount of detail, math language, and symbols.

EXPLAINING A PROCEDURE

Order the numbers 909, 9009, 9909, and 999 from greatest to least. Explain how you ordered them. When explaining a procedure, students could focus on these criteria:

Did you

• show all the steps in order?
• include reasons for the steps?
• show the right amount of detail?
• use math language and symbols?

I put the numbers with 4 digits first. 4-digit numbers are greater.

9009 9909 909 999

I compared the 100s digit of the 4-digit numbers to see which was greater because the 1000s digit is the same   9909 > 9009

I compared the tens digit of the 3 digit numbers because the 100s digits were the same
999 > 909

The order is 9909, 9009, 999, 909

Student Response

This student explains the relationship between two sets of numbers. He or she uses words, rather than symbols involving variables.

EXPLAINING A CONCEPT

Use words to describe the relationship in this table.

1st Column	2nd Column
1	6
2	7
3	8
4	9
5	10
6	11

When explaining a concept, students can focus on these criteria:

Did you

• explain your thinking?
• use diagrams, patterns, or relationships to other ideas to help explain?
• use math language and symbols?

they relate because 1+5=6
2+5=7   3+5=8   4+5=9   5+5=10
5+6=11   in the first column
if you add 5 it eavals the
number the second column.

Providing Exemplars and Scaffolding

When an appropriate opportunity arises for teachers to explain something in writing, they should model the process and product for students. Teachers can do this in two ways: by "thinking out loud" and recording as they go or by providing exemplars of other students' work.

For many students, especially ESL students, it is particularly important to provide some scaffolding, or structured support, for organizing the writing and to provide some of the needed vocabulary.

Fostering Written Communication

The most important consideration when assigning a written task in mathematics is to ensure that the communication is suitable and that the task is as rich as possible. Some of the typical prompts for such tasks are:

- What do you think ... means?
- Tell everything you can about ....
- Tell about a time when ....
- Why is it easy to ...?
- When do you ...?
- How do you know that ...?
- What can you say that is true about all of ...?
- Tell a different way to ....
- ... can mean two different things. Tell about what ... can mean.
- Explain why ....
- What question could you ask to find out about ...?

Tell about a time when you had a difficult time trying to figure out a pattern.

> it was a number pattern and the numbers got bigger but not by the same amount each time. i asked my partner to help me and we asked the teacher for help. she asked us to look at how much was bettween the numbers then we saw a pattern

Student Response

This student was able to explain, in writing, not only why the number pattern was difficult to figure out but how she or he eventually figured it out.

Many teachers encourage the keeping of a math journal, where students respond to questions such as those above.

Free Writing

One specific technique for fostering written communication is free writing. The teacher provides a stimulus—whether a picture, a word, or a manipulative—and then students are asked to write for a certain number of minutes without editing or stopping. With this approach, students are more likely to disclose what they know about a topic. Examples of stimuli are shown on the next page.

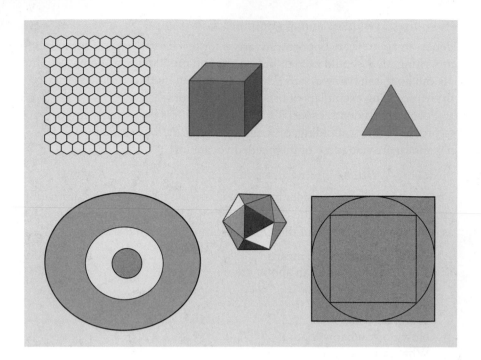

Symbolic and Graphical Communication

Young students need to communicate mathematically even before they have all of the formal tools they need. They should be allowed and encouraged to use invented symbolism to describe their mathematical thinking. Sometimes the symbolism may seem unclear, but it is important to ask what students are thinking as this is an effective way to better understand why they chose the symbols they did, and what meaning those symbols possess specifically for them.

One of the symbols used with older students is a letter of the alphabet to describe an unknown quantity (a variable), for example, $n = 5 \times 7$. For younger students, a box or blank is used instead; for example, $\blacksquare = 5 \times 7$.

Many students find it easier to explain their thinking using diagrams rather than words. This should be encouraged, particularly, but not exclusively, for younger students. Leaving a space instead of blank lines for student responses is one way to indicate to students that their response might include a picture or a graphic element of some kind. Older students might need to be prompted to use words to support their diagrams.

Student Response

This student showed his or her understanding symbolically. You might ask for an oral explanation as well.

a) What is the formula for the perimeter of a rectangle?

$$P = L + L + W + W$$

b) Why does your formula make sense?

$$+ = 10$$

$$5 \qquad 10 \qquad 5$$

$$+ = 20$$

$$10$$

$$20 + 10 = 30$$

This student uses a picture to show her or his ideas about pattern.

Physical Communication

An important part of communication in the math classroom involves physical actions. Physical actions not only show what students do with manipulative materials; they can also be useful for "explaining" many mathematical concepts. For example, a student who has trouble explaining in words what *area* means might find it easier to describe or explain the concept concretely through demonstration, by covering a surface with square tiles.

Students communicate some of their mathematical thinking by performing actions concretely. For example, one of the meanings of *division* is "sharing." Suppose students are asked to solve the division problem shown below. If students physically share 15 counters among 5 groups, they are acting out the operation of division and, at the same time, communicating that they understand that this is a division situation.

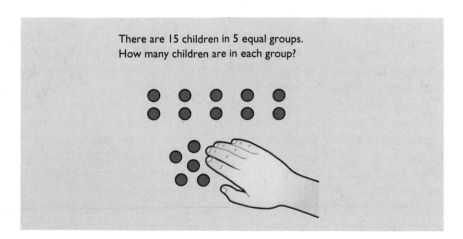

Division can be communicated by the act of sharing manipulatives in equal groups.

Many geometric understandings are best shown using physical communication. This student shows her or his understanding of cones.

Reading Opportunities in Mathematics

Mathematics textbooks often include features not as common in other textbooks, including the following:

- a combination of statements or questions that require action and those that do not
- fairly dense text with little repetition, particularly at the higher grade levels
- a mixture of essential and non-essential diagrams that are not always distinguishable
- material that must be read not only left to right, but also right to left, and top to bottom (for example, parts of problems organized in different ways)
- tables, charts, and graphs
- many symbols and conventions with meanings that might not be defined through context
- many instructions

These features make the textbook hard for students to read without some teacher instruction. It is critical that teachers spend the time to help students learn to read these textbooks.

Besides reading mathematics textbooks, students should have the opportunity to read children's stories related to mathematical concepts in math class. Children's literature is an excellent context for teaching mathematics. It also builds on the positive reaction that most children have to hearing and reading familiar and new stories. Although more books are probably suitable for students in the primary years, many pieces of children's literature can enrich the mathematics classroom and provide reading opportunities for students at all levels. A number of resources describe some appropriate literature, including *Read Any Good Math Lately?* by David Whitin and Sandra Wilde. In many of the chapters in this textbook, relevant children's literature suggestions are provided near the end of the chapter.

Mathematics Vocabulary and Symbols

Vocabulary is an issue in both oral and written mathematical communication. Some people even consider mathematics to be a language of its own. No one disputes that students are expected to become comfortable with vocabulary associated with mathematics when reading, speaking, and writing. Some vocabulary terms are content related and others are process related. For example, students are asked to learn number words like *sum*, *product*, *area*, *pyramid*, and *variable*, but they are also expected to understand what is meant when the words *justify*, *explain*, *estimate*, *extend*, and *solve* are used. These latter terms must be clarified, too.

Another complication in mathematics is the confusion between the symbol and the idea. The terms *number* and *numeral* are used to try to make the distinction, but that distinction is not always clear. For example, the symbol 7 is smaller than the symbol 2, but the number 7 is greater than the number 2. Punctuation marks, such as the colon in a ratio, and grammatical structures, such as saying "8 divided into 2" when we mean 2 ÷ 8 or "8 divided into 2s" when we mean 8 ÷ 2, can also confuse students.

The Importance of Vocabulary

Knowing the right word to use allows students to communicate more effectively and efficiently and, as a result, consolidate their learning. Often, the mathematics cannot really be understood or communicated without reference to appropriate vocabulary.

Strategies for Reinforcing Math Vocabulary

When introducing new terms, many actions can be taken to help solidify this vocabulary, including the following:

- a **word wall**, where words are posted as reminders for students. Math terms are often grouped by concept or topic; for example, all the words associated with operations might be in one group (e.g., *sum*,

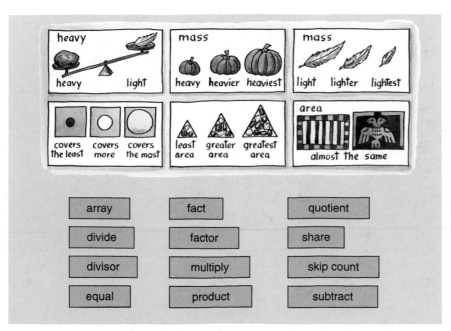

difference, product, and *quotient*), and words associated with geometry would be in another (e.g., *circle* and *triangle*). If the words are on cards, they can be sorted in different ways so students can see the various connections and relationships. They may be illustrated as well.

• a **glossary**, either posted or in a notebook. The glossary can be created in students' own words, rather than the teacher's, although the teacher will want to ensure that students' definitions are correct. A glossary can use pictures or diagrams, along with words to explain. An example or two with each definition is also helpful.

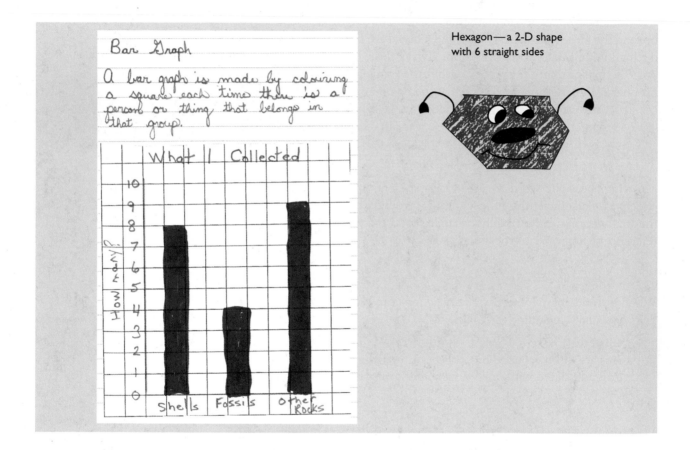

Hexagon—a 2-D shape
with 6 straight sides

• **sentence completion**. For example, "The _____ of 12 and 8 is 20."
• **integrating math and language arts**. Some teachers include mathematics vocabulary words in their language arts spelling and comprehension activities.
• **concept maps** like the Frayer model map (An example is shown on the next page.)

A Sample Frayer Model Map for $\frac{1}{4}$

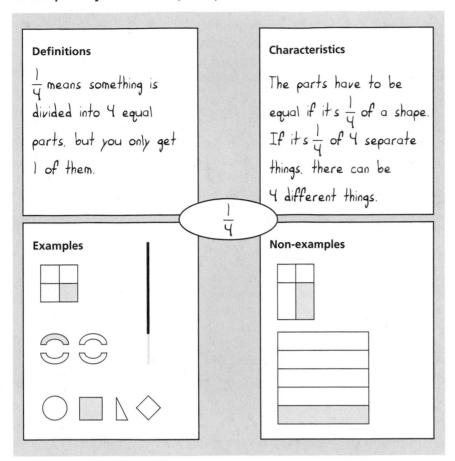

Math Terminology and Everyday Language

One of the additional complications in mathematics is that some words are used differently in mathematics compared to how they are used in everyday situations. Some examples are shown below:

- *Odd* in everyday language can mean unusual.
- *Unknown*, which in everyday language means something you do not know, but mathematically is something that we temporarily do not know, but then actually do know.
- *Mean* can mean unpleasant (rather than an average).
- *Negative* can mean bad.
- *Right* describes a direction.

Mnemonics for Math Vocabulary

In many instances, the formal mathematical meaning of a word can be connected to the everyday meaning, albeit with a bit of imagination and creativity. Making these connections can be a powerful tool to help students remember new vocabulary and also make sense of mathematical language.

Here are some examples:

- When you multiply two numbers, you "produce a product."
- When you pair up students, the expression "the odd one out" could be used to reinforce the fact that, when odd numbers of items are paired, there is always one left over.

As teachers introduce new vocabulary, they should be aware of any potential ambiguity in the meaning of the new term. It is important, though, for teachers to understand the terminology themselves. Teachers should have access to a suitable math dictionary, whether they purchase their own or use the one from the school library. A number of online math dictionaries can be accessed to support both teacher and student understanding.

Engaging Students in Communication

Just as some students are more inclined to communicate than others, students may also be more inclined toward certain types of communication, whether it be oral, written, or physical. Below are some strategies to help engage those students who are less inclined to communicate.

- Adding a personal element to a problem can sometimes make it of particular interest to a student (see Personal Engaging Math Tasks below).

PERSONAL ENGAGING MATH TASKS

- Are you older or younger than a million seconds?
- If each letter has a value (A is 1, B is 2, C is 3, etc.), what is your name worth? Is your given name worth more than your family name?
- Describe your family using fractions.

- Using an interactive white board where students' writing is digitally recorded for future reference and where their handwriting actually turns into printed text, is very intriguing for many students.
- Paying attention to what each student says and writes is critical to making that student want to invest in communication. A classroom where students listen to one another respectfully is an essential component to motivate more communication.
- Handling situations appropriately where students say or write something that is questionable is critical to encourage risk taking. The teacher must address the issue but, at the same time, ensure that the learning environment is a positive one. For example, a student has written the **Student Response** on page 81. Some good thinking is demonstrated in recognizing that multiplication is a "short form" for addition, and that should be acknowledged. The teacher needs to probe further, however, to find out what the student means by, "You use it when you cannot add, subtract, or divide." For example, the teacher might say, "You say that multiplication is a shorter way to add and that is true. But you also say that you multiply when you cannot add. How can both of these statements be true?"
- Allowing students to use multiple forms of communication might make them more willing to take the risk. For example, if they are told they will have an opportunity to explain what they write orally, they might attempt written communication.
- Encouraging students to use pictures when they write can take the pressure off those students with poor writing skills.
- Allowing students to use manipulatives when explaining themselves orally redirects the focus from a shy student to the manipulatives. The use of manipulatives also allows students to use the language of the manipulatives to make communication easier. For example,

Describe what multiplication is all about.

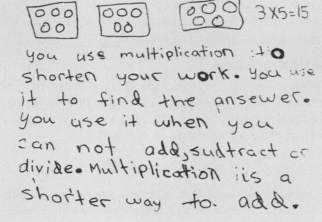

$3 \times 5 = 15$

You use multiplication to shorten your work. You use it to find the ansewer. You use it when you can not add, sudtract or divide. Multiplication iis a shorter way to. add.

Student Response

This student has some good ideas, but further probing is necessary.

a student might struggle with the language necessary to explain place value concepts, such as hundreds, but, when using base ten blocks to explain, he or she might call it the big square block or the flat. The teacher can take this opportunity to model the appropriate language.

Assessing Student Communication

- Make sure to assess communication separately from other processes, content knowledge, or understanding. For example, a student might know the mathematical concept, but not communicate her or his understanding well. On the other hand, a student might communicate quite well, but incorrectly.
- Provide opportunities for students to communicate in different ways, sometimes orally, sometimes in writing, sometimes physically, and sometimes symbolically.
- Share with students the criteria you will be using to assess their communication.

Applying What You've Learned

1. What data skills and what number skills did you use to solve the chapter problem? Did you do a good job of communication? What was good about it or what did it lack?

2. Some teachers who believe in the value of communication expect a student to explain every answer in an exercise. How often would you require explanations? Justify your decision.

3. Choose a grade level and a topic of interest. In what types of situations in the exploration of that topic do you think that written communication is essential? Why?

4. What sorts of questions would you include in an anticipation guide for a lesson in Grade 3 focusing on subtraction?

5. Describe some ways you could infuse creative writing into a mathematics program at a grade of your choice.

6. Create a concept map, for example, a Frayer model, to show what you know about adding fractions.

WebConnect

www.makingmathmeaningful.nelson.com

Visit Nelson's Making Math Meaningful website to find out more about anticipation guides.

Interact with a K–8 Student:

7. Choose a math term appropriate for the student with whom you are interacting, for example, *add* for Grade 1 or *prime number* for Grade 7. Ask the student to tell you as many things as he or she can about that word. Assess the richness of the communication.

Discuss with a K–8 Teacher:

8. Many teachers are nervous about allowing too many students to explain their thinking on a problem just because other students may get confused with too many approaches. Ask the teacher how she or he handles communication in this sort of situation.

Selected References

Altieri, J.L. (2005). Creating poetry: Reinforcing mathematical concepts. *Teaching Children Mathematics,* 12, 18–23.

Anderson, M., and Little, D.M. (2004). On the write path: Improving communication in an elementary mathematics classroom. *Teaching Children Mathematics,* 10, 468–472.

Countryman, J. (1992). *Writing to learn mathematics.* Portsmouth, NH: Heinemann.

Griffiths, R., and Clyne, M. (1994). *Language in the mathematics classroom: Talking, representing, recording.* Portsmouth, NH: Heinemann.

Hiebert, J., and Wearne, D. (1993). Instructional tasks, classroom discourse, and students' learning in second grade arithmetic. *American Educational Research Journal,* 30, 393–425.

Hufferd-Ackles, K., Fuson, K.C., and Sherin, M.G. (2004). Describing levels and components of a math-talk learning community. *Journal for Research in Mathematics Education,* 35, 81–116.

Huinker, D., and Laughlin, C. (1996). Talk your way into writing. In Elliott, P.C., and Kenney, M.J. (Eds.). *Communication in mathematics, K–12 and beyond.* Reston, VA: National Council of Teachers of Mathematics, 81–88.

Lilburn, P., and Rawson, P. (1994). *Let's talk math: Encouraging children to explore ideas.* Portsmouth, NH: Heinemann.

National Council of Teachers of Mathematics. (2000). *Principles and standards for school mathematics.* Reston, VA: National Council of Teachers of Mathematics.

Novak, J.D. (1990). Concept maps and Vee diagrams: Two metacognitive tools for science and mathematics education. *Instructional Science,* 19, 29–52.

O'Connell, S. (2007a). *Introduction to communication, grades PreK–2.* Portsmouth, NH: Heinemann.

O'Connell, S. (2007b). *Introduction to communication, grades 3–5.* Portsmouth, NH: Heinemann.

Pimm, D. (1996). Diverse communication. In Elliott, P.C., and Kenney, M.J. (Eds.). *Communication in mathematics, K–12 and beyond.* Reston, VA: National Council of Teachers of Mathematics, 11–19.

Reinhart, S.C. (2000). Never say anything a kid can say! *Mathematics Teaching in the Middle School,* 5, 478–483.

Shield, M., and Swinson, K. (1996). The link sheet: A communication aid for clarifying and developing mathematical ideas and processes. In Elliott, P.C., and Kenney, M.J. (Eds). *Communication in mathematics, K–12 and beyond.* Reston, VA: National Council of Teachers of Mathematics, 35–39.

Shuard, H., and Rothery, A. (1984). *Children reading mathematics.* London, England: Alden Press.

Small, M. (2005a). *PRIME: Number and operations: Background and strategies.* Toronto: Thomson Nelson.

Small, M. (2005b). *PRIME: Patterns and algebra: Background and strategies.* Toronto: Thomson Nelson.

Small, M. (2006). *PRIME: Data and probability: Background and strategies.* Toronto: Thomson Nelson.

Steinbring, H., Bartolino Bussi, M.G., and Sierpinska, A. (Eds.). (1998). *Language and communication in the mathematics classroom.* Reston, VA: National Council of Teachers of Mathematics.

Whitin, D., and Wilde, S. (1992). *Read any good math lately?* Portsmouth, NH: Heinemann Educational Books, Inc.

Chapter 5

Mathematics for the Younger Learner

IN A NUTSHELL

The main ideas in the chapter are listed below:

1. There is a difference between rote counting (being able to say the number words 1, 2, 3, etc., in the proper order), and meaningful counting (understanding how counting can be used to describe the size of a set).

2. There are many forms of counting that students need to learn, including counting forward, counting back, counting on, and skip counting. Counting is fundamental to further number work.

3. It is critical that students learn to represent numbers in as many ways as they can. Each of these representations broadens the meaning of the number for the student. Numerals are only one form of representation.

4. Numbers are most meaningful to a student when they are related to anchor or benchmark values that are well understood.

CHAPTER PROBLEM

Describe four ways that 6 and 8 are alike and three ways that they are different.

Numbers in the Child's World

Numbers are a part of even a young child's life. He or she wants to know how many of something there are, whether it is how many cookies he or she can eat, how many fingers someone is holding up, or how many candles are on his or her cake. All other work with numbers, whether representing quantities or performing operations, is dependent on children learning to count.

Counting Principles

Before there can be any meaningful counting, students must be able to recite the sequence beginning 1, 2, 3, 4, 5, etc. This is called rote counting. They need to be able to say those numbers in order, even if they do not know what those amounts actually look like. How high they can meaningfully count depends on how much of the sequence they know.

Many, but not all, students can rote count to 10 or even higher, and many can count a small set of objects meaningfully before they begin school. The latter indicates that these students have begun to internalize the following fundamental counting principles.

> **COUNTING PRINCIPLES**
>
> 1. There is one and only one number said for each object (the one-to-one principle).
> 2. There is a consistent set of counting words that never changes (the stable order principle).
> 3. The last number spoken tells how many (the cardinal principle).
> 4. It does not matter what you count; the process for counting remains the same (the abstraction principle).
> 5. It does not matter in which order you count; the number in the set does not change (the order-irrelevance principle).
>
> *(Gelman and Gallistel, 1978)*

Zero and One

When students see the sets below, they are likely to think about how many there are.

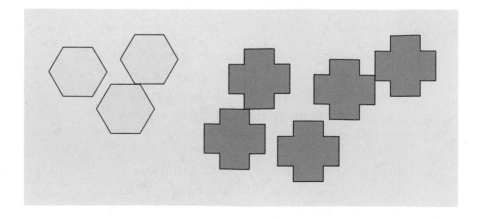

But when they see just one item, for example, the one circle below, they think "circle," not "one."

Students have to be encouraged to see that the number 1 represents the number of circles.

It is even more difficult for students to visualize zero. How do you visualize nothing? One effective technique is to model several different numbers using paper plates with items on them. For example, seven is modelled as a paper plate with seven circles on it or five as a paper plate with five circles on it. Gradually, take the circles off one at a time and ask, "How many are on the plate now? And now?" Once there is only one circle left on the plate, take it off and ask students how many circles are on the plate now. Many will say "none." Introduce the word *zero* as the word you use to tell the number of circles on the plate and show them how it is written as 0.

<aside>
ACTIVITY 5.1

Read a favourite counting book, such as Bert Kitchen's *Animal Numbers* (1988). Invite students to predict the number they will hear and see when you turn the page.
</aside>

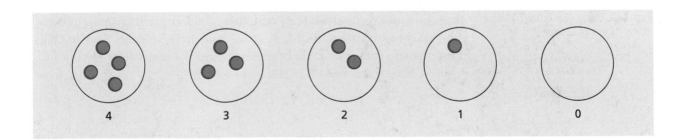

Counting Strategies

Students need to develop a sense of confidence in their counting. For example, if they count out some objects and decide that there are 6 of them, they need to realize immediately that if you rearrange the objects and then ask how many, they do not have to re-count, because the count is still 6. This is often referred to as *conservation of number*.

Students also have to learn physical techniques for counting. For example, children who are good counters usually have strategies for keeping track of what they have counted, such as touching each object and moving it away once it has been counted. Later, they learn to use visual or other kinesthetic motions, like nodding, to keep track of what has been counted. Students normally learn these techniques by copying others who are efficient counters, whether fellow students or the teacher.

<aside>
ACTIVITY 5.2

Have students play board games where they roll a die and have to count the number of spaces to move. Have them think about where they would have been had the number been one more or one less.
</aside>

A number of researchers have elaborated stages of counting. One, the Stages of Arithmetical Learning (SEAL) model, based on work by Steffe (1992), lists 6 stages of counting:

Stage 0: Emergent counting (cannot count visible items)
Stage 1: Perceptual counting (can count perceived items, but not concealed ones)
Stage 2: Figurative counting (can count hidden items, but always from one)
Stage 3: Initial number sequence (can count on to add)
Stage 4: Intermediate number sequence (can count back to subtract)
Stage 5: Facile number sequence (many counting strategies, including skip counting)

Once students make the connection between rote counting and cardinality (or how many), they become more flexible in dealing with larger quantities (Stages 3, 4, and 5). At these stages, students use more sophisticated and efficient approaches to counting such as

- counting on (starting at a number other than 1)
- counting back (e.g., counting back from 10 by ones or from 20 by 2s)
- skip counting (e.g., 2, 4, 6, 8, …)

Counting Back

Counting back is often overlooked by teachers, yet it is an extremely important skill to prepare students for later work in subtraction. Some children's counting books and songs, like *The Right Number of Elephants* (Sheppard, 1992), or *Five Little Monkeys Jumping on a Bed* (Christelow, 1998), provide counting-back opportunities. But teachers can easily create such opportunities themselves. For example, just before starting a new activity, the teacher might begin "10, 9, 8, …" and have students join in. It is important to start at different beginning points, for example, sometimes 10, 9, 8, …, but other times 15, 14, 13, …, or 6, 5, 4, ….

Skip Counting

There is an emphasis in early grade curricula on skip counting by 2s, 5s, or 10s, and later 100s, then 50s, and 25s. The focus of skip counting in these early years seems to be on helping students see the patterns in our place value system as well as to prepare students for work with money.

Highlighting the numbers that are heard when skip counting on a number line helps the student learn the skip counting patterns. Highlighting can be visual, as shown below, but it can also be physical, for example, by clapping when reaching the number that is to be said.

ACTIVITY 5.3

Students can practise skip counting on an animated number line, using software like the Geometer's Sketchpad sketch below.

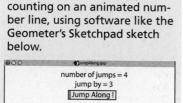
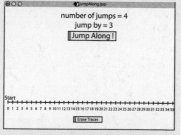

http://dynamicgeometry.com/general_resources/classroom_activities/young_learners/pages/activities_3to5.php

---

1	2	3	4	5	6	7	8	9	10
1	2	3	4	5	6	7	8	9	10

Over time, students should have experiences skip counting both forward and backward, and not always starting with the obvious start number. For example, we often skip count "2, 4, 6, 8, ...," but not as often "1, 3, 5, 7, ...," which would also be helpful to students.

Counting On

Counting on is a critical prerequisite for success in addition. Students must be able to add 4 + 3 by starting at 4, and then saying 3 more numbers: 5, 6, 7. If the student has to start back at 1—1, 2, 3, 4, and then 5, 6, 7—his or her progress with addition will be slow. Students become comfortable with counting on through experience. The teacher might have them stand on a walk-on number line or a hopscotch frame, for example, at 5, and ask them to take two more steps, saying the number stepped on each time: "..., 6, 7."

You might also do a lot of counting on as "sponge" activities, activities you can squeeze in when there is a minute or two to spare. For example, while students are packing up for the day, start saying "7, 8, 9, ..." and have students join in the chant. Many teachers emphasize the ability to say the number 1 or 2 more, or 1 or 2 less than a given one. For example, they might call out a number 6 and ask for the number 2 more; students are expected to think, "6, 7, 8."

One way to help students count on is to "hide" the items that make up the start number, as is shown in **Activity 5.4**.

A Sense of Number

Comparing and Relating Numbers

Many everyday situations provide opportunities for students to compare numbers, such as whether there are enough napkins for all of the children at a table, or whether there are 2 too many or 1 too few. Teachers can quickly create many simple comparing opportunities, for example, by asking students to clap 2 times fewer or more than they do.

ACTIVITY 5.4

Take two groups of objects. Hide one group under a piece of paper and label it with its count. Leave the other group exposed. Ask the student how many objects there are altogether. (As the student is not able to count the individual items in the hidden group, he or she is forced to count on.)

"There are 4 counters hiding, so there are 4, 5, 6, 7 counters altogether."

Students employ two primary strategies for comparing numbers: 1–1 correspondence, and position in the counting sequence.

One-to-One Correspondence

One-to-one correspondence is the real test for comparison. Both numbers are modelled with elements of the two sets matched up. The set that has items left over is the larger set, and the number representing it is the greater number.

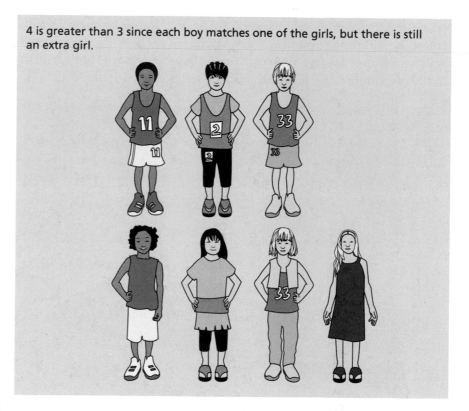

4 is greater than 3 since each boy matches one of the girls, but there is still an extra girl.

An everyday example of the use of one-to-one correspondence revolves around the interpretation of simple bar graphs. If, for example, students get to choose the activity they want to do and they are asked to stack a cube on a stack, depending on their choice, they can easily see whether more students are choosing one activity compared to another.

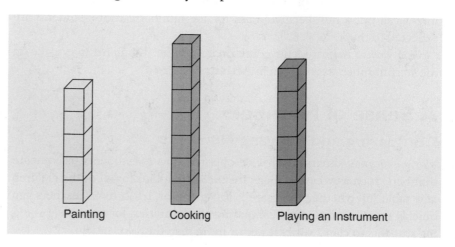

Painting   Cooking   Playing an Instrument

Position in the Counting Sequence

Later, students count the items in both sets separately and compare the position of the two numbers in the number sequence. For example, if one set has 3 items and one has 4, they know that since the number 3 comes before 4 in the counting sequence, 3 is less than 4, and the set of 3 contains fewer items than the set of 4.

Comparison Language

Whenever possible, it is preferable to say "4 is greater than 3" rather than "4 is more than 3" to teach that mathematical language to students. Eventually, they will learn to use the greater-than symbol: $4 > 3$.

Many students have difficulty recognizing that if 4 is greater than 3, 3 is automatically less than 4; they tend to focus on only the "greater than" aspect of the relationship. Make sure that both sides of the relationship are considered.

Spatial Comparison

Bar graphs are one way to compare numbers spatially; using ordinal numbers is another way. Ordinal numbers describe position, rather than cardinality, but there is a relationship between ordinality and cardinality. For example, if you are 2nd in a race, it is because there is only one person ahead of you, making you person number 2. There are many natural classroom opportunities to use ordinal numbers; for example, "I'd like the third person in line to come to the front."

Numbers to 5

Subitizing

A very efficient strategy to tell how many is *subitizing*. Subitizing is a method of determining how many are in a group without specifically counting each item; it depends on an immediate recognition of arrangements or configurations of certain numbers of items. It is a valuable skill for success in mathematics. For example, most people immediately recognize, or subitize, the arrangements for 1 to 5 shown below, as these configurations of dots are commonly used on dice, cards, and other game materials. Which numbers are immediately recognizable varies with students' experiences.

Many teachers use paper plates with stickers attached or dots created by bingo dabbers, and play "pattern flash" games. They show a dot pattern very briefly and students are asked if they recognize it. Although some patterns are more commonly used than others, and these can be the ones that

---

ACTIVITY 5.6

Encourage students to make chains out of plastic links. They might spin a spinner to decide how many links, or they could decide on a number of their own choice. They predict whose chain will be longer and how much longer, and then test to check.

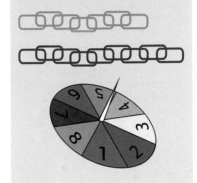

ACTIVITY 5.7

Put out 5 blue counters for students to see.

Tell students to draw a picture of something that comes in 5s.

Now put out fewer red counters for students to see.

Tell students to draw a picture of something that comes in groups of that number.

ACTIVITY 5.8

Students use square tiles, number cards from 1 to 9, and two other cards, one marked More and one marked Less.

They choose a number card to tell how many tiles to use and a More or a Less card. They make a design using a number of tiles that matches what they drew. For example, if they drew less and 7, they might create "an elephant face."

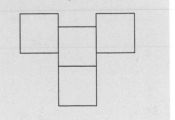

Encourage students to play games that help them to relate numerals to the amounts they represent. A simple game is Concentration.

Concentration

Have students lay a collection of set cards and small number cards face down. Students take turns turning over cards in search of a matching set, where the set card matches the number card. If they find a match, they can remove the pair of cards from play. When they have uncovered all of the pairs, they can count their cards and the player with the most cards wins the round.

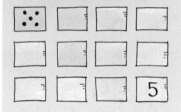

are emphasized, some teachers use a variety of representations often enough that students begin to recognize them right away. For example, below are different representations that might be used for 9.

Some teachers use patterns that emphasize looking at a number as made up of parts. For example, the cards below show that 6 is 3 and 3, and that 5 is 4 and 1.

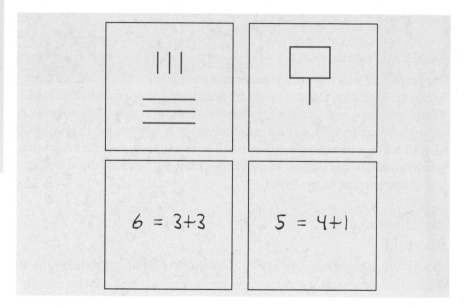

Numbers to 10

5 and 10 as Benchmarks

Many students think of one number in relationship to another; for example, 6 is the number that is 1 more than 5, or 9 is the number that is 1 less than 10. Relating numbers to benchmark numbers can be used as a tool for comparing numbers (as shown below), and should be encouraged. The numbers 5 and 10 often provide the strongest benchmarks for young students.

I know 3 is less than 8 because 3 is less than 5 and 8 is more than 5.

One way to encourage this sort of reference to benchmarks is to use an appropriate visual model. Aside from the obvious model of the fingers on one or both hands, three other models are particularly useful: the 5-frame, the 10-frame, and the beaded number line.

The 5-Frame The 5-frame is a rectangle of 5 squares with each square large enough to hold a counter.

Students learn to *subitize* these representations for 1 to 5, but also think of the numbers 3 and 4 in relation to 5.

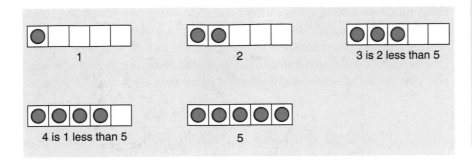

The 10-Frame The 10-frame is a set of two 5-frames put together in two rows. The frame is filled by beginning at the left, filling the top row, and then starting at the left again to fill the bottom row.

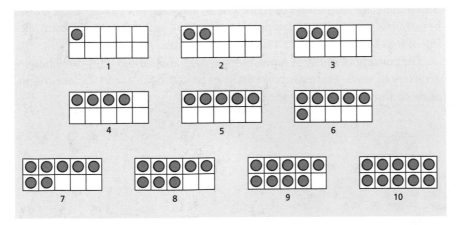

This model focuses students on relationships to 5 and 10, for example, 6 as 1 more than 5, or 8 as 2 fewer than 10.

The Bead Number Line Many teachers use beads to create number lines on strings. They alternate colours every 5 beads.

Initially, they might mark the numbers with stickers on the beads, but later they take the stickers off. This helps students focus on comparisons to a benchmark, for example, 7 as the number 2 past 5.

ACTIVITY 5.10

Students can create and contribute to a visual display of 5. They can

- make pictures of five of their favourite things
- make fingerprint handprints
- print fancy numeral 5s
- print five in different languages

ACTIVITY 5.11

Invite children to make 5 many different ways using square tiles, toothpicks, or buttons.

Making Ten

Put a full set of 10-frame models in a bag. Students must put pairs of frames together to make tens.

For example, they might pair these two models.

Once students are familiar with 10-frame arrangements, teachers might want to play a variety of games with them to practice the arrangements for various numbers.

The Teen Numbers

Many students struggle with the teen numbers, the numbers between 10 and 20, particularly the numbers 13 to 19. One of the reasons offered is that we say the numbers in the English language (this is not the case in many other languages) in a different order than we write them, for example, sixteen, with the "six" part last and the "teen" part first—16. The focus for these numbers should always be on the relationship to 10. 16 is sixteen because it is 6 more than 10. Students need a great deal of experience representing and using teen numbers to become comfortable with their use.

The use of a double 10-frame is helpful for the teen numbers. For example, 15 is shown as below, and is clearly 5 more than 10.

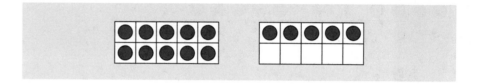

Importance of Multiple Representations

One of the important concepts young students need to learn about number is that there are many ways to represent an amount. For example, the number of arms you have can be represented by the symbol 2, but also by thinking of it as 1 more than 1, or 1 less than 3 or, later, 7 − 5.

The concept of multiple representation can and should be approached in a variety of ways. For example, to model the number 7, the student might draw or show any of the models below:

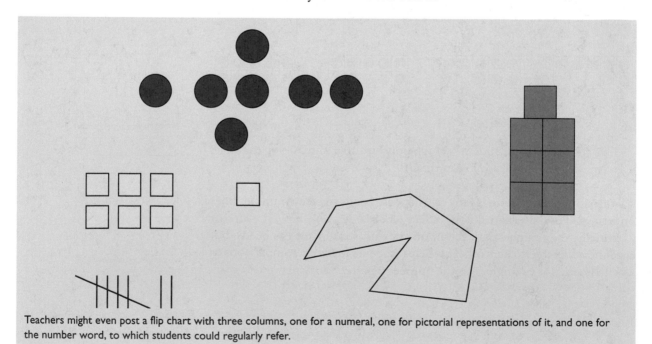

Teachers might even post a flip chart with three columns, one for a numeral, one for pictorial representations of it, and one for the number word, to which students could regularly refer.

The 6 and 1 model using squares above shows what is called a part-part-whole relationship; students view 7, the whole, as being made of two parts, the 6 and the 1. These part-part-whole relationships become the basis for later addition work. As well, if students are shown part of a whole and figure out what the other part is to make the whole, then a foundation for subtraction work is being set.

One particularly important idea to introduce is the meaning of the equals sign as a symbol that tells you that two sets of symbols are representations for the same amount. For example, when you write 3 + 1 = 4, you are saying that another way to represent 4 is as 3 and 1. Similarly, when you write 3 + 2 = 4 + 1, you are saying that another way to represent 3 and 2 is as 4 and 1.

Often, this is modelled by using a pan balance. If, for example, 3 green and 2 blue cubes are placed on one pan, they will balance 4 blue and 1 yellow on the other pan.

ACTIVITY 5.13

Read the book *10 for Dinner* by J.E. Bogart (1989) to students. The pages require students, in a very interesting setting, to think about combinations for 10. Ask students to act out their own scenarios that would fit the story.

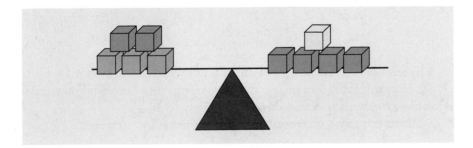

Reading and Writing Numerals

Numerals are one particularly universal way of representing numbers. Children encounter the use of numerals in many everyday situations. For example, a child might receive a birthday party invitation (such as the one shown below) that includes numerals representing different things.

Sara is 7 years old.

Please come to her 7th birthday party.

It's at 4:00 p.m. on Tuesday, March 2nd. It's at 355 Third Avenue.

Call 453-2867 to R.S.V.P.

Numerals can be used to represent age, time, and location, and for identification.

It is important that students recognize numerals and what they represent, and learn to use them. They learn to read them through a variety of opportunities, such as reading storybooks (where they can attend to page numbers and numbers in the story itself). Increasingly, in our digital world, students see "block" form numerals rather than the handwritten forms of numerals that are often taught. It is important that students recognize the variability that is possible. For example, the teacher might show them all of these different versions of the numeral 8 to point out how they are similar and how they are different.

The teacher might follow up with an activity such as Activity 5.14. Students might enjoy a puzzle that helps them focus on what numerals look like as well, such as that shown in Activity 5.15.

Students can gain experience in numeral writing by

- completing prepared dot-to-dots to follow a path to construct numerals
- tracing numerals in the air, following teacher instruction
- forming numerals in soft material like sand or salt or wikki sticks (to allow mistakes to be erased quickly and to provide additional kinesthetic feedback)
- making modelling clay or edible cookies in the shape of numerals
- tracing numerals on one another's backs, using their index finger, and guessing the numbers

In the Appendix are some tools that can be used to help children learn to write numerals. There are also downloadable masters on the Internet that teachers can use to provide numeral writing practice. Teachers must be aware that there is not one correct way to write a numeral, although some ways have proven themselves to be simpler for children than others. No matter what style is used, it is important to focus on where the writing begins, the path to follow, and the end point.

Common Errors and Misconceptions

Many of the common misconceptions and errors related to early number work revolve around not having full comprehension of the counting principles.

Small Whole Numbers: Strategies for Dealing with Common Errors and Misconceptions

COMMON ERROR OR MISCONCEPTION	SUGGESTED STRATEGY
Counting Students do not attend to which objects have been counted and which still need to be counted. They do not keep track of, or they lose track of, the objects they are counting by • skipping some of the objects • counting some of the objects twice • counting one too few when counting on, for example: 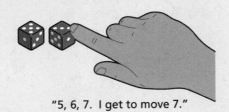 "5, 6, 7. I get to move 7."	• As students count, the teacher should watch to see if they can coordinate their verbal counting with their actions on the objects. • Students should be encouraged to move objects as they count them, one at a time, away from the objects still to be counted. • To minimize the likelihood of incorrect counting on, students should say aloud the number they are counting on from while pointing to that group, and then count on from there, pointing to each item as they count on. For example, to count on to find the sum of a roll of 5 and a roll of 3, students can say "5," while pointing to the die showing 5, and then say "6, 7, 8" as they point to each dot on the other die.
Counting Students who do not conserve number do not recognize the irrelevance of the space occupied by items. For example, they might think that by spreading out 4 counters, they are now a greater number.	Conservation of number is something that comes with experience and maturity. As students mature cognitively, they start to realize that the arrangement of items is irrelevant to the cardinality. Early on, however, it is important for students to have opportunities where they see that when they count, they get the same number both ways.
Counting Some students do not recognize that where you begin to count is irrelevant. For example, in counting the objects below, you could start with the yellow counter, going right and then back to the red and green ones, or you could start with the olive one at the right going left. The count does not change. 	Experience is the best tool in this case. Provide opportunities for students to count a set of objects, starting in several different places, or model how that is done. Ask students whether the total changed. Eventually they come to believe that it will not change.
Cardinal and Ordinal Numbers Students misunderstand the difference between cardinal and ordinal numbers; for example, in this situation, the student was asked to show 5 books. 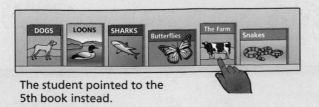 The student pointed to the 5th book instead.	It is through experience that students learn that a number can refer to a group of objects. It may be useful to set up a contradiction that a student will need to deal with. For example, for the situation shown to the left, move the 5th book to the 2nd position, and then ask the student to show you 2 books. If she or he points to the same book, ask, "I thought you said this was 5. It is also 2?"

Appropriate Manipulatives

Manipulatives are critical to the development of early number sense.

COUNTERS

Counters are essential manipulatives in early number work. Many different types of counters are useful:

- counters of different shapes and sizes
- objects of interest to children
- two-sided counters for number activities where random outcomes are desirable. For example, if a child spills 10 two-sided counters, she or he can compare the number of reds and yellows. Each time they are spilled, there could be a different number comparison.

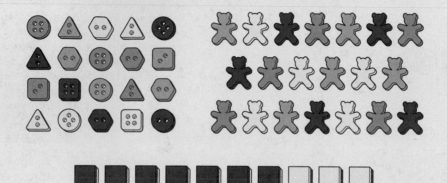

LINKING CUBES

Linking cubes are easy for students to manipulate and group. They are also good for number comparisons, as the attribute of length can help with comparing. If cubes of different colours are used, they can also be used for ordinal work.

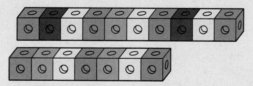

Counting on: "10, 11, 12, 13, 14, 15, 16, 17"
Comparing: "10 is 3 more than 7."
Ordinals: "The 2nd and 8th cubes are red."

DOMINOES AND DICE

Dominoes and dice provide familiar representations for numbers that students can begin to internalize.

Kei: "I recognize 6."

5-FRAMES

5-frames are useful for number comparisons and working with the benchmark of 5.

4 is one less than 5.

10-FRAMES

10-frames are useful for number comparisons and working with benchmark numbers (5 and 10).

8 is greater than 5 because 8 has 3 more than 5.

GAME MATERIALS

Game materials such as dice, cards, and dominoes are useful for the development of subitizing configurations that are associated with certain numbers. They are also useful for counting and encouraging the use of efficient counting strategies.

Subitizing with dice: "I rolled a 3 and a 4."
Counting on with dominoes: "6, 7, 8, 9, 10"
Comparing with cards: "9 is more than 3."

A WALK-ON NUMBER LINE

Walk-on number lines are useful for numeral identification, for early counting, both forward and backward, and for number comparisons.

8 is greater than 5 because it's farther along the number line.

(continued)

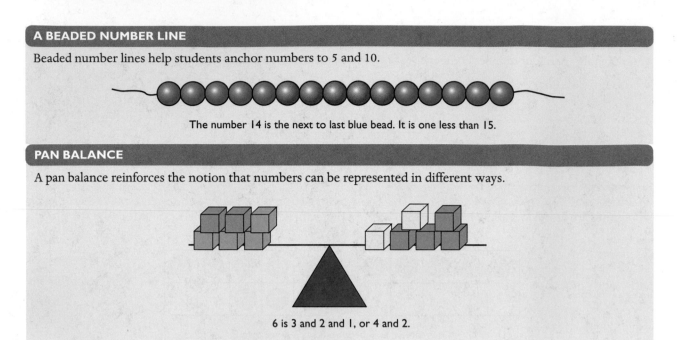

A BEADED NUMBER LINE

Beaded number lines help students anchor numbers to 5 and 10.

The number 14 is the next to last blue bead. It is one less than 15.

PAN BALANCE

A pan balance reinforces the notion that numbers can be represented in different ways.

6 is 3 and 2 and 1, or 4 and 2.

Appropriate Technology

Calculators

Calculators can be used to reinforce and support counting. For early counting work, students would most likely use the repeat, or constant, function of a calculator to count on or back, or skip count forward or backward. Not all calculators have this function, so a teacher may want to give parents some advice on which calculator to choose for those purchased for home use or for those to be brought to school.

Counting on:

5 + 1 = = = 8.

Skip counting backward:

20 − 2 = = = 14.

Computers

Students can also use computers to reinforce and support counting. There are a number of excellent computer software packages for children to support counting. The higher quality programs provide opportunities for students to see many configurations of any one number. In addition, they provide interesting objects for students to count. An "old" standard is *Millie's Math House*. Another commonly used package, *Unifix Software*, allows students to manipulate linking cubes, and another, *Tenth Planet Explores Math: Number Meaning and Counting*, is worth considering. But new, quality programs are being developed all the time.

Assessing Student Understanding

- Observe whether students stumble as they count, whether they count groups of objects efficiently, for example, by counting on, and whether they recognize certain configurations immediately and do not actually need to count them.
- Observe whether students can represent quantities in more than one way. For example, if asked to show 6 items, do they realize that the 6 can be arranged spatially in many ways?
- Some students can compare numbers more easily if they are very different than if they are close in size. Make sure to assess students' ability to compare in both situations.
- There should be little, if any, paper and pencil assessment at this level. Observation is the best tool to get a sense of what students at this age understand.

Appropriate Children's Books

10 Black Dots (Crews, 1992).
The author uses graphic designs based on different numbers of dots. The focus is on the numbers from 1 to 10. For example, the page for 2 talks about how two dots can make the eyes of a fox, and the two dots are visually represented to show this. A teacher might have students then construct their own pictures using different numbers of dots and might, if appropriate, focus on the combinations of dots that make up the total.

Animal Numbers (Kitchen, 1988).
This beautifully illustrated book of animals helps children see how mother animals take care of their young. What is interesting about it mathematically is that each page has one more item on it than the number on the page, since there is one mother animal with the indicated number of baby animals. This can provoke some good discussion.

Twelve Ways to Get to 11 (Merriam, 1996).
A variety of different contexts provide the backdrop for showing different combinations of 11. For example, one picture shows six peanut shells and five pieces of popcorn, and an elephant decked out in circus regalia to model 11 at the circus.

The Right Number of Elephants (Sheppard, 1992).
Original drawings and an unusual story line focus the reader on the sequence of numbers you hear as you count backward. The story line involves a girl deciding how many elephants are needed to help her accomplish various silly tasks.

Applying What You've Learned

1. To solve the chapter problem, you listed some ways that 6 and 8 are alike and different. How frequently might you use an activity like this involving different pairs of numbers? Explain your decision.
2. Some teachers believe it is best to deliver lessons for each number separately, for example, a lesson on 5, a lesson on 6, etc. Argue as to why this might not be the best thing to do.

3. One of the main differences between the walk-on number line and the standard number line is that instead of using numbers to mark points on the number line, the numbers in the walk-on line occupy spaces.

   a) What are the advantages of a number line where spaces are marked?

   b) What are the disadvantages?

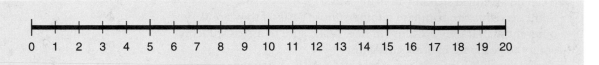

4. Locate five counting books that have particular mathematical merit. What makes each one valuable?

5. Develop a lesson plan around comparing numbers that are 10 or less. Include in the plan what assessment you will use to determine the success of the lesson.

6. a) Describe two or three interesting approaches to numeral writing that you could use with students.

   b) Do you think that numerals should be written as they appear on digital displays? (For example, the loops in 8 would be square rather than round.)

7. Examine several texts at the K and 1 levels. Do these texts emphasize the relationship of other numbers up to 20 to the anchor numbers of 5 and 10? Choose one or two lessons in the text to talk about how that relationship could be strengthened.

Interact with a K–8 Student:

8. Observe a fairly young child counting a set of 5 to 6 objects. What does the child do to keep track of objects to make sure that they are not counted twice? Does this strategy serve him or her well or not?

Discuss with a K–8 Teacher:

9. Ask a Kindergarten or Grade 1 teacher to share his or her knowledge of typical students' comfort with counting when they enter that grade level. Ask how the teacher adapts instruction for those students whose counting is significantly more advanced than that norm.

WebConnect

www.makingmathmeaningful.nelson.com

Visit Nelson's Making Math Meaningful website to find links to counting books.

Selected References

Akers, S. (1990). *What comes in 2's, 3's and 4's?* New York: Simon & Schuster.

Baroody, A.J. (1992a). The development of preschoolers' counting skills and principles. In Bideaud, J., Meljac, C., and Fischer, J.P. (Eds.). *Pathways to number: Children's developing numerical abilities*, Hillsdale, NJ: Erlbaum, 99–126.

Baroody, A.J. (1992b). Remedying common counting difficulties. In Bideaud, J., Meljac, C., and Fischer, J.P. (Eds.). *Pathways to number: Children's developing numerical abilities*, Hillsdale, NJ: Erlbaum, 307–324.

Baroody, A.J., and Benson, A. (2001). Early number instruction. *Teaching Children Mathematics.* 8, 154–158.

Baroody, A.J., and Wilkins, J.L.M. (1999). The development of informal counting, number, and arithmetic skills and concepts. In Copley, J. (Ed.). *Mathematics in the early years.* Reston, VA: National Council of Teachers of Mathematics, 48–65.

Bialystok, E., and Codd, J. (1996). Developing representations of quantity. *Canadian Journal of Behavioural Science, 28*(4), 281–291.

Bogart, J.E. (1989). *Ten for dinner.* Richmond Hill, ON: Scholastic Tab.

Briars, D., and Siegler, R.S. (1984). A featural analysis of preschoolers' counting knowledge. *Developmental Psychology, 20,* 607–618.

Cavanagh, M., Dacey, L., Findell, C.R., Greenes, C.E., Sheffield, L.J., and Small, M. (2004). *Navigating through number and operations in Prekindergarten–grade 2.* Reston, VA: National Council of Teachers of Mathematics.

Christelow, Eileen. (1998). Five little monkeys jumping on the bed. New York: Clarion Books.

Clements, D.H. (1999). Subitizing: What is it? Why teach it? *Teaching Children Mathematics, 5,* 400–405.

Crews. D. (1992). *Ten black dots.* Toronto: Scholastic.

Dacey, L.S., and Eston, R. (1999). *Growing mathematical ideas in kindergarten.* Sausalito, CA: Math Solutions Publications.

Frye, D., Braisby, N., Lowe, J., Maroudas, C., and Nicholls, J. (1989). Young children's understanding of counting and cardinality. *Child Development, 60,* 1158–1171.

Fuson, K.C. (1988). *Children's counting and concepts of number.* New York: Springer-Verlag.

Fuson, K.C., Grandau, L., and Sugiyama, P.A. (2001). Achievable numerical understandings for all young children. *Teaching Children Mathematics, 522–526.*

Fuson, K.C., Secada, W.G., and Hall, J.W. (1983). Matching, counting, and conservation of numerical equivalence. *Child Development, 54,* 91–97.

Gelman, R., and Gallistel, C.R. (1978). *The child's understanding of number.* Cambridge, MA: Harvard University Press.

Kitchen, B. (1988). *Animal numbers.* Cambri0dge, UK: Lutterworth Press.

Merriam, E. (1996). *Twelve ways to get to 11.* New York: Aladdin.

Sheppard, J. (1992). *The right number of elephants.* New York: HarperTrophy.

Small, M. (2005). *PRIME: Number and operations: Background and strategies.* Toronto: Thomson Nelson.

Steffe, L.P. (1992). Learning stages in the construction of the number sequence. In Bideaud, J., Meljac, C., and Fischer, J.P. (Eds.). *Pathways to number: Children's developing numerical abilities.* Hillsdale, NJ: Lawrence Erlbaum, 83–98.

Wright, R.J., Martland, J., and Stafford, A.K. (2006). *Early numeracy: Assessment for teaching and intervention.* London, UK: Paul Chapman Publishing.

Chapter 6

Developing Early Operation Concepts

IN A NUTSHELL

The main ideas in this chapter are listed below:

1. All four operations, addition, subtraction, multiplication, and division, are related.

2. There are multiple meanings for each operation. Students need exposure, over time, to each of these meanings.

3. Different models should be employed to model the operations since some principles are better explained with one model than another.

4. Students need opportunities to use concrete materials and mental strategies to relate facts to one another. They must not be rushed into memorizing facts before they are ready.

CHAPTER PROBLEM

Addition facts describe the results of adding two single-digit numbers. They are often shown in a table like this one:

+	0	1	2	3	4	5	6	7	8	9
0										
1										
2										
3										
4										
5										
6										
7										
8										
9										

Which number appears most often in the table? Why?

How the Four Operations Are Related

The four operations that are the focus of K–8 mathematics are addition, subtraction, multiplication, and division.

They are highly related. The picture below shows the most critical aspects of those relationships.

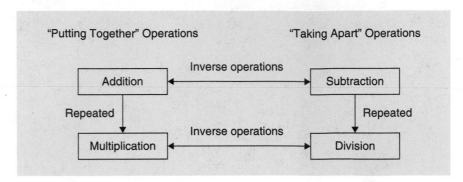

Frequently, the same problem can be viewed using any of the four operations. For example, consider this problem:

Rafi had 12 cookies on a plate. If he ate them 3 at a time, how many times could he go back for cookies?
–Using addition: I'll add 3s until I get to 12: $3 + 3 + 3 + 3 = 12$. Solution: 4 times.
–Using subtraction: I'll subtract 3s until there are 0 cookies left: $12 - 3 - 3 - 3 - 3 = 0$. Solution: 4 times.
–Using multiplication: I'll figure out what to multiply by 3 to get 12. $4 \times 3 = 12$. Solution: 4 times.
–Using division: I'll divide 12 by 3: $12 \div 3 = 4$. Solution: 4 times.

Addition and Subtraction

In Canadian schools, teachers generally introduce addition and subtraction formally before multiplication and division.

Meanings of Addition

Although addition always relates to the situation of combining things, students find it easier to first consider active situations, where a joining actually occurs, and later more static situations, where a whole is made up of two parts. In both cases, the numbers you add are called *addends* and the result is called a *sum*.

MEANING	EXAMPLE
Joining is an active addition situation.	A child has 5 marbles. His mom then brings him 3 new ones. 5 marbles + 3 new marbles = 8 marbles
Part-part-whole is a static addition situation where no action takes place.	A child has 8 marbles; 5 of them are blue and 3 are red. No action occurs, but it is still an addition situation. 5 blue marbles + 3 red marbles = 8 marbles

Meanings of Subtraction

Subtraction is a more complex operation than addition. Most simply, it is the opposite of addition, but there are many nuances.

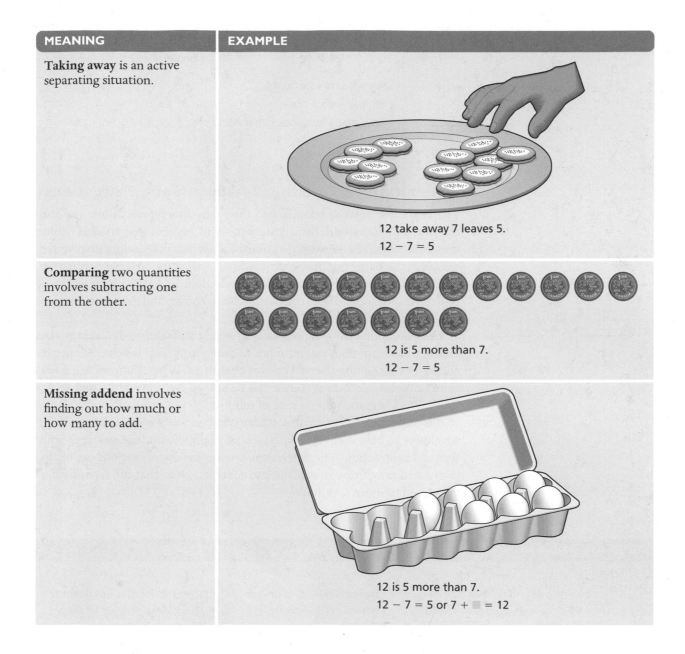

MEANING	EXAMPLE
Taking away is an active separating situation.	12 take away 7 leaves 5. $12 - 7 = 5$
Comparing two quantities involves subtracting one from the other.	12 is 5 more than 7. $12 - 7 = 5$
Missing addend involves finding out how much or how many to add.	12 is 5 more than 7. $12 - 7 = 5$ or $7 + \blacksquare = 12$

It is important for students to realize that these varying meanings for subtraction are related; in other words, it makes sense to apply the same operation in each situation. Therefore, a teacher must ensure that the connections are explored. One example is described below.

How Is Taking Away Like Comparing?

Consider the situation modelled and described below. To compare the number in the top row (*the minuend*) with the number in the bottom row (*the subtrahend*), you are finding how many more are in the top row than in the bottom row. You can take away the 3 counters that match in each row and what is left (*the difference*) is how many more were in the top row. So to compare to find how many more, you can take away.

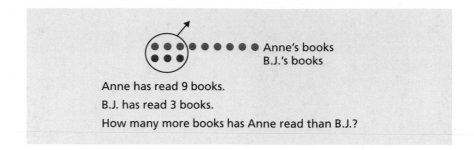

Anne has read 9 books.

B.J. has read 3 books.

How many more books has Anne read than B.J.?

Understanding Addition and Subtraction Situations

The chart that follows summarizes the many different addition and subtraction situations with which students will be required to deal. Some involve actions, like joining or taking away (separating), some involve recognizing the parts that make up a whole, and some involve comparing. Sometimes the whole and one part are known and the other part must be determined; other times the two parts are known and the whole must be determined.

Each situation can be represented by either an addition or a subtraction number sentence with one number missing, and each is solved either by adding or subtracting the two known quantities. What is interesting is that sometimes an addition sentence can be solved by subtracting and sometimes by adding; the same is true of subtraction sentences.

It is important to ensure that students encounter a wide variety of these structures to help them construct a more complete understanding of addition and subtraction. The different meanings for the operations can be distinguished only through appropriate contexts. Note that the term *separating* is used to mean *take away*.

ADDITION AND SUBTRACTION SITUATIONS

Joining situations	1	2	3
	Result (sum) is unknown	Change (addend) is unknown	Start (addend) is unknown
	I have 3 pennies to start with.	*I have 5 pennies to start with.*	*I had some pennies to start with.*
	I get 1 more. How many do I have now?	*I get some more. Now I have 10. How many more did I get?*	*I got 3 more. Now I have 8. How many did I start with?*
	$3 + 1 = \blacksquare$	$5 + \blacksquare = 10$	$\blacksquare + 3 = 8$
	$a + b = \blacksquare$	$a + \blacksquare = c$	$\blacksquare + b = c$
	Add to solve.	To solve, you can subtract $10 - 5$.	To solve, you can subtract $8 - 3$.

ADDITION AND SUBTRACTION SITUATIONS

Separating situations	4	5	6
	Result (difference) is unknown *I had 6 pennies to start with.* *I spent 3. How many do I have left?* $6 - 3 = $ ▨ $c - a = $ ▨ Subtract to solve.	Change (subtrahend) is unknown *I had 6 pennies to start with.* *I spent some. I have 2 left. How many did I spend?* $6 - $ ▨ $= 2$ $c - $ ▨ $= b$ To solve, you can subtract $6 - 2$.	Start (minuend) is unknown *I had some pennies to start with. I spent 4. I have 6 left. How many did I start with?* ▨ $- 4 = 6$ To solve, you can add $6 + 4$.
Part-part-whole situations	**7**	**8**	
	Whole (sum) is unknown *I have 3 pennies and 4 nickels. How many coins do I have altogether?* $3 + 4 = $ ▨ $a + b = $ ▨ Add to solve.	Part (addend) is unknown *I have 7 coins altogether. They are all pennies or nickels; 3 are pennies. How many are nickels?* $3 + $ ▨ $= 7$ $a + $ ▨ $= c$ To solve, you can subtract $7 - 3$.	
Comparing situations	**9**	**10**	**11**
	Difference is unknown *I have 7 pennies and 2 nickels. How many more pennies than nickels do I have?* $7 - 2 = $ ▨ $c - a = $ ▨ Subtract to solve.	Comparing quantity (subtrahend) is unknown *I have 7 pennies and some nickels. I have 2 more pennies than nickels. How many nickels do I have?* $7 - $ ▨ $= 2$ $c - $ ▨ $= b$ To solve, you can subtract $7 - 2$.	Referent quantity (minuend) is unknown *I have some pennies. I have 3 nickels. I have 2 fewer nickels than pennies. How many pennies do I have?* ▨ $- 3 = 2$ ▨ $a = b$ To solve, you can add $2 + 3$.

Solving Addition and Subtraction Number Stories

Students must decode and interpret number stories and not just rely on looking for "clue words" to decide what operation to perform. Notice that the word "more" appears both in Situation 1 in the Addition and Subtraction Situations chart, which involves adding the two given numbers, as well as in Situation 2, which involves subtracting the two given numbers.

Generally, but not always, students find joining and separating (take-away) situations easiest to deal with. If students are encouraged to model number stories as they are presented, however, even young children can deal with part-part-whole and comparing situations.

Relating Addition and Subtraction

Notice that any addition situation can also be viewed as a subtraction one, and vice versa. In fact, what we call a fact family is a set of four number sentences, or equations, that can be used to describe the same situation.

ACTIVITY 6.1

Provide students with a "script," for example, an expression like $4 + 6$ or an equation like $12 - 5 = 7$, and ask them, with a partner, to act out a "play" to show that script. They should be encouraged to use a variety of situations that are meaningful to their own experiences, rather than merely copying a familiar form over and over.

ACTIVITY 6.2

You might provide triangle cards like this one and ask students to describe the four facts in the fact family that go with them. Then ask why sometimes there are only 3 facts (e.g., with 10, 5, and 5).

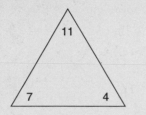

Fact Family for 2, 3, and 5

| | | | | |

3 + 2 = 5   3 blue + 2 red = 5 altogether
2 + 3 = 5   2 red + 3 blue = 5 altogether
5 − 2 = 3   5 altogether; 2 are red, so 3 must be blue
5 − 3 = 2   5 altogether; 3 are blue, so 2 must be red

Addition and Subtraction Principles

There are a number of principles about addition and subtraction that students need to learn and discuss. Some of them are restatements of what mathematicians call properties inherent in our number system; others are built from those properties.

The idea is not to memorize the principles by name, but to be so familiar with our number system, that they are used naturally and informally.

Addition and Subtraction Principles

1. Addition and subtraction "undo" each other. They are related inverse operations. For example, if $4 + 8 = 12$, then $12 - 8 = 4$.

2. You can add numbers in any order (the commutative property). With subtraction, the order in which you subtract the numbers matters.

3. To add three numbers, you can add the first two and then the last one, or the last two and then the first one, to that sum (the associative property). For example, to add $5 + 4 + 3$, you can add $5 + 4$ to get 9 and then add 3, or you can add $4 + 3$ to get 7 and then calculate $5 + 7$. This property exists since addition is actually defined in terms of how to combine two numbers, so rules for three numbers had to be created.

4. You can add or subtract in parts. For example, $2 + 5 = 2 + 4 + 1$; $8 - 5 = 8 - 3 - 2$.

5. To subtract two numbers, you can add or subtract the same amount to or from both numbers without changing the difference. For example, $12 - 7 = (12 + 1) - (7 + 1)$.

6. When you add or subtract 0 to or from a number, the answer is the number you started with.

7. When you add 1 to a number, the sum is the next counting number. When you subtract 1 from a number, the difference is the counting number that comes before.

ACTIVITY 6.3

Students might have visuals of a variety of items with price tags with amounts 10¢ or lower.

They are told they started with 10¢, bought one of the items, and are told how much is left. They have to decide what was purchased.

For example, if 6¢ was left, they had to realize they bought a 4¢ item.

Principle 1: Addition and subtraction "undo" each other. They are related, but inverse, operations.

Mathematicians define subtraction as the inverse operation to addition, that is, it undoes what addition accomplishes. Suppose you start with 4 items, and you add 8 more and end up with 12. How do you get back to where you started at 4? You subtract the 8 you added. Similarly, if you start with 12 items and take away 4, you get back to the starting number, 12, by adding the 4 you took away.

Principle 2: You can add numbers in any order (the commutative property). With subtraction, the order in which you subtract the numbers matters.

The commutative property, or order property, can be modelled and explained using counters. Show a group of 3 counters and a group of 4 counters on a piece of paper, and then turn the paper 180 degrees. It is clear that you have exactly the same counters, so $3 + 4 = 4 + 3$.

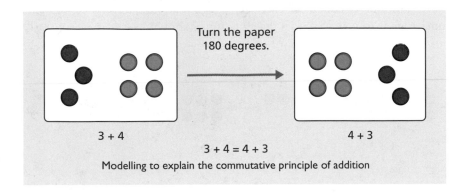

Turn the paper 180 degrees.

3 + 4   4 + 3

3 + 4 = 4 + 3

Modelling to explain the commutative principle of addition

However, order does matter when you subtract. For example, if you take 3 cookies away from 7, you have 4 left. You cannot take 7 cookies away from 3, although later students will learn that you can calculate $3 - 7$, using integers.

Principle 3: To add three numbers, you can add the first two and then the last one, or the last two and then the first one, to that sum (the associative property).

As a consequence of this property, you can take away from one number and add what you took away to the other number without changing the sum. Suppose you are adding 4 counters and 6 counters as shown below; you can move any number of counters from one pile to the other without changing the total. Moving 2 counters from the left pile to the right changes the calculation to $2 + 8$, but does not change the sum. In fact, you have renamed $(2 + 2) + 6$ as $2 + (2 + 6)$.

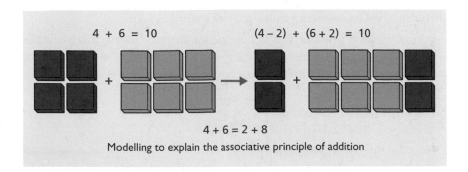

4 + 6 = 10   (4 – 2) + (6 + 2) = 10

+   +

4 + 6 = 2 + 8

Modelling to explain the associative principle of addition

Principle 4: You can add or subtract in parts.

Suppose you want to add 5 objects to a group of objects. It really does not matter if you add all 5 objects at once or if you do it in stages. For example, you can add 3 and then add 2; you are still adding 5 ($2 + 5 = 2 + 3 + 2$). The same is true for subtraction. For example, to subtract 5 objects from a group, you can take away 3 and then take away 2 more ($8 - 5 = 8 - 3 - 2$).

Principle 5: To subtract two numbers, you can add or subtract the same amount to or from both numbers without changing the difference.

If a boy is 12 years old and his brother is 7, the older brother is 5 years older than the younger one. What about next year and the year after that? How much older will he be then? He will always be 5 years older. Because the same amount is added to each age each year, the difference remains unchanged. You could model the situation as shown.

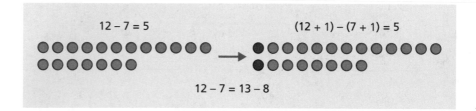

Principle 6: When you add or subtract 0 to or from a number, the answer is the number you started with.

One useful model to show this principle is a walk-on number line:

$3 + 2$ means start at 3 and step 2 spaces forward, ending up on 5.

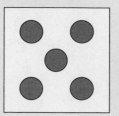
$3 + 0$ means start at 3 and step 0 spaces forward, staying at 3.

Principle 7: When you add 1 to a number, the sum is the next counting number. When you subtract 1 from a number, the difference is the counting number that comes before.

Again, a walk-on number line is helpful for demonstrating this principle since adding 1 means to move 1 space forward, for example, $3 + 1 = 4$, and subtracting 1 means to move 1 space back, for example, $3 - 1 = 2$.

Strategies for Learning Addition and Subtraction Facts

Using the Principles Directly

There are 100 addition facts, from $0 + 0$ to $9 + 9$, as well as 55 related subtraction facts. (There are subtraction facts like $6 - 2$, but not $2 - 6$ [the quantity $2 - 6$ exists, but it is not labelled as a fact], so the number of subtraction facts is less than 100.) The principles that students learn about addition and subtraction can substantially reduce the number of separate facts they need to learn. For example:

Principle	Example
Principle 1 (that subtraction and addition are related) The subtraction facts do not have to be learned as separate facts. The student can always think of the related addition fact.	$8 + 3 = 11$, so $11 - 3 = 8$ and $11 - 8 = 3$
Principle 2 (that numbers can be added in any order) 45 of the addition facts can be related to 45 reverse facts, eliminating the need to memorize them separately.	$4 + 3 = 7$, so $3 + 4 = 7$

Students who become comfortable with the principles articulated on pages 108–110 will recognize which strategies might be useful in which situations to relate an unknown fact to a known one. Typical strategies include:

Strategy	Relevant Principle	Example
Counting on to add 1 or 2	Principle 7	$5 + 1$ Count: (5), 6
Counting back to subtract 1 or 2	Principle 7	$9 - 2$ Count back: (9), 8, 7 A number line is useful for counting on or back since students can see all the numbers in order. 0 1 2 3 4 5 6 7 8
Adding or subtracting 0	Principle 6	$4 + 0 = 4$ There is no more. $3 - 0 = 3$ There is no less.

Using the Principles Indirectly

Many facts can be related so closely to known facts that they never need to be memorized separately.

Building on Doubles Students seem to learn the double facts easily, for example, $3 + 3 = 6$, $7 + 7 = 14$, etc.

Other facts can be related to these.

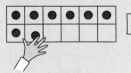

STRATEGY		PRINCIPLE ADDRESSED
$6 + 8 = (6 + 1) + (8 - 1)$ $\quad = 7 + 7$	Move 1 from the 8 to the 6. Now add doubles.	Principle 3
$7 + 8 = 7 + (7 + 1)$ $\quad = (7 + 7) + 1$ $\quad = 14 + 1$, or 15	Recognize that 8 is 7 and 1. First add 7 to make a double. Then add 1.	Principle 3 Principle 7

Making Tens Once students learn the combinations for 10, for example, $4 + 6$, $7 + 3$, etc., they can relate other calculations to these. This is efficient, since to determine $10 + ■$, if ■ is less than 10, does not require addition; it is simply a representation of the number $1■$.

STRATEGY		PRINCIPLE ADDRESSED
$9 + 5 = (9 + 1) + (5 - 1)$ $\quad = 10 + 4$	Move 1 from the 5 to the 9.	Principle 3
$8 + 6 = (8 + 2) + (6 - 2)$	Move 2 from the 6 to the 8.	Principle 3

Subtraction facts can also be related to 10. Again, $1■ - 10$ does not require use of facts.

STRATEGY		PRINCIPLE ADDRESSED
$15 - 9 = (15 + 1) - (9 + 1)$ $\quad = 16 - 10$	Add 1 to both to keep the difference the same.	Principle 5

Getting to 10 along the way is also useful.

STRATEGY		PRINCIPLE ADDRESSED
$7 + 6 = (7 + 3) + 3$ $\quad = 10 + 3$	Add in parts.	Principle 4
$13 - 4 = (13 - 3) - 1$ $\quad = 10 - 1$	Subtract in parts.	Principle 4
For $13 - 9$	Think of subtraction as the opposite of addition.	Principle 1
Think: $9 + 1 = 10$ $\quad\quad 10 + 3 = 13$ So I've added $1 + 3 = 4$	Add up in stages.	Principle 4

It takes time to develop and nurture the thinking strategies that help students learn their facts. Initially, the emphasis is on the development of the many relations among the facts, rather than speed of recall.

One of the best ways to explore facts is in rich problem-solving situations.

Name: _____ Date: _____

What's for Lunch?

Show 3 ways to spend exactly 10¢.

🍌 2¢
🍎 2¢
△ 5¢
🍪 1¢
📦 3¢

The problem above promotes mathematical thinking, but also provides an opportunity to practise facts.

ACTIVITY 6.7

It is important for students to associate each number less than 10 with a partner to add to it to make 10. Create sets of squares with numbers less than 10 on each side. Sides with a sum of 10 can be put together to make a design.

	7	
6		3
	4	

	2	
7		5
	8	

	2	
1		4
	7	

ACTIVITY 6.8

Provide students with small circles with numbers from 0 to 10 on them.

Ask them to arrange six of the circles on the triangle so that each side sums to 10.

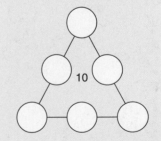

ACTIVITY **6.9**

Provide a game board and game instructions on a laminated card for students to use at a math centre. This game practises addition and subtraction strategies as well as coin relationships.

Lemonade Stand

(for 2 or 3 players)

You will need

number cube

1 paperclip per player

15 pennies per player

4 nickels per player

Lemonade Stand Game Board

How to play

1. Roll the number cube. Move your marker forward or back.

2. If you land on 1¢ or 5¢, take that much money.

3. When you have 12¢ or more, go to the lemonade stand. Who will get there first?

I've got 12¢. I can get lemonade!

Lemonade 12¢

ACTIVITY 6.10

Set up a grid of 2 rows of 9 seats and gather students around them.

Sing the song "The Wheels on the Bus" with students. Pause at various points and indicate how many people are to get on and off the "bus." Some students act the situation out while the other students predict how many will be left on the bus after each situation is acted out.

Common Errors and Misconceptions

Addition and Subtraction: Strategies for Dealing with Common Errors and Misconceptions

COMMON ERROR OR MISCONCEPTION	SUGGESTED STRATEGY
Understanding Open Sentences Students are confused by open sentences with missing addends, and missing subtrahends and minuends. For example, they might interpret $3 + \blacksquare = 8$ as $8 + 3 = \blacksquare$.	Have students explain what the sentence actually says; for example, "A number is added to 3 and you end up with 8." Then ask how they know the missing number has to be less than 8.
Interpreting Walk-On Number Lines Students have difficulty using walk-on number lines to add or subtract. For example, to show $8 - 3$, some students will start at 8 but include 8 as they count back 3, landing on 6 instead of 5.	Encourage students to stand with both feet on the start number of the number step before taking their first step. This will force their first step onto the next square.

Appropriate Manipulatives

Addition

Manipulatives can be used to model both the joining (or active addition) and part-part-whole (or static addition) meanings of addition.

Addition: Examples of Manipulatives

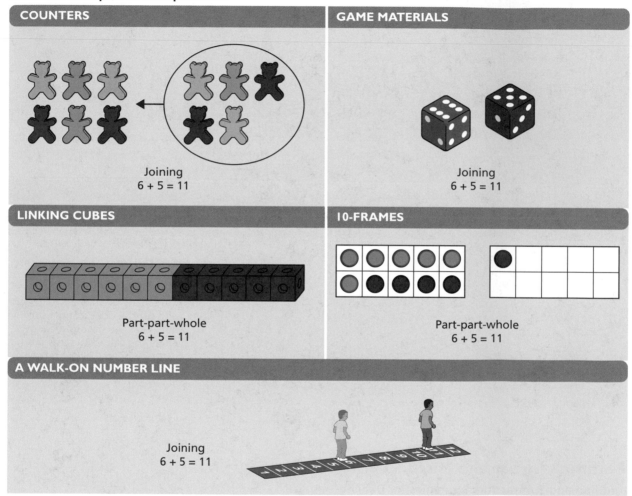

COUNTERS

Joining
6 + 5 = 11

GAME MATERIALS

Joining
6 + 5 = 11

LINKING CUBES

Part-part-whole
6 + 5 = 11

10-FRAMES

Part-part-whole
6 + 5 = 11

A WALK-ON NUMBER LINE

Joining
6 + 5 = 11

Subtraction

Manipulatives can be used to model take-away, comparison, missing addend, and part-part-whole meanings of subtraction. Sometimes the meaning of subtraction is tied to the physical representation, but other times it depends on the words that are said when looking at the model.

Subtraction: Examples of Manipulatives

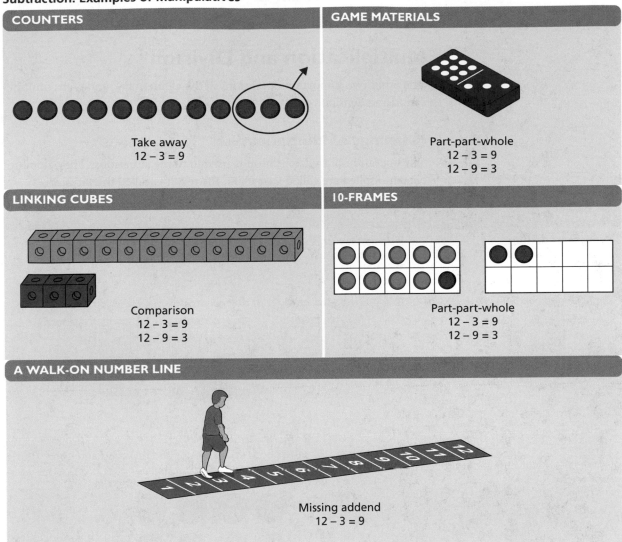

COUNTERS

Take away
12 – 3 = 9

GAME MATERIALS

Part-part-whole
12 – 3 = 9
12 – 9 = 3

LINKING CUBES

Comparison
12 – 3 = 9
12 – 9 = 3

10-FRAMES

Part-part-whole
12 – 3 = 9
12 – 9 = 3

A WALK-ON NUMBER LINE

Missing addend
12 – 3 = 9

Appropriate Technology

Calculators

Calculators can be used to explore patterns involving addition and subtraction. Students might look at the results, for example, of repeatedly adding 9 to a number, as shown right. They will notice how the ones digit decreases by 1 and the tens digit increases by 1, until the ones digit hits 0, and then the tens digit does not change and the 0 becomes a 9.

Calculators can also be used to explore problems involving multiple calculations or calculations using greater numbers for which students do not yet have the skills to calculate. If they have grasped the meanings of addition and subtraction, working with greater numbers should not pose a challenge, as they will know what operation to use.

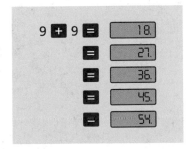

Computers

There are many useful computer software packages available. Some are more conceptual, such as Sunburst's *Combining and Breaking Apart Numbers*; some are for practice, like *Math Blaster*, and others are problem based, like

Ten Tricky Tiles. One that uses animation to see the trading/regrouping actions is Neufeld's *Understanding Math Plus*.

Multiplication and Division

The other two important operations in the elementary grades are multiplication and division.

Meanings of Multiplication

The operation of multiplication is used in many situations. The two numbers multiplied are called *factors* and the result is called the *product*.

MEANING	EXAMPLE
Repeated Addition	The first factor, in this case 3, tells how many times to add the second factor, 4. $3 \times 4 = 4 + 4 + 4$
Equal Groups or Sets	3×4 is the total number of objects in 3 sets of 4. $4 + 4 + 4 = 12$ $3 \times 4 = 12$ This model shows both equal groups and repeated addition.
An Array	3×4 is the total number of items in a 3-by-4 array. $3 \times 4 = 12$ An array of 3 rows with 4 counters in each has 12 counters altogether.
Area of a Rectangle	3×4 is the area of a 3-by-4 rectangle. $3 \times 4 = 12$ A rectangle that is 3 units wide by 4 units long has an area of 12 square units.

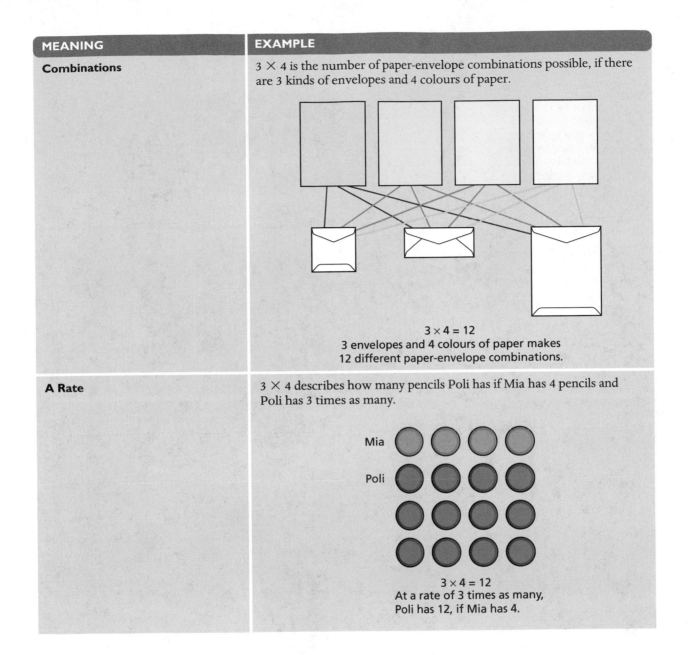

MEANING	EXAMPLE
Combinations	3×4 is the number of paper-envelope combinations possible, if there are 3 kinds of envelopes and 4 colours of paper. $3 \times 4 = 12$ 3 envelopes and 4 colours of paper makes 12 different paper-envelope combinations.
A Rate	3×4 describes how many pencils Poli has if Mia has 4 pencils and Poli has 3 times as many. Mia Poli $3 \times 4 = 12$ At a rate of 3 times as many, Poli has 12, if Mia has 4.

How the Meanings of Multiplication Are Equivalent

Simply knowing the meanings will not help students develop a well-rounded understanding of the operation. It is important for students to understand why these various meanings are equivalent and are, therefore, all related to multiplication. One such relationship is shown below.

How Is a Rate Meaning Really the Same as a Repeated Addition or an Array Meaning? If Mia has 4 items and Poli has 3 times as many items as Mia, then Poli has 12 items (3 items for each 1 item that Mia has). This can be modelled in an array as shown (Poli's array) and can be represented by adding the number in each row using repeated addition: $4 + 4 + 4$.

ACTIVITY 6.11

Draw arrays on cards and cut off a corner so that some counters are missing, but the numbers of rows and columns are clear. Present a card, suggesting that a dog bit it off. Ask how many counters were originally on the card, given that the array was originally complete.

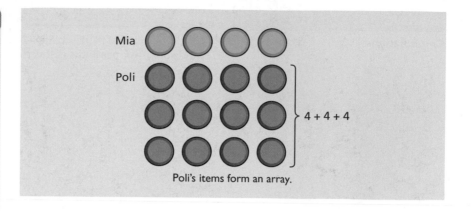

Poli's items form an array.

Meanings of Division

When one number is divided by another, the number being divided is called the *dividend*, the other number is called the *divisor*, and the result is called the *quotient*.

MEANING	EXAMPLE
Equal Sharing (Partitive)	$12 \div 4 = 3$ is the amount each person gets if 12 items are shared equally among 4 people. $12 \div 4 = 3$
Equal Grouping (Quotative)	$12 \div 4 = 3$ is the number of equal groups of 4 you can make with 12 items. $12 \div 4 = 3$
Repeated Subtraction	$12 \div 4 = 3$ is the number of times you can subtract 4 from 12 before you get to 0. $-4 \qquad -4 \qquad -4$ 0 1 2 3 4 5 6 7 8 9 10 11 12 $12 - 4 - 4 - 4 = 0$ $12 \div 4 = 3$

MEANING	EXAMPLE
Width or Length of a Rectangle	$12 \div 4 = 3$ is the width of a rectangle with an area of 12 square units and a length of 4 units. Area is 12 square units 4 units long $12 \div 4 = 3$ units wide

Make up a problem to go with this number sentence:

200 ÷ 10 = 20

Katy has 200 cookies that she is going to share with 9 other friends equaly. How many will each friend get.

Answer - 20

Student Response

Notice how this student has used the sharing meaning of division to create a number story. This meaning is often the first that students tend to use.

How the Meanings of Division Are Equivalent

It is important for students to understand why these various meanings are equivalent and, therefore, all relate to division. One such relationship is shown below.

How Is Equal Sharing Like Equal Grouping? Suppose you want to share 12 items among 4 people. One of the most natural ways to do this is to give each of the 4 people one item, then give each of them a second item, and then a third item, until all the items are gone. After you have given each of the 4 people his or her first item, you have created a group of 4. After you have given each of the 4 people a second item, you have created another group of 4, and so on. So, even though you are sharing, you are also creating equal groups after each round of sharing.

Sharing 12 cookies among 4: as you share equally, you create equal groups.

Understanding Multiplication and Division Situations

As with addition and subtraction, there are many types of multiplication and division situations. Each situation can be represented by either a multiplication or division number sentence with one number missing, and each is solved by either multiplying or dividing the two known quantities. Sometimes a multiplication sentence can be solved by dividing and sometimes by multiplying; the same is true of division sentences.

As with addition and subtraction, it is very important to ensure that students encounter a wide variety of these structures to help them construct a more complete understanding of multiplication and division. The different meanings of multiplication and division can only be distinguished through appropriate contexts.

Equal group situations	1	2	3
	Whole (product) is unknown	Size of group (quotient) is unknown	Number of groups (divisor) is unknown
	I have 3 boxes with 4 tomatoes in each. How many tomatoes do I have?	*I have 12 tomatoes packed equally in 3 boxes. How many tomatoes are in each box?*	*I have some boxes of tomatoes. I have 12 tomatoes altogether, and there are 4 in each box. How many boxes do I have?*
	$3 \times 4 = \blacksquare$	$12 \div 3 = \blacksquare$	$12 \div \blacksquare = 4$
	$a \times b = \blacksquare$	$c \div a = \blacksquare$	$c \div \blacksquare = b$
	Multiply to solve.	Divide to solve.	Divide to solve: $12 \div 4$.
Comparing situations	4	5	6
	Result of comparison (product) is unknown	Size of original group (factor) is unknown	Size of comparison ratio (factor) is unknown
	Meg has 5 pennies and I have 3 times as many as she does. How many do I have?	*I have 15 pennies. I have 3 times as many pennies as Meg. How many does Meg have?*	*Meg has 5 pennies and I have 15. How many pennies do I have for each of Meg's?*
	$3 \times 5 = \blacksquare$	$3 \times \blacksquare = 15$	$\blacksquare \times 5 = 15$
	$a \times b = \blacksquare$	$a \times \blacksquare = c$	$\blacksquare \times b = c$
	Multiply to solve.	Divide to solve: $15 \div 3$.	Divide to solve: $15 \div 5$.
Combination situations	7	8	
	Total (product) is unknown	Size of one set (factor) is unknown	
	I have 3 shirts and 2 pairs of pants. How many shirt-pant outfits do I have?	*I have 8 shirt-pant outfits and 4 shirts. How many pairs of pants do I have?*	
	$3 \times 2 = \blacksquare$	$4 \times \blacksquare = 8$	
	$a \times b = \blacksquare$	$a \times \blacksquare = c$	
	Multiply to solve.	Divide to solve: $8 \div 4$.	

Notice that the sentence $\blacksquare \div 4 = 3$ is not shown in the chart. It is equivalent, though, to Situation 1. For example, the problem might be worded as, "I have some tomatoes. I was able to make 3 boxes of 4 tomatoes. How many tomatoes did I have?" and could be solved by multiplying 3×4.

Solving Multiplication and Division Problems

As with addition and subtraction, students should work with a wide variety of structures to help them construct a more complete understanding of multiplication and division situations. Because students find equal group situations easier to understand, combinations and comparison situations are usually encountered after equal group situations have been explored. As with addition and subtraction, the most difficult situations for students are those represented by $\blacksquare \times b = c$ and $\blacksquare \div a = b$, where the first term is unknown.

Once students are comfortable solving simple multiplication and division number stories, they may want to create their own number stories.

Relating Multiplication and Division

Notice that any multiplication situation can also be viewed as a division situation, and vice versa. In fact, what teachers call a fact family is a set of four number sentences, or equations, that can be used to describe the same situation.

Fact Family for 3, 4, and 12

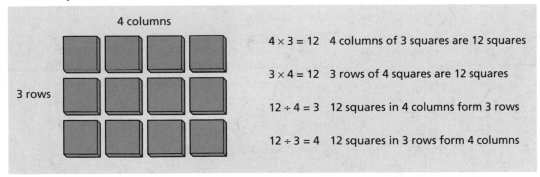

$4 \times 3 = 12$	4 columns of 3 squares are 12 squares
$3 \times 4 = 12$	3 rows of 4 squares are 12 squares
$12 \div 4 = 3$	12 squares in 4 columns form 3 rows
$12 \div 3 = 4$	12 squares in 3 rows form 4 columns

Multiplication and Division Principles

Students need to become familiar with and use a number of principles about multiplication and division. In the explanations of the principles on the following pages, different meanings of multiplication and different models are used each time. Often, one meaning of an operation is much more helpful than another in explaining a particular idea.

As with addition, some properties of multiplication have been named by mathematicians, in particular, the commutative, associative, and distributive properties. These are identified in the chart.

Multiplication and Division Principles

1. Multiplication and division "undo" each other. They are related inverse operations. For example, if $12 \div 3 = 4$, then $3 \times 4 = 12$.

2. You can multiply numbers in any order (the commutative property). With division, the order in which you divide the numbers matters.

3. To multiply two numbers, you can divide one factor and multiply the other by the same amount without changing the product (a variation of the associative property). For example, $8 \times 3 = (8 \div 2) \times (3 \times 2)$.

(continued)

ACTIVITY 6.12

Students can make space creatures using blobs of clay. They roll a die to determine the number of eyes and again to determine the number of toothpick legs. They roll once more to tell how many creatures to make. But before they make them, they predict the total number of eyes and legs.

4. To divide two numbers, you can multiply both numbers by the same amount without changing the quotient. For example, $15 \div 3 = (15 \times 2) \div (3 \times 2)$.

5. You can multiply in parts (the distributive property). For example, $5 \times 4 = 3 \times 4 + 2 \times 4$.

6. You can multiply in parts by breaking up the multiplier. For example, $6 \times 5 = 2 \times 3 \times 5$.

7. You can divide in parts by splitting the dividend into parts, but not the divisor (the distributive property). For example, $48 \div 8 = 32 \div 8 + 16 \div 8$.

8. You can divide by breaking up the divisor. For example, $36 \div 6 = 36 \div 3 \div 2$.

9. When you multiply by 0, the product is 0.

10. When you divide 0 by any number but 0, the quotient is 0.

11. You cannot divide by 0.

12. When you multiply or divide a number by 1, the answer is the number you started with.

Principle 1: Multiplication and division "undo" each other. They are related inverse operations.

Multiplication and division are inverse operations; one "undoes" the other. In fact, division is defined as the "opposite" of multiplication. If you start with 12 items and share them among 3 people, each person gets 4 items. How do you get back to where you started (to 12)? You think of the 3 people, each with 4 items, as a multiplication situation, or 3 groups of 4, which is 12.

Principle 2: You can multiply numbers in any order (the commutative property). With division, the order in which you divide the numbers matters.

If you model 3 groups of 4 as shown below, it is not clear why it is the same as 4 groups of 3.

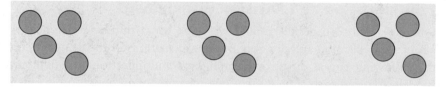

But, if you rearrange the same 12 items in an array, it is obvious why $3 \times 4 = 4 \times 3$. The same model shows both 3 sets of 4 and 4 sets of 3.

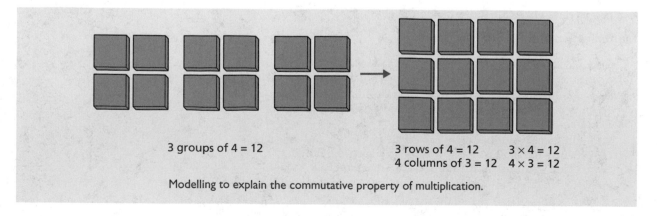

3 groups of 4 = 12

3 rows of 4 = 12 $3 \times 4 = 12$
4 columns of 3 = 12 $4 \times 3 = 12$

Modelling to explain the commutative property of multiplication.

Note that the order does matter when you divide. For example, if you were to divide 12 items into groups of 3, you would have 4 groups of 3. If you were to try to divide 3 items into groups of 12, you would not have even 1 full group.

Principle 3: To multiply two numbers, you can divide one factor and multiply the other by the same amount without changing the product.

The associative property of multiplication suggests that you can multiply $a \times b$ first and then multiply by c, or calculate $b \times c$ first and then multiply by a. For example, $4 \times 2 \times 3 = 8 \times 3$ or 4×6. The property exists since multiplication is only defined for two numbers, and rules had to be created to allow you to deal with more numbers than that.

Consider the 8 groups of 3 (8×3) shown below. If you pair up groups of 3, you will have 6 in each group or twice as many in each group but only 4 groups, that is, half as many groups (4×6).

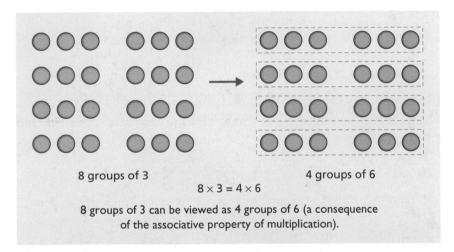

8 groups of 3   4 groups of 6

$8 \times 3 = 4 \times 6$

8 groups of 3 can be viewed as 4 groups of 6 (a consequence of the associative property of multiplication).

To multiply 12×5, Chris thinks "6×10." Explain his thinking.

Its easier to myltiply by 10 in your head and the answer doesn't change anyway because its half of 12 but twice 5.

Student Response

This student demonstrates an understanding of the value of using an equivalent form of a product with numbers easier to multiply mentally.

Principle 4: To divide two numbers, you can multiply both numbers by the same amount without changing the quotient.

For instance, $15 \div 3$ asks how much each person gets if 3 people share 15 items equally. It makes sense that if there are twice as many items to be shared by twice as many people, the share size stays the same. It does not matter what the dividend and divisor are multiplied by. As long as they are multiplied by the same amount, the quotient does not change.

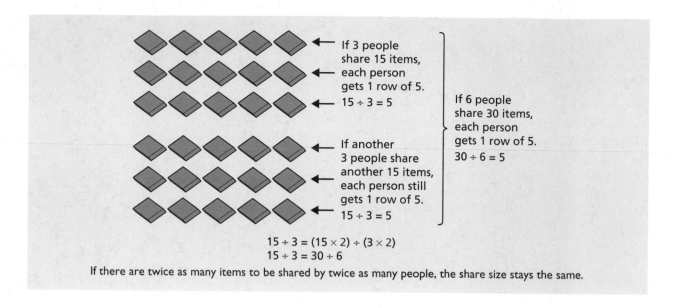

If 3 people share 15 items, each person gets 1 row of 5.

15 ÷ 3 = 5

If another 3 people share another 15 items, each person still gets 1 row of 5.

15 ÷ 3 = 5

If 6 people share 30 items, each person gets 1 row of 5.

30 ÷ 6 = 5

$$15 \div 3 = (15 \times 2) \div (3 \times 2)$$
$$15 \div 3 = 30 \div 6$$

If there are twice as many items to be shared by twice as many people, the share size stays the same.

Principle 5: You can multiply in parts (the distributive property).

For instance, you can separate 5 rows of 4 squares into 3 rows of 4 and 2 rows of 4 ($5 \times 4 = 3 \times 4 + 2 \times 4$) without changing the total number of squares.

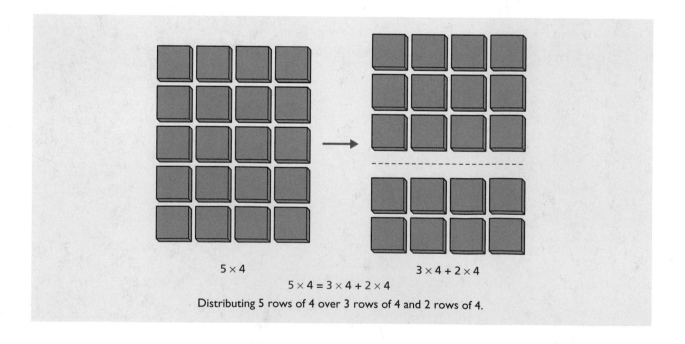

5×4

$3 \times 4 + 2 \times 4$

$$5 \times 4 = 3 \times 4 + 2 \times 4$$

Distributing 5 rows of 4 over 3 rows of 4 and 2 rows of 4.

Principle 6: You can multiply in parts by breaking up the multiplier.

An array is a good way to show this principle. For example, you can easily separate 6 rows of 5 squares into 2 groups, each with 3 rows of 5, without changing the total number of squares.

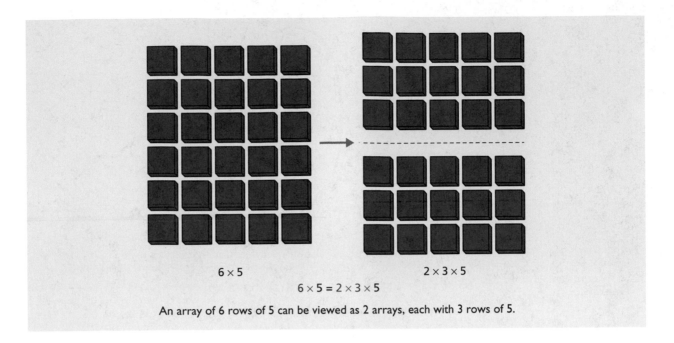

6×5 $2 \times 3 \times 5$

$6 \times 5 = 2 \times 3 \times 5$

An array of 6 rows of 5 can be viewed as 2 arrays, each with 3 rows of 5.

Principle 7: You can divide in parts by splitting the dividend into parts, but not the divisor (a variation of the distributive property).

For example, $48 \div 8$ asks how many items each person gets when 48 items are shared equally among 8 people. It is possible to "distribute" the first 24 among the 8 people, and then "distribute" the other 24 among the same 8 people (hence the name, the distributive property).

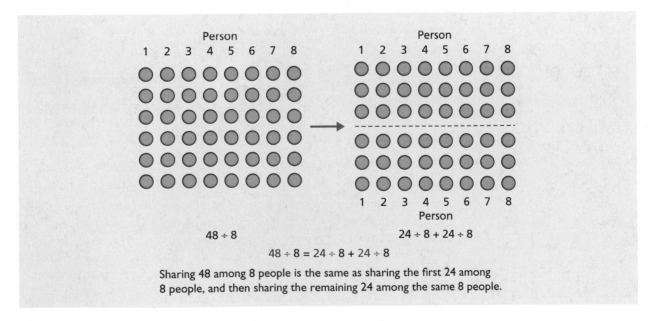

$48 \div 8$ $24 \div 8 + 24 \div 8$

$48 \div 8 = 24 \div 8 + 24 \div 8$

Sharing 48 among 8 people is the same as sharing the first 24 among 8 people, and then sharing the remaining 24 among the same 8 people.

Principle 8: You can divide by breaking up the divisor.

The expression $36 \div 6$ tells how many items there are in each group if 36 items are shared equally among 6 groups. You could share the 36 items among 6 groups ($36 \div 6$), or you could split the 36 items into 2 groups of 18 and then share within each of the 18s, each into 3 smaller groups of 6 (that is, $36 \div 2 \div 3$).

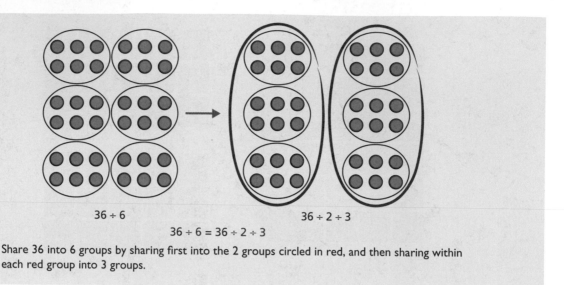

$36 \div 6$

$36 \div 2 \div 3$

$36 \div 6 = 36 \div 2 \div 3$

Share 36 into 6 groups by sharing first into the 2 groups circled in red, and then sharing within each red group into 3 groups.

Principle 9: When you multiply by 0, the product is 0.

To show, say, 5 sets of 0, you might use 5 empty plates. Since there is nothing on any of the plates, the total number of items is 0.

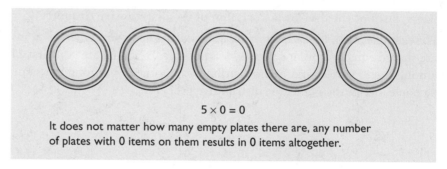

$5 \times 0 = 0$

It does not matter how many empty plates there are, any number of plates with 0 items on them results in 0 items altogether.

Principle 10: When you divide 0 by a number other than 0, the quotient is 0.

For example, $0 \div 5$ asks the share size if 5 people share nothing. The amount is clearly nothing.

Principle 11: You cannot divide by 0.

It is more difficult to explain $5 \div 0$ than $0 \div 5$. How can 5 items be shared among 0 groups? Here a repeated subtraction meaning for division might make more sense to explain the principle. To divide, for example, $15 \div 5$, you can subtract 5 three times from 15, until you get to 0, so $15 \div 5 = 3$. So, to divide $5 \div 0$, you must determine how many times you can subtract 0 from 5 before getting down to 0. There is no answer; you will simply never get to 0. Therefore, $5 \div 0$ is undefined.

As for $0 \div 0$, you can subtract 0 any number of times from 0 to get to 0, so the answer could be 1, 2, 3, or any number. Since there are too many answers, $0 \div 0$ is indeterminate.

Another way to describe this principle is to appeal to the relationship between multiplication and division. If the answer were ■, that is, $5 \div 0 = $ ■, then $0 \times$ ■ $= 5$. Since 0 × anything is 0, there are no answers. If $0 \div 0 = $ ■, then $0 \times$ ■ $= 0$. Here there are an infinite number of answers (any number works). In either case, it makes no mathematical sense to divide by 0.

Principle 12: When you multiply or divide a number by 1, the answer is the number you started with.

The following models explain this principle for multiplication and for division.

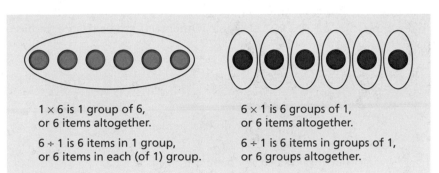

1 × 6 is 1 group of 6,
or 6 items altogether.

6 ÷ 1 is 6 items in 1 group,
or 6 items in each (of 1) group.

6 × 1 is 6 groups of 1,
or 6 items altogether.

6 ÷ 1 is 6 items in groups of 1,
or 6 groups altogether.

Strategies for Learning Multiplication and Division Facts

How Many Facts Are There?

There are 100 multiplication facts, from 0 × 0 to 9 × 9, as well as 90 related division facts (since you cannot divide by 0, the number of division facts is less than 100). However, the principles that students learn about multiplication and division can substantially reduce the number of independent facts they need to learn.

PRINCIPLE	EXAMPLE
By knowing Principle 2 (the commutative property for multiplication), students need only learn about half of the multiplication facts involving different factors.	If students know 6 × 5 = 30, then they know 5 × 6 = 30.
By knowing Principle 1, students realize they do not need to separately learn the division facts, but can use a related multiplication fact instead.	Since 4 × 6 = 24, 24 ÷ 4 = 6 and 24 ÷ 6 = 4
By knowing Principle 12, students do not need to separately memorize facts involving multiplication or division by 1.	▢ × 1 = ▢ 1 × ▢ = ▢ ▢ ÷ 1 = ▢ ▢ ÷ ▢ = 1 no matter what number (except 0) is used for ▢.
By knowing Principle 9, students do not need to separately memorize facts involving multiplication or division with 0.	0 ÷ ▢ = 0 0 × ▢ = 0 ▢ × 0 = 0 no matter what number is used for ▢.

Using Other Principles to Develop Fact Strategies

Students who become comfortable with the principles articulated on pages 124–129 will recognize which strategies might be useful in which situations to relate an unknown fact to a known one.

Building on Doubles Students seem to learn the double facts easily, for example, $2 \times 4 = 8$; $2 \times 7 = 14$, etc. Other facts can be related to these.

STRATEGY	PRINCIPLE
$4 \times 7 = 2 \times (2 \times 7)$. Double 7 first. $\qquad = 2 \times 14$ Double the double, perhaps $\qquad = 14 + 14$ by adding. Every $4 \times$ fact can be calculated by doubling a $2 \times$ fact; every $8 \times$ fact can be calculated by doubling a $4 \times$ fact.	Principle 6

ACTIVITY 6.14

To explore doubles, allow students to use a transparent mirror to see the double of what they put on one side of the mirror.

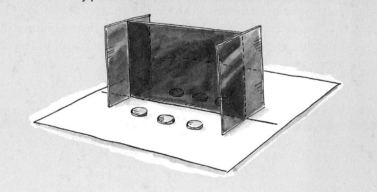

ACTIVITY 6.15

Show students how to multiply by 9 on their fingers.

Number the fingers from 1 to 10 starting at the left.

To multiply 9 by, for example, 7, fold in finger 7. Count the fingers at the left for the tens digit and at the right for the ones digit.

Half/Double If students are multiplying by a number like 6 or 8, they might use a half/double strategy.

STRATEGY	PRINCIPLE
$4 \times 6 = (4 \times 2) \times (6 \div 2)$ Double one factor and $\qquad = 8 \times 3$ halve the other. Notice that the student could have used $(4 \div 2) \times (6 \times 2)$ to get the right answer, although 2×12 might not be as familiar as 8×3.	Principle 3

Add Parts Students can break up a multiplication or division into simpler components.

STRATEGY		PRINCIPLE
$8 \times 6 = (5 \times 6) + (3 \times 6)$ $= 30 + 18$	Treat 8 groups as 6 groups and 3 groups.	Principle 5
$21 \div 3 = (15 \div 3) + (6 \div 3)$ $= 5 + 2$	Share 21 by sharing 15 and then 6.	Principle 7

Easier Tables Two "tables" that students find particularly easy to learn are the $5 \times$ table and the $9 \times$ table. They skip count by fives, sometimes using a clock: 5, 10, 15, 20, ..., to calculate a multiple of 5. To determine a multiple of 9, they observe the pattern where the tens digit goes up by 1 and the ones go down by 1, with the digits totalling 9:

$$9 \quad 18 \quad 27 \quad 36 \quad 45 \quad 54 \quad 63 \quad 72 \quad 81$$

Using these known facts, they can calculate other products. For example,

$$8 \times 7 = 5 \times 7 + 3 \times 7 \text{ or } 8 \times 7 = 9 \times 7 - 1 \times 7$$

ACTIVITY 6.18

Have students play a multiplication fact board game like the one below.

The Product Game

1	2	3	4	5	6
7	8	9	10	12	14
15	16	18	20	21	24
25	27	28	30	32	35
36	40	42	45	48	49
54	56	63	64	72	81

1	2	3	4	5	6	7	8	9

The first player puts his colour of counter on one of the numbers on the strip below the board.

The second player puts his counter on the same or a different number on the strip, multiplies the two, and then puts a counter of his colour on that product on the board.

Player 1 moves one counter, multiplies, and puts his counter on the board on that product.

Play continues until a player gets four of his coloured counters in a row.

It takes time to develop and nurture the thinking strategies that help students learn their facts. Developing the many relations among the facts is the initial emphasis when facts are first being explored, rather than speed of recall.

ACTIVITY 6.16

Encourage students to play the game Metre Race.

Each player chooses a coloured counter and then picks 2 number cards, labelled from 1 to 6.

The first card tells how many jumps to make, and the second card tells how far to jump along the metre stick.

The first player to get to 100 cm wins.

ACTIVITY 6.17

Set up a problem like this one for students to solve:

Julia's school is having a read-a-thon. Julia's goal is to read 100 pages. If she starts on April 1 and reads 5 pages every night, will she get to her goal by the end of the month or before that? Show how you know.

Common Errors and Misconceptions

Multiplication and Division: Strategies for Dealing with Common Errors and Misconceptions

COMMON ERROR OR MISCONCEPTION	SUGGESTED STRATEGY
Generalizing about Products Students incorrectly generalize that the product of two numbers is always greater than the sum of the same two numbers. These students are stymied by expressions like 5×1, 5×0, and 2×2.	More often than not, this misconception arises because it is inadvertently promoted. Teachers tell their students that multiplication makes things "bigger," and they forget about the contradictions to this rule. This can be avoided if teachers are aware of the contradictions, and are careful with their generalizations.
Reversing Dividend and Divisor Students reverse the dividend and divisor when recording a division sentence (and may or may not calculate correctly). For example, to represent the number of groups of 3 in 15, they record $3 \div 15$ instead of $15 \div 3$. This common error should not be surprising, though, as one of the ways students are taught to record this division is as below, where the 3 is to the left of the 15: $3\overline{)15}$ for $15 \div 3$	The connection between words and symbols must be carefully crafted. When writing $15 \div 3$, you should be saying aloud, "How many 3s are in 15?" and writing both forms of the symbolic expression at the same time, as shown: $3\overline{)15}$ for $15 \div 3$
Remainders Students struggle with division problems that have remainders. For example: • They might think an expression like $17 \div 4$ is impossible since you cannot make perfect groups of 4. • They think that an expression like $17 \div 4$ is 4 since you can make 4 groups of 4, or that $17 \div 4$ is 5 since there are 4 groups of 4 and 1 group of 1 for a total of 5 groups.	Students should meet situations involving remainders early on in their work with division. They need to understand that the result need not always be a whole number. Note that these misconceptions about remainders actually lead to correct answers in certain contexts. For example: • 17 marbles shared equally among 4 children: The answer is 4 because you cannot share the leftover marble. • 17 children transported in cars that hold 4 children each: The answer is 5 because you need a fifth car to transport the "leftover" child.

Student Response

This student shows an understanding that you must consider context when discussing a remainder.

There are 80 Grade 5 students going on a field trip.

Each van can seat 6 children.

To find out how many vans were needed, John divided $80 \div 6$.

Why did he say that 14 vans were needed, even though $80 \div 6$ is not 14?

when you divide 6 by 80 it equals 13 and 2 are left so you need one more van which makes 14 vans.

$$6\overline{)80} \quad \begin{array}{r} 13 \\ -6 \\ \hline 20 \\ -18 \\ \hline 2 \end{array}$$

Appropriate Manipulatives

Multiplication

Manipulatives can be used to model many multiplication meanings. (See *Meanings of Multiplication* on page 118 for other examples of ways to use manipulatives to model different meanings of multiplication.)

Multiplication: Examples of Manipulatives

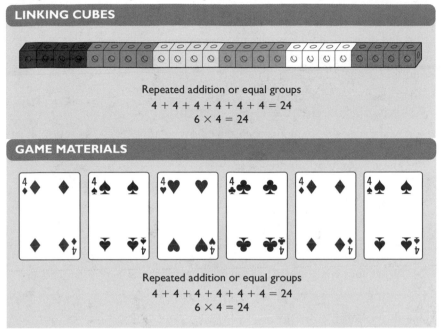

LINKING CUBES

Repeated addition or equal groups
4 + 4 + 4 + 4 + 4 + 4 = 24
6 × 4 = 24

GAME MATERIALS

Repeated addition or equal groups
4 + 4 + 4 + 4 + 4 + 4 = 24
6 × 4 = 24

Division

Manipulatives can be used to model many division meanings. Some examples are shown below. (See *Meanings of Division* on page 120 for other examples of ways to use manipulatives to model different meanings of division.)

Division: Examples of Manipulatives

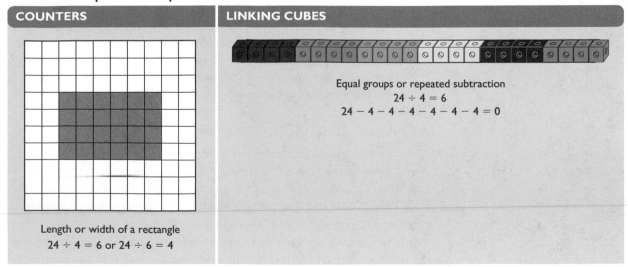

COUNTERS

Length or width of a rectangle
24 ÷ 4 = 6 or 24 ÷ 6 = 4

LINKING CUBES

Equal groups or repeated subtraction
24 ÷ 4 = 6
24 − 4 − 4 − 4 − 4 − 4 − 4 = 0

Appropriate Technology

Calculators

The calculator is useful for showing repeated addition (the basis for multiplication) and repeated subtraction (the basis for division). The repeat, or constant, function makes this particularly easy.

Computers

Many of the computer software packages mentioned on page 117 for use with addition and subtraction also have components involving multiplication and division. Students can also use graphics packages, such as *KidPix*, to stamp equal sets of objects and arrays, which can be used to represent multiplication and division situations.

WebConnect

www.makingmathmeaningful
.nelson.com

Visit Nelson's Making Math Meaningful website to find links to problems you might use with your students.

Assessing Student Understanding

- Make sure that students recognize how to apply each operation in situations that represent different meanings; for example, ask how these two situations are alike:

    I have $4 and need $10 to buy a gift. How much more do I need?

    and

    I am 10 years old and my sister is 4. How much older am I?

- Ask questions that focus on the meanings of the operations. For example:

    What does 4 × 6 mean? instead of, How much is 4 × 6?

Student Response

This student solves the division question using a diagram to explain his or her thinking rather than representing it symbolically. You might follow up by asking how he or she would write this using a sentence of the form [ ] ÷ [ ] = [ ].

> Use 12 counters.
> Write a division sentence that describes this situation:
>
> There are 12 cookies to share among 3 people.
> How many cookies will each get?
>
> each get 4 cookies

- Focus assessment of fact recall on understanding and not speed in the early stages. Even later, although you want students to commit facts to memory, the student can still take a few seconds to use a strategy to recall a particular sum, difference, product, or quotient.
- Encourage students to tell you why a particular strategy is useful to recall a fact. For example, if you want to remember what 7 × 4 is, what other facts could you use to help you? Why?

Appropriate Children's Books

Two of Everything: A Chinese Folktale (Hong, 1993).
A magic pot doubles whatever is put into it. The context of the story can be continued to practice doubling. The teacher puts items into a "pot" and students predict how many items will emerge if the pot doubles its contents.

Counting by Kangaroos (Hulme, 1995).
Australian animals populate this story. Different elements of the story allow the reader to skip count by different amounts. Because skip counting is the basis for multiplication, this will support familiarity with simple products.

Sea Squares (Hulme, 1991).
Students see visual representations of the special products 1×1, 2×2, 3×3, etc., on the attractive pages of this book. They observe that the product of a number and itself can always be modelled as a square.

Sea Sums (Hulme, 1996).
Ocean animals are the "actors" in addition and subtraction stories in this book.

The Doorbell Rang (Hutchins, 1986).
In this engaging and well-known story, students get a chance to use their division skills in predictable situations.

Splash (Jonas, 1995).
Students can use both addition and subtraction to describe the events in this story where creatures jump in and out of a pond.

Bunches and Bunches of Bunnies (Matthews, 1978).
These illustrated spreads use verse to explore the square numbers 1×1, 2×2, etc.

A Remainder of One (Pinczes, 1995).
Twenty-five bugs march in different-sized groups, where there is usually a remainder of 1. This book suits early division work with remainders.

Applying What You've Learned

1. What was your solution to the chapter problem? How could you have predicted the answer without completing the table?

2. How would you help students recognize the relationships between addition and subtraction? Why do you think that your approach might be effective?

3. Teachers often read a subtraction sign saying the words *take away*, for example, $8 - 2$ as *eight take away 2*. Would you? Why or why not?

4. Which of the principles for addition and subtraction could be explained effectively using 10-frames? Why?

5. To calculate $14 - 8$, a students says, "13, 12, 11, 10, 9, 8, 7, 6, 5" as she holds up 8 fingers, one at a time. How would you respond to this approach to the calculation?

6. A parent asks you whether it is a good idea to use flashcards for fact recall for her Grade 2 son. What would your advice be?

7. Which of the principles for multiplication and division do you think are most critical for students to understand? Why?

8. Develop an engaging task that would involve students in exploring some aspect of multiplication. What idea about multiplication would they learn? Why do you think your task would be engaging?

9. How would you help students distinguish between the sharing (partitive) and how-many-groups (quotative) meanings of division?

10. Some teachers are concerned that presenting too many fact strategies for learning the multiplication facts would overwhelm students. What is your opinion? Why?

11. Examine a current text for Grade 3 students. Which multiplication fact strategies do they emphasize? Which is introduced first? Why might that make sense?

Interact with a K–8 Student:

12. Ask a student to show each of these with models (if they are not yet in Grade 3, only use a) and b)). Observe whether they simply show the answer or whether they actually model the expression to show its meaning:

    a) 6 + 7

    b) 13 − 5

    c) 5 × 8

    d) 16 ÷ 2

Discuss with a K–8 Teacher:

13. Ask a teacher whether she or he teaches addition and subtraction at the same time or separately. Ask why she or he takes that approach.

Selected References

Baroody, A.J., and Dowker, A. (**2003**). *The development of arithmetic concepts and skills.* Mahwah, NJ: Lawrence Erlbaum Associates.

Baroody, A.J., and Wilkins, J.L.M. (**1999**). The development of informal counting, number, and arithmetic skills and concepts. In Copley, J. (Ed.). *Mathematics in the early years.* Reston, VA: National Council of Teachers of Mathematics, 48–65.

Buchholz, L. (**2004**). Learning strategies for addition and subtraction facts: The road to fluency and the license to think. *Teaching Children Mathematics, 10,* 362–367.

Carpenter, T.P., Fennema, E., Franke, M.L., Levi, L., and Empson, S. (**1999**). *Children's mathematics: Cognitively guided instruction.* Portsmouth, NH: Heinemann.

Cavanagh, M., Dacey, L., Findell, C.R., Greenes, C.F., Sheffield, L.J., and Small, M. (**2004**). *Navigating through number and operations in prekindergarten–grade 2.* Reston, VA: National Council of Teachers of Mathematics.

Crespo, S., Kyrkiakides, A.O., and McGee, S. (**2005**). Nothing "basic" about basic facts: Exploring addition facts with fourth graders. *Teaching Children Mathematics, 12,* 60–67.

Fosnot, C.T., and Dolk, M. (**2001**). *Young mathematicians at work: Constructing number sense, addition, and subtraction.* Portsmouth, NH: Heinemann.

Ginsburg, H.P. (**1989**). *Children's arithmetic.* Austin, TX: Pro-Ed.

Hedges, M., Huinker, D., and Steinmeyer, M. (**2005**). Supporting teacher learning: Unpacking division to build teachers' mathematical knowledge. *Teaching Children Mathematics, 11,* 478–483.

Hong, L.T. (**1993**). *Two of everything: A Chinese folktale.* Morton Grove, IL: Albert Whitman and Company.

Hope, J.A., Leutzinger, L.P., Reys, B.J., and Reyes, R.E. (**1988**). *Mental math in the primary grades.* White Plains, NY: Cuisenaire/Dale Seymour.

Hulme, J.N. (**1995**). *Counting by kangaroos: A multiplication concept book.* New York: W.H. Freeman & Co.

Hulme, J.N. (**1999**). *Sea squares.* New York: Hyperion Books for Children.

Hutchins, P. (**1989**). *The doorbell rang.* New York: Scholastic.

Isaacs, A.C,. and Carroll, W.M. (**1999**). Strategies for basic-facts instruction. *Teaching Children Mathematics, 5,* 508–515.

Jonas, A. (**1995**). *Splash.* New York: Greenwillow.

Kamii, C., Lewis, B.A., and Booker, B.M. (**1998**). Instead of teaching missing addends. *Teaching Children Mathematics, 4,* 458–461.

Leutzinger, L.P. (**1999**). Developing thinking strategies for addition facts. *Teaching Children Mathematics, 6,* 14–18.

Mathews, L. (**1978**). *Bunches and bunches of bunnies.* New York: Scholastic.

Pinczes, E.J. (**1995**). *A remainder of one.* Boston: Houghton Mifflin.

Postlewait, K.B., Adams, M.R., and Shih, J.C. (**2003**). Promoting meaningful mastery of addition and subtraction. *Teaching Children Mathematics, 9,* 354–357.

Roberts, S.K. (**2003**). Snack math: Young children explore division. *Teaching Children Mathematics, 9,* 258–261.

Small, M. (**2005**). *PRIME: Number and operations: Background and strategies.* Toronto: Thomson Nelson.

Sun, W., and Zhang, J.Y. (**2001**). Teaching addition and subtraction facts: A Chinese perspective. *Teaching Children Mathematics, 8,* 28–31.

Thornton, C.A. (**1990**). Strategies for the basic facts. In Payne, J.N. (Ed.). *Mathematics for the young child.* Reston, VA: National Council of Teachers of Mathematics, 133–152.

Chapter 7

Representing Multi-Digit Whole Numbers

IN A NUTSHELL

The main ideas in this chapter are listed below:

1. The place value system we used is built on patterns to make our work with numbers efficient.

2. To gain an understanding of the place value system, students should initially use proportional materials, ideally materials they can group themselves.

3. Students gain a sense of the size of numbers by comparing them to meaningful benchmarks.

4. Thinking of numbers as factors and/or multiples of other numbers enriches a student's number sense.

CHAPTER PROBLEM

What is the least positive integer that is divisible by 2, 3, 4, 5, 6, 7, 8, 9, and 10? How do you know?

Greater Numbers in the Student's World

As students get older, the numbers they deal with in their everyday lives become more complex. Students need strategies for representing and making sense of these greater numbers. Although it is possible to count, say, 87 items individually, it is not practical. When items are grouped, counting is made easier and probably more accurate.

This becomes very clear when a teacher puts, for instance, 35 items in a disorganized fashion on an overhead projector, allows students to look for a few seconds, and then turns off the projector. Very few students can tell how many items there were. In contrast, if 35 items are shown in 3 groups of 10 and 5 more (as shown below), students find it easier to identify the amount. Grouping is a real help.

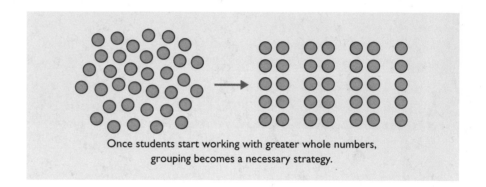

Once students start working with greater whole numbers, grouping becomes a necessary strategy.

Numeration Principles

The most basic principles that students need to learn in order to work with our number system relate to the base ten trading rules and the concept of place value. Base ten is a trading system in which you trade groups of 10 ones for 1 ten, 10 tens for 1 hundred, and so on. Place value is a system in which the position that a symbol (a digit 0 to 9 in the case of our numeration system) occupies in a number has a bearing on the value of that symbol. For example, the 2 in 23 means 20, but the 2 in 42 means 2.

A number of researchers, including Kamii (1986), have expressed caution about moving into place value too quickly. Kamii points out how a number of students read the number 16 and really have no sense of what the 1 really means; they often treat it as 1 rather than 10. She suggests teaching numbers more holistically for longer, for example, thinking of 23 as twenty three, not as 2 tens and 3 ones, until students are ready for the transition, which may be later than some teachers think.

Even when students eventually do get an understanding of the system, there is often a significant period of time between when they are comfortable with numbers in the 100s or even 1000s, and when they have gained a full understanding of the structure of the system going farther to the left or to the right (to decimal values).

One of the difficulties is that a place value system requires students to deal with a multi-unit conceptual structure (Fuson, 1990a). Many students are very focused on single unitary structures.

The base ten place value system is defined by conventions; these conventions are not implicit in what number is all about. Because they are conventions, they must be explicitly taught. Some of the principles that students need to learn are listed below.

NUMERATION PRINCIPLES

1. You group in tens for convenience so that you need only 10 digits (0 to 9) to represent all numbers.
2. Patterns are inherent in our numeration system because each place value is 10 times the value of the place to the right.
3. A number has many different "forms." For example, 123 is 1 hundred, 2 tens, 3 ones, and also 12 tens, 3 ones.
4. A place value system requires a symbol for a placeholder. For example, the 0 in 304 is a placeholder; it pushes the digit 3 over to show that it represents 300 instead of 30.
5. Numbers can be compared when written in standard, or symbolic, form.

Principle 1: You group in tens for convenience so that you need only 10 digits (0 to 9) to represent all numbers.

Students quickly realize how convenient the base ten system is if they are asked to memorize separate symbols for, say, the first 25 different numbers instead of just recognizing 10 digits. But they require a considerable time to internalize the structure of the system.

Many young students have difficulty thinking about the one item that represents a 10 as being worth more than the one item representing 1. For that reason, models that are "proportional," that is, where the 10 looks 10 times as big as the 1, the 100 looks 10 times as big as the 10, etc., are important. Some of these models, showing 23, are

- the 10-frame

- unifix cube stacks

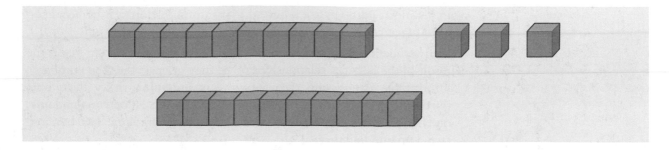

• Popsicle stick bundles

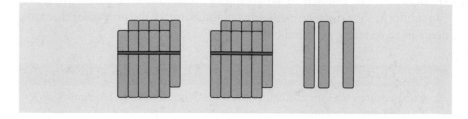

• base ten blocks

Although all of the models presented above can be extended to numbers greater than 100, usually only the base ten block model is extended.

Pre-grouped models like base ten blocks are certainly more convenient to use, but some students do not realize that the value of, say, 2 ten rods and 3 ones is the same as the value of 23 ones. If students group the materials themselves, as would be the case with Popsicle sticks, unifix trains, or 10-frames, it is easier for them to recognize this.

Later, students can use non-proportional materials, such as counters on a place value mat. The place value model below shows 314, but it is not obvious that each red counter is worth more than each blue one.

Hundreds	Tens	Ones
● ● ●	○	● ● ● ●

Principle 2: Patterns are inherent in our numeration system because each place value is 10 times the value of the place to the right.

Many students easily take to the rhythm of the number system that is the result of the base ten relationships (once they get past the teen numbers), for example, twenty-**one**, twenty-**two**, …, twenty-**nine**, thirty, thirty-**one**, thirty-**two**, …, thirty-**nine**, forty. Or **one, two, three**, …, one hundred **one**, one hundred **two**, one hundred **three**, …, two hundred **one**, two hundred **two**, two hundred **three**, ….

The hundreds chart is a useful tool for helping students recognize patterns for numbers up to 100.

0	1	2	3	4	5	6	7	8	9
10	11	12	13	14	15	16	17	18	19
20	21	22	23	24	25	26	27	28	29
30	31	32	33	34	35	36	37	38	39
40	41	42	43	44	45	46	47	48	49
50	51	52	53	54	55	56	57	58	59
60	61	62	63	64	65	66	67	68	69
70	71	72	73	74	75	76	77	78	79
80	81	82	83	84	85	86	87	88	89
90	91	92	93	94	95	96	97	98	99

The circled numbers are read eight, eighteen, twenty-eight, thirty-eight, forty-eight, ...

ACTIVITY 7.3

One powerful way to use the hundreds chart is to cover up some of the numbers and have students use the patterns to figure out what the covered numbers must be.

You might also focus on smaller parts of a 100 chart. For example, students might be asked to print the missing numbers in small sections of the chart like these.

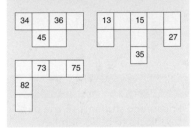

Another important pattern in our system allows us to interpret unfamiliar numerals. Each place value is 10 times the value of the unit to its right. To understand the place values to the right of the decimal point, students learn to think in reverse; that is, each new place value is $\frac{1}{10}$ of the unit to its left.

Thousands 1000	Hundreds 100	Tens 10	Ones 1	Tenths 0.1	Hundredths 0.01	Thousandths 0.001
10×100	10×10	10×1	1	$1 \times \frac{1}{10}$	$0.1 \times \frac{1}{10}$	$0.01 \times \frac{1}{10}$
				$1 \div 10$	$0.1 \div 10$	$0.01 \div 10$

The base ten block models typically used to represent whole numbers are designed to show the 10 times relationship. Below, ten cubes make 1 rod, 10 rods make 1 flat, and 10 flats make 1 thousand cube.

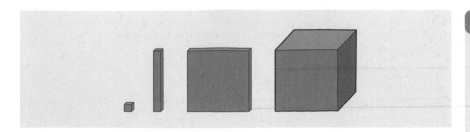

Very large numbers can also be modelled with base ten blocks. A model for 10 000 is a "rod" made of 10 thousand cubes. Similarly, a model for

ACTIVITY 7.4

Pose a problem like this one to students:

How many 2-digit or 3-digit numbers can be modelled with 5 base ten blocks?

Vary the problem by changing the number of digits or the number of blocks.

100 000 is a flat made of 100 thousand cubes, although often there are not enough cubes in a classroom to make the complete model.

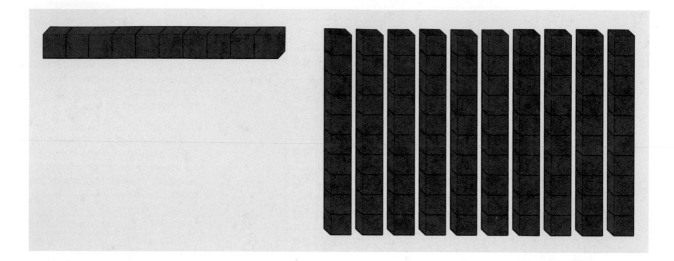

Encourage students to use base ten blocks to build number towers. They might be asked to build two towers with the same height as this one for 1320 and think about what numbers would work.

Another pattern in the system pertains to larger numbers. Numbers are written in pattern groups called periods. For example, 235 235 235 is read as, "two hundred thirty-five million, two hundred thirty-five thousand, two hundred thirty-five" since the digits 235 appear in the millions, the thousands, and the ones periods. Within each perioid, there are hundreds, tens, and ones. For example, 234 123 345 is 234 millions, 123 thousands, 345 (ones). Students need to learn the grouping names in order to read numbers, but then can use the similarity within the groupings to help them deal with numbers they had not previously encountered.

Principle 3: A number has many different "forms."

The ability to rename numbers is fundamental to many of the algorithms involving addition, subtraction, multiplication, and division that students will learn. For example, regrouping 3 hundreds, 1 ten, and 2 ones as 2 hundreds, 10 tens, and 12 ones makes the traditional subtraction algorithm possible for a calculation such as 312 − 178 (see Algorithm 1 on page 167).

When calculating with greater numbers, there are times when students want to rename 1 000 000 as 1000 thousands or as 10 hundred thousands or as 100 ten thousands, for example, to divide 1 000 000 by 1000 or 100 000 or 10 000. Similarly, there are times when it is convenient to write 3 600 000 as 3.6 million, for example, to write a newspaper headline.

Student Response

This student has used Principle 3 to create a "creature" with a value of 321 using 32 tens and 1 one.

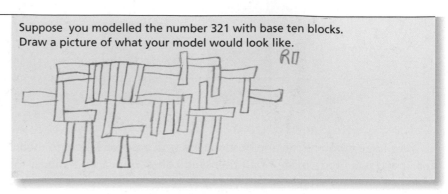

Suppose you modelled the number 321 with base ten blocks. Draw a picture of what your model would look like.

Principle 4: A place value system requires a symbol for a place holder.

When you write a number in its symbolic form using digits, for example, 304, you call the digit 0 a placeholder. But many people cannot really explain what this means. The idea is that, if you did not have the digit 0, the number would be recorded as 34, and you would mistakenly think that the 3 represented 30 instead of 300.

If you always recorded the digits on a place value mat or worked with base ten blocks, as shown below, the digit 0 would not be necessary. In symbolic recordings, however, you need a placeholder.

A place value mat to show 304.

Thousands	Hundreds	Tens	Ones

3   0   4

Principle 5: Numbers can be compared when written in standard, or symbolic, form.

To learn to write numbers in standard form, students must realize that the order in which numbers appear matters. That is, 53 and 35 mean two very different things. For some students, this takes more time than for others. One thing that teachers can do to help is to continue to work on place value mats as long as students benefit from them, and to take the time to make sure that the greater place values always appear to the left from the students' point of view.

Once whole numbers are represented in their standard, or symbolic, form, students can use the number of digits to get a sense of their size in order to compare them. For example, any 3-digit whole number is 100 or greater, but less than 1000. Similarly, any 2-digit whole number is less than 100. Therefore, any 3-digit whole number is automatically greater than any 2-digit whole number.

When two whole numbers have the same number of digits, the leftmost digits matter most when ascertaining the size of the numbers, because that place has the greatest value. Another way for students to think about the role of the various digits in a numeral is to realize that there are digits that are more and less important in the numeral. For example, in 3021, the 3 is quite important; it really gives a sense of the size of the number. The 1 is important, perhaps, in clarifying that the number is odd, but not much at all in terms of the size of the number.

ACTIVITY 7.6

Pose problems like this one to practice place value concepts, while also providing students with opportunities to develop problem-solving abilities.

Rachel chose 6 base ten blocks.

The value of her blocks is more than 200 and less than 220.

Which blocks did Rachel choose?

ACTIVITY 7.7

Provide riddles like these for students to explore:

I'm thinking of a number that fits these clues.

Can you figure out my number?

- It is between 20 000 and 60 000.
- Each digit is even.
- The sum of the digits is 10.

For younger students, the riddles might involve lower numbers.

For example,

I'm thinking of a number less than 100.

The ones digit is greater than the tens digit.

The sum of the digits is 11.

What could the number be?

To create more riddles, simply write a number and make up 3 clues about it.

After some experience with these riddles, students might make up riddles for other students.

COMPARING 3-DIGIT AND 2-DIGIT NUMBERS

423 > 43 because
423 > 100 and 43 < 100.

523 > 489 because
523 > 500 and 489 < 500.

Counting Based on Place Value

Place value work depends on students' ability to count using more than one grouping in the same situation. When you count by ones, twos, fives, or even hundreds, you are counting in a consistent way. But when you count to, for example, 223 by saying 100, 200, 210, 220, 221, 222, 223, this is a complicated form of counting. Students must realize that they can start counting by 100s, and then continue counting differently, that is, by 10s and then by 1s.

Another stumbling block for students in counting is the transition from numbers like xx99 to xx00. You can support students in this by presenting problems like those in **Activity 7.8**.

Estimating Numbers

Often you do not require an exact amount to represent a number, but only an estimate. Students should be comfortable with a variety of ways to estimate numbers, depending on the context and the numbers involved. Estimating is used

- in computation; for example, to estimate 35 + 27, you could estimate 35 as 30 and 27 as 30 to estimate 30 + 30 = 60
- to get a sense of the size of numbers in order to compare them; for example, 389 is about 400 and 315 is about 300, so 389 > 315
- for reporting numbers; for example, about 400 people came to the event

As students share their estimates, you can gain insight into their number sense.

ACTIVITY 7.8

Present problems of interest that involve numbers close to multiples of 100, 1000, or 10000. For example, a problem might be:

The population of a town is 15 197. A new family moves to town. What might the population be now?

Student Response

This student knows that the population of the world is an estimate. It would be interesting to ask the student to explain her or his thinking.

Tell about an estimated number you heard or read about. It could be on the radio, on TV, on the Internet, or in a magazine or newspaper.

how many people in the world

Rounding

One approach to estimating is to round a number to the nearest multiple of 10, 100, 1000, ... To round a number, students can think of a number line as a highway with "gas stations" at the multiples to which the number could be rounded. The rounded number is the location of the closest "gas station." For example, when rounding to the nearest ten, the gas stations appear at multiples of 10. The nearest gas station to 133 is at 130, so 133 rounds to 130.

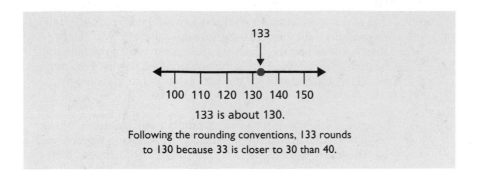

133 is about 130.

Following the rounding conventions, 133 rounds to 130 because 33 is closer to 30 than 40.

If, instead, numbers were rounded to the nearest 100, the gas stations would be at 0, 100, 200, 300, etc., and 133 would round to 100. Note that a number like 135 could be rounded up to 140 or down to 130, when rounding to the nearest ten, because neither 130 nor 140 is closer, although the convention is to round up.

Benchmark Numbers

Other benchmark, anchor, or "comfortable" numbers can also be used to estimate. For example, many people are comfortable with the 25s, likely because of the monetary system. For example, a principal might estimate a class with between 23 and 28 students as having about 25 students instead of estimating it as 20 or 30.

One way to focus students on benchmarks is to use a number line, as in **Activity 7.9**.

To become comfortable with greater benchmark numbers, students might enjoy exploring numbers like 1 million or 1 billion in contextually interesting ways, as described in **Activity 7.10**.

You might want to use some of the David Schwartz books about a million to introduce some of these activities.

Scientific Notation

As students move toward high school, they learn to use the place value system in a new way—writing numbers in scientific notation. The purpose of this notation is to give a quick sense of the size of a number.

For example, 4236 is written as 4.236×10^3 (or 4.236 thousands) to emphasize that the number is in the 1000s (10^3) range. It is the 4 in 4236 that is the most significant digit, and that is why it is the only digit to the left of the decimal point in the multiplier of the power of 10.

Converting numbers to and from scientific notation emphasizes the pattern of the place value system. For example, 123 000 becomes 1.23×10^5 because the digit that was in the place representing 10^5 moves to the ones place (to represent about 1 group of 10^5). Similarly, 3.46×10^7 becomes 34 600 000 because the number is about 3 ten millions, so the 3 must move over 7 places to the ten millions place.

ACTIVITY 7.9

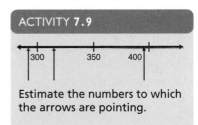

Estimate the numbers to which the arrows are pointing.

ACTIVITY 7.10

Think about 1 million pennies.

How many loonies would it be worth?

How many toonies?

How many $100 bills?

If you lined up 1 million pennies against a wall, how long would the line be?

If you made a square of 1 million pennies lying flat, as close to each other as possible, how long would the side of the square have to be?

How long would it take you to roll 1 million pennies?

How high a stack would 1 million pennies make?

Common Errors and Misconceptions

Greater Whole Numbers: Strategies for Dealing with Common Errors and Misconceptions

COMMON ERROR OR MISCONCEPTION	SUGGESTED STRATEGY
Interpreting 0 Digits Students do not effectively distinguish between numbers like 304 and 3004. In fact, some students think that, since 0 is nothing, there is no difference between the numbers.	One of the ways to deal with this is to model both numbers and ask students if the amounts are the same. Students will likely observe the difference. Then ask students to record the numeral for each. If they record the same numeral, ask which of the two models would better represent that value and to explain why.
Interpreting Teen Numbers Students have trouble with the teen numbers. When hearing "seventeen," they write 71.	Encourage students not to write a number down until they have heard the entire number. For example, when saying "seventeen," ask students to listen without writing anything down, and then say the number again as they record it. As well, ask students to interpret numbers they record or read in terms of tens and ones; for instance, 17 means 1 ten and 7 ones, but 71 means 7 tens and 1 one.
Space Placement Students have difficulty knowing where to locate the space for whole numbers greater than 9999. The conventional practice in English Canada for whole numbers is to write the digits in groups of 3, starting from the right with spaces between those groups, except for 4-digit numerals (for example, 3 123 103, 10 325, and 4123).	Note that students will learn this convention through exposure and practice, but it should also be explicitly taught. It is sometimes helpful to allow students to write numerals by using commas (the previous convention) to show where the spaces should be. Students can then rewrite the numerals with the spaces.

A variety of manipulative materials can support student learning of place value concepts.

Appropriate Manipulatives

Greater Whole Numbers: Examples of Manipulatives

100 CHART	STUDENT-MADE BASE TEN MATERIALS
A 100 chart is one of the most valuable tools you can use in developing early numeration ideas. In a very simple way, it shows how numbers are grouped and the patterns inherent in the system. It also displays all the numbers 0–99 (or 1–100) at a glance.	Students can create their own models using buttons or craft sticks: • craft sticks in bunches of 10 (with elastics around each bunch), each representing 10, and bags with 10 bunches of 10 in them, each representing 100 • buttons in small bags of 10, each representing 10, and larger bags with 10 small bags of 10 in them, each representing 100

0	1	2	3	4	5	6	7	8	9
10	11	12	13	14	15	16	17	18	19
20	21	22	23	24	25	26	27	28	29
30	31	32	33	34	35	36	37	38	39
40	41	42	43	44	45	46	47	48	49
50	51	52	53	54	55	56	57	58	59
60	61	62	63	64	65	66	67	68	69
70	71	72	73	74	75	76	77	78	79
80	81	82	83	84	85	86	87	88	89
90	91	92	93	94	95	96	97	98	99

The 100 chart makes the patterns in the place value system clearer.

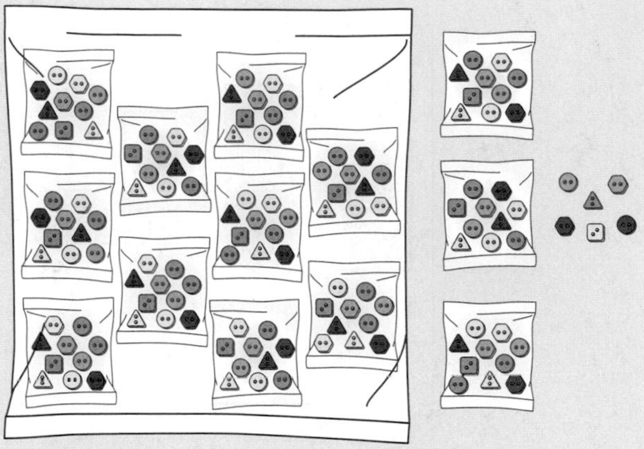

1 hundred, 3 tens, 6 ones
136

Student-made numeration models are excellent for early numeration work and for developing an understanding of the need for a numeration system.

LINKING CUBES

Linking cubes can be grouped in trains of tens; for example, 27 would be modelled with 2 trains and 7 loose cubes. (To introduce the number 100, 10 trains of 10 can be bound together by an elastic into a large bundle.)

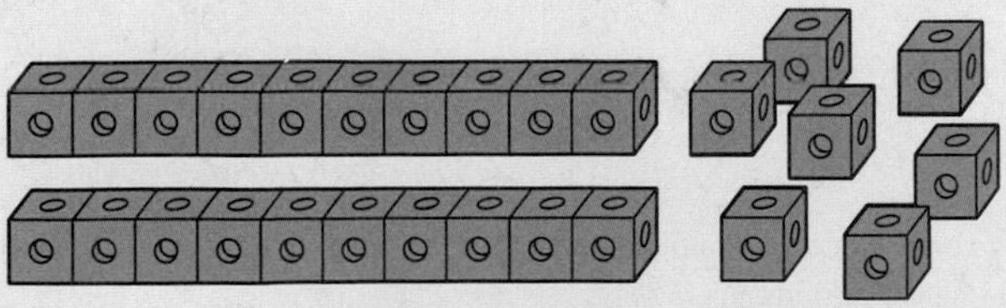

2 tens, 7 ones is 27

A linking cube model is most effective for modelling 2-digit numbers.

BASE TEN BLOCKS

Base ten blocks are an efficient and valuable model. As with the other models described here (buttons, craft sticks, and cubes), base ten blocks are proportional (for example, the ten block is 10 times as big as the one block, and the hundred block is 100 times as big as the one block.) This helps with developing number sense, as a number like 250 is 10 times as big as the number 25.

It is preferable to use blocks that can be physically linked or connected; for example, 10 one blocks can be connected to create 1 ten block, and 10 ten blocks can be connected to form 1 hundred block. This allows students to see that 10 ones is the same as 1 ten and they can more literally perform the trade when instructed to.

Base ten blocks can be used with or without place value mats (the blocks shown on page 148 would represent 1235 no matter what order they are in). However, place value mats allow for a transition from the blocks, which inherently do not require any thought of place value, to numerals, which consist of digits that have place value.

(continued)

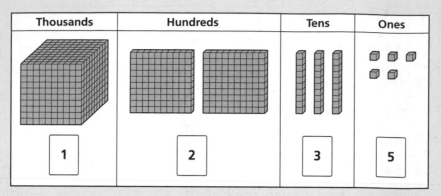

Thousands	Hundreds	Tens	Ones
1	2	3	5

1235

Students can move from modelling with just the blocks, to modelling with the blocks on a place value mat, to working with the blocks and digit cards on a place value mat, to working with just the digit cards on the place value mat, to finally working with just the digit cards.

MONEY

A money model uses dollars (hundreds), dimes (tens), and pennies (ones) to model 3-digit numbers. Note that this is not a proportional model (for example, the dime is not 10 times as "big" as the penny). It is a value model because the dime has a value that is 10 times that of the penny.

Some students find this model easy to work with as they have internalized money concepts. Others need to work with a proportional model, such as base ten blocks.

437

The money model could be used in conjunction with a place value mat to prepare students for the place value concepts underlying the symbolic representation (the numeral) of numbers.

Appropriate Technology

Calculators

Students can use calculators to explore place value concepts. For example, they could add 100 ten times on a calculator to see the pattern: 100, 200, 300, ..., up to 1000. This solidifies the notion that 1000 is 10 hundreds. Similarly, students could divide 4500 by 100 to see that 4500 is 45 hundreds.

Computers

There are a number of computer software programs that allow students to practise work with 100 charts and base ten blocks, for example, Sunburst's *Grouping and Place Value*.

Number Theory

Some Background

Number theory is a study of integers, but often just counting numbers, that focuses on multiplicative and divisive properties of numbers, as opposed to a number's representation in the place value system. Multiplicative thinking is thinking that focuses on how one number is made up of groups of another "unit," as opposed to additive thinking where that is not the case. For example, thinking of 20 as 4 fives is thinking of the 20 being made up of units of 5. Thinking of 20 as $11 + 9$ is valid, but is additive, not multiplicative, thinking. As students work with multiplication and division, they deal with the concepts of divisibility, multiples, and factors.

Even and Odd Numbers

Even before students work with multiplication and division, they learn that the 0, 2, 4, 6, 8, 10, ... pattern represents the even numbers. In fact, many older students will define even numbers as those that end in 0, 2, 4, 6, and 8. The concept of "evenness," however, is a multiplicative idea.

Each even number represents an amount that is a multiple of 2; it can be modelled using groups of 2 with nothing left over. Odd numbers are defined by what they are not; they are the non-even numbers. Students can also represent odd numbers by relating them to even numbers, as either 1 more or 1 less than even numbers.

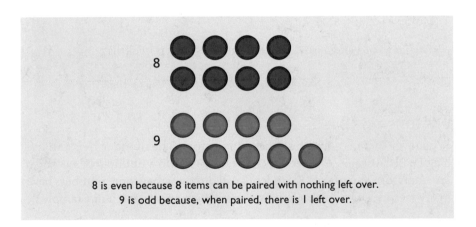

8 is even because 8 items can be paired with nothing left over.
9 is odd because, when paired, there is 1 left over.

Many students wonder whether 0 is an even number. There are two reasons why 0 is considered even: one is that it is part of the pattern of even numbers, and the other is that it is a multiple of 2 (because $2 \times 0 = 0$), and all multiples of 2 are even numbers.

Multiples

A multiple of a number is the product of that number with an **integer** multiplier. For example, 8 is a multiple of 4 since $8 = 2 \times 4$. -8 is also a multiple of 4: -2×4). But even though 9 can also be expressed as the product of 4 and another number ($9 = 2.25 \times 4$), it is not a multiple of 4; the multiplier is not an integer.

Common Multiples

Sometimes you need to find the multiples that two numbers have in common. Common multiples come in handy for solving problems like the one in **Activity 7.11** and for later work with fractions to determine the least common denominator (which is the least common multiple of the numbers in the denominators).

ACTIVITY 7.11

Pose a variety of problems whose solution involves using common multiples or common factors.

One example is:

Kyle bought some $12 shirts. Art bought some $15 shirts.

They each spent less than $200, but they both spent the same amount.

How much could they have spent?

To determine the common multiples of, for instance, 12 and 15, you list the multiples for each, and then look for multiples common to both lists:

> Multiples of 12: 12, 24, 36, 48, 60, 72, 84, 96, 108, 120, 132, ...
>
> Multiples of 15: 15, 30, 45, 60, 75, 90, 105, 120, 135, ...
>
> The common multiples of 12 and 15 are 60, 120, and so on.

There is an infinite list of common multiples of 12 and 15. The least common multiple is 60, but every multiple of 60 is also a common multiple of 12 and 15.

To write the fractions $\frac{2}{3}$ and $\frac{3}{4}$ with the same denominator, you need to find the least common denominator (LCD) of thirds and fourths, that is, the least common multiple (LCM) of 3 and 4:

> Multiples of 3: 3, 6, 9, 12, 15, 18, 21, ...
>
> Multiples of 4: 4, 8, 12, 16, ...
>
> The LCM of 3 and 4 is 12, which means the LCD is twelfths:
> $\frac{3}{4} = \frac{9}{12}$ and $\frac{2}{3} = \frac{8}{12}$.

ACTIVITY 7.12

Allow students to explore what happens if they graph something like $y = \text{LCM}(3, x)$ or $y = \text{LCM}(5, x)$. They can interpret the graph in light of what they know about the least common multiple.

Factors

Whenever there is a multiple, there are factors. The number 18 is a multiple of 6 because $3 \times 6 = 18$, which means 18 is also a multiple of 3; 3 and 6 are, therefore, factors of 18. Students will discover that some numbers have many factors, some have a few, and some have only 1 or 2. For example:

Factors of 24		Factors of 6		Factors of 97	
(8 factors)		(4 factors)		(2 factors)	
1	24	1	6	1	97
2	12	2	3		
3	8				
4	6				

As shown in the chart above, factors come in pairs, although some numbers have an odd number of different factors (square numbers), and the number 1 has only 1 factor (it is the only such counting number). For example:

Factors of 16		Factors of 1	
(5 factors)		(1 factor)	
1	16	1	1
2	8		
4	4		

Determining Factors

Organized lists, like those one page 150, are a way of determining factors in a systematic fashion, beginning with 1 and the number itself, and then 2 or the next possible factor and its factor partner, etc. Another way to organize and display the factors of a number is using a factor rainbow. For example:

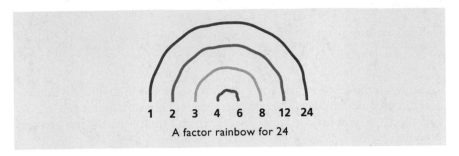

1 2 3 4 6 8 12 24
A factor rainbow for 24

If students attempt to construct a factor rainbow for a number like 100, they will discover that there is a repeated factor.

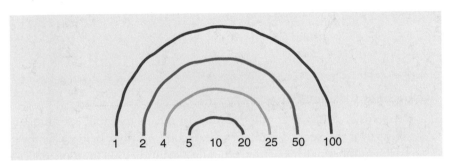

1 2 4 5 10 20 25 50 100

Concrete models and other pictorial models can also be used. For example, to determine the factors of 12, take 12 square tiles and try to arrange them into a rectangle. Record the length and width of each rectangle you can make; these are the factor pairs. This can also be done pictorially by drawing rectangles on grid paper (as shown below). You can use the same strategy as an organized list by approaching this systematically, beginning with a width of 1 unit, and then 2 units or the next possible width that is a factor.

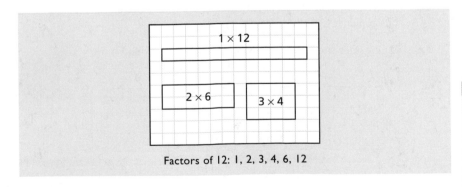

1 × 12

2 × 6   3 × 4

Factors of 12: 1, 2, 3, 4, 6, 12

Common Factors

Sometimes you need to determine the factors that two numbers have in common. Common factors can be used to solve problems such as the one in **Activity 7.13** and for expressing fractions in lowest or simplest terms.

ACTIVITY 7.13

Present this problem: Peter's dad put cookies in bags with the same number in each bag. Peter has 30 cookies altogether in his bags and his brother has 18 cookies altogether in his bags. How many cookies could his dad have put in each bag? Ask students to solve the problem and describe the strategies they used.

ACTIVITY 7.14

Let students explore a graph like this one showing $y = $ GCF (4, x). Have them interpret what the peaks mean and where they will occur.

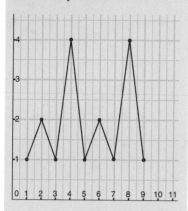

Then let them predict what a graph of $y = $ GCF (6, x) might look like and test their prediction.

To determine the common factors of, for example, 18 and 30, you list the factors for each and then look for factors common to both lists.

Factors of 18: 1, 2, 3, 6, 9, 18

Factors of 30: 1, 2, 3, 5, 6, 10, 15, 30

The common factors of 18 and 30 are 1, 2, 3, and 6.

To write the fraction $\frac{12}{18}$ in lowest terms, you need to divide the numerator, 12, and denominator, 18, by the greatest common factor (GCF). To find the GCF, you list the factors for each, and then look for the greatest common factor:

Factors of 18: 1, 2, 3, 6, 9, 18

Factors of 12: 1, 2, 3, 4, 6, 12

The GCF of 12 and 18 is 6. So $\frac{12}{18} = \frac{12 \div 6}{18 \div 6} = \frac{2}{3}$.

Factors and Divisibility

If a number is divisible by another number, it means that the first number is a multiple of the second number (the second number being a factor). There are a number of tests for determining if a number is a multiple of certain factors. Some of the tests are described below.

Divisibility Tests

RULE	EXPLANATION
Divisibility by 2 A number is divisible by 2 if the ones digit is 0, 2, 4, 6, or 8.	This works because of the pattern of the number system. 2 is automatically divisible by itself. Then every 2nd number follows the pattern 2, 4, 6, 8, x0, x2, x4, x6, x8, x0, with only the digits 0, 2, 4, 6, and 8 appearing in the ones place.
Divisibility by 3 A number is divisible by 3 if the sum of the digits is a multiple of 3.	Consider the number 414 (4 hundreds, 1 ten, and 4 ones): 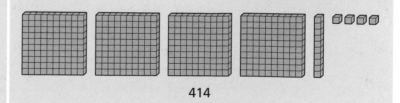 <div align="center">414</div>

- If 1 hundred block is divided into groups of 3, there will be 1 one block left over. So, if the 4 hundred blocks are grouped into 3s, there will be 4 one blocks left over.
- If the 1 ten block is grouped into 3s, there will be 1 one block left over.
- There are already 4 one blocks.
- After grouping the 4 hundreds and 1 ten into as many 3s as possible, there are 9 one blocks left over (since $4 + 1 + 4 = 9$), and 9 can be grouped into 3s because it is a multiple of 3. That makes 414 a multiple of 3. This explanation holds true for any number for which the sum of the digits is a multiple of 3.

Divisibility by 4 A number is divisible by 4 if the sum of twice the tens digit and the ones digit is a multiple of 4.	Every 100, 1000, 10 000, etc., can automatically be divided by 4. So only the tens and ones digits have to be considered. If each 10 is broken up into $8 + 2$, the 8 part is divisible by 4, so only the 2 part needs to be considered. For example, $352 = 100 \times 3 + 5 \times 8 + 5 \times 2 + 2$ 100×3 is a multiple of 4 and so is 5×8. Since $2 \times 5 + 2$ is also a multiple of 4, 352 is a multiple of 4.
Divisibility by 5 A number is divisible by 5 if the ones digit is 5 or 0.	This works because $5 \times 1 = 5$. Further multiples are determined by adding 5. When you add 5 to any number that has 5 as the ones digit, the ones digit is 0. When you add 5 to any number that has 0 as the ones digit, the ones digit is 5.
Divisibility by 6 A number is divisible by 6 if it is even and divisible by 3.	The multiples of 3 are 3, 6, 9, 12, 15, 18, ... Every second multiple of 3 is even (6, 12, 18, ...); these are the multiples of 6.
Divisibility by 8 A number is divisible by 8 if $4 \times$ hundreds digit $+ 2 \times$ tens digit $+$ ones is a multiple of 8.	Every 1000, 10 000, etc., can automatically be divided by 8 since $1000 \div 8 = 125$. So only the hundreds, tens, and ones digits have to be considered. If each 100 is broken up into $96 + 4$, the 96 part is divisible by 8, so only the 4 part needs to be considered. If each 10 is broken up into $8 + 2$, the 8 part is divisible by 8, so only the 2 part needs to be considered. For example, $352 = 3 \times 96 + 3 \times 4 + 5 \times 8 + 5 \times 2 + 2$ $4 \times 3 + 5 \times 2 + 2 = 24$ Since 24 is divisible by 8, the entire number is divisible by 8.
Divisibility by 9 A number is divisible by 9 if the sum of the digits is a multiple of 9.	The same explanation used for divisibility by 3 pertains here.
Divisibility by 10 A number is divisible by 10 if its ones digit is 0.	If a number is divisible by 10, it can be grouped into 10s with 0 ones left over. That means that the tens place or any places to its left can be anything, but the ones place must be 0. *(continued)*

Divisibility by 11

A number is divisible by 11 if the sums of alternate digits are equal, or a multiple of 11.

The powers of 10 alternate between being 1 greater and 1 less than a multiple of 11.

$$1 = 0 + 1 \qquad 10 = 11 - 1$$
$$100 = 99 + 1 \qquad 1000 = 1001 - 1$$
$$10\,000 = 9999 + 1 \quad 100\,000 = 100\,001 - 1$$

Because of this, if you add the digits in the 1s, 100s, 10 000s, … places, and then subtract the sum of the digits in the 10s, 1000s, 100 000s, … places, the values should be equal or else a multiple of 11 (including 0) if the number is a multiple of 11.

For example, 5412 is divisible by 11 since $2 + 4 - (1 + 5) = 0$.

ACTIVITY 7.15

Provide practice in working with multiples by allowing students to play games.

For example, each player might have to choose three cards from a deck of cards and try to arrange them into a number divisible by as many of the numbers 2, 3, 4, 5, 6, 8, 9, and 10 as possible. Their score might be the number of those divisors that their number has.

Prime and Composite Numbers

Numbers with exactly 2 factors have a special name; they are called prime numbers, or primes. There are very small prime numbers such as 2, 3, and 5, but there are also very large ones, for example, 6299. In fact, mathematicians continue to identify greater and greater prime numbers. Note that 2 is the only even prime number. Composite numbers have 3 or more factors. Every whole number other than 1 that is not a prime is called a composite number. The number 1 is neither prime nor composite (mathematicians call it a unit).

Determining Whether a Number Is Prime

There are many ways to decide whether a number is prime. One way, which is very tedious, is to try to divide the number by every possible smaller number to see how many factors it has. This would take a long time, even if done systematically. Another more interesting way is to use a technique called the Sieve of Eratosthenes, as described below.

Use a 100 chart to find the primes from 1 to 100:

Step 1 Place a blue counter on 1.

Step 2 Place red counters on every multiple of 2 but not 2 itself.

Step 3 Place yellow counters on every uncovered multiple of 3 but not 3 itself.

Step 4 Place blue counters on uncovered multiples of 5 but not 5 itself.

Step 5 Place green counters on uncovered multiples of 7 but not 7 itself.

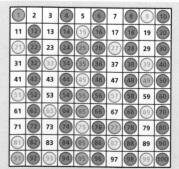

The Sieve of Eratosthenes "catches" the prime numbers.

The remaining uncovered numbers are prime numbers: 2, 3, 5, 7, 11, 13, 17, 19, 23, 29, 31, 37, 41, 43, 47, 53, 59, 61, 67, 71, 73, 79, 83, 89, and 97.

Some students will observe that the only possible final digits for primes greater than 2 and 5 are 1, 3, 7, and 9. This occurs because no other multiple of 2 can be prime (since it has a minimum of 3 factors: 1, 2, and itself), and no multiple of 5 other than 5 itself can be prime (since it has a minimum of 3 factors: 1, 5, and the number itself).

At some point, students will learn that the primes are the "building blocks" of our whole numbers in the sense that each whole number can be broken down into prime factors in one unique way. This is called prime factorization. For example, $36 = 2 \times 2 \times 3 \times 3$. Students often use factor trees to determine these prime factors; what is interesting is that the trees end up with the same factors even if they start differently.

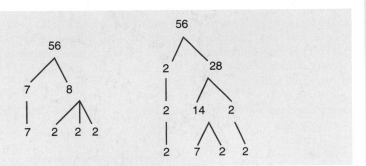

> **ACTIVITY 7.16**
>
> There are many famous conjectures about prime numbers. Ask students whether they think this one (called Goldbach's conjecture) is true:
>
> Every even number can be written as the sum of two primes, e.g.,
>
> $6 = 3 + 3$ $8 = 5 + 3$ $10 = 7 + 3$
>
> Ask students to explore these other conjectures about prime numbers, as well:
>
> • Every odd number is the sum of a prime and a power of 2, e.g.,
>
> $15 = 2^3 + 7$ $101 = 2^6 + 37$.
>
> • There is always at least one prime between consecutive square numbers, e.g., 7 between 2^2 and 3^2 and 101 between 10^2 and 11^2.

Common Errors and Misconception

Number Theory: Strategies for Dealing with Common Errors and Misconceptions

COMMON ERROR OR MISCONCEPTION	STRATEGY
Confusing "Factor" and "Multiple" Students confuse the terms "factor" and "multiple."	To help students remember, you might write a definition and example on a word wall: factor × factor = multiple For example, $3 \times 2 = 6$
Mistaking 1 for Prime Students identify the number 1 as a prime number. The number 1 is not a prime since it has only 1 factor.	Perhaps if 1 had a name, students would be less inclined to call it a prime. It is called a "unit."
0 as a Multiple Students struggle with the notion that 0 can be a multiple of other numbers.	There are two ways to approach this. One is to observe that, for example, $0 = 0 \times 3$, so 0 is a multiple of 3. The other is to use patterns. The multiples of 4 are 4 apart, so going down from 4, you get to 0: 24, 20, 16, 12, 8, 4, 0.
Mistaking Odd Composites for Prime Numbers Students mistake many odd composite numbers for prime numbers, particularly numbers such as 33, 39, and 51, because they do not immediately see how to factor the number.	If students have lots of experience working with hundred charts and calculating multiples, particularly multiples of 3, 7, and 9, they will see that many numbers ending in the digits 1, 3, 7, and 9 are, in fact, composite numbers.
Mistaking Odd Digits for Prime Numbers Students think that if each digit of a number is prime, the number is prime.	Present an example, such as the numbers 25 and 35, which students know are composite but have two prime digits.

Appropriate Manipulatives

Number Theory: Examples of Manipulatives

COUNTERS	100 CHARTS
Counters can be used to show the concept of "even-ness." If the counters can be paired up, the number is even; if they cannot, it is odd (see *Even and Odd Numbers* on page 149). Counters can also be used to form rectangular arrays for working with multiples and factors, if square tiles or grid paper are not available.	100 charts are useful for working with number patterns (even and odd numbers), multiples, and prime numbers.

SQUARE TILES AND GRID PAPER	GEOBOARDS AND SQUARE DOT PAPER
Square tiles and grid paper can be used to form or draw rectangles for working with multiples and factors (see *Determining Factors* on page 151). Tiles are concrete models while grid paper is pictorial. Both have their advantages. Tiles can be manipulated and allow students the opportunity to explore and try different arrangements. Grid paper offers a permanent record. Ideally, the two can be used together, with students using tiles to manipulate, and then drawing what they have done on grid paper.	Geoboards or square dot paper can be used to form rectangles in order to work with even and odd numbers, multiples, factors, and prime and composite numbers. 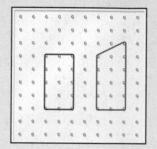 A geoboard for exploring even-ness: 8 squares is even; 9 squares is odd.

Appropriate Technology

Calculators

Students can and should use calculators to test for divisibility of one number by another. For example, when you divide 105 by 3, the result is a whole number. That means 105 is divisible by 3. And, if 105 is divisible by 3, you know that 105 is a multiple of its factor 3, and that it is a composite number. On the other hand, 107 is not divisible by 3 since there is a decimal in the quotient. If you keep dividing 107 by different numbers, you will discover that it is a prime number.

Web Connect

W W W

www.makingmathmeaningful
.nelson.com

Visit Nelson's Making Math Meaningful website to find more explorations of prime numbers.

Computers

There are online divisibility test applets that students can use to test their conjectures, as well as applets to generate prime numbers or test numbers to see whether they are prime. There are also sites that allow students to learn about other divisibility tests.

Assessing Student Understanding

- Frequently, teachers use items like this to test place value understanding:

  234 = ___ hundreds ___ tens ___ ones.

  Even if a student has no idea what the question means, he or she is likely to put the numbers 2, 3, 4 in the blanks in order since it is the only information available. In other words, the item may not tell the teacher what the student really does or does not know. Instead, ask a question like: What digit is in the tens place?

- A good question to determine whether students recognize that a number can be represented in many ways using place value ideas is to ask them to list as many numbers as they can that can be represented with 15 base ten blocks (e.g. 591, 492, ..., but also 15 or 150).

- Students should have assessment opportunities where a model is provided and the number associated with it must be determined as well as asking them to model a given number.

- It is important to encourage flexibility in estimating numbers. If, for example, a student estimates 339 as 300 rather than 340, this should be considered appropriate.

Appropriate Children's Books

The King's Commissioners (Friedman, 1995).
This story is designed, through humour, to show that there are a number of ways to count in groups, including by tens. The concepts developed in the book lead naturally into a discussion of the place value system.

A Million Dots (Clements, 2006).
This book includes a million dots. Its purpose is to give students a sense of the size of 1 million. The groups of dots on individual spreads are also given meaning, for example, a page representing the 525 600 minutes from one birthday to the next.

How Much Is a Million? (Schwartz, 1985).
This beautifully illustrated book (illustrator Steven Kellogg) encourages students to think about a million, billion, and trillion in a number of different contexts, including, for example, the height of a "tower" of 1 million, billion, or trillion children.

Number Sense and Nonsense (Zaslavsky, 2001).
This math-focused book is written for a student to read to learn about and experiment with properties of numbers. It is suitable for those students who are open to exploring number patterns, including divisibility tests.

Applying What You've Learned

1. Describe your process for solving the chapter problem. Which concept in the chapter does it relate to? How?

2. a) Why is the term *place value* appropriate for our number system?

   b) Why is a place value system an efficient one?

3. Explain why proportional materials that require students to create groups of 10 themselves (rather than having the 10s pre-made for them) are important when students are first exploring place value ideas?

4. Look at the hundreds chart shown on page 141. Describe four or five number patterns related to place value that could emerge as students become familiar with the chart.

5. Read one of the suggested appropriate children's books described on page 157. Build a lesson plan around that book that engages students in thinking about the related math concept.

6. Explain how the number line could be an important tool in helping students estimate the size of large numbers.

7. Create a set of two or three problems that you think would be good to assess student understanding of the place value system for numbers beyond the thousands. Describe what aspects of place value are being assessed.

8. Some people would argue that knowing about prime numbers is an unnecessary aspect of the math curriculum. How would you respond? Explain your reasoning.

Interact with a K–8 Student:

9. Ask a student to show you how to model a number with base ten blocks. Then ask them to model the same number a different way. Observe:

   a) Do they start with the digit at the left or the digit at the right?

   b) Do they have difficulty thinking about another way to model or do they fairly immediately replace either a large block with 10 small ones or 10 small ones with a large one? How might your observations influence how you approach the teaching of place value?

Discuss with a K–8 Teacher:

10. Ask a teacher what aspects of place value he or she finds most difficult to teach. Do some research. What ideas do you have that might create more success in teaching that topic?

Selected References

Baroody, A.J. (1990). How and when should place-value concepts and skills be taught? *Journal for Research in Mathematics Education,* 21, 281–286.

Clements, A. (2006). *A million dots.* New York: Simon & Schuster Publishing.

Cotter, J. (2000). Using language and visualization to teach place value. *Teaching Children Mathematics,* 7, 108–114.

Friedman, A. (1995). *The king's commissioners.* New York: Scholastic.

Fuson, K.C. (1990a). Conceptual structures for multiunit numbers: Implications for learning and teaching multidigit addition, subtraction, and place value. *Cognition and Instruction,* 7, 343–403.

Fuson, K.C. (1990b). Issues in place-value and multidigit addition and subtraction learning and teaching. *Journal for Research in Mathematics Education,* 21, 273–280.

Hope, J., Small, M., and Drost, D. (1994). *Interactions 4.* Toronto: Ginn Publishing Canada, Inc.

Jones, G.A., and Thornton, C.A. (1993). Children's understanding of place value: A framework for curriculum development and assessment. *Young Children,* 48, 12–18.

Kamii, C.K. (1986). Place value: An explanation of its difficulty and educational implications for the primary grades. *Journal of Research in Childhood Education,* 1, 75–86.

Kari, A.R., and Anderson, C.B. (2003). Opportunities to develop place value through student dialogue. *Teaching Children Mathematics,* 10, 78–82.

Ross, S. (2002). Place value: Problem solving and written assessment. *Teaching Children Mathematics,* 9, 419–423.

Schwartz, D. (1985). *How much is a million?* New York: HarperCollins.

Small, M. (2005). *PRIME: Number and operations: Background and strategies.* Toronto: Thomson Nelson.

Strauss, S. (1995). *The Sizesaurus.* Toronto: Key Porter Books.

Taylor, A.R., Breck, S.E., and Aljets, C.M. (2004). What Nathan teaches us about transitional thinking. *Teaching Children Mathematics,* 11, 138–142.

Yolles, A. (2001). Making connections with prime numbers. *Mathematics Teaching in the Middle School,* 7, 84–86.

Zaslavsky, C. (2001). *Number sense and nonsense.* Chicago: Chicago Review Press.

Chapter 8
Computation with Whole Numbers

IN A NUTSHELL

The main ideas in the chapter are listed below:

1. There are many procedures, or algorithms, for adding, subtracting, multiplying, and dividing. The traditional one is simply one of these and not necessarily better than the others.

2. It is valuable for students to have opportunities to invent their own procedures.

3. Procedures should always be taught with meaning, referring to the meaning of the operation, principles of the operations, and concrete manipulations that describe the procedure.

4. Students should learn procedures for estimating, not just for calculating.

CHAPTER PROBLEM

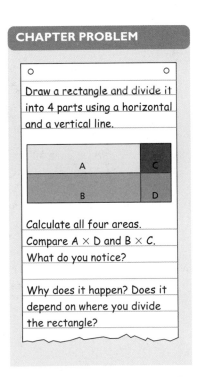

Draw a rectangle and divide it into 4 parts using a horizontal and a vertical line.

Calculate all four areas. Compare A × D and B × C. What do you notice?

Why does it happen? Does it depend on where you divide the rectangle?

Addition and Subtraction Procedures

Estimating Sums and Differences

Estimating sums and differences is valuable as it helps in checking calculations, and predicting answers, and sometimes it is all that is required.

Factors Influencing Estimation

A number of factors come into play when making decisions about estimating, such as the context and the numbers and operations involved.

Context The context will determine

- if an estimate or an exact answer is more appropriate. For example, when a customer wants to know if she or he can afford two items, an estimate might be appropriate. When the clerk is giving the customer change, however, an exact difference is required.
- how close the estimate should be to the exact value. For example, estimating the total number of people at a sports event for a news report would not require as close an estimate as would estimating the total cost of two items.
- whether a high or low estimate is more appropriate. For example, to estimate the total cost of two items, a high estimate is safer than a low estimate. A low estimate is probably better when someone is estimating how many of something he or she can afford to buy.

The Numbers and Operations Involved

- The individual numbers involved matter. For example:

  $836 + 94$ is about $836 + 100 = 936$, rounding 94 to 100 because 100 is close and easy to work with

  $672 - 69$ is about $675 - 75 = 600$, rounding both numbers so that they are compatible

- Whether you are adding or subtracting: Rounding one number up and the other down is usually appropriate for adding, but not necessarily for subtracting; rounding both numbers up or both numbers down is usually appropriate when subtracting, but not when adding. For example:

  $46 + 36$ is about $50 + 30$ (rather than rounding to $50 + 40$)

  $84 - 36$ is about $90 - 40$ (rather than rounding to $80 - 40$)

ACTIVITY 8.1

Ask students to estimate which animals with certain masses can safely cross a set of bridges with particular load limits.

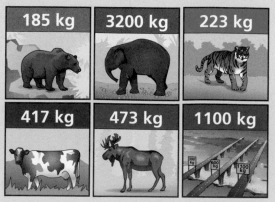

Estimating Strategies

To estimate sums and differences, students might use strategies such as the following:

STRATEGY	EXAMPLE
Round each number to the nearest multiple of 10, 100, 1000, etc.	693 + 458 is about 700 + 500 = 1200 693 − 458 is about 690 − 460 = 230
Round each number to another "round" number.	693 + 458 is about 700 + 450 = 1150 693 − 458 is about 700 − 450 = 250
Round one number but not the other.	693 + 458 is about 700 + 458 = 1158
When adding, round both numbers, one up and one down.	693 + 458 is about 700 + 450 = 1150
When subtracting, round both numbers up or both numbers down.	693 − 458 is about 700 − 500 = 200 693 − 458 is about 650 − 450 = 200
Estimate within a range.	428 + 397 is between 700 (400 + 300) and 900 (500 + 400) 516 − 147 is between 300 (500 − 200) and 500 (600 − 100)
Estimate in terms of money.	385 + 245 is about 3 loonies, 3 quarters + 2 loonies, 2 quarters, which is 6 loonies, 1 quarter, or 625
Estimate by using compatible numbers, which are often not "round" at all.	867 − 471 is about 867 − 467 = 400

Notice that one approach shown in the chart was to estimate within a range. Onslow et al. (2005) suggest that students might estimate the sum of 323 and 428 as a number in the 700s, rather than as a particular single value.

As is evident in many of the estimating examples described above, it is essential that students know the addition and subtraction facts and how to add and subtract multiples of 10, 100, 1000, etc., in order to estimate. There is neither one right strategy nor one right answer when estimating.

Here is what two friends spent each day.

	Tuesday	Wednesday	Thursday	Friday
Jane	$5.96	$12.48	$37.26	$18.95
Ricki	$7.10	$12.50	$37.50	$18.74

To find out who spent more, do you need to calculate an exact answer? _____No_____

Explain.

No, because there's only one time when Jane spends more than Ricki and it's not by very much.

Student Response

This student recognizes that some estimating situations require no calculations at all.

Varied Approaches to Addition and Subtraction

Students, even as early as in Grade 2, are expected to apply what they know about adding and subtracting single-digit numbers ("the facts") and the meanings of those operations for adding and subtracting greater numbers. It is at this point when it becomes useful to learn algorithms or procedures that can be followed to add and subtract greater numbers.

As with estimating sums and differences, before students can work efficiently and flexibly with algorithms, they must

- know their addition and subtraction facts
- understand the basic principles underlying the place value system
- know how to add and subtract multiples of 10, 100, 1000, etc.
- understand the basic addition and subtraction principles, as many algorithms are built on those principles

Invented Algorithms

Students should have early opportunities to develop their own algorithms. These are sometimes referred to as invented algorithms. Research has shown that students can have much greater success if they have opportunities early on to develop their own algorithms, generally using concrete models (Hiebert, 1984; Kamii, Lewis, and Livingston, 1993). The transition to more conventional algorithms is best done when a student is ready and not necessarily according to a teacher's timetable.

Mental Math

Some of the algorithms presented on the next few pages are more appropriate for pencil-and-paper work. Others are mental algorithms. There is great value in using mental algorithms as they are often quicker and easier to use.

Most mental algorithms require students to compose and decompose numbers; for instance, think of $99 + 36$ as $100 + 35$, or think of $111 - 89$ as $100 - 90 + 10 + 2$. Mental computation is about considering which form or representation of a number is most useful for a particular calculation. Students who do mental calculations exercise and further develop their number sense. One of the ways that teachers can encourage students to calculate mentally is to present computations in horizontal, rather than vertical, form. In this way, students do not immediately think in columns. This helps them to remember that, for example, the 2 in 324 is 20 and not 2.

Student Response

This student has performed a mental math algorithm that involves adding "convenient" numbers, and then compensating.

Explain the steps you would follow to add 48 + 17.

I would round 48 to 50
then Add 17 on which is 67
Then subtract 2 which is 65

Alternative Algorithms

Many people find it surprising that there is considerable flexibility in calculating sums and differences, just as there is with estimating. Teachers should be aware of this and be prepared to expose students to multiple algorithms.

Why Encourage Alternative Algorithms?

- One algorithm might make more sense to a student than another.
- One algorithm might be more convenient for a particular set of numbers.
- Some algorithms lend themselves to mental computation, when that is required.
- A student may get help at home from a parent who uses a very different algorithm than what has been taught at school. It is helpful if students are open to both.
- Students who have a repertoire of algorithms to choose from can use one algorithm to perform a calculation, and a different one to check it.
- Some algorithms are actually procedures that a student might "invent." Something a student creates himself or herself is almost always more meaningful to him or her.

Teachers are sometimes disappointed when a student uses the "traditional" algorithm to calculate a computation such as $1000 - 999$, instead of a more "common sense" approach, reasoning that the numbers are only 1 apart, so the answer is 1. It is hardly surprising when you consider that the traditional algorithm is sometimes the only algorithm taught.

TRADITIONAL ALGORITHM	AN ALTERNATIVE ALGORITHM
The "traditional" algorithm focuses on single digits and is recorded: $\begin{array}{r} 9\,9\,10 \\ \cancel{1}\cancel{0}\cancel{0}\cancel{0} \\ -\ \ \ 999 \\ \hline 1 \end{array}$	This alternative algorithm uses number sense and addition principles and lends itself to mental math: $1000 - 999 = \blacksquare \rightarrow 999 + \blacksquare = 1000$ $\qquad\qquad\qquad 999 + 1 = 1000$ $1000 - 999 = 1$

Alternative Addition Algorithms For the traditional algorithm (Algorithm 1) and many others, it is appropriate, initially, to model the algorithm with manipulatives. A written record is not necessary in the early stages of algorithm use, but is important later on, with each step of the algorithm matching a physical action with the manipulatives. No matter what algorithm is used, it is important that students understand and are able to explain why they do what they do. Algorithms suitable for mental calculation will be noted as they are described.

Algorithm 1 Using the traditional algorithm, the digits are combined beginning at the ones place and working left. An example is shown.

Step 1 Model both numbers with blocks, on a place value mat, if available.

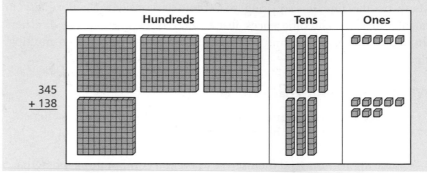

$$\begin{array}{r} 345 \\ + 138 \\ \hline \end{array}$$

Step 2 Add the ones. Trade 10 ones for 1 ten. Record the ones that are left.

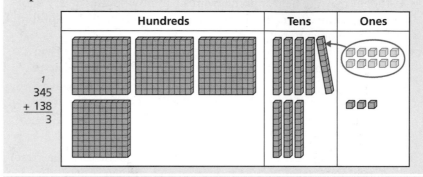

$$\begin{array}{r} {}^{1} \\ 345 \\ + 138 \\ \hline 3 \end{array}$$

Step 3 Add the tens. Record the tens.

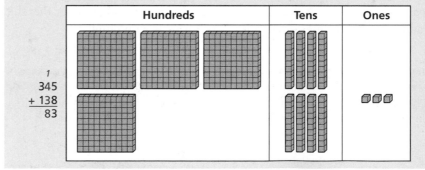

$$\begin{array}{r} {}^{1} \\ 345 \\ + 138 \\ \hline 83 \end{array}$$

Step 4 Add the hundreds. Record the hundreds.

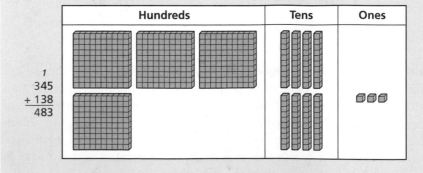

$$\begin{array}{r} {}^{1} \\ 345 \\ + 138 \\ \hline 483 \end{array}$$

ACTIVITY 8.2

Pose problems that require students to use addition, but in more mathematically rich ways. For example, two problems might be:

• Imagine tossing a pair of dice again and again to create two 2-digit numbers, which are then added.

What is the least number of tosses needed for a sum greater than 200?

How do you know?

• A triangle has a perimeter of 45 cm. What could the lengths of the sides be?

Some teachers have students work on a place value mat with three rows, one for the first addend, one for the second, and one for the sum. If there are sufficient blocks, students can even leave the addend blocks in place and use other blocks to show the sum. In this way, there is a complete concrete record of the question.

Algorithm 2 This algorithm involves finding partial sums and then totalling them. For Algorithm 2A (front-end addition), the adding begins at the left (the greatest place value), while, for Algorithm 2B, it begins at the right, or the ones. Each step in the addition is shown as a partial sum. This algorithm lends itself to mental calculation.

ALGORITHM 2A	ALGORITHM 2B
345	345
+ 138	+ 138
400 (Add the hundreds.)	13 (Add the ones.)
70 (Add the tens.)	70 (Add the tens.)
+ 13 (Add the ones.)	+ 400 (Add the hundreds.)
483 (Add the partial sums.)	483 (Add the partial sums.)

Algorithm 2 can be modelled with base ten blocks. Algorithm 2A is shown below.

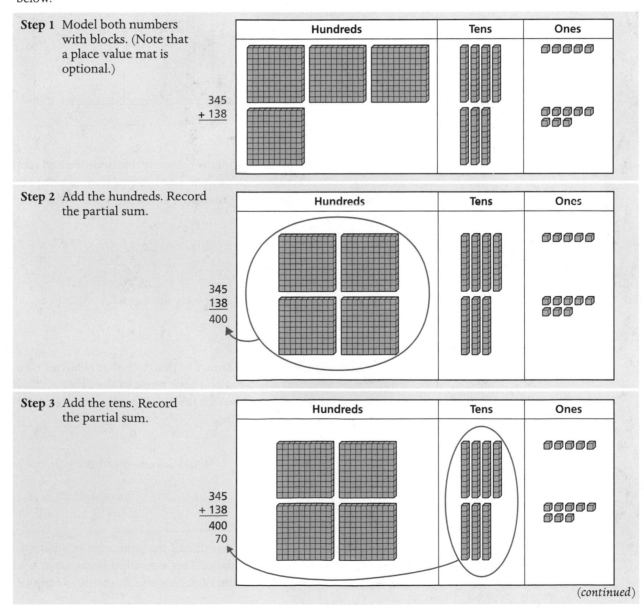

Step 1 Model both numbers with blocks. (Note that a place value mat is optional.)

345
+ 138

Step 2 Add the hundreds. Record the partial sum.

345
138
400

Step 3 Add the tens. Record the partial sum.

345
+ 138
400
70

(continued)

Step 4 Add the ones. Record the partial sum.

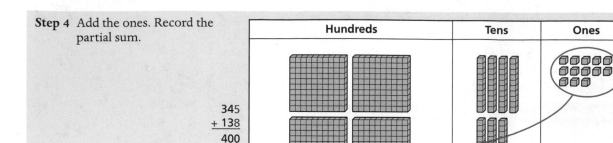

$$
\begin{array}{r}
345 \\
+\ 138 \\
\hline
400 \\
70 \\
13 \\
\end{array}
$$

Step 5 Combine the hundreds, tens, and ones. Regroup 10 ones for 1 ten. Record the sum of the partial sums.

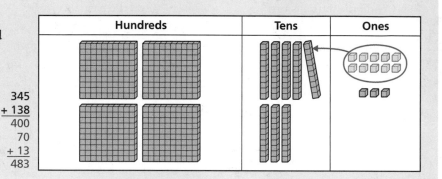

$$
\begin{array}{r}
345 \\
+\ 138 \\
\hline
400 \\
70 \\
+\ 13 \\
\hline
483 \\
\end{array}
$$

Algorithm 3 This algorithm is based on the principle that addition and subtraction "undo" each other. In this case, you add too much in order to get an easier addend to work with, often mentally, and then "undo" what you did by taking away:

$$357 + 597 \rightarrow 357 + (597 + 3) \qquad \text{(Add 3 too many.)}$$
$$= 357 + 600$$
$$= 957 \rightarrow 957 - 3 \qquad \text{(Take away the extra 3.)}$$
$$= 954$$

Algorithm 4 This algorithm is based on the principle that you can take away from one addend and add what you took away to the other addend without changing the sum. This allows for the creation of addends that are easier to calculate with, often mentally.

$$389 + 197 = (389 - 3) + (197 + 3) \qquad \text{(Move 3 from 389 to 197.)}$$
$$= 386 + 200$$
$$= 586$$

Algorithm 5 This algorithm is based on one of the principles of addition, that is, adding can be completed in parts. This algorithm is easiest to use when the adding of subsequent amounts does not affect previous additions as shown below. Note that for a calculation such as 345 + 178, adding the 70 (in 178) requires more than a straightforward adding of the tens digits; regrouping is required to add 70 to 40. This algorithm can often be performed mentally.

ACTIVITY 8.3

Ask students to calculate all possible sums if they hit this dart board three times and never miss.

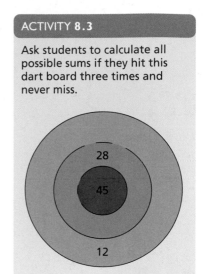

345 + 138
Start with 345 and add 138 in parts:
First add 100: 345 + 100 = 445
Then add 30:   445 + 30 = 475
Then add 8:   475 + 8 = 483

Alternative Subtraction Algorithms Just as with addition, there is a broad range of possible subtraction algorithms. A number of these are described here. Algorithms suitable for mental calculation will be noted.

Algorithm 1 The traditional North American algorithm is not always the easiest for students. One of the reasons is that it proceeds in a left-to-right direction to regroup but in a right-to-left direction to subtract. The algorithm is built around focusing on one place value position at a time and, therefore, often involves several stages of regrouping. At each place value, students have to first decide whether to regroup, and then actually perform the regrouping. This requires students to go back and forth between thinking about regrouping and performing the subtraction.

Step 1 Model the minuend, on a place value mat, if available. (Notice that the subtrahend is not modelled since it is to be taken away from the minuend.)

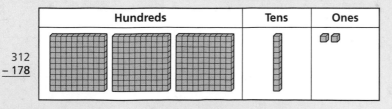

Step 2 Recognize that there are not enough ones to be able to take away 8 ones. Trade 1 ten for 10 ones so you can take away 8 ones. Record the ones that are left.

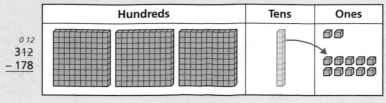

(continued)

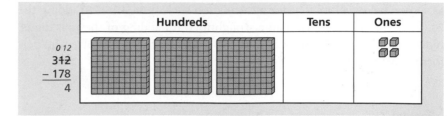

Step 3 Recognize that there are not enough tens to be able to take away 7 tens. Trade 1 hundred for 10 tens so you can take away 7 tens. Record the tens that are left.

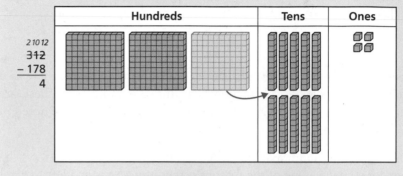

Step 4 Take away 1 hundred. Record the hundreds that are left.

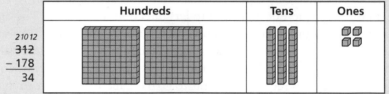

Algorithm 2 Because addition and subtraction "undo" each other, if you subtract too much in order to use a number that makes the calculation easier, you need to "undo" what you did by adding back the amount you subtracted. This algorithm can be performed mentally.

$$414 - 296 \rightarrow 414 - (296 + 4) \qquad \text{(Subtract 4 extra.)}$$
$$= 414 - 300$$
$$= 114 \longrightarrow 114 + 4 \qquad \text{(Add back 4.)}$$
$$= 118$$

Explain the steps you would follow to subtract 50 − 37.

You would round 37 to 40, then subtract 40 from 50, then add 3.

Student Response

This student has subtracted too much and then compensated.

Algorithm 3 This algorithm is based on the principle that you can subtract in parts. You subtract in parts because the parts are easier to subtract mentally.

$$414 - 302 = 414 - 300 - 2 \quad \text{(Subtract 300 and then subtract 2.)}$$
$$= 114 - 2$$
$$= 112$$

Algorithm 4 This subtraction algorithm is built on the principle that, to subtract two numbers, you can add or subtract the same amount to or from both numbers without changing the difference. By selecting appropriate amounts to add or subtract, a student is often able to transform a calculation that she or he would need to do on paper into one that can be accomplished mentally.

$$414 - 296 = (414 + 4) - (296 + 4) \quad \text{(Add 4 to each number.)}$$
$$= 418 - 300$$
$$= 118$$

Algorithm 5 The relationship between addition and subtraction underlies what is sometimes called the "making change" algorithm. When you make change in money situations, you count from the price (the subtrahend) up to the money paid (the minuend) to find the difference. Although the counting up can be done mentally, the "change" must still be added; some students would need to jot down these amounts in order not to forget them.

Step 1 Think of the subtraction as a missing addend number sentence:
$$327 - 158 = \square \rightarrow 158 + \square = 327$$

Step 2 Count up:
Add 2 to get to a multiple of 10: $158 + 2 = 160$
Add 40 to get to a multiple of 100: $160 + 40 = 200$
Add enough to get to the minuend, or total: $200 + 127 = 327$
Add up the "change": $2 \quad + 40 \quad + 127 = 169$

Communicating about Addition and Subtraction Algorithms

Notice that in many of the examples on the previous pages, the terms "regroup," "trade," and "exchange" are used rather than "carry" or "borrow." This is because carrying and borrowing have no real meaning with respect to the operation being performed, but the term "regroup" suitably describes the action the student must take.

Students sometimes use poor math language when they perform algorithms that focus on one place value or digit at a time. For example, in the addition below, in Step 2, you are not adding 2 and 3; you are adding 2 tens and 3 tens, or 20 and 30. It is important for teachers to model the appropriate place value language and expect students to use it.

Step 1 Add the ones:	Step 2 Add the tens:	Step 3 Add the hundreds:

3 2 5   "5 + 4 = 9"
 + 1 3 4
 ———
        9
	3 2 5 "2 tens + 3 tens = 5 tens"
	 + 1 3 4
	 ———
	      5 9
		3 2 5 "3 hundreds + 1 hundred = 4 hundreds"
		 + 1 3 4
		 ———
		 4 5 9

ACTIVITY 8.4

This is called a magic square because the rows, columns, and diagonals all add to the same amount. Ask students to determine which numbers are missing.

	17	22
19		23
20	25	

To create additional magic squares, you can always begin with one that you have, like the one above, and add, subtract, multiply, or divide all entries using the same value. You can also rotate or reflect the square.

ACTIVITY 8.5

Set up a problem-solving centre where students use tiles with the digits 0 to 9 on them, each once, to complete calculations begun for them.

```
  ▨ 3      5 8       6 ▨       ▨ 3
+ ▨ 7    - ▨ ▨     + ▨ ▨     - ▨ 4
 ————     ————      ————      ————
  6 ▨      4 2      1 4 9      1 9
```

Common Errors and Misconceptions

Many of the common errors in performing addition and subtraction algorithms stem from a lack of understanding of the underlying principles (numeration, addition, and subtraction principles). If students continue to make these kinds of errors and do not seem to understand what they are doing wrong, they should be using concrete base ten models to work through the algorithms, while at the same time recording the written algorithms.

Addition and Subtraction Algorithm: Strategies for Dealing with Common Errors and Misconceptions

	SUGGESTED STRATEGY
Regrouping Students forget to regroup when adding, and write a 2-digit number where there should be only one digit. $$\begin{array}{r} 145 \\ +\ 247 \\ \hline 3812 \end{array}$$	Students should be encouraged to estimate to check their answers. In this case, if students rounded up to overestimate $145 + 247$ as $200 + 300 = 500$, they would realize that an answer such as 3812 is much too high.
Regrouping Students remember to regroup, but reverse which digit is recorded in the sum and which is recorded in the regrouping area above; for example, $$\overset{2}{1}45 \quad \text{instead of} \quad \overset{1}{1}45$$ $$\underline{+\ 237} \qquad\qquad \underline{+\ 237}$$ $$391 \qquad\qquad\quad 392$$	If the actual sum and the incorrect sum are close, estimating may not be helpful. Another strategy is to have students use place value mats for recording calculations. This way, when they record or place the number below and above the addition, they are placing it in an identified place value position.
Misunderstanding the Algorithm Students subtract the lesser digit from the greater digit within each column, regardless of whether it is in the minuend or the subtrahend; for example, $$325 \quad \text{instead of} \quad \overset{2\ 11}{\cancel{3}\,\cancel{2}}5$$ $$\underline{-189} \qquad\qquad \underline{-\ 189}$$ $$264 \qquad\qquad\quad 136$$	Estimating may or may not be helpful, depending on how close the actual and incorrect differences are. Students who estimate $300 - 200 = 100$ will suspect there is an error. Students who estimate $300 - 100 = 200$ may not. Another strategy is to appeal to a simpler problem where the error is more obvious. For example, if students subtract incorrectly within columns for a question such as $15 - 9$, they are more apt to notice the error.
Misalignment of Digits Students misalign digits when recording calculations and end up computing incorrectly.	Students can use grid paper or lined paper turned sideways to align digits. $$\begin{array}{c|c|c} 1 & 1 & \\ \hline 5 & 7 & 3 \\ \hline +\ 2 & 4 & 8 \\ \hline 9 & 2 & 1 \end{array}$$

Appropriate Manipulatives

Any of the algorithms described on the previous pages can be initially modelled with manipulatives so that students understand the procedure and why it works.

Addition and Subtraction Algorithms: Examples of Manipulatives

BASE TEN MATERIALS

Base ten materials come in many forms. However, commercial base ten materials are particularly useful because they are sturdy, easy to manipulate, and present a proportional model.

All of the algorithms shown on the previous pages can be modelled using base ten materials.

This model shows Algorithm 4 for addition on page 166 using base ten blocks.

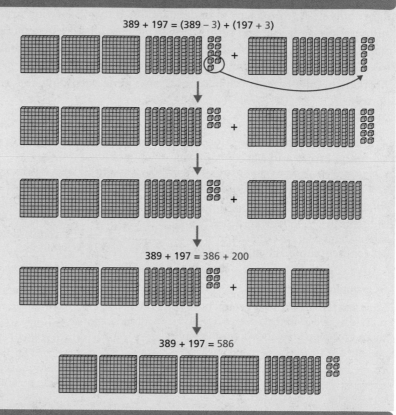

$$389 + 197 = (389 - 3) + (197 + 3)$$

$$389 + 197 = 386 + 200$$

$$389 + 197 = 586$$

PLAY MONEY

Play money is a nonproportional model (sometimes called a value model) and is particularly useful for students who have internalized place value money concepts. (Note that some teachers reserve money for modelling decimal calculations; others use it for both whole number and decimal calculations.)

In a money model, only the loonie, dime, and penny are used: the loonie represents 100, the dime represents 10, and the penny represents 1. All of the algorithms shown on the previous pages can be modelled using the money model in the same way as base ten blocks, with the loonie substituting for the hundred block, the dime for the ten block, and the penny for the one block.

345
+ 138

PLACE VALUE MATS

Place value mats are optional when working with base ten materials or the money model, but they do help reinforce the place value concepts underlying the algorithms. The model at right uses a place value mat for Algorithm 1 for subtraction shown on page 167, using coins instead of blocks.

312
− 178

Hundreds	Tens	Ones

Appropriate Technology

Calculators

Students should always be encouraged to estimate before performing a calculation on a calculator to ensure that an answer makes sense. It is very easy to press a wrong button. There are those who feel that students should estimate before they calculate, and those who feel that the estimating can occur after the calculation. What is important is that students determine the reasonableness of their answers by estimating.

Calculators are particularly useful for work with large numbers, for multiple calculations, or when the focus is on the problem to be solved and not the calculation.

Computers

There is some good problem-solving computer software available. An example is *Ten Tricky Tiles*, in which students must figure out where to put each of the digits 0 to 9 to finish the display of a set of computations, much like **Activity 8.5** on page 170. There are many free Internet sites that allow students to practise addition and subtraction; however, they often require students to input the answer in only one way, thereby forcing a particular algorithm. This is counter to the whole philosophy of encouraging the use of multiple algorithms, and should be used sparingly.

Multiplication and Division Procedures

Multiplying and Dividing Using Powers of 10

Both estimation and calculation of multi-digit products and quotients are based on students knowing multiplication and division facts, and knowing how to multiply and divide with multiples of 10, 100, 1000, etc. The following models can be used to teach and explain these concepts.

Multiplying by 10, 100, and 1000
Using Place Value Concepts

Example 1 This model shows 5×30. It can be extended to 5×300 using base ten hundred blocks, and to 5×3000 using base ten thousand blocks for thousands.

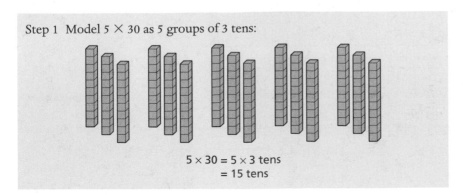

Step 1 Model 5×30 as 5 groups of 3 tens:

$$5 \times 30 = 5 \times 3 \text{ tens}$$
$$= 15 \text{ tens}$$

ACTIVITY 8.6

Students can solve interesting problems involving addition and subtraction.

Examples include:

- Five numbers add to 100. The difference between the least one and greatest one is 12. How do you know that none is greater than 50? What could the numbers be?

- Which numbers between 50 and 100 can be expressed as the sum of four consecutive numbers?

Step 2 Regroup by trading 10 tens for 1 hundred:

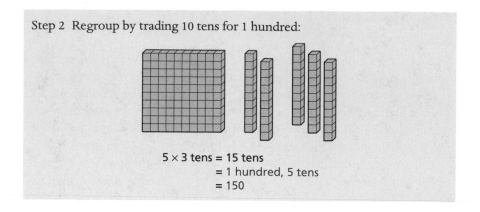

5 × 3 tens = 15 tens
= 1 hundred, 5 tens
= 150

Example 2 This model shows 20 × 30. (Note that students usually find calculations like this, in which both factors are multiples of 10, more difficult than when only one factor is a multiple of 10, for example, 2 × 30.)

Step 1 Model 20 × 30 as 20 groups of 3 tens:

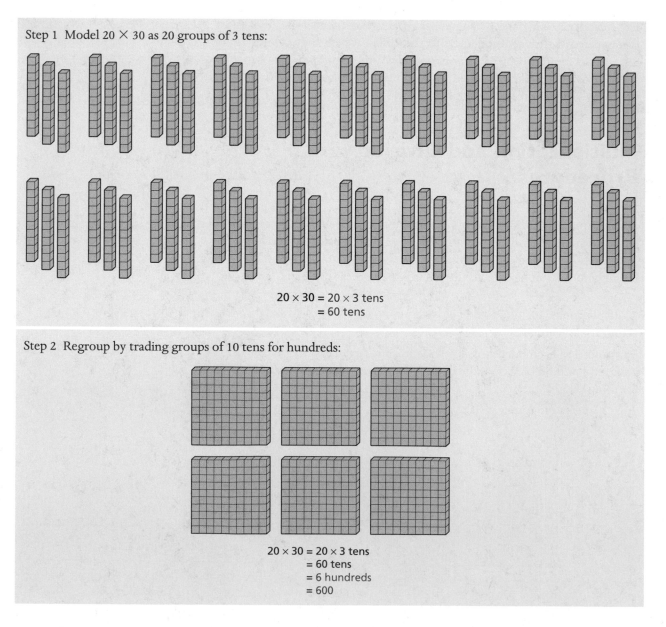

20 × 30 = 20 × 3 tens
= 60 tens

Step 2 Regroup by trading groups of 10 tens for hundreds:

20 × 30 = 20 × 3 tens
= 60 tens
= 6 hundreds
= 600

Multiplying by 10, 100, and 1000 Using Patterns

Example This model uses patterning to multiply.

$2 \times 3 = 6$

$20 \times 3 = 60$ (One factor is 10 times as much, so the product is 10 times as much.)

$20 \times 30 = 600$ (One factor is 10 times as much, so the product is 10 times as much again.)

$200 \times 30 = 6000$ (One factor is 10 times as much, so the product is 10 times as much again.)

$200 \times 300 = 60\,000$ (One factor is 10 times as much, so the product is 10 times as much again.)

$2000 \times 300 = 600\,000$ (One factor is 10 times as much, so the product is 10 times as much again.)

$2000 \times 3000 = 6\,000\,000$ (One factor is 10 times as much, so the product is 10 times as much again.)

Dividing with 10, 100, and 1000 Using Place Value Concepts

Example 1 This model shows $320 \div 8$. It can be extended to $3200 \div 8$, using base ten hundred blocks, and to $32\,000 \div 8$, using base ten thousand blocks for thousands.

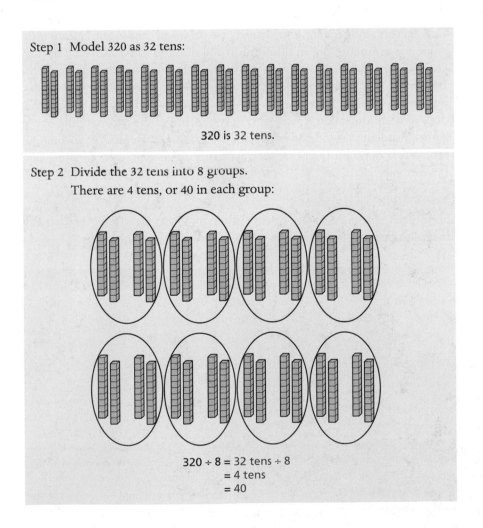

Step 1 Model 320 as 32 tens:

320 is 32 tens.

Step 2 Divide the 32 tens into 8 groups.
There are 4 tens, or 40 in each group:

$320 \div 8 = 32$ tens $\div 8$
$= 4$ tens
$= 40$

Example 2 This model shows $400 \div 80$ and uses place value language instead of concrete models (for example, the word "tens" is used instead of a base ten block).

$$400 \div 80 = 40 \text{ tens} \div 8 \text{ tens}$$
$$= 5$$

Dividing with 10, 100, and 1000 Using Patterns

Example This model uses patterning to divide.

$40 \div 8 = 5$

$400 \div 8 = 50$ (The dividend is 10 times as much so the quotient is 10 times as much.)

$4000 \div 8 = 500$ (The dividend is 10 times as much so the quotient is 10 times as much again.)

$4000 \div 80 = 50$ (The divisor is 10 times as much so the quotient is $\frac{1}{10}$.)

$4000 \div 800 = 5$ (The divisor is 10 times as much so the quotient is $\frac{1}{10}$ again.)

Estimating Products and Quotients

The factors influencing estimation for addition and subtraction also influence estimation for multiplication and division (see *Factors Influencing Estimation* on page 160). However, when it comes to considering the operations involved, it is important to note that estimates involving multiplication and division often tend to be further from the actual values than is the case for addition and subtraction, simply because of the nature of the operations. Students should pay particular attention to whether the estimated product or quotient might be too low or too high (see *Overestimating and Underestimating* on page 177).

Estimating Strategies

To estimate products and quotients, students might use strategies such as the following:

STRATEGY	EXAMPLE
Round one or both numbers to the nearest multiple of 10, 100, 1000, etc.	25×52 is about $25 \times 50 = 1250$ 39×31 is about $40 \times 30 = 1200$ $642 \div 32$ is about $600 \div 30 = 20$
Round numbers such that familiar multiplication and division facts can be used.	$574 \div 9$ is about $560 \div 8 = 70$ $574 \div 9$ is about $540 \div 9 = 60$
When multiplying, round one factor up and the other down.	65×15 is about $60 \times 20 = 1200$
When dividing, round both numbers up or both numbers down.	$337 \div 8$ is about $360 \div 9 = 40$ $337 \div 8$ is about $280 \div 7 = 40$
Round numbers to the nearest multiple of 10, 100, 1000, or 25 to be able to multiply or divide by 25.	389×27 is about $400 \times 25 = 10\ 000$ $612 \div 27$ is about $600 \div 25 = 24$

Overestimating and Underestimating

Students should keep in mind the effect that the operations of multiplication and division have on numbers. They need to consider this when deciding on what strategy to use to ensure that the estimate is reasonable.

When multiplying, rounding one factor has a different effect than rounding the other In the following example, rounding the 8 to 10 has a greater effect on the estimated product than rounding the 68 to 70, even though it is an increase of 2 for each. This is because two extra 68s in 68×10 is more than 8 extra 2s in 70×8.

Multiply exactly: $68 \times 8 = 544$	Round the second factor up: $68 \times 10 = 680$ 680 is 136 greater than 544.	Round the first factor up: $70 \times 8 = 560$ 560 is 16 greater than 544.

When dividing, rounding the dividend has a different effect than rounding the divisor The following example uses the sharing model of division to explain why rounding the dividend up increases the estimated quotient, but rounding the divisor up decreases the estimated quotient.

Divide exactly: $450 \div 7 \doteq 64.3$ 450 items shared among 7 people is 64 items each with a few left over.	Round the dividend up: $450 \div 7$ is about $490 \div 7 = 70$ 70 is greater than the exact quotient since there are more items to share among the same number of people.	Round the divisor up: $450 \div 7$ is about $450 \div 9 = 50$ 50 is less than the exact quotient, 64.3, since there are more people sharing the same number of items.

Jane has $500 to buy 8 games. Each game costs $37.
Jane wonders if she has enough money.

Could she estimate the total cost or should she find the exact total? _she should estimate._

Explain your thinking.

She should estimate because $37 × 10 = $370 but she only buys 8 game so she only has to estimate.

Student Response

This student knows that it is appropriate to estimate given the situation and the numbers involved.

Algorithms for Multiplication and Division

Students usually begin working with multiplication and division algorithms in about Grade 4, after they have started to become proficient with the multiplication facts. For most multiplication and division algorithms, students must

- know their multiplication and division facts
- know how to multiply and divide with multiples of 10, 100, and 1000
- know how to add and subtract
- understand the basic principles underlying the place value system (see *Numeration Principles* on page 138)
- understand the basic multiplication and division principles, as many algorithms are generally built on those principles (see *Multiplication and Division Principles* on page 123)

Alternative and Invented Algorithms There are many good reasons why students should be exposed to multiple algorithms for multiplication and division and be allowed to invent their own algorithms (see *Alternative Algorithms* on page 163).

Student Response

This nontraditional approach by a student reveals considerable number sense.

Find the product of 36 × 14. ___504___

Explain the steps you followed to multiply.

I went 40 x 15 = 600 then subtracted 4 groups of 15 and then subtracted 36 and got 504

Alternative Multiplication Algorithms For the traditional algorithm (Algorithm 1) and many others, it is appropriate to initially model the algorithm with manipulatives. Normally, a written record is not necessary in the early stages of algorithm use, but is important later on, with each step of the algorithm matching a physical action with the manipulatives. No matter what algorithm is used, it is important that students understand and be able to explain why they do what they do.

A number of the algorithms that follow translate well into mental algorithms and will be noted as they are described.

Algorithm 1 The traditional multiplication algorithm is built on the principle that you can multiply in parts. To multiply 5 × 423, the number 423 is broken up into 400 + 20 + 3, and each part is multiplied by 5. In this version of the traditional algorithm, the parts are calculated starting with the smaller values.

Step 1 Model 5 groups of 4 hundreds, 2 tens, and 3 ones. (Note that a place value mat is optional.)

Step 2 Combine the ones. Trade 10 ones for 1 ten. Record the ones that are left.

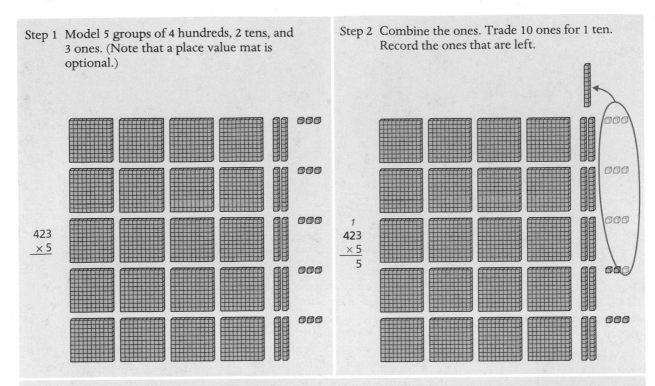

423
× 5

1
423
× 5
5

Step 3 Combine the tens. Trade 10 tens for 1 hundred. Record the tens that are left.

Step 4 Record the hundreds.

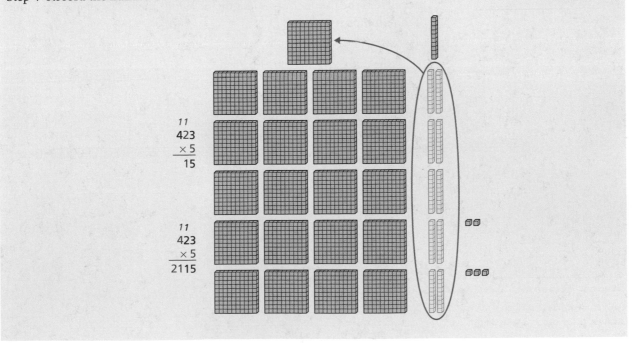

11
423
× 5
15

11
423
× 5
2115

Algorithm 2 This algorithm is sometimes called the partial product algorithm because all partial products are recorded, and then they are added up at the end (as opposed to Algorithm 1, for which partial products are not recorded because students regroup as they go). The multiplying can be done either beginning with the greater values (Algorithm 2A) or the lower values (Algorithm 2B).

ALGORITHM 2A	ALGORITHM 2B
423 × 5 2000 (5 × 400) 100 (5 × 20) + 15 (5 × 3) 2115 (Add the partial products.)	423 × 5 15 (5 × 3) 100 (5 × 20) + 2000 (5 × 400) 2115 (Add the partial products.)

Algorithm 2 for 5 × 423 can be modelled using base ten blocks beginning with 5 groups of blocks, each with 4 hundred blocks, 2 ten blocks, and 3 one blocks (as modelled in Step 1 of Algorithm 1):

- For Algorithm 2A, the next step is to combine first the hundred blocks, then the ten blocks, and finally the one blocks (forming the three partial products in the recorded algorithm). Then, the last step is any final regrouping.
- For Algorithm 2B, the next step is to combine first the one blocks, then the ten blocks, and finally the hundred blocks (forming the three partial products). Then, the last step is any final regrouping.

Algorithm 2 can also be modelled using what is called an area model. This model is based on the area meaning of multiplication; that is, the area of a rectangle is the product of its length and width. Below is a pictorial model of the multiplication.

A PICTORIAL AREA MODEL FOR 5 × 423

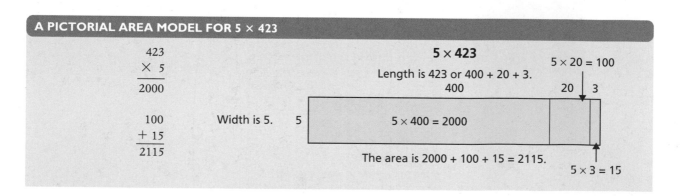

Student Response

This student has described a mental math strategy based on Algorithm 2 (the partial product algorithm).

Explain how to use mental math to multiply 3 × 35.

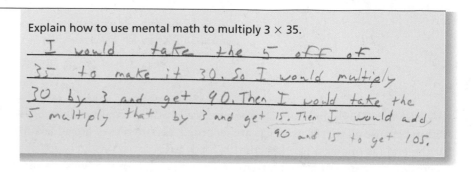

I would take the 5 off of 35 to make it 30. So I would multiply 30 by 3 and get 90. Then I would take the 5 multiply that by 3 and get 15. Then I would add 90 and 15 to get 105.

Algorithms for Multiplying with 5, 25, and 15

ALGORITHM	EXAMPLE

Multiplying by 5
 	
To multiply a number by 5, you can multiply by 10 mentally, and then divide by 2, or vice versa because $5 = 10 \div 2$. This is based on the principle that you can halve one factor and double the other without changing the product.
	$34 \times 5 \rightarrow 34 \div 2 = 17$ (Divide by 2.)
	            $17 \times 10 = 170$ (Multiply by 10.)
	$34 \times 5 \rightarrow 34 \times 10 = 340$ (Multiply by 10.)
	            $340 \div 2 = 170$ (Divide by 2.)

Multiplying by 25
 	
To multiply a number by 25, you can multiply by 100 mentally, and then divide by 4, or vice versa because $25 = 100 \div 4$. This is based on the principle that you can take one fourth of one factor and quadruple the other without changing the product. Many students will think of this as similar to finding the value of 480 quarters. Note that to divide by 4, it is often easier to divide by 2 twice.
	$48 \times 25 \rightarrow 48 \times 100 = 4800$ (Multiply by 100.)
	           $4800 \div 4 = 1200$ (Divide by 4.)
	$48 \times 25 \rightarrow 48 \div 4 = 12$ (Divide by 4.)
	           $12 \times 100 = 1200$ (Multiply by 100.)
	$48 \times 25 \rightarrow 48 \times 100 = 4800$ (Multiply by 100.)
	           $4800 \div 2 = 2400$ (Divide by 2.)
	           $4800 \div 2 = 1200$ (Divide by 2 again.)
	$48 \times 25 \rightarrow 48 \div 2 = 24$ (Divide by 2.)
	           $24 \div 2 = 12$ (Divide by 2 again.)
	           $12 \times 100 = 1200$ (Multiply by 100.)

Multiplying by 15
 	
To multiply a number by 15, you can multiply the number by 10 mentally, and then add on half of the product. The product is essentially found in parts, first by multiplying by 10, and then by 5.
	$36 \times 15 = 36 \times 10 + 36 \times 5$
	         $= 360 + \text{half of } 360$
	         $= 360 + 180$
	         $= 540$

Explain how you would use mental math to solve this problem:

425×5

I would think in money. $4.25 × 5 = $21.25 then take away the decimal and there is your answer.

Student Response

Many children invent algorithms that are based on money concepts. This student may have calculated 5×4 dollars = \$20, then 5 quarters = \$1.25, and then added the partial products.

Multiplying Two 2-Digit Numbers When multiplying two 2-digit numbers, students put together the various ideas already presented. For example, to multiply 32×43, they might use an area model and add the pieces to calculate the total. This duplicates what can be modelled with base ten blocks.

ACTIVITY 8.8

Ask students to determine which digits should replace each letter. The same digit is used each time the letter appears.

$A \times BCB = DAEB$

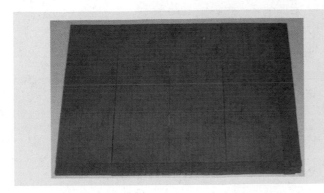
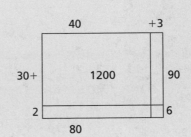
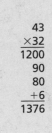

Another approach to multiplying 2-digit numbers is the lattice algorithm.

For example, to multiply 53 × 34, arrange a grid of 4 squares, each divided diagonally with the relevant values around the edge.

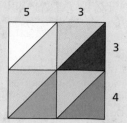

Within the grid, multiply the two outside values. Place the tens digit (if there is one) above the diagonal and the ones digit below.

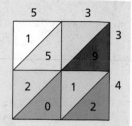

Extend the diagonals and add down diagonally.

The values at the bottom and left (1802) show the product.

This algorithm works since each digit is automatically placed in the right place value column. It is fairly simple for students to follow. However, it does not bring "meaning" to the steps students are taking.

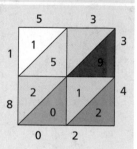

ACTIVITY 8.9

Students enjoy "broken calculator key" activities. For example, they might be asked to come up with a way to multiply 7 × 59 if the 9 key on the calculator is not working. This requires students to use their number sense.

ACTIVITY 8.10

You may want to introduce Egyptian multiplication.

With this process, students only need to double and add.

For example, to multiply 36 × 53, start 2 columns, one beginning with 1 and the other with 53.

Keep doubling until the number in the 1 column is going to be greater than 36.

1	53
2	106
4	**212**
8	424
16	848
32	**1696**

Find numbers in the 1 column that add to 36 and add the corresponding numbers in the 53 column to get the product.

32 + 4 = 36, so 36 × 53 = 1696 + 212 = 1908

Let students try the algorithm using different products.

Alternative Division Algorithms Algorithms suitable for mental calculation will be noted as they are described.

Algorithm 1 This algorithm is built on the numeration principle that a number has many different "forms" and on the division principle that you can divide in parts. This traditional algorithm is best explained using the sharing meaning of division and a concrete base ten model, as shown below. Two alternative written forms of the algorithm are presented.

If 3 people share 346 items, how many would each get?

346 ÷ 3

Step 1 Model 346 with 3 hundred blocks, 4 ten blocks, and 6 one blocks. Draw 3 boxes to represent the "shares" (÷ 3).

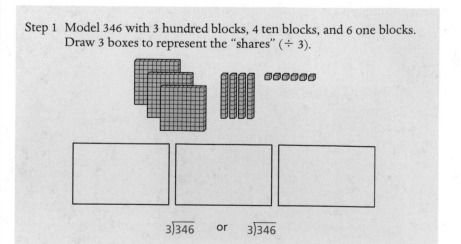

Step 2 Share the 3 hundred blocks. Each share gets 1 hundred block, so record 100 or 1 (hundred). There are 4 ten blocks and 6 one blocks left, so record 46.

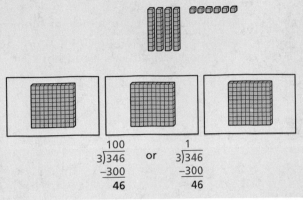

$$
\begin{array}{r}
100 \\
3\overline{)346} \\
-300 \\
\hline 46
\end{array}
\quad \text{or} \quad
\begin{array}{r}
1 \\
3\overline{)346} \\
-300 \\
\hline 46
\end{array}
$$

Step 3 Share the 4 ten blocks. Each share gets 1 ten block, so record 10 or 1 (ten). Trade the leftover ten block for 10 one blocks (to be shared in Step 4). There are 16 one blocks left, so record 16.

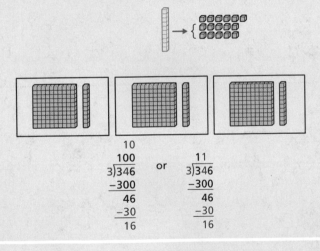

$$
\begin{array}{r}
10 \\
100 \\
3\overline{)346} \\
-300 \\
\hline 46 \\
-30 \\
\hline 16
\end{array}
\quad \text{or} \quad
\begin{array}{r}
11 \\
3\overline{)346} \\
-300 \\
\hline 46 \\
-30 \\
\hline 16
\end{array}
$$

Step 4 Share the 16 one blocks. Each share gets 5 one blocks, so record 5. One block is left over as a remainder.

R 1 ▱

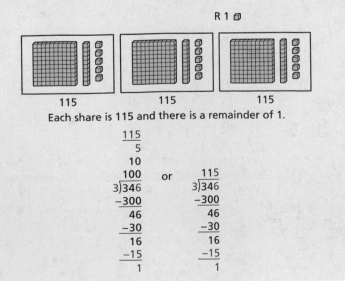

115   115   115

Each share is 115 and there is a remainder of 1.

$$
\begin{array}{r}
115 \\
5 \\
10 \\
100 \\
3\overline{)346} \\
-300 \\
\hline 46 \\
-30 \\
\hline 16 \\
-15 \\
\hline 1
\end{array}
\quad \text{or} \quad
\begin{array}{r}
115 \\
3\overline{)346} \\
-300 \\
\hline 46 \\
-30 \\
\hline 16 \\
-15 \\
\hline 1
\end{array}
$$

Algorithm 2 As with Algorithm 1, this algorithm is based on the principle that you can divide in parts by splitting the dividend into parts. This algorithm makes most sense to model using the equal group meaning of division, as shown.

Algorithm 2B shows how you can underestimate the number of groups and still successfully complete the algorithm, although you end up taking more steps to do it. (This is not the case with Algorithm 1.)

How many groups of 3 are in 346?

$$346 \div 3$$

ALGORITHM 2A		ALGORITHM 2B	
$3\overline{)346}$		$3\overline{)346}$	
-300 100 (100 groups of 3)		-150 50 (50 groups of 3)	
46		196	
-30 10 (10 groups of 3)		-60 20 (20 groups of 3)	
16		136	
-15 5 (5 groups of 3)		-90 30 (30 groups of 3)	
115		46	
		-30 10 (10 groups of 3)	
		16	
		-15 5 (5 groups of 3)	
		1 115	

Algorithm 3 This algorithm is based on breaking up the dividend into comfortable parts, that is, into parts, or numbers, that are easy to divide. The underlying principle is that you can divide in parts by splitting the dividend into parts. This makes sense if you visualize the sharing model of division for the first example shown below: to share 400 among 3 people, you could first share 300 among the 3 people, then 90 among the 3 people, and then the last 10. (See *Appropriate Manipulatives* on page 189 for a base ten block model of this algorithm.)

$$3\overline{)400} = 3\overline{)\begin{array}{ccccc} 100 & + & 30 & + & 3 \\ 300 & + & 90 & + & 10 \end{array}} \qquad 133 \text{ R }1$$
$$400 \div 3 = 133 \text{ R }1$$

$$3\overline{)400} = 3\overline{)\begin{array}{ccccc} 50 & + & 80 & + & 3 \\ 150 & + & 240 & + & 10 \end{array}} \qquad 133 \text{ R }1$$
$$400 \div 3 = 133 \text{ R }1$$

$$3\overline{)400} = 3\overline{)\begin{array}{ccc} 130 & + & 3 \\ 390 & + & 10 \end{array}} \qquad 133 \quad \text{R }1$$
$$400 \div 3 = 133 \text{ R }1$$

Algorithms for Dividing with 5 and 25

ALGORITHM	EXAMPLE
Dividing by 5 This algorithm is based on the principle that to divide two numbers, you can multiply both numbers by the same amount, without changing the quotient. To divide by 5, you can multiply both numbers by 2, in order to change the divisor to 10, which is easy to divide by mentally.	Multiply dividend and divisor by 2: $460 \div 5 = 920 \div 10$ $\qquad\qquad = 92$
Dividing by 25 This algorithm is also based on the principle that to divide two numbers, you can multiply both numbers by the same amount, without changing the quotient. To divide by 25, you can multiply both numbers by 4 in order to change the divisor to 100, which is easy to divide by mentally. Depending on the numbers involved, it may be easier to multiply by 2 twice instead of multiplying by 4.	Multiply dividend and divisor by 4: $3800 \div 25 = 15\ 200 \div 100$ $\qquad\qquad\ = 152$ Multiply dividend and divisor by 2 and then by 2 again: $3800 \div 25 = 7600 \div 50$ $\qquad\qquad\ = 15\ 200 \div 100$ $\qquad\qquad\ = 152$

ACTIVITY 8.11

Students can play a game where they roll two dice to create a dividend and one die to create a divisor. They score 1 point if the remainder is 0 and/or 2 if the quotient is 20 or greater.

ACTIVITY 8.12

Students could solve a number of "personal" division problems. For example, they could

- determine how many times they would have to write their first names to have more than 1000 letters
- determine how long it would take them to walk 1000 paces if they time themselves to walk 10 paces
- determine the "average" distance they can throw a ball by averaging 5 throws, once they know about calculating a mean

Treatment of Remainders When dividing whole numbers, there are sometimes leftover amounts. These form the "remainder." Students need to learn to make sense of the remainder conceptually as well as how to account for the remainder symbolically when using a division algorithm. Context is what determines how the remainder should be treated.

Interpreting Remainders

INTERPRETATION	EXAMPLE
Remainder as a Whole Number Suppose students are using a traditional algorithm to find the share size when 3 people share 34 marbles. Students will end up recording the remainder and reporting the answer as "11 Remainder 1," because each person would get 11 marbles and there would be 1 marble left over. Marbles cannot be divided up, so it makes sense that there would be a whole number remainder given the context.	34 marbles shared among 3 children: $34 \div 3 = 11\ \text{R}\ 1$ It does not make sense to divide 1 marble further. So, each child gets 11 marbles, and there is 1 marble left over. *(continued)*

Remainder as a Fraction

If the problem were the amount of time each person would have to work if 3 people shared a job that took 34 hours total, the quotient could be reported as $11\frac{1}{3}$ hours; the remainder is included in the quotient.

34 hours shared among 3 workers:

$$3 \overline{)34}$$

quotient $11\frac{1}{3}$

$$-33$$
$$\quad 1$$

$\frac{1}{3}$ of an hour makes sense; it is 20 minutes. So, each person works $11\frac{1}{3}$ hours.

Remainder as a Decimal

If the problem were the amount of money each person would get if 3 people shared $34, each person would get $11 and there would be $1 left over. Because of the money context, you would continue to divide the $1 left to find that each person gets $11.33, but there is still 1 penny left over. Again, because of the context, the quotient is reported as a decimal, but only to the hundredths place because it is dollar notation. In this case, the leftover penny remains.

$34 shared among 3 people:

$$3 \overline{)34.00}$$

quotient 11.33

$$-33$$
$$\quad 10$$
$$\quad -9$$
$$\quad\ 10$$
$$\quad\ -9$$
$$\quad\ \ 1$$

It does not make sense to divide 1 cent further as there is no such thing as $11.333. So, each person gets $11.33 (and there is 1 cent left over).

Rounding a Remainder Up

There are contexts when a quotient might be "rounded up," for example, to solve the following problem: How many cars are needed to transport 34 children if 3 children can go in each car?

34 children, at 3 per car: how many cars?

$34 \div 3 = 11$ R 1

An additional car is needed because of the remainder. It does not make sense to leave one child behind, and 11.33 or $11\frac{1}{3}$ cars does not make sense either. So, 12 cars will be needed to transport 34 children.

Communicating about Multiplication and Division Algorithms

As with addition and subtraction, teachers need to be careful with their words and must encourage students to be clear and accurate, too.

- Language such as "3 into 2 doesn't go," for a division such as $3\overline{)214}$, is not appropriate, nor is it correct. In fact, it is 200 and not 2 that you are dividing by 3.
- For a multiplication sentence like 34×25, it is important to use the appropriate place value language and say "2 tens times 3 tens" instead of "2 times 3," when multiplying the tens.
- When multiplying or dividing by powers of 10, it is important to avoid talking about "adding or dropping zeros," but instead to use more meaningful language, such as 3 groups of 4 tens is 12 tens.

Student Response

This explanation by a student shows that a combination of principles and strategies was used to multiply.

Explain the steps you would follow to find the answer to $32 \times 6.$ = 192

first half and double then times 60 x3 it equals 180. then 4 x3 it equals 12. add 12 + 180 it equals 192 and that is your answer.

Common Errors and Misconceptions

Many of the common errors in performing multiplication and division algorithms stem from a lack of understanding of the underlying principles (numeration, multiplication, and division principles). If students continue to make these kinds of errors and do not seem to understand what they are doing wrong, they should be using concrete models to work through the algorithms, while at the same time recording the written algorithms.

Multiplication and Division Algorithms: Strategies for Dealing with Common Errors and Misconceptions

COMMON ERROR OR MISCONCEPTION	SUGGESTED STRATEGY
Multiplying by the Incorrect Amount Students do not multiply by the correct amount when multiplying by a 2-digit number. For instance, as in the example below, a student might multiply the 3 in 34 as a 3 and not as 30. $$\begin{array}{rl} 28 & \\ \times\,34 & \\ \hline 60 & (3 \times 20) \\ 24 & (3 \times 8) \\ 80 & (4 \times 20) \\ +\,32 & (4 \times 8) \\ \hline 196 & \end{array}$$ instead of $$\begin{array}{rl} 28 & \\ \times\,34 & \\ \hline 600 & (30 \times 20) \\ 240 & (30 \times 8) \\ 80 & (4 \times 20) \\ +\,32 & (4 \times 8) \\ \hline 952 & \end{array}$$	Estimating will help here. For example, $30 \times 30 = 900$, and 196 is a long way from 900, so the student should be able to catch his or her error. Another strategy is to have students model the calculation with base ten blocks using an area model (see the base ten block area model for Algorithm 2 on page 180). Sometimes this sort of error is a result of teaching that focuses too much on the digits of the number, rather than on the value of the number. Rather than saying or having students say, "multiply the 3 by the 8, and then the 3 by the 2," instead use "multiply the 30 by the 8, and then the 30 by the 20."
Internal Zeros Students ignore internal zeros in a number; for example, $$\begin{array}{r} 302 \\ \times\,4 \\ \hline 128 \end{array}$$ instead of $$\begin{array}{r} 302 \\ \times\,4 \\ \hline 1208 \end{array}$$	By encouraging students to estimate, this sort of mistake is more likely to be caught. For example, 4×302 is just a bit more than $4 \times 300 = 1200$. So, an incorrect answer like 128 should indicate an error.
Including Incorrect Regrouped Values Students use a regrouped value from a partial calculation in the wrong subsequent calculation. In the example below, the regrouping that resulted from multiplying 4 by 8 (3 tens) was used when multiplying the 30 by 20. $$\begin{array}{r} \overset{3}{2}8 \\ \times\,34 \\ \hline 112 \\ +\,940 \\ \hline 1052 \end{array}$$ instead of $$\begin{array}{r} \overset{2}{\overset{3}{2}}8 \\ \times\,34 \\ \hline 112 \\ +\,840 \\ \hline 952 \end{array}$$	Estimating may or may not be helpful, depending on how close the actual and incorrect products are. Students who use a partial product method (Algorithm 2 for multiplication) are less likely to make this error. This algorithm could also be modelled using an area model and base ten blocks (see the base ten block area model for Algorithm 2 on page 180). $$\begin{array}{r} 28 \\ \times\,34 \\ \hline 32 \\ 80 \\ 240 \\ +\,600 \\ \hline 952 \end{array}$$

COMMON ERROR OR MISCONCEPTION	SUGGESTED STRATEGY
Understanding Principles of Multiplication Students confuse some of the principles of addition with those of multiplication. Multiplication is different from addition in that, in multiplication, the digit in a particular place value in one number is combined with all of the digits in the other number, not just with the digit in the same place value. Many students get confused and end up making errors like those shown below. $\begin{array}{r}\overset{1}{412} \\ \times 8 \\ \hline 6 \end{array}$ ⟶ $\begin{array}{r}\overset{1}{412} \\ \times 8 \\ \hline 426 \end{array}$ $(41 + 1 = 42)$ $\begin{array}{r}36 \\ \times 25 \\ \hline 30 \end{array}$ ⟶ $\begin{array}{r}36 \\ \times 25 \\ \hline 630 \end{array}$ $(2 \times 3 = 6)$	These students might benefit from the partial product algorithm (Algorithm 2): $\begin{array}{r}412 \\ \times 8 \\ \hline 3200 \\ 80 \\ + 16 \\ \hline 3296 \end{array}$ They could also sketch an area model to represent the problem (see the pictorial area model for Algorithm 2 on page 180).
Forgetting Remainders and Regrouping Students forget required regrouping or remainders when dividing; for example: Divide 21 by 4 to get 5 (forgetting the 1). Then divide 5 by 4 to get 1 (forgetting the remainder). $\begin{array}{r}51 \\ 4\overline{)215} \end{array}$ instead of $\begin{array}{r}53 \text{ R } 3 \\ 4\overline{)215} \end{array}$	Estimating will not reveal the error, since $215 \div 4$ is about the same as the most likely estimate, which is $200 \div 4 = 50$. But, if students multiply $4 \times 51 = 204$ to check, they will see that the result is not 215.
Internal Zeros Students ignore internal zeros when dividing; for example, $\begin{array}{r}21 \\ 3\overline{)6003} \end{array}$ instead of $\begin{array}{r}2001 \\ 3\overline{)6003} \end{array}$	Estimation or multiplication would reveal this error: $3 \times 20 = 60$ or $3 \times 21 = 63$ Both 60 and 63 are considerably less than 6003.
Aligning Partial Product Digits Students do not align the digits on the partial products as they record them (see Algorithm 2 on page 180), resulting in an error when they add the partial products.	Students can use grid paper or lined paper turned sideways (see Common Errors and Misconceptions for addition and subtraction algorithms on page 171).

Appropriate Manipulatives

Any of the algorithms described on the previous pages can and should be modelled with manipulatives initially so that students understand the procedure and why it works. Students might be encouraged to continue to use the manipulative language even when they are no longer using the manipulatives.

Multiplication and Division Algorithms: Manipulatives

BASE TEN MATERIALS

All of the algorithms shown on the previous pages can be modelled using base ten materials. (See the discussion about base ten blocks under Appropriate Manipulatives for working with greater whole numbers on page 147.)

This model shows Algorithm 3 for division on page 184 using base ten blocks.

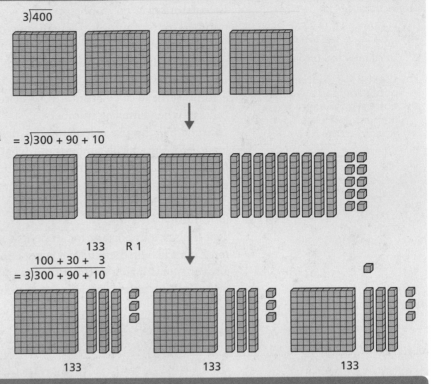

$$3 \overline{)400}$$

$$= 3 \overline{)300 + 90 + 10}$$

$$\begin{array}{r} 133 \quad \text{R 1} \\ 100 + 30 + \ \ 3 \\ = 3 \overline{)300 + 90 + 10} \end{array}$$

133   133   133

PLAY MONEY

Play money, as a substitute for base ten materials, is particularly useful for students who have internalized place value money concepts. (See the discussion about play money on page 172, Appropriate Manipulatives for addition and subtraction algorithms.) This model shows Step 1 of Algorithm 1 for division on page 182, using coins instead of blocks.

346 ÷ 3

PLACE VALUE MATS

Place value mats can be used with base ten materials or money for modelling multiplication algorithms, but they are optional. This model shows Step 1 of Algorithm 1 for multiplication, shown on page 179, using coins instead of blocks on a place value mat.

$$\begin{array}{r} 423 \\ \times \ 5 \end{array}$$

Hundreds	Tens	Ones

ACTIVITY 8.13

Students can try these calculator activities.

a) Enter the number 49. Use only the 4, ☐ ☒ ☐ keys to change the display to 1.

b) Use the 1, 3, 5, 7, and 9 keys once each, and any operation keys. What are the greatest and least numbers you can create?

Appropriate Technology

Calculators

Calculators play an important role when multiplying and dividing large numbers, or for multiple calculations when the focus is on problem solving.

There should be some caution about the fact that many students enter numbers in the wrong order when asked to divide; for instance, they input $6 \div 357$ for $357 \div 6$. Teachers need to be proactive to avoid this common error. Overhead calculators are useful for showing students the correct procedures when entering numbers.

Students who use calculators for division will stumble across decimals long before they fully understand what decimals are. This could actually prove to be a motivation for learning about decimals for some students and the context may, in fact, provide an opportunity for them to figure out what benchmark decimals such as 0.5 and 0.25 mean before they are formally introduced to them.

It is always important for students to estimate when they use a calculator. This will help them in two ways. First, it will help them determine if the answer is reasonable in order to find out if they made a keying error. Second, it will help them understand the meaning behind the decimal.

40 ÷ 3 is just a bit more than 13 ($39 \div 3 = 13$). So, .333333 must mean the answer is a bit more than 13.

WebConnect W W W

www.makingmathmeaningful.nelson.com

Visit the Making Math Meaningful website for links to sites with addition, subtraction, multiplication, and division games.

Computers

The computer is also a useful tool. With the Internet, however, teachers should be aware that many sites that allow students to practise multiplication and division require students to input the answer in only one way, forcing a particular algorithm. Such practice will undermine teachers' efforts to encourage students to choose a procedure or algorithm based on the numbers involved.

Assessing Student Understanding

- Although students are taught many algorithms, it is not necessary that they use all of them. The idea is to use the one or ones that makes the most sense to them.
- Students should sometimes show their understanding by performing the algorithm with manipulatives and not only using pencil-and-paper approaches. They might also explain their thinking verbally.
- Observe whether students use mental algorithms when appropriate. This provides insight into their number sense.

- Ask estimating questions frequently. For example, ask how they know that $356 - 296$ has to be less than 100.

Appropriate Children's Books

Anno's Mysterious Multiplying Jar (Anno, 1983).
This classic story, in a very inventive way, explores the products 1×2, $1 \times 2 \times 3$, $1 \times 2 \times 3 \times 4$, etc. It begins with 1 island, with 2 countries on it, with 3 mountains in each country, etc. Students might make up their own stories based on the book; for example, in 1 village, there were 2 elephants. On top of each elephant were 3 lions, ...

The Rajah's Rice: A Mathematical Folktale from India (Barry, 1994).
This version of the ancient Indian folktale, which can be found under many titles, allows students to explore multiplicative growth as compared to additive growth. Students learn that, eventually, you gain a lot more if you start with less and let it keep doubling than if you start with more and just add a fixed amount repeatedly.

Ten Times Better (Michelson, Baskin, 2000).
This book focuses on multiplying by 10 by using the rate meaning of multiplication, for example, "I'm ten times wetter." The book educates the reader, through watercolour illustrations and text, about various interesting animals. The book also provides some problems for students to explore and lots of visual representations for comparing numbers to 10 times as many, for example, 3 to 30.

In the Next Three Seconds (Morgan, 1997).
This interesting book full of data tells a variety of things that will happen in the next three seconds all over the world, for example, 93 trees will be cut down to make liners for disposable diapers. Students have many interesting calculating opportunities.

One Hundred Hungry Ants (Pinczes, 1999).
This rhyming book explores, in an amusing way, different organizations of 100 ants into equal groups, for example, two groups of 50 or four groups of 25. The setting is the ants' journey to a picnic.

Applying What You've Learned

1. What was your solution to the chapter problem? Were you able to explain why your "rule" worked?

2. Select one of the children's literature suggestions offered. Read the book. Describe how you would follow up its reading to engage students in a valuable mathematical task.

3. Many people argue that base ten blocks are an essential manipulative to explain the algorithms for the four operations. Do you agree or not? Explain.

4. Some parents are concerned when they see a child coming home performing a calculation differently from what the parent knows. How would you handle a complaint about this?

5. To calculate $5002 - 3189$, a teacher suggested changing the question to $4999 - 3189$, and then adding 3 to the answer.

   a) Why might she do this?

   b) Do you think it is a good idea to make that suggestion?

6. Select a current elementary school text. Select a lesson about subtracting or adding multi-digit numbers that you think is particularly well constructed. Explain why you think it is a good lesson.

7. You want to teach students how to approach a 2-digit by 2-digit multiplication problem. How would you introduce the lesson and how would you summarize it?

8. Choose one of the division algorithms. What prerequisite skills would a student need to successfully perform that algorithm? How would you find out if they had those skills?

9. Would your main goal in developing computational algorithms be to foster skill with the paper-and-pencil algorithm, with estimating, or with mental algorithms? Explain your thinking.

10. If you had to assess what your Grade 4 students knew about adding 3-digit and 4-digit numbers and you could only ask three questions, what would they be? Why?

Interact with a K–8 Student:

11. Work with a student who knows how to subtract multi-digit numbers. Ask the student to explain to you how he or she would solve, for example, $91 - 43$, or $901 - 478$.

   a) What kinds of errors, if any, did you observe? Did they surprise you?

   b) If the student did not explain his or her actions, choose one of the steps performed and ask why it was done. See if the student simply repeats rules or if he or she explains why the action makes sense.

Interact with a K–8 Teacher:

12. Talk with a Grade 3 to 7 teacher about whether she or he encourages students to use alternate algorithms, or even invent their own, and why she or he holds that point of view.

Selected References

Anno, M. (1983). *Anno's mysterious multiplying jar.* New York: Putnam Juvenile.

Baek, J.M. (1998). Children's invented algorithms for multidigit multiplication problems. In Morrow, L., and Kenney, M.J. (Eds.). *The teaching and learning of algorithms in school mathematics.* Reston, VA: National Council of Teachers of Mathematics, 151–160.

Baek, J.M. (2005). Research, reflection, practice: Children's mathematical understandings and invented strategies for multidigit multiplication. *Teaching Children Mathematics, 12,* 242–247.

Barry, D. (1994). *The rajah's rice.* New York: W.H. Freeman and Co.

Bass, H. (2003). Computational fluency, algorithms and mathematical proficiency: One mathematician's perspective. *Teaching Children Mathematics, 9,* 322–327.

Carroll, W.M., and Porter, D. (1999). Alternative algorithms for whole-number operations. In Morrow, L., and Kenney, M.J. (Eds.) *The teaching and learning of algorithms in school mathematics.* Reston, VA: National Council of Teachers of Mathematics, 106–114.

Flowers, J., Kline, K., and Rubenstein, R.N. (2003). Developing teachers' computational fluency: Examples in subtraction. *Teaching Children Mathematics, 9,* 330–334.

Fosnot, C.T., and Dolk, M. (2001). *Young mathematicians at work: Constructing number sense, addition and subtraction.* Portsmouth, NH: Heinemann.

Fuson, K.C. (2003). Toward computational fluency in multidigit multiplication and division. *Teaching Children Mathematics, 9,* 300–305.

Hiebert, J. (1984). Children's mathematics learning: The struggle to link form and understanding. *Elementary School Journal, 84,* 496–513.

Huinker, D., Freckman, J.L., and Steinmeyer, M.B. (2003). Subtraction strategies from children's thinking: Moving toward fluency with greater numbers. *Teaching Children Mathematics, 9,* 347–353.

Jacobs, V.R., and Philipp, R.A. (2004). Mathematical thinking: Helping prospective and practicing teachers focus. *Teaching Children Mathematics,* 11, 194–201.

Kamii, C., and Dominick, A. (1999). The harmful effects of algorithms in grades 1–4. In Morrow, L., and Kenney, M.J. (Eds.). *The teaching and learning of algorithms in school mathematics.* Reston, VA: National Council of Teachers of Mathematics, 130–140.

Kamii, C., Lewis, B.A., and Livingston, S.J. (1993). Primary arithmetic: Children inventing their own procedures. *Arithmetic Teacher,* 41, 200–203.

Michelson, R., and Baskin, L. (2000). *Ten times better.* Tarrytown, NY: Marshall Cavendish Children's Books.

Morgan, R. (1997). *In the next three seconds.* New York: Lodestar Books.

Onslow, B., Adams, L., Edmunds, G., Waters, J., Chapple, N., Healey, B., and Eady, J. (2005). Are you in the zone? *Teaching Children Mathematics,* 11, 458–463.

Pinczes, E.J. (1999). *One hundred hungry ants.* Boston: Houghton Mifflin.

Scharton. S. (2004). "I did it my way": Providing opportunities for students to create, explain and analyze computation procedures. *Teaching Children Mathematics,* 10, 278–283.

Small, M. (2005). *PRIME: Number and operations: Background and strategies.* Toronto: Thomson Nelson.

Taylor, A.R., Breck, S.E., and Aljets, C.M. (2004). What Nathan teaches us about transitional thinking. *Teaching Children Mathematics,* 11, 138–142.

Whitenack, J.W., Knipping, N., Novinger, S., and Underwood, G. (2001). Second graders circumvent addition and subtraction difficulties. *Teaching Children Mathematics,* 8, 228–233.

Chapter 9

Fractions

IN A NUTSHELL

The main ideas in this chapter are listed below:

1. Fractions can represent parts of wholes, parts of sets, parts of measures, division, or ratios. A fraction is not as meaningful without knowing what the whole is.

2. Renaming fractions is often the key to comparing them or computing with them. Every fraction can be renamed in an infinite number of ways.

3. Operations with fractions have the same meanings as operations with whole numbers, even though the algorithms are different.

4. There are multiple models and/or procedures for computing with fractions, just as with whole numbers.

CHAPTER PROBLEM

What is the fraction between $\frac{2}{7}$ and $\frac{5}{12}$ with the lowest denominator possible?

Representing Fractions
Fractions in the Child's World

A fraction is a number that describes a relationship between a part (represented by the numerator) and a whole (represented by the denominator). Although students see two numbers, they have to think of one idea, the relationship. As a result, fractions are a challenge for many students and even for many adults.

Fractions are used to represent parts of a region, parts of a measure, and parts of a set (or group); they can also represent division and ratios. Initially, students experience fractions as parts of a region and parts of a set. Later they are introduced to the other meanings of fractions.

The first fraction that students meet is usually $\frac{1}{2}$. Generally, they work next with other unit fractions, such as $\frac{1}{4}$ and $\frac{1}{3}$. Once students have a firm grasp of the commonly used unit fractions, they typically extend their work to other proper fractions, such as $\frac{2}{3}$, $\frac{3}{4}$, and $\frac{5}{8}$. In later grades, they meet improper fractions like $\frac{3}{2}$, and mixed numbers such as $1\frac{1}{2}$ and $2\frac{3}{5}$. Eventually, students work with fraction operations, but usually not until middle or junior high school.

ACTIVITY 9.1

Ask students to draw as many different pictures as they can to show the fraction $\frac{2}{5}$.

See what meanings of fractions they choose to model. By sharing pictures, the notions of multiple representations and multiple meanings are reinforced.

ACTIVITY 9.2

Print the letters of a name on individual cards and display them on a table.

Provide a list of questions students can address about the letters. For example,

What fraction of the letters are

- vowels?
- in the first half of the alphabet?
- capital?
- not F?

Students can make a set of cards for their own name and create questions they can answer about fractions of their name.

Meanings of Fractions

MEANING	EXAMPLE
Set or Group	$\frac{3}{5}$ of the group of counters are red.
Region	$\frac{4}{5}$ of this circular region is blue.
Measure	$\frac{1}{3}$ of the volume of this cube is made up of green cubes.
Division	$7 \div 3 = 2\frac{1}{3}$ If you divide 7 counters among the three equal parts of this circle, there are $2\frac{1}{3}$ counters in each part.
Ratio	The ratio of red hexagons to total hexagons is 2:5, or $\frac{2}{5}$ of this set of hexagons is red.

How the Fraction Meanings Are Equivalent

Because fractions have different meanings, at some point, students will have to put these meanings together and see that they are all equivalent. Some of the methods teachers can use to help students bring some of these meanings together are shown below.

How Is a Fraction of a Set Like a Fraction of a Region?

EXAMPLE 1

Here is a model that shows the relationship between a fraction of a set and a fraction of a region:

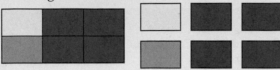

$\frac{1}{6}$ of the rectangular region is yellow.

$\frac{1}{6}$ of the set of rectangles is yellow.

EXAMPLE 2

Here is another model that shows the relationship between a fraction of a set and a fraction of a region:

- To show $\frac{1}{3}$ of a region, divide a rectangle into 3 equal parts and colour 1 part blue.
- To show $\frac{1}{3}$ of a set, or group, divide a group of 15 counters into 3 equal parts and consider 1 part.

The relationship between the two meanings becomes more apparent when you combine them in the same model as shown below.

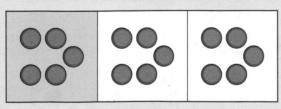

$\frac{1}{3}$ of the rectangle is blue.

$\frac{1}{3}$ of 15 counters is 5.

How Is a Fraction of a Region the Same as Division?

Division is about sharing. To show $\frac{1}{3}$, you take 1 whole and "share" it into 3 parts; thus, the relationship between $1 \div 3$ and $\frac{1}{3}$ is quite easy to see. But the question is how this generalizes to other numerators and denominators, particularly non-unit fractions such as $\frac{2}{3}$. The following model uses the context of sharing 2 rectangular cakes among 3 people ($2 \div 3$) to show why $\frac{2}{3}$ is the same as $2 \div 3$.

ACTIVITY **9.3**

Provide students with circle templates to make fraction wheels, like those shown below.

One circle has a slit from the centre to the edge along a radius. The others are divided into fractional sections and also slit along a radius where two sections meet.

By turning the "wheel," different fractions with that denominator can be shown.

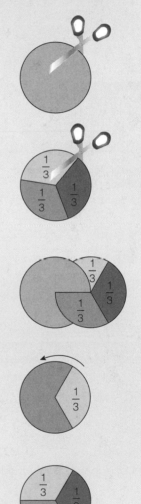

ACTIVITY 9.4

Display circle graphs like this one to students. Ask questions related to fractions about them. For example, about what fraction of the school population is in each grade? How do you know?

How might the graph change if about $\frac{1}{4}$ of the students were in kindergarten?

Students in K to Grade 3 in Valley School

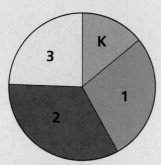

A circle graph is a context for estimating fractions.

FRACTIONS AND DIVISION

$\frac{2}{3}$ is the same as 2 ÷ 3, or 2 shared 3 ways.

Each cake can be divided into 3 thirds. Each of the 3 people sharing gets 1 third from each cake (a blue, a white, and a red piece). This is equivalent to getting 2 thirds of one cake.

Fraction Principles

Some of the important principles that students must learn about fractions are listed below.

FRACTION PRINCIPLES

1. A fraction has a numerator and a denominator.
2. You have to know what the whole is to say what the fraction is.
3. The equal parts into which the whole is divided are equal but do not have to be identical. For parts of a set, this means that the members of the set do not have to be identical.
4. Fraction parts do not have to be adjacent.
5. If the numerator and denominator of a fraction are equal, the fraction represents one whole, or 1. Therefore, all whole numbers can be represented as fractions.
6. Fractions have more than one name.
7. Fractions with numerators greater than their denominators are greater than 1.

Principle 1: A fraction has a numerator and a denominator.

The denominator tells the total number of equal parts in the whole, and the numerator tells the number of parts accounted for.

FRACTION OF A REGION EXAMPLE

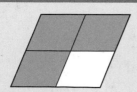

3 of 4 equal parts $\left(\frac{3}{4}\right)$ of the parallelogram are green.

FRACTION OF A SET EXAMPLE

$\frac{3}{4}$ are soccer balls.

SOME FRACTION DEFINITIONS

$\dfrac{3 \rightarrow \text{numerator}}{4 \rightarrow \text{denominator}}$

- the denominator tells how many equal parts the whole has been divided into
- the numerator tells how many there are of the equal parts
- a unit fraction has a numerator of 1, as in $\frac{1}{3}$
- a proper fraction, such as $\frac{4}{5}$, is less than 1

- an improper fraction, such as $\frac{7}{4}$, has a numerator equal to or greater than the denominator
- a mixed number, such as $5\frac{7}{8}$, is a whole number and a proper fraction

Principle 2: You have to know what the whole is to say what the fraction is.

If, for example, we say the blue rectangle below is $\frac{1}{4}$, it is only in relation to the first rectangle, on the left. If it were in relation to the second rectangle, on the right, the blue rectangle becomes $\frac{1}{6}$. In the example of the family below, the fraction used to describe the girl also depends on what is considered the whole.

FRACTIONS OF A REGION EXAMPLE	FRACTIONS OF A SET EXAMPLE
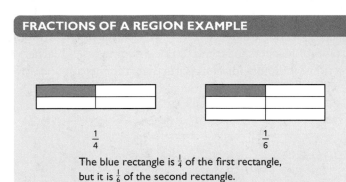	
The blue rectangle is $\frac{1}{4}$ of the first rectangle, but it is $\frac{1}{6}$ of the second rectangle.	This girl is $\frac{1}{2}$ of the children in her family, but $\frac{1}{4}$ of the whole family.

Students might find it interesting to explore how the fraction names change if the whole changes. For example, the blue rhombus is $\frac{2}{3}$ if the red trapezoid is the whole, but if the blue rhombus is the whole, the red trapezoid is $\frac{3}{2}$, the reciprocal.

Principle 3: The equal parts into which the whole is divided are equal but do not have to be identical. For parts of a set, this means that the members of the set do not have to be identical.

The rectangle below on the left is divided into four equal parts, each a fourth, but notice that not all of the fourths are congruent (same size and shape); for example, the yellow fourth is wide and short and the green fourth is narrower and taller. However, they are still equal parts because each fourth has the same area. On the right, below, you can see that the rectangle's yellow and green fourths are both made up of the same two congruent triangles. This shows that the fourths are equal in area.

The green part and the yellow part of the rectangle may not be congruent, but they are equal in area (as each is made up of the same two congruent right triangles). That means that each is a fourth of the rectangle.

In the group of shapes below, $\frac{3}{5}$ are red because, even though each fifth is a different shape and size, the whole is considered the set of 5 shapes, so each shape is 1 fifth.

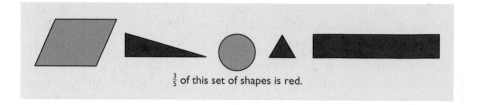

$\frac{3}{5}$ of this set of shapes is red.

Principle 4: Fraction parts do not need to be adjacent.

In this four-coloured rectangle, the two sections that make up the yellow fourth are not adjacent; neither are the two sections that make up the blue fourth. It is important for teachers to attend to this. In some cases, teachers so rarely show fractions with non-adjacent parts that students are uncomfortable when they encounter them.

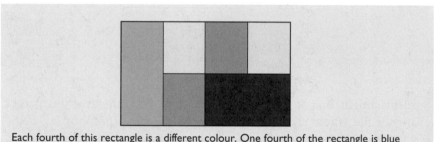

Each fourth of this rectangle is a different colour. One fourth of the rectangle is blue and one fourth is yellow, even though the sections that make up the blue fourth and the yellow fourth are not adjacent.

Principle 5: If the numerator and denominator of a fraction are equal, the fraction represents one whole, or 1. Therefore, all whole numbers can be represented as fractions.

This principle is true for $\frac{2}{2}, \frac{3}{3}, \frac{4}{4}, \frac{5}{5}, \frac{6}{6}$, etc.

FRACTION OF A REGION EXAMPLE	FRACTION OF A SET EXAMPLE
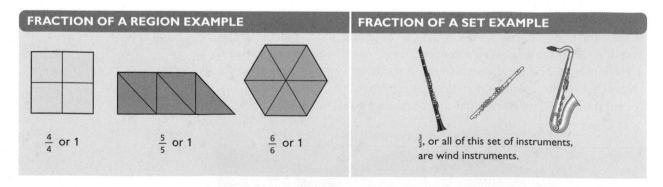	

$\frac{4}{4}$ or 1 $\frac{5}{5}$ or 1 $\frac{6}{6}$ or 1

$\frac{3}{3}$, or all of this set of instruments, are wind instruments.

Principle 6: Fractions have more than one name.

In both examples on page 201, $\frac{1}{2}$ is another name for $\frac{2}{4}$ since the same part of the same whole is represented by both fractions.

FRACTION OF A REGION EXAMPLE   **FRACTION OF A SET EXAMPLE**

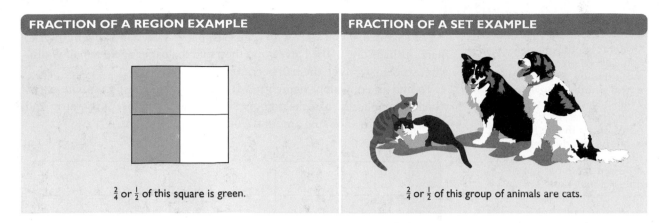

$\frac{2}{4}$ or $\frac{1}{2}$ of this square is green. $\frac{2}{4}$ or $\frac{1}{2}$ of this group of animals are cats.

Principle 7: Fractions with numerators greater than their denominators are greater than 1.

The pair of circles below could be described as $\frac{7}{4}$, or 7 fourths, red if one circle is considered the whole. Since it only takes 4 fourths to make a whole (a circle), 7 fourths must be greater than a whole, or 1. The two egg cartons below could be described as $\frac{17}{12}$, or 17 twelfths, full if one carton is considered the whole. Since one carton is 12 twelfths, 17 twelfths must be greater than a whole, or 1.

Fractions of this type are called improper fractions. Some students assume something is wrong with them because of the term "improper," but this is, of course, not the case.

FRACTION OF A REGION EXAMPLE   **FRACTION OF A SET EXAMPLE**

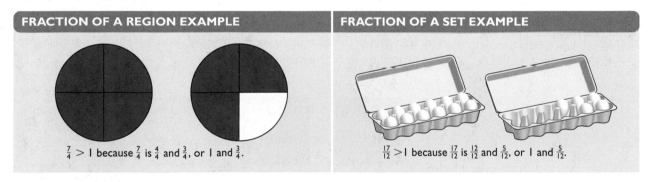

$\frac{7}{4} > 1$ because $\frac{7}{4}$ is $\frac{4}{4}$ and $\frac{3}{4}$, or 1 and $\frac{3}{4}$. $\frac{17}{12} > 1$ because $\frac{17}{12}$ is $\frac{12}{12}$ and $\frac{5}{12}$, or 1 and $\frac{5}{12}$.

Equivalent Fractions

As described above in Principle 6, fractions have more than one name.

Proper Fractions To find an equivalent name for a proper fraction, you can subdivide the existing parts to create more equal-size parts, which symbolically has the effect of multiplying the numerator and denominator by the same amount. For example:

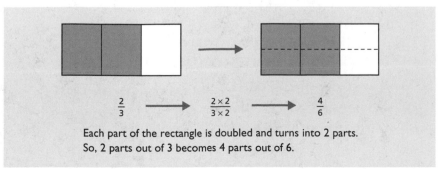

$$\frac{2}{3} \longrightarrow \frac{2 \times 2}{3 \times 2} \longrightarrow \frac{4}{6}$$

Each part of the rectangle is doubled and turns into 2 parts.
So, 2 parts out of 3 becomes 4 parts out of 6.

Students might consider equivalence in terms of musical notes. For example, a whole note is equivalent to 2 half notes, 4 quarter notes, 8 eighth notes, or 16 sixteenth notes. Using this idea, they might be asked to create measures of music with as many different combinations of notes as they can.

Older students can try to use all the digits from 1 to 9 to create a fraction equivalent to $\frac{1}{2}$. This sort of activity exercises students' number sense. For example, they must realize that the numerator must be 4 digits and the denominator 5 digits. They must also recognize that the rightmost digit of the denominator must be even, or the fraction could not be equivalent to $\frac{1}{2}$.

One way to accomplish this is to fold a piece of paper.

For example, if you start with a sheet of paper folded in half lengthwise, mark or shade one of the halves, and then fold the paper again in half widthwise, students will see the half becoming $\frac{2}{4}$.

To find an equivalent name for a fraction, you can also combine parts, which symbolically has the same effect as dividing the numerator and denominator by the same amount. For example:

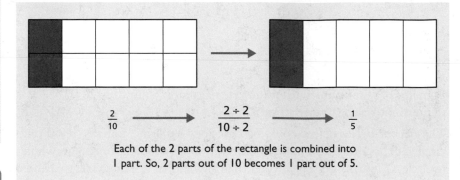

$$\frac{2}{10} \longrightarrow \frac{2 \div 2}{10 \div 2} \longrightarrow \frac{1}{5}$$

Each of the 2 parts of the rectangle is combined into 1 part. So, 2 parts out of 10 becomes 1 part out of 5.

Mixed Numbers and Improper Fractions

One of the equivalences students need to learn about is the relationship between mixed numbers and equivalent improper fractions. For example, $\frac{15}{4} = 3\frac{3}{4}$ since 15 fourths makes 3 wholes (4 fourths + 4 fourths + 4 fourths) and 3 fourths. Symbolically, this has the effect of dividing 15 by 4 to determine the number of wholes. The remainder is the number of fourths in the fraction part of the mixed number. However, students should not rush into the procedure until the meaning is clear.

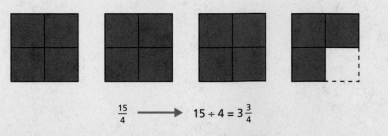

$$\frac{15}{4} \longrightarrow 15 \div 4 = 3\frac{3}{4}$$

Divide the 15 parts by 4 (because there are 4 parts per whole) to determine the number of wholes. The remainder becomes the fraction part of the mixed number.

Student Response

This student renamed the improper fraction as a mixed number in order to compare the fractions. This student also made a very common error in transposing the dividend and divisor when recording the division.

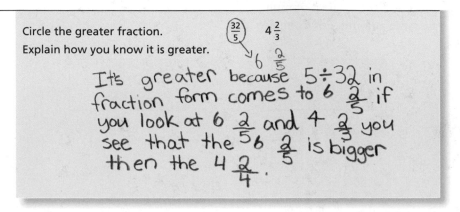

Circle the greater fraction.
Explain how you know it is greater.

It's greater because 5÷32 in fraction form comes to 6 $\frac{2}{5}$ if you look at 6 $\frac{2}{5}$ and 4 $\frac{2}{3}$ you see that the 6 $\frac{2}{5}$ is bigger then the 4 $\frac{2}{4}$.

Visualizing with Fractions

Sometimes you have to estimate fractions when the division into equal parts is either incomplete or not displayed. **Activities 9.8** and **9.9** display that type of situation.

Another useful skill for students is visualizing the whole when given the fraction. The task in **Activity 9.10** is an example of a task that forces students to "think the other way around," that is, instead of working from a known whole and finding the part, students must work from the known part to find the unknown whole.

ACTIVITY 9.8

Post pictures like those below. Ask students to estimate what fraction of each whole is coloured.

Pay attention to students' use of spatial visualization skills. For example, a student might look at the triangle and imagine three more small red triangles filling the white space. This would lead the student to estimate the red section as $\frac{1}{4}$.

ACTIVITY 9.9

Provide tangram sets.

Tell students it costs 5¢ to make one small tangram triangle. Ask how much each other piece would cost to make.

Principles for Comparing Fractions

Some of the important principles that students must understand in order to compare fractions are listed below.

ACTIVITY 9.10

Use the picture of a cube displayed at the right. Tell students that this represents $\frac{1}{3}$ of a cake. The other $\frac{2}{3}$ has been eaten. Ask students: What did the whole cake look like?

Is only one shape possible?

You might follow up by changing the dimensions of the original displayed shape (e.g., use a rectangular prism that is not a cube), or by changing the fraction that it represents.

PRINCIPLES FOR COMPARING FRACTIONS

1. Fractions can be compared only if the whole is known in each case.
2. If two fractions have the same denominator, the one with the greater numerator is greater, for example, $\frac{4}{5} > \frac{3}{5}$.
3. If two fractions have the same numerator, the one with the greater denominator is less, for example, $\frac{3}{5} < \frac{3}{4}$.
4. Some fractions can be compared by relating them to benchmark numbers such as 0, 1, and $\frac{1}{2}$.
5. Fractions can be compared by renaming them with common denominators, or by renaming them with common numerators.
6. No matter what two different fractions are selected, there is a fraction in between. For example, $\frac{3}{6}$ is between $\frac{1}{3}$ and $\frac{2}{3}$.

Principle 1: Fractions can be compared only if the whole is known in each case.

SAME WHOLE

You can easily compare the two fractions shown below, $\frac{1}{3}$ and $\frac{1}{2}$, because they are $\frac{1}{3}$ and $\frac{1}{2}$ of the same whole.

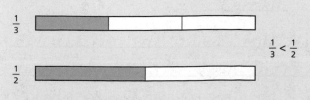

$\frac{1}{3} < \frac{1}{2}$

$\frac{1}{3}$ is less than $\frac{1}{2}$ of the same rectangle.

DIFFERENT WHOLES

Although the fraction $\frac{1}{4}$ is less than the fraction $\frac{1}{2}$, the green square representing $\frac{1}{4}$ is not less than the green rectangle representing $\frac{1}{2}$. This is because the wholes are different in each case.

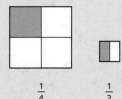

$\frac{1}{4}$ and $\frac{1}{2}$ cannot be compared without considering the wholes.

Student Response

This student can tell from the model that $\frac{2}{3}$ and $\frac{3}{4}$ are not fractions of the same whole, and, therefore, cannot be compared as if they were.

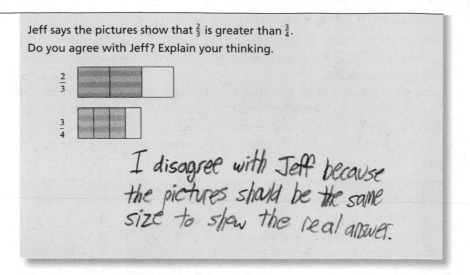

Jeff says the pictures show that $\frac{2}{3}$ is greater than $\frac{3}{4}$.

Do you agree with Jeff? Explain your thinking.

$\frac{2}{3}$

$\frac{3}{4}$

I disagree with Jeff because the pictures should be the same size to show the real answer.

Principle 2: If two fractions have the same denominator, the one with the greater numerator is greater.

This principle assumes that the fractions are fractions of the same whole. The denominator tells the total number of equal parts the whole is divided into, and the numerator tells the number of parts accounted for. If the denominators of two fractions are the same, then the parts are the same. So, the fraction with the greater number of parts accounted for is the greater fraction.

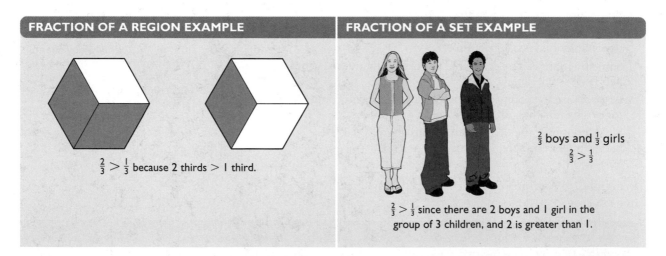

FRACTION OF A REGION EXAMPLE

$\frac{2}{3} > \frac{1}{3}$ because 2 thirds > 1 third.

FRACTION OF A SET EXAMPLE

$\frac{2}{3}$ boys and $\frac{1}{3}$ girls

$\frac{2}{3} > \frac{1}{3}$

$\frac{2}{3} > \frac{1}{3}$ since there are 2 boys and 1 girl in the group of 3 children, and 2 is greater than 1.

Student Response

This student understands why you can compare fractions with the same denominator by comparing their numerators.

Brent eats $\frac{3}{8}$ of a pizza while Harry has the remaining $\frac{5}{8}$.

Who ate more pizza? _Harry_

How do you know?

Because if you divide the pizza into 8 pieces Brent only ate 3 out 8 and Harry ate 5 of the 8 and everybody should know that 5 is bigger than 3.

Principle 3: If two fractions have the same numerator, the one with the greater denominator is less.

This principle assumes that the fractions are fractions of the same whole. The denominator tells the total number of equal parts that the whole is divided into, and the numerator tells the number of parts accounted for. If the numerators are the same, then the number of parts accounted for is the same. But, if the denominators are different, then the fraction with the greater denominator is less, because the greater the number of parts, the smaller the parts.

FRACTION OF A REGION EXAMPLE	FRACTION OF A SET EXAMPLE
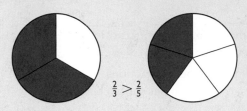 $\frac{2}{3} > \frac{2}{5}$ $\frac{2}{3} > \frac{2}{5}$ because 2 parts of a circle divided into 3 is greater than 2 parts of the same circle divided into 5.	 $\frac{2}{4} < \frac{2}{3}$ since the girls make up less of the whole in the first group than in the second group.

Principle 4: Some fractions can be compared by relating them to benchmark numbers such as 0, 1, and $\frac{1}{2}$.

If one fraction is greater than $\frac{1}{2}$ (or 1) and the other is less, it is easy to compare them.

USING BENCHMARKS TO COMPARE FRACTIONS

Using $\frac{1}{2}$ to compare: $\frac{2}{5} < \frac{3}{4}$ since $\frac{2}{5} < \frac{1}{2}$ and $\frac{3}{4} > \frac{1}{2}$.

Using 1 to compare: $\frac{7}{3} > \frac{3}{4}$ since $\frac{7}{3} > 1$ and $\frac{3}{4} < 1$.

Principle 5: Fractions can be compared by renaming them with common denominators, or by renaming them with common numerators.

Here are two ways to compare $\frac{3}{8}$ and $\frac{4}{10}$. The first method is based on Principle 2, and the second method is based on Principle 3.

RENAMING WITH COMMON DENOMINATORS	RENAMING WITH COMMON NUMERATORS
Comparing $\frac{3}{8}$ and $\frac{4}{10}$: $\quad \frac{3}{8} = \frac{30}{80} \quad \frac{4}{10} = \frac{32}{80}$ $\frac{30}{80} < \frac{32}{80}$ $\frac{3}{8} < \frac{4}{10}$	Comparing $\frac{3}{8}$ and $\frac{4}{10}$: $\quad \frac{3}{8} = \frac{12}{32} \quad \frac{4}{10} = \frac{12}{30}$ $\frac{12}{32} < \frac{12}{30}$ $\frac{3}{8} < \frac{4}{10}$

ACTIVITY 9.11

One tool students can use to compare fractions, whether with the same numerator or denominator or as they relate to 0, $\frac{1}{2}$, or 1, is a fraction tower.

Using the tower shown, students might be asked to describe 5 different fraction comparisons that the tower shows them.

1					
$\frac{1}{2}$			$\frac{1}{2}$		
$\frac{1}{3}$		$\frac{1}{3}$		$\frac{1}{3}$	
$\frac{1}{4}$		$\frac{1}{4}$	$\frac{1}{4}$		$\frac{1}{4}$
$\frac{1}{5}$	$\frac{1}{5}$	$\frac{1}{5}$	$\frac{1}{5}$		$\frac{1}{5}$
$\frac{1}{6}$	$\frac{1}{6}$	$\frac{1}{6}$	$\frac{1}{6}$	$\frac{1}{6}$	$\frac{1}{6}$

The strategy of using common numerators to compare fractions (that is, comparing the denominators of fractions if the numerators are the same) is often overlooked. In fact, students will often rename fractions, for instance, $\frac{2}{3}$ and $\frac{2}{5}$ as $\frac{10}{15}$ and $\frac{6}{15}$ in order to compare them instead of simply comparing the denominators without doing any renaming at all.

Student Response

This student understands that because the denominator of 5 is less, it means the parts are larger, and so there is more of the 2 in each share (Principle 3).

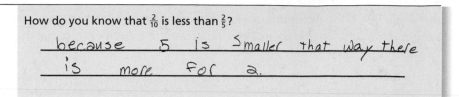

How do you know that $\frac{2}{10}$ is less than $\frac{2}{5}$?

_because   5   is   smaller   that   way   there
is   more   for   a._

Principle 6: No matter what two different fractions are selected, there is a fraction in between.

Between $\frac{3}{5}$ and $\frac{4}{5}$ are an infinite number of fractions. You can rename $\frac{3}{5}$ and $\frac{4}{5}$ with greater denominators to find them, as shown below.

$\frac{3}{5} = \frac{6}{10}$ and $\frac{4}{5} = \frac{8}{10}$, so $\frac{7}{10}$ is between.

$\frac{3}{5} = \frac{12}{20}$ and $\frac{4}{5} = \frac{16}{20}$, so $\frac{13}{20}$, $\frac{14}{20}$, and $\frac{15}{20}$ are between, etc.

Relating Fractions to Decimals

At some point, students will be ready to write a fraction as a decimal quantity. At the K–8 level, students begin by writing fractions like $\frac{3}{10}$ or $\frac{3}{100}$, with denominators as powers of ten, in decimal form. Then they write other fractions, with equivalents in this form, as decimals, for example, $\frac{1}{8} = \frac{125}{1000}$ as 0.125. But eventually, they learn to write any fraction as a decimal, using the division meaning for fractions. Since $\frac{2}{3}$ means $2 \div 3$, then the decimal for $\frac{2}{3}$ is calculated by dividing 2 by 3, usually using a calculator.

Common Errors and Misconceptions

Many of the common errors in fraction work stem from a lack of understanding of the underlying principles. If students continue to make these kinds of errors and do not seem to understand what they are doing wrong, they should be using concrete and pictorial models of the fractions.

Fractions: Strategies for Dealing with Common Errors and Misconceptions

COMMON ERROR OR MISCONCEPTION	STRATEGY
Understanding the Whole in Fractions Students do not understand the importance of the whole in describing a fraction. For example, in the situation below, 2 cakes are each divided into thirds. Even though there are 6 shares, $\frac{1}{3}$ still describes $\frac{1}{3}$ of one cake. Many students see 6 parts and call each part $\frac{1}{6}$.	Students should be encouraged to circle or highlight the whole unit and use language to reinforce the whole. In this case, the green rectangle is $\frac{1}{3}$ of 1 cake. one whole cake

COMMON ERROR OR MISCONCEPTION	STRATEGY
Equal Parts of a Region or Measure Students do not pay attention to the need for all parts to be equal when talking about parts of a region or a measure. (Note that this is not the case when talking about parts of a set.) For example, the blue part of the rectangle below is not $\frac{1}{3}$ even though it is 1 of 3 parts. 	Ensure that students have many opportunities to work with incorrectly divided wholes in context. For the example shown here, you might relate the fraction to a real context, such as a cake divided into 3 pieces. Ask if students think that the recipients will each be happy with their "thirds."
Parts of Sets Can Be Different Students are confused by sets containing different items. For example, students might not recognize the circle below as $\frac{1}{3}$ of the set of shapes.  The circle is $\frac{1}{3}$ of the set of shapes.	Many students do not have enough experience working with parts of sets, having worked only with regions. This can be remedied by providing more of these opportunities. Using pattern blocks for both fractions of a set and region can help; for example, the green block is $\frac{1}{6}$ of the yellow block (fraction of a region) but $\frac{1}{4}$ of the set of 4 blocks below (fraction of a set). 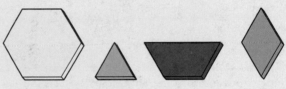 The green block is $\frac{1}{4}$ of this set of blocks.
Increasing the Value of a Fraction Students have the misconception that a fraction always increases in value if the numerator and denominator are increased.	There are specific circumstances when this is true; for example, if both the numerator and denominator of a proper fraction increase by the same amount, the value of the fraction increases. It is only by using a counter-example that students will see that adding (different) amounts to the numerator and denominator does not always increase the value of the fraction. For example: $$\frac{5}{8} \rightarrow \frac{5+1}{8+2} = \frac{6}{10} \qquad \frac{6}{10} < \frac{5}{8}$$
Fractions Can Be Greater Than 1 Students have the misconception that all fractions are less than 1.	Clearly, many fractions are greater than 1. There are many real-world examples of fractions greater than 1, such as $1\frac{1}{2}$ hours and $2\frac{1}{2}$ dozen cookies. Students need many opportunities to work with mixed numbers and improper fractions in a variety of contexts.

Appropriate Manipulatives

Many appropriate manipulative materials are available for work with fractions. It is essential that all students work with at least some of these materials and not rely on pictures. Even older students should be encouraged to use physical representations of fractions.

Fractions: Examples of Manipulatives

FRACTION PIECES

Fraction pieces are shapes, whether plastic, paper, or some other material, that are pre-cut to show various fractions and are used to represent fractions of regions. Usually, the different fractions are different colours. The wholes upon which these fractions are based are not always the same shape. Often they are square, rectangular, or circular.

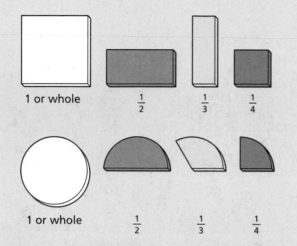

1 or whole $\frac{1}{2}$ $\frac{1}{3}$ $\frac{1}{4}$

1 or whole $\frac{1}{2}$ $\frac{1}{3}$ $\frac{1}{4}$

PATTERN BLOCKS

Pattern blocks provide another model for representing fractions of a region. Pattern blocks work particularly well for showing halves, thirds, and sixths if the yellow hexagon block is considered 1 or the whole.

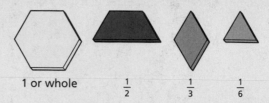

1 or whole $\frac{1}{2}$ $\frac{1}{3}$ $\frac{1}{6}$

Note that the fraction representations can change, depending on which block is considered the whole.

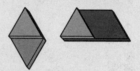

The green block is $\frac{1}{2}$ the blue block.

The green block is $\frac{1}{3}$ the red block.

SQUARE TILES

Square tiles come in different colours, and can be used to show many different fractions of a region. They can also be used to show fractions of a set.

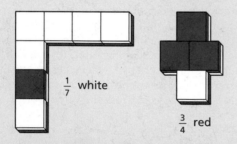

$\frac{1}{7}$ white

$\frac{3}{4}$ red

EGG CARTONS

Egg cartons are useful for showing fractions with denominators that are factors of 12 (halves, thirds, fourths, sixths, and twelfths).

$\frac{3}{12}$, or $\frac{1}{4}$, of the carton is filled.

GEOBOARDS AND SQUARE DOT OR GRID PAPER

Geoboards allow students to represent fractions as parts of regions in a variety of ways. Square dot paper or grid paper can be used to record what is shown on the geoboard or as a pictorial equivalent. One of the advantages of the geoboard is that more unusual shapes and fractions, such as $\frac{2}{7}$, can be shown.

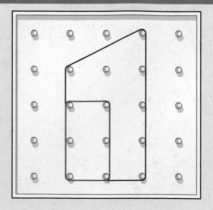

If the whole is 7 squares, 2 squares are $\frac{2}{7}$.

CUISENAIRE RODS

Cuisenaire rods are useful to show the concepts of fraction of a measure (length) and fraction as a ratio. As with pattern blocks, any rod can be considered the whole, so the fraction that each rod represents varies, depending on what is considered the whole, for example:

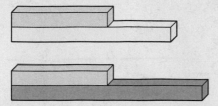

The light green rod is $\frac{3}{5}$ of the yellow rod but $\frac{1}{2}$ of the dark green rod.

The rods can also be used to show improper fractions and mixed numbers, for example:

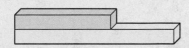

The yellow rod is $\frac{5}{3}$, or $1\frac{2}{3}$ of the light green rod.

COUNTERS

Counters in a variety of colours and shapes can be used to show fractions of sets. Two-sided counters with a different colour on each side are also useful.

$\frac{3}{5}$ of the counters are white.

$\frac{3}{5}$ of the counters are square.

FRACTION BARS

Fraction bars are another length model for showing fractions of a measure. They can be made of plastic or paper and are sometimes called fraction strips. The bars are all the same length, are pre-divided, and are sometimes colour-coordinated to show halves, thirds, fourths, fifths, sixths, eighths, tenths, and twelfths.

MONEY

Money provides a value model that can be very effective for students who have internalized money concepts.

3 quarters is $\frac{3}{4}$ or $\frac{75}{100}$, of a dollar.

4 dimes is $\frac{4}{10}$, $\frac{40}{100}$, or $\frac{2}{5}$ of a dollar.

NUMBER LINES

Number lines are useful for comparing and ordering fractions. Students can place fractions at appropriate spots on a number line using the benchmarks 0, $\frac{1}{2}$, and 1.

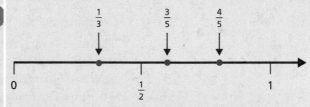

$\frac{4}{5}$ can be placed using its size relative to 0 $\left(\frac{0}{5}\right)$ and $1\left(\frac{5}{5}\right)$.

$\frac{1}{3}$ can be placed using its size relative to 0 and $\frac{1}{2}$.

$\frac{3}{5}$ can be placed using its size relative to $\frac{1}{2}$ and 1.

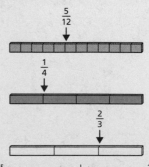

$\frac{5}{12}$ is greater than $\frac{1}{4}$ but less than $\frac{2}{3}$.

Modelling with Manipulatives

MODELLING EQUIVALENCE	MODELLING FRACTIONS GREATER THAN 1
The equivalence of fractions can be shown using manipulatives. For example, using pattern blocks: If the yellow block is 1 or the whole, each green block is $\frac{1}{6}$. So, 3 green blocks make up $\frac{3}{6}$, or $\frac{1}{2}$, of the yellow block. 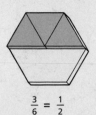 $\frac{3}{6} = \frac{1}{2}$	Fractions greater than 1 can also be modelled using manipulatives. The equivalence of improper fractions and mixed numbers also becomes apparent. For example, using pattern blocks: If the yellow block is 1, then each blue block is $\frac{1}{3}$. So, 5 blue blocks are $\frac{5}{3}$, or $1\frac{2}{3}$, yellow blocks. 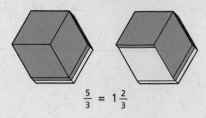 $\frac{5}{3} = 1\frac{2}{3}$

Appropriate Technology

Calculators

Certain calculators can assist struggling students with writing fractions as decimals, mixed numbers as improper fractions, and vice versa, and with simplifying fractions. These devices are useful once students have a conceptual understanding of these topics.

Computers

There are several software programs useful for developing fraction understanding. One is Sunburst's *Fraction Attraction*. "Tutorial" type software, such as *Understanding Fractions* produced by Neufeld Math, is also available. There are also many Internet applets for displaying fractions using different types of wholes and different numbers of sections.

Fraction Operations

Although decimal algorithms closely parallel whole number algorithms, that is not the case with fraction algorithms. For this reason, although many students learn the fraction procedures, they are not comfortable with why they are doing what they are doing. It is essential to continue to help students see that the meaning of the operations has not changed just because students are now working with fractions.

Adding and Subtracting Fractions

As students add and subtract fractions, an appropriate sequence of types of questions might be:

- fractions less than 1 with the same denominator, where the sum, or the minuend, is less than 1, like $\frac{3}{8} + \frac{4}{8}$
- any fractions less than 1 with the same denominator, like $\frac{5}{8} + \frac{7}{8}$
- fractions less than 1 with a sum, or minuend, less than 1, like $\frac{1}{4} + \frac{2}{3}$
- any fractions less than 1, like $\frac{3}{5} + \frac{7}{8}$

One way to begin the topic is to use what students already know about representations. For example, since students know that $\frac{5}{8}$ can be represented as 5 sections out of 8, they can colour different sections to create different addition expressions:

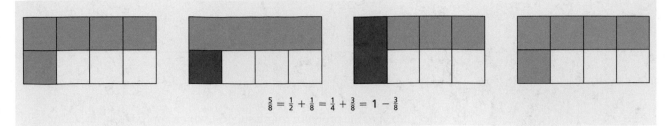

$$\tfrac{5}{8} = \tfrac{1}{2} + \tfrac{1}{8} = \tfrac{1}{4} + \tfrac{3}{8} = 1 - \tfrac{3}{8}$$

Once students see that $\tfrac{5}{8}$ can be represented as $\tfrac{1}{4} + \tfrac{3}{8}$, it makes sense that the sum of $\tfrac{1}{4} + \tfrac{3}{8}$ is $\tfrac{5}{8}$.

Whenever calculating sums and differences, students should be estimating using benchmarks, for example, is the sum closer to $\tfrac{1}{2}$ or 1? Is the difference closer to 0 or $\tfrac{1}{2}$? It is also important that different meanings of subtraction arise in problems that students meet—sometimes take away, sometimes comparison, and sometimes missing addend.

It makes sense to expose students to addition and subtraction of improper fractions after mixed numbers have been introduced, since then it is possible for students to check the reasonableness of the sum or difference. It also makes sense to repeatedly focus on the relationship between addition and subtraction.

Different models and approaches can and should be used to show addition and subtraction of fractions. Some examples are shown below:

Model 1: Think of the denominator as a unit when fractions have the same denominator.

$\tfrac{3}{4} + \tfrac{1}{5}$

Fifths are just like any other unit. Three of them and one more of them is four of them, so 3 fifths + 1 fifth = 4 fifths, or $\tfrac{3}{5} + \tfrac{1}{5} = \tfrac{4}{5}$.

$\tfrac{3}{5} - \tfrac{1}{5}$

Again, think of fifths as the "unit." Three of them are two more than one of them, so 3 fifths − 1 fifth = 2 fifths, or $\tfrac{3}{5} - \tfrac{1}{5} = \tfrac{2}{5}$.

Model 2: Number Lines

$\tfrac{3}{5} + \tfrac{1}{5}$ is the resulting position when a distance of $\tfrac{1}{5}$ is added to the $\tfrac{3}{5}$ position on a number line:

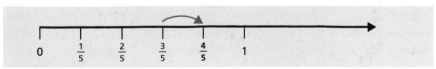

$\tfrac{3}{5} - \tfrac{1}{5}$ can be thought of in two ways:

i) the distance from $\tfrac{1}{5}$ to $\tfrac{3}{5}$ on the number line ($\tfrac{2}{5}$, in this case, represents the length of the arrow).

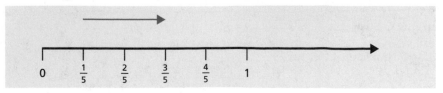

ii) the resulting position when you move $\frac{1}{5}$ to the left instead of the right from the $\frac{3}{5}$ position

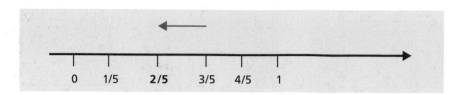

The context of the problem might suggest which approach to use, although either is correct in any subtraction situation.

For example, if the problem were: *I had 1 of the 5 reports done, but I promised 3 of them. What fraction of the work do I have left?*, the first model might make more sense.

If the problem were: *$\frac{3}{5}$ of the work was done. I decided to redo $\frac{1}{5}$ of it. How much did I not have to redo?*, the second model fits better.

Model 3: Fraction Strips

$\frac{2}{3} + \frac{1}{4}$

$\frac{2}{3} + \frac{1}{4}$ is the length of a fraction strip with the same total length as the $\frac{2}{3}$ and $\frac{1}{4}$ strips placed end-to-end.

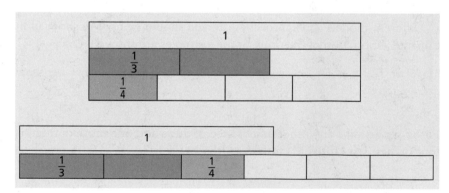

It is not hard to see that the sum is less than 1, but it is hard to see exactly what it is since the pieces are different sizes.

Students might use the idea that thirds and fourths can both be represented as twelfths to complete the problem. 12 was chosen since it is a common multiple of the two denominators.

Before expecting students to add fractions, it is important to be sure that they are comfortable creating equivalent fractions and that they are comfortable with the concept of a common multiple.

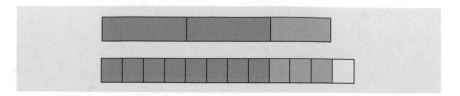

Using equivalent twelfths:

$$\frac{2}{3} + \frac{1}{4} = \frac{8}{12} + \frac{3}{12} = \frac{11}{12}$$

$\frac{2}{3} - \frac{1}{4}$

$\frac{2}{3} - \frac{1}{4}$ can be thought of as how much longer the $\frac{2}{3}$ strip is than the $\frac{1}{4}$ strip. 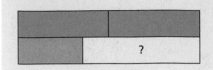	Again, it is hard to see without the equivalent twelfths. 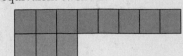 Then it is easy to see that $\frac{2}{3} - \frac{1}{4} = \frac{8}{12} - \frac{3}{12} = \frac{5}{12}$.

Model 4: Grids and Counters

$\frac{3}{5} + \frac{1}{3}$

- Use a 5 × 3 or 3 × 5 grid since it nicely shows both fifths (as columns) and thirds (as rows).
- $\frac{3}{5}$ of the grid is 3 out of the 5 columns; $\frac{1}{3}$ of the grid is one of the 3 rows.
- First model the first fraction: $\frac{3}{5}$.

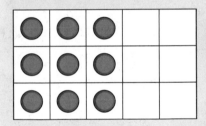

- Adding $\frac{1}{3}$ means adding the number of counters in one row.
- Move some of the $\frac{3}{5}$ counters in order to have room to fill a full row $\left(\frac{1}{3}\right)$.

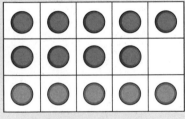

$\frac{14}{15}$ of the grid is full, so $\frac{3}{5} + \frac{1}{3} = \frac{14}{15}$.

Notice that the use of a 5 × 3 grid automatically showed equivalent fractions with a common denominator, the $\frac{3}{5}$ as $\frac{9}{15}$ and the $\frac{1}{3}$ as $\frac{5}{15}$.

This will always be true. So, for example, if students want to add sixths and fifths, they could use a 6 × 5 grid, or for fourths and fifths, a 4 × 5 grid.

$\frac{3}{4} - \frac{2}{3}$

- Use a 4 × 3 grid since the denominators are 4 and 3.
- $\frac{3}{4}$ of the grid is 3 of the 4 columns.
- $\frac{2}{3}$ of the grid is 2 of the 3 rows.
- Model the first fraction, $\frac{3}{4}$, by filling 3 of the 4 columns.

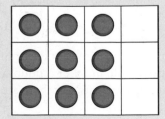

- Subtracting $\frac{1}{3}$ means taking away all the counters in one full row. Subtracting $\frac{2}{3}$ means taking away all of the counters in two full rows.
- Move some of the $\frac{3}{4}$ counters so 2 rows are full.
- Then you can remove all the counters in the two rows and see what is left. It is $\frac{1}{12}$.

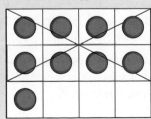

ACTIVITY 9.13

Present pictures of start and end positions for containers where liquid has been drained in some way. Ask students to write subtraction sentences to describe the pictures. For example, the pictures below show how much of a pitcher of lemonade has been poured out and how much of a gas tank in a car has been used.

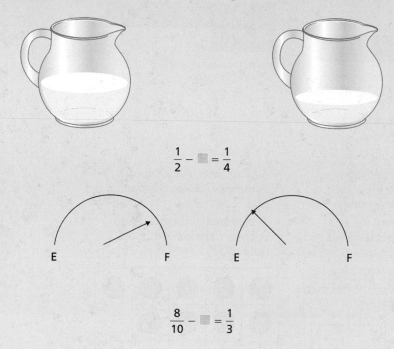

$$\frac{1}{2} - \blacksquare = \frac{1}{4}$$

$$\frac{8}{10} - \blacksquare = \frac{1}{3}$$

ACTIVITY 9.14

Students can explore the sums and differences of fractions that form a pattern. For example, they could calculate the sums for each pair of neighbouring fractions shown below:

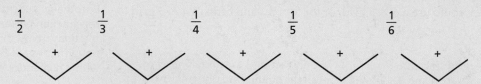

You can create other situations to explore by replacing this fraction pattern with other fraction patterns, for example, $\frac{1}{2}$, $\frac{1}{4}$, $\frac{1}{8}$, $\frac{1}{16}$, ..., or asking students to subtract instead of add.

Adding and Subtracting Mixed Numbers

When adding and subtracting mixed numbers, the same models can be used as with proper fractions. Normally, the whole-number amounts are added or subtracted separately from the fraction amounts, but there are exceptions. For example:

$1 - \frac{2}{3}$

NUMBER LINE	GRID
$1 - \frac{2}{3}$ is the distance from $\frac{2}{3}$ to 1, i.e., $\frac{1}{3}$. 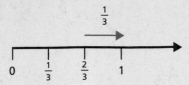	$1 - \frac{2}{3}$ tells how much of a grid is not filled if $\frac{2}{3}$ is filled. Here it is easy to see that it is $\frac{1}{3}$ of the grid. 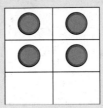 Notice that a grid with 3 rows and 2 columns was used, but any grid with either 3 rows or 3 columns could have been used to model thirds.

$4 - \frac{2}{3}$

NUMBER LINE	EQUIVALENT FRACTIONS
$4 - \frac{2}{3}$ is the combined distance from $\frac{2}{3}$ to 1, and then from 1 to 4. 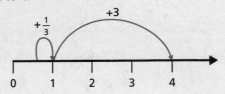 The total jump is $3\frac{1}{3}$.	$4 = \frac{12}{3}$, so $4 - \frac{2}{3} =$ 12 thirds $-$ 2 thirds $=$ 10 thirds or $3\frac{1}{3}$

$1\frac{1}{2} + 3\frac{4}{5}$

The whole-number parts might be added first, and then the fraction parts.

$$1 + 3 = 4$$
$$\frac{1}{2} + \frac{4}{5} = \frac{5}{10} + \frac{8}{10} = \frac{13}{10} = 1\frac{3}{10}$$
$$4 + 1\frac{3}{10} = 5\frac{3}{10}, \text{ so}$$
$$1\frac{1}{2} + 3\frac{4}{5} = 5\frac{3}{10}$$

$3\frac{1}{4} - 1\frac{3}{5}$

ADDING UP USING A NUMBER LINE	REGROUP AND SUBTRACT
Add $\frac{2}{5}$ to get to 2. Add $1\frac{1}{4}$ to get to $3\frac{1}{4}$. 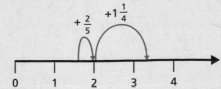 The total move is $\frac{2}{5} + 1\frac{1}{4}$. $\frac{1}{4} + \frac{2}{5} = \frac{5}{20} + \frac{8}{20} = \frac{13}{20}$, so $3\frac{1}{4} - 1\frac{3}{5} = 1\frac{13}{20}$	Because $\frac{3}{5} > \frac{1}{4}$, without using negatives, it is not possible to subtract the whole parts and fraction parts separately. So rename $3\frac{1}{4} = 2 + \frac{4}{4} + \frac{1}{4} = 2\frac{5}{4}$. Now subtract: $2\frac{5}{4}$ $- 1\frac{3}{5}$ $\overline{1\frac{13}{20}}$ (since $\frac{5}{4} - \frac{3}{5} = \frac{25}{20} - \frac{12}{20} = \frac{13}{20}$)

ACTIVITY 9.15

Students can use pattern blocks to create a design, choose a block to call 1, and then name the design using fraction addition. For example, if the yellow block is 1, the design below can be written as $2 + \frac{2}{6} + \frac{2}{3} + \frac{1}{2}$. The student sees that this is equivalent to $2\frac{1}{2}$ by rearranging the blocks.

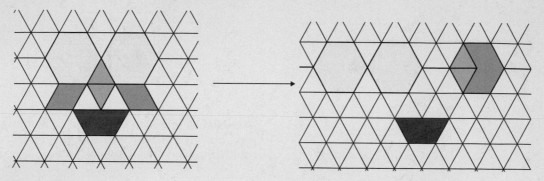

ACTIVITY 9.16

Provide puzzles like these for students to solve:

Use the digits 1 to 6, once each, to make this true.

$$\frac{\blacksquare}{\blacksquare} + \frac{\blacksquare}{\blacksquare} + \frac{1}{\blacksquare} = 6$$

Multiplying and Dividing Fractions

As students multiply and divide fractions, an appropriate sequence of types of problems might be

- multiplying fractions by whole numbers, e.g., $5 \times \frac{2}{3}$
- multiplying two fractions less than 1, e.g., $\frac{2}{3} \times \frac{4}{5}$
- dividing fractions by whole numbers, e.g., $\frac{3}{4} \div 6$
- dividing a fraction less than 1 by a lesser one, e.g., $\frac{3}{4} \div \frac{1}{3}$
- dividing any two fractions, e.g., $\frac{1}{8} \div \frac{2}{5}$
- dividing mixed numbers, e.g., $4\frac{2}{3} \div 1\frac{3}{4}$

Multiplying a Fraction by a Whole Number

Students can interpret the multiplication of a fraction by a whole number as repeated addition. For example, $4 \times \frac{3}{5}$ means 4 sets of $\frac{3}{5}$, so it is $\frac{3}{5} + \frac{3}{5} + \frac{3}{5} + \frac{3}{5} = \frac{12}{5}$ or $2\frac{2}{5}$.

Multiplying Two Fractions

One of the most difficult aspects of multiplying two fractions for students is the fact that the product is less than the factors; this is something they had never experienced using whole numbers and is quite troublesome for some students.

To begin, it is important to help remind students of what multiplication means.

One of the things it means is "of," that is, 3×4 means 3 [sets] of 4, or 8×9 means 8 [sets] of 9.

It only makes sense that the same is true with fractions, that is, $\frac{1}{2} \times \frac{3}{5}$ means $\frac{1}{2}$ [set] of $\frac{3}{5}$.

Using fraction strips helps students see that $\frac{1}{2}$ of $\frac{3}{5}$, or $\frac{1}{2} \times \frac{3}{5}$ means $\frac{3}{10}$.

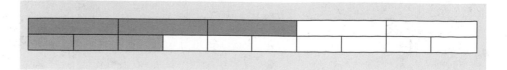

ACTIVITY 9.17

Students can use fraction strips and try to describe a variety of fractions as parts of other fractions. For example, looking at the strips below, they could see that $\frac{1}{6}$ is $\frac{1}{2}$ of $\frac{1}{3}$ or $\frac{1}{3}$ of $\frac{1}{2}$.

1											
$\frac{1}{2}$						$\frac{1}{2}$					
$\frac{1}{3}$				$\frac{1}{3}$				$\frac{1}{3}$			
$\frac{1}{4}$			$\frac{1}{4}$			$\frac{1}{4}$			$\frac{1}{4}$		
$\frac{1}{5}$		$\frac{1}{5}$		$\frac{1}{5}$		$\frac{1}{5}$		$\frac{1}{5}$			
$\frac{1}{6}$		$\frac{1}{6}$		$\frac{1}{6}$		$\frac{1}{6}$		$\frac{1}{6}$		$\frac{1}{6}$	
$\frac{1}{7}$		$\frac{1}{7}$	$\frac{1}{7}$		$\frac{1}{7}$		$\frac{1}{7}$		$\frac{1}{7}$		$\frac{1}{7}$
$\frac{1}{8}$	$\frac{1}{8}$	$\frac{1}{8}$	$\frac{1}{8}$	$\frac{1}{8}$	$\frac{1}{8}$	$\frac{1}{8}$	$\frac{1}{8}$				
$\frac{1}{9}$	$\frac{1}{9}$	$\frac{1}{9}$	$\frac{1}{9}$	$\frac{1}{9}$	$\frac{1}{9}$	$\frac{1}{9}$	$\frac{1}{9}$	$\frac{1}{9}$			
$\frac{1}{10}$	$\frac{1}{10}$	$\frac{1}{10}$	$\frac{1}{10}$	$\frac{1}{10}$	$\frac{1}{10}$	$\frac{1}{10}$	$\frac{1}{10}$	$\frac{1}{10}$	$\frac{1}{10}$		
$\frac{1}{11}$	$\frac{1}{11}$	$\frac{1}{11}$	$\frac{1}{11}$	$\frac{1}{11}$	$\frac{1}{11}$	$\frac{1}{11}$	$\frac{1}{11}$	$\frac{1}{11}$	$\frac{1}{11}$	$\frac{1}{11}$	
$\frac{1}{12}$	$\frac{1}{12}$	$\frac{1}{12}$	$\frac{1}{12}$	$\frac{1}{12}$	$\frac{1}{12}$	$\frac{1}{12}$	$\frac{1}{12}$	$\frac{1}{12}$	$\frac{1}{12}$	$\frac{1}{12}$	$\frac{1}{12}$

Another meaning of multiplication that students used with whole numbers is the notion that multiplication represents the area of a rectangle with given dimensions. That concept can be used to model, for example, $\frac{3}{5} \times \frac{2}{3}$, as below.

A rectangle is created with one dimension $\frac{3}{5}$ and the other $\frac{2}{3}$. This can be done by using grid paper, forming a whole that is 5×3 (since the denominators are 5 and 3), or by folding paper to form thirds in one direction and fifths in the other.

The blue part is a rectangle with dimensions $\frac{2}{3}$ and $\frac{3}{5}$.

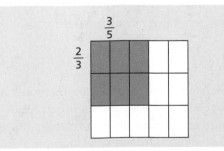

Notice that it is also $\frac{3}{5}$ of $\frac{2}{3}$, as was described above, if you think of the blue rectangle as part of this green one, representing $\frac{2}{3}$.

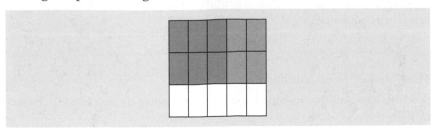

Students observe that the numerator of the resulting fraction is 3 × 2 since there are 3 columns with 2 pieces in each, and the denominator is 5 × 3 since the whole is made up of 5 columns with 3 pieces in each.

In general, when you multiply two fractions, the numerator is the product of the numerators, and the denominator is the product of the denominators. The total grid has b × d sections, and only a × c of them are inside the rectangle formed.

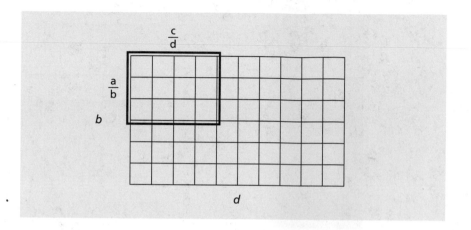

Even if the fractions are greater than 1, this algorithm can be used. For example, to show $\frac{5}{4} \times \frac{2}{3}$, you would make whole grids of 4 by 3. You would create a rectangle, using two of the grids, with dimensions 5 × 2, so there would still be 20 sections in the rectangle and each grid would still be divided into 12.

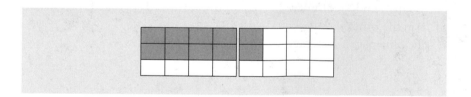

Once students understand how to multiply fractions, it is possible to revisit the concept of creating equivalent fractions in a new way.

Students know that to create an equivalent fraction, they could multiply the numerator and denominator by the same amount. For example, $\frac{2}{3} = \frac{6}{9}$ since both numerator and denominator were multiplied by 3.

Now they can see that they have really completed the question $\frac{2}{3} \times \frac{3}{3} = \frac{6}{9}$.

Since $\frac{3}{3} = 1$, they have actually multiplied by 1, which they know does not change an amount.

Multiplying Mixed Numbers

Students can multiply mixed numbers, either using an area model, or multiplying the equivalent improper fractions.

Example

$2\frac{2}{3} \times 3\frac{1}{3}$

AREA MODEL	**USING IMPROPER FRACTIONS**
$2\frac{1}{2} \times 3\frac{1}{3}$ is the area of a rectangle that has those dimensions.	Use equivalent improper fractions.
Separate the rectangle into four smaller rectangles, separating the whole part and fraction part of each mixed number, and add the four areas.	$2\frac{1}{2} \times 3\frac{1}{3} = \frac{5}{2} \times \frac{10}{3} = \frac{50}{6} = 8\frac{2}{6}$

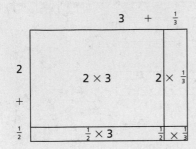

$$\begin{aligned}
\text{Area} &= 6 + \tfrac{2}{3} + \tfrac{3}{2} + \tfrac{1}{6} \\
&= 6 + \tfrac{4}{6} + \tfrac{9}{6} + \tfrac{1}{6} \\
&= 6 + \tfrac{14}{6} \\
&= 6 + 2 + \tfrac{2}{6} \\
&= 8\tfrac{2}{6}
\end{aligned}$$

If students use the improper-fraction approach, they should be encouraged to use mixed-number equivalents to estimate the answer to see if their product is reasonable.

Dividing a Fraction by a Whole Number

Thinking about division as sharing helps students to divide fractions by whole numbers. For example, $\frac{6}{7} \div 3$ means 6 sevenths is shared by 3 people. Each person gets 2 sevenths, so $\frac{6}{7} \div 3 = \frac{2}{7}$. In other words, the numerator is divided by the whole number and the denominator does not change.

Sometimes, the division is not as straightforward. For example, $\frac{6}{7} \div 4$ means 6 sevenths is shared by 4 people. Each person gets $1\frac{1}{2}$ sevenths, but this is awkward to write. If an equivalent for $\frac{6}{7}$ is written where the numerator is divisible by 4, the problem is much easier to grasp.

$$\frac{6}{7} = \frac{12}{14} \quad \text{so} \quad \frac{6}{7} \div 4 = \frac{12}{14} \div 4 = \frac{(12 \div 4)}{14} = \frac{3}{14}$$

This can be modelled:

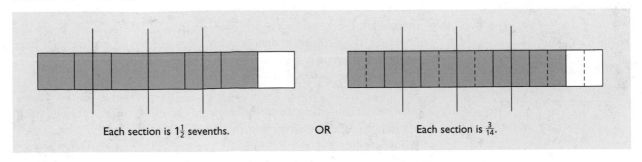

Each section is $1\frac{1}{2}$ sevenths.   OR   Each section is $\frac{3}{14}$.

Dividing Two Fractions

Some division of fraction questions can be very easy for students without knowing any formal procedures. This is particularly the case if the division is "read" to them meaningfully. For example, reading $\frac{1}{2} \div \frac{1}{4}$ as *How many fourths are in $\frac{1}{2}$?* allows students who do not know any formal procedure to calculate a quotient of 2.

With the use of manipulatives and a recognition that $a \div b$ means how many bs are in a, students can easily estimate quotients.

For example, $\frac{2}{3} \div \frac{1}{10}$ means how many $\frac{1}{10}$s are in $\frac{2}{3}$.

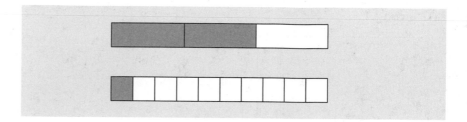

Just looking at the diagram, it is clear that the answer is about 7.

To get the exact answer, though, students need to use more exact procedures.

Algorithm 1: Using Common Denominators Among the easiest types of fraction division for students are questions like $\frac{6}{7} \div \frac{2}{7}$ (*How many 2 sevenths are in 6 sevenths?*) or $\frac{8}{9} \div \frac{2}{9}$ (*How many 2 ninths are in 8 ninths?*), where the denominators are the same and one numerator is a factor of the other. Students readily see that the quotient is simply the quotient of the numerators; the denominator is not used in the computation.

The question is only slightly more difficult if the denominators are the same, but one numerator is not a factor of another.

For example, $\frac{3}{5} \div \frac{2}{5}$.

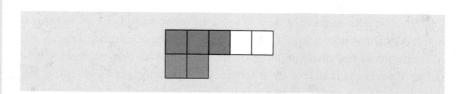

The question is really about how many 2s (in this case, 2 fifths) are in 3 (in this case, 3 fifths). The diagram shows that 1 set of two fifths does not go far enough and you can see that 2 sets would go too far, so an answer of $1\frac{1}{2}$ makes sense. $1\frac{1}{2} = 3 \div 2$, the quotient of the two numerators.

In general: $\frac{a}{c} \div \frac{b}{c} = a \div b = \frac{a}{b}$

Dividing using common denominators works even when fractions have different denominators if equivalent fractions are substituted.

For example, $\frac{3}{4} \div \frac{2}{3} = \frac{9}{12} \div \frac{8}{12} = 9 \div 8$ or $\frac{9}{8}$.

Algorithm 2: Inverting and Multiplying The more traditional algorithm for dividing fractions is inverting and multiplying.

For example, $\frac{3}{4} \div \frac{2}{3} = \frac{3}{4} \times \frac{3}{2} = \frac{9}{8}$.

This algorithm can be explained in several ways. One meaningful approach is this one.

- $1 \div \frac{1}{3} = 3$ since there are 3 thirds in 1.
- $\frac{3}{4} \div \frac{1}{3} = \frac{3}{4}$ of 3 since there can only be $\frac{3}{4}$ as many thirds in $\frac{3}{4}$ as there are in 1.

That is the same as $\frac{3}{4} \times 3$.

- Since $\frac{2}{3}$ is twice as much as $\frac{1}{3}$, only half as many $\frac{2}{3}$s can fit into a whole as $\frac{1}{3}$s, so

$$\frac{3}{4} \div \frac{2}{3} = \frac{1}{2} \text{ of } (\frac{3}{4} \times 3)$$
$$= \frac{3}{4} \times \frac{3}{2}$$

The invert and multiply is the better-known algorithm, probably because it is easier to use in algebraic situations in later grades, but either the common denominator or the invert and multiply algorithms are appropriate for students to use.

Dividing Mixed Numbers

The easiest way to divide mixed numbers is to use the equivalent improper fractions and apply one of the division algorithms to these values.

For example, $2\frac{1}{2} \div 1\frac{1}{3} = \frac{5}{2} \div \frac{4}{3}$
$$= \frac{5}{2} \times \frac{3}{4} = \frac{15}{8} = 1\frac{7}{8}$$

Students should be asked to look back to see if an answer makes sense. This answer does make sense since $1\frac{1}{3}$ is slightly bigger than $1\frac{1}{4}$, and $1\frac{1}{4}$ fits into $2\frac{1}{2}$ twice.

Common Errors and Misconceptions

COMMON ERROR OR MISCONCEPTION	STRATEGY
Students add or subtract numerators and denominators to add or subtract fractions. For example, they add $\frac{3}{5} + \frac{2}{3}$ as $\frac{5}{8}$.	Focus students on the size of the fractions being added. Ask students to estimate: *If you are starting at a number greater than $\frac{1}{2}$ ($\frac{3}{5}$) and adding a number greater than $\frac{1}{2}$ ($\frac{5}{8}$), about how much should the sum be? Is $\frac{5}{8}$ reasonable?*
When students draw diagrams to show the addition of fractions when the result is greater than 1, they forget what the whole is. For example, a student adds $\frac{2}{5} + \frac{4}{5}$ and reports the answer as $\frac{6}{10}$. 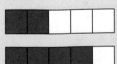	It is easy for students to forget what the whole is. What the student sees in this situation are 6 coloured pieces out of 10, so it is natural to say $\frac{6}{10}$. Encourage students to estimate answers before they begin. For example, ask whether 2 fifths and 4 fifths should be more or less than 1. Then if the error is made, it will be easier to convince the student that there is a problem. Another strategy is to have students circle the whole in their diagrams.
When subtracting mixed numbers, students separately subtract the whole numbers and mixed numbers, but not always in the same direction. For example, a student records: $\begin{array}{r} 4\frac{1}{4} \\ -1\frac{1}{2} \\ \hline 3\frac{1}{4} \end{array}$	Students who calculate using rote procedures and who know that the fractions and whole numbers can be subtracted separately might make this sort of error. Encourage students to estimate. $4\frac{1}{4}$ is about 4. To get from $1\frac{1}{2}$ to 4, go $\frac{1}{2}$ to get to 2 and another 2, so the answer should be about $2\frac{1}{2}$. $3\frac{1}{4}$ is too high. Ask students to model with manipulatives. *(continued)*

ACTIVITY 9.19

Students can play fraction games. For example, they can roll four dice to get two numerators and two denominators. They can then add, subtract, multiply, or divide the fractions to get as close to $\frac{2}{3}$ as possible.

COMMON ERROR OR MISCONCEPTION	STRATEGY
Students believe you must use a common denominator to multiply two fractions. For example, $\frac{2}{3} \times \frac{1}{2} = \frac{4}{6} \times \frac{3}{6} = \frac{12}{36}$	This approach is not efficient, but it is not incorrect. If students draw an area diagram to model the problem, they will see that equivalent fractions are not required.
When dividing fractions, students invert the wrong fraction. For example, $\frac{2}{3} \div \frac{3}{4} = \frac{3}{2} \times \frac{3}{4} = \frac{9}{8}$	Suggest that students read a division problem in terms of "how many," e.g., $\frac{2}{3} \div \frac{3}{4}$ as how many $\frac{3}{4}$s are in $\frac{2}{3}$. Recognizing that $\frac{3}{4}$ is more than $\frac{2}{3}$, the answer of $\frac{9}{8}$ will not seem reasonable.

Appropriate Manipulatives

A variety of manipulatives are useful for work with fractions.

FRACTION STRIPS	NUMBER LINES
Fraction strips can be used to add, subtract, multiply, or divide fractions. For example, $\frac{2}{3} \times \frac{3}{5}$ is $\frac{2}{3}$ of $\frac{3}{5}$.	Number lines can be used to add, subtract, multiply, or divide fractions. For example, to calculate $1\frac{1}{4} - \frac{3}{8}$, jump from $\frac{3}{8}$ to 1, and then another $\frac{1}{4}$, and total the amount jumped.

$\frac{2}{3}$ of $\frac{3}{5}$ is $\frac{2}{5}$.

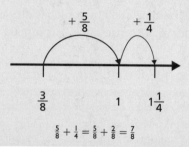

$\frac{5}{8} + \frac{1}{4} = \frac{5}{8} + \frac{2}{8} = \frac{7}{8}$

GRIDS AND COUNTERS	GEOBOARDS
Grids and counters can be used for all four operations. For example, $\frac{5}{8} \div \frac{1}{3}$ tells how many $\frac{1}{3}$s fit in $\frac{5}{8}$. Cover $\frac{5}{8}$ of a 3-by-8 grid. $\frac{1}{3}$ of the grid is 1 row of 8, so the question is really how many groups of 8 counters can be formed.	Geoboards can be used in the same way as grids and counters, but rather than using counters, sections of the geoboard are circled with elastics. For example, $\frac{2}{3} \times \frac{1}{5}$ is shown by using an elastic to enclose a 3×5 rectangle, another elastic to enclose 1 column of the rectangle, and then another to enclose 2 of the 3 rows in that column.

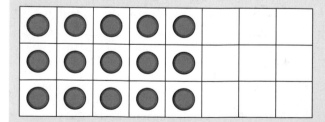

$15 \div 8 = 1\frac{7}{8}$

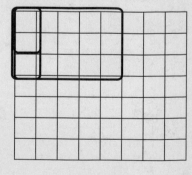

$\frac{2}{3} \times \frac{1}{5} = \frac{2}{15}$

Appropriate Technology

Calculators

Certain calculators have the capability of fraction calculations. Once students have made sense of the fraction operations and have shown competence with them, they should be allowed to use these devices if a large number of calculations are required.

Computers

One valuable piece of software is *Fraction Operations* by Tenth Planet. There is also some tutorial software that allows students to add or subtract fractions, usually with some visual support. There are also some computer applets that students can use. For example, a fraction bar blackjack applet allows students to practise fraction addition.

> **WebConnect** W W W
>
> www.makingmathmeaningful.nelson.com
>
> Visit the Making Math Meaningful website for links to Internet tools that can help students add and subtract fractions.

Assessing Student Understanding

- Although typically teachers ask students to describe the fraction associated with a picture, it is equally important to have students draw a picture for a fraction. This provides insight into a child's understanding of the need for equal parts for fractions of a whole or fractions of a measure.
- Make sure to not only focus on fractions as parts of a whole, but include consideration of fractions as parts of a set. This is supported by the use of a grid-and-counters model for fraction operations.
- It is important to encourage students to use alternative models and alternative algorithms so that when they are assessed on their understanding of fraction concepts or operations, they can select the model or algorithm that makes the most sense to them.
- Assessment of fraction understanding should include an appropriate balance of conceptual, procedural, and problem-solving questions. For example, to find out what students understand about subtracting fractions, include questions where
  - they are asked to draw models to represent a particular subtraction
  - they are given a model and asked to provide the associated computation
  - they explain why a difference might be in a particular range of numbers, for example, why $\frac{3}{4} - \frac{1}{3}$ is between $\frac{1}{2}$ and $\frac{2}{3}$
  - they solve a problem involving subtraction of fractions
  - they create a problem to match a particular subtraction calculation

Appropriate Children's Books

Fraction Action (Leedy, 1996).
Although not a story, this illustrated book uses animal characters to help young students explore the meaning of fractions of a whole and fractions of a set.

Eating Fractions (McMillan, 1991).
The attractive real-life pictures in this book explore situations where students might encounter halves, thirds, and fourths in their everyday experience.

Jump, Kangaroo, Jump! (Murphy, 1998).
A group of 12 kangaroos divide themselves into different numbers of teams for some field-day events. The fractions associated with these groupings are shown visually and symbolically.

Applying What You've Learned

1. Many young children have an understanding of $\frac{1}{2}$ much earlier than other simple fractions, for example, $\frac{1}{3}$ or $\frac{1}{4}$. Why do you think this might be?

2. We often focus on the part-of-a-whole meaning for fractions. Make a case for why the part-of-a-set, part-of-a-measure, division, and ratio meanings are also important to use.

3. Develop a plan for a lesson using pattern blocks to demonstrate the importance of what the whole is in attaching a fraction name to an object.

4. How would you help a student understand why the wholes need to be considered in order to compare two fractions?

5. One of the ways we later use the notion that fractions represent division is to divide a numerator by a denominator to create a decimal equivalent. For example, we get the decimal for $\frac{3}{7}$ by dividing 3 by 7. Set up an activity that would make this approach make sense to a Grade 7 student.

6. Consider each of the fraction operations. In what ways is an understanding of fraction equivalence fundamental to success with each operation? Be as specific as you can.

7. Consider each of the fraction operations. In what ways is visualization fundamental to success with the operations? Be as specific as you can.

8. Which is usually greater: the sum, difference, product, or quotient of two fractions? Explain.

9. Find a journal article either from the reference list or elsewhere that documents the difficulties students have in learning about fractions.

   a) What reasons are proposed for these difficulties?

   b) What remedies are suggested?

10. You are creating an assessment tool focused on multiplication of fractions.

    a) What understandings are important to get at?

    b) How would you make sure these are part of the assessment?

Interact with a K–8 Student:

11. Try Activity 9.8 with students in Grade 4 or higher. What strategies do they use to figure out the fractions? How might you (or did you) intervene to help a student whose estimates are not reasonable?

Discuss with a K–8 Teacher:

12. Ask a teacher what fraction topics cause the most difficulty for his or her students. Ask how he or she tries to avoid some of those difficulties.

Selected References

Armstrong, B.E., and Larson, C.N. (1995). Students' use of part-whole and direct comparison strategies for comparing partitioned rectangles. *Journal for Research in Mathematics Education, 26,* 2–19.

Bay-Williams, J.M., and Martinie, S.L. (2003). Thinking rationally about number and operations in the middle school. *Mathematics Teaching in the Middle School, 8,* 282–287.

Empson, S.B. (2001). Equal sharing and the roots of fraction equivalence. *Teaching Children Mathematics, 7,* 421–425.

Huinker, D. (1999). Letting fraction algorithms emerge through problem solving. In Morrow, L., and Kenney, M.J. (Eds.). *The teaching and learning of algorithms in school mathematics.* Reston, VA: National Council of Teachers of Mathematics, 170–182.

Kieran, T., Davis, B., and Mason, R. (1996). Fraction flags: Learning from children to help children learn. *Mathematics Teaching in the Middle School, 2,* 14–19.

Lamon, S.J. (1999). *Teaching fractions and ratios for understanding: Essential content knowledge and instructional strategies for teachers* (2nd ed.). Mahwah, NJ: Lawrence Erlbaum Associates.

Leedy, L. (1996). *Fraction action.* New York: Holiday House.

Mack, N.K. (1995). Confounding whole-number and fraction concepts when building on informal knowledge. *Journal for Research in Mathematics Education, 26,* 422–441.

Mack, N.K. (1998). Building a foundation for understanding the multiplication of fractions. *Teaching Children Mathematics, 5,* 34–38.

Mack, N.K. (2004). Connecting to develop computational fluency with fractions. *Teaching Children Mathematics, 11,* 226–232.

McMillan, B. (1991). *Eating fractions.* New York: Scholastic Press.

Middleton, J.A., van den Heuvel-Panhuizen, M., and Shew, J.A. (1997). Using bar representations as a model for connecting concepts of rational number. *Mathematics Teaching in the Middle School, 3,* 302–312.

Moss, J., and Case, R. (1999). Developing children's understanding of the rational numbers: A new model and an experimental curriculum. *Journal for Research in Mathematics Education, 30,* 122–147.

Murphy, S. (1998). *Jump, kangaroo, jump!* Toronto: Harper-Collins Canada.

Olive, J. (2002). Bridging the gap: Using interactive computer tools to build fraction schemes. *Teaching Children Mathematics, 8,* 356–361.

Payne, J.N., Tosley, A.E., and Huinker, D.M. (1990). Fractions and decimals. In Payne, J.N. (Ed.). *Mathematics for the young child.* Reston, VA: National Council of Teachers of Mathematics, 175–200.

Perlwitz, M.D. (2005). Dividing fractions: reconciling self-generated solutions with algorithmic answers. *Mathematics Teaching in the Middle School, 10,* 278–283.

Reys, B.J., Kim, O., and Bay, J.M. (1999). Establishing fraction benchmarks. *Mathematics Teaching in the Middle School, 4,* 530–532.

Riddle, M., and Rodzwell, B. (2000). Fractions: What happens between kindergarten and the army? *Teaching Children Mathematics, 7,* 202–206.

Small, M. (2005). *PRIME: Number and operations: Background and strategies.* Toronto: Thomson Nelson.

Tzur, R. (1999). An integrated study of children's construction of improper fractions and the teacher's role in promoting learning. *Journal for Research in Mathematics Education, 30,* 390–416.

Warrington, M.A., and Kamii, C.K. (1998). Multiplication with fractions: A Piagetian constructivist approach. *Mathematics Teaching in the Middle School, 3,* 339–343.

Watanabe, T. (2002). Representations in teaching and learning fractions. *Teaching Children Mathematics, 8,* 457–463.

Chapter 10

Decimals

IN A NUTSHELL

The main ideas in this chapter are listed below:

1. A decimal is an alternative representation of a fraction, but one that allows for calculations that are consistent with whole number calculations.

2. A decimal can be read and interpreted in different ways; sometimes one representation is more useful than another in explaining a computation.

3. Algorithms for computing with decimals are derived directly from algorithms for computing with whole numbers.

CHAPTER PROBLEM

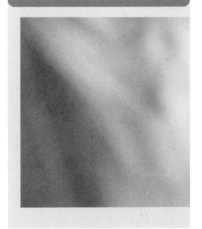

Representing Decimals

Decimals are not unfamiliar to students who have seen prices in dollar-and-cents form even before they get to school. However, students' understanding of this notation, for example, $3.14, is in terms of 3 dollars and 14 cents and not 3 dollars and 14 hundredths of a dollar, which is the underlying decimal meaning.

It is not really possible for students to make sense of decimals without some understanding of fractions. An introduction to decimals requires familiarity with the concept of fraction tenths. It is natural to begin with items that come in tens to begin renaming fraction tenths as decimal tenths.

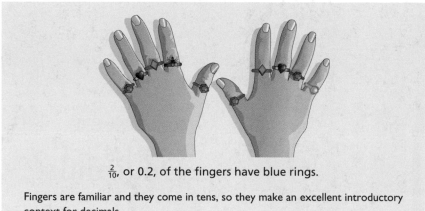

$\frac{2}{10}$, or 0.2, of the fingers have blue rings.

Fingers are familiar and they come in tens, so they make an excellent introductory context for decimals.

Some students who are fairly comfortable with decimal tenths and hundredths become less comfortable with decimal thousandths. It is important not to hurry the introduction of thousandths until students are ready, or at least to use concrete or pictorial support.

A good pictorial representation of thousandths is possible using thousandths grids like the one below.

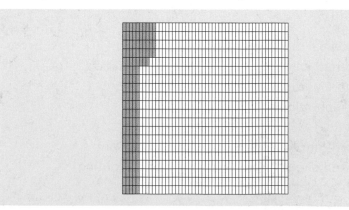

Decimal Contexts

Some valuable contexts that can be used to teach decimals are

- fingers and toes (for tenths)
- items that are packaged in tens, such as pencils (for tenths)
- food that can be shared in tenths, for example, pizza and cake
- money: dollars as the whole, dimes as tenths, and pennies as hundredths

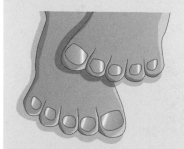

- the metric system: the metre as the whole or 1, decimetres as tenths, centimetres as hundredths, and millimetres as thousandths
- gas prices, which are posted to the tenth of a cent (Note that prices are shown to the thousandths of a dollar on the pumps.)
- scores that are in decimal form in various sports events

Decimal Principles

Some of the important principles that students must learn about decimals are listed below.

DECIMAL PRINCIPLES

1. Using decimals extends the place value system to represent parts of a whole.
2. Our base ten place value system is built on symmetry around the ones place.
3. Decimals can represent parts of a whole, as well as mixed numbers.
4. Decimals can be read in more than one way.
5. Decimals can be renamed as other decimals or fractions.

Principle 1: Using decimals extends the place value system to represent parts of a whole.

Decimals are an extension of whole numbers. The convention of writing the tenths after the decimal point must be explicitly addressed since it is simply a convention. It is important, though, to show why this convention makes sense, given the way whole numbers are written. If you follow the base ten relationship from left to right, a pattern appears.

Hundreds	Tens	Ones	Tenths
100	$\frac{1}{10}$ of 100, or 10	$\frac{1}{10}$ of 10, or 1	$\frac{1}{10}$ of 1, or 0.1

Each time you move one place to the right, the value decreases by a factor of $\frac{1}{10}$. It makes sense that the next place after the ones is $\frac{1}{10}$ of 1, or 0.1.

Students should also be led to see why there must be some demarcation (called a decimal point) to separate the tenths from the ones. Otherwise, you might assume that 42 means 42 ones, even if 4 ones and 2 tenths (4.2) had been intended. Note that in some systems, for example in Québec, a comma is used instead of a decimal point.

Principle 2: The base ten place value system is built on symmetry around the ones place.

The base ten system is built on symmetry. The tens and the tenths and the hundreds and the hundredths are "reflections" across the line of symmetry.

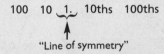

100   10 ‿1.‿   10ths   100ths

"Line of symmetry"

There is symmetry in our place value system. The "line of symmetry" includes the ones place and the decimal point.

Principle 3: Decimals can represent parts of a whole, as well as whole numbers or mixed numbers.

Decimals can be used to represent improper or mixed fractions or whole numbers. For example, 3.2 means $\frac{32}{10}$ or $3\frac{2}{10}$, and 3.0 means $3\frac{0}{10}$ or 3.

ACTIVITY 10.2

Students can colour designs on a decimal grid and give the design a decimal value.

For example, this animal is worth 0.27.

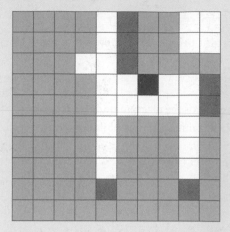

Students can also be given a value and asked to draw something to match it.

Principle 4: Decimals can be read in more than one way.

Decimals can be renamed just as can whole numbers. Students should become comfortable both reading and representing decimals in alternative forms. The first example below uses a full 10-frame as the whole, or 1. As with fractions, it is critical that the whole be identified.

ACTIVITY 10.3

Students can use egg cartons with the last two compartments cut off to represent wholes and tenths. For example, a student could fill 1 carton and 0.8 of another to see that 1.8 is 18 tenths.

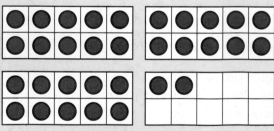

3.2 = 32 tenths

If one 10-frame is the whole, or 1, this model shows that 3.2 is 3 ones and 2 tenths, or 32 tenths.

In this example, the base ten block that is used to represent 100 when modelling whole numbers is now used to represent the whole, or 1 (see *Appropriate Manipulatives* on page 242). For some students, this is a difficulty, and using a new colour of block, if available, might be helpful.

Representing 2.35 in Different Ways

2 ONES, 3 TENTHS, 5 HUNDREDTHS	23 TENTHS, 5 HUNDREDTHS

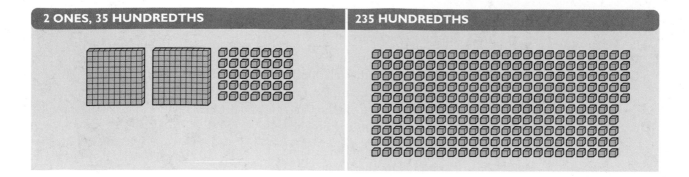

| 2 ONES, 35 HUNDREDTHS | 235 HUNDREDTHS |

Principle 5: Decimals can be renamed as other decimals or fractions.

Just like fractions, decimals have multiple names, including both fraction and decimal equivalents.

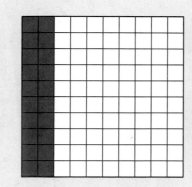

20 out of 100 squares of this grid are red.

$\frac{20}{100}$ or 0.20, $\frac{2}{10}$ or 0.2, or $\frac{1}{5}$

Equivalent Decimals

Explaining Equivalence of Decimals

USING FRACTIONS	USING PLACE VALUE
One way to explain equivalence of decimals is to appeal to fraction descriptions for each decimal. $0.2 = \frac{2}{10}$ $\frac{2}{10} = \frac{2}{10} \times \frac{10}{10}$ $\quad = \frac{20}{100}$ $\frac{20}{100} = 0.20$ Therefore, $0.2 = 0.20$.	Another way to explain equivalence of decimals is to use place value language and expanded notation. $0.2 = 2$ tenths $0.20 = 2$ tenths $+ 0$ hundredths Since the 0 hundredths has no effect, 0.20 must be the same as 0.2.

Equivalent Decimals and Precision

It should be noted that, when you speak about measurement units, you cannot equate, for example, 3.2 m and 3.20 m, since different levels of precision are implied by the use of more decimal places. The measurement 3.20 m indicates that the length could be anywhere between 3.195 m and 3.205 m (the range of values that could be rounded to 3.20); whereas 3.2 m could be anywhere between 3.15 m and 3.25 m (the range of values that could be rounded to 3.2), which makes 3.2 m less precise than 3.20 m.

Equivalent Fractions and Decimals

Simpler Fractions

Decimals are first introduced as tenths or hundredths, so students immediately recognize the relationship between decimals and fraction tenths or hundredths: for example, $\frac{2}{10}$ is 0.2, and 0.34 is $\frac{34}{100}$. But often it is convenient to take advantage of other fraction and decimal relationships. For example, you want students to know that

- 0.5 or 0.50 is another name for $\frac{1}{2}$
- 0.25 is another name for $\frac{1}{4}$
- 0.125 is another name for $\frac{1}{8}$
- 0.333... is another name for $\frac{1}{3}$

Knowing these relationships helps students interpret decimals meaningfully. For example, they see 0.48 and realize that it is almost $\frac{1}{2}$.

Explaining Equivalence of Decimals and Fractions

USING A MONEY MODEL	USING DIVISION
One way to explain equivalent fractions and decimals is using a money model. For example: • Since a quarter is 25¢, or $\frac{25}{100}$, of a dollar, and 4 quarters make a dollar, 0.25 is $\frac{1}{4}$.  • A dime is $\frac{1}{10}$ ($\frac{10}{100}$), or 0.1 (0.10), of a dollar. 	Another way to explain equivalent fractions and decimals is to use the quotient or division meaning of fractions. For example: You can think of $\frac{1}{2}$ as $1 \div 2$. When you divide 1 by 2 on a calculator, the display reads 0.5. You read this as "5 tenths" and realize that this makes sense since 5 out of 10 is half. 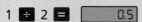 $\frac{1}{2}$ as $1 \div 2$ makes sense because 0.5 is 5 tenths, 1 is 10 tenths and 5 is half of 10.

More Complex Fraction/Decimal Relationships

In about Grade 7 or 8, students are asked to apply the fraction/decimal relationship even when fractions are not as easy to interpret as decimals.

For example, students are asked to think of $\frac{1}{3}$ as a decimal.

In general, you use the division meaning of fraction to make this make sense.

Since $\frac{1}{3} = 1 \div 3$, students use either a calculator or a pencil-and-paper algorithm to see that $\frac{1}{3} = 0.3333...$. Students observe that, unlike other decimals they had met before, this decimal **repeats**, and does not **terminate**. Students will accept this because the calculator shows it, but they can use logical reasoning to make sense of this as well.

Imagine trying to divide 1 whole so that 3 people can share it.

Each person cannot get a whole, so rename the whole as 10 tenths.

Now each person gets 3 tenths, but there is 1 tenth left over that cannot be shared.

So rename the 1 tenth as 10 hundredths.

Now each person gets 3 hundredths, but there is 1 hundredth left over that cannot be shared.

So rename the 1 hundredth as 10 thousandths ....

Students soon see that every time there will be one piece left over, so the process will never end. They also see that every time, each person sharing gets 3 of the new and smaller unit.

$\frac{1}{3} = 0.333...$ makes sense.

At this point, you usually introduce notation for a repeating decimal. For example, you can write 0.3333 as $0.\overline{3}$ or as $0.\dot{3}$.

In later grades, students learn how to convert a repeating decimal to a fraction.

ACTIVITY 10.6

Have students play a concentration game where they use a deck of turned-over cards, some with decimals and some with fractions. Their job is to make matches by turning over two cards. They keep the cards if they match. They turn them back over if they do not match.

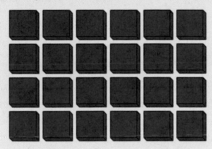

A card set might include $\frac{1}{10}, \frac{1}{5}, \frac{1}{4}, \frac{1}{2}, \frac{3}{4}, \frac{7}{10}, \frac{1}{100}, \frac{1}{50}, \frac{1}{25}, \frac{3}{5}, \frac{4}{5}, \frac{9}{10}$.

And 0.1, 0.2, 0.25, 0.5, 0.75, 0.7, 0.01, 0.02, 0.04, 0.6, 0.8, 0.9.

Rounding and Estimating Decimals

Students should be able to round decimals to simpler decimals, such as 2.567 to 2.6 or 2.567 to 3. The conventions, or rules, for rounding are just like the ones for whole numbers. For example:

Rounding Decimals

Decimal	Nearest Thousandth	Nearest Hundredth	Nearest Tenth	Nearest Whole
2.9375	2.938	2.94	2.9	3
6.0693	6.069	6.07	6.1	6

You might round decimals when you are describing measurements with different units. For example, suppose a wall is 2.367 m long. The length can be estimated as 2.37 m (2 m and 37 cm) or 2.4 m (2 m and 4 dm) or as 2 m. These would be meaningful examples of rounding to the nearest hundredth, tenth, and whole, respectively.

Student Response

This student has rounded to "convenient" numbers that are easy to calculate with mentally.

Round each number to estimate.

32.46 − 17.48 is about __30.50__ − __20.50__ = __1600__

Students should also have the opportunity to estimate decimals using simple fractions; for example, 3.24 is about $3\frac{1}{4}$, and 2.17 is almost $2\frac{1}{5}$. To do this type of estimating, the common fraction–decimal equivalents below come in handy. Students can "round" the decimal to the nearest common fraction–decimal equivalent; for example, 5.81 is about 5.75, or $5\frac{3}{4}$.

Some Common Fraction–Decimal Equivalents

$\frac{1}{5}$	$\frac{1}{4}$	$\frac{2}{5}$	$\frac{1}{2}$	$\frac{3}{5}$	$\frac{3}{4}$	$\frac{4}{5}$
0.2	0.25	0.4	0.5	0.6	0.75	0.8

Reading and Writing Decimals

Reading Decimals

Students should read a decimal like 3.2 as "3 and 2 tenths," not as "3 point 2" or "3 decimal 2." Reading a decimal like 7.23 as "7 and 23 hundredths" reveals the important connection between fractions and decimals, but the language "seven point two three" does not.

However, you rarely read decimals with more than 3 digits after the decimal place in this meaningful way, although you could. For example, a decimal number like 0.4578 could be read as "four thousand five hundred seventy-eight ten thousandths," but is more likely to be read as "point four five seven eight." Once students are working comfortably with decimals of this many digits, the value of reading the decimal as a fraction is no longer as great.

Note that the decimal point is represented by the word "and." That is why it is recommended that students be taught to read whole numbers without using "and"; for example, it might be preferable to read 547 as "five hundred forty-seven" rather than "five hundred *and* forty-seven," although using "and" in this case is not incorrect. As well, teachers and students should also be careful to read the digit 0 as "zero," not "oh," in order to emphasize its mathematical "value."

Writing Decimals

Decimals can be greater than 1 or less than 1. For this reason, encourage students to record decimals less than 1 using a zero in the ones place, for example, 0.2, rather than just .2. This reinforces that the decimal is less than 1 and eliminates the confusion when decimal points are written indistinctly. Note that, for assessment purposes, writing 0.2 as .2 is not incorrect unless the purpose of the assessment is to determine if the student can apply the convention of recording a 0 in the ones place. Numbers such as 3 can be written as 3 or as 3.0, depending on the context and level of precision required.

Comparing Decimals

Strategies for comparing decimals relate more closely to strategies for comparing whole numbers than to strategies for comparing fractions. This is, in fact, one of the reasons that a decimal system is used—to make comparison easy. The trick, as with whole numbers, is to ensure that values in the same places are being compared. In the examples below, each decimal pair is compared two different ways.

0.78 > 0.39 since 7 tenths > 3 tenths	43.8 > 8.27 since 4 tens > 0 tens
0.78 > 0.39 since 78 hundredths > 39 hundredths	43.8 > 8.27 since 43 ones > 8 ones

Note that with whole numbers, you can rely on the number of digits to provide a sense of the relative size of numbers—a 3-digit whole number is always greater than a 2-digit whole number. This is not the case with decimals. When comparing decimals, the number of digits is irrelevant; it is the place value of the digits that matters. For example:

> 0.021 < 0.2 because 0 tenths < 2 tenths
> 0.021 > 0.01 because 2 hundredths > 1 hundredth

Many students find it easier to compare decimals if the number of digits is the same. This is always possible using equivalent decimals. For example:

> 0.34 > 0.3 because 0.34 > 0.30 (34 hundredths > 30 hundredths)
> 8.302 < 8.32 because 8.302 < 8.320 (302 thousandths < 320 thousandths)

ACTIVITY 10.7

Students can represent decimal tenths using base ten blocks. If the flat is worth 1, they might observe that 2.3 can be represented with fewer base ten blocks than 1.8, even though it has a greater value.

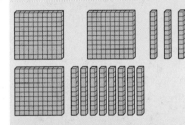

Ask students to build as many decimals as they can that are less than 2.3 but require more than 5 base ten models to represent them.

Creating In-between Decimals

Sometimes, students need to determine a decimal value between two other values. This is always possible with decimals, as it is with fractions (see Principle 6 on page 206). For example:

BETWEEN 3.2 AND 3.6	BETWEEN 3.2 AND 3.3	BETWEEN 3.2 AND 3.21
To create decimals between 3.2 and 3.6 is simple because there are decimal tenths in between:	To create decimals between 3.2 and 3.3 requires looking to the hundredths:	To create decimals between 3.2 (3.20) and 3.21 requires looking to the thousandths:
3.2, 3.3, 3.4, 3.5, 3.6	3.2, 3.21, 3.22, 3.23, ..., 3.29, 3.3	3.2, 3.201, 3.202, ..., 3.209, 3.21

Decimal Operations

As students learn to add, subtract, multiply, and divide with decimals, they should be using what they learned about whole numbers.

- Each principle related to whole number operations continues to apply (see page 108 for *Addition and Subtraction Principles,* and page 123 for *Multiplication and Division Principles*).
- Each algorithm students learned for whole numbers continues to apply (see page 162 for *Algorithms for Addition and Subtraction,* and page 178 for *Algorithms for Multiplication and Division*). There are virtually no changes to the explanations for the algorithms when dealing with addition and subtraction of decimals rather than whole numbers. The changes required to deal with multiplication and division with decimals relate more to the subtleties of how things are said than to changes in how the procedures are carried out.
- What students learned about estimating whole numbers also applies to decimals (see page 160 for *Estimating Sums and Differences,* and page 176 for *Estimating Products and Quotients*).

Adding and Subtracting

Just as with whole numbers, students have a choice of algorithms for adding and subtracting decimals. Many of the following algorithms translate well into mental algorithms, depending on the numbers involved.

The Traditional Algorithm for Addition

This algorithm follows the same steps as it does for whole numbers (see Algorithm 1 for Addition on page 163). Step 1 of the procedure has been modelled below to show how the algorithm could be modelled for decimals.

Step 1 Model both numbers with blocks, on a decimal place value mat, if available.

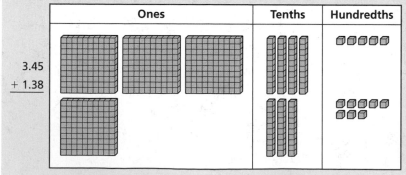

3.45
+ 1.38

Note how the values of the blocks have changed with respect to what they represent:

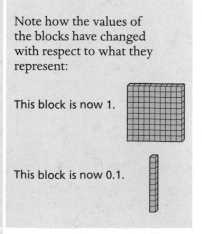

This block is now 1.

This block is now 0.1.

Steps 2 to 4 See Algorithm 1 for Addition on page 163.

ACTIVITY 10.8

Provide decks of cards to students with each of the numbers 0.1, 0.2, ..., 0.9 on a card.

Ask students to choose three cards to add to various values, for example, 1.2.

The Traditional Algorithm for Subtraction

As with addition, this subtraction algorithm follows the same steps as it does for whole numbers (see Algorithm 1 for Subtraction on page 167). Step 1 of the procedure has been modelled on page 237 to show how the algorithm could be modelled for decimals using base ten blocks.

Step 1 Model the minuend, on a decimal place value mat, if available.

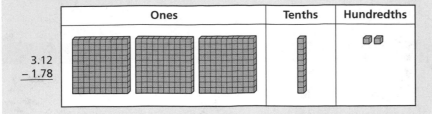

	Ones	Tenths	Hundredths
3.12 − 1.78			

Steps 2 to 4 See Algorithm 1 for Subtraction on page 167.

Alternative Algorithms

All of the other algorithms available to students for adding and subtracting whole numbers can be applied to those operations with decimals. Here are a few examples.

"Making Change" to Subtract Students can add on to subtract (see Algorithm 5 for Subtraction on page 169). For example:

Step 1 Think of the subtraction as a missing addend number sentence:
$50 − 22.8 = \blacksquare$, so $22.8 + \blacksquare = 50$

Step 2 Count up:
a) Add 0.2 to get to the next whole number: $22.8 + 0.2 = 23$
b) Add 7 to get to a multiple of 10: $23 + 7 = 30$
c) Add 20 to get to the minuend, or total: $30 + 20 = 50$
d) Add up the "change": $0.2 \quad + 7 \quad + 20 = 27.2$

Adding Too Much and Then Subtracting to Compensate Students can also use the compensating algorithms that they use for whole numbers (see Algorithm 3 for Addition on page 166). For example:

$4.25 + 3.97 \rightarrow 4.25 + (3.97 + 0.03)$ (Add 0.03 too many.)
$= 4.25 + 4$
$= 8.25 \rightarrow 8.25 − 0.03$ (Take away the extra 0.03.)
$= 8.22$

Describe the steps you would follow to add $4.87 + 3.154$.

I would round 4.87 to 5 and add that to 3.154. Then take away 0.13 that I added on and get 8.024.

Student Response

This student is adding too much and then subtracting to compensate.

ACTIVITY 10.9

Encourage a huff-and-puff contest where two students blow a cotton ball across a table and measure how much farther, in hundredths of a metre, one cotton ball went than another.

ACTIVITY 10.10

Encourage students to bring in grocery receipts. They can sort the items into categories of their choosing and figure out how much was spent in the various categories.

ACTIVITY 10.11

Encourage students to compare sports statistics, for example, batting averages for baseball players, using adding and subtracting.

Adding or Subtracting in Parts Students can also add and subtract in parts (see Algorithm 5 for Addition on page 166 and Algorithm 3 for Subtraction on page 169), for example:

ADDING IN PARTS

$5.68 + 3.2$

Start with 5.68 and add 3.2 in parts:
First add 3: $5.68 + 3 = 8.68$
Then add 0.2: $8.68 + 0.2 = 8.88$

SUBTRACTING IN PARTS

$8.46 - 3.7$

Start with 8.46 and subtract 3.7 in parts:
First subtract 3: $8.46 - 3 = 5.46$
Then subtract 0.4: $5.46 - 0.4 = 5.06$
Then subtract 0.3: $5.06 - 0.3 = 4.76$

Often students are taught that to add and subtract decimals, the critical thing to remember is to line up the decimal points. Notice that this is not an issue with many of the alternative algorithms.

Multiplying and Dividing Decimals

Multiplying by Powers of 10

Before students begin multiplying with decimals, it is useful to look at patterns with respect to the effect of multiplying whole numbers by 0.1 and 0.01, and decimals by 10, 100, and 1000.

Multiplying Whole Numbers by Decimal Powers of 10

MULTIPLYING 400 BY 0.1 AND 0.01

$100 \times 400 = 40\,000$
$10 \times 400 = 4000$ (One factor is $\frac{1}{10}$ as much, so the product is $\frac{1}{10}$ as much.)
$1 \times 400 = 400$ (One factor is $\frac{1}{10}$ as much, so the product is $\frac{1}{10}$ as much again.)
$0.1 \times 400 = 40$ (One factor is $\frac{1}{10}$ as much, so the product is $\frac{1}{10}$ as much again.)
$0.01 \times 400 = 4$ (One factor is $\frac{1}{10}$ as much, so the product is $\frac{1}{10}$ as much again.)

Multiplying Decimals by Whole Number Powers of 10

MULTIPLYING 2.5 BY 10, 100, OR 1000

$1 \times 2.5 = 2.5$ (One factor is 10 times as much, so the product is 10 times as much.)
$10 \times 2.5 = 25$ (One factor is 10 times as much, so the product is 10 times as much again.)
$100 \times 2.5 = 250$ (One factor is 10 times as much, so the product is 10 times as much again.)
$1000 \times 2.5 = 2500$ (One factor is 10 times as much, so the product is 10 times as much again.)

Moving Digits, Not the Decimal Note that multiplying or dividing by powers of 10 does not change the digits of a number, only the position of each digit within the number. If, for example, you begin with 3.4, dividing by 10 or multiplying by 0.1 decreases the value of each part of the number by a factor of 10, and so the digits in the product change value and move over one place to the right. 3 ones are now 3 tenths; 4 tenths are now 4 hundredths. It is actually the digits that move, not the decimal point.

Alternative Multiplication Algorithms

Many of the multiplication and division algorithms for whole numbers can also be applied to decimals, often with the same models. Many of the following algorithms translate well into mental algorithms, depending on the numbers involved.

Modelling Multiplication of Decimals This algorithm follows the same steps as it does for whole numbers (see Algorithm 2 for Multiplication on page 179). As with whole number multiplication, this algorithm, too, can be modelled using the area model and base ten blocks.

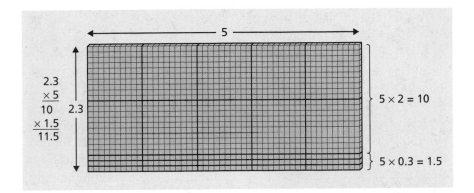

"Ignoring" the Decimal Often students pretend that the decimal is not there while calculating, and then compensate at the end. This is appropriate since the digits do not change; only their placement within the number changes. The algorithm shown below could be performed mentally, depending on the numbers involved.

"IGNORE" THE DECIMAL (× 10)	COMPENSATE (÷ 10)	ESTIMATE TO CHECK
$5 \times 2.3 \to 5 \times 23 = 5 \times 20 + 5 \times 3$ $= 100 + 15$ $= 115 \longrightarrow$	$115 \div 10 = 11.5$	5×2.3 is a bit more than $5 \times 2 = 10$. 11.5 is a bit more than 10.

To multiply 8×0.25, Jeff thought of it as 8 fourths. How might that help him multiply?

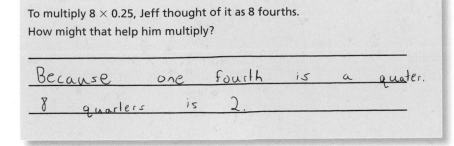

Because one fourth is a quater.
8 quarters is 2.

Student Response

This student uses her or his understanding of fractions and money to multiply decimals.

When multiplying two decimals rather than a decimal and a whole number, students use the same approaches as above, but must interpret what the factors mean. For example, 0.2×0.4 means two-tenths of four-tenths. Since 0.1×0.4 is $\frac{1}{10}$ of $\frac{4}{10}$, or $\frac{4}{100}$, then 0.2×0.4 must be twice as much, or 0.08.

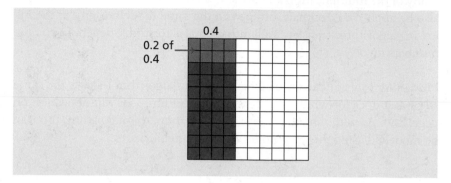

ACTIVITY 10.12

Students can solve problems of the form $13.25 \div 0.25$ by thinking about how many quarters are in $13.25. Pose a variety of questions like this involving dividing by 0.10 (to count dimes), 0.05 (to count nickels), or 0.25 (to count quarters).

ACTIVITY 10.13

Students can calculate the averages (means) of a variety of measurements that are in decimal form. For example, to figure out how far they can jump, they might jump 5 times, measure in decimal amounts of metres, and calculate their average.

ACTIVITY 10.14

Students might use decimal calculations to try to determine how much C$1 is worth in U.S. dollars if the Canadian dollar is worth US$0.98. Use the most current exchange rate, if possible.

Alternative Division Algorithms

As with multiplication, many of the whole number division algorithms can also be applied to decimals, often with the same models. Many of the following algorithms also translate well into mental algorithms.

Written Division Algorithms The algorithms shown below follow the same steps as they do for whole numbers (see Algorithms 1 and 2 for division on pages 182–184). Because some students experience difficulty in lining up the partial quotients correctly using the algorithm on the right, many teachers prefer the one on the left when dealing with decimals.

$$
\begin{array}{r}
2.6 \\
6\overline{)15.6} \\
-12.0 \\
\hline
3.6 \\
-3.6 \\
\hline
0
\end{array}
\qquad
\begin{array}{r|l}
6\overline{)15.6} & \\
-12.0 & 2.0 \\
\hline
3.6 & \\
-3.6 & 0.6 \\
\hline
0 & \\
\hline
& 2.6
\end{array}
$$

Mental Math Algorithms for Decimals

There are many division algorithms that lend themselves to mental math. For example:

USING PLACE VALUE CONCEPTS	USING A DIVISION PRINCIPLE
Renaming each decimal:	Multiplying both numbers by the same amount:
$3.0 \div 0.6 = 30$ tenths $\div$ 6 tenths	$3.0 \div 0.6 = (3.0 \times 10) \div (0.6 \times 10)$
$\quad = 5$	$\quad = 30 \div 6$
$3.2 \div 0.08 = 32$ tenths $\div$ 8 hundredths	$\quad = 5$
$\quad = 320$ hundredths $\div$ 8 hundredths	$3.2 \div 0.08 = (3.2 \times 100) \div (0.08 \times 100)$
$\quad = 40$	$\quad = 320 \div 8$
	$\quad = 40$

Common Errors and Misconceptions

Decimals: Strategies for Dealing with Common Errors and Misconceptions

COMMON ERROR OR MISCONCEPTION	SUGGESTED STRATEGY
Models for Whole Numbers versus Decimals Students struggle with using the same models for whole numbers as for decimals. If the flat represents 100 with whole numbers, they have difficulty switching to a flat representing the whole, or 1, for decimals. 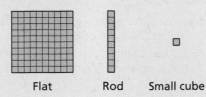 Flat Rod Small cube Whole numbers: The flat is 100, the rod is 10, and the small cube is 1. The large cube is not used. Decimals: If the flat is 1, the rod is 0.1, and the small cube is 0.01.	Ensure that students do not refer to the flat as 100 but as 1 whole. Relate the flat to everyday items such as one whole cake. In this case, the rod becomes a slice that is one tenth of the cake, and the small cube becomes a piece that is one tenth of the slice and one hundredth of the whole cake. If possible, try to use a set of blocks of a different colour to differentiate decimal blocks from whole number blocks. If students struggle with this model for decimals, they might feel more comfortable working with hundredths grids instead.
Switching the Model for 1 Students struggle with switching from using a flat to represent 1 to using a large cube to represent 1. This switch is often done when students begin working with thousandths, for which they need a model that has different blocks for 1, 0.1, 0.01, and 0.001. 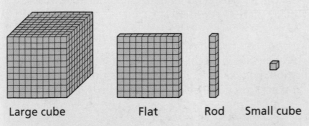 Large cube Flat Rod Small cube For thousandths: If the large cube is 1, the flat is 0.1, the rod is 0.01, and the small cube is 0.001. For hundredths: The flat is 1, the rod is 0.1, and the small cube is 0.01. The large cube is not used.	It is helpful to use real-life analogies, for example, by thinking of the large cube as a big piece of cheese, the flat as a wide slice, the rod as a thin slice, and the small cube as a bite or piece. However, if students are struggling, it may be preferable to switch to a different model, such as thousandths grids.
Counting in Tenths Students have difficulty counting in tenths as they bridge whole numbers; for example, instead of 0.8, 0.9, 1.0, 1.1, 1.2, many students write 0.8, 0.9, 0.10, 0.11, 0.12 and read them incorrectly as 8 tenths, 9 tenths, 10 tenths, 11 tenths, and 12 tenths.	If students read 0.10 as 10 tenths, present them with a 10-by-10 grid, and ask them to show you 10 hundredths and to write the decimal. Have them look at the decimal that they read as 10 tenths to see and hear the contradiction.
Reading Decimals Students do not recognize the difference between decimals like 3.04 and 3.004.	If students are encouraged to read decimals meaningfully, this is less likely to occur: 3.04 would be read as "3 and 4 hundredths." 3.004 would be read as "3 and 4 thousandths." *(continued)*

COMMON ERROR OR MISCONCEPTION	SUGGESTED STRATEGY
Interpreting Decimal Digits Students think that decimal numbers with a greater number of digits or with digits that are greater are "bigger" than they really are. For example, when comparing 0.8211 and 23, a student might think that 0.8211 is greater because of the digit 8 or because it has more digits.	Place value language and estimation is helpful here. The focus for students should be on thinking of 0.8211 as about 8 tenths (not even 1 whole) and 23 as more than 2 tens, or 20 wholes. Another strategy is to allow students to record zeros to align the numbers along the decimal: <div align="center">00.8211 23.0000</div>
Understanding and Comparing Decimals Students do not see the difference between 3.05 and 3.50. This is natural, particularly if they had been told that you can "add zeros after the decimal point" without changing the answer.	Students can use place value language and expanded notation to understand and compare the numbers: 3.05 is 3 ones, and 0 tenths, 5 hundredths. 3.50 is 3 ones, and 5 tenths, 0 hundredths.
Aligning Digits Students forget to line up the decimals when adding and subtracting. Consequently, the answer does not make sense; for example: <div align="center">4.2 +15 —— 5.7</div>	Students should be given exercises in horizontal form, for example, 1.5 + 1.85 + 1.787, so they can practise aligning digits when calculating. As well, estimating is particularly important in this situation to help determine the reasonableness of an answer. For example, if a student adds 4.2 + 15 as shown to the left, an estimate of 15 + 4 = 19 should indicate an error.
Renaming Decimals Students do not know how to handle a question like 3.4 × 100 since there are not enough digits in 3.4 to easily move the digits over 2 places, as is necessary when multiplying by 100.	Students who have lots of experience renaming decimals, for example, 3.4, 3.40, and 3.400, will know that 3.4 can be written as an equivalent decimal with as many places as desired.
Interpreting Division Students use place value to calculate, but they interpret division incorrectly. For example: <div align="center">30 tenths ÷ 6 tenths = 5 tenths</div> instead of <div align="center">30 tenths ÷ 6 tenths = 5</div>	A comparison might be made to a more familiar situation. For example, if you ask how many groups of 2 trucks are in 4 trucks, the answer is 2, not 2 trucks. <div align="center">4 trucks ÷ 2 trucks = 2</div>

Appropriate Manipulatives

Decimals: Examples of Manipulatives

10-FRAMES

10-frames can be used to show decimal tenths, both less than 1 and greater than 1, as shown below.

1.2 is 12 tenths.

DECIMAL SQUARES

Decimal squares are a commercial product that models specific decimals. Students can easily compare decimals using these models. They are sometimes available so that tenths, hundredths, and thousandths are different colours. In this case:

- The yellow ones show thousandths and go up by 0.125: 0.125, 0.250, 0.375, ..., 1.000.
- The green ones show hundredths and go up by 0.05: 0.05, 0.10, 0.15, ..., 0.95, 1.00.
- The red cards show tenths: 0.1, 0.2, ..., 0.9, and 1.0.

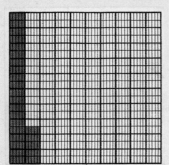  

BASE TEN BLOCKS

Base ten blocks can be used to model decimals.

If it is necessary to model thousandths, the large cube can be treated as the whole. If it is only necessary to model hundredths, the flat can be treated as the whole. (See *Common Errors and Misconceptions* on page 241.)

DECIMAL GRIDS

Decimal grids divided into one hundred squares can be used to model decimal hundredths and show equivalent decimals and fractions. Decimal grids can also be used for tenths and thousandths.

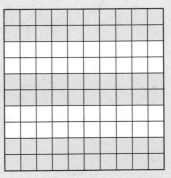

White: 0.40, 0.4, $\frac{40}{100}$, $\frac{4}{10}$, $\frac{2}{5}$

Yellow: 0.60, 0.6, $\frac{60}{100}$, $\frac{6}{10}$, $\frac{3}{5}$

NUMBER LINES

Number lines are useful for comparing and relating numbers. Students can relate decimals to benchmark numbers such as 0, 0.5, 1.5, and 2.0:

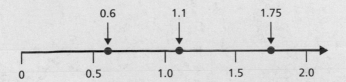

(continued)

MONEY

Coins can be used to model decimals. A loonie could represent 1, a dime for 0.1, and a penny for 0.01.

| 1 | 0.1 | 0.01 |

MEASUREMENT MODEL

Metre sticks and base ten blocks can be used to model decimals:

- The metre could be the whole, or 1, and is modelled with a metre stick.
- The decimetre would be a tenth (represented by a rod, which is 1 dm long).
- The centimetre would be a hundredth (represented by a small cube, which is 1 cm long).

1.11 m
1 m, 1 dm, 1 cm

PLACE VALUE MATS

Place value mats, which up until now have been used for whole numbers, can be extended to include decimals to the thousandths place. Both money and base ten blocks can be modelled on the mat.

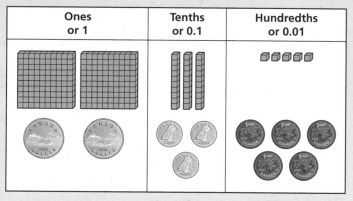

| Ones or 1 | Tenths or 0.1 | Hundredths or 0.01 |

2.35

Hundredth Circles Circles divided into 10 sections but with small tick marks dividing each tenth into 10 are useful to model both tenths and hundredths.

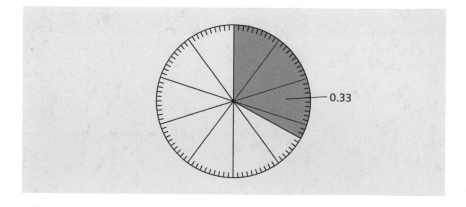

0.33

Finish colouring the grid so that seventeen hundredths of the grid is shaded altogether.

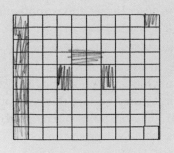

Student Response

This student has used a decimal hundredths grid model to show that he or she understands that a decimal does not have to be modelled as adjacent parts.

Appropriate Technology

Calculators

Calculators are an essential tool when exploring the relationship between decimals and fractions. Students will divide the numerator by the denominator to determine the decimal representation for the fraction. They can also use calculators to explore decimal patterns such as multiplying and dividing by powers of 10 (see page 173). Calculators are also useful for decimal computations involving complicated numbers, multiple calculations, and problem solving.

Computers

Software programs such as the *Mathville Series* are good for decimal practice.

Assessing Student Understanding

- Make sure to assess student's conceptual understanding of decimals and not just their ability to perform algorithms. For example, a student might know that you can calculate 1.3×1.4 by multiplying 13 by 14 and placing the decimal point so that the answer is about 2, but not know why this is appropriate.
- Avoid questions like 3.25 = ___ ones + ___ tenths + ___ hundredths. Even students who do not understand place value are likely to put the number 3, 2, and 5, respectively, in the correct spaces.
- Make sure that students understand the effect of multiplying and dividing by decimals. For example, you might ask which of these is true:

  ▪ $\times$ 0.4 is less than ▪
  ▪ $\div$ 0.4 is less than ▪
  ▪ $\times$ 1.4 is less than ▪
  ▪ $\div$ 1.4 is less than ▪

Appropriate Children's Books

10 for Dinner (Bogart, 1989).
This humourous book about a very interesting group of 10 children provides an excellent context for dealing with decimal tenths. The decimals could describe subgroups of the 10 children.

WebConnect W W W

www.makingmathmeaningful.nelson.com

Visit the Making Math Meaningful website for links to sites involving decimals.

The Father Who Had Ten Children (Guettier, 1999).
As with *10 for Dinner*, this is another book that focuses on a group of 10 children. These children can form the basis for problems related to tenths.

If the World Were a Village: A Book about the World's People
(Smith, Armstong, 2002).
Students have an opportunity to use decimal hundredths in a meaningful context as they explore this book that describes the demographics of our world. They can follow up on a variety of websites that explore similar activities where village sizes of both 100 and 1000 are used.

Applying What You've Learned

1. What was your solution to the chapter problem? What would a student need to understand about decimals to solve this problem?

2. What ideas about fractions do you think students should understand before you introduce decimals? Why?

3. We often introduce decimal tenths before decimal hundredths. Some people believe that we should start with hundredths first since students are familiar with prices. What would your position be? Why?

4. Some people believe that it confuses students to use base ten blocks as decimal representations when they had previously been used for whole numbers. How would you argue that they are still an important manipulative for understanding and carrying out decimal operations?

5. How would you first introduce multiplication by a decimal less than 1?

6. Describe a task involving the representation of decimal thousandths that you think would be both engaging and instructive to introduce that topic. After describing the task, describe its strengths.

7. Some teachers believe that the best way to approach a question like $4 - 1.23$ is to have students set it up as $4.00 - 1.23$, and then regroup using the traditional algorithm. Argue why it might be a good idea, and also argue why it might not.

Interact with a K–8 Student:

8. Many counting books for young children that focus on the numbers from 1 to 10 can provide a context for working with decimal tenths. Choose such a book and create some problems that a child who has been introduced to decimals might grapple with. What do you observe about that child's understanding of decimals?

Discuss with a K–8 Teacher:

9. Ask a teacher of Grades 3 to 8 students what sorts of problems her or his students experience with decimals. Ask the teacher to talk about how these problems might be avoided.

Selected References

Baturo, A., and Cooper, J. (1997). Reunitising hundredths: Prototypic and non-prototypic representations. In Pehkonen, E. (Ed.). *Proceedings of the 21st Conference of the International Group for the Psychology of Mathematics Education,* Lahti, Finland: PME, 2-57–2-64.

Behr, M., Harel, G., Post, T., and Lesh, R. (1992). Rational number, ratio and proportion. In Grouws, D. (Ed.).

Handbook of Research on Mathematics Teaching and Learning. New York: MacMillan, 296–333.

Bogart, J.E. (1989). *10 for Dinner.* Richmond Hill, Ontario: North Winds Press.

Brown, M. (1981). Place value and decimals. In Hart, K. (Ed.). *Children's Understanding of Mathematics, 11–16.* London: John Murray, 48–65.

Carpenter, T., Corbitt, M., Kepner, H., Lindquist, M., and Reys, R. (1981). Decimals: Results and implications from national assessment. *Arithmetic Teacher, 28,* 34–37.

Causley, C. (1986). High on the wall. In *Early in the morning.* London: Puffin.

Glasgow, R., Ragan, G., Fields, W.M. (2000). The decimal dilemma. *Teaching Children Mathematics, 7,* 89–93.

Grossman, A.S. (1983). Decimal notation: An important research finding. *Arithmetic Teacher, 30,* 32–33.

Guettier, B. (1999). *The Father Who Had Ten Children.* East Rutherford, NJ: Dial/Penguin.

Hiebert, J., Wearne, D., and Taber, S. (1991). Fourth graders' gradual construction of decimal fractions during instruction using different physical representations. *The Elementary School Journal, 91,* 321–341.

Irwin, K.C. (2001). Using everyday knowledge of decimals to enhance understanding. *Journal for Research in Mathematics Education, 32,* 399–420.

Martinie, S.L., and Bay-William, J.M. (2003). Investigating students' conceptual understanding of decimal frac-tions using multiple representations. *Mathematics Teaching in the Middle School,* 8, 244–247.

Nesher, P., and Peled, I. (1986). Shifts in reasoning: The case of extending number concepts. *Educational Studies in Mathematics, 17,* 67–79.

Oppenheimer, L., and Hunting, O. (1999). Relating fractions and decimals: Listening to students talk. *Mathematics Teaching in the Middle School,* 4, 318–321.

Resnick, L.B., Nesher, P., Leonard, F., Magone, M., Omanson, S., and Peled, I. (1989). Conceptual bases of arithmetic errors: The case of decimal fractions. *Journal for Research in Mathematics Education, 20,* 8–27.

Small, M. (2005). *PRIME: Number and operations: Background and strategies.* Toronto: Thomson Nelson.

Smith, D.J., and Armstrong, S. (2002). *If the World Were a Village: A Book about the World's People.* Toronto: Kids Can Press.

Thompson, P. (1992). Notations, conventions, and constraints: Contributions to effective uses of concrete materials in elementary mathematics. *Journal for Research in Mathematics Education, 23,* 123–147.

Chapter 11
Ratio, Rate, and Percent

IN A NUTSHELL

The main ideas in this chapter are listed below:

1. Proportional thinking involves the use of a rate, ratio, or percent to solve a problem. The relationships are multiplicative ones.

2. Ratios, rates, and percents, just like fractions and decimals, are comparisons of quantities. A rate compares quantities with different units, for example, distance to time, or price to number of items. A percent always compares a quantity to 100.

CHAPTER PROBLEM

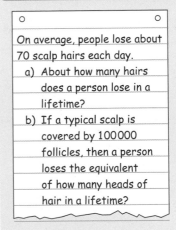

On average, people lose about 70 scalp hairs each day.
a) About how many hairs does a person lose in a lifetime?
b) If a typical scalp is covered by 100000 follicles, then a person loses the equivalent of how many heads of hair in a lifetime?

Proportional Thinking

Proportional reasoning focuses on how two amounts are related multiplicatively. For example, thinking of 6 as two 3s instead of as 4 + 2 contrasts multiplicative thinking to additive thinking. Developing proportional reasoning is one of the goals of Grades 4 to 8 mathematics instruction. It is only when students can deal with multiplicative relationships that fractions, decimals, ratios, rates, and percents make sense. Proportional reasoning is also essential for students to have a full understanding of other concepts such as measurement with units, the concept of scale (e.g., on maps), geometric notions of similarity, and division. Post, Behr, and Lesh (1988) also point out that proportional reasoning involves qualitative thinking. For example, a student who recognizes that a person who runs 7 km/min finishes a 10-km run faster than one who runs 8-km/min is thinking proportionally.

Proportional reasoning is an obstacle many young learners have difficulty overcoming (Lesh, Post, and Behr, 1988). This is reasonable; students have to look at a relationship between numbers instead of looking at one number in isolation. The difficulties students have has been of interest to researchers. The Rational Number Project, a long-standing project in the United States, has been devoted to fostering and reporting this research. Research reports as far back as 1979 and as recently as 2003 are covered on its website. Another important site for research on proportional reasoning has been the University of Alberta, under the leadership of Tom Kieren.

This chapter focuses on a subset of the topic of proportional reasoning: concepts of rate, ratio, and percent.

Ratio

A ratio is a comparison between two numbers. For example, 3:4 is the ratio of blue to red circles. It can be read *three to four* and denotes that for every three blue counters there will be four red counters. The 3 is called the first term of the ratio and the 4 the second term. Notice that a colon is used between the numbers to represent the ratio.

Unless the comparison referred to can be presumed to continue, a ratio should not be used. For example, if, in a pile of counters, there are always four blue counters for every three red ones, a ratio is appropriate. If the number of blues per red is more random, then it does not make sense to use a ratio.

Whenever a situation can be described by one ratio, it can be described by several ratios. For example, the picture on page 251 shows that for every three boys, there are two girls. All of these ratios describe the situation:

- 3:2 describes boys:girls.
- 3:5 describes boys:runners.
- 2:5 describes girls:runners.
- 2:3 describes girls:boys.
- 5:3 describes runners:boys.
- 5:2 describes runners:girls.

The two ratios in the first line are called part-to-part ratios. These ratios compare two parts of something. The two ratios 3:5 and 2:5 are called

part-to-whole ratios. They compare one part of something to the whole thing—in this case the whole group of runners.

Any ratio can also be described as a fraction, for example, 3:5 as $\frac{3}{5}$.

If the second term in the ratio describes the whole, the fraction tells what fraction of the whole group the part represents. But even expressing the ratio 3:2 as the fraction $\frac{3}{2}$ is meaningful. It says that there are $\frac{3}{2}$ as many boys as girls.

Although ratios are often not formally introduced until Grade 6, they are actually considered much earlier, in informal ways. For example, to teach a student about number in Kindergarten, you often describe 2 by saying that there are 2 eyes for every person; this is a ratio. When multiplication is introduced in Grade 2 or 3, ratio is implicit. For example, if you ask students how many wheels are on 5 bicycles, they are using the ratio of 2:1 to solve that problem.

Equivalent Ratios

Two ratios are equivalent if they represent the same relationship. For example, 3:4 and 6:8 represent the same relationship since if there are 4 red counters for every 3 blue ones, there would have to be 8 red ones for every 6 blue ones.

Calculating equivalent ratios is handled in the same ways as calculating equivalent fractions. To help students make sense of those equivalents, you can use ratio tables. The tables can be either vertical or horizontal. For example, to clarify the ratio 2:3, think about 2 red counters for each 3 blue ones.

If there are ... red ones	there are ... blue ones
2	3
4	6
6	9
8	12
10	15

Students initially focus on the fact that the values in each column change by adding, but eventually realize that the relationship is really a multiplicative one. Each row is a multiple of every other row.

Students can also use graphs to represent ratios. For example, the graph below represents the ratio 1:3, comparing the number of cans of juice concentrate to cans of water to make orange juice from frozen concentrate.

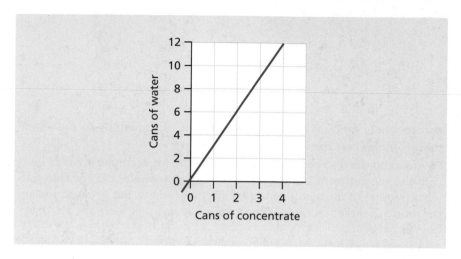

The graph can be used to write other equivalent ratios. Each ordered pair representing a point on the line describes terms of a ratio equivalent to 1:3.

Students can use ratio tables or graphs to solve simple problems. For example, suppose the ratio of red counters to blue ones is 3:5. You can use ratio tables to calculate the number of red counters if there are 45 blue ones.

A Table Built on Doubles

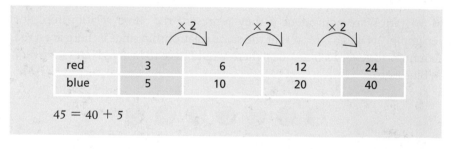

$45 = 40 + 5$

There are (24 + 3) 27 reds if there are 45 blues.

A Table Built on Equivalent Ratios That Are Not Necessarily Doubles

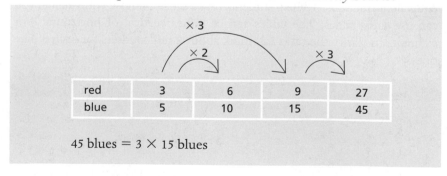

45 blues = 3 × 15 blues

so the number of reds = 3 × 9
= 27 reds

You can also look for the y-coordinate on a graph of $y = \frac{3}{5}x$, where x represents the number of blue counters and the corresponding y represents the corresponding number of red counters. This latter approach is more likely to be used at higher grade levels.

ACTIVITY 11.2

Students can use multiplication tables to look for equivalent ratios. For example, ratios equivalent to 3:4 (6:8, 9:12, etc.) are found by looking at numbers in the same column of the ×3 and ×4 rows of the table:

×	0	1	2	3	4	5	6
0	0	0	0	0	0	0	0
1	0	1	2	3	4	5	6
2	0	2	4	6	8	10	12
3	0	3	6	9	12	15	18
4	0	4	8	12	16	20	24
5	0	5	10	15	20	25	30
6	0	6	12	18	24	30	36

Relating Ratios

As with fractions, we often compare ratios with the same second term. For example, if the ratio of skiers to the population of a school is 189:410, and the ratio of snowboarders to the population of that school is 72:410, it would make sense to compare the two ratios.

Part-part ratios are often compared to the benchmark ratio 1:1 (which represents $\frac{1}{2}$). For example, the ratio of skiers above is less than the benchmark ratio 1:1.

Any ratios can be compared, treating the ratios as fractions. Whether the comparison is meaningful depends on the context.

Solving Ratio Problems

Ratios can be used to solve a variety of problems.

Some teachers begin using problems that do not involve numbers. The idea is for students to get a sense of what the situations actually mean. For example, a student is presented with two glasses of liquid. One is made using 1 part orange juice to 1 part water, and the other is 1 part orange juice to 2 parts water. Students are asked which will taste sweeter.

In a similar way, although the numbers are more evident, Kent, Arnosky, and McMonagle (2002) cite a problem where students are asked to identify which parking lot is "more full."

ACTIVITY 11.3

Recipes provide a relevant and meaningful context for students to explore ratio ideas. Provide students with recipes, indicating how many servings they are meant for, and have students adjust the recipes to serve more or fewer people. Initially, use multiples and factors of the intended number of servings, but later make the problems more complex, for example, revising a recipe for 6 to serve 8.

ACTIVITY 11.4

One of the most "famous" ratios is the number π, which is the ratio of the circumference to the diameter for any circle. Ask students to measure around a number of circular objects of different sizes and, in each case, to compare that measurement to the diameter of the object. Have them notice that, in each case, the result is the same value, slightly greater than 3.14. The ratio of diameter to circumference could be written 1: 3.14 or 1:π.

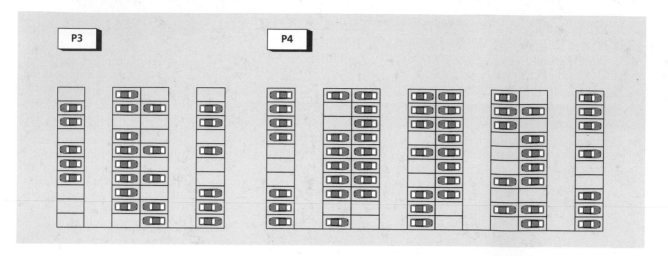

Students cannot just count cars since the lots are of different sizes; they must use proportional thinking.

Different Types of Ratio Problems

Different researchers catagorize ratio problems in different ways. For example, Lamon (1993) categorizes such problems into four types: "well-chunked measures," "part-part-whole," "associated sets," or "stretchers and shrinkers." Examples of each are listed below.

Well-Chunked Measures These types of problems involve the comparison of two or more measures that result in another meaningful measure.

Example 1: After 2, 5, and 7 hours of driving, distances travelled were 260 km, 650 km, and 890 km. Did the three drivers travel at the same rate?

Example 2: Casey spent $37.38 for 42 L of gasoline. At that rate, could she get another 40 L for less than $35?

Part-Part-Whole These types of problems involve the number of items in a subset of a larger group.

Example 1: Which shape is more blue?

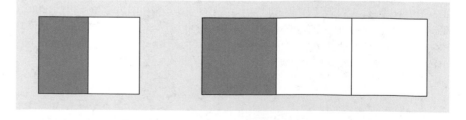

Example 2: A teacher divided her 25 students into 5 equal size groups. Each group had 3 girls in it. How many boys are in the class?

Associated Sets These types of problems involve creating a connection between two groups that might, initially, seem unconnected.

Example 1: 7 girls are sharing 3 vegetarian pizzas. 3 boys are sharing 1 pepperoni pizza. Who gets more pizza, a boy or a girl?

Example 2: Two children bought 3 balloons for $2. How much would it cost to buy enough balloons for their whole class of 28 students?

Stretchers and Shrinkers These problems involve growth, usually linear growth.

Example 1: Which tree has grown the most?

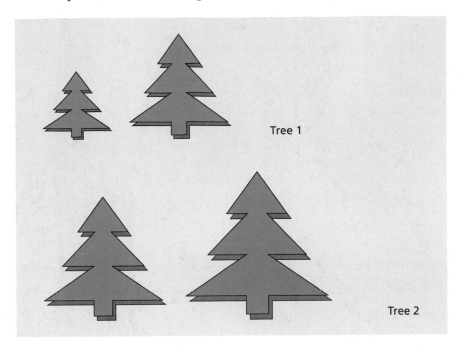

Example 2: Is an 8 × 10 enlargement of a 5 × 7 picture exactly the same as the original picture?

Other Ratio Problems

The problems below are provided to give you a fuller sense of the kinds of problems that Grades 6 to 8 students are likely to confront based on current Canadian curricula.

Problem 1 You know that the ratio of boys to girls in a Grade 5 class is 5:4. The problem is to determine how many students could be in the class.
   Solution: Because the ratio is 5:4 and it is a part-to-part ratio, that means for every 5 boys, there are 4 girls. Each group of 5 boys and 4 girls contains 9 people. That means the class has to consist of 9, 18, 27, 36, 45, ... people, that is, a multiple of 9. Based on common practice in Canada, the class probably has 18 or 27 students.

Problem 2 Suppose you learned that, on average, there are 105 males born in Canada for every 100 females. Officials in Calgary predicted about 15 000 births in 2007. About how many of these babies would be boys?
   Solution: The problem can be solved in a variety of ways.

Multiplying by an Appropriate Fraction or Decimal If there are 105 males for every 100 females, the fraction of babies that are male is $\frac{105}{205}$. You can multiply this fraction by 15 000 to estimate the number of boys.

$\frac{105}{205} \times 15\,000 = \frac{1\,575\,000}{205} = 7682.93$, so about 7683 are likely to be boys.

You could also have written $\frac{105}{205}$ as the decimal 0.5122 and multiplied to get the same result.

Setting Up a Proportion The ratio of boys to total births must be equivalent to $\frac{105}{205}$. You can set up an equation saying that the two ratios are equivalent; this is called a proportion:

$$\frac{x}{15\,000} = \frac{105}{205}$$

To solve it, you can multiply both sides of the equation by 15 000 and, again, you get a result of about 7683 boys.

Problem 3 Sometimes, a problem involves combining ratios. For example, suppose you know that in one class the ratio of boys to girls is 3:4, and in another it is 4:3. You are asked what the ratio of boys to girls is in the whole group.

If the groups are the same size, you can actually add first terms and second terms. For example, if both classes had 28 students, the ratio of boys to girls would be 7:7, which is the same as 1:1, in the total group. You can explain this visually:

Class 1		Class 2	
BBB	GGGG	BBBB	GGG
BBB	GGGG	BBBB	GGG
BBB	GGGG	BBBB	GGG
BBB	GGGG	BBBB	GGG

Combined, there are four groups of

BBB   GGGG   BBBB   GGG, which is the same as

BBBBBBB   GGGGGGG.

You can see that if the sizes of the classes were different, this would not be the case. For example, if there were an extra 7 students in Class 2, there would be a total of 32 boys and 31 girls. The ratio is no longer 1:1.

The fact that terms of ratios can be added actually creates difficulties for students since numerators and denominators of fractions cannot normally be added. Over-emphasis of the relationship between ratios and fractions can actually create learning difficulties.

Problem 4 Ratios are often used in geometric situations. In fact, shapes are similar only if the linear measures of one are proportional (in the same ratio) to the linear measures of the other. **Activities 11.5** and **11.6** provide examples of geometric problems based on ratio.

Rates

Some mathematicians define a rate as like a ratio, only with different units. For example, a rate could be $5.50/person to represent the cost of a movie, 6 for $5 to represent the cost of an item, or 12 oranges/litre to represent the number of oranges that have to be squeezed to make 1 L of orange juice. Other mathematicians do not make a distinction between rates and ratios. The notion is that although the units may be different, the mathematics used to talk about rates is identical to the mathematics used to talk about ratios.

ACTIVITY 11.5

Ask students to enlarge a picture of this dog so that it is twice as wide and twice as high.

ACTIVITY 11.6

Tell students that the ratio on a map of the world is marked as 1:50 000 000. Canada is about 11 cm wide on the map from its most easterly to most westerly point. Ask: How wide is Canada, really?

ACTIVITY 11.7

Encourage students to learn about the typical body ratios that artists use for drawing. For example, the ratio of head height to total height is usually 1:7. They might try to draw a body using those ratios.

Rates have two terms, just as ratios do. They represent comparisons, just as ratios do, and can and usually are written as fractions, as ratios can be. There are equivalent rates, for example, 6 for $5 is equivalent to 3 for $2.50, and rates can be compared.

Problems involving rates can be solved using the same technique as problems involving ratios. There is more emphasis, though, in solving rate problems on what is called the unit rate.

Using Unit Rates

A unit rate is an equivalent rate where the second term is 1. For example, if you drive 30 km in 20 minutes, the unit rate is 1.5 km/min. The second term is 1 minute.

Unit rates are not the only way to solve rate problems, but they are often used.

For example, consider the problem: Which is the better buy: 3.6 L of dishwashing soap for $3.69 or 4 L for $4.29?

If you think of the rate as litres/dollar, you want to know how many litres you can buy for $1 in each case. If you get more litres for your dollar, it is a better buy.

If 3.6 L cost $3.69, you need to divide 3.6 by 3.69 to see how much you get for $1.

$3.6 \div 3.69 = 0.9756$ L

If 4 L cost $4.29, you divide 4 by 4.29 to see how much you get for $1.

$4 \div 4.29 = 0.9324$ L

The first soap is the better buy—you get more for each $1.

You could have written the rate as dollars/litre and solved the problem by determining how many dollars 1 L of each costs.

If $3.69 gets you 3.6 L, then 1 L costs $3.69 \div 3.6 = 1.025, about $1.03.
If $4.29 gets you 4 L, then 1 L costs $4.29 \div 4 = 1.0725, about $1.07.

> **ACTIVITY 11.8**
>
> Pose this problem to students:
>
> A baby grows from a birth height of 55 cm to an adult height of 189 cm over 18 years.
>
> What was the daily growth rate?

Fermi Problems

One set of problems that people find interesting are called Fermi problems. They are problems that require realistic estimates to solve, and they always relate to objects in the real world. They are named after the physicist Enrico Fermi. An example is: Choose a tree in the school yard in the spring-time or summertime. Estimate the number of leaves on the tree.

To solve these problems, students use ratios. For example, they might count the number of branches, count the number of leaves on one branch, and multiply. They are assuming the ratio of leaves to branch is constant.

Another problem might be to estimate how large an area $10 000 worth of loonies, laid out flat on a floor, would cover. The ratio here is the ratio of value to a given area.

Percent

Some Background

Percents are a special sort of ratio, a ratio where the second term is 100. The concept of 50% or 100% is rarely new to students. They are familiar with both from talk about test scores and everyday situations like weather reports. In fact, some teachers choose to teach percent before they teach other ratios. Some students may note the connection to the word "cent," where a cent is $\frac{1}{100}$ of a dollar, just like 1 cm is $\frac{1}{100}$ of 1 m.

Principles for Percent

PRINCIPLES FOR PERCENT

1. A percent is a ratio or a comparison of a number to 100 and can be written as ■:100 or $\frac{[\,]}{100}$ or as an equivalent decimal. It can be represented with a variety of models.
2. The actual amount that a percent represents is based on the whole of which it is a percent.
3. Comparing percents is as easy as comparing decimals, as in many instances, you only need to compare whole number values.
4. Percents can be as low as 0, but can go higher than 100.
5. Sometimes percents are used to describe change.
6. There are a variety of strategies appropriate for solving any problem involving percent.

These principles can be explored using a variety of approaches.

Principle 1: A percent is a ratio or a comparison of a number to 100 and can be written as ■:100 or $\frac{[\,]}{100}$ or as an equivalent decimal. It can be represented with a variety of models.

Early on, any model for a percent should involve something that has 100 parts; this will reinforce the meaning of percent as a comparison to 100. One obvious model is a base ten block flat. To show, for example, 22%, you can cover a base ten block with 2 tens and 2 ones.

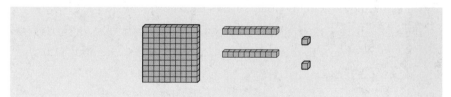

Adults often think of percents as sections of a circle, because of the prominence of pie charts or circle graphs. Nonetheless, a decimal hundredths grid is an excellent model for percents, particularly if grids have been used previously to model decimal hundredths.

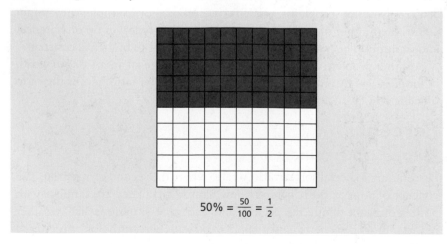

$$50\% = \frac{50}{100} = \frac{1}{2}$$

Eventually, students can simply sketch models. For example, a student might represent 30% like this:

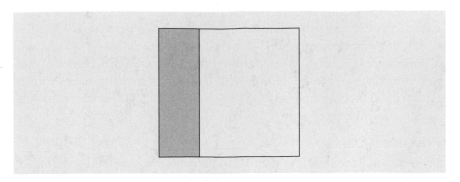

A percent can always be written as a decimal, or vice versa. For example, 48% is the same as 0.48; both mean 48 hundredths. If a number is written as a decimal, the first two places to the right of the decimal point can be written as a whole number percent. For example, 0.235 can be written as 23.5%.

Initially, students should relate certain percents to some comfortable fractions, for example, 50% to $\frac{1}{2}$, 25% to $\frac{1}{4}$, 10% to $\frac{1}{10}$, and perhaps 33% to about $\frac{1}{3}$. Later, students use relationships to relate a broader group of percents to related fractions or fractions to related percents. For example, the fraction $\frac{3}{4}$ is related to 75% since it is the same as three groups of $\frac{1}{4}$, or $3 \times 25\%$.

ACTIVITY 11.9

Ask students which of these make sense and why:

- The percent of males in the world is 42%.
- The percent of the floor in a living room covered by furniture is usually 50%.
- The percent of red on the Canadian flag is 75%.

Principle 2: The actual amount that a percent represents is based on the whole of which it is a percent.

1% can be a lot or a little; it depends what it is 1% of. For example, 1% of all the water on the planet is a lot of water, but 1% of a juice glass full of water is not very much water at all.

The same quantity can represent different amounts depending on the whole. For example, 20 is 50% of 40, but it is 100% of 20 and only 10% of 200.

Principle 3: Comparing whole number percents is as easy as comparing two decimals or two whole numbers.

Although comparing two fractions with different numerators and denominators is not always straightforward, comparing two percents is as easy as comparing whole numbers or decimals.

For example, although the fraction $\frac{27}{40}$ is greater than the fraction $\frac{21}{32}$, it is not immediately obvious. However, if they are both written as decimals (0.675 and 0.65625) or percents (67.5% and 65.625%), it is clearer that the first fraction is greater.

Principle 4: Percents can be as low as 0, but can go higher than 100.

Fractions and decimals less than 1 can be compared to 100. For example, 0.5% means half of 1%. It actually represents the fraction $\frac{1}{200}$ since there would be 200 half-squares and only 1 is coloured.

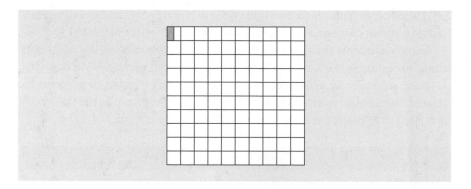

To show more than 100%, it is necessary to use more than one grid, assuming each single grid is defined as 100%.

For example, the diagram below shows 125%.

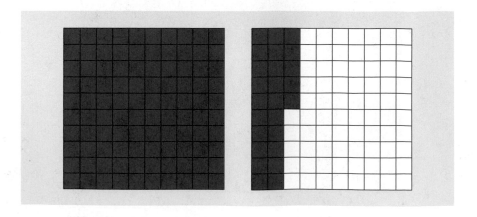

Principle 5: Sometimes percents are used to describe change.

A newspaper headline might read, "Population grew by 8%." One of the important ideas for students to understand is that the 8% represents the change, but the new population is actually 108% of the old one. The ability to represent a percent increase (or decrease) has many practical everyday applications. For example, tax has to be added to the price of an item that you purchase. It is the new price, not just the tax, that you are interested in; the new price might be 114% of the marked price, depending on taxes.

Sometimes prices are decreased. For example, a store is having a sale and marks 40% off. A customer should realize that the new price is actually 60% of the original price in order to make a quick estimate of the new price.

One of the situations where percents are used to describe change is currency conversion. If C$1 is worth US$0.92, you can use rates or percents to figure out the appropriate conversion. If the Canadian dollar is worth only 92% of the U.S. dollar, a dollar amount in Canadian dollars must be multiplied by 0.92 to determine its worth in U.S. dollars. On the other hand, a U.S. dollar amount must be divided by 0.92 to determine its worth in Canadian dollars. It turns out that US$1 is worth $1.09 at this exchange rate. Many students, and adults, are surprised that you do not gain the same number of cents as you lose when you make a currency conversion. The reason is based on **Principle 2** above. The whole that you are taking a percent of has changed; in one case, the whole is the Canadian dollar, but in the other case, it is the U.S. dollar, which is worth more—a greater whole.

Principle 6: There are a variety of strategies appropriate for solving any problem involving percent.

Sometimes, in solving a percent problem, you want to calculate the percent. Other times, you want to calculate the amount the percent represents, and still other times the value of the whole.

Problem 1 For example, the price of a $60 item has been reduced by 20% and you want to know your savings. You must calculate 20% of $60. One way is to write 20% as the decimal 0.2 and multiply by 60.

0.2 × 60 = 12.0. You save $12.

Another way is to think of 20% as $\frac{1}{5}$. You can divide 60 by 5 or multiply 60 by $\frac{1}{5}$ to calculate the savings.

Another way to calculate your savings is to use a ratio table. Your goal is to have a percent of 20 in the bottom row and to find the corresponding price in the top row. You can divide both terms by 5, and read off the $12 saved.

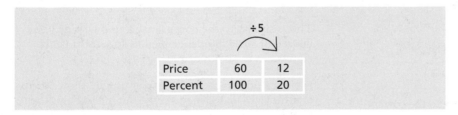

Problem 2 During another sale, you know that you paid $50 for an $80 item. You want to know what the discount was.

You know you saved $30, so you could compare 30 to the original price of 80. (You compare to the original price since the discount is applied to that price.) Since $\frac{30}{80} = 0.375$, the savings is 37.5%.

Another way to solve this is to realize that an $8 savings is a 10% discount. But you saved $30. Since 30 ÷ 8 = $3\frac{3}{4}$, the percent you want is 10% × $3\frac{3}{4}$ = 37.5%.

Yet another strategy is to solve the proportion: $\frac{30}{80} = \frac{x}{100}$. To solve the proportion, you can multiply $\frac{30}{80}$ by 100.

Problem 3 Suppose, at yet another sale, the discount was 40% and you know that you saved $50. You want to know what the original price was.

You can use strategies similar to those described for the other two problems. You might realize that if a discount of 40% is worth $50, then a discount of 20% is worth $25. If 20% is $25, then the original price, which is 100%, must be 5 times as much, or $125.

You might divide 50 directly by 0.4 since the original price was multiplied by 0.4 to get 50. The result is still $125.

You could set up a ratio table and manipulate the values to get 100% in the bottom row; 100%, the original price, would be $125.

	÷2		×5	
Amount	50	25		125
Percent	40	20		100

ACTIVITY 11.10

Students might keep track of their calories over the course of a day or week and create a percent graph that shows the percent in various food groups.

Or, again, you can set up and solve a proportion: $\frac{40}{100} = \frac{50}{x}$. To solve, you can multiply both sides of the equation by 100x and then divide by 40, and the result is, again $125.

Common Errors and Misconceptions

Percent Strategies for Dealing with Common Errors and Misconceptions

COMMON ERROR OR MISCONCEPTION	SUGGESTED STRATEGY
Percents Greater than 100% Students get confused with percents greater than 100%. Some students who are focused on the concept of "out of 100" find these percents difficult to deal with. A percent greater than 100 would be equivalent to an improper fraction.	Students might look at hundredths grids where first 10, then 20, then 30, ... up to 100 squares are coloured. Then bring out a second grid and colour another 10 squares in that grid. Talk about how this is 100% and another 10%, so the total would be 110%.
Writing Decimals Students write a decimal like 0.5 as 0.50%.	This is similar to the confusion around writing 0.25¢ instead of $0.25. Students need to know that 0.5 is equivalent to 50 out of 100, or 50%.
Describing Percent Change Students sometimes do not relate to the correct whole (or 100%) when describing a percent change. For example, when calculating the original price after a discount of 20% that results in a price of $40, they forget that the 20% discount was based on a different whole than a 20% increase of $40 would be based on.	Having students check an answer usually shows them that they calculated incorrectly. But it also helps them to always identify what 100% represents before they perform any calculation.
Relating Percent to Multiplication Inappropriately Some students solve the problem 4 = __ % of 8, by noticing that 8 = 2 × 4, so they write 2% instead of 50%.	When students first consider a percent problem, they should focus on meaning. For example, in this case, if the answer were 100%, it would be all of the 8. If it were 10%, it would be less than 1 since 10% of 10 is 1. In this way, they would see that an answer of 2% does not make sense. Help students see that it is because 8 = 4 × 2 that 4 is half of 8, and thus 50% of it.

Appropriate Manipulatives

COUNTERS

Counters can be used to represent ratios.

For example, the counters below show the ratios 6:4, 4:6, 4:10, 10:4, 6:10, and 10:6.

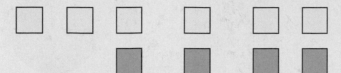

DECIMAL HUNDREDTHS GRIDS

Decimal hundredths grids are particularly appropriate to represent percents and some ratios. For example, this hundredths grid shows clearly why 75%, or 75 out of 100, is the same ratio as 3 out of 4:

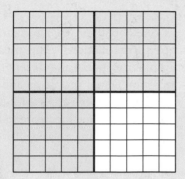

75% is 75:100, or 3:4.

DECIMAL SQUARE HUNDREDTHS CARDS

Decimal square hundredths cards are ready-made models for 5% (0.05), 10% (0.1), 15% (0.15), ..., 95% (0.95), and 100% (1.0).

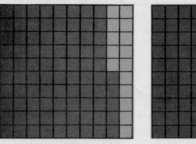

These cards show hundredths and, indirectly, percents.

PERCENT CIRCLES

Percent circles can be used to model percent. Ideally, if the circle is large enough, the ticks could be placed around the circumference to show each hundredth, or at least every 5 hundredths. This model is a good one to show the relationship between percent and fractions.

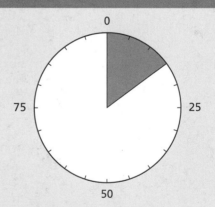

This circle shows that the 15% that is blue is less than $\frac{1}{4}$.

Appropriate Technology

Calculators

Calculators will be essential for solving many ratio, rate, and percent problems, that is, all but those with the simplest values involved. A four-function calculator is all that is required since students can equate percents to the equivalent decimals or fractions.

Computers

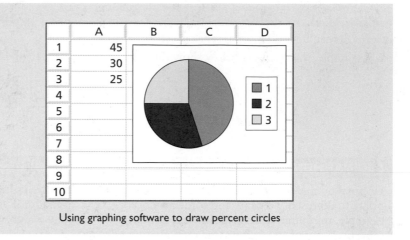

Using graphing software to draw percent circles

Students might use Geometer's Sketchpad or an alternate dynamic geometry software package and perform dilations. The measurement menu allows them to measure ratios of corresponding side lengths.

The Internet is an excellent source for Fermi problems and problems requiring the use of ratio and scale. There are online applets for percentage calculations, even automatic percent increase and decrease calculations. Students might also enjoy solving rate problems relating to download speeds for songs and other files.

Assessing Student Understanding

- Make sure to focus on students' reasoning in assessing their proportional thinking. Reasoning is fundamental to proportional thinking. For example, pose a question like this: In a certain class, the ratio of boys to girls was 4:5. In another class, the ratio was 6:5. What would the ratios be if a boy and a girl from the second class move to the first class?

- Encourage students to use a variety of strategies to solve problems, not always a single strategy. For example, if they solve one problem using a unit rate, ask them to solve the next problem a different way.

- Ask students to describe situations where rates, ratios, and proportions are used to show that they have a sense of when these mathematical concepts apply.

- Make sure students can relate various rates, ratios, and percents to known benchmarks. For example, you might ask them to draw a sketch to show what the ratio 4:9 might mean and what that ratio might really describe.

Appropriate Children's Books

How Many Candles? (Griffith, 1999).
In this story, different animals' lifespans are compared with the typical human lifespan. For example, students can figure out how old a dog would be in human years.

One Inch Tall (in *Where the Sidewalk Ends*) (Silverstein, 1973).
Shel Silverstein invites you to imagine what the world would be like if you were only an inch tall. This is one of many pieces of children's literature that explore the notion of human size relative to the sizes of other objects in the world. Another is, of course, *Alice in Wonderland* by Lewis Carroll.

If Dogs Were Dinosaurs (Schwartz, 2005).
This book compares the relative sizes of items. For example, it says, "If your hair were as thick as spaghetti, the meatballs would be as big as bowling balls." Most of the comparisons are surprising and interesting. Schwartz actually includes the calculations at the back of the book to explain his thinking.

If You Hopped like a Frog (Schwartz, 1999).
This book also allows students to explore relative proportions. For example, if a person jumped as high, proportionally, as a flea, the person could reach the torch of the Statue of Liberty. It compares how much a person could eat compared to a shrew and even compares growth rates of people during the nine months before they were born to their growth rate after birth.

Applying What You've Learned

1. Some students are troubled by a problem like the chapter problem since there is some ambiguity; they worry that it is not definitive how long a lifetime actually is.

   a) What are the advantages and disadvantages of this sort of ambiguity?

   b) Were you surprised by the solution to the problem? Explain why or why not.

2. a) Describe three different ways that you might solve this problem: 72% of students in a school participated in the food drive. If 198 students participated, how many students are in the school?

   b) Which of those ways do you personally find most comfortable? Why?

3. Many students struggle with the introduction of percents greater than 100% and that is why the topic is usually left until Grade 8. List one or two ways to introduce these percents that you think will make their use more meaningful to students.

4. It was mentioned in the chapter that there is some informal proportional thinking that happens in Grades K to 5. Cite as many examples as you can think of and explain how several of them really are about proportional thinking.

5. What are some of the advantages of differentiating between $a:b$ and the fraction $\frac{a}{b}$? Explain your thinking.

6. Create a lesson plan built around a piece of children's literature related to ratio and proportion. What ideas about proportion does your lesson plan bring out? How?

7. There are some educators who advocate the introduction of percent prior to formal work with ratios of the form $a:b$. What might be some arguments for this? What might be some arguments against this?

Interact with a K–8 Student:

8. Prepare a set of percent statements with which a Grade 5 to 8 student can agree or disagree. See how reasonable this student's responses are. An example might be: 20% of Grade 5 students play sports.

Discuss with a K–8 Teacher:

9. Ask a teacher to share with you one or two of his or her favourite problems that require the use of ratio, rate, and percent. Ask why he or she particularly likes these problems. What is your response to the problems?

Selected References

Abrahamson, D., and Cigan, C. (2003). A design for ratio and proportion instruction. *Mathematics Teaching in the Middle School, 9,* 493–501.

Attia, T.L. (2003). Using school lunches to study proportion. *Mathematics Teaching in the Middle School, 9,* 17–21.

Beckmann, C.E., Thompson, D.R., and Austin, R.A. (2004). Exploring proportional reasoning through movies and literature. *Mathematics Teaching in the Middle School, 9,* 256–262.

Billings, E.M.H. (2001). Problems that encourage proportion sense. *Mathematics Teaching in the Middle School, 7,* 10–14.

Cramer, K., and Post, T. (1993). Making connections: A case for proportionality. *Arithmetic Teacher, 60,* 342–346.

Griffith, H.V. (1999). *How many candles?* New York: Greenwillow Books.

Heller, P., Post, T., Behr, M., and Lesh, R. (1990). Qualitative and numerical reasoning about fractions and rates by seventh- and eighth-grade students. *Journal for Research in Mathematics Education, 21,* 388–402.

Kent, L.B., Arnosky, J., and McMonagle, J. (2002). Using representational contexts to support multiplicative reasoning. In Litwiller, B., and Bright, G. (Eds.). *Making sense of fractions, ratios, and proportions: 2002 yearbook.* Reston, VA: National Council of Teachers of Mathematics, 145–152.

Lamon, S.J. (1993). Ratio and proportion: Connecting content and children's thinking. *Journal for Research in Mathematics Education, 24,* 41–61.

Langrall, C.W., and Swafford, J. (2000). Three balloons for two dollars: Developing proportional reasoning. *Mathematics Teaching in the Middle School, 6,* 254–261.

Lesh, R., Post, T., and Behr, M. (1988). Proportional reasoning. In Hiebert, J., and Behr, M. (Eds.). *Number concepts and operations in the middle grades.* Reston, VA: Lawrence Erlbaum and National Council of Teachers of Mathematics, 93–118.

Lo, J.J., Watanabe, T., and Cai, J. (2004). Developing ratio concepts: An Asian perspective. *Mathematics Teaching in the Middle School, 7,* 362–367.

Martinie, S.L., and Bay-Williams, J.M. (2003). Using literature to engage students in proportional reasoning. *Mathematics Teaching in the Middle School, 9,* 142–147.

Miller, J.L., and Fey, J.T. (2000). Proportional reasoning. *Mathematics Teaching in the Middle School, 5,* 310–313.

Moss, J., and Case, R. (1999). Developing children's understanding of the rational numbers: A new model and an experimental curriculum. *Journal for Research in Mathematics Education, 30,* 122–147.

Moss, J., and Caswell, B. (2004). Building percent dolls: Connecting linear measurement to learning ratio and proportion. *Mathematics Teaching in the Middle School, 10,* 68–74.

Pagni, D. (2005). Angles, time, and proportion. *Mathematics Teaching in the Middle School, 10,* 436–441.

Parker, M. (1999). Building on "Building up": Proportional reasoning activities for future teachers. *Mathematics Teaching in the Middle School, 4,* 286–289.

Parker, M., and Leinhardt, G. (1995). Percent: A privileged proportion. *Review of Educational Research, 65,* 421–481.

Post, T., Behr, M.J., and Lesh, R. (1988). Proportionality and the development of prealgebra understandings. In Coxford, A.F., and Shulte, A.P. (Eds.). *The ideas of algebra, K–12.* Reston, VA: National Council of Teachers of Mathematics, 78–90.

Schwartz, D. (1999). *If you hopped like a frog.* New York: Scholastic Press.

Schwartz, D. (2005). *If dogs were dinosaurs.* New York: Scholastic Press.

Silverstein, S. (1973). One inch tall. In *Where the sidewalk ends.* New York: HarperCollins Children's Books.

Slovin, H. (2000). Moving to proportional reasoning. *Mathematics Teaching in the Middle School, 6,* 58–60.

Small, M. (2005). *PRIME: Number and operations: Background and strategies.* Toronto: Thomson Nelson.

Thompson, C.S., and Bush, W.S. (2003). Improving middle school teachers' reasoning about proportional reasoning. *Mathematics Teaching in the Middle School, 8,* 398–403.

Chapter 12

Integers

IN A NUTSHELL

The main ideas in this chapter are listed below:

1. The negative integers are the "opposites" of the whole numbers. Each integer is the reflection of its opposite across a line perpendicular to and cutting the number line at 0.

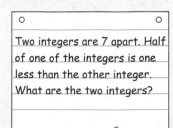

Two integers are 7 apart. Half of one of the integers is one less than the other integer. What are the two integers?

2. Integer operations are based upon the zero principle, the fact that $(-1) + (+1) = 0$.

(*continued*)

CHAPTER PROBLEM

Two integers are 7 apart. Half of one of the integers is one less than the other integer. What are the two integers?

Some Background

The concept of negative integers is introduced near the end of the elementary school years or in early middle/junior high school. Many students, even younger ones, are quite comfortable interpreting these numbers, particularly because of their familiarity with negative temperatures, although operations with integers may be less familiar.

Integer Contexts

Useful contexts for making work with integers meaningful, depending on the interest and experience of students, include

- temperatures
- floors below and above a main floor
- being in debt or not
- below and above sea level or ground level
- golf scores that are below and above par

ACTIVITY 12.1

Have students bring in clippings from newspapers that include negative numbers.

They can discuss the variety of situations they have found by sharing their findings.

They might also listen to weather reports and attend to how the negative numbers are read, whether as "minus 5" or "negative 5."

Student Response

This student has an interesting interpretation of the number −2.

ACTIVITY 12.2

Pose this problem to students:

Make a coordinate grid.

Plot points for which the first coordinate is the opposite of the second one. Join the points.

What do you notice?

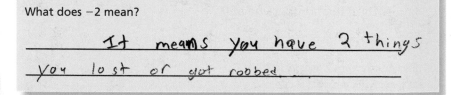

What does −2 mean?

It means you have 2 things you lost or got robbed.

Reading and Writing Integers

It is desirable to use either a raised + or − sign or brackets around the number to write an integer, to make the distinction between these symbols and the operations symbols for addition and subtraction. However, even though making this distinction is helpful when students are first working with integers, later on they will learn that there is a connection between subtraction and the negative symbol and between addition and the positive symbol; for example, $^-3$ or (-3) is $0 - 3$, and $^+3$ (or $+3$) is $0 + 3$. Students can use the + symbol to indicate a positive integer, even though it is not necessary to do so, as the symbol is assumed if there is no integer symbol.

Comparing Integers

When comparing integers, it is helpful if students think about the placement of each integer on a number line rather than trying to memorize rules. In this way, students are much less likely to make the mistake of thinking that $-9 > -7$.

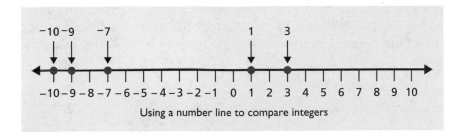

Using a number line to compare integers

PRINCIPLES FOR COMPARING INTEGERS

1. Any negative integer is always less than any positive integer.
2. A positive integer closer to 0 is always less than a positive integer farther away from 0; for example, $+1 < +3$.
3. A negative integer closer to 0 is always greater than a negative integer farther away from 0; for example, $-7 > -10$.

These principles can be explained easily using the number line.

Principle 1: Any negative integer is always less than any positive integer.

Every negative value is to the left of 0. Every positive value is to the right. Since the number line is built so that greater numbers are to the right, any positive integer must be greater than any negative integer.

Principle 2: A positive integer closer to 0 is always less than a positive integer farther away from 0.

0 is to the left of all of the positive integers. So a positive integer closer to 0 is farther to the left than one farther from 0. Since it is farther to the left, it is less.

Principle 3: A negative integer closer to 0 is always greater than a negative integer farther away from 0.

0 is to the right of all of the negative integers. So a negative integer closer to 0 is farther to the right and, therefore, greater.

The Zero Principle

Mathematicians have defined (-1) as the number that you add to $+1$ to result in 0; that is, by definition, $(-1) + (+1) = 0$. This is referred to as the zero principle and is the foundation for computations involving negative numbers. As a consequence of this definition, any number can be added to its opposite to result in a value of 0. For example, $(-3) = (-1) + (-1) + (-1)$ and $(+3) = (+1) + (+1) + (+1)$. So $(-3) + (+3) = (-1) +$

> **ACTIVITY 12.3**
>
> Provide students with For and Against hockey scores for various teams. They can use positive numbers for goals scored and negative numbers for goals against and rank the teams based on these scores.

$(-1) + (-1) + (+1) + (+1) + (+1)$. The order of adding numbers is irrelevant, so the total is the same as $[(-1) + (+1)] + [(-1) + (+1)] + [(-1) + (+1)]$. The sum of zeros is just zero.

Adding Integers

Just as with whole numbers, adding means putting together. Therefore, adding $(+3) + (-5)$ means putting together an amount representing $+3$ with an amount representing (-5). This can be modelled in several ways:

• using a number line

Start at (-5) and move 3 forward. You land at (-2).

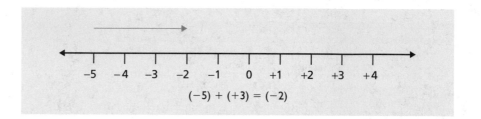

$(-5) + (+3) = (-2)$

• using counters where one colour, for example, blue, represents (-1) and another colour, for example, red, represents $(+1)$.

Use the fact that $(-1) + (+1) = 0$ to simplify $(-5) + (+3)$ to (-2).

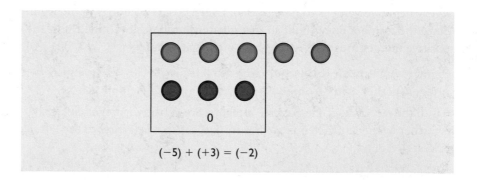

$(-5) + (+3) = (-2)$

PRINCIPLES FOR ADDING INTEGERS

1. The sum of two negatives is negative.
2. The sum of two positives is positive.
3. The sum of a negative and a positive can be either positive or negative. The sum takes the sign of the number that is farther from 0.

Principle 1: The sum of two negatives is negative.

By modelling with counters, students see that they are putting blue counters together with other blue counters. The result is blue counters.

Principle 2: The sum of two positives is positive.

Principle 3: The sum of a negative and a positive can be either positive or negative. The sum takes the sign of the number that is farther from 0.

For example, $(-3) + (+4)$ is positive since there are more reds than blues, so a red is left over when 0s are created by pairing up reds and blues. But $(+3) + (-4)$ is negative since there are more blues than reds, so a blue is left over when zeros are created.

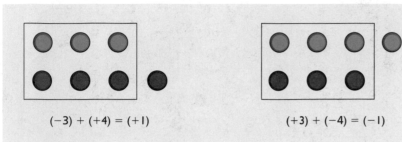

$(-3) + (+4) = (+1)$ $(+3) + (-4) = (-1)$

- symbolically:

  Since $(+1) + (-1) = 0$, any number and its opposite add to 0.

  You can break up (-5) into a (-3) piece and a (-2) piece. The (-3) piece can be added to the $(+3)$ to result in 0.

  $$(-5) + (+3) = (-2) + (-3) + (+3)$$
  $$= (2) + 0$$
  $$= (-2)$$

ACTIVITY 12.4

Integrate integer work with probability. Have students toss a coin. If the coin lands heads, they gain a point $(+1)$. If it lands tails, they lose a point (-1). After students have tossed 20 times, they indicate their final score.

Ask how many tails someone whose final score is -2 could have tossed and why.

ACTIVITY 12.5

Offer the following activity for students to try:

a) Copy the diagram shown below. Start with $+5$ in the top circle. Fill in the other circles by following the arrows and adding the indicated integers.

b) Why is the final sum $+5$ after you finish the last additions?

c) Why is the final sum $+5$ whether you add in either a clockwise direction or a counterclockwise direction?

d) Copy the diagram again. Replace the numbers on the arrows with four different 2-digit integers, so that you still end up with a sum of $+5$.

ACTIVITY 12.6

Invite students to play this game.

YOU WILL NEED

Integer cards numbered -10 to $+10$ (two of each) OR a standard deck of cards including two jokers, with face cards removed.

INTEGRO

When using a standard deck of cards, aces count as 1, numbered cards count as their face values, and jokers count as 0. Red cards are positive, and black cards are negative.

Number of players: 2 or 4

HOW TO PLAY

1. If there are four players, remove the jokers. Shuffle the cards. Deal the cards equally to all the players.

2. In a round, each player places one card face up on the table.

3. The first player to call out the sum of the cards wins all the cards in the turn. These cards go into the player's bank pile.

(continued)

ACTIVITY 12.6 (continued)

4. If there is a tie, the tied players play additional rounds until one of them wins.

5. When a player runs out of cards, the player shuffles his or her bank pile and continues playing. If the player's bank is empty, the player is out of the game.

6. The game ends when one player has won all the cards.

ACTIVITY 12.7

Display a number line. Ask students to determine how to get from 2 to −3 if the only allowable moves are moving left 2 spaces or right 8 spaces. Then ask students to use a number sentence to describe what they did.

Encourage students to use a variety of mental math strategies when adding two or more integers. For example, to add $(-32) + (-39) + (42) + (30)$, it might make sense to combine $(+42) + (-32)$ to get $(+10)$ to add to (-9), the result of adding (-39) and $(+30)$.

Subtracting Integers

As with adding integers, it is important for students to have a conceptual understanding of the principles that underpin integer subtraction.

PRINCIPLES FOR SUBTRACTING INTEGERS

1. To subtract an integer, you can use either a take away meaning or a missing addend meaning.

2. To subtract an integer, you can use the zero principle to add enough to the minuend (the starting amount) to take away the subtrahend.

3. To subtract an integer, you can determine what to add to the subtrahend to get to the minuend; sometimes you need to use the zero principle.

4. To subtract an integer, you can add its opposite.

Principle 1: To subtract an integer, you can use either a take away meaning or a missing addend meaning.

As with whole numbers and decimals, subtraction can mean take away or how much must be added to one number to get another.

You might model subtraction of integers with two-coloured counters using either a take away model or a missing addend model.

- $(-5) - (-2)$ means you have 5 blues and you want to take away 2 of them. 3 blues are left.

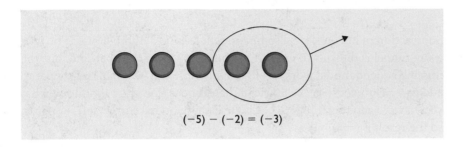

$$(-5) - (-2) = (-3)$$

- $(-5) - (-2)$ tells how much to add to (-2) to get to (-5) (just as $4 - 3$ tells how much to add to 3 to get to 4). If you already have (-2), 2 blues, you have to add 3 more blues (-3) to get to (-5). Again, $(-5) - (-2) = (-3)$.

Principle 2: To subtract an integer, you can use the zero principle to add enough to the minuend (the starting amount) to take away the subtrahend.

Both meanings of subtraction can also be used to subtract numbers like $(-2) - (-6)$ or $(+2) - (-6)$, where taking away is not immediately possible. (If you only have 2 blues, how do you take away 6?)

- $(-2) - (-6)$ can mean you have 2 blues, but want to take away 6 blues. To get more blues to take away, you can add four pairs of 0 in the form of $(+1) + (-1)$, that is, 4 reds and 4 blues. Because you are adding 0, you are not changing the total, but now there are 6 blues to take away. Once they are removed, the result is 4 reds, or $(+4)$.

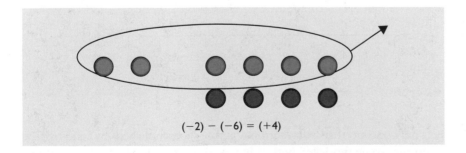

$$(-2) - (-6) = (+4)$$

- $(+2) - (-6)$ tells how much to add to (-6) to get to $(+2)$. That means you start with 6 blues and want to figure out what to add to end up with 2 reds. You want to add 8 reds (to pair up with the 6 blues) and still have two blues left.

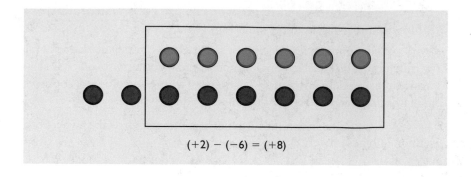

$$(+2) - (-6) = (+8)$$

Subtraction of integers can also be modelled using a number line. The take away model is difficult to explain meaningfully on a number line, but the missing addend model works well. For example, $(-7) - (-1)$ tells what to add to (-1) to get to (-7). Start on the number line at (-1) and see what you have to add to get to (-7). It is clear that you have to go left, 6 spaces, so the result is (-6).

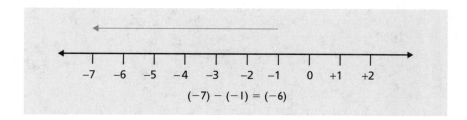

$$(-7) - (-1) = (-6)$$

Principle 3: To subtract an integer, you can add its opposite.

When you subtract a negative from a positive, it is easy to see, using the number line model, why you can add the opposite to subtract.

$(+4) - (-5)$ tells what to add to (-5) to get to $(+4)$. It is clear that you need to move 5 to the right to get to 0, and another 4 to the right to get to $(+4)$, so the total amount to be added is $4 + 5$.

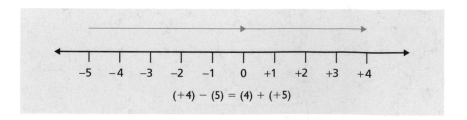

$$(+4) - (5) = (4) + (+5)$$

The concept that subtraction can be accomplished by adding the opposite can be modelled with other types of questions, too, for example, $(-3) - (-2)$, but it tends to be a little less obvious.

Some teachers teach subtraction of integers as just a rule: adding the opposite. For example, to model $(-3) - (-5)$, they simply encourage students to rewrite the question as $(3) + (+5)$. Although the correct answer is achieved and students will accept the rule, it is not really clear to most students why the rule works. The rule can be justified using equations:

Start with $(-3) - (-5) = $ ▪

Since this is a subtraction, it can be rewritten as an addition:

$(-3) = $ ▪ $+ (-5)$

Add $+5$ to both sides.

$(-3) + 5 = $ ▪ $+ (-5) + 5$

But $(-5) + 5 = 0$, so

$(-3) + 5 = $ ▪ $+ 0$

$= $ ▪

This latter explanation, although correct, is highly symbolic and may be more difficult for many students than using the number line, or counters (as described in the section for Principle 2).

ACTIVITY 12.8

Provide a magic square partially filled in. All columns, rows, and diagonals add to the same total. Ask students to complete the square.

+8		−5	+5
	+3	+2	
	−1		+4
−4			−7

Multiplying Integers

Although the rules for multiplying integers are fairly easy for students to learn, explaining why those rules make sense is a greater challenge.

PRINCIPLES FOR MULTIPLYING INTEGERS

1. Integers can be multiplied in any order without affecting the product.
2. The product of a positive and a negative is negative.
3. The product of two positives or two negatives is positive.
4. The distributive principle applies to multiplication and addition of integers, that is, $a(b + c) = ab + ac$.

Principle 1: Integers can be multiplied in any order without affecting the product.

Mathematicians have defined the set of integers to ensure that they obey the same properties as the set of whole numbers. One example is the commutative property. For example, $(+3) \times (-2) = (-2) \times (+3)$. Knowing this property will be key to explaining Principle 2.

Principle 2: The product of a positive and a negative is negative.

A variety of models can be used to explain why a positive multiplied by a negative is negative. For example, one can model $3 \times (-2)$ as 3 groups of (-2) using either counters or the number line.

Clearly 3 groups of (-2) is modelled by the same number of counters as 3×2, but the counters are all blue, so the product is negative.

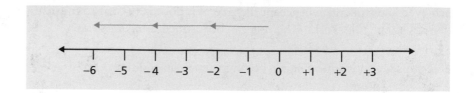

The number line model is based on repeated addition, that is, $3 \times (-2) = (-2) + (-2) + (-2)$, and so the result has to be negative.

It is harder to model $(-3) \times (+2)$ since it is not clear what (-3) groups means. However, using the commutative principle, $(-3) \times (+2)$ can be represented as $(+2) \times (-3)$, and 2 groups of (-3) can be modelled.

Another way to model $(-3) \times (+2)$ is symbolically through patterns.

$$(+3) \times (+2) = (+6)$$
$$(+2) \times (+2) = (+4)$$
$$(+1) \times (+2) = (+2)$$
$$(0) \times (+2) = (0)$$
$$(-1) \times (+2) = (?)$$
$$(-2) \times (+2) = (?)$$
$$(-3) \times (+2) = (?)$$

A student observes that the product decreases by 2 as the left-hand factor decreases by 1. This makes sense: each time there is one less 2. If the pattern were to continue, the products would be (-2), (-4), and then (-6).

Principle 3: The product of two positives or two negatives is positive.

One of the most comfortable ways for students to understand why, for example, $(-3) \times (-2) = (+6)$ is to build that concept through patterns.

You can set up a pattern that will ultimately include the desired factors. For example:

$$(+3) \times (-2) = (-6)$$
$$(+2) \times (-2) = (-4)$$
$$(+1) \times (-2) = (-2)$$
$$(0) \times (-2) = (0)$$
$$(-1) \times (-2) = (?)$$
$$(-2) \times (-2) = (?)$$
$$(-3) \times (-2) = (?)$$

The student would notice that as the first factor decreases by 1, the product increases by 2. This makes sense since each time there is one less (-2) to bring down the product. If the pattern were to continue, the products would be $(+2)$, $(+4)$, and $(+6)$, so $(-3) \times (-2) = (+6)$.

Some teachers use "stories" to explain why two negatives make a positive. Generally, although they capture students' attention, the logic on which they are based is a little vague for the student. One example is the idea of a videotape: $(+2) \times (+3)$ means a tape is fastforwarded 3 frames a minute for 2 minutes. You are 6 frames ahead.

$(+2) \times (-3)$ means a tape is rewound 3 frames a minute for 2 minutes. You are 6 frames behind the starting point, so the result is (-6).

$(-2) \times (+3)$ means a tape is fastforwarded 3 frames a minute. You want to know where you were 2 minutes ago (-2 represents a time of -2). You would be 6 frames behind where you are now, so the product is (-6).

$(-2) \times (-3)$ means a tape is rewound 3 frames a minute. You want to know where you were 2 minutes ago. You would be 6 frames ahead of where you are now, so the product is $(+6)$.

The "vagueness" in this story is why the first negative sign means time forward and time backward. It is simply stated, but some students might wonder why the first negative sign means something different than the other one does (running forward or backward).

Principle 4: The distributive principle applies to multiplication and addition of integers, that is, $a(b + c) = ab + ac$.

Students are likely simply to assume that this principle holds. It is useful in a situation like this one: The student knows that $-2 \times 34 = -68$ and wants to calculate -2×37. He or she would think of this as $-2 \times 34 + (-2) \times 3$, and would add the two values together. Indeed, this principle does hold for integers.

Dividing Integers

PRINCIPLES FOR DIVIDING INTEGERS

1. Division of integers can be modelled using a sharing, a grouping (measurement), or an inverse multiplication meaning.
2. The rules for assigning signs to the quotient of two integers are based on the rules for products.
   - The quotient of two positives or two negatives is positive.
   - The quotient of a positive and a negative is negative.

Principle 1: Division of integers can be modelled using a sharing, a grouping (measurement), or an inverse multiplication meaning.

One of the meanings of a quotient like $14 \div 2$ is the size of the share if 2 people share 14. That approach can also be used to describe the quotient of a negative divided by a positive. For example, $(-10) \div 2 = (-5)$.

- 10 blue counters can be shared by 2 people. Each gets 5 blue counters.

$(-10) \div 2 = (-5)$

• a jump on the number line of 10 to the left can be divided into 2 jumps of 5 to the left

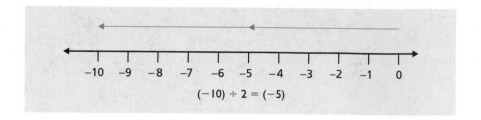

$(-10) \div 2 = (-5)$

Another meaning of division is grouping or measurement. It is useful to explain a positive divided by a positive, or a negative divided by a negative. For example, $(-10) \div (-2)$ can mean how many groups of (-2) can be found in a group of (-10). There are 5 groups.

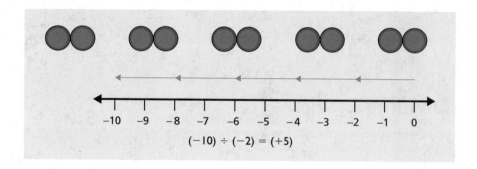

$(-10) \div (-2) = (+5)$

A third meaning of division is inverse multiplication. The quotient of two numbers is the number you must multiply the divisor by to achieve a product that is the dividend. For example, $12 \div 2 = 6$ since $6 \times 2 = 12$. It is this meaning of division that best explains the quotient of integers with different signs.

For example, $(-12) \div 2$ describes the number by which you must multiply 2 to get a product of (-12). From the rules for multiplying, it is clear that the number is negative.

$(-12) \div 2 = -6$ since $2 \times (-6) = (-12)$.

Principle 2: The rules for assigning signs to the quotient of two integers are based on the rules for products.

• The quotient of two positives or two negatives is positive.
• The quotient of a positive and a negative is negative.

ACTIVITY 12.10

Students can practise division of integers by calculating the average score per hole in a golf game if the values are reported as scores above and below par.

Because of the relationship between multiplication and division, the sign rules are the same for division as for multiplication.

For example, $(-12) \div (-4)$ must be $(+3)$ since $(-4) \times (+3) = (-12)$.

$(-12) \div (+4)$ must be (-3) since $(+4) \times (-3) = (-12)$.

$(+12) \div (-4)$ must be $(+3)$ since $(-4) \times (+3) = (-12)$.

Mystery Integers

Select four integers. Do not tell anyone what they are. Make up a set of eight clues that will allow someone to guess the integers you chose. All eight clues must be necessary.

The clues must

- use all four operations somewhere in the eight clues
- include comparing integers

For example, suppose that your integers are −8, 7, 5, and −3. Here are three possible clues:

- The sum of the four integers is 1.
- If you order the integers from least to greatest, the product of the two middle integers is −15.
- If you subtract the least integer from the greatest integer, and divide the difference by 3, the quotient is 5.

What eight clues can you write to describe your four integers?

A. The three clues above do not give enough information to figure out the integers. What five additional clues would give enough information?

B. Select any four integers of your own, and make up eight clues. Remember that all the clues must be necessary. It should not be possible to figure out all the integers with only some of the eight clues.

Common Errors and Misconceptions

COMMON ERROR OR MISCONCEPTION	STRATEGY
A student assumes $(-9) > (-4)$ since $9 > 4$.	Focus students on the number line model for integers. Some students respond better to a vertical number line than a horizontal one. It seems clearer to them that "up" means greater. When asked to compare numbers, students can locate both numbers and then look for the one that is farther up.
A student adds $(-3) + (-8)$ and gets 11. He says that the rule is "two negatives make a positive."	Frequently, to simplify the mathematics for students, "rules" are created for them to remember. This student remembered, all too well, that two negatives make a positive. He or she did not think about when that rules applies (for multiplication and division, not addition and subtraction). Rather than memorizing rules, students should always be thinking about what the operation means. They should be reading this as "(-3) and another (-8)", rather than simply as "(-3) plus (-8)."
A student subtracts $(-3) - (-8)$ and gets $+11$. She or he reasons that you add when there are two negatives, so $8 + 3 = 11$.	Again, the student is applying a rule where it does not apply. The student should be reading $(-3) - (-8)$ as "How far is it from (-8) to (-3)?" Then the error is much less likely.

ACTIVITY 12.11

Offer students a mystery integers task to complete (see page 279).

Appropriate Manipulatives

Integers: Examples of Manipulatives

NUMBER LINES

The negative of a number is defined to be the number equally distant from zero as its positive opposite. Because of this, integers are usually modelled first with a number line, whether horizontal or vertical. The vertical number line more closely resembles a thermometer, making it perhaps a more "contextual" model if students are working with a context such as temperature or altitude.

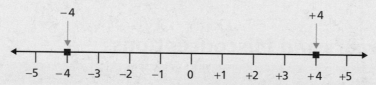

This number line shows that −4 is the opposite of +4.

INTEGER TILES

Another common model for integers is two-sided coloured tiles, where one colour represents a positive (usually white) and a different colour represents a negative (usually red). In later work, when adding integers, students pair up negative tiles and positive tiles to create pairs with a value of 0, and what is left over is the sum.

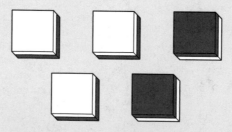

+3 and −2 are modelled with
white positive and red negative tiles.

Two colours of counters can be used in the same way as integer tiles. For example, $(-3) + (+8)$ is modelled as below.

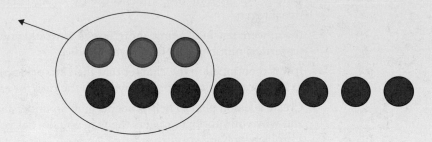

Appropriate Technology

Calculators

Calculators vary in terms of how negative numbers are entered. Students will need to learn how to appropriately use their calculators.

For example, on the TI-15, the computation $(+6) - (-5)$ is entered as $6, -, (-), 5, =$. Students have to distinguish the subtraction sign from the negative sign as applied to integers.

Computers

There are a number of Internet tools that students can access to work with integers. These can be accessed through this book's website.

Assessing Student Understanding

- Observe how students handle situations where integers are used in context. For example, you can use temperature change for some questions involving addition and subtraction.
- Include conceptual and problem-solving questions in your assessment plan. For example, a conceptual question might be: *Explain why the product of two negative integers has to be greater than their sum.* An example of a problem-solving question might be: *A certain negative integer fits these clues:*
  – greater than -20
  – less than -4
  – farther from -4 *than* -20.
  What is the greatest value it could be?
- Rather than asking for a series of calculations, ask questions "backwards." For example, indicate that you had added 3 integers and the result was (-16). Ask what those integers could have been and why. Similarly, you could ask why 2 integers could have been subtracted, multiplied, or divided to result in (-16), and ask why.
- Have students reflect on how operations with integers are like those with whole numbers, and how they are different.

Applying What You've Learned

1. There are two solutions to the chapter problem—one involving positive integers and one involving negative integers. What assumptions

WebConnect

www.makingmathmeaningful
.nelson.com.

Visit the Making Math Meaningful website for links to Internet tools that students can access to work with integers.

do you have to make about the two integers in the problem to get the negative solution?

2. What do you see as the advantages and what do you see as the disadvantages of insisting that students use the + sign in describing positive integers?

3. If you were teaching a unit about integers, would you use a horizontal or vertical number line? Justify your choice.

4. It was mentioned in the chapter that the zero principle is fundamental to all four operations. Show why this is the case for each operation.

5. Create a lesson plan to help students gain an understanding of how and why you subtract integers the way you do. Set your lesson plan in a problem-solving context.

6. A game was offered in the chapter for adding integers. Find or create a game that involves other integer operations. Comment on the value of the goal in terms of practising skills and/or developing or assessing understanding.

Interact with a K–8 Student:

7. Select one of the activities in the unit or the game that you created for question 6. Try it out with a student. Report on what you observed about student understanding of integers in the course of playing the game or completing the activity.

Discuss with a K–8 Teacher:

8. Ask a middle school/junior high teacher what struggles her or his students have in learning integer operations and how she or he handles those challenges. Think about the teacher's choices and describe what you might do differently and why.

Selected References

Chang, L. (1985). Multiple methods of teaching the addition and subtraction of integers. *Arithmetic Teacher, 33,* 14–19.

Cooke, M.B. (1993). A videotaping project to explore the multiplication of integers. *Arithmetic Teacher, 41,* 170–171.

Crowley, M.L., and Dunn, K.A. (1985). On multiplying negative numbers. *Mathematics Teacher, 78,* 252–256.

Kent, L.B. (2000). Connecting integers to meaningful contexts. *Mathematics Teaching in the Middle School, 6,* 62–66.

Lamb, L.C., and Thanheiser, E. (2006). Understanding integers: Using balloons and weights software. In Alatorre, S., Cortina, J.L., Sáiz, M., and Méndez, A. (Eds.). *Proceedings of the 28th Annual Meeting of the North American Chapter of the International Group for the Psychology of Mathematics Education, 2,* 163–164.

Linchevski, L., and Williams, J. (1999). Using intuition from everyday life in "filling" the gap in children's extension of their number concept to include the negative numbers. *Educational Studies in Mathematics, 39,* 131–147.

McAuley, J. (1990). Please sir, I didn't do nothin. *Mathematics in School, 19,* 45–47.

Petrealla, G. (2001). Subtracting integers: An affective lesson. *Mathematics Teaching in the Middle School, 7,* 150–151.

Reeves, C.A., and Webb, D. (2004). Balloons on the rise: A problem solving introduction to integers. *Mathematics Teaching in the Middle School, 9,* 476–482.

Small, M. (2005). *PRIME: Number and operations: Background and strategies.* Toronto: Thomson Nelson.

Streefland, L. (1996). Negative numbers: Reflections of a learning researcher. *Journal of Mathematical Behavior, 15,* 57–77.

Chapter 13

3-D and 2-D Shapes

A mirror was placed on the original shape to create each of the other three shapes. Each time, indicate where the mirror was placed and how you know.

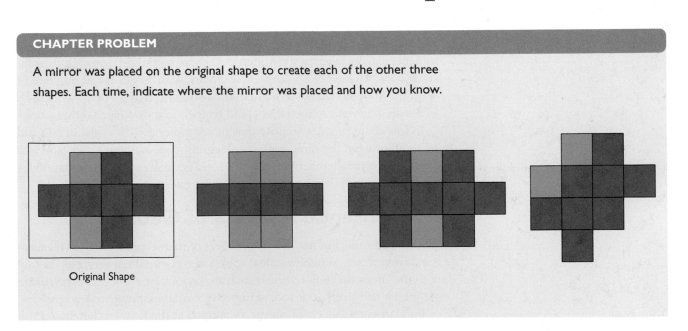

Original Shape

> **IN A NUTSHELL**
>
> The main ideas in this chapter are listed below:
>
> 1. Researchers have described a taxonomy of geometric development that elaborates growth from the least sophisticated to the most sophisticated geometric understanding.
>
> 2. Properties and attributes of geometric shape become the object of study in geometry. Many of the same properties and attributes that apply to 2-D shapes apply to 3-D shapes. The fact that every shape can be "cut up" and rearranged into other shapes is a fundamental part of this study.
>
> 3. Many geometric properties and attributes are related to measurements, for example, whether two sides are the same length, two faces the same area, lines equally distant apart, etc.

Geometry, which encompasses the study of shapes and spatial relationships, is an area of study that many students and teachers enjoy because it offers such a wide range of opportunities for hands-on exploration. K–8 students usually begin by examining 3-D shapes, and then broaden their investigations to include 2-D shapes and work with location and movement on grids. At higher levels of mathematics, students may go on to work with 3-D grids, or even explore what could happen in more than 3 dimensions.

In this chapter, you will note that many topics are discussed in 2-D and 3-D situations in the same sections. Helping you, as the teacher, and students see the parallels between 2-D and 3-D geometry is important; it helps focus on the underlying mathematical principles.

Fundamental Aspects of Geometry

Geometry is one, but not the only, aspect of mathematics where visualization is important. Whiteley (2004) speaks about visual reasoning as "seeing to think." Because visualization is such an obvious aspect of geometry, using geometric thinking as one tool to improve visual reasoning makes sense.

Fundamental aspects of geometry studied at the K–8 level include:

- recognizing, describing, and making predictions about 3-D shapes, including their role in building structures
- recognizing, describing, and making predictions about 2-D shapes, including the representation of 3-D shapes in two dimensions
- exploring location and position, for example, using coordinate systems or map grids, and developing an understanding of relative position
- recognizing, describing, and making predictions about the effects of transformations on shapes, for example, predicting what a shape will look like after it is turned
- using visualization and spatial models to explore mathematical topics
- using reasoning to compare and contrast shapes, and to draw conclusions about them

- using geometric models and concepts to solve problems
- using mathematical language to communicate about geometric concepts
- representing shapes in different ways
- recognizing how geometric ideas connect to each other, and how they connect with other strands of mathematics and other subject areas

Some of these topics will be examined in this chapter and some in Chapter 14.

Development of Geometric Thinking

It is important to note that children's ability to conceptualize shape develops through different stages, and that this development is fostered by each child's experience. Two researchers who explored these stages of development are Pierre van Hiele and Dina van Hiele-Geldof, who developed a taxonomy of geometric thinking (Teppo, 1991). At the initial level, Level 0: Visualization, students focus on what individual shapes "look like." A child at this level may identify a circle only because it "looks like" a circle. By Level 1: Analysis, children are ready to conceive of shapes as part of a group of similar shapes, and to begin taking note of their properties. By Level 2: Informal Deduction, they have a greater ability to apply "if-then" reasoning and are ready to consider simple logical arguments about shape properties. Van Hiele Levels 3 and 4 (Deduction and Rigour) apply to students in high school and beyond, and involve more formal work in which students are expected to use traditional Euclidean and also non-traditional axiom (premise) structures from which to deduce properties of shapes.

Van Hiele's Taxonomy of Geometric Thought

LEVEL 0: VISUALIZATION	
	Which shapes are triangles? Tell how you know.

LEVEL 1: ANALYSIS	
	How can you determine which side of a triangle is the longest if you know all three angle measurements?

(continued)

LEVEL 2: INFORMAL DEDUCTION

Do you think every triangle is half of a parallelogram? Explain.

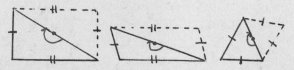

LEVEL 3: DEDUCTION

(not applicable to elementary school students and very few Grades 7–8 students)

What is the sum of the angles in a triangle? How can you use parallel lines and transversals to show that every triangle will have the same angle sum?

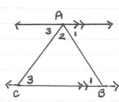

- The angles labeled 1 are equal because the line through A and side CB are parallel and side AB is a transversal.
- The angles labeled 3 are equal because the line through A and side CB are parallel and side AC is a transversal.
- Angles 1, 2, and 3 at the top form a straight angle so they have a sum of 180°.
- Therefore, angles 1, 2, and 3 inside the triangle have a sum of 180°.

LEVEL 4: RIGOUR

(not applicable to elementary school students)

Draw a triangle on a globe by joining the North Pole to two points on the equator. Show that the sum of the interior angles of this triangle is greater than 180°.

Two of the angles in the triangle meet the equator at right angles, so they add up to 180°. This means that the sum of the triangle's three angles has to be greater than 180°.

Identifying, Naming, and Classifying Shapes

Younger students identify and name shapes on an intuitive level—they just know that it is a "ball" (sphere) or a "box" (rectangle-based prism) or a square or a triangle. As students develop mathematically, they are increasingly able to identify and name a shape by examining its properties and using reasoning. For example, a student might say, "Both of these shapes are triangles because each has 3 straight sides. All shapes with 3 straight sides are triangles." This student recognizes that having 3 straight sides is a property of the class of shapes called triangles.

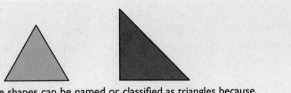

Both of these shapes can be named or classified as triangles because they have 3 straight sides.

Later, students' ability to identify and name/classify shapes becomes more sophisticated. These students are able to consider more and more geometric properties and more specific classifications. For example, a more advanced student might say, "The red triangle is a right isosceles triangle because it has 3 straight sides and two of them are equal, and it has a right angle."

Identification of 2-D and 3-D Shapes

One way to provide experience with identifying shapes is to organize a shape hunt or a WebQuest, as described in **Activity 13.1** below. A shape hunt or WebQuest is a good way to connect geometry with everyday life. For example, students can observe and identify shapes in their environment, shapes in books they are reading, shapes in works of art, shapes in architectural structures, etc.

ACTIVITY 13.1

Young students can identify 3-D shapes by taking part in a shape hunt or geometry walk in the classroom, school, or playground, or at home. Older students can identify 2-D shapes by taking part in a WebQuest on the Internet.

Shape Hunt	
Shapes we looked for	Names of things we found
Cube	
Cylinder	

(continued)

- Click some links on some of the Web links. Find pictures of triangles.

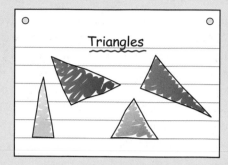

- Print and cut out the pictures.
- Make a booklet or a poster about your triangles.

Grade 4 or higher students can work with shape classifications and geometric properties by creating a 2-D shape collage to fit the rules given below:

Use cutout shapes to make this collage.

1. All the shapes are quadrilaterals.

2. Two shapes have parallel sides, but are not rectangles.

3. Three shapes have lines of symmetry.

As students become more familiar with basic shape identification, they can participate in activities that focus increasingly on the geometric properties that define or classify certain shapes. For example, in **Activity 13.2** in the margin, students are working with shape classifications (quadrilaterals and non-rectangles) that are associated with certain geometric properties (4 sides, parallel sides, and no right angles), as well as other properties such as symmetry.

Exploring Geometric Attributes and Properties

Young students can take part in activities where they explore the attributes of shapes. For 2-D shapes, they might consider whether the sides of a shape are rounded or straight, or whether the shape is open or closed. For 3-D shapes, they might consider whether the shape can or cannot roll. The focus at this point is on exploring and comparing shapes, rather than fitting them into formal classifications.

As students become more familiar with geometric attributes, they gradually gain an awareness of the specific attributes that define each class of shape, that is, the properties of shapes. A *property* is an attribute that applies to all the shapes of a certain class. For example, the class of shapes called rectangles has these properties: 4 straight sides, 2 pairs of equal sides, and 4 right angles. Quadrilaterals (a class of shapes that includes rectangles) also have 4 straight sides but only some quadrilaterals have 4 right angles. So, having 4 right angles is a property of all rectangles, but not of all quadrilaterals, although it is an attribute of some quadrilaterals.

Comparing Shapes

In the Student Response on page 289, the student has focused on properties of the shapes—the number and shape of the faces—in order to compare them. Other properties that differentiate these two classes of shapes could be the number of vertices or the number of edges. If asked how these shapes are the same, the student would have to refer to those properties that make these shapes part of a higher classification. The student might notice, for example, that all the faces are *polygons*, so both shapes are *polyhedrons*.

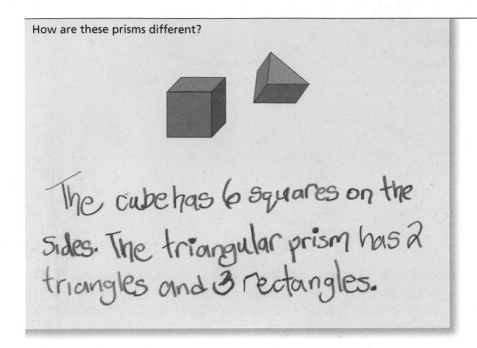

How are these prisms different?

The cube has 6 squares on the sides. The triangular prism has 2 triangles and 3 rectangles.

Student Response

This student recognizes that cubes are different from triangle-based prisms because they have a different number of faces and different face shapes. Note that the student is still using the informal term "side" rather than the formal mathematical term "face."

In **Activity 13.3**, students compare 2-D shapes. Suppose the student drew a rectangle. In order to differentiate it from the triangle, a student might mention the number of sides: 4 sides (a property of rectangles) versus 3 sides (a property of triangles), or he or she might draw a shape that is much bigger or a triangle that is tilted over, focusing on size or orientation. In order to find similarities, students may look for properties that the shapes share. In this case, a student might note that both have straight sides, which is a property of the class of shapes called *polygons*.

Sorting and Patterning to Explore Geometric Attributes

Most curricula in Canada require elementary school students to sort and construct 2-D and 3-D shapes. One of the main purposes of sorting shapes and creating patterns with them is to focus students' attention on geometric attributes that they can use to classify the shapes, for example, sorting a group of 2-D shapes to separate those with 3 sides from those with 4 or more sides.

Sorting Shapes

In the sort below, some prisms have been sorted according to how many *faces* they have. Through a sort like this, students will begin to discover some of the geometric properties of triangle-based and rectangle-based prisms, for example, all triangle-based prisms have 5 faces and all rectangle-based prisms have 6 faces.

ACTIVITY 13.3

a) Copy this shape.

b) Now draw a shape that is different from the shape in one way, but the same in another way.

c) How are they different? How are they alike?

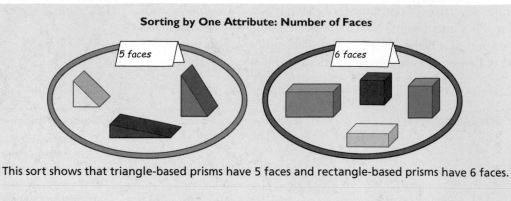

Sorting by One Attribute: Number of Faces

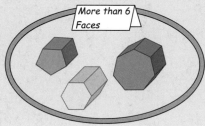

This sort shows that triangle-based prisms have 5 faces and rectangle-based prisms have 6 faces.

Students can also use sorting to investigate properties of 2-D shapes. The Venn diagram below shows that having right angles is an *attribute* of some parallelograms, but it is not a *property* of them because some parallelograms have no right angles. Note that the orange shape is outside the circles because it is not a parallelogram and it has no right angles.

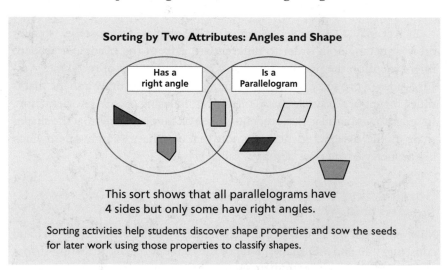

Sorting by Two Attributes: Angles and Shape

This sort shows that all parallelograms have 4 sides but only some have right angles.

Sorting activities help students discover shape properties and sow the seeds for later work using those properties to classify shapes.

Patterning to Explore Geometric Attributes and Properties

Shape patterns are founded on experience with sorting and classifying according to attributes and properties. Sorting items using attributes such as the direction in which a shape is pointing, or the properties such as number or lengths of sides (for 2-D shapes) or flat versus curved surfaces (for 3-D shapes), prepares students for patterning. It helps students focus on what makes one element in a pattern like or different from another. This then makes it possible to identify, describe, compare, and extend the pattern.

Young students usually begin with simple repeating patterns like the one shown at the top of page 291.

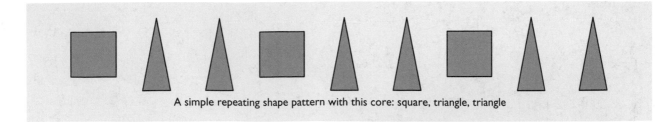

A simple repeating shape pattern with this core: square, triangle, triangle

As students gain more experience with shape patterns, they gain the ability to interpret, extend, and create increasingly complex patterns. These include patterns with multiple attributes, growing/shrinking patterns, and grid patterns that change in two directions. Patterns may also involve transformations.

More Challenging Shape Patterns

A REPEATING TWO-ATTRIBUTE PATTERN

In this pattern, not only do the shapes change, but the orientation of the shapes changes as well.

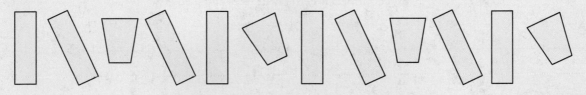

Pattern rule 1: rectangle, rectangle, trapezoid, ...
Pattern rule 2: vertical, turned, ...

A GROWING TWO-DIMENSIONAL PATTERN

In this growing pattern, both the length and the width of the square increase by 1 square each time.

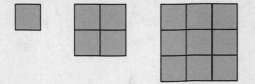

A MULTI-DIRECTIONAL PATTERN

Patterns are visible in rows, columns, and diagonals on this grid.

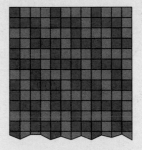

Types of 3-D Shapes

A number of 3-D shapes are either so familiar or of sufficient mathematical interest that they have special names.

Polyhedrons, Spheres, Cones, and Cylinders

A polyhedron is any 3-D shape whose faces are all polygons. Polyhedrons can have as few as 4 faces or they can have many more. Each face can have as few as 3 sides. All prisms and pyramids are polyhedrons (or polyhedra). Spheres, cones, and cylinders are not polyhedrons as their surfaces are not polygons, but they are shapes students are expected to become familiar with.

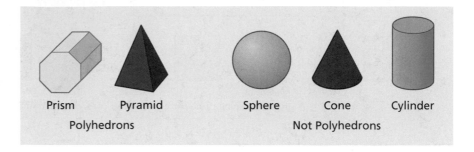

Prism   Pyramid   Sphere   Cone   Cylinder

Polyhedrons   Not Polyhedrons

Components of 3-D Shapes

In order to describe the properties of 3-D shapes, and to classify them, students need to understand their components. Components are the individual parts that go together to make a shape—*faces*, *curved surfaces*, *edges*, and *vertices*.

Concrete models of 3-D shapes allow students to explore these components in a very hands-on way. For example, a student would be able to manipulate a model of a triangle-based prism to view, touch, and count all 5 faces—2 triangles and 3 rectangles. He or she would also be able to touch and count each of the 6 vertices and 9 edges.

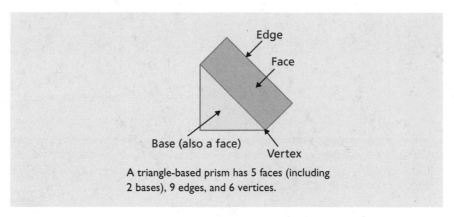

A triangle-based prism has 5 faces (including 2 bases), 9 edges, and 6 vertices.

One way to familiarize students with 3-D shapes is to provide information about the properties of a particular shape (or have students provide this information for one another), and have students figure out what the shape might be. Some students might be able to do this by visualizing; others will need concrete materials to help them.

Activities with 3-D shapes can often provide realistic and meaningful reasons for studying 2-D shapes. In fact, most teachers prefer to begin their study of shapes with 3-D shapes, which provides a natural context for studying the 2-D shapes that form their faces.

Using Properties to Classify 2-D Shapes

As with 3-D shapes, certain 2-D shapes are met regularly in elementary school curricula.

Polygons and Circles

A *polygon* is a closed 2-D shape whose sides are straight line segments that intersect only at the vertices. A circle is defined as a set of points that are the same distance from a given point, the centre.

ACTIVITY 13.4

Tell students that a certain 3-D shape has 8 vertices. Ask what it could be.

Components of 2-D Shapes

To describe the properties of 2-D shapes, and to classify them, students can use descriptions of their components. Components are the individual parts that go together to make a shape—straight sides, curves, and angles.

Components of 2-D Shapes

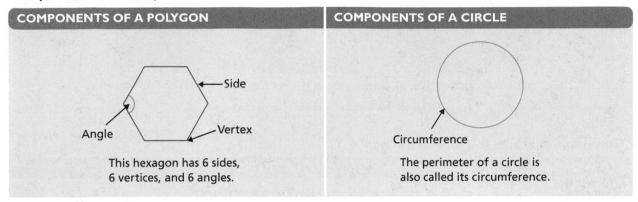

COMPONENTS OF A POLYGON	COMPONENTS OF A CIRCLE
This hexagon has 6 sides, 6 vertices, and 6 angles.	The perimeter of a circle is also called its circumference.

Types of Polygons

NAMING POLYGONS

Sample polygons	Number of sides	Name	Sample polygons	Number of sides	Name
	3	**tri**angle		8	**octa**gon
	4	**quadri**lateral		9	**nona**gon
	5	**penta**gon		10	**deca**gon
	6	**hexa**gon		11	**hendeca**gon
	7	**hepta**gon		12	**dodeca**gon

Although most polygons are called "…gons," triangles and quadrilaterals are not. For some students, that makes it less likely for them to include these shapes as types of polygons.

Relating Polygon Vertices and Sides

An interesting property of polygons is that the number of vertices is always equal to the number of sides. The example on page 294 demonstrates why.

In a polygon, each vertex is formed by the endpoints of 2 line segments, so the number of vertices will be equal to the total *number of separate endpoints* ÷ 2 or *n* vertices. Each of the shapes below has 5 sides, so there are 10 end points altogether, which meet at 10 ÷ 2 or 5 vertices.

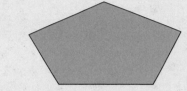  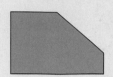

5 sides and 5 vertices   5 sides and 5 vertices   5 sides and 5 vertices

Polygons have the same number of sides as vertices.

Classifying 2-D Shapes by Properties: Polygons

CLASS OF 2-D SHAPE AND DISCUSSION	PROPERTIES

Triangles

Triangles are 3-sided polygons. They are usually classified in terms of the relationship of their side lengths. *Equilateral triangles* have all 3 sides equal; *isosceles triangles* have 2 sides equal; and *scalene triangles* have 3 sides of different lengths.

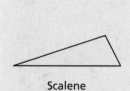

Scalene   Isosceles   Equilateral
                                     Equiangular

Classifying triangles by side length

Some say that, because there are 2 equal sides in an equilateral triangle, it is a special type of isosceles triangle.

Alternative Classifications

A different way to classify triangles is in terms of their angles. If a triangle has one square corner (or right angle or 90° angle), then the triangle is called a *right triangle*. If all three angles are less than 90° (all acute angles), the triangle is called an *acute triangle*. If one angle is greater than 90° (an obtuse angle), it is called an *obtuse triangle*. If all three angles are equal (each having a measure of 60°), it is called an *equiangular triangle*.

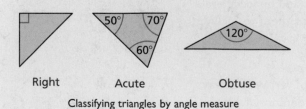

Right   Acute   Obtuse

Classifying triangles by angle measure

Basic Properties

All triangles are polygons with:

3 straight sides

3 vertices (3 angles)

The properties of special types of triangles are listed in the chart below.

Class of Triangle	Properties
equilateral	3 equal sides
equiangular	3 equal angles, each 60°
isosceles	2 equal sides
	2 equal angles
scalene	3 sides of different lengths
	3 angles of different measures
right	1 right angle
acute	3 acute angles
obtuse	1 obtuse angle

Related/Other Properties

- In order to form a triangle, the sum of the lengths of the two shorter sides must be greater than the longest side.

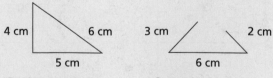

Can form a triangle   Cannot form a triangle

- The side opposite the greatest angle is always the longest side. Similarly, the side opposite the smallest angle is always the shortest side.

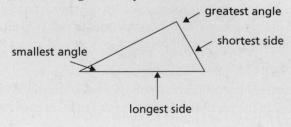

CLASS OF 2-D SHAPE AND DISCUSSION

Students can use dynamic geometry software to see how the side lengths, overall shape, and angle measures change when one vertex is moved.

Unlike other polygons, triangles are rigid structures. This is why triangles are frequently used in construction.

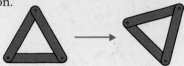

When pushed, a triangle does not change its shape because it is a rigid shape.

When pushed, a rectangle becomes a non-rectangular parallelogram.

PROPERTIES

- If two angles of a triangle have the same measure, then the sides opposite them are of equal length (and vice versa).
- The sum of the 3 angles is always 180°.
- A triangle can never have more than one obtuse angle (an angle greater than 90°) because the 3 angles in a triangle always add to 180°.

A triangle with two right angles is impossible.

A triangle can never have two 90° angles because, if it did, the sides opposite those angles would be parallel, and would not meet at a vertex.

QUADRILATERALS

Quadrilaterals are 4-sided polygons. Although rectangles are the most common quadrilateral that you see in everyday life, students will soon discover that there are many classes of quadrilaterals. The quadrilateral family includes parallelograms, kites, and trapezoids, along with other four-sided shapes.

The diagram below shows how different classes of quadrilaterals are related to one another. An alternate way to classify quadrilaterals is based on their symmetries (Whiteley, 2006).

Classifying Quadrilaterals

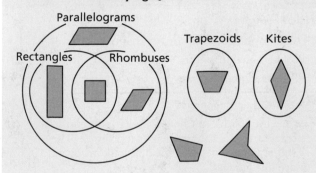

Some mathematicians consider a parallelogram to be a special type of trapezoid, since it has one pair of parallel sides (as well as another pair). In that case, the parallelogram circle above would be inside the trapezoid circle.

PROPERTIES

Basic Properties

All quadrilaterals are polygons with:

4 straight sides

4 vertices (4 angles)

The properties of special types of quadrilaterals are listed in the chart below.

Quadrilateral	Properties
Parallelogram	A quadrilateral with two pairs of parallel sides
Rhombus	A parallelogram with all sides equal in length
Rectangle	A parallelogram with four right angles.
Square	A rectangle with all sides equal in length.
Trapezoid	A quadrilateral with one pair of parallel sides. If 2 sides are equal, the shape is called an *isosceles trapezoid*.
Kite	A quadrilateral with two pairs of equal adjacent sides.

(continued)

Similarly, some would consider a rhombus to be a special kind of kite, since it has 2 pairs of equal adjacent sides (even though both pairs are the same). In this case, the kite circle would need to include the rhombus circle.

Different definitions are possible for many quadrilaterals, and students at later developmental phases can explore these. For example:

- A parallelogram is typically described as a quadrilateral with two pairs of parallel sides. It can also be described as a quadrilateral where opposite sides are equal in length, since this is only possible where there are two pairs of parallel sides.

- A rectangle is typically described as a parallelogram with 4 right angles, but it can also be described as a parallelogram with at least 1 right angle, since this is only possible if the other angles are also right angles.

Related/Other Properties

- Every quadrilateral has 2 diagonals.

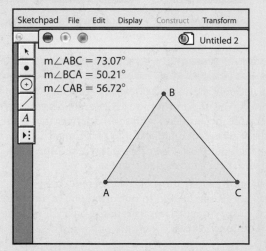

- Because a diagonal divides a quadrilateral into two triangles, the sum of the angles in a quadrilateral is always 180° + 180° or 360°.

Angle sum = 180°   Angle sum = 180°

Angle sum = 360°

This latter concept can be explored by creating the shape using dynamic geometry software, which will measure the angles for the student.

Sketchpad   File   Edit   Display   Construct   Transform

Untitled 2

m∠ABC = 73.07°
m∠BCA = 50.21°
m∠CAB = 56.72°

CLASS OF POLYGON AND DISCUSSION

Regular Polygons

In a *regular polygon*, all the sides are the same length and all the angles are the same size. Equilateral triangles and squares are examples of regular polygons.

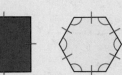

Equilateral triangle   Square   Regular hexagon

The word "regular" sometimes creates confusion for students, since they may think of something "regular" as something that's "ordinary." From that perspective, students may view common shapes such as circles or rectangles as "regular," but this is not the mathematical definition.

PROPERTIES

Basic Properties

All regular polygons are convex shapes that have

- all sides equal in length
- all angles equal in size

Related/Other Properties

- As the number of sides on a regular polygon increases, so does the angle at each vertex. The result is a series of polygons that look more and more like circles.

3 sides   4 sides   6 sides   12 sides
60° angles   90° angles   120° angles   150° angles

When you add another side to a regular polygon, the angle at each vertex increases.

Planes

Although planes are often not addressed in K–8 formally, students discuss planes informally when working with many aspects of geometry. A plane is a 2-D or flat surface that goes on forever in two directions not on the same line. The faces of 3-D shapes are parts of planes. Planes can be *parallel* or they can *intersect*.

RELATING PLANES AND 3-D SHAPES

- Each face is on a different plane.
- Edges are where two planes intersect.
- Vertices are where three or more planes intersect.
- Adjacent faces of a cube are parts of intersecting planes, and opposite faces are parts of parallel planes.

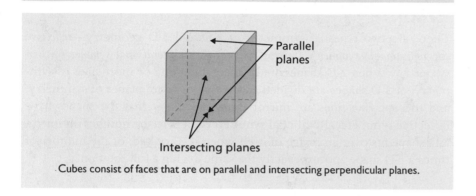

Cubes consist of faces that are on parallel and intersecting perpendicular planes.

Lines, Segments, and Rays

It is normally taken for granted that students know what *lines* are, but the term is often used interchangeably with *ray* and *line segment*. The usual way of naming a line, line segment, or ray is to locate and name two points on it (usually indicated with a dot). The standard convention for showing the difference between lines, line segments, and rays is to use an arrow to indicate where a line extends indefinitely and to use a dot to indicate an end point.

LINE	LINE SEGMENT	RAY
A line is something straight and "infinitely thin" that extends forever in two directions.	A line segment is a "piece of a line," with two defined endpoints.	A ray has one defined endpoint and extends infinitely from it.

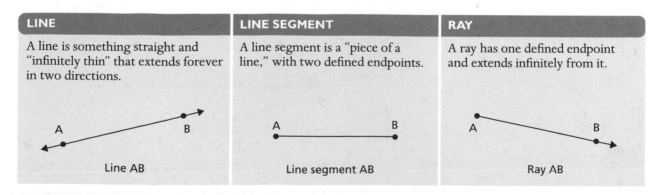

Lines, line segments, and rays can be *parallel* or they can *intersect*. Parallel lines, line segments, and rays never meet, as they remain a constant distance apart. Whenever two lines intersect, they meet at a single point. When lines intersect at a 90° angle, they are said to be *perpendicular*.

PARALLEL	INTERSECTING	PERPENDICULAR
Parallel lines do not meet. The distance between parallel lines remains constant.	Intersecting lines meet at a single point. The distance between the lines increases as you move from that point.	Perpendicular lines are intersecting lines that meet at a right angle.

Symmetry

There are two types of symmetry in 2-D and 3-D geometry—*reflective* (or *reflectional*) *symmetry* (*mirror symmetry*) and *rotational symmetry* (*turn symmetry*). When 2-D shapes are divided along one or more lines of symmetry, or 3-D shapes are divided across one or more planes of symmetry, and the opposite sides are mirror images, you say that the shapes have reflective symmetry. Rotational symmetry refers to the number of times a 2-D shape fits over an image of itself when it is rotated, or the number of times a 3-D shape appears exactly the same during a full rotation.

Reflective Symmetry of 2-D and 3-D Shapes

A shape has *reflective symmetry* if one half of the shape is a reflection of the other half. Both 2-D and 3-D shapes can have reflective symmetry. In a 2-D shape, the reflection occurs across a line. In a 3-D shape, it occurs across a plane.

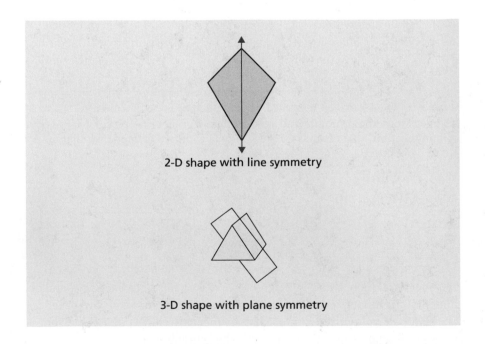

2-D shape with line symmetry

3-D shape with plane symmetry

2-D Shapes: Understanding and Determining Line Symmetry

When one half of a shape reflects onto the other half across a line, the line is called the *line of symmetry*. Shapes can have one or more lines of symmetry. In fact, a circle has an infinite number of lines of symmetry.

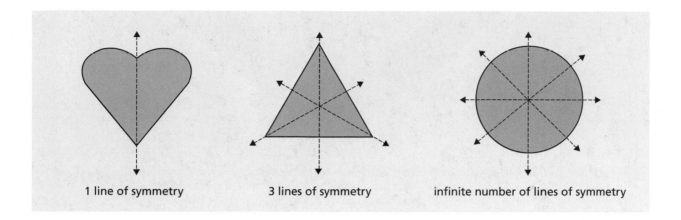

| 1 line of symmetry | 3 lines of symmetry | infinite number of lines of symmetry |

Students are often surprised to find that a shape can have more than one line of symmetry. Note that the more sides there are on a regular polygon, the more lines of symmetry there will be. This is because the shape is getting more and more like a circle. In addition, the number of lines of symmetry in a regular polygon is always equal to the number of vertices.

Students can test the symmetry of a 2-D shape either by folding it to see if the halves match, or by placing a transparent mirror (or a commercial tool called a *Mira*) on the shape. In each case, if the shape is symmetrical along the fold line or where the Mira has been placed, the image of one side of the shape will fall right on top of the other side of the shape.

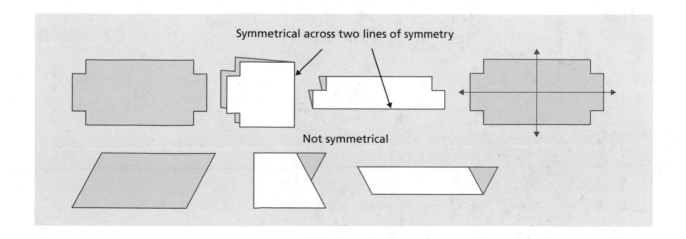

Symmetrical across two lines of symmetry

Not symmetrical

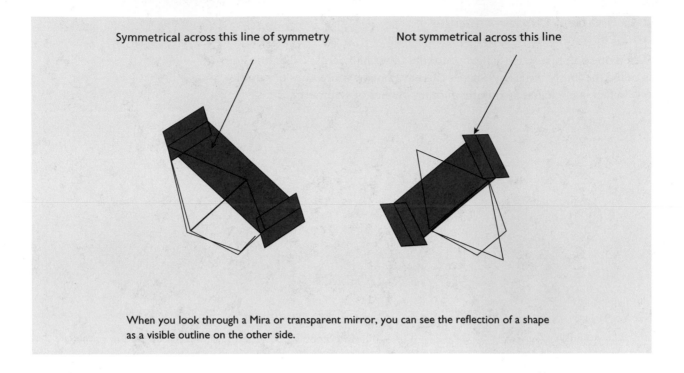

Symmetrical across this line of symmetry   Not symmetrical across this line

When you look through a Mira or transparent mirror, you can see the reflection of a shape as a visible outline on the other side.

Cut a simple shape out of a picture in a magazine. Fold your shape in half, and then cut along the fold line.

Glue your picture to a piece of paper and draw the missing half.

2-D Shapes: Constructing Shapes with Line Symmetry

There are a number of different ways for students to construct shapes with line symmetry. Students can build designs with square tiles or pattern blocks, use folded paper, use a Mira, use geoboards or grid paper, or use technology tools such as a drawing program or dynamic geometry software. Another approach is described in **Activity 13.5**.

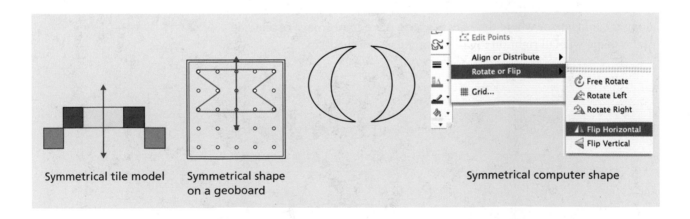

Symmetrical tile model   Symmetrical shape on a geoboard   Symmetrical computer shape

3-D Shapes: Understanding and Determining Plane Symmetry

When one half of a 3-D shape reflects onto the other half across a plane, the plane separating the halves is called the *plane of symmetry*. This is why reflective symmetry in 3-D shapes is called *plane symmetry*.

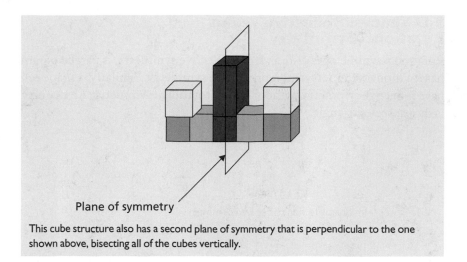

Plane of symmetry

This cube structure also has a second plane of symmetry that is perpendicular to the one shown above, bisecting all of the cubes vertically.

It is sometimes difficult to test 3-D shapes for symmetry, since the shapes cannot be folded and overlapped. However, they can often be represented with modelling clay or linking cubes, and then divided in half. Then students can examine and manipulate the halves to see if one half looks like the exact "reverse" of the other half.

There are a number of different ways for students to construct shapes with plane symmetry. These include building structures with linking cubes, stacking shape blocks, and using modelling clay. Block stacks can be tested for symmetry with a Mira, while modelling clay shapes can be cut through the centre with a strand of dental floss.

Rotational Symmetry of 2-D and 3-D Shapes

A shape has rotational symmetry if, when you turn it around its centre point, it fits over a tracing of itself (or into an outline of itself) at least once before it has completed a full rotation. Both 2-D and 3-D shapes can have rotational symmetry.

2-D Shapes: Determining Rotational Symmetry

One way to test for rotational symmetry is to trace the shape, and then turn it around a pencil point to see whether it fits over itself. For example, a rectangle fits over itself twice—once after a half turn, and again after a complete turn.

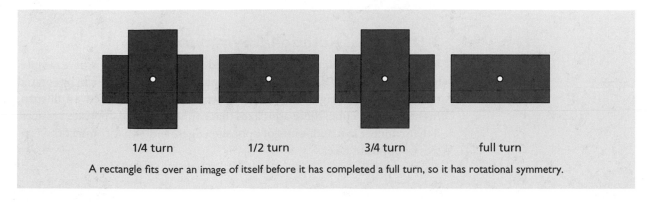

1/4 turn   1/2 turn   3/4 turn   full turn

A rectangle fits over an image of itself before it has completed a full turn, so it has rotational symmetry.

2-D Shapes: Reflective versus Rotational Symmetry

Rotational symmetry is distinct from reflective symmetry. A parallelogram has rotational symmetry but no reflective symmetry. Similarly, a shape can have reflective symmetry without having rotational symmetry. An example is this isosceles triangle.

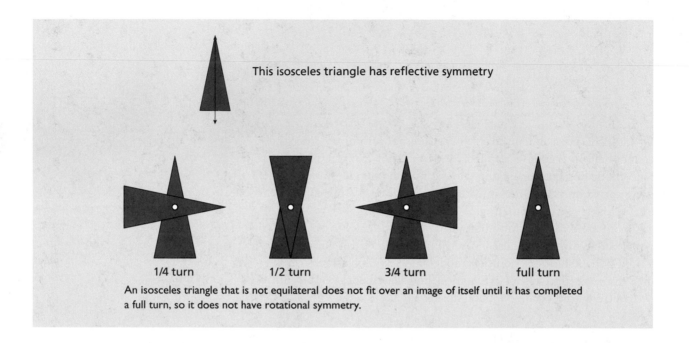

This isosceles triangle has reflective symmetry

| 1/4 turn | 1/2 turn | 3/4 turn | full turn |

An isosceles triangle that is not equilateral does not fit over an image of itself until it has completed a full turn, so it does not have rotational symmetry.

Although the two types of symmetry are distinct, there are relationships. For example, if a shape has two or more lines of mirror symmetry, it also has rotational symmetry.

2-D Shapes: Measuring Rotational Symmetry

The number of ways that a shape fits over its outline is called its *order of rotational symmetry*. For example, for an equilateral triangle, the order of rotational symmetry is 3 because it fits over its image 3 times within a full turn. For a circle, the order of rotational symmetry is infinite, because it fits over its image an infinite number of times as it turns through 360°.

3-D Shapes: Rotational Symmetry

Rotational symmetry is also associated with 3-D shapes. For example, a cube has 13 *axes of symmetry*—lines around which the shape can be rotated to reproduce its original orientation before it has completed a full turn. In the case of a cube, there are 4 axes that connect pairs of opposite vertices, 6 that connect the midpoints of opposite edges, and 3 that connect the centres of opposite faces.

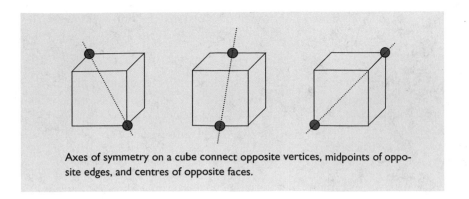

Axes of symmetry on a cube connect opposite vertices, midpoints of opposite edges, and centres of opposite faces.

Representing Shapes

Creating representations of shapes is a good way for students to use their visualization skills. It is also an area of geometry that is closely linked to other curriculum areas, especially the visual arts.

Representations can take many forms, including modelling clay or linking cube models, skeletons, nets, and various types of drawings. As students develop geometrically, their representations will appear more and more like the real shapes they represent. As well, they will be able to create more sophisticated representations, for example, moving from simple sketches of 3-D shapes to isometric drawings.

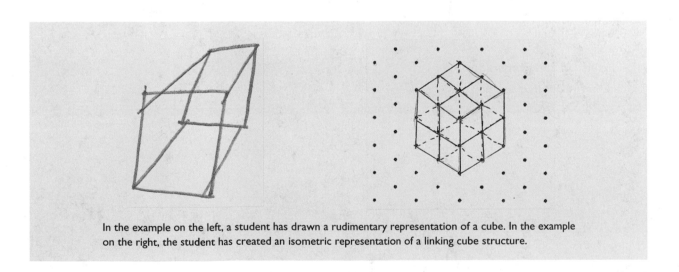

In the example on the left, a student has drawn a rudimentary representation of a cube. In the example on the right, the student has created an isometric representation of a linking cube structure.

Modelling Shapes

One way to represent shapes is to make concrete models. Making models allows students to explore shape properties in a very hands-on way.

As with any mathematics activity, students are more likely to be engaged if the activity is presented in context. For example, students could make cookies or decorations for a special occasion.

Some possible contexts for modelling 3-D shapes are shown in **Activities 13.6** and **13.7**.

Concrete Models

An appropriate activity for younger students involves using modelling clay to model shapes they can see and handle. To make the models, students can either form the clay by hand or use a mould.

For 2-D shapes, students can use cookie cutters with modelling clay or trace stencils onto paper. For 3-D shapes, students can use geometric solids or recycled materials (cans, boxes, cardboard tubes, etc.) as models, or they can work with commercial materials such as *Polydrons*.

A very concrete way for students to explore the properties of 2-D shapes is for them to form the vertices of the shapes with their own bodies. For example, provide a group of students with a large loop of yarn. Ask three of them to hold the yarn using one finger and tell you what shape they have made (a triangle). Discuss the properties of the triangle—3 sides and 3 vertices. Then ask a fourth student to join the group so the four make a rectangle. Ask how the properties of the shape have changed. Then continue to have more and more students join the group of yarn holders until they have formed a 20-sided shape. Finally, ask the students to describe the shape they have made. Most will see something very close to a circle.

In this hexagon, the students themselves are forming the vertices.

For older students, teachers can use activities such as **Activity 13.8** to prompt critical thinking about shapes, in this case triangles, and their properties.

Skeletons

Another type of model is a *skeleton*—a physical representation of just the edges and vertices of a 3-D shape, or just the sides and vertices of a 2-D shape. Materials for constructing skeletons include toothpicks and small balls of modelling clay, wiki sticks, or straws connected with bent pipe-cleaner segments. Toothpicks are especially useful for modelling regular shapes because they have a uniform length. There are also commercial construction toys, such as *Tinkertoys, K'nex, Zoob, Geomag,* and *D-stix,* that are suitable for constructing skeletons.

ACTIVITY 13.6

This 3-D shape was made by stacking pattern blocks.

a) What other shapes can you make this way?

b) Which of your shapes has the most faces?

ACTIVITY 13.7

This rectangle-based prism was built from linking cubes.

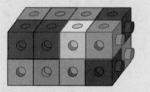

a) Use linking cubes to make a different rectangle-based prism.

b) Tell three things that are different about the prisms.

c) Tell three things that are the same about the prisms.

ACTIVITY 13.8

Which types of triangle combinations are possible? Use straws for sides.

	Acute	Obtuse	Right
Equilateral			
Isosceles			
Scalene			

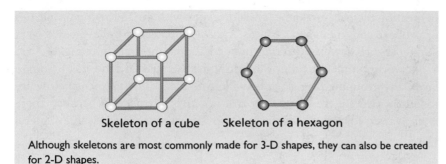

Skeleton of a cube   Skeleton of a hexagon

Although skeletons are most commonly made for 3-D shapes, they can also be created for 2-D shapes.

In order to construct the skeleton of a shape, many students need to have the shape in front of them. This way, they can look at and touch the edges, and vertices (focusing on the properties of the shape), to develop a mental picture of how many there are, and where they belong. Others are comfortable working from a picture of the shape, and still others can sometimes use just the verbal descriptions.

Skeletons help students see familiar shapes in a different way. When they are working with solid shapes, students often tend to focus more on the faces than on other components. The process of making a skeleton, where the faces are implicit, helps students become more aware of other components, such as edges, vertices, and angles. It also helps them create a mental image of the shape, which will stay with them even when they no longer have concrete models to look at. For example, when asked for the number of edges on a cube, a student might visualize the cube skeleton and mentally count the edges.

Activity 13.9 shows how a task involving skeletons can be used to help students learn more about the edge and vertex properties of 3-D shapes. For this activity, you may want to provide some samples of 3-D shapes for students' reference.

Nets

A net is a 2-D representation of a 3-D shape that can be folded to re-create the shape. When students make nets, they focus particularly on the faces, and how the faces fit together to form the shape.

It is important for students to realize that there are often many different nets for a single shape. Even though the faces do not change, they can be connected in different ways. For example, all of the nets below can be folded to make a cube.

Possible Nets for a Cube

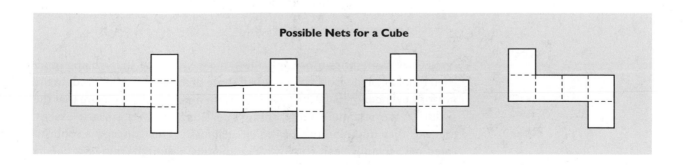

In creating the net for a cube, students work with the following properties of a cube: 6 congruent square faces, 3 pairs of opposite parallel faces, 3 faces joining at each vertex, and congruent edges that meet at right angles.

However, students cannot assume that because a cube has 6 square faces, any grouping of 6 squares will create a net. The patterns below are made from 6 squares, but they are not nets for a cube because there is no way to fold them to create a top face, a bottom face, and 4 lateral faces.

Not Nets for a Cube

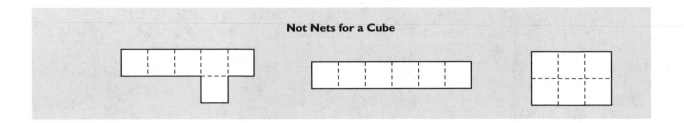

Creating Nets Although nets are a focus of study mainly for students in Grade 4 or higher, they can also be introduced to younger children. Students can roll a shape and trace all the faces onto a sheet of paper, or can connect squares from a set of Polydrons. When students compare results, they will see that their nets do not all look the same, even though all the nets can be folded to produce the shape they started with.

Later, students can use more sophisticated techniques. To create a net for a pyramid, students can draw the base, and then draw congruent isosceles triangles on each side, making sure that the height of each triangle is sufficient to reach farther than the centre of the base. Many students are surprised to find that pyramids with different heights can be created on the same base.

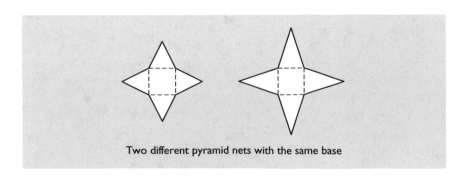

Two different pyramid nets with the same base

Nets are sometimes more difficult to make when the shape being modelled is not a polyhedron, that is, when some of the edges are curved. In the net for a cylinder on page 307, it is important for students to ensure that the width of the rectangle representing the lateral curved surface exactly matches the circumference of the circular base. This concept is sophisticated and generally dealt with by older students, although younger students can cut out pre-made nets and observe this property.

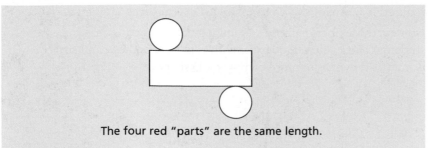

The four red "parts" are the same length.

For a cylinder net to work, the width of the rectangle representing the lateral curved surface must match the circumference of the circular base.

Drawing 3-D Shapes

Another way to represent a shape is with a picture. Before students can draw a shape, they need time to examine it. For example, to make perspective drawings of prisms, they need to focus on parallel bases and edges, as well as on face shapes.

Face Maps

In an introductory activity for young students, a teacher might provide a set of 3-D shapes and a "map" that shows all the faces of one of the shapes. The students' task is to identify the shape represented by the map. Later, students can make their own face maps of various 3-D shapes by tracing the faces one at a time.

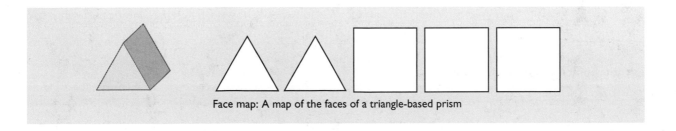

Face map: A map of the faces of a triangle-based prism

Isometric Drawings of Simple Shapes

An isometric drawing does not distort parallel lines the way a perspective drawing does. It is drawn on equilateral triangle dot paper, or isometric dot paper. Edges that are parallel on the original shape are represented by parallel lines in the drawing.

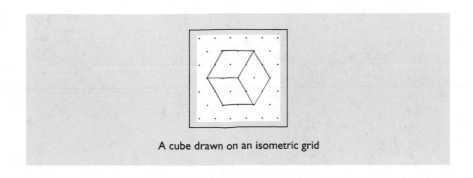

A cube drawn on an isometric grid

Isometric Drawings of Composite 3-D Structures

Isometric drawings of cubes and linking cube structures are the easiest for students to draw first. However, with experience, they can learn to create isometric drawings of more complex 3-D shapes.

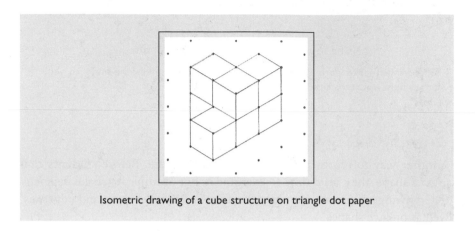

Isometric drawing of a cube structure on triangle dot paper

Orthographic Drawings of Simple 3-D Shapes

Orthographic drawings show what a shape looks like from the front, top, and sides. Draftsmen often create various views of a 3-D shape in order to help someone else build it.

When students are ready to begin drawing views of their own, they might start with a simple 3-D shape, such as a prism. View drawings can also be done for shapes with curved sides (like the cylinder shown below). When sides are curved, the view shows a flat representation of what the curved surface looks like.

Orthographic Drawings of 3-D Shapes

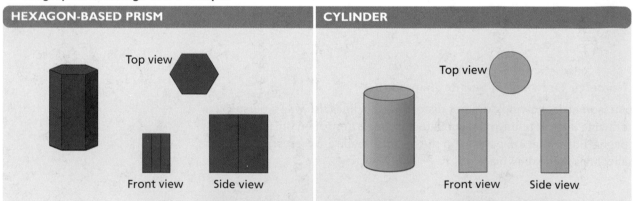

HEXAGON-BASED PRISM	CYLINDER
Top view / Front view / Side view	Top view / Front view / Side view

Base Plans

A base plan is another way of mapping a cube structure. The base plan is a view of the structure's base that uses numbers to indicate the height of each part of the structure. For example, the base plan illustrated on page 309 shows that the 2 rows at the back of the structure are 3 cubes high, while the front row is only 1 cube high.

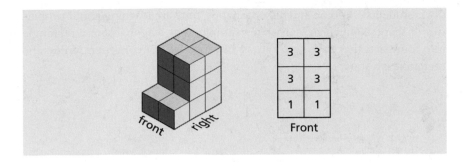

Drawing 2-D Shapes

To draw a 2-D shape on paper, students may need to apply some measurement skills, such as measuring lines and angles. Luckily, there are many everyday classroom tools that can help. Younger students can use tools such as fraction circles, grid paper, and pattern blocks to help them draw 2-D shapes.

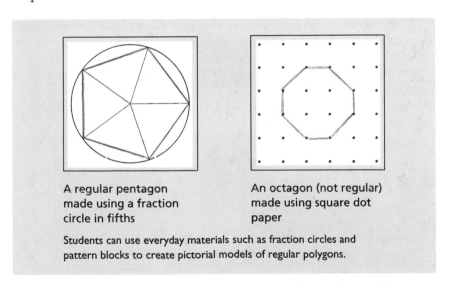

A regular pentagon made using a fraction circle in fifths

An octagon (not regular) made using square dot paper

Students can use everyday materials such as fraction circles and pattern blocks to create pictorial models of regular polygons.

Older students are ready to use math tools such as protractors and compasses to construct 2-D shapes.

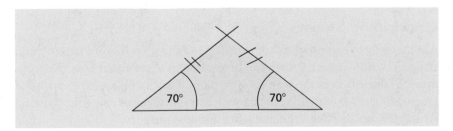

Combining and Dissecting Shapes

One of the key concepts in geometry is that any shape can be created by either combining or dissecting other shapes. Students are working with this concept when they are putting shapes together to make another shape, a picture, a design, or a structure, or when they are cutting a shape into pieces.

As students combine and dissect shapes, they are learning about properties of shapes. They can learn, for example, that diagonals cut a rectangle into four parts that have equal areas, but that are not congruent unless the rectangle is a square.

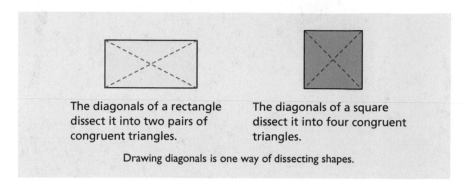

The diagonals of a rectangle dissect it into two pairs of congruent triangles.

The diagonals of a square dissect it into four congruent triangles.

Drawing diagonals is one way of dissecting shapes.

The ability to combine and dissect shapes also supports the development of measurement formulas. For example, cutting a parallelogram apart and reassembling it to form a rectangle can help students see why the area of a parallelogram can be determined by multiplying its base length by its height.

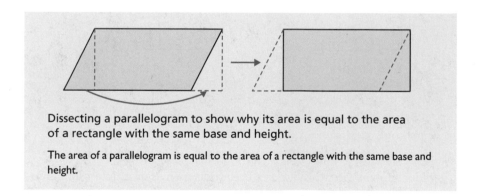

Dissecting a parallelogram to show why its area is equal to the area of a rectangle with the same base and height.

The area of a parallelogram is equal to the area of a rectangle with the same base and height.

Combining Shapes

Another way to explore the properties of 3-D shapes is to use them to build structures. Building structures can help students learn about how the properties of shapes affect the way you use them. For example, shapes with flat faces can be stacked while shapes with curved surfaces can roll. Building structures can also help students learn about symmetry.

Students can practise communicating about geometry as they describe how two structures are the same and different.

After some time for experimentation, students will be ready to build a structure to match a picture, or to fit a list of specifications. Younger students might be challenged to build a tall structure that is not wide, or a clay model with a point. They might discover, for example, that various mea-

ACTIVITY 13.10

Use toothpicks and marsh-mallows to build a 3-D shape with 6 vertices.	Stack pattern blocks to build 3-D shapes with 8 vertices. How many different shapes can you make?	Combine linking cubes to build two different symmetrical structures using 24 cubes that look like this from the left. 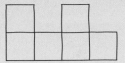

surements of a 3-D shape are independent of one another. Older students could complete tasks such as those in **Activity 13.10**.

Making pictures with 2-D shapes (either cutouts or stickers) can also be instructive for younger students. In creating the pictures, students are led to focus on how the shapes they learn about in school relate to shapes in their world.

Teacher: What can you tell me about your picture?
Student: I made a house and a tree.
Teacher: What shapes did you use?
Student: I used a rectangle and a triangle to make the house and I put a circle on top of a stick to make the tree.

Student Response

This student is beginning to recognize and name shapes, but does not yet realize that the "stick" is also a rectangle. This is a good opportunity for the teacher to focus the student's attention on geometric properties of rectangles by asking, "Which other shape in the picture is most like the stick shape? Why?"

Using Pattern Blocks

The pictures students create can also be made with concrete materials like pattern blocks. For example, the illustration shows 3 of the many composite 2-D shapes that students can make with 4 triangle blocks.

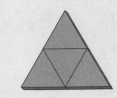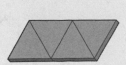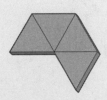

Different composite shapes made from 4 pattern-block triangles

ACTIVITY 13.11

How many different shapes can you make by combining two pattern block pieces?

ACTIVITY 13.12

Fit pattern blocks together to fill this outline.

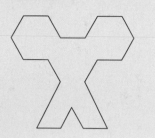

Students also enjoy solving shape puzzles where they have to fit shapes into an outline to create a picture or cover a design.

Working on puzzles provides a context to explore many geometric concepts. For example, very young students can learn that a shape is defined by its sides and vertices, but not by its orientation. Students also have the opportunity to see what a shape looks like when it is turned, or to attend to the sharpness of the angles.

The easiest puzzles show an outline for each block, and the child simply places each block where it belongs on the picture or design. More complex puzzles have outside outlines for students to fill in, but the individual blocks are not outlined. Many students enjoy creating puzzles like these to exchange with classmates.

PATTERN BLOCK PUZZLES

With each block outlined

With only an outside outline

Using Tangrams

Tangram pieces (sometimes called *tans*) are formed by dissecting a square into 7 smaller shapes as shown below. The pieces can then be combined to reconstruct the original square (a challenge best reserved for older students), as well as to create many other shapes.

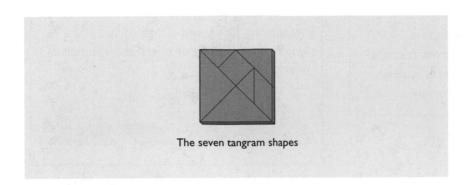

The seven tangram shapes

Like pattern blocks, tangrams can be used to illustrate both shape combinations and shape dissections. As with pattern blocks, the easiest tangram puzzles show individually outlined pieces, while the more difficult puzzles show only the outline of the shape as a whole.

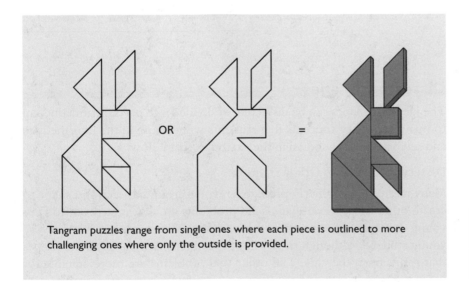

Tangram puzzles range from single ones where each piece is outlined to more challenging ones where only the outside is provided.

ACTIVITY 13.13

Use your tangram pieces to create other tangram animals.

Students can combine tangram pieces to create geometric shapes, as well as to make pictures as in **Activity 13.14**.

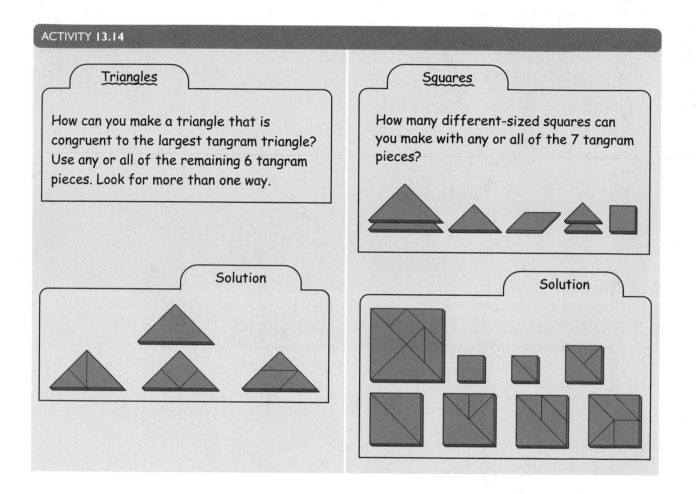

ACTIVITY 13.14

Triangles

How can you make a triangle that is congruent to the largest tangram triangle? Use any or all of the remaining 6 tangram pieces. Look for more than one way.

Solution

Squares

How many different-sized squares can you make with any or all of the 7 tangram pieces?

Solution

Dissecting Shapes

The idea that shapes can be dissected, or divided into parts, is fundamental to many geometry concepts that students will explore in the intermediate and senior grades, as shown in the examples that follow.

Dissecting to Create Other Shapes

Many interesting geometry problems revolve around dissecting a shape to create other shapes, and many such problems are accessible even to very young students. For example, the problem below is accessible to very young students, although they will not yet be able to name all the shapes that result from the cuts. The other two problems are more suitable for older students.

SAMPLE DISSECTING PROBLEMS

What shapes can you make by cutting a rectangle into 2 parts with straight cuts?

SAMPLE DISSECTING PROBLEMS

What shapes can you make by cutting a square into 4 pieces?

How can you cut a triangle into pieces so the pieces will make a square?

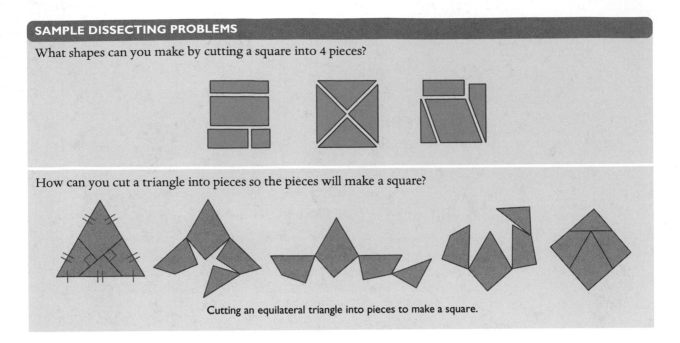

Cutting an equilateral triangle into pieces to make a square.

Dissecting to Calculate Angles

Students will learn that they can calculate the angle size for any regular polygon by dissecting the shape into triangles.

Calculating Angles in a Regular Octagon

There are six triangles that go together to form a regular octagon. The sum of the angles in each triangle is 180°, so the sum of the angles in a regular octagon is 6 × 180° or 1080°.

Since the eight angles in a regular octagon are all equal, each one measures 1080° ÷ 8 or 135°.

Congruence and Similarity

Congruence and similarity are geometric concepts that apply to both 2-D and 3-D shapes, although work with these concepts at the K–8 level is mainly limited to 2-D shapes.

Two shapes are considered to be congruent if one can be transformed into the other through a series of flips, slides, and/or turns. One fits exactly over the other (in the case of 2-D shapes).

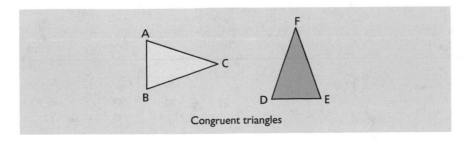

Congruent triangles

The word *congruent* is not only used to describe whole shapes, but also specific components of shapes, such as sides and angles. For example, these two triangles have a pair of congruent sides and a pair of congruent angles, but they are not congruent shapes.

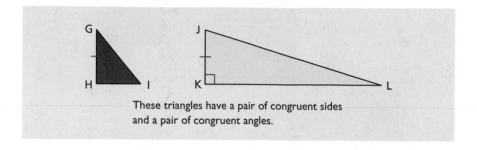

These triangles have a pair of congruent sides
and a pair of congruent angles.

Congruence can also be used to describe the properties of a single shape. For example, an equilateral triangle has 3 congruent sides and 3 congruent angles.

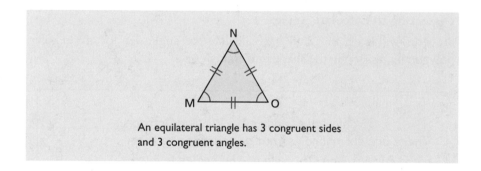

An equilateral triangle has 3 congruent sides
and 3 congruent angles.

Two shapes are said to be *similar* if they have the same shape, with sides in proportion to one another. Congruent shapes are similar, but so are two shapes where one is an enlargement or reduction of the other.

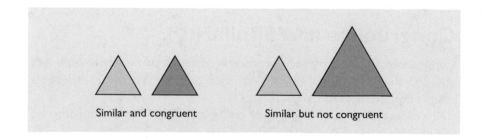

Similar and congruent   Similar but not congruent

Congruence of 2-D Shapes

Two 2-D shapes are congruent if they are identical in shape and size—that is, if one is an exact duplicate of the other. Students sometimes do not understand the difference between the math term *congruent* and the everyday term *the same*. It is important to recognize that the term *congruent* applies only to shape and size. Thus, figures can be different colours, or oriented in different ways, and they will still be congruent as long as they are the same shape and the same size.

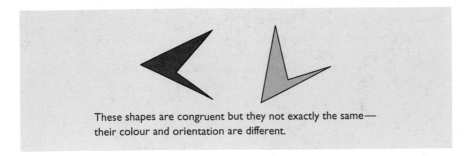

These shapes are congruent but they not exactly the same—
their colour and orientation are different.

One interesting way to explore congruence is to use optical illusions, as illustrated by the examples below.

OPTICAL ILLUSIONS

Which picture has a larger circle in the centre?

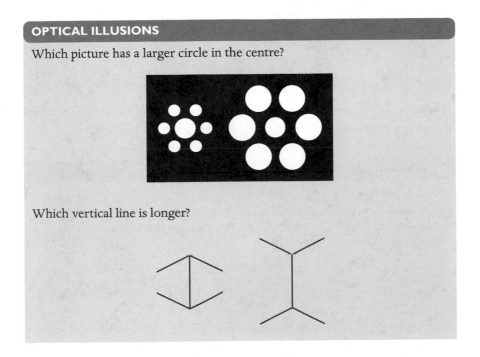

Which vertical line is longer?

Determining Congruence of 2-D Shapes

There are many ways to test for congruence, some more sophisticated than others.

WAYS TO TEST FOR CONGRUENCE

Superimposing

The easiest way to test 2-D shapes for congruence is simply to put one shape on top of the other to see if the outlines can be made to match exactly.

(continued)

Measuring Corresponding Sides and Angles

A more sophisticated strategy (and one that works for shapes in any orientation) is to measure the sides and angles in both shapes and compare the results. On congruent shapes, all the corresponding side lengths and angle measures will match.

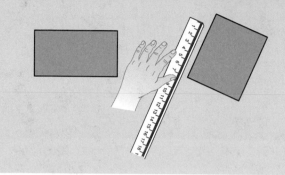

Constructing Congruent 2-D Shapes

Once students understand the nature of congruence, they can begin making congruent shapes of their own, using a wide variety of materials.

WAYS TO CONSTRUCT CONGRUENT SHAPES

Using a Geoboard

Students can use geobands to form congruent shapes on a geoboard. Using a geoboard helps to focus students' attention on the fact that congruent shapes have the same side lengths.

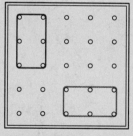

Congruent rectangles
on a geoboard

Measuring

Once students understand that congruent shapes have congruent side lengths and angle measures, they can use rulers and protractors to construct congruent shapes.

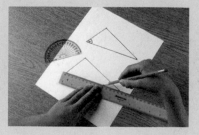

WAYS TO CONSTRUCT CONGRUENT SHAPES

Using Technology

Technology makes it possible for even younger students to construct congruent shapes. (See *Appropriate Technology* on pages 329–331.)

Congruence of 3-D Shapes

In the case of 3-D shapes, it is much more difficult to determine congruence. If two shapes simply look the same, this may be enough for some children to assume congruence. However, testing congruence requires the ability to use measurements to compare shapes—a characteristic of more mathematically sophisticated students. Structures made of standard linking cubes might be easier to test, since the cubes can be counted in order to make comparisons.

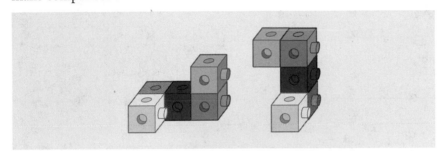

ACTIVITY 13.15

Measure the side lengths and angles on this triangle.

Write the shortest description you can to tell someone else how to make a triangle that is congruent to this one.

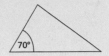

Similarity of 2-D Shapes

Figures that have the same shape, but not necessarily the same size, are said to be *similar*. Congruent shapes are similar, but so are reductions and enlargements of a shape. When shapes are similar, corresponding angles are congruent, and corresponding side lengths are all enlarged or reduced by the same factor.

In the case of the similar rectangles below, the ratio of the length to the width is the same in both rectangles. This is not true in the non-similar rectangles, where the ratio of length to width for the rectangle on the right is less than for the rectangle on the left.

RECTANGLES THAT ARE AND ARE NOT SIMILAR

Similar Rectangles

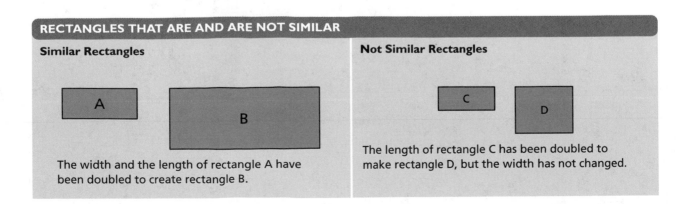

The width and the length of rectangle A have been doubled to create rectangle B.

Not Similar Rectangles

The length of rectangle C has been doubled to make rectangle D, but the width has not changed.

Determining Similarity of 2-D Shapes

If two shapes are similar, the following statements are true:

- Corresponding angles in both shapes are congruent.
- You can multiply or divide all the side lengths in one shape by the same amount to describe the corresponding side lengths of the other shape.
- The ratio between one side length and another on one shape is the same as the ratio between the corresponding side lengths on the other shape.

Angle measures alone cannot be used to test two shapes for similarity. For example, a square and a long, thin rectangle both have four 90° angles, but they are not similar shapes. To determine similarity, students need to look at the side lengths of the shapes. Some tests for similarity are outlined below.

TESTING FOR SIMILARITY

Measuring Side Lengths

To test the two rectangles below for similarity, students can measure the side lengths to see if they have been increased or decreased by the same proportion. Or, they can compare the length to the height in each shape to see if the relationship is the same.

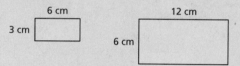

The width and length of the second rectangle are twice as long as the width and length of the first rectangle, so the rectangles are similar.

Another test for similarity involves comparing side lengths within each shape. For example, when you divide the length of each rectangle above by its height, the answer is 2. Both rectangles are twice as long as they are high, so the rectangles are similar.

Using Diagonals to Test Rectangles

There is a special and easy way to test rectangles for similarity. First, place the rectangles one on top of the other so the smaller one fits into the bottom left corner of the larger one. Then draw the diagonal of the larger rectangle so it passes through both shapes. If the diagonal of the large rectangle is also a diagonal of the small one, then the rectangles are similar.

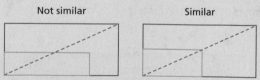

This test works because similar rectangles have the same ratio of length to height.

Constructing Similar 2-D Shapes

Once students understand the relationships that make two shapes similar, some may want to try constructing pairs of similar shapes on their own. The methods they use will depend on their mathematical knowledge, as shown in the table on page 321.

WAYS TO CONSTRUCT SIMILAR SHAPES

Using Square Grids

Square grids are good tools for students to use when they are first learning to construct similar shapes. They can begin by constructing a shape on a square grid, and then copy the shape onto another grid with larger (or smaller) squares.

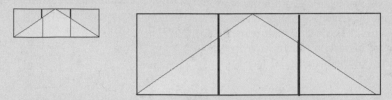

Similar shapes constructed on different-sized square grids

Measuring Sides and Angles

Older students may be ready to construct simple shapes—mainly rectangles—with rulers and protractors. Working with rectangles allows students to focus on measuring the side lengths, and then multiplying or dividing each length by the same amount. With other shapes, it will be necessary to measure and construct angles with a protractor.

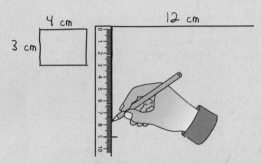

Enlarging a square by tripling the side lengths.

Using Technology

Technology makes it possible for students of all ages to construct similar shapes. For example, students could use dynamic geometry software to construct a shape and then reduce it.

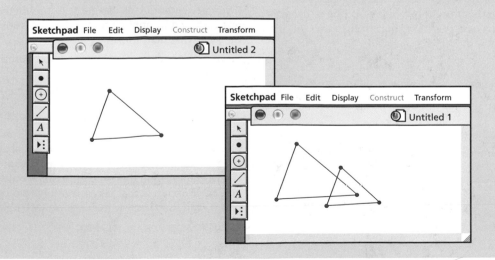

Common Errors and Misconceptions

3-D Shapes: Common Errors, Misconceptions, and Strategies

COMMON ERROR OR MISCONCEPTION	SUGGESTED STRATEGIES
2-D and 3-D Vocabulary Students frequently confuse the vocabulary associated with 2-D and 3-D shapes. For example, students who have been asked to look for rectangles in the classroom might point to a tissue box. (If this happens, first ask students to elaborate in order to make sure they are not simply pointing out the rectangular faces.)  Because a rectangle-based prism has faces that are rectangles, students and even adults will often describe it as a rectangle.	Make sure students have opportunities to compare and contrast shapes that are likely to be confused. For example, present a square and a cube. Ask students to tell how they are different. Make sure that students attach the correct name to each shape. 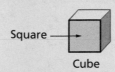Square Cube Formal names for 3-D shapes can be confusing for some young students, so teachers often introduce simple everyday names for these shapes. For example, a sphere is often called a "ball" and a rectangle-based prism is often called a "box." Most students are comfortable with the more precise language.
Components of 3-D Shapes Because students are familiar with the word *side* in the context of 2-D shapes, they may mistakenly apply the same term to the flat surfaces on 3-D shapes. 3-D shapes have faces, not sides.	Help students see that the word *side* could be confusing if it were applied to 3-D shapes. Emphasize that the flat surfaces on a 3-D shape are called *faces*, and that the places where the faces meet are called *edges*. Edge Face Correct terminology for 3-D shapes
Counting Components on 3-D Shapes Students may have trouble counting faces, edges, and vertices on 3-D shapes because they lose track of which components have already been counted. They may also not be sure whether the apex of a cone counts as a vertex (there are contrasting views on this), or whether the curved edge of a cone or cylinder counts as an edge (there are contrasting views on this).	Encourage the students to mark a starting point for counting and to count in a systematic way, perhaps from the base up. Since a cone and a cylinder are not polyhedrons, it is not usually useful to include them in component-counting activities. However, if a student is not sure about the definition of *vertex* or *edge* (even mathematicians disagree about whether these terms should be applied to non-polyhedrons), review the following definitions: • On a polyhedron, a vertex is a point common to three or more faces. • On a polyhedron, an edge is a line segment formed where two faces intersect.
Identifying the Base of a Prism Students sometimes have difficulty identifying the base of a prism, particularly when the prism is a short one. Students may misidentify this as a square-based prism because the lateral faces are square.	Having students build prisms from stacks of pattern blocks may help them see that the block shape they use to start and end the prism is the base, and that the lateral faces on this type of prism are always rectangles. Emphasize that there are only two bases on a prism, and they may or may not be rectangles. Prisms have two parallel bases.

COMMON ERROR OR MISCONCEPTION	SUGGESTED STRATEGIES
Congruent Edges on Nets Students who create nets simply by "eyeballing" a shape may find that their nets do not fold properly because they have not taken into account the need to match congruent edges. 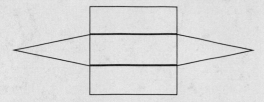 This net for a triangle-based prism cannot be folded because the sides of the triangle are too long.	Encourage students to measure the edges of the shape they plan to duplicate in order to ensure that the resulting net will fold properly. For example, on the net shown below, the three rectangular faces are congruent so the bases must be equilateral triangles, not isosceles.  When this net is folded, the sides of the triangles will match the sides of the rectangles.

2-D Shapes: Common Errors, Misconceptions, and Strategies

COMMON ERROR OR MISCONCEPTION	SUGGESTED STRATEGIES
Attributes versus Properties Students confuse attributes of shapes with their properties. An attribute applies to only some of the shapes in a group, while a property applies to all of them. For example, students may assume that since a particular rectangle has long sides and short sides, then all rectangles must have long sides and short sides. Rectangles 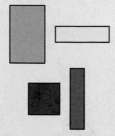 Students often assume incorrectly that rectangles have long and short sides and do not recognize a square as a rectangle.	Students need opportunities to explore each class of shape in many different forms. For example, when parallelograms are introduced, provide opportunities for students to examine and sort some parallelograms and non-parallelograms, and to talk about how they can tell if a shape belongs in the parallelograms group. 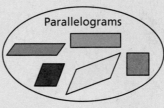  Students need opportunities to work with many different types of parallelograms
Changes in Orientation Students think that the way a shape is oriented is part of what defines it. For example, while younger children will usually recognize the yellow shape on page 324 as a triangle, they may describe the red one as an "arrow" or a "flag," since it is oriented differently from what they think a triangle should look like. This misconception can affect an older student's	Working with concrete shape models, such as pattern blocks and attribute blocks, can help students see that shapes can be oriented in different ways and still maintain their shape properties.

(continued)

ability to perceive congruence, since the student may not recognize that shapes are congruent when they are oriented differently.

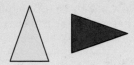

Congruent triangles can face in different directions

Flipping or turning a triangle does not change its shape properties.

Orientation of Perpendicular Lines

Students sometimes assume that lines can only be perpendicular if one is horizontal and the other is vertical. A student with this misconception would recognize the first pair of line segments shown here as perpendicular, but not the second.

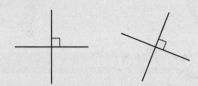

Examples of perpendicular line segments

Remind students that angles can be "tipped" or turned without changing their size. It might help to show a square, and establish that the sides are perpendicular by placing a cutout square corner in the corner. Then turn the square 45° and ask if the sides are still perpendicular; students could replace the square corner to check. Students could also look around the classroom to see if they can find any examples of perpendicular lines that are *not* vertical and horizontal.

Wrong Scale on the Protractor

Students use the wrong scale on a protractor to measure an angle. For example, a student might record the size of this angle as 120°.

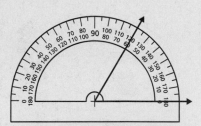

A student might misread this angle measure as 120°.

Encourage students to look at the starting arm of the angle to see which 0° mark it points to, and remind them to use that scale to make the measurement.

It is also important to remind students to use estimation to check angle measures. For example, the angle shown to the left is obviously less than 90°, so a 120° measurement does not make sense. A 60° measurement, on the other hand, seems much more reasonable.

Colour and Reflective Symmetry

Students mistakenly assume that shapes cannot be symmetrical if the colours or decorations do not match. For example, a student might not recognize that this shape is symmetrical, because the halves are different colours.

This shape has reflective symmetry because one half matches the other half exactly when folded along or reflected across the line of reflection.

Provide students with many opportunities to test for symmetry using folding when possible and a transparent mirror when not possible to fold.

Reinforce that matching exactly when folded along, or reflected across, the line of reflection is what defines reflective symmetry.

Parallelograms and Reflective Symmetry

Students often think that a diagonal of a parallelogram is a line of symmetry. This, of course, is correct for rhombuses and squares, but not for other parallelograms, including rectangles. This common error stems from the fact that the two triangles on the sides of the diagonal are congruent.

A shape can have congruent halves and not be symmetrical.

Reflective versus Rotational Symmetry

Students make incorrect assumptions about reflective symmetry and rotational symmetry. For example, they think that a shape with reflective symmetry must also have rotational symmetry.

This triangle has reflective symmetry, but not rotational symmetry.

Provide many opportunities to test for symmetry by folding and using a transparent mirror.

Students need opportunities to work with each shape type:
- shapes with reflective symmetry, but not rotational symmetry
- shapes with rotational symmetry, but not reflective symmetry
- shapes with both types of symmetry

 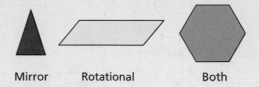

Mirror   Rotational   Both

Appropriate Manipulatives

2-D and 3-D Shapes: Examples of Manipulatives

PLASTIC SHAPES	EXAMPLE
Plastic shapes come in a wide variety of forms and from a wide range of manufacturers. They include attribute blocks (2-D shapes that vary in thickness, colour, and size) and 3-D shape models. Plastic shape blocks can be used for a number of different activities, including sorting and classifying, building structures, exploring shape properties, and patterning.	This pattern shows how the number of faces on a pyramid increases by 1 each time the number of sides on the base is increased.

3 sides on the base
4 faces

4 sides on the base
5 faces

5 sides on the base
6 faces

(continued)

Blocks

Wooden, plastic, or foam blocks can be used to build structures in order to explore the properties of 3-D shapes, including stability.

Building towers with cylinders, prisms, and cones provides an opportunity for students to explore the relative stability of different structures.

Linking Cubes

Linking cubes can be joined to construct simple 3-D shapes and structures. They are especially useful for exploring topics such as properties of rectangle-based prisms (see page 304), plane symmetry (see page 301), and congruence of 3-D shapes (see page 319).

Linking cube structures allow students to explore how a structure looks from different perspectives.

Cube Structure   Front view   Right view

Toothpicks and Modelling Clay

Toothpicks can be combined with small balls of modelling clay or marshmallows to make skeletons of 2-D and 3-D shapes in order to focus attention on the sides, vertices, and angles of 2-D shapes and the edges and vertices of 3-D shapes. (See page 305.)

These toothpick shapes show that each time you want to increase the number of sides on the base of a prism by 1, you need to add 3 toothpicks in all to the prism.

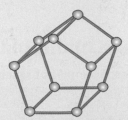

Pentagon-based prism with 10 vertices and 15 edges

Polydrons

Polydrons are regular polygons that can be linked along hinged edges in order to build 3-D shapes and nets. They are particularly useful for exploring the properties of 3-D shapes.

Polydrons make it easy even for young children to make nets that they can fold into 3-D shapes.

Commercial Building Toys

Building toys such as *Lego, K'nex, Tinkertoys, Zoob, Geomag,* and *D-stix* can all be used to build and explore skeletons of 2-D and 3-D shapes. Building skeletons focuses attention on the sides, vertices, and angles of 2-D shapes and the edges and vertices of 3-D shapes. (See page 305.)

Geomag, Tinkertoys, Zoob, K'nex, and *D-stix* can all be used to create skeletons of 3-D shapes.

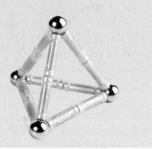

Pattern Blocks

Pattern blocks are wooden or plastic models that young children can use to explore the properties of simple and composite 2-D shapes and prisms (see page 311), for combining and dissecting 2-D shapes, and for patterning activities.

These pattern blocks show a shape pattern.

Geostrips

Geostrips are plastic strips of different lengths that can be connected at the ends. They are useful for investigating side lengths and angles of polygons. Home-made geostrips are strips of card stock that can be attached with paper fasteners.

Making triangles with geostrips can help students discover that a triangle can be made from any set of strips in which the two shortest sides have a combined length that is greater than the longest side.

Straws and Pipe Cleaners

Straws and pipe cleaners can be used to make 2-D as well as 3-D skeletons to explore properties of shapes related to sides, edges, and vertices. They can be cut to different lengths and connected to each other with small pieces of pipe cleaner that are slid inside the straw ends.

This is one of many quadrilaterals students can make with straws and pipe cleaners.

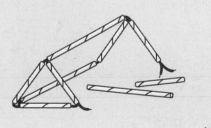

(continued)

Geoboards

On a geoboard, students use geo-bands to create polygons. There are many different sizes of square geoboards.

Geoboards have a wide range of uses, for example, to examine the properties of polygons, and to explore symmetry, congruence, and similarity.

Square geoboards are used most often, but triangular and circular geoboards are also available; the latter are particularly useful for exploring properties of circles and dividing circular regions into congruent parts.

Geoboards are helpful for solving problems such as the following.

I am a triangle with one square corner. Two of my sides are congruent. What do I look like?

If two triangles have the same height and base length, are they congruent?

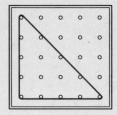

I am a triangle with one square corner. Two of my sides are congruent. What could I look like?

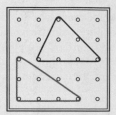

If two triangles have the same height and base length, are they congruent?

Protractors

Protractors are used to measure and construct angles, perpendicular lines, and polygons. They come in semicircular and circular forms, and some circular protractors are available with a single scale (which can be less confusing for students).

The circular form reinforces the concept that angles are parts of a circle and allows students to get a better feel for what angles look like when they are greater than 180°.

Either of these types of protractors could be used to determine if two line segments are perpendicular, but only a circular protractor can be used to directly measure angles greater than 180°.

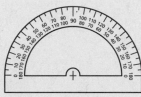

Semicircular protractor

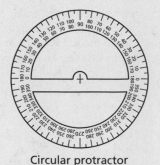

Circular protractor

Mirrors

Both ordinary flat mirrors and transparent mirrors (Miras) are invaluable for determining symmetry, creating symmetrical shapes, creating congruent shapes, and in some instances, determining congruency.

With a transparent mirror, students can reflect a given shape to create a symmetrical shape.

PLASTIC SHAPES	EXAMPLE
Tangrams A tangram is a square puzzle made of 7 pieces. Tangrams can be used to explore combining and dissecting shapes. (See page 313.) The seven tangram shapes	This illustration shows one way to combine tangram pieces together to form a triangle. It also shows how a right isosceles triangle can be dissected into a square and two smaller congruent right isosceles triangles. A square and 2 right triangles combine to form a larger right triangle.
Pentominoes Pentominoes are made of 5 congruent squares that have been joined along full sides. Students can use 3 (triominoes), 4 (tetrominoes), or all 5 (pentominoes) to create different shapes. Teachers can buy them commercially or make their own. Pentominoes are most often used as a context for a geometry activity in which students look for all the possible ways to combine 5 squares to make composite shapes. However, these figures can also be used to explore congruence (e.g., if one pentomino can be flipped or turned to fit over another, then the two are considered to be the same shape), as well as other geometric properties, such as line symmetry.	Some pentominoes have line symmetry and some do not. 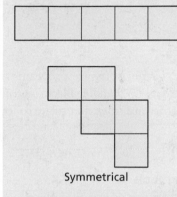 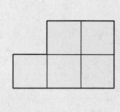 Symmetrical Not Symmetrical

Appropriate Technology
Computers

There are a number of software packages that students can use to explore shapes. Most simply, they can use the drawing programs of word processors to create and manipulate shapes for a variety of purposes. (See pages 330–331.) Students can also use programs such as *Kid Pix*, where they can explore shapes and make designs.

In addition to this, there are many types of software created especially to allow students to explore shapes. One example is *The Geometer's Sketchpad*. Here is a sampling of the geometry concepts that can be explored using this software program:

- helping students distinguish ray, angle, line segment
- dissecting shapes
- exploring congruence and similarity
- determining the sum of the angles in a polygon

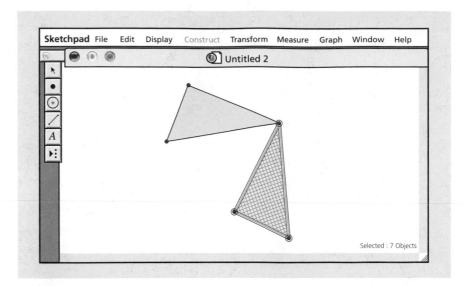

Other software programs that promote thinking about shapes include *Shape Up, Building Blocks*, and *aspexTabsMST*. (Page 360 lists some additional software titles that relate to location and movement.)

Possible Applications for Drawing Tools

MANIPULATING 2-D SHAPES

The drawing tools in most word-processing programs have a rich potential for geometry activities. With these tools, students can explore pre-made basic shapes. For example, a drawing program might provide a ready-made equilateral triangle with a moveable dot at the *apex* (top vertex). Students can move that dot from side to side to create other triangles that look different, but still have the same base and height.

CHANGING A 2-D SHAPE TO A 3-D SHAPE

Once students have made a 2-D shape, they can apply various effects in order to develop it into a 3-D shape. For example, a student could transform a trapezoid into any of the following shapes.

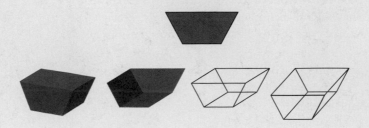

EXPLORING PARALLEL AND PERPENDICULAR LINE SEGMENTS

Drawing tools can also be used to explore and create different types of line segments. These tools make it easy to create parallel and perpendicular lines, and usually include a rotation feature that allows students to turn line segments in order to orient them differently.

To create parallel lines with a drawing program, you can draw a line, and then copy and paste it. When you draw a horizontal line and a vertical line, the computer uses a background grid to make sure the lines are exactly perpendicular.

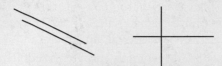

Computer-created parallel and perpendicular lines

EXPLORING SYMMETRY

To create symmetrical shapes, students can use a drawing program to create, copy, and flip a shape, and then position the two halves opposite each other. (See page 300.)

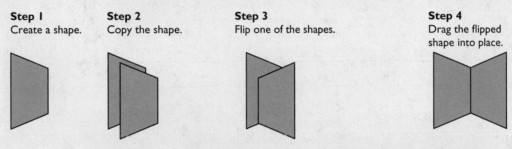

Step 1
Create a shape.

Step 2
Copy the shape.

Step 3
Flip one of the shapes.

Step 4
Drag the flipped shape into place.

Using technology to make a symmetrical shape

EXPLORING CONGRUENCE

Technology offers a number of useful tools for exploring congruence. These range from simple drawing programs that allow students to draw, copy, and re-orient shapes, to dynamic software, such as *Shape Up*, created especially for the purpose of creating and transforming congruent shapes. (See Chapter 14 for more information about transformations.)

EXPLORING SIMILARITY

Most drawing programs make it easy for students to explore similarity by drawing, copying, and stretching or reducing familiar 2-D shapes.

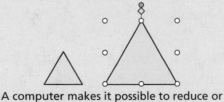

A computer makes it possible to reduce or
enlarge a shape by clicking and dragging.

When you enlarge a computer-drawn shape, it is important to stretch the shape horizontally and vertically at the same time, or the result will not be similar to the original. (On some programs, holding down the shift key while you stretch allows you to do this.)

The Internet

The Internet is a fertile source of geometry investigations for children. Many sites offer not only activity ideas, but also virtual tools for exploration. Examples include pattern blocks, tangrams, square grids, dot grids, and geoboards.

Assessing Student Understanding

- Many of the skills and concepts addressed in this chapter are best assessed through observation of students working directly with physical materials. In that way, it is possible to see, for example, how students cut up a shape and rearrange it into other shapes.

- Many geometric problems require a reasonable amount of precision in the placement of lines, angles, or 3-D components; often students do not have the motor ability to be that precise. It may be necessary to assist, while allowing the student to take the lead in discussing what needs to be done.

- Everyday use of geometric language sometimes interferes with student understanding. For example, it is so rare in everyday life that a student sees a square identified as a rectangle that it is reasonable that he or she would not believe it is a rectangle. Make sure to take these obstacles into account when preparing instruction and assessing student understanding.

Appropriate Children's Books

The Greedy Triangle (Burns, 1994).
This amusing story focuses students on the various sorts of polygons and how they are alike and different. There is also an opportunity to see where those shapes are typically found.

So Many Circles, So Many Squares (Hoban, 1998).
Tana Hoban's beautiful photographs help students see where they can find squares and circles in the world around them.

Captain Invincible and the Space Shapes (Murphy, 2001).
This cartoon-like story built around 3-D shapes takes place in a spaceship returning to Earth. Readers focus on six 3-dimensional shapes, including a cone, a cube, and a pyramid, which the "astronauts" use to battle their way to safety.

Grandfather Tang's Story (Tompert, 1990).
This tale, based on the ancient Chinese tangram puzzle, revolves around the relationship between a grandfather and granddaughter. The illustrations tell the story using pictures based on tangram designs.

Applying What You've Learned

1. Would you assign the chapter problem to a Grade 6 student to solve without providing a mirror? Explain your position on this.

2. Read an article in a journal about the van Hiele model of geometric development.

   a) Briefly summarize the article.

   b) Why do you think it might be important, as a teacher, to know about the van Hiele model?

3. A distinction is made between properties and attributes of shapes. Why is that distinction a useful one?

4. Many primary teachers prefer to begin with 2-D geometry rather than 3-D geometry because they believe it is simpler and more accessible. How could you convince them that starting with 3-D work in geometry might be more appropriate?

5. There is an increasing push to use technology to explore all mathematical topics, including geometry, yet many people believe that geometry needs to be hands-on. List three concepts that you think might be better explored with technology; argue as to why this would be preferable in these situations.

6. Middle school or junior high teachers often spend time teaching students how to perform ruler and compass constructions to bisect angles and segments and create perpendiculars and parallels.

   a) Find out what properties of shapes are explored using these types of constructions.

   b) Would similar constructions with other tools like a computer or transparent mirror evoke the same learning? Explain.

7. A significant amount of time is spent on geometry learning related to symmetry. Argue as to why, or whether, this is an appropriate central topic in the study of geometry.

8. One of the key ideas in geometry is that every shape can be viewed as a part of or a combination of other shapes.

   Why might this be a useful unifying idea in the study of geometry?

Interact with a K–8 Student:

9. Provide a student with a set of pattern blocks.

   a) Ask the student how the different coloured shapes are alike and how they are different, other than in terms of colour.

   b) Ask the student what other shapes he or she could make by combining the provided shapes.

   c) What geometric understandings did the student display as he or she completed parts (a) and (b)?

Discuss with a K–8 Teacher:

10. Many teachers do not spend much time during the school year teaching geometry.

    a) Ask how much time this teacher spends on the topic and what his or her main emphasis is.

    b) Ask whether this teacher would like to spend more time teaching the topic or whether he or she thinks the topic does not warrant more time.

    c) What do you think is an appropriate proportion of the year to spend on spatial work? Why?

11. Ask whether students who have difficulty in number ever do better in geometry, or whether some with difficulty in geometry do better in number, and whether the teacher finds this to be unusual or not. Why do you think this might occur?

Selected References

Battista, M.T. (1999). The importance of spatial structuring in geometric reasoning. *Teaching Children Mathematics, 6,* 170–177.

Bruni, J.V., and Seidenstein, R.B. (1990). Geometric concepts and spatial sense. In Payne, J.N. (Ed.). *Mathematics for the young child.* Reston, VA: National Council of Teachers of Mathematics, 202–227.

Burger, W., and Shaughnessy, J.M. (1986). Characterizing the van Hiele levels of development in geometry. *Journal for Research in Mathematics Education, 17,* 31–48.

Burns, M. (1994). *The greedy triangle.* New York: Scholastic Press.

Clements, D.H. (1999). Geometric and spatial thinking in young children. In Copley, J. (Ed.). *Mathematics in the early years.* Washington, DC: National Council of Teachers of Mathematics and National Association for the Education of Young Children, 66–79.

Clements, D.H. (2000). Geometric and spatial thinking in young children. In Copley, J.V. (Ed.). *The young child and mathematics.* Washington, DC: National Association for the Education of Young Children and National Council of Teachers of Mathematics.

Clements, D.H., and Battista, M.T. (1992). Geometry and spatial reasoning. In Grouws, D.A. (Ed.). *Handbook of research on mathematics teaching and learning.* New York: Macmillan Publishing Co., 420–464.

Clements, D.H., and Sarama, J. (2000a). The earliest geometry. *Teaching Children Mathematics, 7,* 82–86.

Clements, D.H., and Sarama, J. (2000b). Young children's ideas about geometric shapes. *Teaching Children Mathematics, 6,* 482–487.

Copley, J.V. (2000). *The young child and mathematics.* Washington, DC: National Association for the Education of Young Children and National Council of Teachers of Mathematics.

DelGrande, J. (1990). Spatial sense. *Arithmetic Teacher, 37,* 14–20.

Delgrande, J., and Morrow, L. (1993). *Geometry and spatial sense: Addenda series grades K–6.* Reston, VA: National Council of Teachers of Mathematics.

Ernst, B. (1987). *Adventures with impossible figures.* Norfolk, UK: Tarquin Publications.

Findell, C.R., Small, M., Cavanagh, M., Dacey, L., Greenes, C.E., and Sheffield, L.J. (2001). *Navigating through geometry in prekindergarten–grade 2.* Reston, VA: National Council of Teachers of Mathematics.

Fox, T.B. (2000). Implications of research on children's understanding of geometry. *Teaching Children Mathematics, 6,* 572–576.

Gavin, M.K., Belkin, L.P., Spinelli, A.M., and St. Marie, J. (2001). *Navigating through geometry in grades 3–5.* Reston, VA: National Council of Teachers of Mathematics.

Granger, T. (2000). Math is art. *Teaching Children Mathematics, 7,* 10–13.

Hannibal, M.A. (1999). Young children's developing understanding of geometric shapes. *Teaching Children Mathematics, 5,* 353–357.

Hershkowitz, R., Parzysz, B., and Van Dormolen, J. (1997). Shape and space. In Bishop, A.J., Clements, M.A., Keitel, C., Kilpatrick, H., and Laborde, C. (Eds). *International handbook of mathematics education.* Springer International Handbooks of Education. Dordrecht, Germany: Kluwer Academic Publishers.

Hoban, T. (1998). *So many circles, so many squares.* New York: Greenwillow Books.

Jacobson, C., and Lehrer, R. (2000). Teacher appropriation and student learning of geometry through design. *Journal for Research in Mathematics Education, 31,* 71–88.

Jenkins, L., Laycock, M., and McLean, P. (1988). *Geoblocks and geojackets.* Hayward, CA: Activity Resources Co.

Lehrer, R., and Chazan, D. (Eds.). (1998). Designing learning environments for developing understanding of geometry and space. In *Studies in mathematical thinking and learning.* Mahwah, NJ: Lawrence Erlbaum Associates, Inc.

Lehrer, R., Fennema, E., Carpenter, T., and Ansell, E. (1994). Review of NCRSME research. *NCRSME research review: The teaching and learning of mathematics.* Madison, WI: National Center for Research in Mathematical Sciences Education Research, Wisconsin Center for Educational Research, 10–13.

Maccarone, G., and Neuhaus, D. (1997). *Three pigs, one wolf, seven magic shapes.* New York: Cartwheel Books.

Murphy, S. (2001). *Captain Invincible and the space shapes.* New York: HarperTrophy.

Oberdorf, C.D., and Taylor-Cox, J. (1999). Shape up! *Teaching Children Mathematics, 6,* 340–345.

Piaget, J., and Inhelder, B. (1967). *The child's conception of space.* New York: W.W. Norton & Co.

Pugalee, D.K., Frykholm, J., Johnson, A., Slovin, H., Malloy, C., and Preston, R. (2002). *Navigating through geometry in grades 6–8.* Reston, VA: National Council of Teachers of Mathematics.

Roper, A. (1990). *Primary cooperative problem solving with pattern blocks.* Sunnyvale, CA: Creative Publications.

Sarama, J., and Clements, D.H. (2003). Building blocks of early childhood mathematics. *Teaching Children Mathematics, 9,* 480–484.

Selke, D. (1999). Geometric flips via the arts. *Teaching Children Mathematics, 5,* 379–383.

Small, M. (2007). *PRIME: Geometry: Background and strategies.* Toronto: Thomson Nelson.

Teppo, A. (1991). Van Hiele levels of geometric thought revisited. *The Mathematics Teacher, 84,* 210–221.

Tompert, A. (1990). *Grandfather Tang's story*. New York: Crown Publishers.

VanCleave, J. (1994). *Geometry for every kid: Easy activities that make learning geometry fun*. New York: John Wiley.

Wheatley, G.H., and Reynolds, A.M. (1999). Image maker: Developing spatial sense. *Teaching Children Mathematics*, 2, 374–378.

Whiteley, W. (2004). Visualization in mathematics: Claims and questions toward a research program [Online]. Available: http://www.math.yorku.ca/Who/Faculty/Whiteley/Visualization.pdf. Cited 2007 Apr. 22.

Whiteley, W. (2006). Exploring the parallelogram through symmetry [Online]. Available: http://dynamicgeometry.com/general_resources/user_groups/jmm_2006/download/ExploringParallelograms.doc.

Chapter 14

Location and Movement

IN A NUTSHELL

The main ideas in this chapter are listed below:

1. Although properties of shapes are often the focus of attention in geometry, development of skills in describing and predicting location is also an important aspect of spatial sense.

2. There is a continuum of simple to much more sophisticated systems to describe location. Even the youngest elementary school student can use a simple system.

3. The study of transformations and the use of constructions provide an excellent vehicle for exploring geometric properties of both position and shape.

CHAPTER PROBLEM

A triangle on a coordinate grid is rotated and then reflected. After the two moves, the vertices are located at (−8, −3), (−2, −3), and (−2, +5). Describe 2 possible sets of coordinates where the triangles might have started. Explain your thinking.

Location and Movement

Geometric experiences involving location and movement support the development of spatial sense and positional vocabulary. Students should learn to

- describe the positions of objects in structures and pictures
- read and draw maps
- plot points and describe paths on coordinate grids
- transform and construct shapes

Developing Positional Vocabulary

A child's earliest spoken language might include terms such as "up," "down," "in," and "out"—terms that describe spatial relationships. As the child grows, so does his or her spatial understanding and related vocabulary.

Using Dance, Song, and Play

Many dances, songs, games, and toys for young children provide opportunities to build spatial sense and positional vocabulary, and often link well with investigations in other subject areas, such as physical education or social studies. Examples include games such as "Simon Says" and action songs such as "The Hokey Pokey."

Sports and imaginative play are also important vehicles for this type of development. Parents and teachers can help by modelling positional vocabulary—words that describe how one object's location relates to another's—as children play. For example, an adult observing a child who is playing with blocks and toy farm animals might ask:

- Why did you put the cow *inside* the fence?
- What animals are still *outside*?
- What block could you put *on top of* this one to make your fence higher?

Word Walls

A good way to build positional vocabulary is to record terms on a Math Word Wall as they come up in classroom activities. To help students see relationships among positional words, it may help to group words that belong together, such as "over" and "under."

Words That Tell Where Things Are

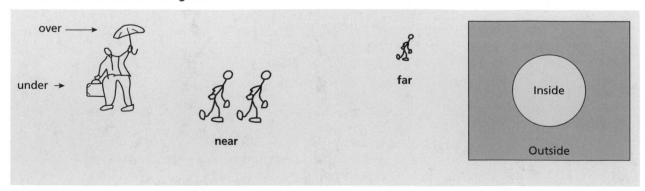

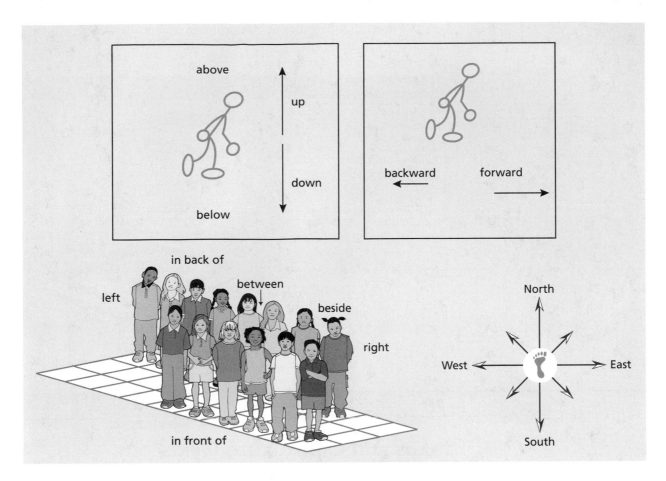

As students use and discuss these terms, they will learn that by combining terms or modifying them, they can give a more exact idea of where an object is located. For example, younger students might discuss why, although it is true to say that the Slinky on the table below is *behind* the duck, it is more useful to say that the Slinky is *behind the duck and to the right*.

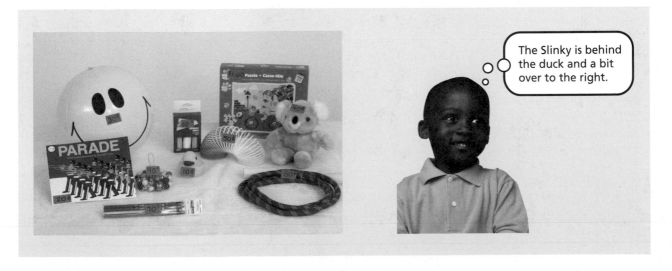

Another approach to developing positional vocabulary also supports the development of visual memory, that is, the ability of students to recall what they saw once it is out of view. As children mature mathematically, they can be asked to recall the relative positions of more shapes in somewhat more complex spatial arrangements.

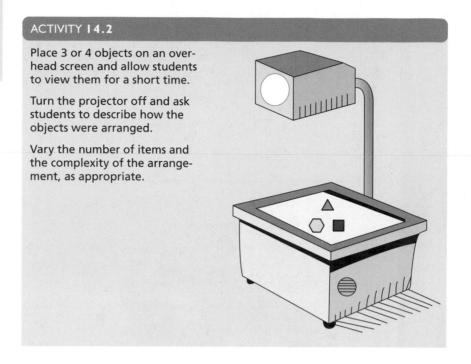

Maps and Coordinate Grids
Drawing and Interpreting Maps

Maps make it possible to record and describe how objects are located relative to one another. Even young students can make simple maps of their environment. However, as students develop better spatial sense, their maps better reflect the geometric features of objects in their surroundings, and give a more accurate impression of the proportional distances between objects. For example, a younger student might draw a classroom map similar to this one.

Student Response

This map illustrates a student's recognition of how one object should be positioned relative to others nearby.

Working with Grids

At some point, students are ready to use a grid system to identify locations on a map, or to describe how to get from one map location to another.

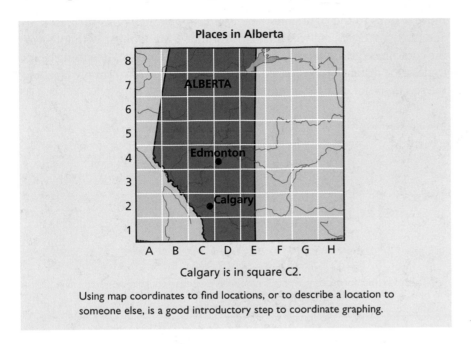

Places in Alberta

Calgary is in square C2.

Using map coordinates to find locations, or to describe a location to someone else, is a good introductory step to coordinate graphing.

Students can also create designs on grids, and then describe their designs by identifying grid squares to colour. Alternatively, students can be given grid locations and colours and asked to show the design on a grid.

Simple Four-Quadrant Grids

Although students do most of their work with coordinate grids after Grade 4, it is possible to introduce some grid-related ideas in earlier years. Younger students, for example, might simply identify the location of an object on a grid like the one shown below.

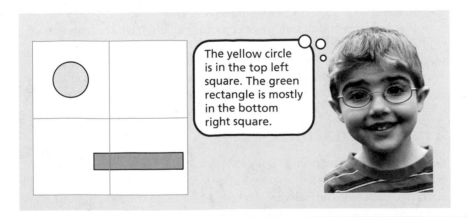

The yellow circle is in the top left square. The green rectangle is mostly in the bottom right square.

Number Coordinates

After some time working with grids like city maps where locations are designated using a letter and a number to describe a horizontal and vertical space in which they are found, students learn to use the conventional number-number code for identifying locations where two grid lines intersect. At this stage, it becomes important for students to recognize that, by convention, the first number indicates the distance across from the vertical axis and the second the distance up from the horizontal axis. For example, to reach point (2, 3), you begin at (0, 0), where the two reference axes meet, move 2 steps to the right, and then 3 steps up. Designations such as (0, 0) and (2, 3) are called *ordered pairs*. Once students are familiar with integers, the coordinate grid is extended to four quadrants. The switch to using labels to describe distance travelled along the axes as opposed to simply labelling the square is not easy for some students.

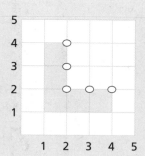

This system for plotting points is called the Cartesian coordinate system, in honour of mathematician René Descartes.

Games and Activities for Coordinate Grids There are many games and activities to help students learn how to use coordinate systems. Some are commercial games, such as *Battleship*, while others are teacher-made or student-made. An example of one teacher-made activity is shown in **Activity 14.3**.

Other games and activities include the following:

- Introduce coordinate graphing by using masking tape to make a large grid on the floor. Use cards to label the axes with coordinates. Invite a student to stand at a point on the grid: "Aaron, please come and stand on point (3, 5)." Then that student can invite another student to stand on a different point, and so on.
- Place objects at different points on the grid and have students use coordinates to describe their locations.
- In a variation of Twister, one student gives a partner directions for placing both feet and both hands on coordinates on a floor grid. Then the students trade roles and play again.

Transformations

Geometric transformations are motions that affect a shape in some specified way. K–8 students work with transformations because many mathematical concepts, such as symmetry, are described best using transformations.

Euclidean Transformations— Slides, Flips, and Turns

There are three transformations that change the location of an object in space, or the direction in which it faces, but not its size or shape. These transformations, called *Euclidean transformations*, result in images that are

---

ACTIVITY 14.3

a) Ask students to follow this path on a grid.

- Plot Point A at (3, 2).
- Go right 5 to plot Point B.
- Go right 2 and up 2 to plot Point C.
- Go up 2 to plot Point D.
- Go left 2 and up 2 to plot Point E.
- Go left 5 to plot Point F.
- Go left 2 and down 2 to plot Point G.
- Go down 2 to plot Point H.
- Go right 2 and down 2 to re-plot Point A.

b) Have students connect the points in the order they were plotted. Ask what shape was made.

c) Have students create directions for their own secret shape.

ACTIVITY 14.4

Ask students how many paths there are from A to B if you always have to move right or down. Ask what the paths have in common.

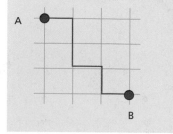

---

congruent to the original object. The three types of Euclidean transformations are *slides* (or *translations*), *flips* (or *reflections*), and *turns* (or *rotations*).

In the examples that follow, a dotted green line is used to indicate the original shape, while a solid green line is used for the transformation image, and red is used for slide arrows, flip lines, and turn centres.

Slides, Flips, and Turns

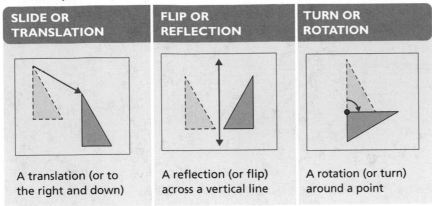

SLIDE OR TRANSLATION	FLIP OR REFLECTION	TURN OR ROTATION
A translation (or to the right and down)	A reflection (or flip) across a vertical line	A rotation (or turn) around a point

Transformations on Simple Grids

When students first begin learning about slides, flips, and turns, they work with concrete shapes on a flat surface. Later, they might work with simple coordinate grids like the one shown below. Working with transformations, especially slides, on a simple grid helps younger students learn to describe motions with mathematical language.

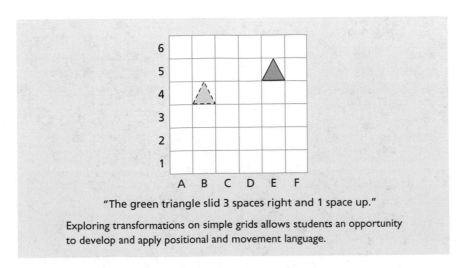

"The green triangle slid 3 spaces right and 1 space up."

Exploring transformations on simple grids allows students an opportunity to develop and apply positional and movement language.

Transformations on Coordinate Grids

In later grades, students begin to explore Euclidean transformations on Cartesian coordinate grids like the one shown on page 344. Here, students can look not only at how a transformation affects the direction in which a shape is facing, but also at how it changes the coordinates of the vertices. For example, the rectangle shown was slid right 4 units and down 1 unit. As a result, the first coordinate of each vertex increased by 4. The second coordinate decreased by 1.

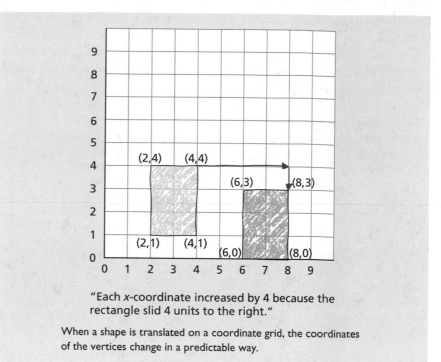

"Each *x*-coordinate increased by 4 because the rectangle slid 4 units to the right."

When a shape is translated on a coordinate grid, the coordinates of the vertices change in a predictable way.

Slides

A slide (or translation) moves a shape left, right, up, down, or diagonally without changing the direction in which it faces in any way. This type of transformation is one of the easiest for students to recognize. For example, the picture below shows 3 different slides of the same triangle. Each one is completely defined by a "slide arrow" that links a point on the original shape to the matching point on the image. Slide arrows could be drawn between each pair of corresponding vertices, but one slide arrow is all that is required to show the slide.

Slide Directions

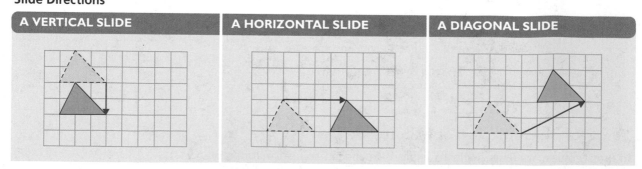

| A VERTICAL SLIDE | A HORIZONTAL SLIDE | A DIAGONAL SLIDE |

Describing Slides

A diagonal slide can be separated into its right-left and up-down components. This becomes useful when students are working with slides on coordinate grids.

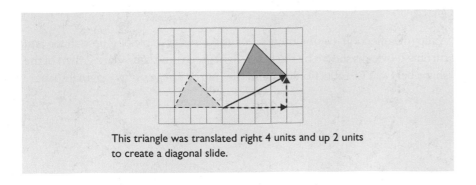

This triangle was translated right 4 units and up 2 units to create a diagonal slide.

Describing Slide Images

Mathematicians often use letter notation to show how each vertex on the original shape is matched to a vertex on its slide image.

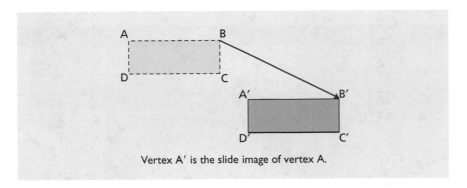

Vertex A′ is the slide image of vertex A.

Properties of Slides

SLIDE ARROWS	ORIENTATION
No matter where slide arrows are drawn to link matching points on an original shape and its image, these arrows (shown here in red) are all exactly the same length and parallel. In addition, the sides on the image are parallel to the corresponding sides on the original shape.	The way a shape faces does not change with a slide. If point C is below and to the right of point A on the original shape, then the image of point C is below and to the right of the image of point A on the slide shape.

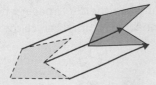

The slide arrows that define a particular translation are all the same length and parallel.

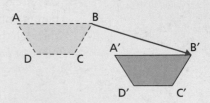

Flips

A flip (or reflection) can be thought of as the result of picking up a shape and turning it over, as shown by the front (light green) and back (dark green) of the shape below. The reflection image is the mirror image of the original shape.

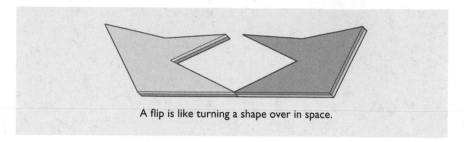

A flip is like turning a shape over in space.

Flip Lines

A flip is always made across a line called the *flip line* or *line of reflection*. A flip line can be vertical, horizontal, or diagonal.

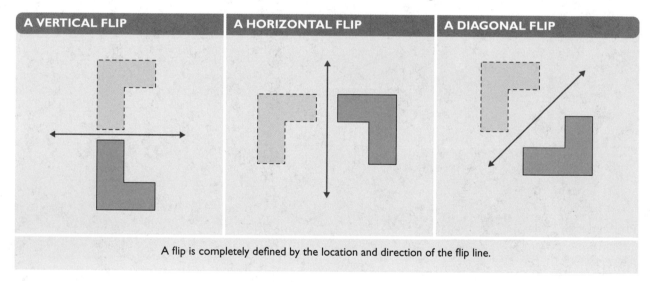

| A VERTICAL FLIP | A HORIZONTAL FLIP | A DIAGONAL FLIP |

A flip is completely defined by the location and direction of the flip line.

Transparent Mirrors

While students generally have little difficulty flipping a shape horizontally or vertically, flips across a diagonal line can be more difficult to perform. In this situation, a transparent mirror (or Mira) can be very helpful. In a transparent mirror, students can actually see the flip image when they look through the plastic, so it becomes possible to simply trace the image onto a piece of paper.

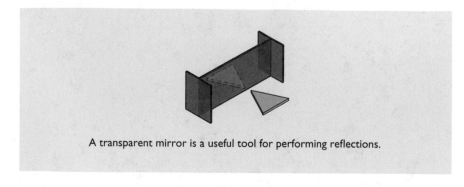

A transparent mirror is a useful tool for performing reflections.

ACTIVITY 14.5

Ask students where to put the mirror on the original shape to create the two images.

original

A transparent mirror not only allows students to flip a shape across a diagonal line with ease, it also makes it possible to flip across a line drawn *through* the original shape. In this case, a student actually has to perform two flips, first flipping one side of the shape, and then the other.

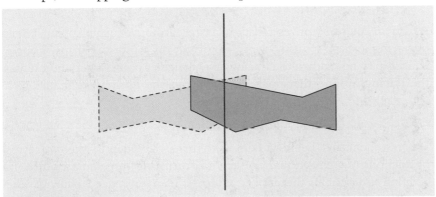

Properties of Flips

FLIPPING A SHAPE ACROSS A SIDE	FLIPPING A SHAPE ACROSS A LINE OF SYMMETRY
If a 2-D shape is flipped across one of its own sides, the result is a symmetrical 2-D shape. The only points in the original shape that do not move are those that are located along the flip line.	If a shape is flipped across one of its own lines of symmetry, then the flip image will fit exactly over the original shape.

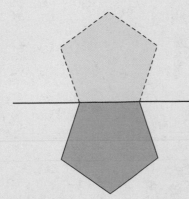

A symmetrical octagon created by flipping a pentagon across one side.

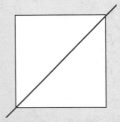

A square flipped across one of its lines of symmetry.

(continued)

DISTANCE FROM THE FLIP LINE	ANGLE AT THE FLIP LINE
Each point on the image is exactly the same distance from the flip line as its counterpart on the original shape.	When any point on the original is joined to its counterpart on the flip image, the connecting line is perpendicular to the flip line.

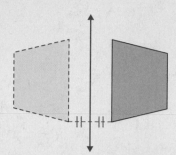

Corresponding points are the
same distance from the flip line.

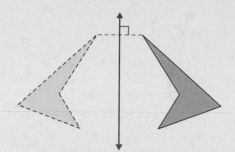

A line connecting corresponding points
is perpendicular to the flip line.

Turns

A turn (or rotation) moves a shape in a circle around a turning point. Think of tracing a shape, putting the tracing right on top of the shape, using a pencil tip to hold down the tracing at a particular point, and then rotating the tracing around that point (as shown in the illustration in the next paragraph).

Describing Turns Using Fractions of a Circle

When students first begin working with turns, they identify them in terms of fractions of a circle: quarter turn, half turn, and three-quarter turn. In addition to describing the amount of turn, students also need to identify the turn direction (clockwise or counterclockwise). Sometimes clockwise and counterclockwise are abbreviated as "cw" and "ccw."

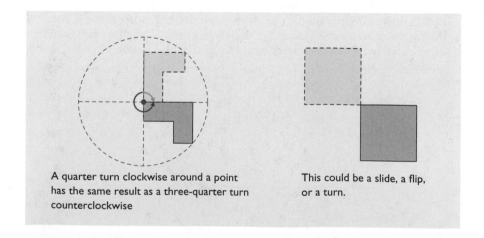

A quarter turn clockwise around a point
has the same result as a three-quarter turn
counterclockwise

This could be a slide, a flip,
or a turn.

Describing Turns Using Angles

Later, students learn that turns can also be identified in terms of degrees. For example, the picture on page 349 shows the same shape turned 90° (a quarter turn) clockwise, and 180° (a half turn) counterclockwise. As students turn shapes, they may find it helpful to think of hands on a clock face. This way, they can focus on the change of position for one side of the shape, as shown below.

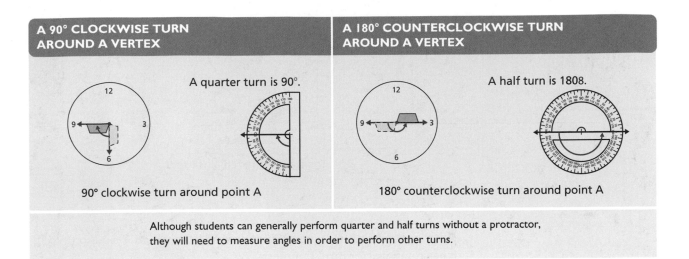

A 90° CLOCKWISE TURN AROUND A VERTEX	A 180° COUNTERCLOCKWISE TURN AROUND A VERTEX
A quarter turn is 90°.	A half turn is 1808.
90° clockwise turn around point A	180° counterclockwise turn around point A

Although students can generally perform quarter and half turns without a protractor, they will need to measure angles in order to perform other turns.

Turn Centres

A shape can be turned around any point—not just around a vertex or its centre point. The turn centre can be inside the shape, outside the shape, or on the perimeter of the shape. When a shape is turned on a grid, its final location depends not only on the size and direction of the turn, but also on where the turn centre is located. This happens because the turn centre remains fixed, while all the other points on the shape move in a circle around that point.

The location of the turn centre, however, does not influence the direction in which the image will face. For example, each image below shows the result of turning a triangle $\frac{1}{4}$ turn clockwise around a different turn centre: the orientation of the image is the same in each case, even though its location on the grid is different.

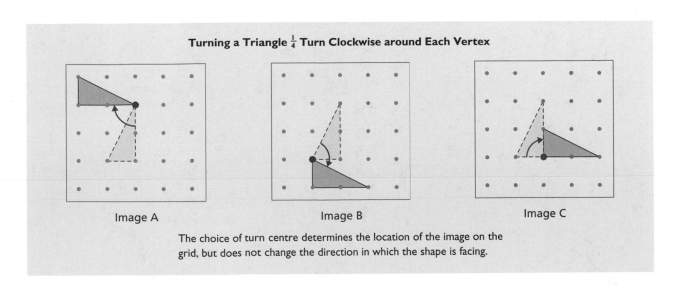

Turning a Triangle $\frac{1}{4}$ Turn Clockwise around Each Vertex

| Image A | Image B | Image C |

The choice of turn centre determines the location of the image on the grid, but does not change the direction in which the shape is facing.

Properties of Turns

FIXED TURN CENTRE

When a shape turns on a plane, only one point, the turn centre, stays fixed.

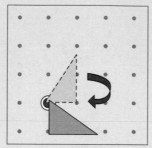

The turn centre remains fixed.

When a shape is turned part of a turn around its centre and "lands on" itself, it has rotational, or turn, symmetry.

For example, a square can be turned $\frac{1}{4}$ turn around its centre and fit right back on its original outline.

A Non-Euclidean Transformation—Dilatation

There are also non-Euclidean transformations that change the size of the shape. Only one of these, the *dilatation*, is introduced, in some jurisdictions, at the K–8 level. A dilatation increases or decreases the size of the original figure without changing its shape. The result of a dilatation is an image whose angle measures match those in the original, and whose side or curve lengths have all been multiplied or divided by the same amount. This results in an image that is a similar shape. For example, the green triangle below was transformed by doubling the length of each side.

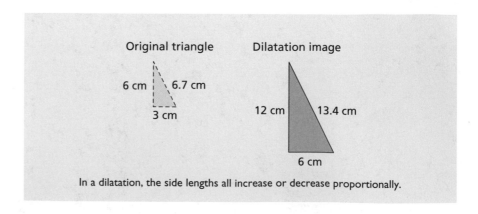

In a dilatation, the side lengths all increase or decrease proportionally.

Dilatations are called *similarity transformations* because the image is always similar to the original shape.

Creating a Dilatation Image by Measuring

STEP I

Choose a point outside the original shape. This is sometimes called a *dilatation point* or *centre of dilatation*.

STEP 2

Connect that point to each vertex on the original shape.

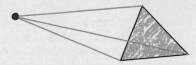

STEP 3

Measure the length of each connecting line.

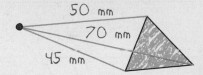

STEP 4

Increase or decrease the length of each connecting line in the same proportion (called the *scale factor*).

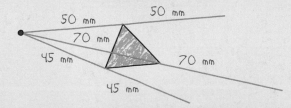

STEP 5

Join the ends of the connecting lines to form the image.

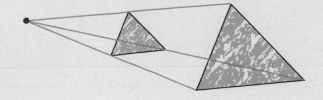

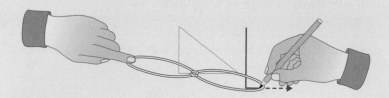

ACTIVITY 14.6

Students can explore the properties of dilatations as they experiment with this method for enlarging a shape.

1. Make a knot to tie the ends of two rubber bands together.
2. Draw a triangle on a piece of paper.
3. Hold down one end of your double rubber band near your triangle. Place a pencil inside the other end.
4. Slowly move the knot along the sides of your triangle.
5. Draw a line with your pencil as you move the knot. What happened?

CREATING A DILATATION IMAGE ON GRID PAPER

To create a dilatation image on grid paper, students might count the spaces along each side of the original shape, and then multiply or divide each side length by the same number to determine the lengths of the corresponding sides on the image. For example, the side lengths of this red rectangle were divided by 2 to create the green image.

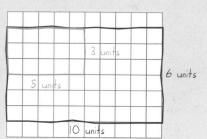

Properties of Dilatations

SIMILARITY	INCREASE IN AREA

SIMILARITY

The image is always similar to the original.

A dilation image is always similar to the original.

Every square is a dilatation image of every other square because, by definition, the sides are all increased or decreased by the same proportion. This is true for any group of regular polygons.

INCREASE IN AREA

When an image is enlarged or reduced, the area increases or decreases by the square of the scale factor.

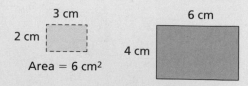

Area = 6 cm²

Area = 24 cm²

When the side lengths are multiplied by 2, the area is multiplied by 2^2 or 4.

Tessellations

Tessellations are included in many mathematics curricula because they provide an opportunity for students to focus on properties of shapes, especially side lengths and angle measures.

Relating Tessellations and Transformations

Tessellations (or *tilings*) involve translating, reflecting, and/or rotating a shape (a *tile*) or a combination of shapes in order to cover a plane surface so there are no gaps or overlaps between the tiles.

2-D Shapes That Tile

Most students realize that squares or rectangles will tile a surface, and many know that regular hexagons will also work because of their experience with square counters or tiles, attribute blocks, and pattern blocks.

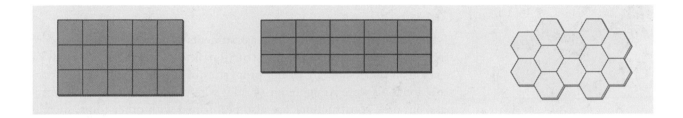

Students may be more surprised to learn that any triangle or quadrilateral can tile. This is because the sum of the measures of the interior angles is 180° in a triangle and 360° in a quadrilateral. Shapes will tessellate if the angles that meet at a central point fill a total of 360°.

In the examples below, congruent angles are colour-coded inside each shape to show how the angles combine at a centre point to fill 360°. In the first figure, each angle from the triangle occurs twice in the centre, for a total of 180° × 2, or 360°. In the second figure, all four angles from the trapezoid meet at the centre, for a total of 360°. Side lengths are also important—in a tessellation, congruent sides are matched to one another.

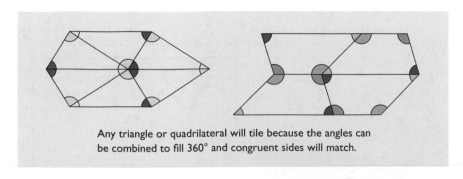

Any triangle or quadrilateral will tile because the angles can be combined to fill 360° and congruent sides will match.

ACTIVITY 14.7

Older students can explore the angle properties of regular polygons through tiling.

Ask them which of these regular shapes will serve as a good tile.

Regular polygons

In **Activity 14.7**, students explore the regular polygons to see which ones will tile a surface on their own. This activity will help them discover that the equilateral triangle, the square, and the hexagon work, because their interior angle measures can be combined to fill 360° (6 × 60°, 4 × 90°, and 3 × 120°).

Since the interior angle measures of the other regular polygons are not factors of 360°, they will not tile a surface unless they are combined with other shapes.

Students might also explore what happens when they try to tile with irregular shapes, or when they combine regular and irregular shapes. For example, some irregular pentagons will tile, depending on their interior angle measures, and regular octagons will tile if they are combined with squares.

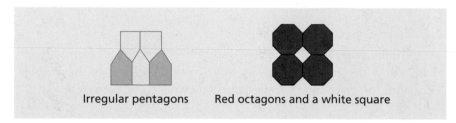

Irregular pentagons   Red octagons and a white square

Constructions

Usually in Grades 7 or higher, you ask students to perform geometric constructions. The purpose of the constructions is to allow students to apply or develop an understanding of the properties of shapes. Traditionally, construction tools were straightedge (a ruler with no numbers on it) and compass, but now constructions are also performed with other tools, such as Miras or dynamic geometry software.

Typically, students might learn to construct:

• the perpendicular to a line
• a line parallel to another line
• the perpendicular bisector of a line segment
• a circle with a given centre
• a circle that goes through 2 or 3 given points
• an angle bisector

By combining these ideas, students might also learn to construct angles of particular sizes, for example, a 45° or 60° angle, an equilateral triangle, a regular hexagon, a circle touching the 3 sides of a triangle, etc.

For example, below are shown constructions of a perpendicular to a line using ruler and compass, a Mira, and Geometer's Sketchpad.

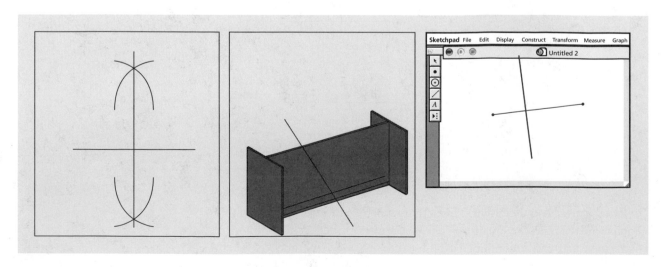

The first construction focuses students on recognizing that the perpendicular bisector of a segment is the set of points equidistant from both end points. The second construction focuses on the notion that the line of reflection is perpendicular to any segment joining a pre-image to its image. The third construction is one that is automatically performed by the software, but requires students to identify a point on the line and the line to which the constructed line will be perpendicular.

Common Errors and Misconceptions

Location and Movement: Strategies for Dealing with Common Errors and Misconceptions

COMMON ERROR OR MISCONCEPTION	SUGGESTED STRATEGY
Meaning of *Above* Students sometimes misinterpret the term *above*, thinking that it must mean *directly above*. For example, they would not recognize that the cloud shown here is not just above the house, but also above the car. 	Students require opportunities to hear teachers use the term *above* in situations where one item is not directly above the other.  A teacher might ask, "Could you get me the red book from the shelf above my desk?"
DIAGONAL FLIPS	**SUGGESTED STRATEGY**
Students may think that flips have to be horizontal or vertical (as shown here), and may not recognize that flip lines can also be diagonal. The green triangle has been flipped horizontally and then vertically. The green triangle has been flipped diagonally.	This misconception arises because teachers often focus on horizontal and vertical flips, since these are easier to perform. In addition, most computer draw programs readily perform vertical and horizontal flips, but not diagonal ones. Make sure to use illustrations of other flips as the topic is being discussed. When students are performing diagonal flips, they will find it helpful to use a Mira. *(continued)*

CONFUSING QUARTER-TURNS WITH HALF-TURNS

A student who has been asked to perform a half-turn often performs a quarter-turn. He or she is likely thinking that a full turn is only half way around.

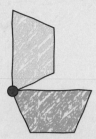

Incorrect representation of a $\frac{1}{2}$ turn

SUGGESTED STRATEGY

A good way to deal with this misconception is to have students use their own bodies to explore turns. A half-turn means turning from front to back. A quarter-turn means turning right or left. You might use a large "wooden" protractor found in high school classrooms by placing it on the floor and having students rotate accordingly.

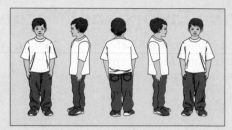

A full turn is the same as four quarter-turns.

Later, students can check their turns by focusing on how one side of the shape, or even one point, moved. It also helps to connect the turn centre to a point on the original shape and a corresponding point on the image. The angle formed will indicate the amount of turn.

A straight angle, so a $\frac{1}{2}$ turn

CONFUSING FLIPS AND TURNS

To a student, a flip and a 180° turn can look very much the same.

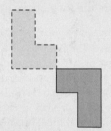

Diagonal flip or 180° turn?

SUGGESTED STRATEGY

If students match vertices on the original shape with the corresponding vertices on the image, this will help them distinguish between a flip and a turn.

As well, they could either visualize or draw a line from one of the original vertices that crosses what they think is the flip line at a right angle. They will see that the corresponding vertex is not along that line and, therefore, the transformation is not a flip.

Vertex A′ is not a flip image of Vertex A across the line, so the transformation is not a flip.

Students should always be encouraged to model a transformation to test their idea about what motion was performed. For example, a student who models a flip of the green shape across the diagonal line will find that the image looks like this:

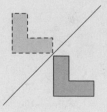

LOCATING POINTS ON A GRID

Students may count lines rather than spaces when they are creating coordinate grids and locating points on a coordinate grid. For example, a student who wants to locate (4, 2) may count the first line as "1" (both horizontally and vertically) and, as a result, mislocate the point as shown here. Although it is at (4, 2) on this grid, it should be labelled as (3, 1).

Incorrect grid lables and
location for point (4, 2)

SUGGESTED STRATEGY

Encourage students to include 0 on each axis, since this will help them count correctly.

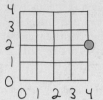

Correct grid and location
for point (4, 2)

INVERTING COORDINATES

Students mix up the order of the Cartesian coordinates when plotting points on a Cartesian grid; for example, they plot point (3, 4) by counting up 3 and then right 4, instead of right 3 and up 4.

SUGGESTED STRATEGY

Encourage students to memorize the positions of (1, 0) and (0, 1) to remind them which number tells them to go right and which number tells them to go up. Since (1, 0) is 1 to the right, that means they go right first. Since (0, 1) is up, that means they go up last.

Appropriate Manipulatives

Manipulatives for Geometry Work

2-D SHAPE MODELS

When students first begin learning about slides, flips, and turns, they work with concrete shapes, such as pattern or attribute blocks. The disadvantage of many of these shapes is that they are symmetrical, and transformations can be more difficult to identify when they are done with symmetrical shapes. Therefore, it is important to use other, less symmetrical shape pieces. Shape models can also be used for tessellations and pattern work.

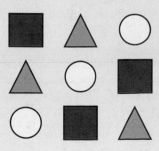

EXAMPLE

2-D shape models can be used for making transformation patterns. In the pattern below, a yellow dot is used to indicate the orientation of each triangle.

Making a pattern by turning and tracing a pattern block

(continued)

GEOBOARDS

Geoboards provide a hands-on model for transformations with 2-D shapes. Younger students can make a shape with an elastic, and then physically turn the geoboard (or flip it, if the geoboard is transparent). Older students can use one elastic to show the original shape and another for the transformation image. Dot paper grids (5-by-5) are useful for recording the results of geoboard activities.

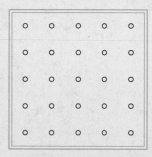

EXAMPLE

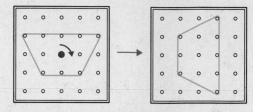

Performing a turn by rotating a geoboard

PROTRACTORS

Protractors are used for measuring angles for the purpose of turning particular amounts.

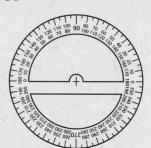

Circular protractor

EXAMPLE

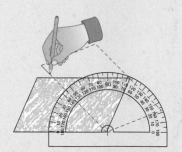

Using a regular protractor to turn a parallelogram 45° clockwise

MIRRORS AND MIRAS

Either traditional mirrors or transparent ones (Miras) are invaluable for identifying and modelling flips.

A transparent mirror

EXAMPLE

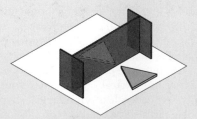

The bottom edge of the Mira represents the flip line.

A transparent mirror makes it easy to see where a flip image is located.

GRID PAPER

Grid paper is needed for work with coordinate graphing and is a useful tool for exploring slides, flips, and turns. (See page 343.) Like dot paper, it can also be used for dilatations. (See next page.)

EXAMPLE

When students flip a shape on a grid, they can count grid squares to locate the flip image of each vertex. They can also discover that lines drawn to link each original vertex with its flip image form a 90° angle with the flip line.

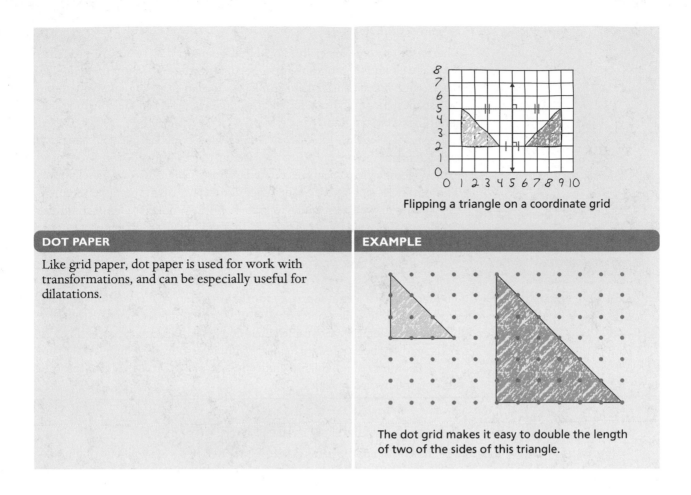

Flipping a triangle on a coordinate grid

DOT PAPER

Like grid paper, dot paper is used for work with transformations, and can be especially useful for dilatations.

EXAMPLE

The dot grid makes it easy to double the length of two of the sides of this triangle.

Appropriate Technology

Computers

There are a number of ways to use computers to help students build an understanding of motion geometry.

Draw Programs

Many computer drawing programs will allow students to reflect or rotate shapes. For example, the green triangle below has been flipped horizontally and then vertically. The green rectangle has been turned 45° clockwise. Some programs have default flip lines (vertical or horizontal flip lines parallel with a side) and turn centres (around the centre point of the shape).

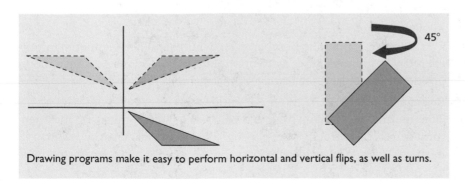

Drawing programs make it easy to perform horizontal and vertical flips, as well as turns.

Geometry Software

There is also some specially developed geometry software for students. Several well-known programs are *Shape Up*, produced by Sunburst, *Building Blocks*, and *Tesselmania*. For example, with *Shape Up*, students can stamp 2-D shapes and apply transformations. The available models include pattern blocks and tangrams.

Geometer's Sketchpad and *Cabri Geometry* are two examples of very powerful dynamic geometry software. Using these tools allows students to explore geometric conjectures related to transformations and tessellations. There is increasing attention being paid to their use in the upper elementary grades as well as secondary grades. For example, students could use *Geometer's Sketchpad* to create a shape that will tile a surface.

WebConnect W W W

www.makingmathmeaningful
.nelson.com

Visit the Making Math Meaningful website for links to sites with activities and applets related to motion geometry.

Internet

The Internet is a fertile source of motion-geometry investigations for children. Many sites offer not only activity ideas, but also virtual tools for hands-on exploration. Examples include pattern blocks, square grids, dot grids, and geoboards. A particularly valuable source is the Math Forum K–12 Geometry site, which includes lesson plans, projects, links to other sites, problems, and puzzles.

Assessing Student Understanding

- It is most appropriate to assess students' knowledge of and ability to use positional vocabulary in everyday situations, not just in designated math times.
- Many of the skills and concepts addressed in this chapter are best assessed through observation of students working directly with physical materials. In that way, it is possible to see, for example, how tools like a protractor or Mira are used.
- Performing transformations on grid paper often requires less sophistication than performing those same transformations on plain paper. Decide which you think is more appropriate for students in terms of assessing them.
- Some provinces introduce transformations in a much later grade than other provinces. Where this is the case, some of the simpler ideas should be both presented and assessed in a somewhat more sophisticated way.

Appropriate Children's Books

All About Where (Hoban, 1991).
Tana Hoban is a prolific photographer who brings the geometry in our everyday world to children's attention. In this book, students think about positional vocabulary, such as *above, under, behind, between,* etc.

Round Trip (Jonas, 1983).
This unusual black-and-white picture book is "read" through, and then turned upside down and "read" through upside down and backwards to tell its story. This book provides an opportunity to think about transformations in a unique way.

The Mirror Puzzle Book (Walter, 1985).
This book, which comes with a mirror, allows students to explore the effects of reflection. Although the book was published in the mid-1980s, the content is not at all dated. The focus is on solving puzzles by using a mirror to create particular designs.

Applying What You've Learned

1. What information about transformations did you use to solve the chapter problem?

2. Positional vocabulary is usually introduced to young children. Which terms would you use earliest and which would you delay? Why?

3. Explain why numbering grid lines on the two axes to describe point locations is more sophisticated than using the typical city map system of letters in boxes on one axis and numbers in boxes on the other axis.

4. At what point do you think it would be appropriate to use terms like *translation, rotation,* and *reflection* as opposed to *slide, turn,* and *flip*? Explain your thinking.

5. Search the Internet for a transformation applet. Why might using that applet be better than drawing shapes on the board?

6. Search for three "fun" activities that students could do with a Mira. In each case, indicate what mathematics students are learning and discuss whether that activity is a good way to approach the math.

7. What task would you assign a Grade 6 student to find out what she or he understands about rotating shapes?

8. A computer language called Logo was very popular 15 to 20 years ago for young students to explore geometry. It is still available both for free on the Web and through a company based in Canada. Find an article about Logo and discuss your opinion of its potential value for exploring geometric ideas.

Interact with a K–8 Student:

9. Ask a student to draw a "map" of the room where you are talking with him or her. Does he or she pay attention only to relative position of articles in the room or to relative distances between them as well? How can you tell?

Discuss with a K–8 Teacher:

10. Do some research on the game Tetris. Ask a teacher how she or he would feel about using Tetris as a vehicle for exploring transformational geometry. Describe your reaction to what you heard.

Selected References

Andrews, A.G. (1996). Developing spatial sense—a moving experience. *Teaching Children Mathematics, 2*, 290–293.

Battista, M.T., and Clements, D.H. (1988). A case for a logo-based elementary school geometry curriculum. *Arithmetic Teacher, 36*, 11–17.

Bruni, J.V., and Seidenstein, R.B. (1990). Geometric concepts and spatial sense. In Payne, J.N. (Ed.). *Mathematics for the young child*. Reston, VA: National Council of Teachers of Mathematics, 202–227.

Clements, D.H. (1999). Geometric and spatial thinking in young children. In Copley, J. (Ed.). *Mathematics in the early years*. Washington, DC: National Council of Teachers of Mathematics and National Association for the Education of Young Children, 66–79.

Clements, D.H. (2000). Geometric and spatial thinking in young children. In Copley, J.V. (Ed.). *The young child and mathematics*. Washington, DC: National Association for the Education of Young Children and National Council of Teachers of Mathematics.

Clements, D.H., and Battista, M.T. (1992). Geometry and spatial reasoning. In Grouws, D.A. (Ed.). *Handbook of research on mathematics teaching and learning.* New York: Macmillan Publishing Co., 420–464.

Clements, D.H., and Sarama, J. (2000a). The earliest geometry. *Teaching Children Mathematics,* 7(2), 82–86.

Clements, D.H., and Sarama, J. (2000b). Young children's ideas about geometric shapes. *Teaching children mathematics,* 6(8), 482–487.

Findell, C.R., Small, M., Cavanagh, M., Dacey, L., Greenes, C.E., and Sheffield, L.J. (2001). *Navigating through geometry in prekindergarten–grade 2.* Reston, VA: National Council of Teachers of Mathematics.

Gavin, M.K., Belkin, L.P., Spinelli, A.M., and St. Marie, J. (2001). *Navigating through geometry in grades 3–5.* Reston, VA: National Council of Teachers of Mathematics.

Giganti, P., Jr., and Cittadinto, M.J. (1990). The art of tessellation. *The Arithmetic Teacher.* 37, 6–16.

Hoban, T. (1991). *All about where.* New York: Greenwillow Books.

Hutchins, P. (1971). *Rosie's walk.* New York: Aladdin Paperbacks.

Jonas, A. (1983). *Round trip.* New York: Mulberrry Books, a division of William Morrow & Co.

Pugalee, D.K., Frykholm, J., Johnson, A., Slovin, H., Malloy, C., and Preston, R. (2002). *Navigating through geometry in grades 6–8.* Reston, VA: National Council of Teachers of Mathematics.

Rubenstein, R.N., and Thompson, D.R. (1995). Making connections with transformations in grades K–8. In House, P.A., and Coxford, A.F. (Eds.). *Connecting mathematics across the curriculum.* Reston, VA: National Council of Teachers of Mathematics, 65–78.

Selke, D. (1999). Geometric flips via the arts. *Teaching Children Mathematics,* 5(6), 379–383.

Sharman, L. (1994). *The amazing book of shapes.* New York: Dorling Kindersley Publlishing.

Small, M. (2007). *PRIME: Geometry: Background and strategies.* Toronto: Thomson Nelson.

Walter, M. (1986). *The mirror puzzle book.* St. Albans, UK: Tarquin.

Chapter 15

Measurement: A Focus on Length and Area

IN A NUTSHELL

The main ideas in this chapter are listed below:

1. Measurement is the process of assigning a qualitative or quantitative description of size to an object based on a particular attribute. It is always a comparison of the size of one object with another, so the same object can be described using different measurements. Therefore, knowledge of the size of certain benchmarks assists you in measuring.

2. The use of standard measurement units is meant to simplify and clarify communication about the size of objects. The use of measurement formulas is meant to simplify measurement calculations.

(continued)

CHAPTER PROBLEM

A right triangle has a perimeter of 36 cm and an area of 54 cm². What are its dimensions?

IN A NUTSHELL (*continued*)

3. Measurement instruction is best approached by beginning with a definition/comparison stage, followed by a stage involving nonstandard units, followed by a stage involving standard units. Problem solving should be part of all stages.

4. Tools, units of measure, and degree of precision for a measurement should be appropriate to the context and purpose for that measurement.

Fundamental Notions about Measurement

Children are naturally curious about measurement. They are interested in how tall, how big, how heavy, how long, how hot, or how cold things are. Initially, they accept answers that describe comparisons: "An elephant is about twice as tall as my teacher." Gradually, they come to understand that measurement is a tool that can help them answer questions more precisely.

The Nature of Measurement

Measurement is about assigning a numerical value to an attribute of an object, relative to another object called a unit. Usually, you measure to have a sense of the size of an object compared to other objects whose size you know. A greater measurement implies that one object has "more" of a particular attribute than another. In elementary and middle school, measurement is typically about length, area, capacity, mass, volume, time, temperature, and angles.

There are a number of principles that underlie any type of measurement.

MEASUREMENT PRINCIPLES

1. No measurement of a continuous attribute can ever be exact, as there is always a smaller, more precise unit.
2. There is always value in estimating a measurement, sometimes because an estimate is all you need, and sometimes because an estimate is a useful check on the reasonableness of a more precise measurement.
3. Familiarity with certain measurement referents helps you estimate.
4. Any measurement can be determined in more than one way.
5. There is more than one possible unit that could be used to measure an item, but the unit chosen should make sense for the object.
6. In order to measure, a series of uniform units must be used or a single unit must be used repeatedly.

7. The unit chosen for a measurement affects the numerical value of the measurement; a bigger unit results in a smaller number of units.

8. Sometimes you want a more precise measurement; in that case, a smaller unit should be used.

9. Sometimes you measure directly and sometimes you use indirect means.

10. Different measurement attributes of the same object are not always related, so it is possible for an object that is large in one way to be small in another.

Students will gradually come to recognize these principles as they gain experience with measurement, and it is important for teachers to recognize opportunities to bring them out through classroom discussion.

Opportunities to Address Measurement Principles in the Classroom

MEASUREMENT PRINCIPLE 1

No measurement of a continuous attribute can ever be exact, as there is always a smaller, more precise unit.

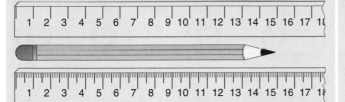

"It's 15 when I measure in centimetres, but it's 149 when I measure in millimetres."

MEASUREMENT PRINCIPLE 2

It is always useful to estimate a measurement, sometimes because an estimate is all you need, and sometimes because it is a useful check on the reasonableness of a more precise measurement.

> It's 3 km to the pool. It takes me about 10 min to walk to school and that's about 1 km. It will probably take us about half an hour to walk to the pool.

Sometimes an estimate is all you need.

> The plum's mass is 135 g. That makes sense because the peach was about 300g, and the plum is about half as heavy as the peach.

Sometimes an estimate helps you decide if a measurement makes sense.

MEASUREMENT PRINCIPLE 3

Familiarity with certain measurement referents helps you estimate.

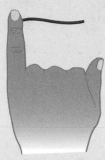

"My finger is 1 cm wide, so this string must be 1, 2, 3, 4, 5 cm long."

MEASUREMENT PRINCIPLE 4

Any measurement can be determined in more than one way.

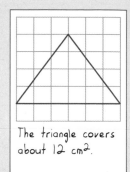

The triangle covers about 12 cm².

Area = base × height ÷ 2
= 6 × 4 ÷ 2
= 12 cm²

"I figured out the area by putting a grid down over the triangle and counting squares. Sarah used a formula."

MEASUREMENT PRINCIPLE 5

There is more than one possible unit that could be used to measure an item, but the unit chosen should make sense for the object.

"I would use the cup to measure how much the pitcher holds because it's not too small or too big."

MEASUREMENT PRINCIPLE 6

In order to measure, a series of uniform units must be used, or a single unit must be used repeatedly.

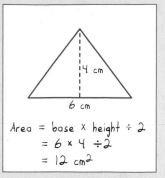

"When you measure, you have to use the same tool again and again."

MEASUREMENT PRINCIPLE 7

The unit chosen for a measurement affects the value of the measurement; a bigger unit results in a smaller number of units.

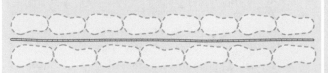

"Our rope is the length of eight of John's shoes, but only seven of Ani's shoes because Ani's shoes are bigger."

MEASUREMENT PRINCIPLE 8

Sometimes you want a more precise measurement; in that case, a smaller unit should be used.

"They're pretty close. I need to use a millimetre ruler to see how much longer."

MEASUREMENT PRINCIPLE 9	MEASUREMENT PRINCIPLE 10
Sometimes you measure directly and sometimes you use indirect means. For example, there are two different ways to find the measure of the red angle in the diagram below.	Different measurement attributes of the same object are not always related, so it is possible for an object that is large in one way to be small in another.

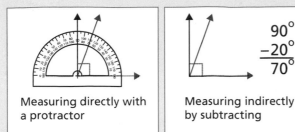

Measuring directly with a protractor   Measuring indirectly by subtracting

$$\begin{array}{r} 90° \\ -20° \\ \hline 70° \end{array}$$

"I could measure the red angle with a protractor or I could measure the smaller angle and subtract 20° from 90°."

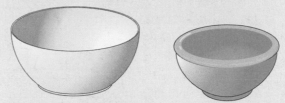

"The yellow bowl is bigger, but the green one is heavier."

Stages of Measurement Instruction

For most types of measurement, there are three stages that teachers typically move through with students:

- **Definition/Comparison:** Students begin to learn to define the measurement, and become aware of and apply a process for comparing items with respect to that measurement, without using units.
- **Nonstandard Units:** Students continue to define the measurement while they learn to measure with nonstandard units, such as scoops of water (for capacity) or linking cubes (for length).
- **Standard Units:** Students learn to use measurement tools to measure with standard units, such as centimetres and grams.

These three stages apply to most, but not all, types of measurement. While students generally move through all three stages in their work with length, area, capacity, volume, mass, and time, they do not typically do so in their work with temperature, money, and angles.

The Three Stages of Measurement Instruction

DEFINITION/COMPARISON

In this stage, students learn what a particular type of measurement is all about by using a comparison process (either direct or indirect) to determine which of two items has more of that measure. For example, to compare two vegetables directly to see which is longer, a student would line up the vegetables at one end to see which one "sticks out."

Indirect comparison is less concrete than direct comparison, but is sometimes used when direct comparison is not possible. For example, a student might cut a string to match the length of a carrot in his or her refrigerator at home, and bring it to school to compare with carrot strings cut by other students. In this case, carrot lengths are being compared indirectly because students are using representations of carrots, rather than the carrots themselves. Whether the comparison is direct or indirect, the process for comparing is the same.

While the same thinking applies to other types of measurement besides length, the processes used to compare the items are different. Students' understanding of each type of measurement develops implicitly as they discuss how to decide which of two items has more of that measure.

(continued)

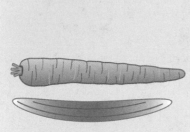

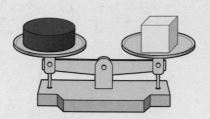

"I know the carrot is longer because it sticks out more."

"I know the blocks have the same mass because the pans balance."

"I know the clear container holds more than the blue container because there's still space after you pour everything from the blue container into it."

NONSTANDARD UNITS

When familiar objects are used as units for measuring, these are typically referred to as nonstandard units since there is no universal meaning that can be attached; there is, for example, no single standard length of a block, capacity of a can, or mass of a cube. Although there are some researchers who have found evidence that it is appropriate to use standard tools and standard units right away, as long as meaning is emphasized over procedure (Stephan and Clements, 2003), most experts continue to believe that students need time to work with nonstandard units before they will be ready for standard units and tools.

Using nonstandard units helps to reinforce important measurement concepts. For example, with length, the use of nonstandard units reinforces the notion that measuring is about determining the distance between two points and not just about identifying the point on a ruler where the length ends.

In the nonstandard unit stage, it is important for students to choose a unit that is appropriate for the type of measurement and the object being measured. For example, if the student is measuring length, the units should

- be uniform (all the same size and shape)
- be smaller than the object being measured (so a reasonable degree of precision is possible)
- combine to create something long and thin that fits along the distance to be measured

"The carrot is 16 cubes long."

The nonstandard unit stage is also relevant for other types of measurement. Whether students are learning to measure capacity, mass, area, volume, or even time, they need time to work with various nonstandard units before standard units are introduced in order to understand what each measurement type is all about.

STANDARD UNITS

In the standard unit stage, students are ready to use a standard unit, and eventually a variety of standard units, to measure. They soon learn that this makes it easier to compare and communicate about measurements. For example, if someone says that a carrot is 22 cm long, everyone knows exactly how long that is. A description with nonstandard units, such as "16 cubes long," would be more difficult to interpret.

At this stage, students learn to use standard tools for measuring. These include such things as rulers, measuring tapes, and trundle wheels (circles with a fixed circumference, usually 1 m, on a stick to allow rolling) for measuring length, measuring cups and spoons for measuring capacity, and gram and kilogram masses for measuring mass. This is more sophisticated than working with direct or indirect comparison or with nonstandard units because it requires students to have an abstract understanding of what is represented by the marks on a ruler or measuring cup, or the size of a standard mass.

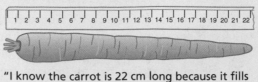

"I know the carrot is 22 cm long because it fills up the space from 0 to 22 along the ruler."

The Metric System of Measurement

Over 30 years ago, Canada adopted the International System of Units (called SI, for Système International) as its official measurement system. The rationale for adopting the metric system included the fact that this system is already used by most countries around the world, and especially in the scientific community, because of its ease of use.

Clearly, one of the attractions of the metric system is its consistency with the place value system. This is particularly valuable when units are renamed, or converted. For example, 3.56 m can easily be renamed as 356 cm without any complicated calculations.

SI Base Units

While the old imperial system of measurement required Canadians to memorize a wide range of unrelated numbers—12 inches in a foot, 3 feet in a yard, 1760 yards in a mile, etc.—the adoption of the metric system meant that people would simply need to learn a few base units and a series of prefixes that could be applied to these base units.

At the K–8 level, students are introduced to three of the seven SI base units—the metre, the kilogram, and the second. It may seem odd that the kilogram is called the base unit when the metric prefixes are attached to the word "gram," not "kilogram." In fact, the gram was actually a base unit in the older CGS system of measurement, but was superseded by the kilogram, which was considered more convenient for practical purposes.

Each of the three base units is based on a precise measurement associated with a science-related situation. While these situations may be of interest to teachers, it is not necessary to teach them, or the term "base unit," to students.

SI Base Units Introduced in Elementary School

Unit	Attribute Measured	Symbol	Definition
metre	length	m	One metre is the length of the path travelled by laser-generated light in a vacuum during the time interval of 1/299 792 458 of a light-second.
kilogram	mass	kg	One kilogram is a mass equal to the international prototype of the kilogram (about the mass of 1 dm³ of water at 4°C).
second	time	s	One second is the duration of 9 192 631 770 periods of radiation corresponding to the transition between the two hyperfine levels of the ground state of the cesium-133 atom at 0 kelvin.

SI Derived and Customary Units

The International System of Units also uses a number of *derived units*—units that were created by applying arithmetic operations to the SI base units. Derived-unit measures used in elementary school mathematics include square metres for area, cubic metres for volume, metres per second for speed or velocity, and *degrees Celsius* for temperature. There are also other derived-unit measures that are not typically dealt with in elementary school. One example is the kilogram per cubic metre, which is used to describe density.

In addition, there are a number of widely used *customary units* that are considered to be outside the International System of Units, but are accepted for use with SI. These include the *litre* to describe capacity, the *tonne* (metric ton) to describe mass, *minute, hour,* and *day* to describe time, and the *degree* to describe angle arc.

Metric Prefixes

Metric prefixes allow the user to begin with a unit and create larger and smaller units. There are actually 20 prefixes—10 to create larger units, and 10 to create smaller units—but you commonly use only about half of these.

Metric Prefixes in Common Use

giga-	mega-	kilo-	hecto-	deca-	unit	deci-	centi-	milli-	micro-	nano-
1 billion units	1 million units	1000 units	100 units	10 units	1 unit	0.1 units	0.01 units	0.001 units	0.000001 units	0.000000001 units

Common Metric Prefixes for Length

kilo-	unit	deci-	centi-	milli-
1000 m	1 m	0.1 m	0.01 m	0.001 m

ACTIVITY 15.1

A day is defined as 24 hours. How long should a deciday be? How long should a centiday be?

Note that the smaller units in the tables above are described with decimals rather than fractions. Decimals are used in the International System of Units because of the relationship of the metric prefixes to the place value system. Using decimals makes it particularly easy to rename a recorded measurement in terms of another unit. For example, to change centimetres to millimetres, you simply need to multiply by 10, which moves each digit one place to the left: 2.4 cm = 24 mm.

Measuring Length

We use the term *length*, or *linear measure*, to describe measurements in one dimension. Linear measurements include height, width, length, depth, distance, and perimeter. Ideas about length are introduced even in preschool, probably since estimating and measuring length is something people do often in everyday life. For example, a student might want to know if a pair of pants is long enough, if a distance is too far to walk, or how the heights of family members compare.

How Concepts of Length Can Be Introduced

Ideas about length can be introduced through the same three stages as many other measurement concepts—definition/comparison, nonstandard units, using standard units). With length, the second stage is usually introduced fairly soon after the first.

How Concepts of Length Can Be Introduced

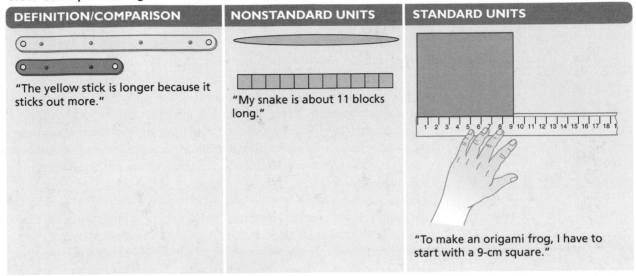

DEFINITION/COMPARISON	NONSTANDARD UNITS	STANDARD UNITS
"The yellow stick is longer because it sticks out more."	"My snake is about 11 blocks long."	"To make an origami frog, I have to start with a 9-cm square."

Length: The Definition/Comparison Stage

At this stage, students explore the notion that one item is longer than another if, when the items are lined up to start at a common base line, one sticks out (or up) farther than the other. In the process, students begin to develop vocabulary for comparing lengths—terms such as "longer than" and "shorter than," or, if they are comparing more than two items, terms such as "longest," "second-longest," "shortest," etc.

Direct and Indirect Comparison

Sometimes, lengths are compared directly by placing the items to be compared side by side. For example, students might use *direct comparison* to compare the lengths of snakes they have made from modelling clay to see whose is longest. At other times, they will need to use *indirect comparison*. With indirect comparison, students compare actual-size representations of objects, rather than the objects themselves. Indirect comparison is usually used when direct comparison would be difficult. For example, students might cut strings to represent the length of their hand-spans and compare the strings with other body lengths, such as their foot lengths or their elbow-to-wrist distances. Comfort with this sort of indirect method is predicated on a student's understanding of *transitivity of measure*, that is, if measure A = measure B and measure B = measure C, then measure A = measure C. Students usually need lots of experience with direct comparison before indirect comparison situations are presented.

Comparison activities, whether direct or indirect, can also be part of larger investigations, such as finding out whether people with longer feet also tend to have wider hand spans. **Activity 15.2** suggests examples of direct and indirect comparison activities for young students.

Length: The Nonstandard Unit Stage

Teachers can introduce work with nonstandard units when students realize that, rather than aligning objects directly or indirectly to compare their lengths, they can use uniform units to assign a numerical value to the length of each object. This makes it possible to compare lengths simply by comparing these values.

Appropriate Nonstandard Units for Length

Nonstandard units are handy everyday items of uniform length, such as unsharpened pencils, new crayons, new erasers, toothpicks, craft sticks (Popsicle sticks), plastic links, paper clips, Cuisenaire rods, and straws. Students can also use body measurements, such as hand-spans, foot lengths, paces, etc. Although students might want to use items such as sharpened pencils or used erasers, these are not ideal since they are not uniform.

For length, it helps students to use items that are long and thin, so there will be no ambiguity about which attribute is being measured. Therefore, items like recipe cards are not ideal, even though one of their dimensions could be used as a unit.

Initially, you want students to use units that are meaningful to them. If, for example, they hear that something is 5 new pencils long, this gives them a good feel for its length because they have a good mental image of a pencil's length.

As they work with nonstandard units, students can discover these important notions:

- Any measurement can be determined with a variety of different units.
- When you use the same unit to measure different lengths, the results are easy to compare.
- Measurements can be determined either by laying out multiple uniform units end to end, or by repeatedly using and moving a single unit along the length to be measured.

Measuring the Same Length with Different Units

It is important for students to have opportunities to measure the same length with different units. This will help them discover that the same item can be described in different ways. It will also help them discover that, as the size of the unit increases, the number of units decreases. For example, the same item might be 56 paper clips long but only 8 straws long. Experiences like the ones represented in **Activity 15.3** and in the teacher-student interview that follows not only help students learn about using different units to measure the same length; they also help them discover that it is more efficient to use longer units to measure longer lengths and shorter units to measure shorter lengths.

ACTIVITY 15.3

Ask each student to have a partner help them cut a string that matches their height. They can then look for some different kinds of units to use to measure their height by measuring the string.

- What are some different ways to tell someone how tall you are?

- Which unit was easiest for you to use? Why?

Student Response

This student is learning that the number of units required to measure a length can be different if a different unit is used.

Teacher: This table is 6 pencils long. Suppose I measure the table again but with crayons like this. Do you think I'll get the same number of units?

(continued)

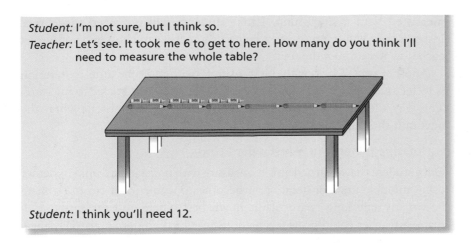

Student: I'm not sure, but I think so.

Teacher: Let's see. It took me 6 to get to here. How many do you think I'll need to measure the whole table?

Student: I think you'll need 12.

Measuring Different Lengths with a Constant Unit

Just as it is important for students to have opportunities to measure a constant length with different units, it is also important for them to measure different lengths with the same unit. This will give them measurement data that can readily be compared and graphed, and will also help them build their estimation skills.

Learning to Iterate

One of the first things students learn about measuring length in nonstandard units is that the units are uniform objects that are used repeatedly. Initially, students measure by lining up the required number of units along the object to be measured. For example, they might observe that a table is about 8 craft sticks long. Later, they learn to use a single item to *iterate*, that is, they move the unit from one position to another along the length of the object and count the number of times it fits along the length. Through experience, students will learn that some units lend themselves to iteration more easily than others. A new pencil, a paper clip, or a foot length will iterate easily, for example, while an arm length might not.

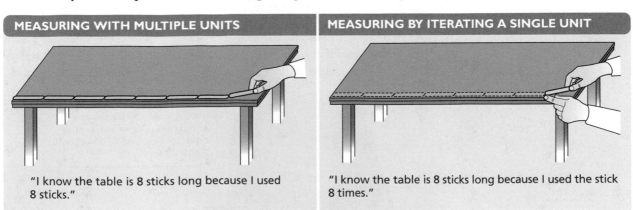

MEASURING WITH MULTIPLE UNITS	MEASURING BY ITERATING A SINGLE UNIT
"I know the table is 8 sticks long because I used 8 sticks."	"I know the table is 8 sticks long because I used the stick 8 times."

To help students make the transition from using multiple uniform items to using iteration, a teacher might place a strip of modelling clay along the length to be measured so students can make end-to-end imprints of the unit until the entire distance is covered. Students need to practise this in order to ensure that each imprint starts exactly where the old one left off, with no space left out and no overlap. With this form of iteration, the imprints give the impression that multiple units were used when, really, the length was measured with a single unit. Later, students will not need to do this. Instead, they will learn to use a finger as a marker to show where to start each new iteration of the unit.

Another way to help with the transition from multiple units to iteration is to let students use two units, for example, two craft sticks, to measure. This way, there is always a unit in place, making it easy to locate where the next unit should be placed.

Estimating Lengths in Nonstandard Units

Once students have learned how to measure with nonstandard units, whether using multiple units or iteration, it becomes possible for them to estimate how many units long a particular item will be. To help students learn to estimate, a teacher could provide situations in which an item is partially measured; the student's task is to estimate how many units it will take to measure the full length. Eventually, students will adopt a similar strategy themselves, using partial measurements as an aid to making reasonable estimates.

Students can estimate length by laying out, or iterating, a few units along the length to be measured, and then using the partial length to estimate the full length.

Another opportunity for estimation is to have students use a measurement for one object to estimate the length of another object. For example, a student who knows that a doorway is 15 erasers wide can use this information to estimate the widths, in erasers, of other objects that are wider or narrower.

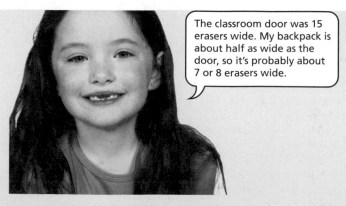

The classroom door was 15 erasers wide. My backpack is about half as wide as the door, so it's probably about 7 or 8 erasers wide.

Students can estimate the length of Object A by measuring Object B, and then using that measurement and the relationship between Objects A and B to estimate the length of Object A.

Students can also measure in one unit, and then use the measurement to make an estimate involving another unit. For example, a student could use dark green Cuisenaire rods to measure a length, and then predict how many of the light green rods (which are half the length of the dark green rods) it would take to measure the same length. Initially, it is best to work with units that are simple multiples of each other, for example, units in a 1:2 or 1:3 or 1:4 ratio. These sorts of tasks help students see that as the unit size decreases, the number of units required to measure a length increases.

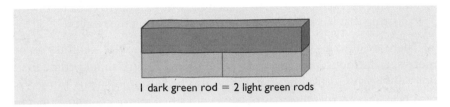

1 dark green rod = 2 light green rods

Nonstandard Unit Rulers

To help students make the transition to using a standard ruler, teachers can have them make their own nonstandard "rulers" by connecting uniform units, such as plastic links, linking cubes, or paper clips.

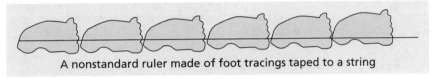

A nonstandard ruler made of foot tracings taped to a string

These "rulers" help students learn that the same tool can be used to measure many different things without having to actively iterate.

Nonstandard Units and Scale Drawings

Scale drawings are representations of objects or spaces that can be larger, smaller, or the same size as what they represent, and that are drawn in proportion to the original dimensions. The amount that the linear dimensions of the original dimensions are multiplied or divided by to create a scale drawing is called the *scale factor*.

The topic of scale drawings bridges the geometry and measurement strands because it deals with shapes as well as with measuring lengths (and sometimes angles). Although students do most of their work with scale drawings in Grades 6 or 7 and beyond, younger students work with maps (which are fundamentally scale drawings), and may also explore enlargements and reductions in the context of geometry activities or in art.

Although, typically, scale drawings are introduced once students use standard units—for example, letting 1 cm represent 1 m—the notion of scale can be very effectively introduced using nonstandard units. You can invite young students to choose two nonstandard units—one small and one large. Students could use the larger unit to measure the dimensions of a fairly large object or space, and then make a scale drawing by using one small unit to represent each large unit in the measurement.

Length: The Standard Unit Stage

Students can be introduced to standard units when they realize that, rather than measuring lengths in nonstandard units, which can mean different things to different people, they can use standard units that everyone will understand.

Introducing Standard Units of Length

Standard units are best introduced in a context that helps students see their value and efficiency. For example, a teacher might

- read a story such as *How Big Is a Foot?* by Rolf Myller (1991), which describes the confusion that ensues when a king uses his own foot to measure the dimensions for the queen's new bed
- use an everyday classroom measurement situation to illustrate how confusion can result from using nonstandard units to describe lengths, for example, by asking each of two students to cut a piece of string that is 5 shoes long, and then comparing the results

There are differing perspectives about which metric unit, centimetres or metres, to introduce first. Some believe that the metre should come first, not only because it is a base unit, but also because measuring in metres results in fewer errors due to problems with small motor coordination. On the other hand, it may be more convenient for the teacher if all students in a class can work on measurement activities at the same time, and this usually necessitates measuring smaller items using the smaller centimetre unit.

Learning about Metric Units of Length

CENTIMETRES

Introducing the Centimetre

Measuring with centimetre cubes provides a bridge from nonstandard units to standard units. These "act like" nonstandard units because students can physically line up cubes along the distance to be measured, or perhaps even link them, but the measurement can be reported in a standard unit-centimetres. Whether metres or centimetres are introduced first, students should have the experience of seeing 100 centimetre cubes lined up along a metre stick.

Introducing Centimetre Rulers

It is important to begin with a ruler that will not confuse students. Primary rulers with alternating coloured stripes work well, or students can use rulers that show only numbered centimetres, and not inches or millimetres. Some primary rulers have both (as shown below). Lining up centimetre cubes along the ruler helps students see that the stripes or numbers correspond to the number of centimetre cubes that can fit along the same distance.

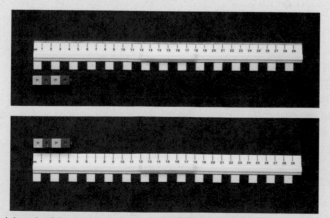

A length of 4 cm is the distance between 0 cm and 4 cm on the ruler. It is not just about the 4 cm mark on the ruler where the length ends.

METRES AND KILOMETRES

Introducing the Metre

Many students are already familiar with the metre stick and will quickly be able to develop a personal sense of the length of a metre. Some teachers find that this personal sense develops more quickly if students make their own tools for measuring 1 m. These might include lengths of string or strips of Bristol board. They can use these "tools" to find objects in their environment that are about a metre long, less than a metre long, and longer than a metre. These tools let them focus on the metre as a unit instead of being distracted by the cm or mm markings that are usually found on metre sticks.

Tools for Measuring in Metres

To measure lengths in metres, students can use multiple metre sticks (or measuring tapes), or they can iterate the metre stick (or tape). Measuring tapes are particularly handy for measuring lengths that are not straight lines.

Trundle wheels are good for measuring longer distances in metres. A trundle wheel has a wheel circumference of 1 m, usually marked off in centimetres. As the wheel turns, it makes a click for each metre travelled. Because

When students begin using rulers with numbers, they need to be taught to line up the 0 mark with one end of the object to be measured. This can be difficult if the 0 mark is implicit (as on the ruler shown on page 376), or if the label is not right at the edge of the ruler.

Once students are comfortable using a ruler, the following situations can be introduced gradually:

- the length of an object falls between two centimetre markings (Students initially round to the nearest centimetre. Later, they use millimetres to measure more precisely.)

- the length is greater than 30 cm (The ruler is used more than once— or multiple rulers are used—and the results are added.)

- the distance to be measured is not a straight line (Students measure indirectly with string, or they use a measuring tape or add the lengths of pieces.)

- the ruler is "broken" and doesn't start at 0 (Students determine the difference between two lengths by measuring from one number on the ruler to another, for example, measuring from 3 cm to 8 cm by counting up from 3 to 8 or by subtracting $8 - 3 = 5$.)

metre sticks, measuring tapes, and trundle wheels usually have cm markings, they can also be used to measure somewhat more precisely, for example, the room is 10 m and 17 cm long.

Introducing the Kilometre

Measuring with a trundle wheel is a good way to introduce the concept of the kilometre. Too often, students are introduced to kilometres in a fairly abstract way—the distance you can walk in 12 minutes, or the distance between the school and the park. Students can gain a more concrete and personal understanding of the size of a kilometre if they actually use a trundle wheel and go for a 1-km walk, counting out 1000 turns of the wheel.

Another option is to measure a 100-m running track with a 10-m piece of rope, and then run the track 10 times.

DECIMETRE (dm)

Introducing the Decimetre

Because a decimetre is in between a centimetre (1 dm = 10 cm) and a metre (1 dm = 0.1 m), it is a handy unit for measuring objects in the classroom when the centimetre might be too small and the metre too big. As well, the base ten rod, used for place value work, is exactly 1 dm long and can serve as a referent for developing a sense of the length of a decimetre and for estimation. (The rod can also be used to measure objects in decimetres in the same way that centimetre cubes can be used to measure objects in centimetres.) However, the decimetre has never caught on as a commonly used unit.

Introducing Decimetre Rods and Marked Metre Sticks

Decimetre rods are good tools to use to show the relationship between decimetres and centimetres.

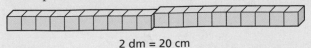

2 dm = 20 cm

MILLIMETRES

Introducing the Millimetre

The time to introduce millimetres is after students have had a lot of experience using centimetres and when a particular measurement falls between two numbers on the centimetre ruler.

Millimetres become necessary when a measurement falls between two numbers on a centimetre ruler.

Introducing Rulers Marked with Millimetres

Introduce rulers marked with millimetres when students are ready to deal with the abstraction of working with tick marks on a ruler, rather than needing the numbers on the ruler to define each mark. Students can look at the millimetre markings to see that there are 10 millimetres in 1 centimetre.

(continued)

Another useful tool is a metre stick with 10-cm increments marked off in alternating colours to show their relationship to the metre.

One of the reasons the decimetre might be introduced in K–8 math is the place value aspect of measurement—it sets up a pattern students will later see extended when they learn about millimetres.

Metre	Decimetre	Centimetre	Millimetre
1 m	0.1 m	0.01 m	0.001 m

A ruler marked in millimetres

Some students may be able to measure in millimetres, if properly instructed, before they actually realize that the purpose of using millimetres is to gain required precision in a measurement situation. At some point, students should have an opportunity to think about how many millimetres make up a metre. To do this, they will need to visualize (or see on a metre stick) 100 cm, with 10 mm making up each centimetre, so there are 1000 mm in all.

Referents for Estimating Standard Units

Referents are familiar objects of particular lengths that students can use to help them estimate. For example, a centimetre is about the width of a baby finger, a decimetre is a bit shorter than a craft stick, and a metre is about the height from the floor to a doorknob. Eventually, many of these referents are internalized so that students can call upon visual images of them when estimating.

Many educators advocate the use of referents that are personally meaningful, since these are easier for students to remember and eventually internalize or visualize. For example, the student who wrote the response below has used the familiar height of a 3-m diving board to visualize a length of 4 m and compare it to 1 km.

Student Response

This student has used a personal referent—the height of a familiar diving board—to estimate how long 4 metres would be in comparison to 1 kilometre.

Chris told Ben he walked 4 kilometres to school. Suppose Chris had told Ben the distance using metres instead of kilometres.

a) Which of these statements is true?

Circle one: The distance would be more than 4 metres.
The distance would be less than 4 metres.

b) Explain your thinking.

Because a diving board at the pool is 3 metres high but a kilometre would be way higher than the roof.

ACTIVITY 15.4

Ask students to find something that is about 1 dm long. Then, cover it up.

- Have them use a mental picture of the object to cut a length of yarn that is as close to 4 dm long as possible.

- Have them compare the length of yarn to the object to see how close they were.

To encourage students to develop referents, teachers can use activities such as the one in **Activity 15.4**.

Renaming Measurements

Part of learning about metric units is learning about the relationships between one unit and another. For example, students need to know that there are 100 centimetres or 10 decimetres in a metre, and 1000 metres in a kilometre. Once students have learned these relationships, they will be able to express a measurement in more than one way. For example, they will understand that 300 cm is another name for 3 m, or that 21.6 cm could also be written as 216 mm.

The ability to rename measurements is useful for
- expressing units in a form that is easier to visualize; for example, a measure of 1.1 m is easier to visualize than 110 cm because it is readily apparent that it is just a little longer than 1 m
- comparing measurement; for example, if two heights are reported in centimetres and metres, respectively, it is easier to compare them if one is renamed
- calculating with measurement formulas; for example, if a rectangle's dimensions are reported in decimetres and centimetres, one of the dimensions has to be renamed to use the area formula
- working with scale; for example, if a map uses 1 cm to represent 1 km, the student needs to rename 1 km as 100 000 cm in order to understand that the map scale is actually 100 000:1

Measuring with More Precision

Once students have a range of standard units at their disposal, they need to learn how to choose the appropriate unit (or combination of units) for the task at hand. This choice depends on

- the magnitude of the length to be measured
- the level of precision required by the task

Some students believe that you use very small units only when you want to measure very small things. It is important for students to understand that you can also use small units to help you measure large things if you want the measurement to be more precise.

Students who are measuring in metres will soon find that by combining metres with centimetres, they can measure more precisely. For example, young students who are not yet renaming units can use a combined measurement such as 5 m and 10 cm to give a more precise record of the length of a piece of playground equipment than a rounded measurement of 5 m. (Note that combining measurements also helps people get a better idea of a length. The measurement 510 cm may be equivalent to 5 m and 10 cm, but it is easier to visualize the combined measurement of "5 m and 10 cm more" than it is to visualize "510 cm.")

The need for precision has a bearing on when new units are introduced. For example, if metres are introduced first to students, centimetres can be introduced by setting up a situation where a measurement falls between metres and a more precise measurement is required. The requirement should be such that simply rounding to the nearest metre or using estimation language, for example, "between 2 m and 3 m," will not be sufficient.

There is a mathematical convention associated with precision that older students will eventually need to understand. The way a measurement is recorded indicates the level of precision that was used in measuring. For example, if you record a measurement of 3 cm, this indicates that the measurement has been measured and rounded to the nearest centimetre, and could be anywhere between 2.5 cm and 3.5 cm. However, if you record 3.0 cm, then the distance has been measured and rounded to the nearest millimetre, and could be anywhere between 2.95 and 3.05 cm. As a result, a recorded measurement of 3.0 cm is considered to be more precise than a recorded measurement of 3 cm.

To understand the importance of precision, students need to encounter situations where it is important to measure very accurately. There are opportunities in many subject areas, such as art and science, where students need to measure carefully and precisely with small units. Hobbies such as sewing and woodworking can also provide such contexts.

Measuring Perimeter

Although measuring perimeter is often perceived to be distinct from linear measurement, it is really only a variation in which students measure a linear distance that is not a straight line. The perimeter of an object can be reported using either nonstandard or standard units, depending on how the side lengths are reported.

Measuring Perimeter

MEASURING INDIRECTLY

Initially, students will learn to measure the perimeter of a shape by fitting a string around the shape, cutting it to that length, and then measuring the length of the string. Initially, students may find it more comfortable to refer to the perimeter as the "distance around" the shape, rather than using the more formal term.

Measuring perimeter indirectly with a string helps students see that perimeter is still a type of length measurement—it is the length around an object.

MEASURING AND ADDING SIDE LENGTHS

Later, students will measure each side of a shape individually and add the side lengths to calculate the perimeter.

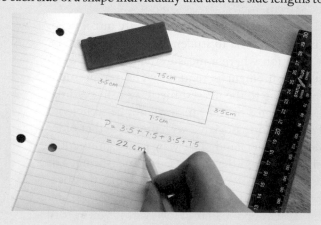

MEASURING AND USING A FORMULA

Using addition to calculate perimeters will inevitably lead to the discovery that there are "shortcuts" people can use to calculate the perimeter of shapes with some equal sides, such as rectangles, squares, equilateral triangles, and parallelograms. These shortcuts lead to formulas.

One of the key concepts in measurement includes the notion that formulas are used to simplify measurement calculations.

Perimeter of a Circle (Circumference)

The perimeter of a circle is called its *circumference*. The topic of circumference is usually dealt with in grades 6 and up, although younger students are certainly capable of understanding the notion of measuring around curves.

When the concept of circumference is first introduced, students generally experiment with string or measuring tapes and a variety of circle sizes to discover that the distance around any circle is always about triple the distance across the circle through its centre (the *diameter*). This presents an opportunity to introduce the concept of π (pi). The circumference is actually π, or $3.1415926...$ times the length of the diameter. (If students use a circle with a diameter of 10 cm, they can derive π by dividing the cirumference by 10.) Some sources say that this value is named π because, in the Greek alphabet, π is the first letter of the Greek word for perimeter.

It is difficult to be accurate when measuring around a circle unless the circle can actually be cut and straightened out. Therefore, it is helpful that there is a relationship between the diameter and circumference to allow us to calculate the circumference of a circle from its easier-to-measure diameter. Students can multiply the diameter by the approximation 3.14. Or, to get a more precise answer, they can use the π key on a calculator.

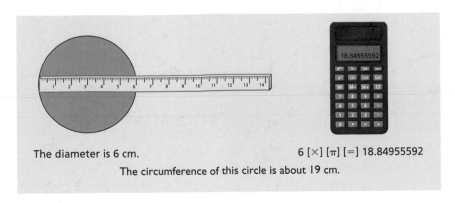

The diameter is 6 cm.   6 [×] [π] [=] 18.84955592

The circumference of this circle is about 19 cm.

Common Errors, Misconceptions, and Strategies

Length and Perimeter: Strategies for Dealing with Common Errors and Misconceptions

COMMON ERROR OR MISCONCEPTION	SUGGESTED STRATEGY
Not Allowing for Hidden Parts Some students at the definition/comparison stage may think that when one length is partly hidden and another is not, the item they can see more of must be longer. For example, some students may think the first stick shown here is longer because they can see all of it. In fact, both lengths are the same.  "The top stick is the longest."	Show two objects that are the same length, and allow students to see that they are equal. Then hide part of one object behind a container and ask which is longer now. Move the container and ask again. Talk about whether students think the length of the object has changed while it was behind the container. (The belief that the length of the object has somehow changed indicates that students cannot yet conserve length.)
Comparing Lengths That Do Not Align Some students at the definition/comparison stage may try to compare lengths without aligning the objects first. These students will often think that length is determined by where an object ends, rather than by the distance from start to end. For example, a student may believe that the lower stick shown here is longer because it sticks out farther. 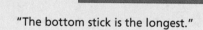 "The bottom stick is the longest."	Show two sticks so they are not aligned at one end. Ask which stick is longer. Then move the bottom stick to the left to line up with the top stick and ask again. Talk about whether the student thinks the length of the stick changed when it was moved.
Measuring Curved Lengths Some students at the definition/comparison stage may not take curves into account when deciding which of two lengths is longer. For example, a student may believe the green piece of yarn is longer because it extends farther from left to right.  "The green yarn must be longer. It sticks out more."	Show a curved piece of yarn, and a straight piece that is shorter, but that extends farther. Ask which piece of yarn is longer. Then straighten the curved piece and ask again. Ask whether the student thinks the amount of yarn has changed, and discuss why the piece that looked shorter before looks longer now.

Problems with Iteration

When students first begin to measure lengths by moving a single nonstandard unit along the distance, they may find it difficult to keep track of where one iteration of a unit ends and the next one begins. This results in gaps or overlap between units and, therefore, incorrect measurement.

Students need opportunities to see that, if they do not begin each new unit where the old one ended, they might get a different measurement each time they measure the same object. This will become evident if the teacher asks them to measure the same object twice and the results are different.

A strategy for helping students learn to iterate correctly is imprinting the units in a strip of modelling clay or letting them use two units initially (see *Learning to Iterate* on page 373).

Teachers should model how to iterate correctly by using a finger or thin stick to mark the end of each unit to help position the next unit.

Ruler Placement

When students first learn to use a centimetre ruler, some will mistakenly begin measuring from points other than the 0-cm mark. Beginning partway along the ruler can indicate that the student has not yet learned that the measurement represents the whole length of the object, from where it begins to where it ends, rather than just the endpoint. Beginning from the 1-cm mark may indicate that the student does not realize that the scale on the ruler actually begins at 0 cm, or simply that the student assumes you always start at 1. This problem often occurs if the 0-cm end is not labelled. As well, students sometimes begin from the opposite end of the ruler, rather than at the 0 mark.

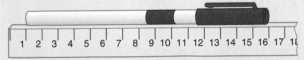

Measuring from the 1-cm mark instead of the 0 mark

To help students who begin measuring from the wrong location along the ruler, a teacher might move the item to a new position along the ruler and ask if the student believes that the item actually got shorter (or longer) now that the end point is a lesser (or greater) number.

If the problem is that the student is unaware of the 0-cm mark, it is useful to line up centimetre cubes along the ruler to show that 1 cube reaches from 0 cm to 1 cm, two cubes stretch from 0 cm to 2 cm, etc.

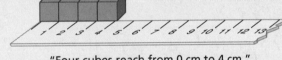

"Four cubes reach from 0 cm to 4 cm."

Renaming Units

A common misconception about metric units is that all smaller units relate to larger ones in the same way. It is especially common for students to believe that there are always 100 smaller units in a larger unit, possibly because the first relationship they learn is that 1 m = 100 cm, and this idea stays with them. For example, a student might say that there must be 100 mm in a metre, 100 g in a kilogram, or 100 mL in a litre.

The time to dispel this misconception is when new units are being introduced. For example, when students are ready to begin using millimetres, the teacher can use a metre stick with millimetre markings to point out that there are far more millimetres in a metre than there are centimetres. It would also be helpful to post a chart so students can check relationships they are not sure of.

Using Small Units

Some students think that you use small units only to measure small items. This is not surprising since it is efficient to use a larger unit to measure a longer item. However, if you want to be more precise, you need to supplement your use of a large unit with the use of a small unit.

Ask students to use metre-long sticks or lengths of string to compare two lengths that cannot be compared directly and that are both between, for example, 3 m and 4 m. Students will see that just using metres does not allow them to make the comparison. Encourage them to finish the task by using a ruler or metre stick to measure the part of the distance that exceeds the last whole metre.

(continued)

Distinguishing between Units

When students begin to measure with precision, for example, measuring a distance in centimetres and then combining it with millimetres (see *Measuring with More Precision* on page 379), they sometimes do not distinguish the units when reporting the measurement. For example, a student might measure a distance of 3 cm and 2 mm and report it as 5 cm because he or she counted on from 3 cm: "1, 2, 3, ..., 4, 5."

If a student reports that an item is, for example, 5 cm long rather than 3 cm and 2 mm, provide a centimetre ruler and ask the student to point to the 5-cm mark on the ruler. Then have the student re-measure the length of the object to see that it is not 5 cm.

Discuss a parallel situation with larger units. For example, an item that is 3 m and 2 cm long is just barely over 3 m long, while an item that is 5 m long is quite a bit longer than 3 m.

Describing Any Part of a Unit as a Half

Some students have trouble reporting measurements that fall between two units on a ruler. For example, they might report both measurements below as "7 and a half centimetres" because they use the term "half" in an informal way to include anything that is not whole.

Ensure students understand that the term "half" has a unique meaning and is the point halfway between two points on a ruler. Have students mark the halfway point between each pair of centimetre markings on a ruler or metre stick. When they measure, encourage them to discuss whether the partial unit at the end of a measurement represents more or less than half of the unit.

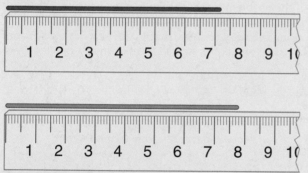

A student might say that both lines are 7 and a half centimetres long.

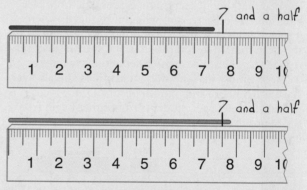

"Neither line is 7 and a half centimetres long—one's a bit more than 7 and the other's a bit less than 8."

Implicit Information in a Diagram

When some of the measurements in a diagram are labelled and others are not, students sometimes forget to include the measures of the unlabelled sides in calculating the perimeter.

Before students begin to calculate the perimeter of a shape, encourage them to label any side lengths that do not already have labels. Discuss why these labels were not originally provided on the diagram (you can tell by just looking at what the lengths are because they are equal to other lengths in the shape), but emphasize that the perimeter is the entire distance around the shape.

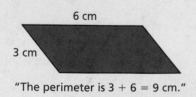

"The perimeter is 3 + 6 = 9 cm."

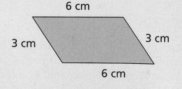

Appropriate Manipulatives

Length and Perimeter: Examples of Manipulatives

STRING, YARN, OR ROPE

String, yarn, and rope are handy tools for many measurement purposes. Students can simply measure pieces that have been cut to different lengths, or they can use these as tools for measuring other lengths. For example, a string that is exactly 1 m long can be used to measure distances in metres. String, yarn, and rope are also useful for measuring distances that are not straight lines, such as curved lines or perimeters, and for comparing lengths indirectly. (See *Direct and Indirect Comparison* on page 371.)

EXAMPLE

A string is useful for comparing lengths or for measuring distances that cannot easily be measured directly with a ruler or metre stick.

Students can create their own 1-m tool from string to find objects that are less than a metre, about a metre, and greater than a metre around.

NONSTANDARD UNITS

Nonstandard units are everyday objects that can be used to measure lengths. These should come in uniform sets, and, ideally, should have or combine to have a long, thin shape. Students will need some longer and shorter units, since different units are suitable for measuring different distances. Good items to have on hand include toothpicks, straws, paper clips, unsharpened pencils, crayons, markers, plastic links, craft sticks (Popsicle sticks), and linking cubes.

EXAMPLE

A child might connect plastic links or paper clips to create a nonstandard unit measuring tool (see *Nonstandard Unit Rulers* on page 375). Students should be aware that using links and paper clips in this way, as opposed to lining them up end to end, will result in slightly different measurements because of the overlap between units.

CENTIMETRE CUBES OR SQUARES

Centimetre cubes are not easy for young students to work with because they are so small. However, centimetre cubes that link together are useful for helping students make the transition between measuring with nonstandard units and measuring with a centimetre ruler (see *Centimetres* on pages 376–377). An alternative is to use a strip of centimetre squares cut from a centimetre grid.

EXAMPLE

Centimetre cubes or squares can be used to create early centimetre "rulers" to introduce the centimetre as a standard unit and introduce the standard centimetre ruler. Students can place their rulers beside standard rulers to see that each marking on the ruler represents 1 cm.

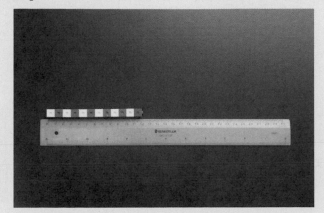

A centimetre cube ruler helps with the transition from nonstandard units to standard units.

(*continued*)

CUISENAIRE RODS

Cuisenaire rods (sometimes called "counting rods") come in lengths ranging from 1 cm to 10 cm. Each length is colour-coded.

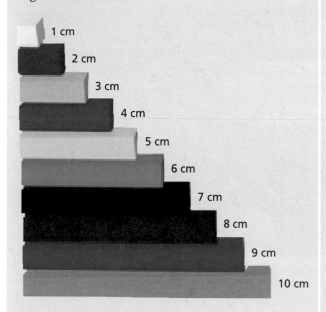

EXAMPLE

Students can use Cuisenaire rods to measure distances in nonstandard units.

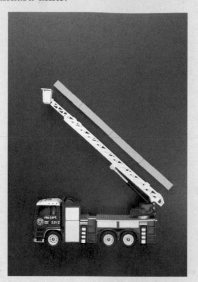

"This toy fire truck is 4 yellow rods long."

Students can also use Cuisenaire rods to measure distances in centimetres.

"Pink is 4 cm, orange is 10 cm, and green is 6 cm, so the fire truck is 20 cm long."

BASE TEN BLOCKS

Unit cubes from a set of base ten blocks are exactly 1 cm long, and 10-rods are exactly 10 cm long. Because the rods have unit markings along their length, they can be used to measure lengths in centimetres as well as in decimetres.

EXAMPLE

By combining 10-rods and unit cubes, students can measure lengths fairly precisely.

"My footstep is 1 dm and 6 cm long. That's 16 cm."

RULERS, METRE STICKS, MEASURING TAPES, AND TRUNDLE WHEELS	EXAMPLE
After students are introduced to standard units, they are ready to begin measuring with standard measurement tools, such as rulers, metre sticks, measuring tapes, and trundle wheels. Initially, students should use tools without millimetre markings. Tools with millimetre markings are introduced when students are ready to measure more precisely. (See *Learning about Metric Units of Length* on pages 376–378.)	Like strings, measuring tapes and trundle wheels are useful tools for measuring distances that do not follow a straight line.

Appropriate Technology

Computers

There are fewer examples of computer software available for measurement than for other strands. After all, measurement is meant to provide real data about real objects. In addition, many software programs come from the United States, and many American materials are not appropriate for Canadian students because they use Imperial units.

For students beyond Grade 3 or 4, the most natural link between measurement and computers involves the use of spreadsheet software. Spreadsheets can be used to record, organize, analyze, and often graph measurement data that students have collected. In addition, a spreadsheet makes it easy to make changes to the data because, when students change one piece of data, the program automatically updates the rest of the data to reflect what was changed. This makes it possible, for example, for students to record measurements in decimetres, and then rename all the measurements in centimetres by entering a simple formula.

Another important tool that allows for measurement is *Geometer's Sketchpad*, or other dynamic geometry software. *Sketchpad* allows students to calculate lengths and areas of drawn shapes. The sketch below shows that a side length, an angle, and an area were all measured automatically.

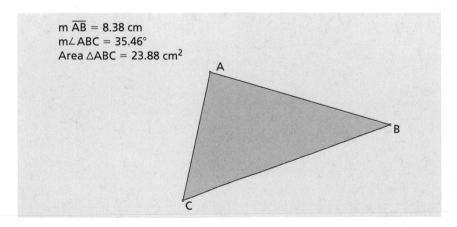

m $\overline{AB}$ = 8.38 cm
m∠ABC = 35.46°
Area △ABC = 23.88 cm^2

The Internet

Because of the issue of Imperial versus metric units, teachers need to be cautious about searching the Internet for sites with length-related activities. However, there are some sites that support work with standard metric

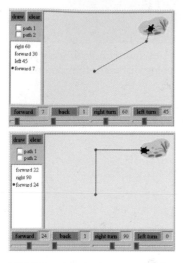

LOGO involves both nonstandard linear measurement and angle measurement.

units. There are also a number of sites with activities involving nonstandard units, for example, ordering objects by length, using nonstandard rulers, and estimating distances or calculating perimeters.

Another avenue to explore involves a computer language called LOGO that was popular in the 1980s and 1990s. Although LOGO is less widely used today, there are still related activities that students can access online. For example, students can experiment with the LOGO problem to draw paths on the screen, using nonstandard units of length. There is an NCTM site where students can readily access the drawing tools shown below.

In the first path shown below, the cursor, called a turtle, has been programmed to move forward 22 units, turn right 90 degrees, and then move forward 24 units. In the second path, the turtle turned right 60 degrees, moved forward 30 units, turned left 45 degrees, and then moved forward 7 units.

Measuring Area

While length describes a one-dimensional attribute of a shape, *area* describes a two-dimensional attribute—the amount of two-dimensional (flat) space that a shape covers or, in the case of a 3-D shape, the amount of flat space that forms the surface of the shape (*surface area*). Because of its two-dimensional nature, area is usually expressed in square units, such as square centimetres and square metres.

Student Response

This student likely has a better sense of length than of area. She or he does not yet understand that area measurement involves covering a space, not measuring a length.

You will need 12 centimetre cubes or tiles for this question.
This shape has an area of 12 square centimetres. Place 12 cubes or tiles on the shape to show that the area is 12 square centimetres.

a) Use the cubes. Make a different shape in the space below that has an area of 12 square centimetres. Trace your shape.

The area of this shape is 12 square centimetres.

b) How do you know your shape has an area of 12 square centimetres? Because I used 12 Square cm.

How Concepts of Area Can Be Introduced

Ideas about area can be introduced through the same three stages as other measurement concepts—definition/comparison, using nonstandard units, and using standard units. (See *Stages of Measurement* on pages 367–369.)

How Concepts of Area Can Be Introduced

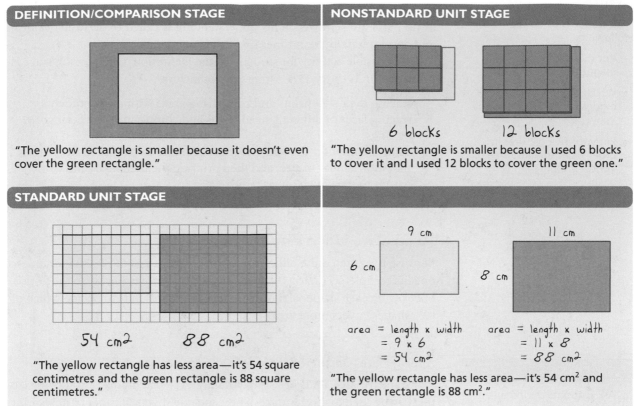

DEFINITION/COMPARISON STAGE

"The yellow rectangle is smaller because it doesn't even cover the green rectangle."

NONSTANDARD UNIT STAGE

6 blocks   12 blocks

"The yellow rectangle is smaller because I used 6 blocks to cover it and I used 12 blocks to cover the green one."

STANDARD UNIT STAGE

54 cm²   88 cm²

"The yellow rectangle has less area—it's 54 square centimetres and the green rectangle is 88 square centimetres."

9 cm   11 cm
6 cm   8 cm

area = length x width   area = length x width
= 9 x 6   = 11 x 8
= 54 cm²   = 88 cm²

"The yellow rectangle has less area—it's 54 cm² and the green rectangle is 88 cm²."

Area: The Definition/Comparison Stage

At this stage, students explore the notion that one item has more area than another if you can cover one shape with the other and there is still some part that is uncovered.

Sometimes, one shape does not fit completely on top of the other. When this happens, students may find they need to dissect one of the shapes in order to make a direct comparison. In the example shown here, a student tried unsuccessfully to fit the orange rectangle over the blue one, and eventually discovered that cutting the orange rectangle in half made it easier to see that the blue rectangle was larger.

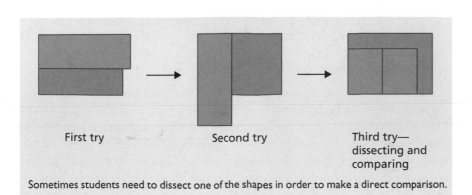

First try   Second try   Third try—
dissecting and comparing

Sometimes students need to dissect one of the shapes in order to make a direct comparison.

Ask students to do the following:

• Cut five pictures out of a magazine.

• Which picture covers the biggest area? How do you know?

• Put your five pictures in order from smallest area to largest area.

In order for students to use this dissection method, they need to understand that the area of a shape does not change when it is dissected, as long as no parts are removed. This understanding is called *conservation of area*, and develops at different times in different students.

One possible activity for students at the Definition/Comparison stage is described in **Activity 15.5**. Others might include

• tracing their shoeprints and comparing areas with other students
• tracing faces of different-sized boxes and comparing or ordering the tracings
• using a computer drawing program to create two different rectangles that look similar in size, and then printing the rectangles and comparing to see which one is larger

Area: The Nonstandard Unit Stage

Because it is often quite difficult to compare the areas of two shapes unless one fits completely on top of the other, students move quickly to the notion of covering each shape with the same nonstandard units to decide which of two shapes covers more area.

Appropriate Nonstandard Units for Area

Nonstandard area units are simply handy everyday items of uniform size that can be used to tile a surface. These include sheets of paper or newsprint (to cover big areas), pattern blocks, square tiles, attribute blocks, and ink stamps.

One possible activity for students at the nonstandard unit stage is described in **Activity 15.6**.

Other activities might include

• using sheets of newspaper to compare the areas of two bulletin boards or windows
• using nonstandard units to determine the areas of different shapes that can be outlined with the same piece of yarn
• cutting a piece of wrapping paper that is the right size to wrap a gift, and then measuring the area of the paper with nonstandard units
• using a box to make a house for a mouse, and then writing a description of the house that includes the floor area, along with features of the home that a mouse might like
• making a paper shape that can be covered by exactly 100 items (100 pennies, 100 cubes, 100 seeds, 100 craft sticks, etc.)
• determining the area of a shape (in nonstandard units) in order to share it equally in two parts
• determining the greatest possible area that can be covered with a rolled-out piece of modelling clay

• Ask students to find an envelope that is big enough to hold a folded piece of letter-sized paper. (It does not matter how the paper is folded.)

• Have them take the envelope apart, flatten it, and use square tiles to measure the amount of paper that was used to make it.

• Ask them: Can you design a different envelope that uses less paper?

From time to time, it is important for students to have opportunities to make choices about which unit to use to measure an area. These situations help students build their understanding of area concepts and provide concrete experience that will support them later when they move on to work with standard units. The examples that follow illustrate some of the area concepts that can be developed through work with various types of units.

Nonstandard Units: Developing Area Concepts

MEASURING AREA WITH UNITS THAT DO NOT TILE

Students should measure area with units that do not tile—that is, that do not fit tightly together—only during introductory work with area, when they are exploring why some units work well for measuring area and others do not. When students use units that do not tile, they learn that much of the area is not counted in the measurement, and that different students can get different results for the same area, depending on how they arrange the units.

 The area is 10 pennies.

 The area is 9 pennies.

When you measure area with circles, the spaces in between are not counted in the measurement.

COMBINING ESTIMATES WITH MEASUREMENTS

Even when units do tile, there are sometimes parts of a shape that cannot be covered with those units. Situations like these help students learn to combine estimating with measuring to get a better approximation of the area. Students need to estimate to add on parts of an area that cannot be covered with units.

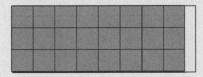

"That's 24 whole squares and about $1\frac{1}{2}$ more, so the area is about $25\frac{1}{2}$ squares."

At other times, students subtract to compensate for units that extend beyond the shape being measured.

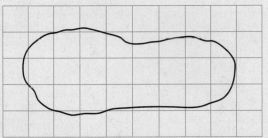

"There are 50 squares with about 29 not covered, so my shoe covers about 21 squares."

USING UNITS THAT TILE, BUT ARE NOT SQUARES

When students use units that tile, they learn that it is important to fit the units together with no spaces between them. Otherwise, there are large amounts of area that are not counted in the measurement.

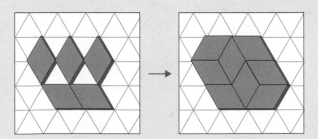

Working with non-square units helps students learn that squares are not the only shapes you can use to measure area.

Student Response

This student was not initially sensitive to the fact that circles do not fit together to cover an area completely; however, when presented with the issue of whether the whole envelope was covered, the student realized the problem.

Teacher: Here are some circles, some triangles, some squares, and some trapezoids. I want you to pick whichever shape you want and tell me how many shapes like that it takes to cover the envelope.

Student: I think I'll pick the circles. *(Covers the envelope.)* It took 18 circles to cover the envelope.

Teacher: Why did you pick the circles?

Student: Because I like circles.

Teacher: Did you cover the whole envelope or is part of it still showing?

Student: There's just a little showing—not very much.

Teacher: So is the area of the envelope 18 circles?

Student: Sort of, I guess.

Teacher: Do you think some of the envelope would still show if you covered it with squares?

Student: I'm not sure—I have to try.

Strategies for Measuring with Nonstandard Units

Students need to recognize that there is never just one way to measure an area. For example, to determine the area of an equilateral triangle, students at the nonstandard unit stage could do any of the following:

- cover the triangle with concrete units, such as triangle pattern blocks, and count how many units it takes to cover the triangle, estimating as necessary to account for regions not covered by the blocks
- place a transparent grid over the triangle and count how many full and how many partial grid squares fit within the shape
- place a transparent grid over the triangle, determine the area of a rectangle that encloses the triangle, and subtract any full or partial grid squares that are inside the rectangle but outside the triangle

Measuring the Same Area with Different Units

Students need to have opportunities to measure the same area with different units to help them discover that the area can be described in different ways. It will also help them discover that, as the size of the unit increases, the number of units decreases. For example, an area that covers 49 squares on a centimetre grid could also be covered with only about 8 square pattern blocks. Experiences like this also help students discover that it is more efficient to use larger units to measure larger areas and smaller units to measure smaller areas.

Measuring Different Areas with the Same Unit

Not only do students benefit from opportunities to explore area by covering the same shape with different units, they also benefit from using the same unit to measure different areas. A common unit is especially useful when the areas are to be compared, as illustrated in **Activity 15.7**.

Iteration and Area

As with length, students who are learning to measure areas with nonstandard units are most comfortable using multiple copies of a unit, such as a set of square tiles. However, there may be times when it is necessary or simply convenient to iterate by moving a single unit from one location to another. This may occur, for example, if there are not enough units to cover the entire space.

ACTIVITY 15.7

Give small groups of students a set of nonstandard units for measuring area and several sheets of notepaper of different sizes. Some sheets should be rectangular, and some should have other shapes. Pose this problem:

- If you wanted to write a long letter, which piece of notepaper would give you the largest area to write on? Tell how you know.

After students have solved the problem, ask:

- Would you have been able to solve the problem if you had measured each page with a different unit? Explain.

In order to measure area by iterating, students need to move the single unit both horizontally and vertically to cover a 2-dimensional space. This task takes both physical and visual coordination, since students need to keep careful track of where one iteration of the unit ends and the next one starts, in two directions.

Initially, a student might use a transition such as the one suggested for length on page 373 — leaving impressions of single units as they are iterated. For example, a student might use impressions from a cookie cutter to measure the area of a flat piece of modelling clay that has been placed over the area to be measured, or use an ink stamp to measure an area outlined on paper. The advantage of using impressions is that they make it easier to see where to place the unit for each new iteration, and easier to keep track of the total number of units.

Like other area units, units used to leave impressions should fit together to cover the surface with no spaces between them.

Eventually, students will learn to use their knowledge of multiplication to simplify the task of iterating.

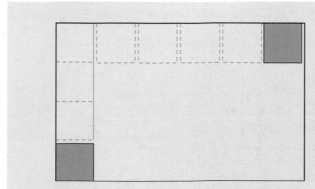

"I measured 6 squares across. Then I measured 4 squares down."

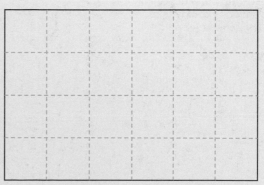

"There's room for 4 rows of 6. That's 24 squares altogether."

Measuring Area with a Transparent Grid

Just as a ruler provides a pictorial model for measuring length, a transparent grid provides a pictorial model for measuring area. The grid removes the need for students either to use many individual units or to face the daunting task of iterating the entire space.

A transparent grid can be placed on top of a shape, making it possible to count the number of grid units that are filled or partially filled by the shape. Like the ruler, the grid allows students to measure different shapes with the same tool. Although a transparent grid usually has square units, there are times when a triangular grid might also be used.

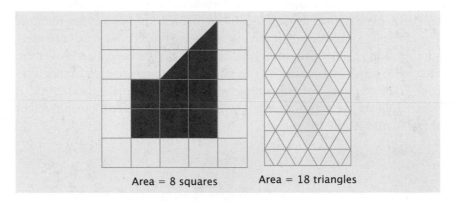

Area = 8 squares   Area = 18 triangles

ACTIVITY 15.8

Ask students to use an elastic on a geoboard to create each shape described below. They can record their work on dot paper.

Make each shape

- a shape that touches 10 pins and has room for exactly 4 full squares of area inside

- a shape that touches 8 pins and has room for exactly 6 full squares of area inside

Write a description of a different shape someone could make following the same rules.

Measuring Area on a Geoboard

Geoboards, which are also grids, are useful for exploring areas measured in nonstandard units, as shown below and in **Activity 15.8**.

An interesting approach to calculating the areas of shapes on geoboards is to view the shapes as combinations of rectangles and "half-rectangles." For example, to calculate the area of this irregular trapezoid, a student would

- look for the biggest rectangle they can inside the trapezoid
- calculate the area of this rectangle
- imagine a rectangle that encloses the rest of the trapezoid
- use this rectangle to determine the area of the rest of the trapezoid
- add these two areas

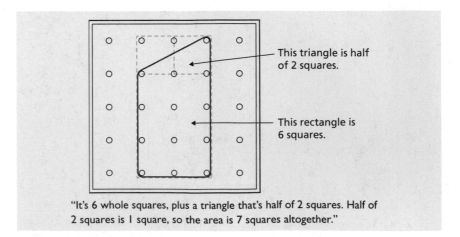

This triangle is half of 2 squares.

This rectangle is 6 squares.

"It's 6 whole squares, plus a triangle that's half of 2 squares. Half of 2 squares is 1 square, so the area is 7 squares altogether."

Estimating Areas in Nonstandard Units

Students must learn to estimate area measurements, as well as to measure them. To help students learn to estimate, teachers might provide situations in which a surface is partially measured; the student's task is to estimate how many units it will take to measure the full area. Eventually, students will adopt a similar strategy themselves, using partial measurements as an aid to making reasonable estimates.

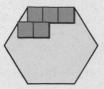

"If it takes 5 squares to cover this much area, then the area of the whole shape must be about 15 squares."

To help students build their understanding of units, it is important for them to have opportunities to measure in one unit, and then use that measurement to make an estimate involving another unit. An example activity is described in **Activity 15.9**.

Area: The Standard Unit Stage

Students can be introduced to standard units when they realize that, rather than measuring areas with nonstandard units, which can mean different things to different people, they can use units that everyone will understand.

Introducing Standard Units of Area

The first standard unit of area that students encounter is usually the square centimetre. They then move on to working with square metres, and finally square kilometres. There are also other standard units of area measure, such as the square millimetre and the square decimetre, but these are rarely used.

Although the standard units of area measure are often described in terms of squares with that area, students need to understand that these squares can be dissected and rearranged to form many different shapes, all representing the same area. For example, a shape with an area of 1 square metre could be a square, but it could also be a triangle, a rectangle, or any other shape that covers the same area. A square metre (or cm or km) has no defined shape—it is a measure of area and, as a result, is a somewhat abstract notion.

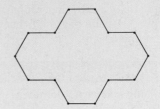

ACTIVITY 15.9

Give students a shape made by tracing 4 yellow pattern blocks.

Ask

- How many yellow pattern blocks can fit on this shape?

- Choose a different pattern block. Estimate how many will fit on the shape (including whole blocks and part blocks). Then check by measuring.

- Repeat with each other kind of pattern block.

Standard Units of Area

SQUARE CENTIMETRE (CM2)	SQUARE METRE (m²)
Defining a Square Centimetre	**Defining a Square Metre**
A square centimetre is an area equivalent to the area of a square with a side length of 1 cm.	A square metre is an area equivalent to the area of a square with a side length of 1 m.
Introducing the Square Centimetre	**Introducing the Square Metre**
Initially square centimetres are introduced in a concrete way, using materials such as centimetre cubes (base ten units), and then pictorially, using centimetre grid paper and transparent centimetre grids. The cubes and grids provide a good transition from non-standard units because students can simply cover a shape with cubes and count to measure the area without focusing on the fact that it is a standard unit. Larger areas can be measured using base ten flats, which cover 100 cm2, or by combining flats, rods (10 cm2), and cubes.	The square metre can be modelled by arranging four metre sticks so that they form the side lengths of a square. The square metre is the space inside. A piece of newspaper or wrapping paper can be assembled to fit the space inside, and then can be used as a transportable square metre unit to locate objects in the room that are smaller than, about the same size as, or larger than 1 m². Once students have had time to work with the model square, it is important for them to realize that the area

(continued)

Square Centimetre Referents

Students should develop personal referents for square centimetres to help develop a sense of the unit and also to help with estimating. For example, a fingernail or the tip of a baby finger might be a good referent for 1 cm². The palm of a child's hand might serve as a referent for 100 cm².

SQUARE KILOMETRE (km²)

Defining a Square Kilometre

A square kilometre is an area equivalent to the area of a square with a side length of 1 km.

Introducing the Square Kilometre

This is a unit that is harder for students to get a sense of because of its size. It may be useful for them to associate it with a familiar place.

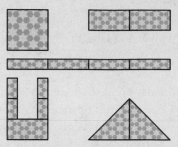

A square kilometre is about the size of Lakeview Park.

can be rearranged into different shapes. Small groups can dissect and rearrange part of a square metre made out of paper to create different shapes, each with an area of 1 m².

Shapes with an area of 1 m²

Square Metre Referents

Students might look for an object in their classroom that covers about 1 m², for example, about half of a small rug, or they might visualize a square metre as an area in which a certain number of students can comfortably stand.

ACTIVITY 15.10

Have students create designs with pattern blocks and measure the areas first in green pattern blocks, but then in square centimetres.

ACTIVITY 15.11

Ask students to create as many different shapes as they can on a grid with an area of 12 cm².

ACTIVITY 15.12

Ask students to determine the amount of gift wrap they use to cover a box.

Recording Area Measures in Standard Units

It is important for students to realize that, when they begin to measure with standard units, they need to report measurements in *square units*. This is different from measuring in nonstandard units, where an area might be reported, for example, as 10 blue pattern blocks. Initially, the units should be spelled out, for example, "12 square metres."

Eventually, students will be ready to write the units in an abbreviated form using exponents. With standard units, the exponent 2 is used to indicate that the units have two dimensions. For example, if an area is 12 square centimetres, we write "12 cm²."

Using a Centimetre Grid

Centimetre grid paper and transparent centimetre grids are useful when students are first beginning to measure areas in square centimetres. For example, they might complete any of **Activities 15.10**, **15.11**, or **15.12**.

Like geoboards, centimetre grids are especially useful for dealing with areas of irregular shapes. For example, to estimate the area of the irregular shape on page 397, students might overlay a transparent centimetre grid, and then count the number of squares that are completely covered and the number of squares that are mostly covered. They add these together, and check to see if the squares with only a little covered seem to balance the missing parts in the squares that are mostly covered. They can then either increase or decrease their estimate appropriately.

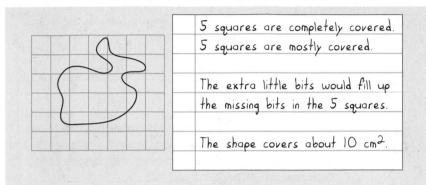

5 squares are completely covered.
5 squares are mostly covered.

The extra little bits would fill up the missing bits in the 5 squares.

The shape covers about 10 cm².

The area of an irregular shape is estimated by counting full and mostly full squares, and by making any necessary adjustments.

Formulas for Calculating Areas of Shapes

During K–8 instruction in math, students normally have an opportunity to develop and use formulas for determining the areas of rectangles, parallelograms, triangles, circles, and trapezoids.

All too often, formulas are seen as rote procedures for calculating a measurement such as volume. A formula actually describes the shape in terms of relationships among its component measurement attributes. The formula for calculating the area of a rectangle, for example, describes the area in terms of an array of squares: *Area = number of rows × number in each row*, or *Area = length × width*, or *Area = width × length*.

Students who do not understand the nature of a formula may apply it to the wrong shape or measurement attribute without knowing why this is incorrect, for example, applying the rectangle formula to the side lengths of a parallelogram or confusing area with perimeter. As well, students who do not understand will have difficulty rearranging the formula to find something other than area, for example, using the area and length of a rectangle to calculate its width. The best way to help students understand and recall each formula is to let them play a role in developing the formula for themselves.

Area of a Rectangle

The first area formula introduced at the elementary level is usually the formula for calculating the area of a rectangle:

Area of a rectangle = length × width, or A = l × w, or A = w × l

Using an Array Model The best way to introduce the formula is to have students work with rectangles created with square tiles, so that the rectangles are basically arrays of squares. From earlier work with multiplication and the array meaning or model of multiplication, students will know that, to determine the total number of squares, you multiply the number of rows of squares by the number of squares in each row. In the consolidation discussion, the teacher might ask:

- What does the length of this rectangle tell you about the number of squares in the rectangle? (the number of rows of squares)
- What does the width tell you? (the number of squares in each row)
- What does the area tell you? (the number of squares altogether)
- If you could not see each square, how could you use just the length and width of a rectangle to figure out its area?

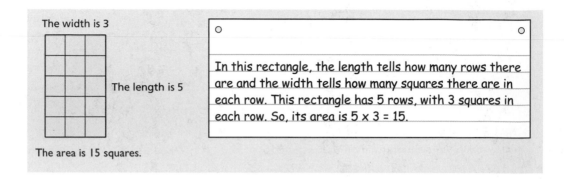

The width is 3

The length is 5

The area is 15 squares.

In this rectangle, the length tells how many rows there are and the width tells how many squares there are in each row. This rectangle has 5 rows, with 3 squares in each row. So, its area is 5 × 3 = 15.

Using Relationships Another way to introduce the formula is to have students create some different-sized rectangles on grid paper and determine the length, width, and area of each rectangle by counting grid spaces and grid square side lengths, recording the data in a table.

Rectangle	Length (cm)	Width (cm)	Area (cm^2)
A	8	2	16
B	5	3	15
C	7	4	28

Students can then look for relationships in the table among the length, width and area, which will lead to the formula, *Area = length × width*. They might also notice that they can find the length by dividing the area by the width, or the width by dividing the area by the length.

Because the formula for determining the area of a rectangle is usually introduced before any other area formulas, it is a common misconception that the formula *Area = length × width* can be applied to determine the area of shapes other than rectangles. When students develop the formula in a concrete way using arrays and using relationships, they are less likely to have this misconception.

Area of a Square

The formula for calculating the area of a square, *Area = side length × side length* ($A = s × s$) is a special case of the rectangle formula since *length × width* in this case is the same as *side length × side length*. Students can create different squares on grid paper and record data about the squares in a table such as that shown. They will soon realize that the area of a square is its side length multiplied by itself.

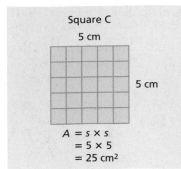

Square	Side length (cm)	Area (cm²)
A	8	64
B	7	49
C	5	25

Square C
5 cm
5 cm

$A = s \times s$
$= 5 \times 5$
$= 25 \text{ cm}^2$

Area of a Parallelogram

Once students have a solid understanding of the rectangle formula, they are ready to learn that a related formula—*Area = base length × height*—can be used to calculate the area of a parallelogram. To explore this idea, the teacher can demonstrate that it is possible to transform a parallelogram into a rectangle with the same base length and height by cutting a triangle from one side of the parallelogram and moving it to the opposite side, or by cutting to create two trapezoids that can be similarly rearranged.

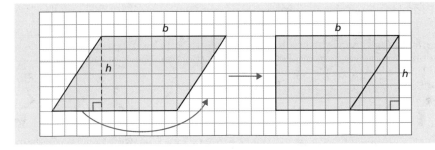

Students can then construct and cut out some other parallelograms and test them to see if they can all be transformed the same way. They may notice that the fact that the opposite sides of a parallelogram are equal is the reason why the triangle that is cut off on one side can always be attached to the other side. It is also important for students to recognize that

- the base that is cut remains the same length because the part removed from one end is added to the other end
- the height is measured at right angles to the base
- a single cut along the height forms both sides of the rectangle

For these reasons, the parts of a parallelogram can always be reassembled to form a rectangle with the same base length and height.

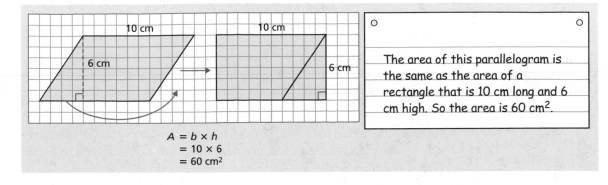

$A = b \times h$
$= 10 \times 6$
$= 60 \text{ cm}^2$

The area of this parallelogram is the same as the area of a rectangle that is 10 cm long and 6 cm high. So the area is 60 cm².

Some students will be interested to note that either side length of the parallelogram can be used as the base, and that they can measure the height from either inside or outside the boundaries of the parallelogram. As long as they measure the height from the side they are using as the base length, the formula will produce the correct area.

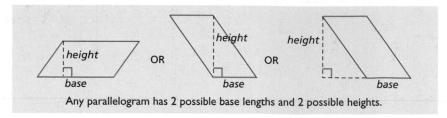

Any parallelogram has 2 possible base lengths and 2 possible heights.

An activity that will help students understand how the base length and height of a parallelogram relate to its area is described in **Activity 15.14** below. This activity indirectly demonstrates the independence of perimeter and area—the perimeter remains the same as the area decreases.

ACTIVITY 15.14

Have students form a rectangle out of Geostrips or cardboard strips hinged together at the four vertices with butterfly clips or pipe cleaners. Each side should be a whole number of centimetres long. Ask them to place the rectangle on grid paper and record a sketch of the shape, the base length, the height, and the area.

Then have students adjust the rectangle to change the height several times to form a series of other parallelograms (with the base anchored on the same location on the grid paper each time). They can record the information about each shape in a table like the one shown here.

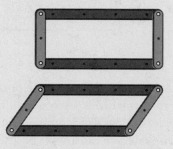

Sketch of Shape	Base	Height	Area
	8 cm	5 cm	40 cm²
	8 cm	3 cm	24 cm²

Area of a Triangle

Once students have developed and worked with the parallelogram area formula, the next step is usually the introduction of the formula for determining the area of a triangle:

$$Area = base \times height \div 2$$

This formula is derived from the parallelogram formula and works because every triangle, no matter what type of triangle it is, can be shown to be half of a parallelogram with the same base and height.

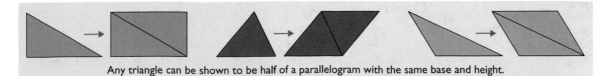

Any triangle can be shown to be half of a parallelogram with the same base and height.

The triangle formula can also be written as $Area = \frac{1}{2} \times base \times height$ or $Area = \frac{base \times height}{2}$, but it makes more sense to use $Area = base \times height \div 2$ until the students learn to multiply with fractions.

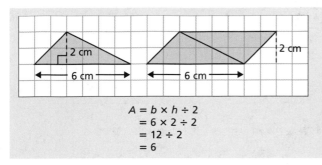

$$A = b \times h \div 2$$
$$= 6 \times 2 \div 2$$
$$= 12 \div 2$$
$$= 6$$

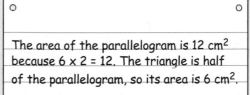

The area of the parallelogram is 12 cm² because 6 × 2 = 12. The triangle is half of the parallelogram, so its area is 6 cm².

The idea that two triangles with the same base and height must have the same area, even if they look different, is very difficult for some students to understand. This can be modelled on a geoboard, where base lengths and heights can be determined by counting horizontal and vertical units. For example, all three of the triangles below have the same base (3 units) and the same height (4 units), so they must also have the same area.

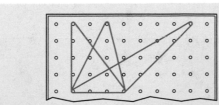

Each triangle has a base length of 3 units and a height of 4 units, so the area of each triangle is 3 × 4 ÷ 2 or 6 square units.

Areas of Other 2-D Shapes

Areas of Trapezoids and Circles

AREA OF A TRAPEZOID	AREA OF A CIRCLE
A trapezoid can always be viewed as half of a parallelogram. The height of the parallelogram is the same as the height of the trapezoid, and the base length of the parallelogram is equal to the sum of the two bases of the trapezoid. (On a trapezoid, the bases are considered to be the two parallel sides.)	A circle can be divided up into many sectors (pie slices) to help students see that these pieces can be formed into an "almost" parallelogram, where the height is the radius of the circle and the base is half the circumference of the circle.

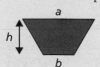 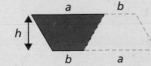

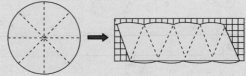

The area of the parallelogram is *base × height* or $(b + a) \times h$, so the area of the trapezoid (which is half the parallelogram) is $(b + a) \times h \div 2$.

Sectors of a circle can be reformed into an "almost" parallelogram.

(continued)

The area of any trapezoid can be calculated using the formula $A = h \times (a + b) \div 2$, where h is the height of the trapezoid, and a and b are the lengths of the bases.

The area of the parallelogram is *base $\times$ height* or, in this case, *(circumference $\div$ 2) $\times$ radius*. If the students already know that the circumference is equal to $2 \times \pi \times radius$, then they can simplify the formula to $A = \pi \times radius \times radius$.

Area of Irregular Shapes

To calculate areas of irregular shapes, students can apply area formulas for more familiar shapes drawn inside or outside the shape in question. For example, this student recognized that square and triangle areas could be used to calculate the area of this irregular hexagon.

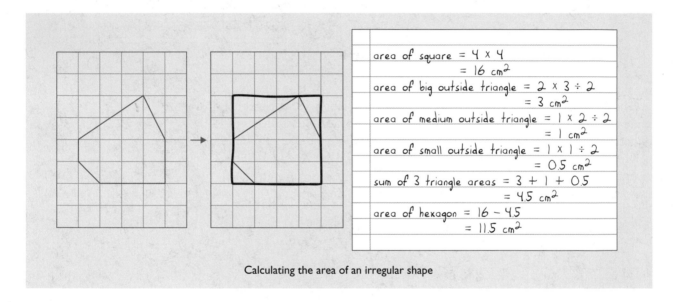

area of square = 4 × 4
　　　　　　　= 16 cm²
area of big outside triangle = 2 × 3 ÷ 2
　　　　　　　　　　　　　= 3 cm²
area of medium outside triangle = 1 × 2 ÷ 2
　　　　　　　　　　　　　　　= 1 cm²
area of small outside triangle = 1 × 1 ÷ 2
　　　　　　　　　　　　　　　= 0.5 cm²
sum of 3 triangle areas = 3 + 1 + 0.5
　　　　　　　　　　　　= 4.5 cm²
area of hexagon = 16 − 4.5
　　　　　　　　= 11.5 cm²

Calculating the area of an irregular shape

Area and Perimeter

Students are often surprised to find that shapes with the same area can have different perimeters, and that shapes with the same perimeter can have different areas.

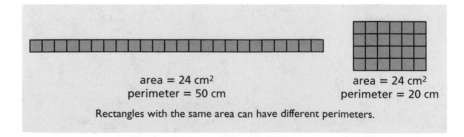

area = 24 cm²
perimeter = 50 cm

area = 24 cm²
perimeter = 20 cm

Rectangles with the same area can have different perimeters.

Exploring the perimeters of rectangles with the same area, as illustrated in **Activity 15.15**, can help students make an important discovery—the perimeter of a shape increases as the area is "stretched out" and decreases as the parts are "pushed together" or become more like a circle. The rectangle with the least perimeter for a given area is a square; the *shape* with the least possible perimeter for any given area is always a circle.

ACTIVITY 15.15

Students use 36 square tiles to make as many rectangles as they can. They work systematically, starting with a rectangle with a width of 1 unit, and record the data in a table such as that shown below:

Width (cm)	Length (cm)	Area (cm²)	Perimeter (cm)
1	36	36	74
2	18	36	40
3	12	36	30
4	9	36	26
6	6	36	24
9	4	36	26

Surface Area

Students in Grades 6 or 7 and up work with the surface areas of 3-D shapes, usually beginning with prisms, and then moving on to pyramids and other shapes. The surface area of a 3-D shape is the sum of the areas of all the faces.

Prisms with bases that are rectangles and triangles are introduced first, since students know how to calculate the areas of these shapes.

Surface Areas of Prisms

RECTANGLE-BASED PRISM	TRIANGLE-BASED PRISM

The rectangle-based prism below has 3 pairs of faces that are congruent rectangles. Nets provide an excellent model to work with when calculating the surface area of a 3-D shape.

The triangle-based prism below has two faces that are congruent triangles and 3 faces that are rectangles. The net makes this easier to see.

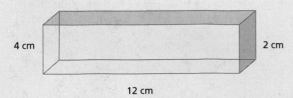

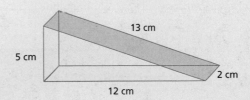

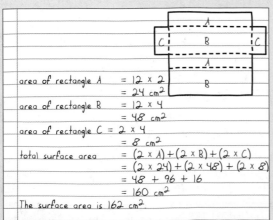

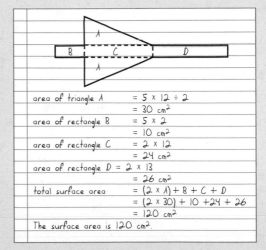

The surface area of a square-based prism would be simpler to calculate as it is covered by 4 congruent lateral rectangle faces and 2 congruent square bases. A cube has the easiest surface area to calculate because it has 6 congruent square faces.

The surface area of an equilateral-triangle-based prism would be simpler to calculate as it is covered by 3 congruent lateral rectangle faces and 2 congruent equilateral triangle bases.

Common Errors and Misconceptions

Area: Strategies for Dealing with Common Errors and Misconceptions

COMMON ERROR OR MISCONCEPTION	SUGGESTED STRATEGIES
Confusing Length with Area Some students continue to focus on linear dimensions of an object to decide which has a greater area. 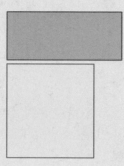 "I think the green rectangle is bigger."	Students have to be reminded that area tells how much flat space objects take up or how many units can cover the object. In the example situation shown to the left, students at the definition/comparison stage could compare by dissecting one of the shapes and rearranging the parts on top of the other shape. Students at the nonstandard unit stage could cover each shape with square tiles to see which shape has the greater area. 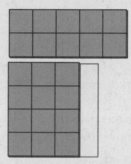 "It only takes 10 squares to cover the green rectangle but it takes more than 12 squares to cover the yellow shape."
Comparing with Different Units When students are using nonstandard units to compare areas, some may rely on number alone, without considering the size of the units. 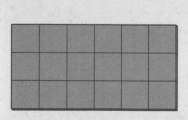 "The red one is bigger because it has room for 28 squares and the blue one only has room for 18 squares."	Make a rectangle that can be covered by two large squares. Cover it and ask students what the area is. After students indicate the area is 2 squares, cover the same space with 8 small squares (each one fourth of the size of the large square). Ask for the area again. Discuss how the amount of space did not change, but the units did. The same space can be covered by many little squares or by fewer big ones. Now tell students that another shape is covered by 6 squares. Ask if it is bigger or smaller than the rectangle they just looked at. Help students to see that they can only tell which is larger if they know whether big squares or small squares were used. The shape is bigger if the area was 6 bigger squares, but smaller if it was 6 smaller squares.
Disregarding Spaces Many students place area units on a surface in a disorganized way, ignoring the fact that some parts of the surface are left uncovered. "I think the area is 3 squares."	To determine area, you need to figure out how many units it takes to cover a whole surface without any gaps. Otherwise, people will get different measurements for the same area. 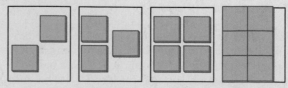 Using units that tile ensures that everyone will get the same area measurement.

If there are parts that cannot be covered, you need to estimate those areas as well. For example, the uncovered area on the last rectangle above might be about $1\frac{1}{2}$ more squares, bringing the total area to about $7\frac{1}{2}$ squares.

Dealing with Partial Grid Squares

Some students ignore partial squares altogether, while others describe the area of any partial square as one half, and, as a result, consider the sum of the area of any 2 partial squares to be 1 whole square.

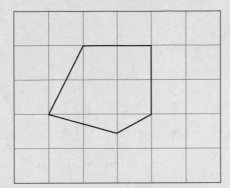

"There are 4 full squares and 2 halves and 3 more halves. That's $6\frac{1}{2}$ altogether."

If students ignore partial squares, remind them that these are also part of the area and they need to be counted. If they count all partial squares as half squares, invite them to compare the areas of the 2 rectangles like the ones shown below. They should recognize that the areas are different, so they can't both be $1\frac{1}{2}$ squares.

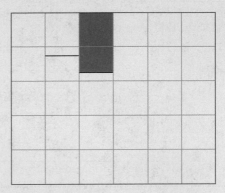

"Yellow is about $1\frac{1}{4}$ squares and blue is more like $1\frac{3}{4}$ squares."

While combining parts to make whole squares is one counting strategy, there are also others. For example, students can visualize the partial squares inside rectangles. Below, the partial squares in the blue rectangle cover about half of 2 squares, or 1 full square. The parts in the red rectangle cover less than half of 3 squares, or about 1 square.

"There are 4 whole squares plus 1 whole square plus 1 more. That's about 6 squares."

Shape of a Square Metre or Square Centimetre

Many students assume that a square centimetre or a square metre has to be square-shaped. In fact, it simply has to cover the same area as the square.

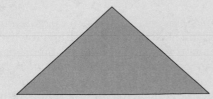

A triangle could cover 1 square metre.

A square unit can be any shape that covers the required area.

A good way to introduce this idea is to use a tangram square. Have students cut out the pieces and rearrange them to form different shapes that use all 7 pieces. Ask, "Whose arrangement covers the most area?" Students should realize that the arrangements all cover the same area because they are all made from pieces of the same original square.

Point out that the same is true for a square metre (or square centimetre). Even if you cut the square into parts and rearrange the parts, they will still cover the same area as the original square.

(continued)

Converting Square Metres to Square Centimetres

Students, and even many adults, are surprised when they realize that 1 m² is not the same amount of space as 100 cm². People tend to assume that since there are 100 cm in 1 m, there must also be 100 cm² in 1 m².

To determine the number of square centimetres in a square metre, ask students to begin covering the square metre with centimetre cubes. They can start at the bottom and begin to cover the bottom row. They probably will not complete the row since it would take 100 cubes, but they can fill in enough to get an idea that 100 cm² is nowhere near enough to cover the whole square. This is because the sides of the square are 100 cm long, so the square is actually made up of 100 rows of 100 cm², or 10 000 cm² altogether.

Multiplying Length × Width for a Non-Rectangle

A student might mistakenly apply the *length × width* formula to calculate the area of a shape that is not a rectangle. This error often occurs with parallelograms when adjacent side lengths are labelled.

Students need to understand that the *length × width* formula works for a rectangle because it describes how square units can be arranged in rows to cover the space.

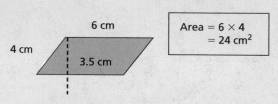

This area has been calculated incorrectly.

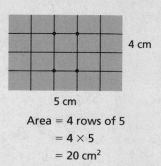

Area = 4 rows of 5
     = 4 × 5
     = 20 cm²

In the case of the parallelogram, students should be able to see that an array of squares will not match the shape of the area to be covered. However, if the parallelogram is changed by cutting a triangle from one side and moving it to the other side, then the resulting rectangle *can* be covered with rows of squares.

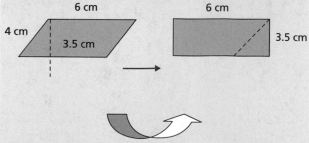

This parallelogram can turn into a 6-cm-by-3.5-cm rectangle, so the area is 6 cm × 3.5 cm = 21 cm².

Another strategy is to have students sketch the parallelogram on grid paper and count squares to check the area.

Not Recognizing the Need for Common Units

Some students will calculate the area of the blue rectangle on page 407 as 70 cm² or as 70 m².

Many times, students simply do not pay attention to the units, and need to be reminded about what the measurements mean. For example, you might ask, "How much area of the blue rectangle would 1 square centimetre cover? If I had 70 square centimetres, would they be enough to cover the whole shape? How do you know?"

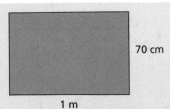

70 cm

1 m

Errors often occur when side lengths are provided in different units.

Students will soon realize that 70 centimetre squares would only be enough to make one column of 70 squares down the side of the rectangle, while there's actually room for 100 columns this size.

Confusing Area with Perimeter

Sometimes students do not make the distinction between perimeter and area, and calculate the area instead of the perimeter (or vice versa), often using whichever formula they know best.

Remind students that the area of a shape is the amount of flat space it covers, and the perimeter is the distance around it. It might help students to think of a garden (the area) surrounded by a fence (the perimeter). It may also help to remind them of the definition when posing a problem, for example, "What is the area of this shape? Remember—area is about how many units it would take to cover this much flat space."

One good way to help students distinguish between perimeter and area is to teach the two topics separately. Perimeter measure is actually a linear measure, and it makes sense to teach about perimeter in a unit on length. Later, when students learn about area, they can review perimeter in the context of solving problems that relate the two measures.

Appropriate Manipulatives

Area: Examples of Manipulatives

ITEM	EXAMPLE
Square Tiles Square tiles make good nonstandard units for measuring area, since they fit together (tile) to cover shapes. Square tiles are also available in square-centimetre size and can be used to introduce students to the square centimetre as a standard unit. However, young children may have difficulty manipulating them.	The area of the rectangle below is 10 square tiles. 
Geoboards Geoboards, which are available in various sizes, can be used to make shapes whose areas can then be described in square geoboard units.	Geoboards provide an opportunity for students to explore partial as well as whole square units. For example, students could create different shapes with an area of 6 square units. 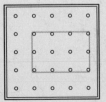 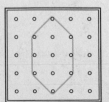 Both of these shapes have an area of 6 square units. *(continued)*

Sheets of Paper

Sheets of construction paper or newsprint can be used to determine the area of larger spaces.

The bulletin board has an area of about 9 sheets of paper.

Measuring an area with sheets of paper

Cookie Cutters

Cookie cutters not only provide an interesting way to measure area, but also allow students to iterate with a single unit. Note that shapes that do not tile are fine for introducing the concept of area, but students should soon realize that they are not very useful for measuring because of the spaces between them. On the other hand, irregular shapes can provide a basis for making estimates.

Working with modelling clay or even real cookie dough gives students an opportunity to use a cookie cutter to determine area.

Students use a single unit over and over when they use a cookie cutter to measure rolled-out modelling clay.

Afterwards, the cutout "cookies" can be placed side by side to estimate the area of a cookie tray.

Ink Stamps and Ink

A variety of interesting stamp shapes can be used to allow students to measure areas by iterating—stamping multiple copies of a single unit. As with cookie cutters, it is important to choose stamps with shapes that will tile when the goal is measurement.

Students can determine the area of a piece of paper by counting the number of stamps they can fit on it.

"I think it will take about 25 stamps to cover the paper."

Pattern Blocks

Because pattern blocks fit together to tile a surface, and they come in uniform sets, they make good units for measuring area.

Students can use one type of pattern block to measure a surface, and then use the results to estimate the number of blocks of a different type that it would take to cover the same surface.

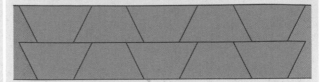

"It took 10 blue blocks and there's a little bit not covered. I can put 3 greens on every blue, so I think I can fit 30 and a few more, maybe 34 greens altogether."

Tangram Pieces

Plastic or wooden tangram pieces can be used as non-standard units for measuring area. (Students can trace a single piece over and over to measure a paper shape.) Students can also use tangram pieces to create two or more shapes with the same area, or they can compare the area of one piece with the area of another.

Students can explore area relationships as they build shapes with pieces from multiple tangram sets.

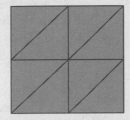

"I can build the same square with 8 small tangram triangles or 2 big ones. That means each big triangle must have the same area as 4 small ones."

Grid Paper and Transparent Grids

Grid paper, and especially a transparent grid photocopied onto acetate, is useful for determining the areas of shapes by counting grid squares. For example, students can trace their footprints onto grids, or place a transparent grid over an area to be measured. Grids come in a variety of sizes, some of which are measured in square centimetres, so they can be used for work with either nonstandard or standard units.

Transparent grids are especially useful for estimating the areas of irregular shapes.

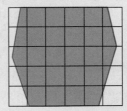

"This hexagon covers about 25 square centimetres. There are 20 whole squares inside, and there are enough part squares to cover about another 5 square centimetres."

Base Ten Blocks

Base ten blocks make it easy to measure areas quickly and accurately in square centimetres.

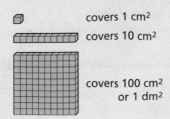

covers 1 cm²

covers 10 cm²

covers 100 cm²
or 1 dm²

A student could use base ten blocks to measure the area of an envelope.

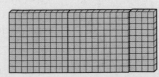

"I used 2 hundreds and 4 tens to cover almost all of the envelope, so the area is about 240 square centimetres."

(continued)

Rulers, Metre Sticks, and Measuring Tapes

Once students have learned formulas for calculating the areas of polygons, they can use rulers, metre sticks, and tape measures to measure the lengths they need to know in order to apply the appropriate area formula.

A student could measure the base and height of a parallelogram with a ruler and multiply *base × height* to determine its area.

Appropriate Technology

Computers

Multimedia programs such as *PowerPoint* and many word-processing programs have drawing features that allow students to create and copy shapes. Students can use this feature to create a large shape, and then paste a number of uniform smaller shapes on top of it to determine its area. There are also software programs such as *Kidpix* that allow students to stamp shapes onto a surface.

Older students could use the "ruler" feature of a drawing program (set to measure in centimetres, not inches) to measure heights and side lengths of rectangles, parallelograms, and triangles so they can apply formulas to determine the areas of these shapes.

Students might also try to create shapes with a given area in nonstandard or standard units. For example, younger students could use drawing software to create a shape they can cover with 10 pictures stamped from a clip art file, while older students could use the ruler in the software to create various rectangles with an area of 24 cm^2.

As well, students can use dynamic geometry software, such as *Geometer's Sketchpad*, to measure lengths and areas of shapes, as described on page 387.

The Internet

As with length, there are problems locating Internet sites that allow students to explore area in nonstandard or metric units. However, there are sites that do offer suitable activities for helping students develop area concepts. Many of these involve measuring areas on a grid, or using grids or geoboards to create different shapes with the same area.

Assessing Student Understanding

- When assessing student understanding of measurement ideas, it is important that teachers attend to both skill and concept understanding, as well as to problem solving. For instance, to determine if a student understands perimeter, you might
  - provide a shape and ask students to measure to determine the perimeter
  - provide a shape with measures given and ask students to calculate to determine the perimeter
  - ask how perimeter would change in particular situations, for example, if the lengths were all doubled
  - ask students to construct a shape with a particular perimeter
  - ask students to determine the cost of a material required to "fence" in a shape

WebConnect

www.makingmathmeaningful
.nelson.com

Visit the Making Math Meaningful website for links to Internet sites that can help students develop area concepts.

Similarly, assessment of student knowledge related to measurement formulas should revolve around application of the formula as well as its development.

- Assessment opportunities should include those where only one measurement is the focus, but also those where multiple measurements are involved, for example, determining areas for different shapes with the same perimeter.
- Students should, in many circumstances, be given a choice of what tool to use to accomplish a measurement.
- Students should have opportunities to exhibit their understanding of when particular types of measurements are appropriate to use, for example, responding to a question such as, "You are getting a new rug for your bedroom. Why might you want to know its area? Why might you want to know its perimeter?"

Appropriate Children's Books

How Tall, How Short, How Far Away? (Adler, 1999).
This book focuses on the history of measurement and talks about many different units of measure, from measurements in ancient Egypt to the metric system.

Counting on Frank (Clement, 1991).
This amusing story about a boy who asks lots of hypothetical questions about measurement and his very unusual dog presents very interesting measurement comparisons.

How Big Is a Foot? (Myller, 1991).
This funny story motivates the need for a standard unit of length measure. The story appeals to many age levels.

Sir Cumference and the Isle of Immeter (Neuschwander, 1997).
This book in the Sir Cumference series focuses students on the perimeter and area in order to solve a mystery.

If You Hopped Like a Frog (Schwartz, 1999).
This story compares human and animal behaviours, and focuses on the use of scale or proportion to consider measurement situations.

Applying What You've Learned

1. What problem-solving strategy did you use to solve the chapter problem? How can you be sure there are no other solutions?

2. a) Describe three interesting activities not already listed in the chapter that are appropriate for students at each of the three stages of teaching length.

   b) Repeat this for the three stages of teaching area.

3. It is important for students to develop strategies for estimating length and area. What are some of the things you can do to help them develop those strategies?

4. Describe some everyday situations where nonstandard units are just as appropriate as standard units.

5. Some educators argue that the importance of measurement in the mathematics curriculum is that it is the content that brings together the two main branches of math—number and geometry. How central a role do you think measurement should play in the curriculum? Explain your answer.

6. a) Make a list of each step that you would need to use to measure the length of the edge of a table that is longer than your ruler.

   b) Why might it be advisable to delay the introduction of ruler use?

   c) How can you help students make the link between measuring with units and using a ruler?

7. Some teachers argue that you cannot teach about area until students know about length. Why might that not be true?

8. Many students believe that you cannot measure the areas of any shapes other than squares using the unit square centimetres. How would you convince them that this is not true?

9. Locate a current Canadian textbook.

   a) Describe a lesson on measuring area that you think is particularly strong. Indicate its strengths.

   b) Describe a lesson measuring length that you think is weak. Indicate its deficits.

Interact with a K–8 Student:

10. Ask a student to tell you as many items as he or she can that might be a certain measurement, for example, about 50 cm long or about 100 cm^2 in area. What measurement understanding did he or she display?

Discuss with a K–8 Teacher:

11. Ask a teacher to share with you a lesson he or she has taught for measuring length that has been particularly successful and engaging. Ask him or her to explain what made the lesson work so well.

Selected References

Adler, D. (1999). *How tall, how short, how far away?* New York: Holiday House.

Barrett, J.E., Jones, G., Thornton, C., and Dickson, S. (2003). Understanding children's developing strategies about concepts for length. In Clement, D.H., and Bright, G. (Eds.). *Learning and teaching measurement.* Reston, VA: National Council of Teachers of Mathematics, 17–30.

Battista, M.T. (1999). The importance of spatial structuring in geometric reasoning. *Teaching Children Mathematics, 6,* 170–177.

Battista, M.T., and Clements, D.H. (1998). Students' understanding of three-dimensional cube arrays. Findings from a research and curriculum development project. In Lehrer, R., and Chazan, D. (Eds). *Designing learning environments for developing understanding of geometry and space.* Mahwah, NJ: Erlbaum, 227–248.

Battista, M.T., Clements, D.H., Arnoff, J., Battista, K., and Van Auken Borrow, C. (1998). Students' spatial structuring of 2D arrays of squares. *Journal for Research in Mathematics Education, 29,* 503–532.

Bloomer, A. (1997). *Getting into area: Grades 3–6.* Palo Alto, CA: Dale Seymour Publications.

Clement, R. (1991). *Counting on Frank.* Milwaukee: Gareth Stevens Publishing.

Clements, D.H. (1999). Teaching length measurement: Research challenges. *School, Science and Mathematics, 99,* 5–11.

Clements, D.H., Battista, M.T., and Sarama, J. (1998). Development of geometric and measurement ideas. In Lehrer, R., and Chazan, D. (Eds.). *Designing learning environments for developing understanding of geometry and space.* Mahwah, NJ: Erlbaum, 201–225.

Clements, D.H., and Bright, G. (2003). *Learning and teaching measurement.* Reston, VA: National Council of Teachers of Mathematics.

Copley, J.V., Glass, K., Nix, L., Faseler, A., De Jesus, M., and Tanksley, S. (2004). Measuring experiences for young children. *Teaching Children Mathematics, 10,* 314–319.

Dacey, L., Cavanagh, M., Findell, C., Greenes, C., Sheffield, L.J., and Small, M. (2003). *Navigating through measurement, prekindergarten–grade 2.* Reston, VA: National Council of Teachers of Mathematics.

Hiebert, J. (1981). Cognitive development and learning linear measurement. *Journal for Research in Mathematics Education, 12,* 197–211.

Joram, E., Gabriele, A. J., Bertheau, M., Gelman, R.I., and Subrahmanyam, K. (2005). Children's use of the reference point strategy for measurement estimation. *Journal for Research in Mathematics Education, 36,* 4–23.

Joram, E., Hartman, C., and Trafton, P.R. (2004). "As people get older, they get taller": An integrated unit on measurement, linear relationships and data analysis. *Teaching Children Mathematics, 10,* 344–351.

Kribs-Zaleta, C.M., and Bradshaw, D.L. (2003). A case of units. *Teaching Children Mathematics, 9,* 397–399.

Lee, M., and Miller, M. (2000). *50 fabulous measurement activities.* New York: Scholastic.

Lehrer, R. (2003). Developing understanding of measurement. In Kilpatrick, J., Martin, W.G., and Schilfter, D. (Eds.). *A research companion to principles and standards for school mathematics.* Reston, VA: National Council of Teachers of Mathematics, 179–192.

Lehrer, R., Jacobson, C., Kemeny, V., and Strom, D. (1999). Building on children's intuitions to develop mathematical understanding of space. In Fennema, E., and Romberg, T.A. (Eds.). *Mathematics classrooms that promote understanding.* Mahwah, NJ: Lawrence Erlbaum Associates, 63–87.

Lehrer, R., Jenings., M., and Osana, H. (1998). Longitudinal study of children's reasoning about space and geometry. In Lehrer, R., and Chazan, D. (Eds). *Designing learning environments for developing understanding of geometry and space.* Mahwah, NJ: Erlbaum, 137–167.

McClain, K., Cobb, P., Gravemeijer, K., and Estes, B. (1999). Developing mathematical reasoning within the context of measurement. In Stiff, L., and Curcio, F.R. (Eds.). *Developing mathematical reasoning in grades K–12.* Reston, VA: National Council of Teachers of Mathematics, 93–106.

Moyer, P.S. (2001). Using representations to explore perimeter and area. *Teaching Children Mathematics, 8,* 52–59.

Murphy, E. (2004). A mathematical measurement mystery. *Teaching Children Mathematics, 11,* 54–64.

Myller, R. (1991). *How big is a foot?* New York: Yearling.

Neuschwander, C. (2006). *Sir Cumference and the Isle of Immeter.* Watertown, MA: Charlesbridge Publishing.

Nitabach, E., and Lehrer, R. (1996). Developing spatial sense through area measurement. *Teaching Children Mathematics, 2,* 473–476.

Outhred, L.N., and Mitchelmore, M. (2000). Young children's intuitive understanding of rectangular measurement. *Journal for Research in Mathematics Education, 31,* 144–167.

Schwartz, D. (1999). *If you hopped like a frog.* New York: Scholastic Press.

Small, M. (pre-press publication). *Professional resources and instruction for mathematics educators: Measurement.* Toronto: Nelson Education Ltd.

Sophian, C. (2002). Learning about what fits: Preschool children's reasoning about effects of object size. *Journal of Research in Mathematics Education, 33,* 290–302.

Stephan, M., Bowers, J., Cobb, P., with Gravemeijer, K. (2003). *Supporting students' development of measuring conceptions: Analyzing students' learning in social context.* Reston, VA: National Council of Teachers of Mathematics.

Stephan, M., and Clements, D.H. (2003). Linear and area measurement in prekindergarten to grade 2. In Clements, D.H., and Bright, G. (Eds.). *Learning and teaching measurement.* Reston, VA: National Council of Teachers of Mathematics, 3–16.

Wilson, P., and Rowland, R. (1993). Teaching measurement. In Jensen, R.J. (Ed.). *Research ideas for the classroom: Early childhood mathematics.* New York: Macmillan, 171–194.

Wright, T., Mokros, J., and Russell, S. J. (1997). *Bigger, taller, heavier, smaller. A grade 1 unit in investigations in number, data, and space.* Palo Alto, CA: Dale Seymour Publications.

Chapter 16

Measuring Capacity, Volume, Mass, Time, and Angle

IN A NUTSHELL

The main ideas in this chapter are listed below:

1. The stages for measuring capacity, volume, time, and angle are the same as those for length and area. Normally, you skip the nonstandard stage for temperature.

2. Capacity and volume are related concepts, but not identical.

3. The attributes of mass and volume or capacity are independent.

4. Measuring time and telling time are different processes.

CHAPTER PROBLEM

Use centimetre grid paper. Cut out a 10 cm × 6 cm rectangle. Then cut one square out of each corner and fold to make an open box. How many centimetre cubes will it hold? How does your answer change if you cut 2 × 2 squares out of each corner? Why might you expect this?

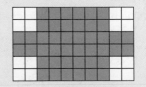

Introduction

Capacity, volume, and mass are all measures that are attached to 3-D objects. The examples that follow show how students might conceptualize each measure at the nonstandard unit stage.

Capacity is the amount that a container can hold.	**Volume** is the amount of space occupied by an object.	**Mass** is the amount of matter in an object. It is what causes the object to feel light or heavy.

"It takes 48 linking cubes to match the amount of space my box takes up."

"It takes 15 pennies to balance my bear."

How Concepts of Capacity Can Be Introduced

You use capacity to describe how much of a pourable substance, such as water or sand, would fit inside a container such as a cup, a pail, a swimming pool, or even a room.

Ideas about capacity can be introduced through the same three stages as other measurement concepts—definition/comparison, nonstandard units, and standard units. As with length, the second stage is usually introduced fairly soon after the first stage.

How Concepts of Capacity Can Be Introduced

DEFINITION/COMPARISON

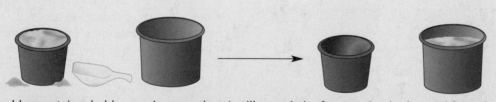

"The blue container holds more because there's still room in it after pouring in the sand from the red container."

NONSTANDARD UNITS

"The blue container holds more because it holds 5 scoops of sand and the red one only holds 3 scoops."

STANDARD UNITS

"The blue container has a greater capacity because it holds 500 mL of sand and the red one only holds 300 mL."

Capacity: The Definition/Comparison Stage

At this stage, students explore the idea that you can compare the capacity of two containers by filling one of the containers with a pourable material, such as water, sand, rice, or small peas, and then pouring the contents into the other container. Through comparing, students can discover that the capacity of a container is determined not only by its height, but also by the area of its base and the configuration of its sides. To this end, students should have opportunities to compare containers that differ in only one dimension, and also to compare containers that differ in more than one way.

When only one dimension of the containers differs ...

capacity = 20 small scoops

capacity = 15 big scoops
= 30 small scoops

"This container holds more."

... it is easy to compare visually to see at a glance which holds more, as long as the containers are of similar thickness.

When the dimensions differ in more than one way ...

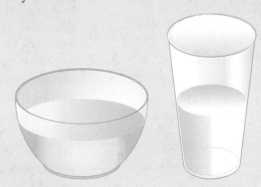

... students can compare visually to estimate which container holds more, but unless the differences are very obvious, they will need to pour the contents of one into the other to be certain.

In the course of measuring capacity, students will use a variety of measurement terms such as *holds more, holds less, full,* and *empty.*

Appropriate activities for students at the definition/comparison stage might include comparing the capacities of empty drink containers (perhaps collected from students' lunches), comparing the capacities of cooking pots, or deciding what bag sizes to use for a class popcorn sale. Students should begin by comparing only two containers, but will soon be ready for the greater challenge of putting three, or perhaps even more than three, containers in order. Although the activity described in **Activity 16.1**

ACTIVITY 16.1

- Provide a container and mark it with an "X."

- Provide several other containers of varying capacities and shapes, including some that hold about the same amount as the container marked "X."

- Ask students to predict how each container might compare with the marked one, measure to check, and then record the results with words or pictures on a chart like the one shown here.

Comparing Containers		
Less	Same	More

involves several containers, it is simpler than an ordering activity because students need to compare only two containers at a time. With younger students, a sand or water table is a good place for comparing capacities.

Capacity: The Nonstandard Unit Stage

At this stage, students learn to measure capacity with nonstandard units such as cups or spoons. Nonstandard units make it possible to assign a number to a container's capacity, allowing students to record the capacities of many containers so they can be compared without having to refill them repeatedly.

Nonstandard units also help students develop referents they can use for estimating. For this reason, students need many opportunities to measure with familiar units such as water bottles, yogurt cups, cereal bowls, and teaspoons. A student who knows, for example, that a container holds 4 teaspoons of sand has a good feel for the capacity of this container.

At this stage, students can use multiple units to measure capacity, or they can use the same unit over and over. It may be more practical, though, to use one unit repeatedly.

Appropriate Nonstandard Units for Capacity

Tools for measuring capacity are handy everyday items of uniform size, such as spoonfuls, cupfuls, and small containers. These are generally filled with water, or with a pourable solid such as sand or rice; these amounts serve as the nonstandard units.

If students are measuring boxes, cubes make good nonstandard units because they pack. In the early stages of work with definition/comparison, teachers may want to let students experiment with units that suit a particular context, but do not pack. For example, students could figure out how many apples will fit in a basket, or how many pennies or jelly beans will fit in a jar. However, whenever these materials are used, the discussion that follows the activity should bring out the idea that some of the space in the container was not measured because the units did not fit tightly together. As a result, these units might not be good ones to use if the purpose of the activity is to compare the capacities of two containers that are similar in size.

Estimating Capacity with Nonstandard Units

In the definition/comparison stage, estimating was simply used to determine which of two containers would hold more. Now students are able to estimate how many units a container might hold. As with other types of measurement, it helps students to compare unknown amounts with amounts they know. For example, a student at this stage might determine that it takes 5 big spoons to fill a container, and then estimate how many little spoons it would take to fill the same container. It is also appropriate at this stage to partially fill a container, for example, to approximately $\frac{1}{4}, \frac{1}{3},$ or $\frac{1}{2}$ of its capacity, and then ask students, "About how many units would it take to fill the container?"

About how many apples will it take to fill this pail?

In order to use a partial measurement to make an estimate, students need to think, "How many times will this quantity fit into the whole amount I have to measure?"

ACTIVITY 16.2

Students at the nonstandard unit stage can practise estimating capacity as they complete this task.

- Show a large pail and a small mixing bowl. Ask each student to estimate how many bowls of sand or water it would take to fill the pail.

- Have individual students record their estimates by attaching name cards to the appropriate categories in the graph.

- Give students a chance to change their estimates after they have seen all the estimates.

- Pour one bowl of sand into the pail, and then give students another chance to change their estimates.

- Fill the rest of the pail and count the number of bowls needed.

	How many bowls will fill the pail?		
		Mahmoud	
		Lachlan	
		Nadia	
		Jordan	Ravi
Dale		Liz	Billy
Devica		Sayada	Julie
Estela		Carmen	Gord
1 to 3	4 to 6	7 to 9	more than 9
	Number of bowls		

Making Nonstandard Measuring Tools

A good way to help students understand the importance of uniformity in nonstandard units is to let them measure out equal amounts in order to make their own measuring tools. For example, a student can make a measuring cup from a large transparent cup or glass (preferably cylindrical rather than tapered) by filling it repeatedly from a smaller container and marking the side of the cup to show the level after each new measure is added. The student can then use the cup to measure the capacity of various bowls.

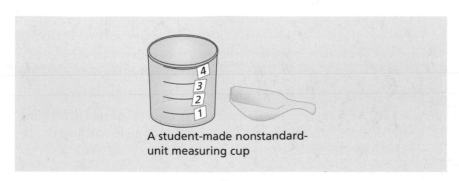

A student-made nonstandard-unit measuring cup

Capacity: The Standard Unit Stage

Students can be introduced to standard units when they realize that, rather than measuring capacity in nonstandard units, which can mean different things to different people, they can use units that everyone will understand.

Introducing Standard Units of Capacity

The litre tends to be introduced early in work with capacity. This is, in part, because litre containers are such a familiar part of everyday life. Products such as milk and ice cream often come in litre containers. This familiarity also helps students understand that litre containers can look different; after all, a milk carton looks quite different from an ice cream tub.

Metric Units of Capacity

LITRES (L)	MILLILITRES (mL)
Defining a Litre	**Defining a Millilitre**
A *litre* is the amount of liquid it would take to fill a cubic container that is 10 cm by 10 cm by 10 cm.	A *millilitre* is $\frac{1}{1000}$ or 0.001 of a litre.
Litre Referents	**Millilitre Referents**
Aside from familiar referents such as 1-L milk cartons and water bottles, students can also refer to a thousand cube from a base ten block set.	For a millilitre referent, students can refer to the amount of liquid it would take to fill a hollow unit cube from a base ten block set.

If a 10 cm thousand cube were hollowed out, its capacity would be 1 L.

If a unit cube were a container, its capacity would be 1 mL.

Because a millilitre is so small, students should also have millilitre referents that represent multiple units, such as teaspoons (5 mL) and tablespoons (15 mL). Graduated medicine cups also make good referents for amounts measured in millilitres.

There are, of course, other metric units of capacity, such as decilitres, kilolitres, and centilitres, but these are rarely used in everyday life.

Standard Tools for Measuring Capacity

Just as a ruler helps students learn that they can use a single tool to measure different lengths, a measuring cup illustrates that a single tool can also be used to measure different capacities. A measuring cup is like a ruler in other ways, too. For example, students need to estimate amounts that fall between the marks on the cup, such as 130 mL. They also need to learn to combine full cups with partial ones to measure quantities greater than the capacity of the measuring cup.

A measuring cup shares many
characteristics with a ruler.

Other standard tools for measuring capacity include measuring spoons, measuring scoops, and graduated cylinders.

Activities for Measuring Capacity

There are many activities teachers can use to provide practice with measuring in millilitres and litres. For example, students could

- estimate the capacities of a variety of containers, and then check by measuring
- prepare recipes that require them to measure quantities in millilitres and litres
- compare several cereal bowls to see how much a typical bowl can hold
- estimate the number of pieces of popcorn it would take to fill a litre container

There are also a number of environmental issues that provide contexts for measuring capacity at home.

How Concepts of Volume Can Be Introduced

The volume of a shape is a measure that describes how much space the shape occupies. Many students and adults interchange the terms *volume* and *capacity*. This is not surprising since people sometimes measure capacities, such as how much a moving truck holds, in units of volume (cubic metres).

ACTIVITY 16.3

Ask students to explore these environmental issues:

- Estimate how many litres of water you could save by having a shower instead of a bath. Describe how you found out.

- Place a container under a dripping tap for 1 hour and estimate how much water is wasted in one day, one week, and one month.

In order to understand volume, a student benefits from a clear understanding of the measurement process, as well as considerable experience with measuring length, area, and capacity.

Ideas about volume can be introduced through the same three stages as other measurement concepts—definition/comparison, using nonstandard units, and using standard units.

How Concepts of Volume Can Be Introduced

DEFINITION/COMPARISON	NONSTANDARD UNITS

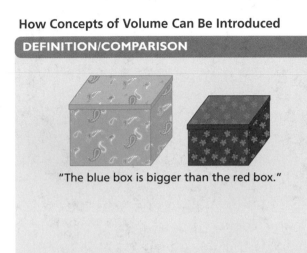

"The blue box is bigger than the red box."

"The blue box is bigger—it took 3 layers of 12 to build it. That's 36 cubes. The red box is 2 layers of 9. That's 18 cubes."

STANDARD UNITS

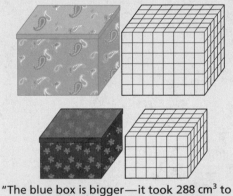

"The blue box is bigger—it took 288 cm³ to build a model of it and the red box only took 144 cm³."

Volume = Area of base × height

Blue box	Red box
$V = 8 \times 6 \times 6$	$V = 6 \times 6 \times 4$
$= 48 \times 6$	$= 36 \times 4$
$= 288 \text{ cm}^3$	$= 144 \text{ cm}^3$

"The blue box is bigger—it's 288 cm³ and the red one is only 144 cm³."

Volume: The Definition/Comparison Stage

At this stage, students explore the notion that one item has more volume than another if the object is "bigger" (occupies more space) than another object. Initially, comparisons should be made with items that are easy to compare directly visually (as shown above). However, when the difference in volume is not obvious—for example, one prism might be taller and wider than another but not as deep—this visual direct comparison method is limited. This situation facilitates the progression to the nonstandard unit stage. A rapid transition to nonstandard units is possible for most students because, by the time volume is introduced, students will have had considerable experience with measurement in general.

Volume: The Nonstandard Unit Stage

Nonstandard units make it possible to assign a number to an object's volume, allowing students to record the volumes of many objects so they can be compared without having to be measured repeatedly.

Generally, students work with rectangular-prism-shaped objects for measuring volume. To measure the volume of a small box, students would measure (count) the number of blocks it takes to build a full-size model of the box. Students generally need to use multiple copies of a unit since it is very difficult to measure volume by iteration (using a single unit over and over).

Appropriate Nonstandard Units for Volume

Students generally measure volume using uniform units that pack (that is, fit together with no overlap or spaces). The size of the blocks does not matter as long as they are uniform. Examples include centimetre cubes, linking cubes, and building blocks. (Even though centimetre cubes are a standard unit (1 cm³), this has no significance for students at the nonstandard unit stage, so these students are able to use centimetre cubes as nonstandard units.)

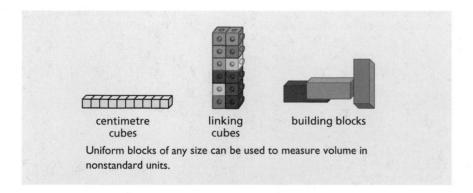

centimetre   linking   building blocks
cubes   cubes

Uniform blocks of any size can be used to measure volume in nonstandard units.

Rectangular blocks are often used for volume, but other shape units can work just as well, depending on the shape of the object to be measured.

"The jar is just a bit smaller than 11 yellow blocks."

Volume and Shape

Students at the nonstandard unit stage are often surprised to find that shapes that look very different can have the same volume.

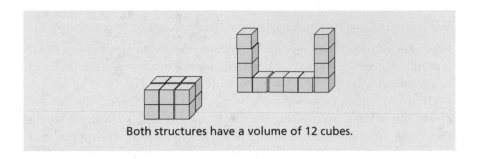

Both structures have a volume of 12 cubes.

To help students explore this concept, a teacher can pose problems that involve making different shapes with the same number of blocks or cubes, or ask questions such as the one illustrated below.

Student Reponse

This student recognizes that the volume of a structure depends on the number of cubes that were used to build it, and is not influenced by how the cubes are arranged.

Use 11 linking cubes to build a cube structure like the one shown here.

A different cube structure has the same volume but it's taller than this one.

How can that be possible? Use words and a picture to explain.

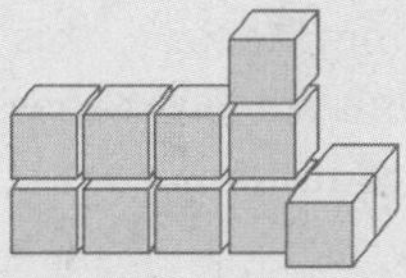

The volume of this structure is 11 cubes.

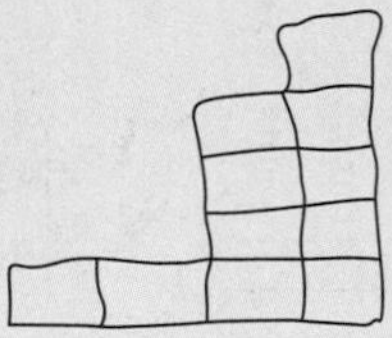

The picture of the structure has the same volume as the one above.
I know because I have counted. It does not matter about the shape and size of the structure, but that it has the same volume.

Estimating Volume with Nonstandard Units

In the definition/comparison stage, estimating was simply used to determine which of two objects took up more space. Now students are able to estimate how many units of space an object might fill. As with other types of measurement, it helps students to compare unknown amounts with amounts they know. For example, a student at this stage might determine that it takes 15 linking cubes to match the size of a small box, and then estimate how many linking cubes it would take to match the size of a larger box. It is also appropriate at this stage to use cubes to model the base of a box, and then ask students, "About how many cubes do you think it would take to match the size of the whole box?"

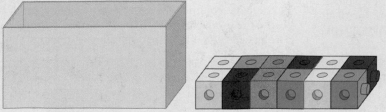

How many cubes would it take to build a box this size?

"It looks like it will take 3 layers this size to build the box, so I think the volume is about 36 cubes."

ACTIVITY 16.4

Have students build a box with green Cuisenaire rods.

Ask,

- How many rods did you use?
- How many yellow rods would you need to build the same-size box?

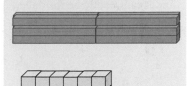

Build this box with linking cubes.

- How many cubes did you use?
- How many cubes would you need to build the same-size box with Centicubes?

Volume: The Standard Unit Stage

Standard units of volume are related to standard units of length. However, while length is measured in units that are straight lines, volume is measured in cubic units. This is because cubic units represent a space that has three dimensions.

Introducing Standard Units of Volume

Generally, the cubic centimetre is introduced first. This is partly because centimetres are familiar to students, and partly because cubic centimetres are a suitable size for measuring many shapes that are easy for students to handle. In addition, concrete models in the form of Centicubes or unit cubes from a set of base ten blocks are readily accessible in many classrooms.

Metric Units of Volume

CUBIC CENTIMETRES (cm³)	CUBIC METRES (m³)

Defining a Cubic Centimetre

A cubic centimetre is a volume equivalent to the space occupied by a cube with a side length of 1 cm. It is important for students to realize that an object with a volume of 1 cm³ is not necessarily cube-shaped, as illustrated by the prisms below.

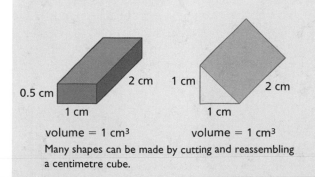

volume = 1 cm³   volume = 1 cm³

Many shapes can be made by cutting and reassembling a centimetre cube.

Defining a Cubic Metre

A cubic metre is a volume equivalent to the space occupied by a cube with a side length of 1 m. Students should realize that an object with a volume of 1 m³ does not have to be cube-shaped. It simply has to occupy the same amount of space as the cube.

Cubic Metre Referents

A good way to model a cubic metre and provide a referent is to make 12 rolls of newspaper, each 1 m long, and tape them together to form the edges of a cube. If the cube were solid, it would have a volume of 1 m³.

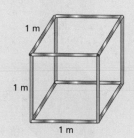

Filled volume is 1 m³

(continued)

Cubic Centimetre Referents

Students can refer to Centicubes or base ten block unit cubes. A base ten rod serves as a referent for 10 cm³, a flat for 100 cm³, and a thousand cube for 1000 cm³.

Students can use this model to find objects in the classroom and outside that have a greater volume, about the same volume, or a lesser volume. They might also use the model to estimate the volumes of familiar objects, such as a shed or a garbage dumpster.

CUBIC DECIMETRES (dm³)

The cubic decimetre is another unit of volume that is useful for students in the elementary grades. Its size is suitable for measuring classroom objects, and it can readily be modelled using a thousand cube from a set of base ten blocks.

Volume = 1 dm³

Other standard units of volume include cubic millimetres and cubic kilometres, but these are rarely used in everyday life.

Recording Standard Units of Volume It is important for students to realize that, when they begin to measure volume with standard units, they need to report measurements in *cubic units*. (This is different from measuring in nonstandard units, where a volume might be reported, for example, as 20 blocks or 17 linking cubes.)

Initially, the units should be spelled out, for example, "12 cubic metres." Although this is not formally correct metric usage, it serves to help students build an understanding of the unit before they begin using symbols. Eventually, students will be ready to write the units in an abbreviated form using exponents, for example, 12 cm³. With standard units, the exponent 3 is used to indicate that the units have three equal dimensions.

Relating Units of Volume Students need opportunities to discuss how one cubic unit relates to another. Just as students who are learning about area may be surprised to discover that 1 m² = 10 000 cm² (and not 100 cm²), students who are learning about standard units of volume may be even more surprised to find that 1 m³ = 1 000 000 cm³.

Relating Units: Linear, Area, and Volume

Linear	1 m	$\overline{}$ 100 cm	100 cm
Area	1 m²	▪ 100 cm × 100 cm	100 cm × 100 cm = 10 000 cm²
Volume	1 m³	▪ 100 cm × 100 cm × 100 cm	100 cm × 100 cm × 100 cm = 1 000 000 cm³

Formulas for Measuring Volume

In K–6, students deal with formulas, if at all, mainly in the context of working with prisms, and especially rectangular prisms. In Grades 7 to 9, they learn formulas for calculating the volumes of other shapes, usually more general prisms, pyramids, cones, cylinders, and spheres. Although volume formulas are officially introduced at the standard unit stage, the notion of a formula or shortcut can be introduced at the nonstandard unit stage.

Volume of a Prism or Cylinder When students build cube models of prisms, many will notice that, instead of counting each cube to find the volume, they can multiply the number of cubes in each layer, the area of the base, by the number of layers, or the height.

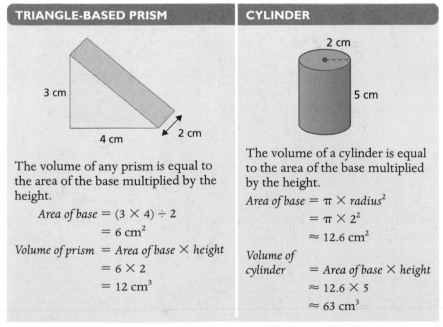

volume = number of cubes in bottom layer
        x number of layers
      = 20 x 3
      = 60 cubes

Volume Formulas for Prisms and Cylinders

TRIANGLE-BASED PRISM	CYLINDER

3 cm
4 cm
2 cm

2 cm
5 cm

The volume of any prism is equal to the area of the base multiplied by the height.

$$\text{Area of base} = (3 \times 4) \div 2$$
$$= 6 \text{ cm}^2$$
$$\text{Volume of prism} = \text{Area of base} \times \text{height}$$
$$= 6 \times 2$$
$$= 12 \text{ cm}^3$$

The volume of a cylinder is equal to the area of the base multiplied by the height.

$$\text{Area of base} = \pi \times \text{radius}^2$$
$$= \pi \times 2^2$$
$$\approx 12.6 \text{ cm}^2$$
$$\text{Volume of cylinder} = \text{Area of base} \times \text{height}$$
$$\approx 12.6 \times 5$$
$$\approx 63 \text{ cm}^3$$

Volume of Other Shapes Later on, students will learn that they can use the volumes of prisms to calculate the volumes of related shapes, such as pyramids, cones, and spheres.

Relating Volume Formulas

VOLUME OF A PYRAMID	VOLUME OF A CONE	VOLUME OF A SPHERE
The volume of a pyramid is $\frac{1}{3}$ of the volume of the prism with the same base and height.	The volume of a cone is $\frac{1}{3}$ of the volume of the cylinder with the same base and height.	The volume of a sphere is $\frac{2}{3}$ of the volume of the cylinder that fits exactly around it. The height of the cylinder is double the radius, r, so the volume of the cylinder is $(\pi \times r^2) \times 2r$ or, in simplified form, $2 \times \pi \times r^3$. The volume of the sphere is $\frac{2}{3}$ as large, so it is $\frac{4}{3} \times \pi \times r^3$. (This formula is generally introduced much later than the other volume formulas.)
		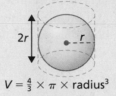
$V = \frac{1}{3} \times base\ area \times height$	$V = \frac{1}{3} \times base\ area \times height$	$V = \frac{4}{3} \times \pi \times radius^3$

Volume and Surface Area At the nonstandard unit stage, students learned that objects with the same volume can have different shapes. Now they can explore the idea that objects with the same volume can also have different surface areas. They might also discover that, as the shape becomes more like a cube, the surface area decreases.

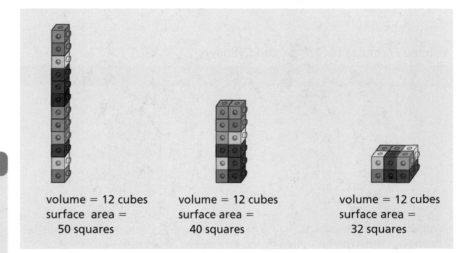

volume = 12 cubes
surface area =
50 squares

volume = 12 cubes
surface area =
40 squares

volume = 12 cubes
surface area =
32 squares

ACTIVITY 16.6

Have students use centimetre grid paper.

They make nets for two prisms that have the same volume, but different surface areas.

They record the volume and surface area of each prism.

ACTIVITY 16.7

Have students roll a sheet of loose-leaf paper both vertically and horizontally. The two "containers" have the same surface area if the bases are not considered, but students can fill them to discover they have different volumes.

The activities described in **Activity 16.6** and **Activity 16.7** can help students see that a short, wide shape has more surface area than a more compact, but taller, shape with the same volume.

Relating Volume to Capacity through Displacement

When an object is completely immersed in water, it displaces an amount of water that is equal to its own volume. At the definition/comparison stage, students can compare the volumes of two objects simply by immersing each object in the same amount of water and checking to compare the changes in the water level. The more the water level rises, the greater the volume of the object.

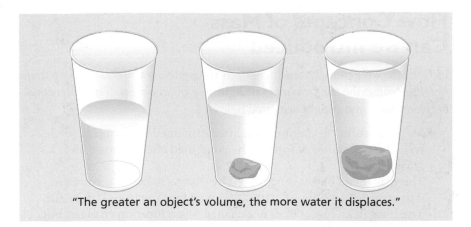

"The greater an object's volume, the more water it displaces."

Although displacement is a fairly simple concept, it is usually not introduced until after students have had some experience with measuring length, area, and capacity. Students require a fairly sophisticated understanding of measurement in order to understand the indirect relationship between the object and the displaced water.

Students often expect a heavier object to displace more water than a light one. For example, a student might be surprised to find that a large plastic bottle displaces more water than a smaller stone. To help students see that volume depends on size, not mass, teachers need to set up displacement experiments with objects that are made of different materials. They might, for example, compare the volumes of a variety of balls.

At the standard units stage, students are ready to learn that metric units of volume are related not only to one another, but also to standard units of capacity. This is why familiarity with units of capacity is a helpful prerequisite for work with volume displacement. When students immerse 1 cm³ of material in water, it displaces exactly 1 mL of liquid. When they immerse 1000 cm³ (1 dm³), this displaces exactly 1 L. As a result, students can use displacement not only to compare volumes, but also to calculate the volumes of irregularly shaped objects in standard units.

"The water level went from 100 mL to 135 mL, so the volume must be 35 cm³."

The same relationship (1 cm³ = 1 mL) can be used to estimate the capacity of a container with a known volume (assuming the sides of the container are not too thick). For example, if the volume of a box is 560 cm³, then the box has a capacity of about 560 mL.

ACTIVITY 16.8

Have students research the volumes of moving trucks.

Ask, *What is a reasonable estimate for the volume of all of the furniture in a school or in a house?*

How Concepts of Mass Can Be Introduced

In Canada, we generally teach children to use the term *mass*, rather than *weight*, to describe the heaviness or lightness of an object. The differences between mass and weight are listed below:

- Mass measures the amount of matter contained in an object, while weight is a measure of force—the combined effect of mass and gravity.
- The mass of an object is measured by using a balance to compare it to a known amount of matter, but weight is measured on a scale.
- The mass of an object does not change when location changes, but the weight can change with a change in location.

In everyday use, the terms *mass* and *weight* are interchangeable; in fact, we often tell a student to weigh an object to determine its mass, although some more advanced scientific and technological applications require that the distinction between the two terms be carefully made.

How Concepts of Mass Can Be Introduced

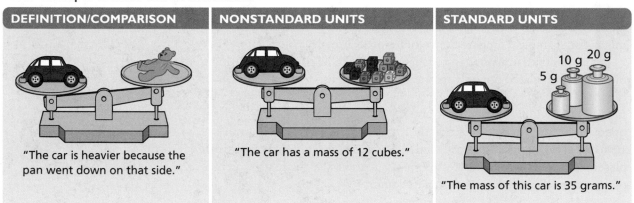

| DEFINITION/COMPARISON | NONSTANDARD UNITS | STANDARD UNITS |

"The car is heavier because the pan went down on that side."

"The car has a mass of 12 cubes."

"The mass of this car is 35 grams."

Mass: The Definition/Comparison Stage

At this stage, students use a pan balance to compare the masses of two objects. The balance then acts like a teeter-totter, with the object whose mass is greater pulling its side of the balance down (as shown above for Definition/Comparison).

Activities for students in the definition/comparison stage might include comparing the masses of different types of fruit, or hunting for objects that have less mass (or more mass) than a given object.

Students at this stage sometimes find it difficult to estimate which of two objects has more mass, since they cannot rely on size. Sometimes a smaller object has a greater mass than a large one. Therefore, students need to be able to physically handle the materials they are comparing. As students are developing their ability to estimate in order to make mass comparisons, they will benefit from opportunities to handle and compare a wide range of materials.

Another way to help students learn to estimate masses is to encourage them to use their own bodies like pan balances. To do this, students take an item in each hand, stretch out their arms, and try to feel which item is heavier. Then they move their arms to show how a pan balance would look if the items in their hands were on the balance.

Using Pan Balances to Compare Mass Directly

While students can make their own pan balances, for example, by using string and a paper clip to connect a paper cup to each end of a coat hanger, it is also practical to have some commercial models on hand.

Before using a pan balance, it is important to level the balance, that is, to make sure the empty pans balance exactly. Pan balances tend to slip out of balance when they are not levelled regularly. An unlevelled balance will result in inaccurate measurements and may foster misconceptions about mass. Most classroom pan balances are suited for a fairly limited range of masses, usually up to 1 kg or 2 kg.

A STUDENT-MADE PAN BALANCE	COMMERCIAL PAN BALANCES
	Some commercial balances have a flat plate on each side, making it easy to see the objects being measured. Others have a removable container, often clear, on each side, making it possible to balance liquids, or small items that might otherwise roll away. 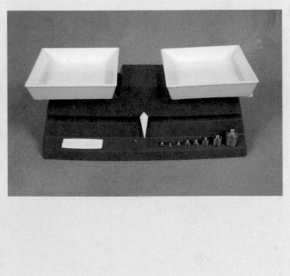

Mass: The Nonstandard Unit Stage

Nonstandard units make it possible to assign a number to an object's mass, allowing students to record the masses of many objects so they can be compared without having to be measured over and over.

To measure an object's mass with nonstandard units, a student places the object on one side of a pan balance, and then counts how many uniform units must be placed on the other side to make the pans balance. For example, it might take 8 blocks to balance the mass of a pet rock.

My pet rock's mass is 12 cubes.

Appropriate Nonstandard Units for Mass

Students can measure mass with nonstandard units such as marbles, coins, linking cubes, base ten blocks, ball bearings, unused erasers, or other small counters. For practical reasons, the unit should have a reasonable amount of mass—not too much or too little. For example, if ping pong balls were used, you would need a significant number of them to measure the mass of even a light object, such as an apple, making them an impractical unit. A unit with too much mass, such as a book, would not allow for much precision in measuring mass.

Measuring Mass with Different Units

Work with nonstandard units provides an opportunity for students to explore the concept that using a bigger unit to measure mass results in a smaller number of units. It is important for students to have opportunities to balance a particular object with several different types of units and to

I think I would need about 10 square pattern blocks to balance this apple.

record the results each time. Work with different units also helps students develop personal referents that they can use to estimate masses.

| I measured the tennis ball |||
What I Used	My Guess	How Many?
pennies	15	21

ACTIVITY 16.9

Provide various small units for measuring mass, such as square pattern blocks, pennies, linking cubes, marbles, etc. Have students use some different units to estimate and measure the mass of a small ball. They can record the results on a chart like the one to the left.

Measuring Different Items with the Same Unit

It is also important for students to have opportunities to balance different items against a common unit. For example, students could use linking cubes to balance a series of small toys. Using the same nonstandard unit for each item allows students to compare masses to see which item has a greater mass, and also to determine the amount of difference.

Activities that provide a context for measuring different items with the same unit might include hunting for items with a particular mass, such as "10 marbles," or putting a series of objects in order according to mass.

Estimating Mass with Nonstandard Units

In the definition/comparison stage, estimating was simply used to determine which of two objects had more mass. Now students are able to estimate how many units it might take to balance a particular object. As with other types of measurement, it helps students to compare unknown amounts with amounts they know. For example, a student at this stage might determine that it takes 10 linking cubes to balance a small object, and then estimate how many linking cubes it would take to balance a larger one.

Estimating the mass of an object is more difficult than estimating other measures because there is no direct relationship between the object's size and its mass. To estimate size (length, area, capacity, or volume), students simply need to visualize how many units will fit along or inside what is being measured. With mass, students need to think about how the unit feels. It is not an easy task to feel one unit and imagine what two units, or ten units, might feel like.

Mass: The Standard Unit Stage

Introducing Standard Units of Mass

The first standard unit of mass that students usually encounter is the kilogram. Students should be given the opportunity to make a kilogram mass of their own. Students might, for example, fill a plastic container with sand until it exactly balances a 1 kg mass on a pan balance.

Metric Units of Mass

KILOGRAMS (kg)	GRAMS (g)

Defining a Kilogram

One *kilogram* is a mass equal to the mass of 1 dm³ of water at 4 °C.

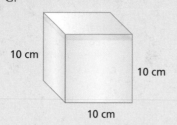

10 cm

10 cm

10 cm

Defining a Gram

A *gram* is $\frac{1}{1000}$ or 0.001 of a kilogram.

Kilogram Referents

A kilogram is the mass of 1 L of water or milk.

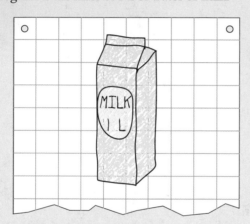

Gram Referents

A *gram* is the mass of 1 mL of water, or the mass of a Centicube (or a unit cube from some sets of base ten blocks). A raisin or paper clip is another useful referent for 1 g.

Because a gram is so small, students should also have referents that represent multiple units, such as a wooden pattern-block square for 5 g and a wooden base-10 rod for 10 g.

Measuring with Kilograms

A pan balance is the preferred tool for measuring mass. However, since classroom pan balances seldom have the capacity to measure beyond 1 or 2 kg, it is sometimes necessary to use a scale to measure larger masses in kilograms. Scale measures may differ slightly from mass measurements depending on where, in relation to sea level, the scale is being used. (At sea level, weight and mass are about the same.) Many scales have a feature that allows users to adjust for differences in altitude.

Measuring with Grams

Due to the small size of a gram, students typically work with pan balances that have masses of 5 g, 10 g, 20 g, 50 g, and 100 g. However, there are some sets that include 1 g, 2 g, 100 g, 200 g, and 500 g masses.

There are other units of mass that students eventually need to understand, but that cannot be measured with a classroom pan balance. *Milligrams* are thousandths of a gram, and are used to measure objects with very little mass. *Tonnes*, on the other hand, are used to measure objects with a lot of mass. One tonne is 1000 kg. While students need not measure with these units, they should be able to say whether milligrams, grams, kilograms, or tonnes would be appropriate in a particular situation. Grams, for example, would be the best unit to use to measure the mass of raisins in a package, while tonnes would be better for measuring the mass of a truck.

There are, of course, other metric units of mass, such as centigrams, decigrams, and hectograms, but these are rarely used in everyday life.

Tools for Measuring Mass in Standard Units

While a pan balance is the tool students should use most often to measure mass, a bathroom scale is also useful, especially when the object's mass exceeds what the pan balance can accommodate. For example, a student could determine the mass of a book by reading his own mass on a scale, first without the book, and then again while holding it. The mass of the book represents the difference between the two readings.

Note that, for younger students, a bathroom scale is a less appropriate tool because it simply involves reading a number, while the pan balance makes it possible to actually see the mass that balances a particular object.

ACTIVITY 16.10

Ask students to try one of these activities:

- Compare the masses of different types of balls, such as baseballs, ping pong balls, etc. Are balls that are bigger usually heavier?

- What is the mass of your backpack? Is it safe for you to carry that much?

- Check 3 products on your pantry shelf. Are the masses reported on the packages accurate?

- How much would 1 kg of pennies be worth? What about 1 kg of quarters?

- If you had to pay for a meal based on your mass, would a fee of 10¢ per kilogram be a good deal?

Common Errors and Misconceptions

Capacity, Volume, and Mass: Common Errors, Misconceptions, and Strategies

COMMON ERROR OR MISCONCEPTION	SUGGESTED STRATEGIES
Judging Capacity by Height Alone Many children at the definition/comparison stage believe that a container that is taller will also have a greater **capacity**, or that if two containers are the same height, they must hold the same amount.	Students need opportunities to compare objects of varying heights and widths in order to learn that a container that is large in one way can be small in another. A good time to do this is when students are comparing two containers, or putting several containers in order according to their capacity. For example, students could be asked to compare a shorter object that holds more (e.g., a wide bowl) with a taller object that holds less (e.g., a plastic glass), or to compare several containers that are about the same height, but that vary in terms of base shape or width, or that have curved sides.
Measuring Capacity Inconsistently When measuring **capacity**, some students do not fill the measuring tool in a consistent way. As well, they sometimes switch to partial units when a container is nearly full.  Measurement units are meaningful only when they are uniform.	Students may need to be reminded that units are useful only if they are uniform. If you know a bottle holds 6 spoonfuls of sand, you can compare this bottle with another only if you know how big the spoons were, and how full they were. To demonstrate, use two transparent containers. Show what happens when you pour 5 full scoops of water into one, and 5 partial scoops of water into the other. Elicit the importance of measuring each scoop of water in the same way. To help students learn to measure with uniform units, encourage them to fill spoons or scoops to the top, and to level them off if necessary.

(continued)

COMMON ERROR OR MISCONCEPTION	SUGGESTED STRATEGIES

Assuming a Longer Object Has More Volume

Some students will use the length of an object as the only basis for extrapolating other measures. For example, a student might decide that the green prism shown here has more **volume** than the red one because the green prism is longer.

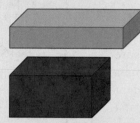

Length is only one of the factors that determine the volume of a shape.

Emphasize that volume tells how much space an object takes up, or how many units it would take to create a model of the object. In this case, students might reconstruct each prism with centimetre cubes, making it readily apparent that it takes more cubes to build the red prism than the green one.

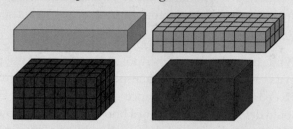

Reconstructing these prisms with cubes shows that the red prism has the greater volume.

Learning to Conserve Volume

Some younger students believe that if you move cubes around in a cube structure, the volume of the structure will change. This misconception becomes apparent when the same blocks are used to build a second structure and the student recounts the cubes.

Students develop their ability to conserve volume through experience. To move beyond this misconception, they will need to do some activities that involve building a cube structure, counting the cubes to determine its volume, and then rearranging the cubes and counting them again. Through discussion, the teacher can help students recognize that the number of cubes does not change unless cubes are added or removed.

Converting Cubic Metres to Cubic Centimetres

Students, and even many adults, are surprised when they realize that 1 m³ is not the same **volume** as 100 cm³. People tend to assume that since there are 100 cm in 1 m, there must also be 100 cm³ in 1 m³.

To determine the number of cubic centimetres in a cubic metre, model a cubic metre with edges made of newspaper rolls and ask students to begin covering the bottom of the metre cube with centimetre cubes. They should realize quite quickly that 100 cm³ is nowhere near enough to fill the whole cube. This is because each edge of the cube is 100 cm, so there are actually 100 layers with 100 rows of 100 in each layer, or 1 million cubes altogether.

Using Inconsistent Units in Volume Calculations

Some students will not attend to the fact that one side of this prism is measured in metres, while the other two sides are measured in centimetres. These students are likely to calculate the **volume** of the prism by multiplying $1 \times 30 \times 50$ and reporting the result as 1500 cm³ or 1500 m³.

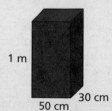

1 m

30 cm

50 cm

The volume of this prism can be calculated in either cubic metres or cubic centimetres, but the units cannot be combined.

To remind students what they are calculating, a teacher might ask,

- How many centimetre cubes will it take to model the bottom layer of the prism? (1500)

- How many layers this size would it take to fill in the entire prism? (100)

- How many cubes is that altogether? ($1500 \times 100 = 150\,000$ cubes in all)

COMMON ERROR OR MISCONCEPTION	SUGGESTED STRATEGIES
Assuming a Larger Object Has More Mass Many students believe that if one object is larger (or longer) than another, then it must also have more **mass**.	To help a child learn that it is possible for an object that is large in one way to be small in another, provide opportunities to compare a small heavy object (e.g., a stone) with a larger object that is lighter (e.g., an empty can). 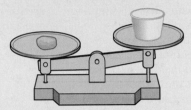 Sometimes the small object is heavier than the large one.
Learning to Conserve Mass Some younger students believe that if you break an object into parts, its **mass** will change. 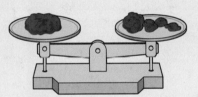 Breaking an object into parts does not change its mass.	An interesting experiment to do with younger students involves two identical balls of modelling clay. Show students that the balls balance each other, and then break one ball up into several smaller balls. Ask, "If I put this ball on one side of the pan balance and these smaller balls on the other side, what do you think will happen?" Use the pan balance to demonstrate that breaking the ball into parts did not change its mass. Experiments like this can help students develop the ability to conserve mass.
Misinterpreting Standard Masses Students who are just beginning to use standard masses may not realize that each **mass** represents different amounts. For example, a student may balance an object with a 20-g mass and a 10-g mass, and then record the mass as 2 g because 2 masses were used. 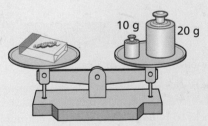 10 g 20 g The crayons have a mass of 30 g, not 2 g.	Initially, students could use a consistent unit, such as the 5-g mass, for determining mass. Later, when they are more comfortable with standard masses, they can add more sizes. Using a set of masses with a different colour for each size may help students keep track of the values. Different colours will also make it easier for students to record and label the masses they used to solve a particular problem.

Appropriate Manipulatives

Capacity, Volume, and Mass: Examples of Manipulatives

MEASURING CUPS, SPOONS, AND SCOOPS

EXAMPLES

When students are learning to measure **capacity**, it is useful to have on hand some transparent and opaque measuring cups, scoops, and spoons. These can be used to measure in nonstandard units until students are ready to measure in litres and millilitres. Students will also need some pourable material, such as sand or coloured water, to use with these measuring tools. (See *How Concepts of Capacity Can Be Introduced* on page 416.)

Cups, spoons, and scoops can be used as tools for measuring with nonstandard units.

"If half of it is 6 scoops, then it must hold 12 scoops."

Standard measuring tools can be used for classroom cooking activities. Commercial sets of containers are also useful for older students.

Play Dough	
500 mL flour	
125 mL salt	
250 mL water	
60 mL cream of tartar	

"I'll need a 250-mL measuring cup and a 15-mL measuring spoon."

VARIOUS CONTAINERS AND BOXES

EXAMPLES

Containers and boxes of varying sizes and shapes are versatile materials for measuring. Students can measure their **capacity**, **mass**, **and/or volume**, and can also use smaller containers as units for measuring larger ones.

Students can measure the capacity of containers with different sizes and shapes.

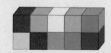

"This bowl holds 10 yogurt cups of popcorn."

A small box can be used as a unit for measuring the volume of a larger box.

"I wonder how many small boxes I would need to make this big box."

LINKING CUBES

EXAMPLE

Linking cubes can be used as units for measuring **capacity or mass**, or students can use them to explore the **volumes** of rectangular prisms. (See *Volume: The Nonstandard Unit Stage* on page 423.)

Students could use cubes to build different rectangular prisms with a given volume.

"Both prisms have a volume of 10 cubes."

BLOCKS

EXAMPLE

Although you most often use rectangular prisms for measuring **volume**, any uniform blocks that pack (combine to fill space without gaps or overlap) work just as well. Examples include building blocks and pattern blocks.

Students can stack pattern blocks to build prisms, and then count blocks to determine their volume. This experience will help them later when they are introduced to the formula for calculating the volume of a prism or cylinder: *Volume = Area of base × height.*

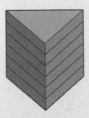

"This triangle-based prism has a volume of 6 triangle blocks."

GEOMETRIC SOLIDS

Commercial geometric solids can be measured in order to determine their **volume** and **mass**.

EXAMPLE

Sets of solids contain several different types of prisms. Students can calculate their volumes by measuring the dimensions, and then multiplying the base area by the height. Students can also use nonstandard or standard units to determine and compare the masses of solids in nonstandard units or in grams.

"This pyramid has a mass of 15 pennies."

CENTICUBES

Centicubes are a commercial brand of linking cubes with a side length of 1 cm and a **volume** of 1 cm³. These cubes have a **mass** of 1 g and, if they were empty, would have a **capacity** of 1 mL. Thus, Centicubes can be excellent referents for **volume**, **mass**, and **capacity**.

There are also other centimetre cubes available, including base ten unit cubes, but they do not always link and their mass is not always 1 g.

EXAMPLE

A student who has built a prism out of Centicubes can simply count the cubes to determine its volume or mass. Thus, working with Centicubes can help students move from the nonstandard unit stage to the standard unit stage with regard to these measures.

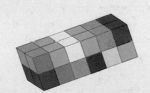

"This prism has a volume of 24 cm³ and a mass of 24 g."

BASE TEN BLOCKS

The basic unit in a set of base ten blocks is a cubic centimetre, so these blocks are good tools for measuring **volume** and **capacity**. Some sets can also be used to measure **mass** (if the unit cube has a mass of 1 g).

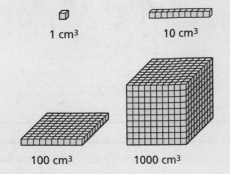

1 cm³ 10 cm³

100 cm³ 1000 cm³

EXAMPLE

A student could measure the **volume** of a box by making a model with base ten blocks.

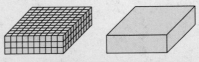

"It took 3 flats and 3 rods to build the model of the box, so it has a volume of 330 cm³."

(continued)

RULERS, METRE STICKS, AND TAPE MEASURES

Rulers, metre sticks, and tape measures can be used to measure lengths in order to make **volume** calculations with formulas. (See *Formulas for Measuring Volume* on page 427.)

EXAMPLE

A student can use a ruler to measure the edges of a rectangular prism, and then apply the formula *Volume = Area of base ×* *height*.

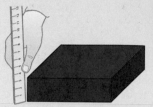

"Once I know the height, I can multiply it by the area of the bottom of the box to figure out the volume."

PAN BALANCES

Student-made or commercial pan balances can be used to compare **masses** or to measure masses with nonstandard or standard masses. (See *How Concepts of Mass Can Be Introduced* on page 430.)

EXAMPLE

Students could use standard masses on a pan balance to find something that has a mass of about 120 g.

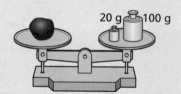

"The plum has a mass of 120 g."

BATHROOM SCALES

Scales with kilogram measures can be used to determine the weight of objects that are too large to fit on a pan balance. As noted earlier, weight diverges from mass as the scale's location diverges from sea level. (Many scales have a feature that compensates for this.)

EXAMPLE

To calculate the weight of a heavy box, a student can use a bathroom scale to determine his or her own weight, with and without the box, and subtract to find the difference.

"The scale went from 41 kg to 44 kg, so the box I'm holding must be 3 kg."

Measuring Time, Temperature, and Angle

Time and temperature are measurement topics that play important roles in students' everyday lives. From very early on, children are aware that the temperature influences what they wear, that there are things they do at certain times of the day, week, and year, and that some events take longer than others.

How Concepts of Time Can Be Introduced

Time can be represented using a linear model. For example, a student can sequence pictures of events by arranging them in a line and, to calculate elapsed time, he or she can visualize a timeline (see *Measuring and Calculating Elapsed Time* on page 447). Although time is often referred to as cyclical and can be modelled that way, time itself is actually linear. It is simply our descriptions of time—names of the hours in a day, names of the days of the weeks, names of the months and seasons, etc.—that cycle.

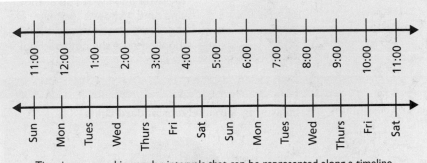

Time is measured in regular intervals that can be represented along a timeline.

Although timelines are linear, they can be cut out and folded into a circle to show the cyclical nature of the names we use for hours and days. A "time circle" is a good tool to use for calculating elapsed time.

Time, as a measurement, is about duration, or how long an event takes from beginning to end. To measure duration, students not only need to develop a personal understanding of how long time units last; they also need to learn to use time measurement tools such as clocks and calendars. Note that reading clocks or telling time has little to do with actually measuring time, except in circumstances where you must read a clock at the beginning and end of an event to figure out its duration.

Ideas about time can be introduced through the same three stages as other measurement concepts—definition/comparison, nonstandard unit, and standard unit.

DEFINITION/COMPARISON

Students focus on sequencing familiar events and on comparing durations by starting two events simultaneously and comparing the end times.

Sequencing Events

"After I wake up, I eat breakfast, and then I walk to school."

Comparing Durations

"My sister and I woke up at the same time. I know it took her longer to get ready and walk to school because she got to school after me."

NONSTANDARD UNITS

Students use tools such as hourglasses or pendulums to measure time in nonstandard units.

Measuring Time in Nonstandard Units

"My mom timed me while I got dressed. She turned the egg timer over 4 times from when I started till when I was done."

STANDARD UNITS

Students learn to measure time in minutes, hours, and seconds.

Reading a Stopwatch

"It took me 1 hour and 13 minutes to get ready and walk to school."

Calculating Elapsed Time

Woke up   Arrived at school

"It took me 1 hour and 13 minutes to get ready and walk to school."

Time: The Definition/Comparison Stage

At the definition/comparison stage, students focus on the sequencing of events. These students often enjoy activities where they draw or organize a sequence of pictures to tell a story. The story might be about what happens before and after school, or after school and before supper. Students might also tell oral stories about what happened first, then next, then next, etc.

At this stage, students also compare the durations of two events to see which takes longer. Without units, the only way to compare durations is to start both events simultaneously and wait to see which one keeps going when the other is over. Many students will see the parallel to the measurement of length; the longer event extends farther than the shorter one.

Students in the definition/comparison stage are building vocabulary they can use to talk about time. They might tell what happened *first*, *last*, *next*, *before*, or *after*, or they might identify one event as *longer*, *shorter*, *faster*, or *slower* than another.

Time: The Nonstandard Unit Stage

Although students in the early grades are introduced to standard units such as hours and minutes, because these are used in everyday life, it still benefits them to work with nonstandard units to measure time duration before they begin using standard units to measure time. A broad experience with measuring in different ways will encourage students to build a better understanding of what it really means to measure time.

There are many nonstandard tools that students can use to measure duration, or elapsed time, including sand timers of various sizes, pendulums, and metronomes. For example, a student could use the number of pendulum swings to measure how long it takes someone to walk down the hall and back.

An advantage of many of the tools used for measuring time in nonstandard units is that they can be adjusted to measure time in a wide variety of unit sizes. Traditional metronomes, for example, can be reset for different speeds by adjusting the position of the weight. Pendulums can be adjusted by using longer or shorter strings, and sand clocks can be made with varying amounts of sand and different dimensions. Making adjustments like these helps students build a better understanding of the factors that influence how the size of the unit affects the resulting measurement.

Appropriate Nonstandard Units for Time

As with all other types of measurement, the key notion behind nonstandard units for measuring time is that the units must be uniform and appropriate. When using tools for measuring in nonstandard units, it is important for students to know that the tools must be used consistently to ensure uniformity. Very young children can use units such as claps or counting to measure time; however, students will eventually realize that it is not possible to ensure uniformity with units that vary from person to person. Tools such as metronomes, sand timers, and pendulums provide these uniform units. Shorter units are used to measure short durations or to increase precision, while longer units are used to measure longer durations.

Ask students to estimate how many times they can do each action in the time it takes to empty a sand timer. They check by doing the action:

- how many steps they can take
- how many jumping jacks they can do
- how many times they can write their names

etc.

Action	My estimate	My result
Steps	50	90
Jumping jacks		

Estimating Time with Nonstandard Units

It is valuable for students to learn to estimate time measurements, as well as to measure them. In order to learn to estimate, students require many opportunities to predict and check how many time units are necessary to accomplish a variety of tasks. As with other measurements, they can use activities with known durations as referents for estimating. For example, students might learn that a pendulum swings 7 times while they write their first name. Students could then use this information to estimate how many times the pendulum will swing as they write their full name or as they copy a sentence from the board.

A possible estimation activity is described in **Activity 16.11**.

Time: The Standard Unit Stage

The Système International (SI) standard metric unit of time is the second, but minutes and hours are usually introduced first because students use them more often in everyday life. Standard units of time should always be introduced in a way that relates them to students' own experiences, since personal experiences will give students a sense of what the units mean and help them establish referents they can use to estimate duration.

Standard Units of Time

MINUTES (min)

Defining a Minute

A *minute* is equal to 60 seconds. It is also $\frac{1}{60}$ of an hour.

Minute Referents

To help students get a feel for one minute, a teacher might use an estimating activity. First, students watch as the teacher times 1 minute. Then they put their heads down, the teacher tells them to start timing, and they raise their hands when they think 1 minute is over.

Other activities that will help students establish personal referents include problems such as the following:

- How many times can you write your name in 1 minute?
- How many times can you clap your hands in 1 minute?
- How high can you count in 1 minute?
- How far can you go saying the letters of the alphabet in 1 minute?

HOURS (h)

Defining an Hour

An *hour* is equal to 60 minutes.

Hour Referents

To help students establish personal referents for 1 hour, a teacher might pose problems such as the following:

- What takes you about 1 hour to do?
- How far could you walk in 1 hour?

Familiar referents for 1 hour might include the amount of time students spend in math class, the length of a favourite TV show, or how long they have for lunch and recess.

SECONDS (s)

Defining a Second

A *second* is the basic SI metric unit of time (see page 369).

Second Referents

To help students establish personal referents for seconds, a teacher might pose problems such as the following:

- What is something that takes about 1 second to do?
- What is something that takes about 10 seconds to do?
- How many seconds does it take you to walk 100 m? to run 100 m?

There are also other standard units that are used to measure longer spans of time. These include days, weeks, months, years, decades (10 years), centuries (100 years), and millennia (1000 years).

Standard Tools for Measuring Time

Students need to learn to tell time on both analog and digital clocks. The world is increasingly digital, but there are still many analog clocks in use. In addition, understanding analog time helps students make sense of common time-related terms. The analog clock makes it apparent why 9:15 can also be read as "a quarter past 9," as the minute hand has literally moved a quarter of the way around the clock. For a student to relate to 9:15 on a digital clock as a quarter past the hour, he or she would have to employ a considerable amount of number sense, realizing that 15 minutes is $\frac{1}{4}$ of 60 minutes.

Students need to work with analog clocks to develop basic concepts about reading clocks and telling time.

Most students are readily able to read the time on a digital clock, but teachers need to be aware that, without an understanding of clock time, the times may not have much meaning for students. For example, a student might see 7:54 and read "seven fifty-four" without recognizing that this means that it is almost 8:00.

For students to make sense of digital times, they need to understand that

- there are 24 hours in a day and they are numbered from 1 a.m. to 12 noon, and again from 1 p.m. to 12 midnight (24-hour time is introduced later)
- there are 60 minutes in 1 hour

Initially students learn that there are two hands on an analog clock—the minute hand and the hour hand—and that the minute hand is longer. Some teachers have students make their own paper-plate clocks with the hands labelled. (For teacher modelling, a geared clock is more suitable because it shows the movement of the hour hand as well as the movement of the minute hand.) Students usually have little difficulty telling time to the hour with an analog clock. Times that fall between the hours are more challenging until students have learned more about how these clocks work.

What Students Need to Know about Analog Clocks

MOVEMENT OF THE HANDS

As the minute hand travels around the clock during each hour, the hour hand moves much more slowly from one number to the next. For "in-between" times, the hour hand does not point directly at the number you need to say.

At 6:25, the hour hand does not point to the 6.

CLOCK NUMBERS AND MINUTES

The numbers on a clock (1, 2, ..., 12) correspond to the hours, not to the minutes. For example, when the minute hand points to the 1, you say the time is "5 after" not "1 after."

The ability to interpret the number of minutes after the hour depends on students' comfort with counting by 5s.

DIFFERENT MEANINGS FOR DIFFERENT HANDS

We say different words when different hands point to the same number on the clock. For example, if the hour hand points to the 6, we say *six*, but if the minute hand points to the 6, we say *thirty*. As a result, students need to be very attentive to the hand lengths as well as the numbers.

6:00

12:30

TIMES WITH MORE THAN ONE NAME

If the time falls more than halfway through the hour, we can read it as a number of minutes after one hour, or as a number of minutes before the next.

We can read this time as "3:40" or as "20 to 4."

ACTIVITY 16.12

Clock Hands

Ask students what time it might be if

- the minute hand is pointed to a spot between 3 and 4
- the hour hand is pointed to a spot between 1 and 2
- the hour hand and minute hand are both pointed directly at numbers

Because of these difficulties, teachers usually sequence work with analog time so students learn to tell time to the hour, then to the half hour, the quarter hour, to the nearest 5 minutes, and finally to the nearest minute. If a clock also has a second hand, telling time to the minute can be especially challenging because students need to observe the position of the second hand as well as the minute and hour hands.

Teachers should be aware that setting the time on a digital or analog clock is a different skill from simply reading the time. Most curriculum expectations/outcomes are about reading clocks, so this should be the focus of classroom activities. However, it is a useful life skill to be able to set a watch or clock. For some students, this will come later. Many interesting problems can be set related to the position of hands on a clock.

A.M. and P.M.

Time is usually described in ordinary speech using the 12-hour clock, in which the hours cycle from 1:00 in the morning until 12:00 noon, and then repeat the cycle from 1:00 in the afternoon until midnight. Since having two times with the same name in a single day has the potential to be confusing, you can specify whether you mean morning or evening by using the acronyms "a.m." and "p.m." These stand for the Latin words *ante meridiem* and *post meridiem*, which mean "before noon" and "after noon," respectively. A good way to introduce the concept of a.m. and p.m. is to use a full-day timeline.

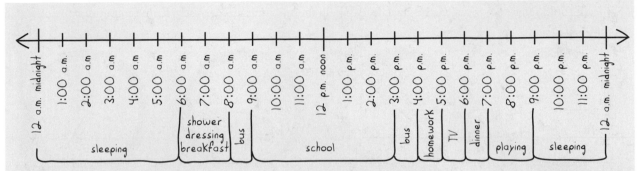

A full-day timeline can help students to become familiar with and to use a.m. and p.m. notation correctly. It can also help students who confuse 12 a.m. with 12 p.m.

24-Hour Time

Eventually, it is important for students to learn about the 24-hour time system, since they will encounter it in everyday life, particularly when they travel. Airports often post times using the 24-hour clock, and students may find that their own watches or computer clocks offer them the option of using 24-hour time. The convention for reporting times in the 24-hour system is to use 4 digits, so times that occur before noon are usually reported with a 0, for example, 04:35 for 4:35 a.m.

The 24-hour clock is used because it eliminates ambiguity—there is only one 11:23 in the day, not two. This can help to ensure that passengers arrive for a plane at the right time, but people often find it convenient to convert 24-hour times that occur after noon to more familiar 12-hour times. The conversion process is simple once students understand that they can simply subtract 12 hours—16:20 is the same as 4:20 p.m.

Measuring and Calculating Elapsed Time

Sometimes students measure elapsed time using tools such as stopwatches. This is usually when the duration is short. For longer durations, it is often necessary to determine the duration of an event from two reported times. For example, a student who arrived at a game at 6:45 and left at 8:25 might want to find out how much time he or she spent at the game. There are a number of approaches for calculating elapsed time.

Ways to Calculate Elapsed Time—from 6:45 to 8:25

USING A TIMELINE

Students could sketch or visualize a timeline as an aid in helping them "count up" (or back) from one time to the other.

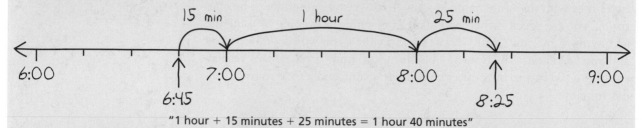

"1 hour + 15 minutes + 25 minutes = 1 hour 40 minutes"

USING A CLOCK FACE

Students could refer to or visualize the clock face to help them "count up" (or back) from one time to the other.

Counting Up

| 6:45 | 7:45 | 8:15 | 8:25 |

"6:45 to 7:45 is 1 h. 7:45 to 8:15 is half an h. 8:15 to 8:25 is 10 min. That's 1 h and 30, ..., 40 min."

Counting Back

| 6:45 | 8:45 | 8:25 |

"6:45 to 8:45 is 2 h. 8:45 back to 8:25 is 20 min. 2 h subtract 20 min is 1 h and 40 min."

ACTIVITY 16.13

You might choose to introduce students to the notion of time zones. It is interesting to try to measure elapsed time when time zones are crossed. For example, you might ask what time a plane will land if a 1.5-hour flight from Toronto to Winnipeg leaves Toronto at 8:10 a.m.

How Concepts of Temperature Can Be Introduced

Temperature is usually considered linear because of the tool used most often to measure it—the linear analog thermometer (see next page).

Temperature measurement is usually taught quite differently than other types of measurement. Rather than introducing work with temperature through the three stages that have been discussed for each of the other measurements, teachers usually only work through the definition/comparison

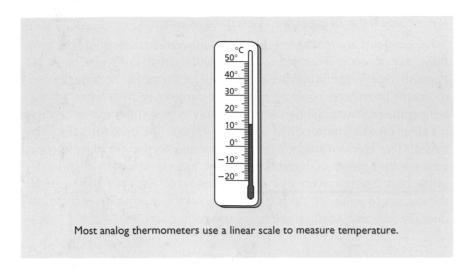

Most analog thermometers use a linear scale to measure temperature.

stage and the standard unit stage (because it would be difficult to create nonstandard units). Those stages can be handled quite efficiently in the context of work students do in other subject areas, especially science. It can be included in work with the calendar and the seasons as well.

How Concepts of Temperature Can Be Introduced

DEFINITION/COMPARISON	USING STANDARD UNITS
Students talk about how hot (or cold) something feels by making reference to personal experiences such as outdoor temperatures or familiar foods.	Students learn to use a typical thermometer and are introduced to degrees Celsius, although they rarely have a sense of what a degree is. However, they do come to recognize that one item is warmer than another if the line of colour inside the thermometer reaches farther along the number line.

"The water in the red glass is warm, like bathwater. The other water is cold, like juice out of the fridge."

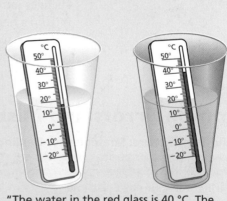

"The water in the red glass is 40 °C. The other water is much colder—it's 15 °C."

Interpreting Negative Temperatures

When students are measuring the daily temperature throughout the year, they may sometimes encounter temperatures that are less than 0 °C. Because these temperatures are meaningful for them, and because the thermometer provides a concrete model for comparing these with warmer temperatures, young children are often ready to read and compare negative numbers on a thermometer long before integers have been formally introduced. The children might begin by referring to these temperatures in terms of the number of degrees below zero. For example, a cold winter day might have a temperature of "5 degrees below 0." This is a good time for the teacher to point out the negative signs on the thermometer and introduce the idea that another way to say this is "negative 5 °C."

Estimating Temperatures

To estimate temperatures in degrees Celsius, students need to develop personal referents for certain benchmark temperatures. They should know that

- it is cold enough to freeze water when the temperature reaches 0 °C
- it is a nice spring day if the temperature is 20 °C
- a person's body temperature is about 37 °C
- water boils at 100 °C

These referents can then be used as points of comparison for other temperatures. For example:

- "The hot water from the tap feels warmer than my body temperature but it's certainly not hot enough to boil, so it must be between 37 °C and 100 °C."
- "There was ice on the puddle in the morning so the temperature must have dropped below 0 °C last night."

Measuring and Calculating Temperature Change

Students might use a vertical number line, which relates directly to a thermometer scale, to measure temperature change. Many students find changes in temperature particularly difficult to interpret when the change is from a negative temperature to a positive one. For example, you can use a vertical number line to show that if the temperature is -3 °C in the morning and $+7$ °C in the afternoon, the temperature has increased by $3 + 7 = 10$ degrees.

Common Errors and Misconceptions

Time and Temperature: Strategies for Dealing with Common Errors and Misconceptions

COMMON ERROR OR MISCONCEPTION	SUGGESTED STRATEGY
Comparing Durations by End Time Some young children look at end times to compare the duration of events, but do not consider the start times. For example, they say that something took more time because it ended at 8:30 instead of 8:00.	To help students recognize that elapsed time measures the length of time from start to end, a teacher might show two wind-up toys and ask students to predict which will run longer. The teacher could then start one toy, wait for a noticeable amount of time, and then start the other. Many students will recognize that this is not a fair test unless the toys are started at the same time. The teacher could then ask a student to help by winding one of the toys so both can be started at the same time.

COMMON ERROR OR MISCONCEPTION	SUGGESTED STRATEGY

Misusing a Sand Timer

When students measure time with a sand timer, some do not wait for the timer to empty completely before turning it over, while others wait too long.

Ask students to watch a sand timer as you time an event and to raise their hands when it is time to turn it over. Afterwards, discuss what would have happened if you had turned the timer too soon (the event would have been measured with a greater number of units), or if you had forgotten to turn the timer when the sand stopped (the event would have been measured with a fewer number of units). Remind students that whenever they measure, it is important to use units that are all the same size. Turning a sand timer at the moment when the sand runs out ensures that the time units will all be the same.

A sand timer being turned too early

Locating the Hour Hand

Students do not position the hour hand on a clock to reflect the number of minutes after the hour.

Students need to discuss how the hour hand moves over the course of each hour. Some teachers use a clock with only an hour hand, showing students how it is possible to estimate the amount of the hour that has passed by looking at just the hour hand.

Incorrect hour-hand position for 7:45

about 4:00   about 4:30   about 4:55

Misinterpreting Minutes on a Clock Face

Students who are learning to tell time on an analog clock may have trouble reading the number of minutes before or after the hour.

This happens because the numbers on a clock directly identify the hour, but the minutes have to be determined by counting by 5s.

Students need to know that there are 60 minutes in one hour, and they need lots of practice reading clocks in the context of everyday classroom activities, not just during math class. For example, a teacher might ask, "What time is it now? How many minutes do we have for tidying up before recess starts?" Teachers must explicitly model how they tell time by talking out loud and pointing to the clock. For example, a teacher might say, "The hour hand is pointing to just past the 1—that means it's just after 1 o'clock. The minute hand is pointing here—that's 5, 10, 15 minutes after the hour. It's 15 minutes after 1."

Some analog clocks and watches have small minute numbers around the edge of the clock face. If the classroom clock does not have these numbers, a teacher could attach sticky notes (5, 10, 15, etc.) around the circumference of the clock face.

1:15

"It's 3 after 1."

(continued)

COMMON ERROR OR MISCONCEPTION	SUGGESTED STRATEGY
Number of Seconds in an Hour Students think that there are 60 seconds in an hour.	This may happen because there are 60 seconds in 1 minute and 60 minutes in 1 hour, so students mistakenly assume that there are always 60 smaller time units in a larger one. If a student responds this way, ask the student to suggest an event that might take about an hour, such as a TV program. Then, with the student, watch a second hand on a clock complete 60 seconds. Ask, • That was 60 s. Was that the same as an hour? • If it wasn't an hour, then what was it? (minute) Through discussion, help the student see that there are 60 seconds in 1 minute, and 60 groups of 60 seconds, or 3600 seconds, in 1 hour.
Confusing 12 a.m. and 12 p.m. Many people confuse 12 a.m. and 12 p.m., thinking that because a.m. means morning, 12 a.m. must be noon.	A timeline is a good tool for helping students remember that, by convention, 12 a.m. represents midnight and 12 p.m. represents noon. (See *A.M. and P.M.* on page 447.)
Interpreting a 24-Hour Clock To convert a 24-hour clock time such as 16:20 to a 12-hour equivalent, students will often subtract 10 hours rather than 12 hours because of their familiarity with the place value system for numbers.  16:20 "16:20 must mean 6:20 p.m."	Make a timeline that shows the 24-hour times aligned with their 12-hour equivalents. Then have students align equivalent times to see that, beginning after noon, there is always a difference of 12 hours between 24-hour times and their 12-hour equivalents. 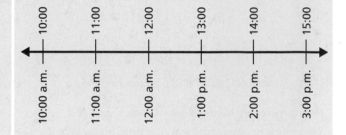
Misinterpreting Times Shown with Decimals Although people usually do not use decimals with times, students might encounter times written this way, for example, 7.5 hours. A student might think that this means 7 hours and 5 minutes.	Use a clock face to show the decimal part of the hour. Remind students that 0.5 means 5 tenths, or half, so 7.5 hours means 7 hours and another half hour, or 7 hours and 30 minutes.
Calculating Elapsed Time across the Hour Students sometimes have difficulty calculating elapsed times that bridge from one hour to the next. For example, one student might mistakenly determine that an event lasting from 7:25 p.m. until 8:15 p.m. lasts 1 hour and 10 minutes (since 8 h − 7 h = 1 h and 25 min − 15 min = 10 min), while another student might say it lasts 1 hour and 50 minutes (because there are 50 minutes from 25 after until a quarter after, and 1 hour from 7 till 8).	Teachers can use a geared clock or a time line to help students visualize how much time actually passes.  "35 minutes to 8 o'clock and another 15 minutes to 8:15 is 50 minutes."

COMMON ERROR OR MISCONCEPTION	SUGGESTED STRATEGY
Reading Temperatures between Scale Numbers Most students find it easier to read temperatures that are labelled on the scale, such as 10 °C or 20 °C, than temperatures that fall between scale numbers, such as 37 °C.  "The temperature is 30.7 °C.	Provide blackline master thermometers with every 10 °C labelled, and with space for students to label smaller scale marks in between in 1° increments. Discuss what the unlabelled scale marks mean and have the students label them. Then ask students to point to where given temperatures would be on the thermometer. For example, 35 °C would be halfway between 30 °C and 40 °C, but 30.5 °C would be halfway between 30 °C and 31 °C.
Misreading Negative Temperatures When reading negative temperatures, students may incorrectly interpret temperatures that fall between the labelled increments. 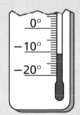 "It's right below −10 °C so it's −9 °C."	In the early grades (before integer number lines have been introduced), any work with negative temperatures should be very informal, and should be directly related to a meaningful context, such as the outdoor temperature. At this stage, students may find it useful to refer to negative temperatures in terms of the number of degrees "below 0." If they count down from 0, they will see that the temperature shown at left is actually 11 degrees below 0, not 9. Once integers have been introduced, some students may be used to seeing negative numbers on a horizontal number line (rather than on the vertical number line represented by a typical thermometer). These students may find it easier to compare temperatures if they turn the thermometer on its side.

Appropriate Manipulatives

Time and Temperature: Examples of Manipulatives

NONSTANDARD TIMERS	EXAMPLE	
Tools such as sand timers, pendulums, and metronomes are useful for measuring time in uniform nonstandard units. These tools can be adjusted so the units are longer or shorter, depending on what is being measured.	The weight on a metronome can be adjusted to create a variety of different units for measuring duration. For example, students might use a longer unit to measure how long it takes to eat a snack. A shorter unit could be used to measure how long it takes to walk from the front of the room to the back.	

A metronome

(continued)

KITCHEN TIMERS

Kitchen timers are useful for working with minutes because they can be set to go off at the end of a given time period.

EXAMPLE

Kitchen timers are especially useful for estimating activities and for developing personal referents for short periods of time. (See *Minute Referents* on page 444.) For example, students can establish personal referents for 1 minute by finding out how many steps they can take in 1 minute, or how many times they can repeat the alphabet in 1 minute.

A kitchen timer

DIGITAL AND ANALOG CLOCKS

Digital and analog clocks, including an alarm clock, can be used to provide contexts for solving problems, to provide practice with telling time, and to give students a sense of the duration of various lengths of time.

EXAMPLE

Clocks can be used to introduce the standard units of time. A teacher might set an alarm clock to go off every hour, or invite students to sit still as one minute passes on a digital or analog clock.

STOPWATCHES

Stopwatches can be used to determine the duration of various events.

EXAMPLE

Students can work in pairs to time each other as they complete activities, such as printing their full names. Then they can compare the results to see who took less time.

LEARNING CLOCKS

Learning clocks, made by attaching card-stock hands to a paper plate with a metal fastener, can be used to provide practice with reading and setting analog times. The process of making the clock ensures that each student will recognize the parts of an analog clock.

Commercial learning clocks are available as well, some with gears that move the hour hand with the minute hand.

Demonstration learning clocks are handy for both the teacher and students to show a large group a specific time.

EXAMPLE

Students can be asked to set their clocks to times they have drawn out of a hat.

THERMOMETERS

Students will need easy-to-read linear analog thermometers to practise reading temperatures. There are also large demonstration thermometers and overhead thermometers that teachers and students could use to, for example, show the temperature outside.

It is also useful to provide blackline master versions of thermometers that students can colour to show different temperatures.

EXAMPLE

A student might use a thermometer to measure and keep a record of the outside temperature at the same time every day.

"It's a bit more than 10 °C—maybe about 12 °C."

STUDENT-MADE THERMOMETERS	EXAMPLE
Student-made thermometers, made by inserting a ribbon that is coloured part white and part red into a cardboard thermometer outline, can be used to provide practice with showing different temperatures.	Students can be asked to set their thermometers to benchmark temperatures, such as the temperature at which water freezes (0 °C) or standard body temperature (37 °C). 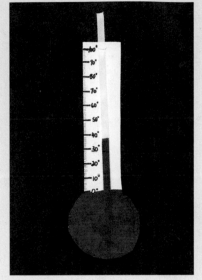

This student recognized that, to show 37 °C, he had to move the string so the red ended just below the 40 °C mark.

Appropriate Technology

Computers

As with other types of measurement, it can be difficult to find software that uses appropriate units, in this case, degrees Celsius. However, there are a few computer software programs that provide practice activities that will help students learn to tell time and count coins. These include

- *Animated Clock* (Flix Productions)
- *Stickybear Time* (Optimum Resource Inc.)

The Internet

Web-based activities with time might include reading digital and analog clocks, matching digital times to analog times or to words (e.g., ten to nine), and measuring the duration of events. Other sites involve practice with reading thermometers.

Measuring Angles

The measurement of angles is considered to be a geometry topic in some curriculums and a measurement topic in others. In some curriculums, certain aspects of the topic of angles are found in both strands.

One important reason for learning how to measure angles is that angle comparisons are integral to many geometry concepts. For example, students might measure angles in order to determine whether a triangle is *acute* or *obtuse*, whether two shapes are *congruent* or *similar*, or whether a four-sided shape has four right angles, making it a rectangle.

An angle is formed by 2 line segments or rays with a common endpoint, which is referred to as the *vertex* of the angle. The line segments or rays are called the *arms* of the angle.

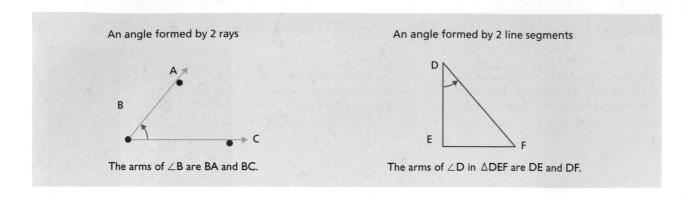

An angle formed by 2 rays

The arms of ∠B are BA and BC.

An angle formed by 2 line segments

The arms of ∠D in △DEF are DE and DF.

Like volume, angle measurement is generally introduced later than some other types of measurement.

Because angles in 2-D are defined as two rays with a common endpoint, the question is—how can you measure them? You do not want to use the area inside the angle as a measure, since you want angles to have the same measure whether their arms are long or short.

Two other approaches avoid this problem. One approach is to think of the measure of an angle in terms of what fraction of a circle it is.

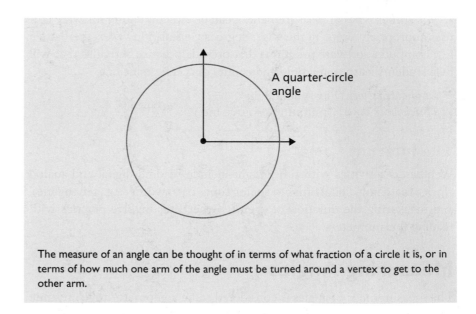

A quarter-circle angle

The measure of an angle can be thought of in terms of what fraction of a circle it is, or in terms of how much one arm of the angle must be turned around a vertex to get to the other arm.

The other approach is to think of the measurement this way: Imagine attaching two thin strips of card stock with a paper fastener and positioning them so one is exactly on top of the other. Then imagine rotating the top arm counterclockwise around the joint (called the vertex) until it reaches the correct position; what you measure is the amount of rotation.

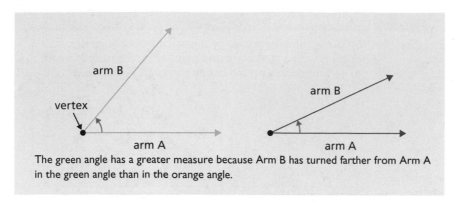

The green angle has a greater measure because Arm B has turned farther from Arm A in the green angle than in the orange angle.

To build an understanding of the connection between angles and turns, students benefit from opportunities to model angles by physically turning arms made from cardboard strips or commercial Geostrips (see page 465) fastened together at one end or by physically all moving in unison in response to teacher directions.

How Angle Concepts Can Be Introduced

Ideas about angles can be introduced through the same three stages as other measurement concepts—definition/comparison, nonstandard unit, and standard unit. Since angles are introduced later than some other types of measurement, students can move fairly quickly through the first two stages. Many teachers bypass the first two stages, but each stage provides students with experiences that will help them develop a better understanding of angle measure.

How Angle Concepts Are Introduced

DEFINITION/COMPARISON

Students compare angles by aligning one arm of one angle with the corresponding arm of the other. The angle that "sticks out" is larger. They can do this directly, by superimposing one angle on top of the other, or indirectly, by creating a model of one angle and comparing it to the other angle.

Direct Comparison

"The blue angle is bigger because the red one fits inside it and there's still room left over."

Indirect Comparison

"The blue angle is bigger because the model of the red angle fits inside it and there's still room left over."

(continued)

NONSTANDARD UNITS	STANDARD UNITS
Students compare angles by measuring both angles with nonstandard units and comparing the measurements to determine how much larger one angle is than the other.	Students compare angles by measuring both angles in degrees with a protractor and comparing the measurements to determine how much larger one angle is than the other.

"The angle on the left is bigger because it has room for 2 pattern block corners, and the angle on the right only has room for 1 of the same block."	"The blue angle is 60° and the red angle is only 35°, so the blue angle is greater."

Angles: The Definition/Comparison Stage

To determine which of two angles is greater, students at the definition/comparison stage can compare angles directly or indirectly. If the angles are "concrete" angles in, for example, pattern block shapes, a direct comparison is simple. If the angles are pictorial, students can either compare directly by cutting out one angle and placing it on top of the other, or they can use cardboard arms (fastened with a paper fastener at one end) to create a model of one of the angles, and then compare the model with the other angle.

Comparing angles indirectly by using a concrete model

Using concrete materials to model angles is important at this stage, since it helps students develop a definition of what an angle is, and how it is created by rotating one arm away from the other. This is also the stage at which students learn to use the vocabulary terms *vertex* and *arm* to refer to the parts of the angle.

Angles: The Nonstandard Unit Stage

Nonstandard units make it possible to assign a number to an angle measurement, allowing students to record the measurements of many angles so they can be compared without having to be tested repeatedly.

Students can use a paper angle model of any size as a nonstandard unit for measuring. For example, if the unit selected were the red model shown below at the left, the measures of the angles on the right would be 2 reds, 3 reds, and $1\frac{1}{2}$ reds respectively.

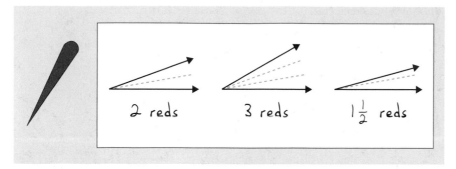

Although nonstandard units for measuring angles are easy to cut out of card stock or waxed paper, it also makes sense to use readily accessible angles such as the vertices of commercial geometric shapes. Pattern blocks, green and tan blocks in particular, make excellent nonstandard units and are readily available in many classrooms. The smaller angle of the tan block is 30°, so this block can be used to measure with a reasonable amount of precision. The relationship between the angles in the green and tan blocks makes them good tools for measuring the same angle with different units.

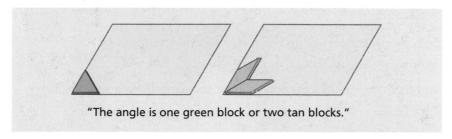

"The angle is one green block or two tan blocks."

A Nonstandard Unit Protractor

Students can create their own nonstandard unit protractors out of transparent paper, such as waxed or parchment paper. They simply cut out a large circle, perhaps about 12 cm in diameter, and then fold it in half and in half again until they have folded four times. When they unfold the paper, students have a transparent circular protractor that can be used to measure angles in nonstandard units.

Start with a large circle. Fold four times.   Use the "protractor" to measure
                                                 angles in nonstandard units.

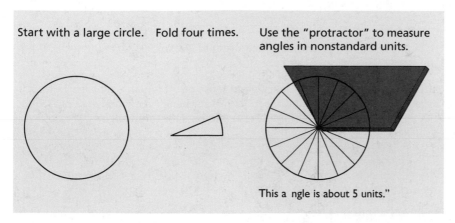

This a ngle is about 5 units."

Using a Full Turn as a Nonstandard Unit

Students at the nonstandard unit stage can interpret angles as fractions of a full turn. In essence, the full turn is being used as the nonstandard unit. Thinking of angles this way provides a good foundation for the later introduction of degrees, and for the use of a circular protractor.

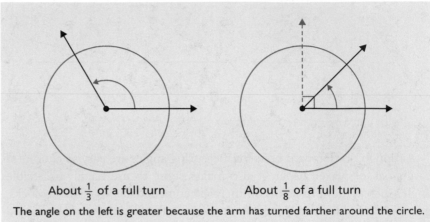

About $\frac{1}{3}$ of a full turn · About $\frac{1}{8}$ of a full turn

The angle on the left is greater because the arm has turned farther around the circle.

Angles: The Standard Unit Stage

The first standard unit angle students usually encounter is the *right angle*, or 90° angle. If students look around the classroom, they can usually find many examples. Students learn to test angles to see if they are right angles by measuring them against the corner of a ruler or a square block.

Standard Units for Measuring Angles

At the K–8 level, students only use one standard unit to measure angles—the degree.

Standard Units for Measuring Angles

DEGREES (°)

Defining a Degree

A degree is $\frac{1}{360}$ of the amount of turn needed to complete a full circle.

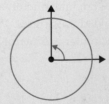

This turn measures $\frac{1}{4}$ of 360° or 90°.

Degree Referents

Most students do not have a very good sense of 1°, which is a barely perceptible angle, but they often develop referents for benchmark angles such as 90°, 45°, and 60°. Pattern blocks are useful referents for these angles.

90°

45°

60°

DEGREES (°)

An analog clock face is another useful aid for establishing angle referents:
- 30° is the size of an angle formed between adjacent numbers.
- 60° is the size of an angle formed between numbers that are 2 apart.
- 90° is the size of an angle formed between numbers that are 3 apart.

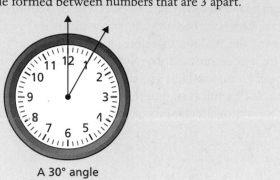

A 30° angle

ACTIVITY 16.14

Tell students that the hands of a clock are forming an angle of 30°. Ask what time it might be.

Classifying Angles

Angles can be classified by how they relate to a 90° angle, a 180° angle, or a 360° angle. Note that, while an angle is usually marked with an arc (to indicate its relationship to a turn), a special notation (a small square) is used to indicate a 90° angle.

Classifying Angles

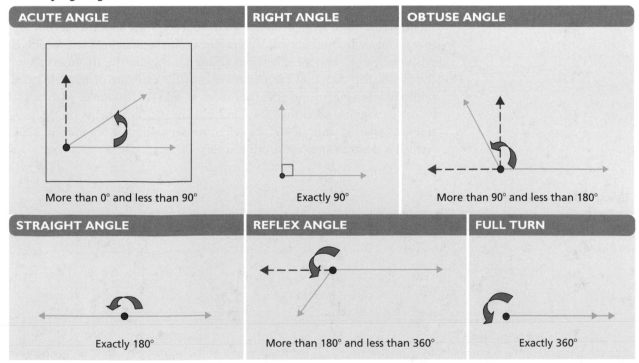

ACUTE ANGLE	RIGHT ANGLE	OBTUSE ANGLE
More than 0° and less than 90°	Exactly 90°	More than 90° and less than 180°

STRAIGHT ANGLE	REFLEX ANGLE	FULL TURN
Exactly 180°	More than 180° and less than 360°	Exactly 360°

Tools for Measuring Angles in Standard Units

Because $1°$ represents $\frac{1}{360}$ of the amount of turn needed to complete a full circle, you use a circular or semicircular device called a protractor to measure angles.

There are two scales on most protractors because the amount of turn can be measured in either a clockwise or a counterclockwise direction. This can, however, be confusing for students if they always choose to measure from the $0°$ line; therefore, it may be easier for students to begin with single-scale protractors. (Note that either arm of the angle can be used as a base for measuring.) The circular protractor will help students see angles as parts of a full turn, but if they are measuring only angles less than $180°$, then a semicircular protractor would be just as convenient.

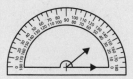

To measure an angle, place one arm of the angle on the $0°$ line, and use the scale to determine the number of degrees that fall between the two arms.

Later, students will be able to use the more common protractor, with two sets of numbers around the edge. To choose the correct scale, students should use estimation skills to compare the angle with a benchmark angle such as $180°$, $90°$, or $45°$, and then look at the scale to see which measurement makes more sense. It also helps if students think about what they are measuring—the number of degrees between the starting arm, which is positioned at $0°$, and the other arm. (If they recognize the $10°$ intervals on the protractor, then they can make a reasonable estimate of an angle's size without referring to the scale numbers at all. For example, each angle below is obviously less than $90°$, and fills six $10°$ increments on the protractor, so a measure of $60°$ makes more sense than a measure of $120°$ (which is the measure on the other scale).

Using a Double-Scale Protractor

USING THE INNER SCALE	USING THE OUTER SCALE
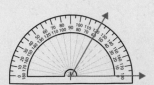	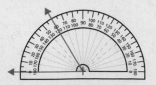
The blue angle is $60°$	The blue angle is $60°$
The starting arm of the angle points to $0°$ on the inner scale, so the inner scale is used to measure this angle at $60°$.	The starting arm of the angle points to $0°$ on the outer scale, so the outer scale is used to measure this angle at $60°$.

ACTIVITY 16.15

- Ask students to cut out the shapes shown.
- Have them put the shapes in order according to how many sides they have.
- They then measure the angles at the vertices of each shape. Ask what they notice.

Students can also relate angles to images of familiar turns, such as quarter-turns and half-turns, in order to get a better sense of benchmark angles such as 90°, 180°, 270°, and 360°. For example, once students learn that there are 360° in a full turn, it becomes clearer to them why a quarter turn is sometimes called a 90° turn.

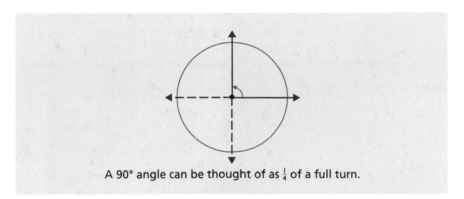

A 90° angle can be thought of as $\frac{1}{4}$ of a full turn.

Common Errors and Misconceptions

Angles: Strategies for Dealing with Common Errors and Misconceptions

COMMON ERROR OR MISCONCEPTION	SUGGESTED STRATEGIES
Confusing Angle Measure with Arm Length Some students may think that arm length has something to do with the size of an angle.  "The blue angle is bigger." This misconception can be particularly problematic when students are working with geometric shapes. For example, a student might think that one angle is bigger than another simply because it is located inside a triangle with a larger area.	Through working with angles of different arm lengths, students learn that it is the amount of turn and not the length of the arm that is important in describing the measurement of the angle. It may help to demonstrate with two pairs of Geostrips—one short pair and one long pair, each attached at one end. Fit the pairs one over the other, and then turn both the same amount at the same time.  Even though the yellow and green angles have arms of different lengths, the amount of turn is the same. *(continued)*

COMMON ERROR OR MISCONCEPTION	SUGGESTED STRATEGIES
Wrong Scale on the Protractor Students use the wrong scale on a protractor to measure an angle. For example, a student might record the size of this angle as 120°. 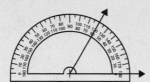 "It says this angle is 120°."	The ability to choose the correct scale depends on the student's conceptual understanding of what is being measured. If a student realizes that the measurement represents a turn through part of a 360° circle, and if the student thinks about known benchmark angles such as 90° and 180°, then it is easy to tell which scale to use. For example, the angle at left is obviously less than 90°, so a 60° measure makes sense but a 120° measure does not. If students are having difficulty with standard protractors, it may be preferable to offer them a circular protractor, ideally one with a single scale. However, it is even more important to make sure that students understand what the degree markings on the protractor really mean.
Misaligning the Protractor Sometimes a student measures an angle incorrectly by lining up the base of the angle along the edge of the protractor rather than the 0° line. 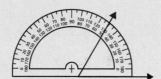 "It says this angle is 50°."	If students are misaligning the protractor, remind them that the crosshairs on the protractor represent the centre of a full turn, and that this is where they should place the vertex of the angle to measure the turn of the angle in degrees. Point to the 0° mark and emphasize that it is useful to align one arm with 0° in order to find out how far it would have to turn to reach the other arm. It may also help to ask a student to compare his or her measurement of an angle with one obtained by another student, and to talk about why the two measurements are different.
Misinterpreting "Right" Angles A student who usually sees right angles presented in the same orientation may think that the term "right" has something to do with the direction in which the arms are pointing. This student might not recognize a differently oriented angle as a right angle, and might even refer to it as a "left" angle. 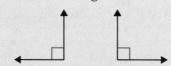 "Both are right angles, even though they face in different directions."	For some students, it may be preferable to use the term "square corner," rather than right angle. Students also need to see right angles (and non–right angles) in many different positions before they will fully grasp the concept. 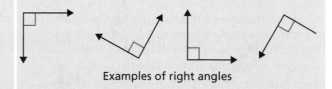 Examples of right angles
Not Recognizing 180° Angles as Angles Many students cannot accept that the picture below shows an angle and not just a line. 	Connect two Geostrips so they form an angle of 0°. Start turning one of the two strips as students observe. They will see that, as the strip turns, the size of the angle moves from 0° through a series of other angles, including 90°, until it finally reaches 180° (halfway around a full circle). Discuss how it makes sense that if 90° represents a quarter turn, then 180° represents a half turn. Let a student check with a protractor to see that the straight angle measures 180°. A straight angle represents a half turn.

COMMON ERROR OR MISCONCEPTION	SUGGESTED STRATEGIES
Angles That Do Not Reach the Protractor Scale Sometimes students have difficulty measuring an angle whose arms are too short to reach the protractor scale. 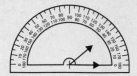 "I can't tell how big it is."	Students will often encounter situations like this one, especially if they are measuring angles in a textbook or angles inside geometric shapes. It is important to talk about these situations, and to discuss possible strategies. For example, if the angle is on paper, students may be able to extend the arms with a ruler and pencil. If it is in a textbook, they can trace the angle on paper and then extend the arms. If the angle cannot be extended directly, a student could position one arm along the base line, and then align a ruler with the other arm so the ruler meets the scale. If the angle does not need to be measured precisely, then the student may simply be able to "eyeball" the measurement.

Appropriate Manipulatives

Angles: Examples of Manipulatives

GEOSTRIPS	EXAMPLE
Geostrips are strips that can be connected to form angles and/or polygons. Similar tools can be created from strips of card stock connected with paper fasteners, or students can simply use a bent pipe cleaner. When students are using these tools to measure angles, emphasize that it is important to measure against the angle formed inside the two strips, rather than the one formed outside, because the inside angle has a more obvious vertex.	Students can use Geostrips to practise their angle estimation skills. For example, when a teacher calls out a measure such as 45°, students try to create that angle with Geostrips, and then check by measuring the results.  "45° is half as big as a right angle, so I think it looks like this."

PATTERN BLOCKS AND OTHER POLYGONS	EXAMPLE
A variety of pattern blocks and other polygons should be on hand so students can compare their interior angles or use them as nonstandard units for measuring angles.	Students at the standard unit stage could measure all the different angles they can make by putting two pattern-block corners together.   2 green corners = 120° a green corner and a large red corner = 180° Combining pattern blocks to make angles

FRACTION CIRCLES

Fraction circles are circles that are divided into equal parts through the centre. Students can cut out sectors from different circles and compare the angles by superimposing or measuring. These sectors could also be used as nonstandard units for measuring other angles.

EXAMPLE

Students might also use fraction circles to explore what happens to the central angles as a pizza is sliced into more and more pieces.

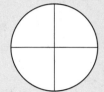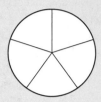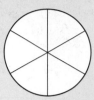

As the number of slices increases, the central angle gets smaller.

PROTRACTORS

Protractors are used to measure and construct angles and polygons. (See page 458.) They come in semicircular and circular forms, and some are available with a single scale.

The circular form reinforces the concept that angles are parts of a circle and allows students to get a better feel for what angles look like when they are greater than 180°.

Although you generally think of protractors as tools for measuring in standard units, it is also possible for students to make nonstandard-unit protractors.

EXAMPLE

Either type of protractor could be used to measure angles less than 180°, but only the circular protractor could be used to directly measure angles greater than 180°.

ANGLE RULER

The angle ruler can be bent to measure angles or straightened to measure straight lines. It includes markings for measuring length as well as a protractor for measuring angles.

EXAMPLE

An angle ruler is a handy tool for measuring side lengths and angles in triangles.

GEOBOARDS AND SQUARE DOT PAPER

On a geoboard, students use elastics to create angles and polygons. They can keep a record of their work by drawing shapes they have created on square dot paper.

There are many different sizes of square geoboards. Their "dimensions" are determined by the number of pins.

Geoboards have a wide range of uses, for example, to create and measure angles, to examine the angle properties of polygons, and to explore similarity and congruence. (See page 318.)

Square geoboards are used most often, but triangular and circular geoboards are also available. The latter are particularly useful for dividing circular regions into congruent parts in order to explore the angles at the centre of shapes to the vertices.

EXAMPLE

Students who are using standard units might want to see how many different angles (less than 180°) they can create on a square geoboard of a given size. They can draw pictures of the angles on dot paper and record the measure of each angle, identifying it as acute, right, or obtuse.

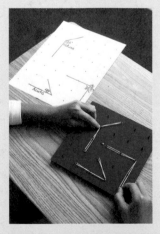

Geoboards are good tools for exploring angles.

Appropriate Technology

Computers

There are a number of software programs that allow students to measure or construct angles. These include *Photoshop*, *The Geometer's Sketchpad* (*GSP*), and *Measure 2.0*, which allows students to measure angles on screen.

The GSP sketch below shows an angle measured automatically by the software.

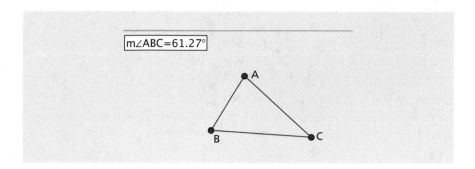

The Internet

There are also a number of Internet sites that students can visit to explore angle measurement. Some involve practice with a protractor, others hone estimation skills, and still others focus on sorting angles by type.

Assessing Student Understanding

- Because size is not a good visual cue for mass, it is important that most assessments involving mass be performance tasks and not paper-and-pencil tasks.

- Part of the assessment of capacity, volume, mass, and angle should involve estimation. Students might be asked to estimate the measure of one object if they are given the measure of another object that they can use as a benchmark. For example, if students are shown an object with a volume reported as 20 cm^3, they might estimate the volume of another object that is larger or smaller.

- Students should be asked to relate measurements to their everyday world. For example, you might ask, What object might have a mass of about 5 kg? What kind of container might have a capacity of 100 mL?

- Part of assessment of capacity, volume, mass, time, temperature, or angle measurement should involve observing students' use of tools. Do they use the tools correctly? Do they use them comfortably or only with difficulty?

- Make sure to appropriately balance attention to analog and digital clocks in assessment situations. Also distinguish between tasks that require students to read time and those that require them to set a clock to show a time; these are different skills.

- Once students have met angles greater than 90°, it is important that assessments provide the opportunity for students to show that they can distinguish between angles more and less than 90°, and use their protractors accordingly.

Appropriate Children's Books

The Dragon's Scales (Albee, 1998).
A young girl challenges a dragon by asking questions about comparing weights. She wins the challenge.

Mr. Archimedes' Bath (Allen, 1980).
This picture book tells the story of Archimedes, who figured out the relationship between volume and capacity using water displacement. The story is told by using animals who get in and out of a bathtub and cause the water to spill over.

Clocks and More Clocks (Hutchins, 1994).
Mr. Higgins notices that different clocks in his house seem to show different times. He discovers, the hard way, that the hands of the clock just keep moving. The story is told with cartoon illustrations.

Measuring Penny (Leedy, 2000).
A child measures her dog in a variety of ways, including measurements involving capacity and time, and standard and nonstandard units.

Applying What You've Learned

1. The problem at the start of the chapter is one of a class of problems called optimizing problems, for example, What is the greatest area for a given perimeter? the greatest volume for a given surface area? etc. Why might these problems be important for students to meet?

2. Describe an interesting activity not already listed in the chapter that is appropriate for students at each of the three stages of teaching one of these measurements: capacity, volume, mass, time, or angle.

3. Create a lesson plan that would be of use in teaching students how the volume of a pyramid relates to the volume of an associated prism.

4. Study the curriculum documents for your region. At what grade level is each of these introduced?
   – standard units for capacity, volume, and mass
   – measurement of angle
   – relating volume and capacity units
   – volume and area formulas
   Do these particular grade levels seem reasonable to you? Explain why or why not.

5. Do you think it might be useful to teach volume and mass together, or do you think they should be taught separately? Explain.

6. The mass of 1 L of water is 1 kg. Create three problems that might be of interest to a student to solve using that information.

7. Both time and angle measures are based more on the Imperial system of measurement than on the metric system. What numbers skills does work with each set of measurements (Imperial and metric) support? Explain.

8. The clock is sometimes used as a "compass." For example, you might say that someone is at 2 o'clock. Do you think this use of the clock enhances or detracts from students' understanding of telling time? Explain.

Interact with a K–8 Student:

9. Observe as a student solves one of these problems:

   Older student: What is the mass of a single sheet of paper?

Younger student: How many paper clips would it take to balance your eraser?

What measurement understandings do you observe?

10. Create a game that you think would be useful to practise angle measurement. Try out the game with some students. What aspects of it would you change? Why?

Discuss with a K–8 Teacher:

11. Ask a teacher to share a successful activity for measuring volume or capacity, and what she or he thinks made it successful.

Selected References

Albee, S. (**1998**). *The dragon's scales*. New York: Random House Books for Young Readers.

Allen, P. (**1980**). *Mr. Archimedes' bath*. New York: Harper-Collins.

Battista, M.T. (**1999**). Fifth graders' enumeration of cubes in 3D arrays: Conceptual progress. *Journal for Research in Mathematics Education*, 30, 417–448.

Battista, M.T. (**2003**). Understanding students' thinking about area and volume measurement. In Clement, D., and Bright, G. (Eds.). *Learning and teaching measurement*. Reston, VA: National Council of Teachers of Mathematics, 122–142.

Battista, M.T., and Clements, D.H. (**1998**). Students' understanding of three-dimensional cube arrays. Findings from a research and curriculum development project. In Lehrer, R., and Chazan, D. (Eds). *Designing learning environments for developing understanding of geometry and space*. Mahwah, NJ: Erlbaum, 227–248.

Burns, M. (**1978**). *This book is about time*. Boston: Little, Brown and Company.

Clarke, D., Cheeseman, J., McDonough, A., and Clark, B. (**2003**). Assessing and developing measurement with young children. In Clement, D., and Bright, G. (Eds.). *Learning and teaching measurement*. Reston, VA: National Council of Teachers of Mathematics, 68–80.

Clement, R. (**1994**). *Counting on Frank*. Boston: Houghton Mifflin School.

Dacey, L., Cavanagh, M., Findell, C., Greenes, C., Sheffield, L.J., and Small, M. (**2003**). *Navigating through measurement, prekindergarten–grade 2*. Reston, VA: National Council of Teachers of Mathematics.

Friederwitzer, F.J., and Berman, B. (**1999**). The language of time. *Teaching Children Mathematics*, 6, 254–259.

Hutchins, H. (**2004**). *A second is a hiccup: A child's book of time*. Toronto: North Winds Press.

Hutchins, P. (**1994**). *Clocks and more clocks*. New York: Aladdin.

Kamii, C.K., and Long, K. (**2003**). The measurement of time: Transitivity, unit iteration, and conservation of speed. In Clement, D., and Bright, G. (Eds.). *Learning and teaching measurement*. Reston, VA: National Council of Teachers of Mathematics, 169–180.

Leedy, L. (**2000**). *Measuring Penny*. New York: Henry Holt and Company, Inc.

Lehrer, R. (**2003**). Developing understanding of measurement. In Kilpatrick, J., Martin, W.G., and Schilfter, D. (Eds.). *A research companion to principles and standards for school mathematics*. Reston, VA: National Council of Teachers of Mathematics, 179–192.

Maida, P., and Maida, M. (**2006**). How does your doughnut measure up? *Mathematics Teaching in the Middle School*, 11, 212–219.

Merz, A.H., and Belzer, S. (**2003**). Hurry up and weight. *Teaching Children Mathematics*, 10, 8–15.

Moone, G., and de Groot, C. (**2005**). Investigations: Time is of the essence. *Teaching Children Mathematics*, 12, 90–98.

Pagni, D.L. (**2005**). Angles, time and proportion. *Mathematics Teaching in the Middle School*, 10, 436–441.

Small, M. (**pre-press publication**). *Professional resources and instruction for mathematics educators: Measurement*. Toronto: Nelson Education Ltd.

Sophian, C. (**2002**). Learning about what fits: Preschool children's reasoning about effects of object size. *Journal of Research in Mathematics Education*, 33, 290–302.

Wells, R.E. (**1996**). *How do you lift a lion?* Morton Grove, IL: Albert Whitman & Co.

Chapter 17

Data Display and Analysis

IN A NUTSHELL

The main ideas in this chapter are listed below:

1. Different types of data displays are appropriate for different situations. The choice of organization and display should reflect the purpose for collecting the data. As with other mathematical situations, concrete data displays should precede semi-concrete or symbolic ones.

2. When data are displayed, either visually or in a table or chart, they can be analyzed to look for patterns, make predictions, make comparisons, draw inferences, and make decisions.

3. Graphs are powerful data displays since visual displays quickly reveal information about data.

CHAPTER PROBLEM

In a big city, there are 100 schools. The graph below shows the enrolments in those 100 schools, but the vertical scale is missing. About how many schools have fewer than 200 students?

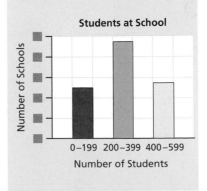

Students at School

Number of Schools

0–199 200–399 400–599
Number of Students

Purposes of Data Display

Sometimes a *data display*, such as a graph, is used to solve a problem. For example, if a city is planning to adjust a set of traffic lights, and the planners need to know if there is a relationship between the frequency of cars on the road and the time of day, they could collect the data by counting cars over a period of time. They could then graph the data in a scatter plot, and then look for a pattern. The graph itself is used to solve the problem because it is easier to get a sense of the data by presenting the data visually.

In other cases, a data display is used to communicate information. Most people find that information presented graphically is more accessible and easier to read at a glance, as long as it is presented effectively and accurately.

Data Display and Organization

Data display, like data collection, involves the organization of data so that the data can be used to solve a problem and/or communicate about a situation. Some display formats require a particular kind of organization. For example, to create a stem-and-leaf plot (see page 486), you must order the data from least to greatest within each data interval. Other formats allow for some variation in how the data are organized.

Data Display Formats

Just as students need to consider their audience when they design survey questions, they need to consider both the audience and the nature of the data to decide about the type of data display they plan to construct. It is important to choose a format that suits the data, and to include clear titles and labels to guide the audience, or reader, in interpreting it.

The first data displays children usually create are tally charts and concrete graphs made from real objects. They then move on to recording numerals in frequency tables or charts. As students begin to recognize that the number of real objects in each category can be represented in other ways, they progress to graph types characterized by increasing levels of complexity and abstraction—from graphs made with pictures of real objects (picture graphs), to graphs that use symbols (pictographs), and, finally, to more abstract graphs (bar graphs, broken-line graphs, and stem-and-leaf plots).

Tally Charts

One of the simplest types of data display is the *tally chart*. Students use tally marks to count the frequency of responses or items in different categories. Using tally marks grouped in 5s makes it easier for students to quickly count the number in each category. Notice how the tallies are aligned across the columns for easy comparison. From this tally chart, it is easy to see at a glance that more people chose the first story than the second one. Note that, with a tally chart, it is important to include a title that clearly explains the meaning of the data.

Which story should
we read today?

I Want a Dog	If You Give a Mouse a Cookie
ⅡⅡ	ⅡⅡ
ⅡⅡ	‖‖
‖	

ACTIVITY 17.1

Ask students to do a survey of 10 students on the playground to see whether they prefer crunchy cookies or chewy cookies. They can make a tally chart and then a picture graph, using cookie pictures.

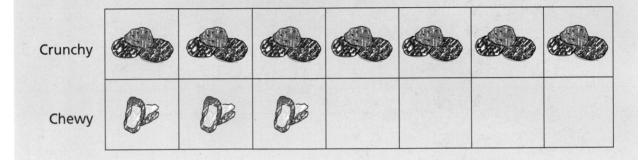

Frequency Tables

Eventually, tally charts can be replaced by *frequency tables,* in which the number of responses or items in each category is recorded in the form of a numeral instead of tally marks. A tally chart is easier to use while a set of data is being collected. However, a frequency table is more useful as a summary table after all the data have been collected and counted.

Colours of Cars in the Parking Lot

Colour	Tally	Number of Cars
Blue	ⅡⅡ ⅡⅡ	10
Green	‖‖	4
Black	ⅡⅡ ‖	6
White	ⅡⅡ ‖‖	7
Silver	ⅡⅡ	5
Gold	‖‖	3

Colours of Cars in the Parking Lot

Colour	Number of Cars
Blue	10
Green	4
Black	6
White	7
Silver	5
Gold	3

A frequency table can be an extension of a tally chart, or students can record the numerical data directly in a frequency table.

ACTIVITY 17.2

Ask students to arrange themselves into a concrete "people graph" to compare the number of students wearing long sleeves with those wearing short sleeves. Ask why it is easy to tell which group is greater once students are lined up in the graph.

Concrete Graphs

Initially, students use real objects to display the results of a sorting in a graph. Graphs made with real objects are called *concrete graphs*. At first, the graphs are arrangements of the actual objects being sorted. Later, other concrete materials are used to model, or represent, the real objects.

It's easy to see that there are 4 more students with long sleeves than short sleeves.

A concrete "people graph" can be used by students to answer a simple question about themselves.

Notice that students in the concrete graph are lined up on a large floor graphing mat, which is a large square grid. This aligns students so that comparisons are easy to make. "People graphs" are usually formed in a way that parallels a pictograph or bar graph with one-to-one correspondence across the categories. However, a concrete "people graph" can also take the form of a circle graph. (See *Ways to Make Circle Graphs* on page 490.)

Concrete Graphs Using Models After students have gained some experience with concrete graphs made with real objects, they will be ready to begin making graphs from concrete models that represent the real objects. This adds a level of abstraction because the model is one step removed from the object it represents.

For example, to represent the information from the sleeve-length concrete "people graph," students could move away from the floor graphing mat, leaving items such as clothespins or linking cubes to hold their place. They could then put the clothespins or cubes together to create a concrete graph. When the students sit down, the model will help them recall the information from their concrete "people graph."

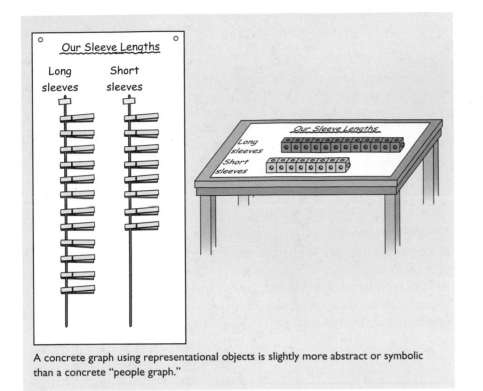

A concrete graph using representational objects is slightly more abstract or symbolic than a concrete "people graph."

As models of concrete graphs are introduced, teachers have an opportunity to talk about why it helps if each object is the same size or if the objects are placed on a grid. Doing so ensures that the objects are equally spaced within each row or column and aligned across the categories, allowing for easy counting and comparisons. Providing cubes of different sizes can help make this point. For example, if students were to place different-sized cubes in categories on a concrete representational graph to show whether they have cats, they would discover that quick visual comparisons are impossible.

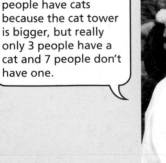

It looks like more people have cats because the cat tower is bigger, but really only 3 people have a cat and 7 people don't have one.

When objects are used to create a concrete graph, and there is no grid, it is important that the objects be the same size and shape.

IMPORTANT POINTS ABOUT CONCRETE GRAPHS

- The first person or concrete object in each category is at the same level or baseline.
- The people or objects in each category are equally spaced.
- The people or objects in each of the categories are spaced the same way or are the same size so that each person or object is aligned with its counterpart in the other categories.
- Concrete graphs can be vertical or horizontal.
- It is important to include labels and a concise but meaningful title to help the reader understand the graph.

Picture Graphs

Before long, students learn that concrete graphs can be unwieldy and difficult to keep intact, and discover that it is more convenient to use pictures to represent data in a *picture graph*. As well, using pictures also allows a display to be more permanent. The same basic principle of concrete graphs applies: the reader should be able to make comparisons at a glance.

In a picture graph, each picture is unique to the object or person it represents. Picture graphs form a bridge between concrete graphs and the more abstract pictographs and bar graphs.

When the pieces of data (represented by pictures) in a picture graph are lined up one to one across the categories, it is easy to read the graph.

Because it is important that the corresponding items in the picture graph be aligned, grid paper is often used to help place the pictures. If the pictures are all the same size, the grid paper is not as important. For example, the use of grid paper for the pictograph above was optional.

IMPORTANT POINTS ABOUT PICTURE GRAPHS

- Each picture is unique to the individual object or person it represents.
- The first picture in each category is at the same level or baseline.
- The pictures in each category are equally spaced.
- The pictures in each of the categories are spaced the same way or are the same size so that each picture is aligned with its counterpart in the other categories.
- Picture graphs can be vertical or horizontal.
- It is important to include labels and a concise and meaningful title to help the reader understand the graph.

Pictographs

A *pictograph* is one step farther than a picture graph along the continuum from concrete to symbolic. Symbols are used to represent data, and sometimes these symbols are picture-like representations. The same symbol is used throughout the pictograph (or, for "early" pictographs, the same symbol is used for each category), making it different from a picture graph, which uses different pictures throughout. The same basic principles of concrete and picture graphs apply: the reader should be able to interpret the graph at a glance by comparing rows or columns.

The following pictograph shows that 10 children were surveyed about their favourite fruits, and 6 children chose strawberries. The same symbol, a happy face, is used to represent each of the 10 children, although a different colour has been used for each category.

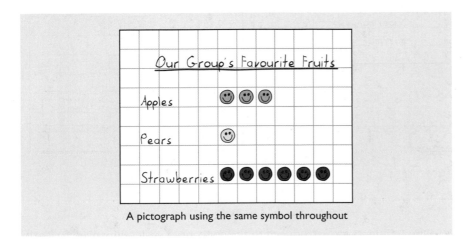

A pictograph using the same symbol throughout

Choosing Symbols Students enjoy choosing symbols for their pictographs, but there is a challenge involved in choosing something that is representative of all the categories. The symbol used to make a pictograph does not have to reflect the context, but choosing a meaningful symbol makes a graph more interesting, and also provides some immediate information about the data. In the pictograph above, a symbol of a particular type of fruit would not be suitable; in fact, it might be misleading. A symbol such as an empty circle would be acceptable, but would not provide as much information as the happy face. With the happy face, it is obvious that each symbol represents a child. Another possibility might be a T-shirt or stick figure.

Choosing an appropriate symbol can be achieved through group discussion and trial and error. The teacher can present some data to students to graph and invite suggestions for possible symbols. Small groups can discuss some possibilities and then present their ideas and justifications to the larger group. The class can then talk about why one symbol would be more appropriate than another, or why a certain symbol would be inappropriate.

One important thing to consider in choosing a symbol for a pictograph is the ease with which the symbol can be drawn and copied. Materials such as stamps, stickers, and stencils can help students create pictographs quickly and efficiently.

Scale or Many-to-One Correspondence As students begin to work with greater amounts of data, it becomes inconvenient to draw a symbol to represent every piece of data. Using a scale allows a single symbol to represent a number of items, a situation referred to as many-to-one correspondence. In the example below, it is easier to draw a graph with 10 comic book symbols than with 50.

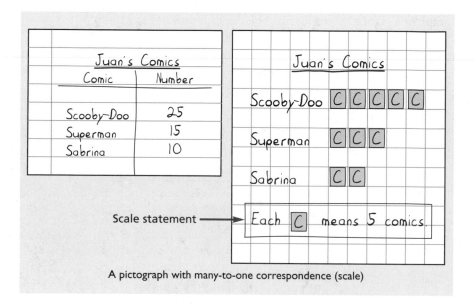

A pictograph with many-to-one correspondence (scale)

Once students are introduced to the concept of scale, they need to learn how to choose one that is appropriate for a given situation. In the example above, students with knowledge of multiplication facts might immediately notice that each number is a multiple of 5 and realize that having each symbol represent 5 comics would make the graph easy to create and interpret. However, a scale of 1 to 5 is not the only possibility.

Scale and Partial Symbols If, in the comic book example above, each symbol represented 2 comics, it would mean using partial symbols for two of the categories. If each symbol represented 4 comics, partial symbols would have to be used for all three categories. Obviously, once scale is introduced, choosing the right symbol becomes more complicated, as the symbol must allow for partial symbols that are easy to read. Thus, a circle or square shape is often the easiest to use.

Partial symbols are introduced when students are confronted with data where there is no obvious common factor other than 1. The best time to introduce this idea is when most of the pieces of data are even, but there is one odd number. Then each symbol represents 2 items, and students will need a half-symbol to represent the odd number of items.

In the following example, partial symbols are unavoidable because there is no common factor for 8, 2, and 5 (other than 1) that can be used as a scale for this data. In this pictograph, the choice of a rectangle as a symbol is appropriate because it is easy to represent 1 game using half of a rectangle.

Number of Soccer Games Played	
Student	Number of games
Lyn	8
Sharleen	2
Juan	5

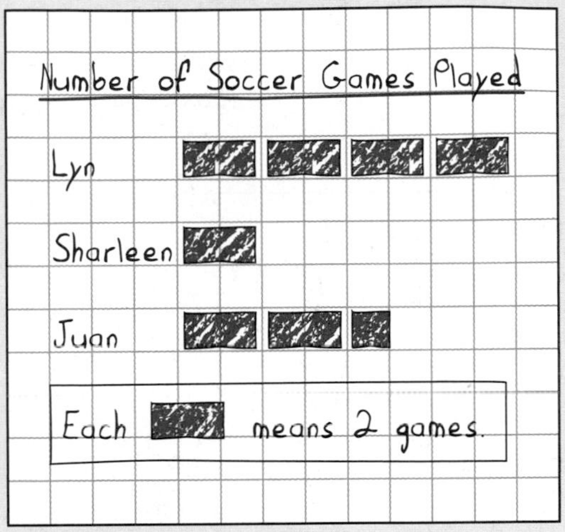

Number of Soccer Games Played

Lyn ▨ ▨ ▨ ▨

Sharleen ▨

Juan ▨ ▨ ▨

Each ▨ means 2 games.

A symbol shape such as a rectangle is a good one to use for a scale of 1 to 2 as it can easily be divided into half symbols.

If the pieces of data are greater numbers, for example, mostly beyond 20, it is more efficient to use symbols that represent more than 2 items. For example, suppose a student planned to graph the hockey card data shown below. Students might decide that a scale of 1 symbol to 4 cards would work, since it would be relatively easy to show 38 as $9\frac{1}{2}$ symbols, 22 as $5\frac{1}{2}$ symbols, and 17 as $4\frac{1}{4}$ symbols. The next task is to choose a symbol that can easily be partitioned into halves and fourths. In this case, a circle works better than a rectangle since the quarter and half symbols are more obvious.

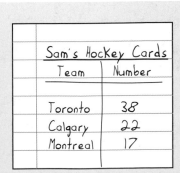

Sam's Hockey Cards	
Team	Number
Toronto	38
Calgary	22
Montreal	17

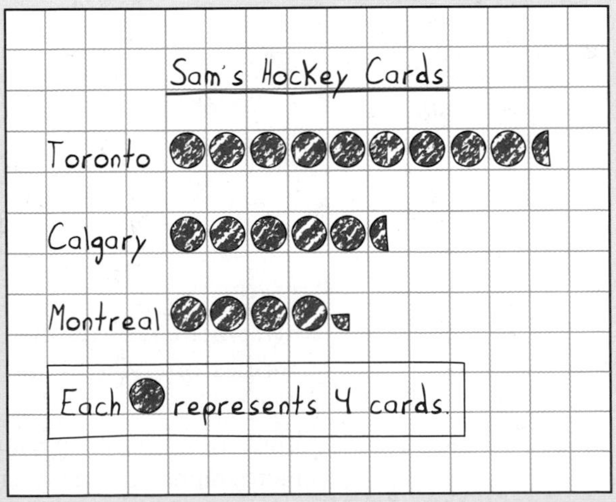

Sam's Hockey Cards

Toronto ●●●●●●●●●◖

Calgary ●●●●●◖

Montreal ●●●●◔

Each ● represents 4 cards.

A circle is the ideal symbol, as it can easily be divided into quarter and half symbols that are easy to interpret.

Often, students are keen to use a symbol that is thematically connected to the data, for example, a picture of a hockey card for Sam's Hockey Cards graph shown above. This advantage has to be balanced against the disadvantage of using a symbol that makes it difficult to represent fractions.

However, there is still room for some creativity, for example, drawing black circles to represent hockey pucks. The pizza graph below illustrates the importance of choosing a symbol that can be divided easily to show fractional parts.

Student Response

This student has the idea of using a partial symbol to represent 2 pizzas. (In the first week, 18 pizzas were sold.) However, the student should have chosen a whole symbol that lends itself more readily to showing fractions.

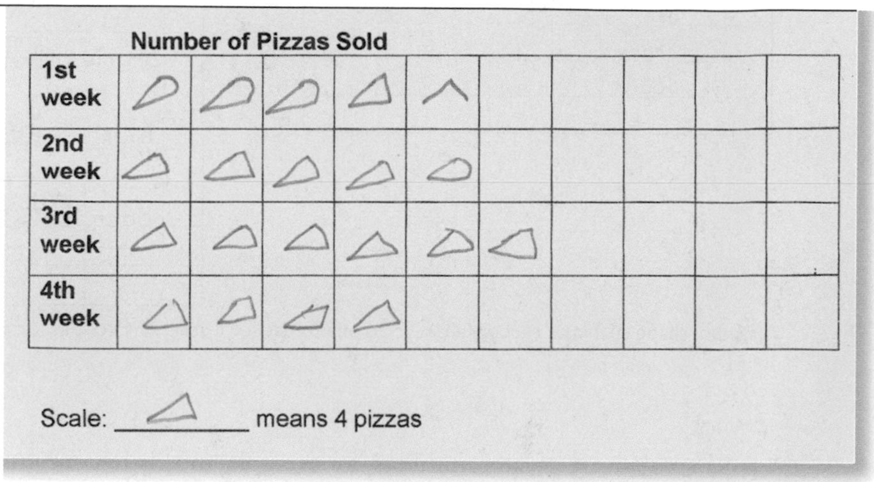

Number of Pizzas Sold

1st week										
2nd week										
3rd week										
4th week										

Scale: _____ means 4 pizzas

IMPORTANT POINTS ABOUT PICTOGRAPHS

- The same symbol is usually used throughout the graph (although some "early" pictographs use the same symbol for each category). This symbol may or may not reflect the context of the data.
- The first symbol in each category is at the same level or baseline.
- The symbols in each category are equally spaced.
- If many-to-one correspondence or scale is used, the scale must be clearly stated in a scale statement, or legend.
- If a scale is used, the symbol chosen should allow for partial symbols that are easy to interpret.
- Pictographs can be vertical or horizontal.
- It is important to include labels and a concise but meaningful title to help the reader understand the graph.

ACTIVITY 17.3

Provide data about the number of visitors to various museum exhibits. Make sure the data involves a variety of 3-digit numbers, not all multiples of 100. Ask students to choose an appropriate scale for the data.

Bar Graphs

Bar graphs are displays that use the lengths or heights of bars to represent quantities, often the frequencies of particular responses to a data collection activity. These are a natural extension of the concrete representational graphs made with linking cubes and the use of square pictures and symbols in pictographs. Normally, students should work on grid paper to draw bar graphs, thereby ensuring that all the squares are the same size.

Scale With bar graphs, as with pictographs, students begin with situations in which each square represents a frequency or quantity of one. Later, when they begin working with greater data values, students learn to use a scale along the axis, as shown in the graph on page 478. (See page 479 for a discussion of the use of many-to-one correspondence with pictographs.) Initially, students tend to choose scales of 2, 5, and 10. This is likely because they feel comfortable skip counting with these numbers. As with pictographs, it is important for students to think about which scale would be best suited to the data, and how they will show amounts that fall between two numbers in the scale.

The bar graphs shown below display the same data, vertically and horizontally. Both use a scale of 10 (as indicated on each numbered axis). Dividing squares horizontally or vertically shows partial amounts. The number of roller coaster riders, 45, is easy to interpret because it is halfway between 40 and 50. The number of merry-go-round riders, about 12 or 13, is more difficult to identify. However, you do not need to know the exact number of riders to make general comparisons with other bars.

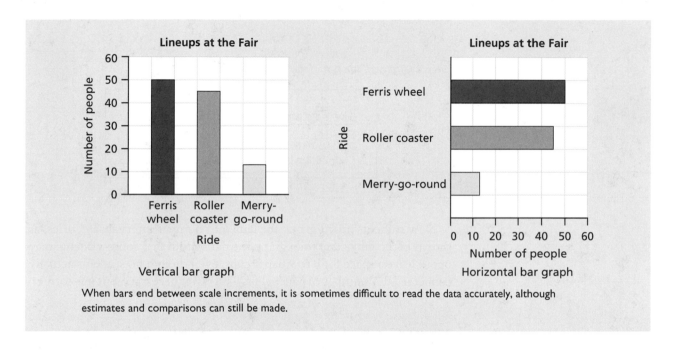

When bars end between scale increments, it is sometimes difficult to read the data accurately, although estimates and comparisons can still be made.

Notice that the bars are spaced an equal distance apart and not connected, making it easier to read each graph. The separation of the bars also shows that each bar represents a separate or discrete category. (See page 485 for a discussion of histograms—graphs where the bars touch because they represent intervals in a continuous number sequence.) Notice also that the horizontal axis of the graph on the left has both labels (one per bar) and an axis heading, "Ride." For many graphs, including both labels is necessary for clarity. In the case of this graph, the axis heading "Ride" is optional as the labels are self-explanatory.

Intervals For some types of data, such as data about fair rides, birthday months, or pets, the categories are discrete, and a bar graph is fairly easy to make and interpret. One axis shows the category names and the other shows a numbered scale. However, when the pieces of data themselves are numerical, things become more complex, and two numbered axes are needed. In this case, it is often useful to group the data into *intervals* before making the display. For example, suppose 27 students in a Grade 4 class conducted an experiment to determine how many paper clips each student can link in two minutes.

Step 1 Collect the data.

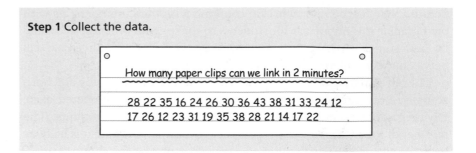

How many paper clips can we link in 2 minutes?

28 22 35 16 24 26 30 36 43 38 31 33 24 12
17 26 12 23 31 19 35 38 28 21 14 17 22

The next step is to organize the data in order from least to greatest to highlight any patterns. Students can readily find the least and greatest numbers, along with any results that occurred more than once.

Step 2 Organize the data from least to greatest.

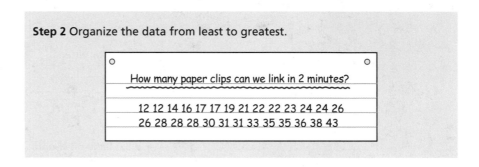

How many paper clips can we link in 2 minutes?

12 12 14 16 17 17 19 21 22 22 23 24 24 26
26 28 28 28 30 31 31 33 35 35 36 38 43

Now students might group the data into number-interval categories, as shown in the table, and then graph the data. Note that some students may opt to leave a space for 0 to 9 paper clips, even though no students actually connected this number of paper clips. This is not necessary, but it is correct.

Step 3 Group the data into intervals.

Step 4 Graph the data.

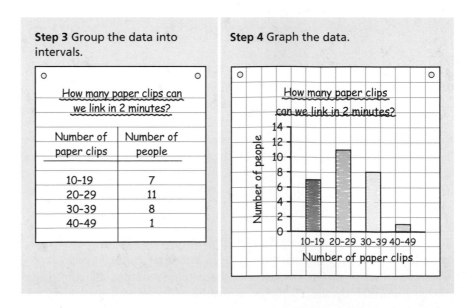

How many paper clips can we link in 2 minutes?

Number of paper clips	Number of people
10–19	7
20–29	11
30–39	8
40–49	1

Imagine what the bar graph would look like if intervals were not used. There would have been 18 bars or more—one for each number of paper clips linked in 2 minutes. This would not be a practical way to display the data. Note that the bars are separated because the data can still be described as discrete. For example, there is no bar to represent quantities between 19 and 20 because you cannot link $19\frac{1}{2}$ clips.

Choosing Intervals The choice of interval categories will depend on the data. For example, if the pieces of data are quite spread out and there are to be only four categories or bars, each interval in the group will include a greater range of numbers. The graphs below show how using different intervals affects the appearance of the paper clip data. The smaller the intervals, the more you can learn about the detail of the data from the graph. However, there is a point where the number of bars becomes excessive.

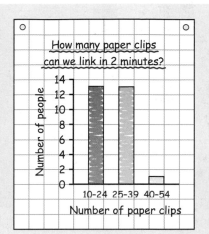 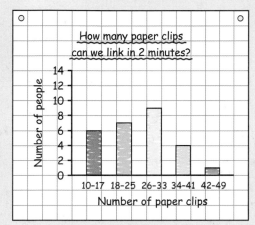

Changing the way data values are grouped in intervals can make the same data look very different.

IMPORTANT POINTS ABOUT BAR GRAPHS

- A grid square is used to represent the same quantity throughout.
- If a many-to-one correspondence is used, the scale must be clearly shown along a numbered vertical or horizontal axis.
- Bars should be separated to indicate that they represent discrete data, although it is not incorrect if there are no spaces between the bars.
- If there are no pieces of data for a category or interval, a space can be left where the bar would be, although it is not required.
- Bar graphs can be vertical or horizontal.
- Both axes should be labelled. Each bar should have a category label, which might be a discrete topic name or a numerical interval. The other axis, the scale axis, is labelled numerically.
- Axis headings should be used, as necessary, for clarity.
- It is important to include a concise but meaningful title to help the reader understand the graph.

ACTIVITY 17.4

To connect data work to probability work, ask students to roll a pair of dice and keep track of the values of the differences of the numbers rolled. Students then display the data in a bar graph.

Variations of Bar Graphs

Double-Bar Graphs Sometimes it is useful to look at two sets of data simultaneously, for example, to compare the number of sisters that classmates have with the number of brothers. To show how two different sets of data are alike or different, it would be appropriate to create a *double-bar graph*.

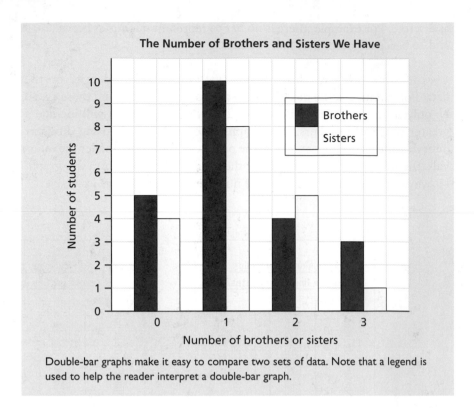

Double-bar graphs make it easy to compare two sets of data. Note that a legend is used to help the reader interpret a double-bar graph.

Line Plots A *line plot* is similar to a bar graph. It shows the frequency of data by organizing the information along a number line. Usually, an X symbol is used to represent each piece of data. To collect the data for the line plot below, someone asked 22 people how many visits they made to a convenience store last week. The line plot, in this instance, serves as both the data display as well as the data collection and organization tool. Notice that this is like a pictograph or bar graph with one-to-one correspondence; each X is like a symbol or one grid square. Because they are based on a number line, line plots are applicable only in situations where the categories are numbers.

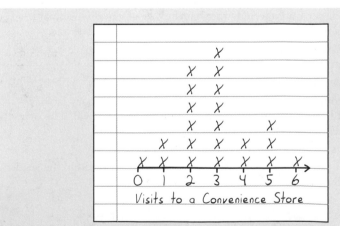

A line plot is a graph that uses a number line as its base.

ACTIVITY 17.5

Students can create a pair of line plots to compare the heart rates of two groups of students.

Each X on the line plot above represents a person. It appears that most of the people visited a convenience store two or three times, and only a few people went a different number of times. The graph shows this pattern visually.

Histograms A *histogram* is basically a bar graph that has been adapted to show data when there are continuous sequences of data. The categories along the horizontal axis are always continuous number intervals (intervals with no gaps between them), and the bars touch to show the continuity. The heights of the bars show how many pieces of data are in each interval (the frequency).

Suppose the following data were collected about the height in centimetres of each student in a math class. The data could be displayed in a bar graph to show the height of each student. In this case, the categories are discrete and the bars would not touch.

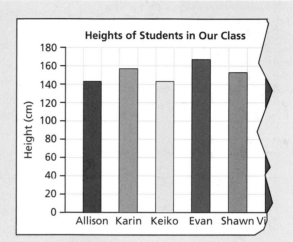

Heights of Students in Our Class

Allison	143	Karin	157
Keiko	143	Evan	167
Shawn	153	Victoria	145
Jessie	168	Rashid	152
Christie	141	Lucie	149
Ahmed	150	Cam	147
Sam	157	Peter	151
Julie	148	Lois	143
Jose	156	Nicole	154
Luigi	155	Sheldon	158

In a bar graph, the spaces between the bars indicate that the data categories are discrete.

To make the graph more concise, the data could be organized into intervals as shown in the frequency table below, and then displayed in a histogram.

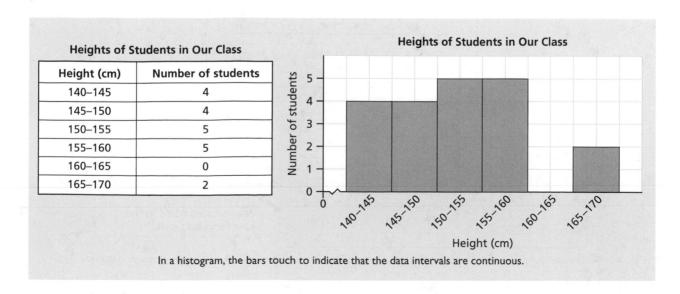

Heights of Students in Our Class

Height (cm)	Number of students
140–145	4
145–150	4
150–155	5
155–160	5
160–165	0
165–170	2

In a histogram, the bars touch to indicate that the data intervals are continuous.

Note that the intervals in the table (and on the graph) appear to overlap; for example, it appears as if 145 cm belongs in both the first and second intervals. By convention, pieces of data that are "on the border" between two intervals are counted in the higher interval. A 145-cm height, for example, is included in the 145- to 150-cm interval rather than in the 140- to 145-cm interval.

IMPORTANT POINTS ABOUT HISTOGRAMS

- Histograms are used to show data in continuous number intervals.
- Histograms always describe frequencies or show how many are in each interval.
- The bars should touch to show the continuity of the data.
- If there are no pieces of data for an interval, a space is left where the bar would be.
- Histograms are usually oriented vertically.
- Each bar should have a label, which will be a numerical interval.
- Both axes should have headings.
- It is important to include a concise but meaningful title to help the reader understand the graph.

ACTIVITY 17.6

Students might conduct a traffic survey and record the number of vehicles that pass a particular busy intersection during each hour during the school day. The data would be displayed in a histogram since time is continuous.

Stem-and-Leaf Plots A *stem-and-leaf plot* is a way of both organizing and displaying numerical data. It is similar to a horizontal bar graph, except that each piece of data is displayed in its original form. Numbers are grouped together by place value: the "stem" is determined by the digit(s) of greater place value when the number is written in standard form; the "leaves" are determined by the digit(s) of lesser place value. For example, using the data about paper clips, students begin by ordering the pieces of data they collected, and then they group the numbers to make the stem-and-leaf plot as shown below.

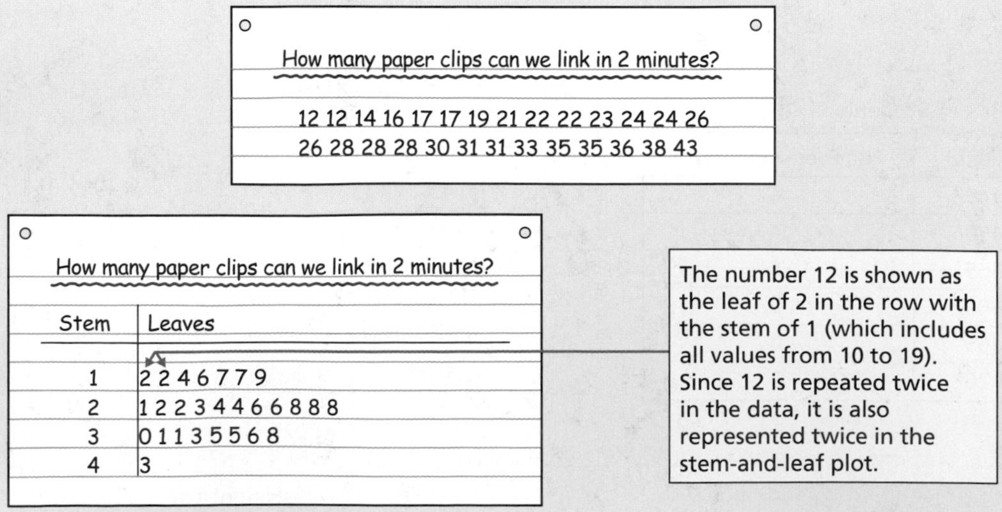

How many paper clips can we link in 2 minutes?

12 12 14 16 17 17 19 21 22 22 23 24 24 26
26 28 28 28 30 31 31 33 35 35 36 38 43

How many paper clips can we link in 2 minutes?

Stem	Leaves
1	2 2 4 6 7 7 9
2	1 2 2 3 4 4 6 6 8 8 8
3	0 1 1 3 5 5 6 8
4	3

The number 12 is shown as the leaf of 2 in the row with the stem of 1 (which includes all values from 10 to 19). Since 12 is repeated twice in the data, it is also represented twice in the stem-and-leaf plot.

A stem-and-leaf plot is like a horizontal bar graph where the data values themselves create the shape of the graph.

The stem-and-leaf plot on page 486 allows students to compare frequencies for different decades. For example, it is easy to see that the greatest number of students had results in the twenties, but only one student had a result in the forties.

If the stem-and-leaf plot above were recorded on grid paper, it would look like a horizontal bar graph that shows the frequency of the data in each of the intervals 10–19, 20–29, 30–39, and 40–49. The advantage of the stem-and-leaf plot, though, is that you can easily see each individual piece of data. Without going back to the original list of data values, students can determine

- the range (from 12 to 43, so the range is 31)
- the mean (add the values and divide by 27 to get 25.6)
- the median (the 14th value from either end, which is 26)
- the mode (28)

In the stem-and-leaf plot shown, the stems are the tens digits and the leaves are the ones digits. In other stem-and-leaf plots, the stems might be the hundreds and tens digits together (for example, 10 for 106), and the leaves would be the ones digits (6 for 106); or the stems might be ones and tenths (for example, 1.2 for 1.23), and the leaves the hundredths (0.03 for 1.23). The choice of stem depends on the nature of the data and the purpose for which it is being organized.

IMPORTANT POINTS ABOUT STEM-AND-LEAF PLOTS

- Each number in the data set is represented by a leaf placed in a row beside a stem.
- The stems are determined by the greater place value(s).
- The data values by stem are in order vertically, usually from least to greatest.
- The data values in each stem (the leaves) are in order horizontally, from least to greatest, and are aligned from stem to stem.
- If there are no data for a stem, the stem is still included with no data values (leaves) recorded beside it.
- It is important to include a concise but meaningful title to help the reader understand the graph.

Line Graphs

Line graphs are used to show trends in data, usually over time. They are sometimes called *broken-line graphs* since they appear jagged or crooked, consisting of connected plotted points that are not in a straight line. The points are plotted to show *relationships* between two *variables*—one of which is often time—and the points are joined with a line to make it easier to see trends. Like bar graphs, line graphs have a title, labelled categories, axis headings, and a clear scale.

Scatter Plots

A *scatter plot* is also designed to show trends and to indicate whether there is a relationship between two variables. Often the data are first recorded in a T-chart or a table of values, and then the points are plotted on a coordinate grid. (More information on coordinate grids is found in Chapter 20 on

ACTIVITY 17.7

Invite students to perform long jumps and record the distances jumped in a stem-and-leaf diagram. Notice that the data below shows jump distances between 172 cm and 230 cm.

Long-Jump Distances (cm)	
Stem	Leaf
17	2 3 5
18	5 6 6 7 8 9
19	3 3 6 8
20	0 2 5 5 6 7 8
21	2 2 2 4 5 5 8
22	0 1 1 2 3 7 8 9
23	0

ACTIVITY 17.8

Students enjoy interpreting line graphs that tell a story. For example, ask students to describe this graph showing Marc's hike.

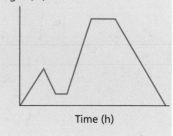

page 589.) The points tend to be scattered on the graph, which is why the graph is called a scatter plot. However, if there is a relationship between the variables, the scattering will actually form a pattern. If there is no relationship, the points will form a random scattering.

For example, the table and scatter plot below show a pattern in the test scores of students who studied for different lengths of time.

Are Study Hours Related to Test Scores?

Hours of study	Test score
2	70
5	90
3	80
6	85
7	90
1	60
7	85
6	80
1	50

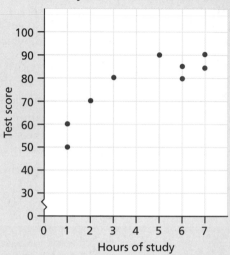

Are Study Hours Related to Test Scores?

Scatter plots are used to look for trends and to determine if there is a relationship between two variables. The scattering of plotted points can be random or it can form a pattern indicating a trend or relationship.

ACTIVITY 17.9

Students might create a scatter plot to relate the cost of a phone call to different numbers of minutes the call might take.

From the data points, it is easy to see that there is a trend or relationship: more study generally led to higher grades. However, if you continue to examine the graph, you will notice that students who study the same amount, for example, 7 hours, can still get quite different scores.

Dependent and Independent Variables Broken-line graphs and scatter plots are examples of graphs that show *relationships* between two variables. In a relationship, changing one variable can result in a change to the other. For example, as growth time increases, so does the height of a bean plant. (See the Height of a Bean Plant graph on page 493.) In mathematics, the variable that changes "independently" (in this case, the plant's growth time) is called the *independent variable*. The variable that is affected by or "depends" on this change (in this case, the height of a plant) is called the *dependent variable*.

By mathematical convention, the independent variable is usually plotted along the horizontal axis, and the dependent variable along the vertical axis. Another example is the scatter plot above, where the amount of study time might influence test scores, so the horizontal axis is labelled "Hours of study" (the independent variable) and the vertical axis is labelled "Test score" (the dependent variable).

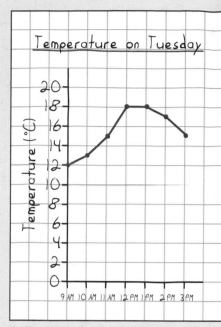

When I made my temperature graph, I put the time of day on the horizontal axis. That way the shape of my line made a picture of how the temperature went up (increased) and down (decreased) during the day.

The convention of plotting the independent variable along the horizontal axis makes it easier to see relationships and trends.

Circle Graphs

Another familiar type of graph is a *circle graph*. Like other types of graphs, a circle graph is based on categorizing data, but its function is primarily to show relationships among the parts of a whole and, at the same time, show relationships between each part and the whole. This type of graph makes the most sense when it is important to see how a total amount is distributed.

For example, a circle graph might show the proportions of

- a budget spent on different categories
- books in a library of different genres or for different age groups
- a day spent on different activities
- a class of students who chose each type of hot lunch

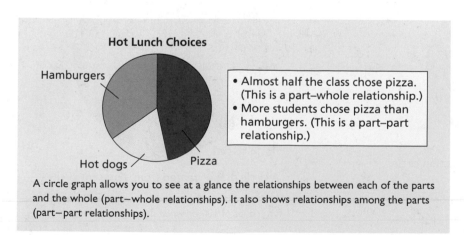

Hot Lunch Choices

- Almost half the class chose pizza. (This is a part–whole relationship.)
- More students chose pizza than hamburgers. (This is a part–part relationship.)

A circle graph allows you to see at a glance the relationships between each of the parts and the whole (part–whole relationships). It also shows relationships among the parts (part–part relationships).

Creating Circle Graphs With a circle graph, it is especially important that no piece of data belong to more than one category, since the sum of the data pieces must be equal to the whole.

Ways to Make Circle Graphs

MAKE A CONCRETE CIRCLE GRAPH WITH PEOPLE

Ask students a question and have them stand in lines that represent their answers. For example, you might ask, "Do you own a dog?" Give a label to the first student in each line.

Bring the ends of the lines together so the children are standing in a circle, but are still in their places in the sequence. To create the circle graph, stretch a string from the centre of the circle to each student who is holding a label. Then move the labels into the sectors you have marked off with the strings.

A concrete circle "people graph"

USE FRACTION CIRCLES

Fraction circles are useful tools for creating circle graphs. Initially, students can use fraction circles that match their data (for example, a circle divided in tenths to represent 10 people), and simply colour the appropriate fractions on the circle.

Once students understand the concept of percent, they can graph data for groups of 100 or percent data using a percent circle (a fraction circle whose circumference is divided into hundredths). For example, if 7 out of 33 students wear glasses, students would calculate that 7 out of 33 is about 21%, so they would colour $\frac{21}{100}$ of the circle to represent these students. (When students round percents, they may sometimes need to adjust the rounding to make sure the results add to exactly 100%.)

A circle graph created from a fraction circle in tenths

Fraction circles can be used to create circle graphs for data representing groups of certain sizes.

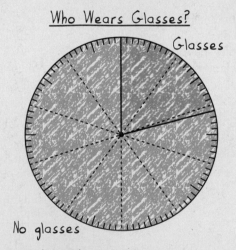

A circle graph created from a percent circle

Percent circles can be used to create circle graphs for groups of 100 or when data are in percent form.

USE ANGLES

Older students can use the fact that there are 360° in a circle to create sectors of a circle that accurately represent groups of data as described below.

Step 1   Draw a circle using a compass or template.

Step 2   Calculate the percent of the whole group represented by each category.

Step 3   Calculate the angle that represents the corresponding percent of 360°.

Step 4   Use a protractor and a ruler to draw the angle and sector to the nearest degree.

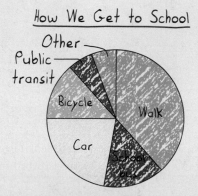

VARIATION OF A CIRCLE GRAPH

A variation of the circle graph is a hundredth grid. Students count the squares on a grid to construct or read the graph. A hundredth grid is similar to a circle graph because, like a circle graph, it shows the relationships of the parts to the whole, as well as the relationships among the parts. The grid here, for example, shows that 50% of the members of the team were on the team last year, 33% were on a different team last year, and 17% are new to the sport.

Where Our Team Members Played Last Year

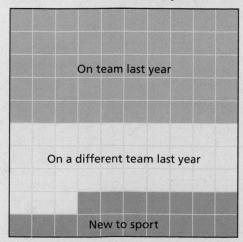

In a hundredth grid, it is easy to count to find the percent for each part.

A hundredth grid is a simple, suitable alternative to a circle graph for showing percent data.

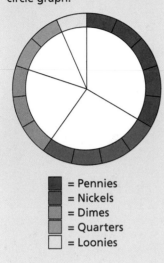

ACTIVITY 17.10

Have students examine the coins in their pockets. They can colour a strip graph to show the number of coins of each denomination. Then they can convert the strip into a circle graph.

■ = Pennies
■ = Nickels
■ = Dimes
■ = Quarters
□ = Loonies

Box Plots

A box plot is used, usually in Grades 8 or up, to show how a set of data is distributed. The data are divided into four quartiles, each containing 25% of the data. For example, the box plot below shows that 25% of students scored between 30 and 60 on a test, 25% between 60 and 70, 25% between 70 and 85, and 25% between 85 and 100. The middle 50% of the data are included in a box divided at the median, and the upper and lower 25% of the data are described by "whiskers," That is why this is often also called a box and whisker plot.

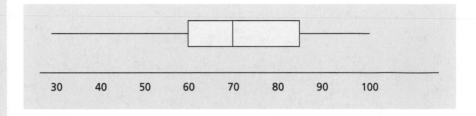

Appropriate Use of Data Display Formats

One of the important things students need to learn is which graph is most appropriate in a given circumstance. There is often more than one good choice, but there can be inappropriate choices as well.

When to Use Each Type of Data Display

PICTOGRAPHS AND BAR GRAPHS

Pictographs and bar graphs are appropriate for quickly and visually comparing frequencies of data in different categories, no matter how great or small those frequencies are. The data categories can be either non-numerical (as in the pictograph shown here), or numerical (as in the interval bar graph).

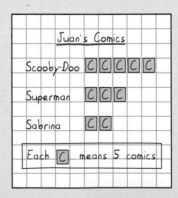

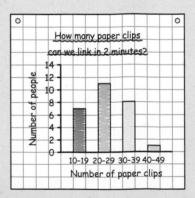

HISTOGRAMS

Histograms are suitable when the data are continuous, that is, when the data categories are number intervals with no gaps between them and the bars show the frequency for each category. Graphs like these are often used to show measurement data. Histograms are not generally introduced until later grades.

HISTOGRAMS

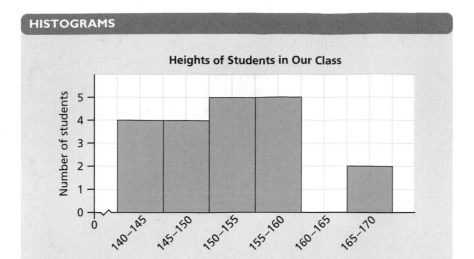

Heights of Students in Our Class

STEM-AND-LEAF PLOTS

Stem-and-leaf plots are used when numerical data are best organized by place value, in intervals or stems of 10 or 100 or some other power of 10. They show the frequency of data in each interval, as well as each individual piece of data (the leaves), making the stem-and-leaf plot a source of raw data and a data display. Seeing individual pieces of data displayed in order is useful for determining the range, mode, and median.

Test Scores

7	1 2 2 7 8 9
8	0 3 4 4 5 8 9 9 9
9	0 0 0 0 1 1 2 2 3 3 3 5 5 8

BROKEN-LINE GRAPHS

Broken-line graphs are used to display a trend or relationship. A broken-line graph can show how something changes, usually over time. When a solid line is used between plotted points, the data can be discrete or continuous. If the line is dashed, it indicates that the data are discrete.

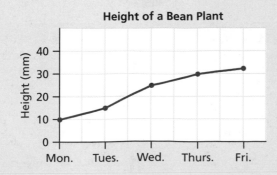

Height of a Bean Plant

SCATTER PLOTS

Scatter plots are used to look for trends and determine if there is a relationship between two variables. For example, a scatter plot might help students determine if there is a relationship between test scores and hours of study.

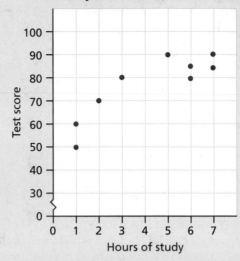

Are Study Hours Related to Test Scores?

CIRCLE GRAPHS

Circle graphs show how a whole set of data can be subdivided into categories. They allow the viewer to compare the frequencies of categories, but do not usually show the actual values of those frequencies. Circle graphs should not be used if there is no meaning to the total set of data. For example, a circle graph showing how many children have a sibling is not meaningful unless all the children surveyed represent a group, such as all the children in a classroom.

Do You Have a Brother?

BOX PLOTS

Box plots are used to show how data vary. Using a box plot, it is easy to see where most of the data lie.

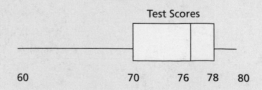

Test Scores

Common Errors and Misconceptions

Data Display: Strategies for Dealing with Common Errors and Misconceptions

COMMON ERROR OR MISCONCEPTION	SUGGESTED STRATEGY
Aligning Categories When making concrete and picture graphs, students do not ensure a consistent baseline for each category line and do not ensure that the items in the lines are equally spaced.	Use a large grid so that items are automatically placed to align with items in the other categories. For larger items or people graphs, a graphing floor mat can be used. Large grid for aligning objects or pictures
Aligning Pictures on Graphs When students create picture graphs or pictographs, they do not ensure that the pictures are lined up, one right below or beside the other.  Misaligned pictures	Provide large grid paper on which students can create their graphs. If the cells are large enough, students can draw their pictures inside each cell. 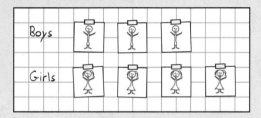
Different Pictograph Symbols When students create pictographs, the symbols might be different sizes and the spacing might be irregular. For example, they might use a different-sized ball for each sport as shown below. 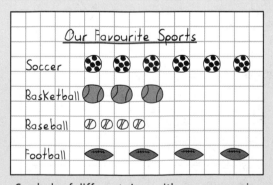 Symbols of different sizes with uneven spacing	There is some debate as to whether using different symbols is actually incorrect. Early pictographs often use a different symbol for each category. These early pictographs introduce students to the notion of using a consistent symbol. They serve as a transition from picture graphs that use a different picture for each object or person to later pictographs that use one symbol throughout. To show why it is a good idea to use a consistent symbol, show a pictograph that uses symbols of different sizes and irregular spacing, and talk about how using the same-size symbol and equal spacing might make the graph easier to read and be less misleading. For example, using the pictograph to the left, you might ask, "Can you tell, without counting symbols, which sport was chosen by the fewest students?"
Irregular Scales When students create bar graphs, they use an irregular scale based on the actual data values instead of an evenly spaced number line. For example, suppose 6 students (A to F) are asked how many times they have used the Internet in the last	Students should look at the greatest value first. They estimate how many squares high they want their graph to be, and then decide how much each square has to represent. They then skip count and record the axis scale before they actually begin making their bars. *(continued)*

COMMON ERROR OR MISCONCEPTION	SUGGESTED STRATEGY
month. The data values for the number of times they logged on are as follows: 35, 60, 6, 8, 22, and 16. A student might graph the data as shown below.	For example, for the use-of-Internet data, students need to go to at least 60, so they might decide to have each square height represent either 5 or 10, depending on how large they want the graph to be. They should create the bars only after the scale is recorded.

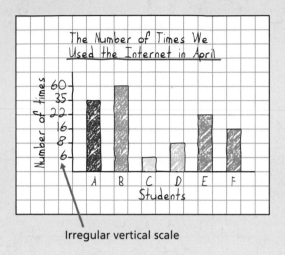

Irregular vertical scale

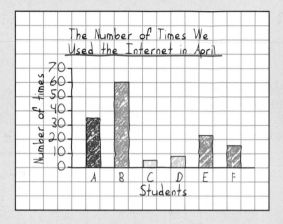

Omitting Repeated Values

When creating stem-and-leaf plots, students omit repeated data values.

Ask students to create a stem-and-leaf plot for each set of data shown below:

Set 1: 21, 21, 21, 21, 21, 21, 21, 22, 31, 32

Set 2: 21, 31, 32

If students create the same stem-and-leaf plot, have them look back at the data. Ask what they notice about the first set (there are a lot of 21s), and ask whether the stem-and-leaf plot reflects this.

Omitting Categories

Students omit a bar on a histogram or a stem row on a stem-and-leaf plot if there are no pieces of data within that interval.

Students always need to check that the numbers are continuous as they read down the list of stems for a stem-and-leaf plot or across the intervals for a histogram. (This is not the case with other graphs that show discrete data, such as bar graphs or pictographs.)

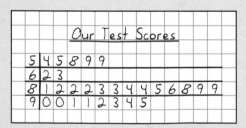

Missing stem row for 7

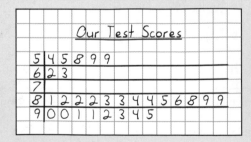

COMMON ERROR OR MISCONCEPTION	SUGGESTED STRATEGY

Leaves Out of Order

When creating stem-and-leaf plots, students do not put the leaves in order within each stem.

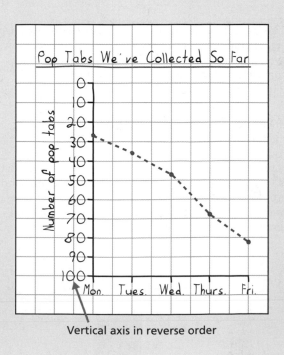

Leaves are not in order

Remind students to double-check their values in each stem for order. Some students prefer to create a working stem-and-leaf plot by recording all the data values within each stem in the order that the data appear or occur; they then create a final stem-and-leaf plot by putting the leaves in order.

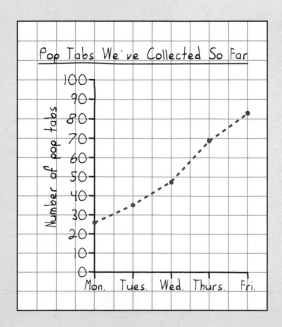

Students can also order the data in a list before constructing the stem-and-leaf plot. Making an ordered list can also be helpful for determining the range in order to establish appropriate stems.

Axes in Reverse Order

When students are making bar graphs or line graphs, they number the vertical axis from top to bottom, rather than from bottom to top. If a student numbers the vertical axis from top to bottom, then the data appear in inverted form.

Vertical axis in reverse order

In the graph to the left, there appears to be a decline in the number of pop tabs, when the collection is actually increasing. Discuss with students why this happened, and remind them that both the vertical and the horizontal axes on a grid should be labelled from the bottom-left corner.

(continued)

COMMON ERROR OR MISCONCEPTION	SUGGESTED STRATEGY
Numbering the Wrong Axis	At the elementary level, it is not necessary for students to understand independent and dependent variables, although it is a good idea for teachers to model a correct approach. Invite students to predict what the graph to the left would look like if the number of pop tabs were graphed on the other axis. Talk about how this would make it easier to see the "shape" of the data.

When students are making line graphs or stem-and-leaf plots, they plot the independent variable along the vertical axis instead of the horizontal axis. A student who has plotted the variables in the reverse positions may have difficulty interpreting the graph. In the example below, the slope of the line makes it appear that the number of pop tabs rose quickly on Monday and Tuesday, and the increase tapered off on Wednesday and Thursday. In actual fact, the greatest increase occurred from Wednesday to Thursday. See the corrected graph in the right column.

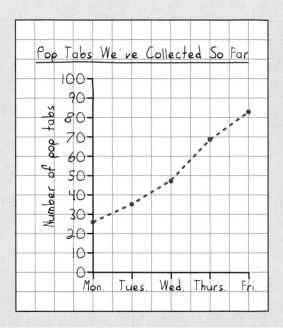

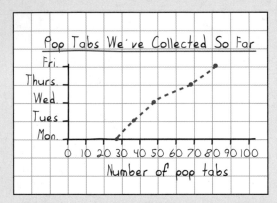

The days of the week should be along the horizontal axis

Not Including "0" on Axes	The "0" is considered optional. Many mathematicians create graphs without the "0," as it is assumed. However, encourage students to make their graphs as complete as possible and model the inclusion of "0" when creating graphs.
Students do not include the "0" along numbered axes.	

Percents Do Not Add to 100%	Encourage students to check their work by adding the final percents in the circle graph. If students are rounding percents to make the graph, then the rounding process can sometimes result in a sum that is very close to, but not exactly, 100%. Students who are using the percents to determine angle measures may need to adjust some measures by rounding differently so the angles will total 360°.
If the percents shown in a circle graph do not add to 100%, there may be an error somewhere in their calculations or it may be due to rounding.	

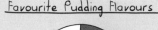

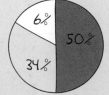

Percents do not add to 100%

Appropriate Manipulatives

Data Display: Examples of Manipulatives

GRAPHING MATS

A graphing mat is a large sheet of vinyl divided into cells by equally spaced horizontal and vertical lines. Ideally, each grid space should be large enough for a person to stand on. A graphing grid can also be created on the floor using masking tape.

EXAMPLE

A graphing mat ensures that students align themselves or objects when working with concrete graphs.

A graphing floor mat helps keep people and large objects aligned when making concrete graphs.

CONCRETE GRAPH MATERIALS

Materials that can be used to create concrete graphs include
- linking cubes
- counters
- clothes pins
- square tiles
- square blocks
- paper clips
- links made from paper, plastic, etc.

Using square counters or blocks to create concrete graphs is a helpful transition from concrete graphs to bar graphs.

EXAMPLES

Linking materials provide a quick way to create concrete graphs that are accurate and easy to read.

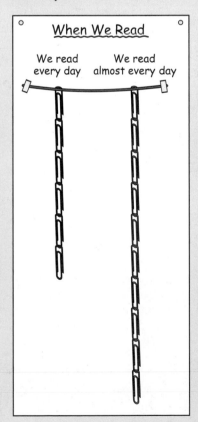

(continued)

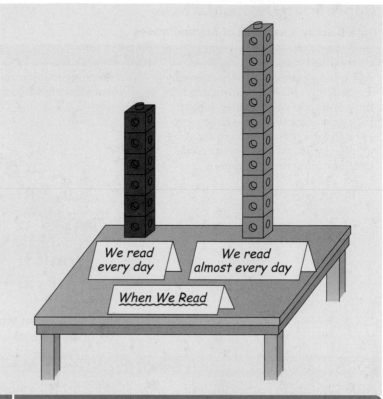

GRID PAPER AND FRACTION CIRCLES

Grid paper in various sizes is used to create graphs. Fraction circles (including percent circles) can be used to create circle graphs.

EXAMPLES

- Using grid paper to create bar graphs helps students keep bars the same size and evenly spaced, and provides a guide for a consistent scale.

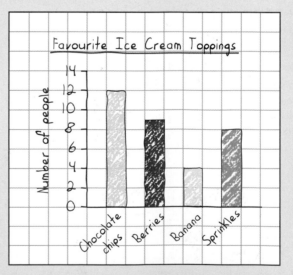

- A piece of grid paper that measures 10 by 10 can be used as a hundredths grid. See page 491 for an example of a circle graph alternative made with a hundredths grid.
- Fraction circles divided according to the data group size make it easy to make circle graphs. See page 491 for an example of a circle graph created using a fraction circle in tenths to graph data about a group of 10 students.

PICTURE AND PICTOGRAPH MATERIALS	EXAMPLE
Students can use stickers, photos, magazine cutouts, stencils, or stamps to create interesting picture graphs and pictographs.	Stickers make interesting pictographs and are often appropriate for scales of 2 to 1 because they can usually be cut in half. 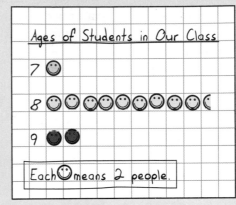 A pictograph using stickers

Appropriate Technology

In today's world, students have many tools available to them to make data displays more engaging and accessible. Once students understand the concept of a graph, the use of technology can allow them to focus on what they want to do with it. There may be a problem they want to solve, and/or they may want to use the graph to communicate information. Technology allows them to focus on the data, instead of worrying about drawing straight lines and plotting points correctly. Even young students can use specially designed software to create bar graphs and pictographs. Students in later grades can and should use graphing tools that are available as part of simple spreadsheet programs. These tools allow them to create many types of graphs, including bar graphs, pictographs, and circle graphs.

Once students have a conceptual understanding of picture graphs or pictographs, they can begin using technology to create graphs. Even very young students can choose a clip art image and paste it into a basic word processing program document. Initially, students may paste pictures randomly, but they will soon learn the importance of pasting symbols in lines (perhaps inside a table) and using same-size pictures to make the graph easier to interpret. Word processing functions make it easy for them to title and label their graphs. For example, the following pictograph uses clip art inserted into a simple table to show the preferences of seven children with regard to two sports.

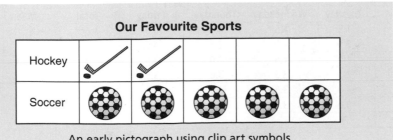

An early pictograph using clip art symbols

To create simple graphs without a grid (with or without a scale), students can create a square with a simple drawing program and fill it with colour. They can then copy as many squares as they need, and drag them to where they belong in the graph. The squares will automatically snap into alignment within each category. The following pictograph (or early bar graph) shows the favourite sports of 35 students.

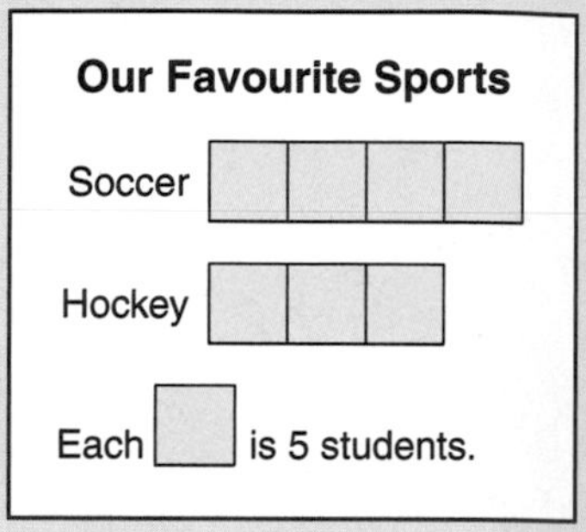

Our Favourite Sports

Soccer

Hockey

Each ☐ is 5 students.

A pictograph using square symbols created in a draw program

Some commercial software programs are also useful. Examples are *Graphers* (distributed by Sunburst), *The Graph Club* (distributed by Tom Snyder), *Data Management & Probability K–3* (distributed by Gamco), and, particularly, Tinkerplots, distributed by Key Curriculum Press, which allows students to import data and easily organize it in many formats. Data from the Census for Schools project, and other data files, for example, based on sports statistics, can be imported and analyzed by students.

Spreadsheets

Spreadsheets allow students not only to organize data, but also to use the technology to perform calculations and to create graphs. In addition, a spreadsheet simplifies making changes to the data because, when students change one piece of data, the program will automatically update the rest of the data to reflect what was changed.

The spreadsheet below shows information about hours of television viewing for a group of students. To calculate the totals and averages, students can insert formulas that will perform the calculations for them. For example, the formula for calculating the total for Monday has been entered into cell B8. Students can change the data easily to compare totals and averages over different weeks.

B8	▼	fx	= B2 + B3 + B4 + B5 + B6 + B7				
	A	B	C	D	E	F	G	H
1	Student's name	Monday	Tuesday	Wednesday	Thursday	Friday	Total	Mean
2	Rishi	3.0	1.5	1.5	4.0	5.0		
3	Justin	2.0	2.5	2.0	2.5	4.0		
4	Ben	1.5	1.0	1.5	2.0	2.5		
5	Christine	0.0	2.5	2.5	3.0	3.5		
6	Cameron	4.0	4.0	3.5	4.0	4.5		
7	Tyler	3.0	0.0	3.0	4.5	4.5		
8	Total	13.5						
9	Mean							

Many spreadsheet programs provide tools to allow students to graph data they have entered. For example, the spreadsheet below shows how many candies of each colour are in a package. With graphing tools, students can create a bar graph or a circle graph to show the data.

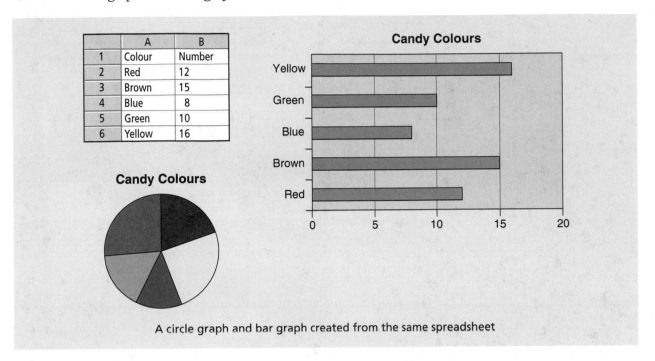

A circle graph and bar graph created from the same spreadsheet

Using the Internet

There are many computer applets for creating any type of graph, whether a bar graph, a circle graph, a stem-and-leaf plot, or even a box plot.

Data Analysis

Reading Graphs

When students interpret graphs constructed by others, they learn to appreciate the features that can help them make sense of a visual display of data. A good graph should communicate some overall impressions of the data to the reader "at a glance." This goal is facilitated by the choice of a graph type that suits the data, clear labelling and titling, and accuracy in representing the data.

The following sample graphs represent different levels of complexity. Each is constructed to make it easy to read the information.

Interpreting Different Types of Graphs

CONCRETE GRAPHS

This concrete graph allows the reader to quickly see that there are more green cubes than red or black ones because it

- uses cubes of the same size in all categories
- starts each row of cubes on a common baseline
- is clearly labelled

(continued)

WebConnect

www.makingmathmeaningful
.nelson.com

Visit the Making Math Meaningful website for links to Internet tools that can help students create different types of graphs.

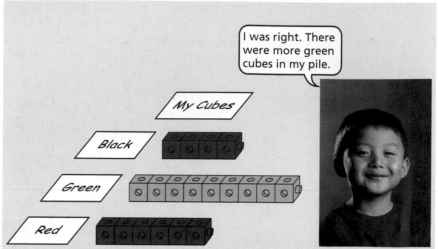

A well-constructed concrete graph makes it easy to compare categories.

PICTURE GRAPHS

This picture graph allows the reader to easily extract all the data because it

- uses a grid to make sure the pictures in each category are equally spaced
- starts each column of pictures on a common baseline
- is clearly labelled
- includes a title that clearly explains what the graph shows

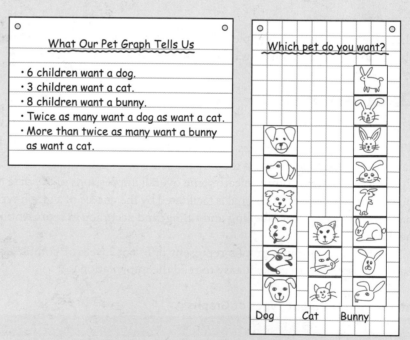

A well-constructed picture graph makes it easy to extract information.

PICTOGRAPHS

This pictograph allows the reader to interpret the symbols because it
- uses the same symbol throughout
- includes a scale statement
- starts the symbols in each row on a common baseline
- uses a symbol that is easily divided in half to represent 1 movie
- is clearly labelled
- includes a title that clearly explains what the graph shows

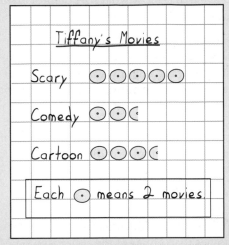

A well-constructed pictograph makes it easy to interpret partial symbols.

LINE GRAPHS

This line graph allows the reader to quickly determine any trends in rainfall over the year because it
- uses dashed lines to indicate to the reader that the data between the plotted points has no meaning and, therefore, cannot be interpolated
- includes labels on both axes that allow the reader to easily estimate the amount of precipitation in each of the 12 months
- includes a title that clearly explains what the graph shows

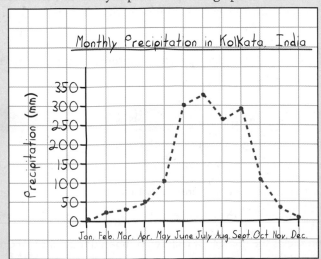

A well-constructed broken-line graph makes it easy to interpret the data and see trends.

Drawing Inferences from Graphs

One of the reasons teachers use visual displays of data is to "paint a picture" of the data in such a way that the display tells more about the data than numbers alone. You want students to be able to read specific pieces of information or facts from a graph and also work with multiple facts, for example, to make comparisons. Eventually, you want them to make inferences about what they see on the graph with appropriate justification.

Below are some examples, based on the graphs in the Reading Graphs chart on pages 503–505, that show what sort of information can be gleaned from graphs, including possible inferences.

The *Which pet do you want?* graph (page 504)

- A young student would report one or two facts from this graph; for example, 8 students want a bunny and 3 want a cat.
- A slightly older student might also conclude that more children want a bunny than either a dog or a cat.
- A student in Grades 5 to 8 might also infer that more people want a bunny because dogs and cats are more typical pets, and many of those students picking a bunny may already have a dog or cat. Note that making inferences often involves personal knowledge and experience.

The *Tiffany's Movies* graph (page 505)

- A student in Grades 2 to 4, even without knowing how to interpret the scale, would be able to conclude from this graph that Tiffany has more scary movies than either of the other two types.
- A possible inference for a student in Grades 5 to 8 might be that, assuming Tiffany bought all the movies herself, she prefers scary movies.

The *Monthly Precipitation* graph (page 505)

A student in Grades 4 to 8 would likely use this graph to

- report that, in the year this set of data was collected, the heavy rain months were from June to September, with a peak in July, and that there was very little rain from November to April, with a low point in December and January
- infer that, assuming this is a typical precipitation pattern, the rainy season in Kolkata is usually from June to September

Inference Activities

Even young students have the capacity to interpret graphical information and make inferences.

ACTIVITY 17.11

Provide an untitled and unlabelled graph, and ask students to come up with different sets of data that might realistically be represented by the graph. For example:

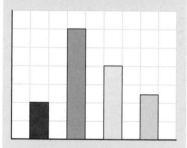

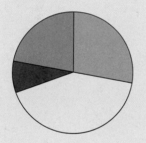

The bar graph might represent

- the number of students in a class with each hair colour: red, brown, black, and blond (using a scale of 2)
- the number of books read by four family members over the summer

The circle graph might represent

- the amount of time spent in a day sleeping (green), at school (blue), eating and snacking (red), leisure time (yellow)
- the favourite leisure activities of students in a class: watching TV (green), sports (yellow), reading (blue), listening to music (red)

ACTIVITY 17.12

Show students two bar graphs without titles or labels:

- Graph A has two bars: one bar is 24 squares high, and the other bar is 1 square high.
- Graph B also has two bars, but one bar is 10 squares high, and the other bar is 14 squares high.

Explain that

- one graph shows the number of children compared to adults in a Grade 2 classroom
- one graph shows the number of 7-year-olds compared to 6-year-olds in a Grade 2 classroom

Ask students to decide which graph is which and why.

Inferring Relationships

Line graphs are particularly well suited for inferring a relationship between variables. For example, the graph below shows running times for Olympic winners for the 100-m women's race from 1948 to 2004.

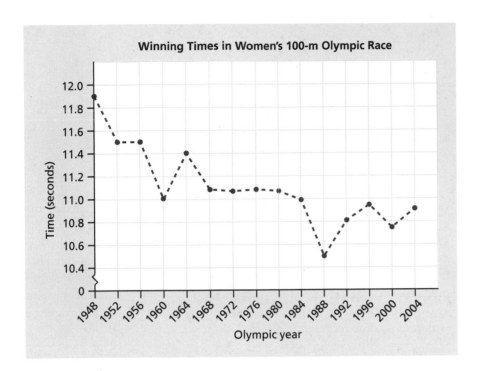

You can infer from this graph that there is a relationship between time and speed; that is, the times to complete the race have been improving over time. However, this improvement has not been continuous, since there is a slight backslide starting in 1992. As well, you can also predict that, as the times get closer to 10 s, the rate of decrease will get less and less.

Interpolation and Extrapolation

One specific way to make inferences from a graph is *interpolation*. Interpolation happens when the reader makes a judgment about values between two given or known values on a graph or in a table.

This broken-line graph shows that the size of the ozone hole has been increasing since 1980, with the sharpest increase from 1980 to 1985. No data were plotted for 1995, but students might estimate that the size of the hole in 1995 was between 18 million km^2 and 26 million km^2—perhaps about 22 million km^2. As with other inferences, it is important to give students a chance to justify their interpolations.

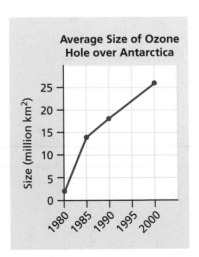

Sometimes students also *extrapolate*—they predict what would happen next. For example, a student might notice that the ozone hole increased in size by roughly 4 million km^2 every 5 years until 2000, and predict that this increase would continue. The student would then predict that the size of the hole would be 30 million km^2 in 2005, and 34 million km^2 by 2010. Again, justification should accompany any extrapolation.

Generally, students are less comfortable with extrapolation than with interpolation and this is reasonable. It is important to emphasize that when line graphs display discrete data, interpolation is inappropriate because there are no data between the known data points. Many line graphs do not use dashed lines even if the data are discrete, so students should be cautioned to analyze line graphs carefully before making any assumptions about interpolating.

Misleading Graphs

One of the main points students need to understand is that it is important to be careful when they are creating and interpreting visual displays. Graphs can be misleading, sometimes deliberately, but more often accidentally.

The following types of errors can lead to misleading graphs.

Misuse of Pictures or Symbols

A typical misleading graph involves the use of pictures or symbols that are not of a consistent shape or size. For example, a student has created the graph below to show the shoe sizes of students. In an attempt to convey the idea that the size 13 shoes are bigger than the size 11 and 12 shoes, the student has used different-sized pictures to represent each shoe size, which has inadvertently misled the reader. It appears that the same number of students wear size 13 as size 11 because the length of each line is the same. It also appears that more students are wearing size 12 than size 11 because the length of the line representing size 12 is longer.

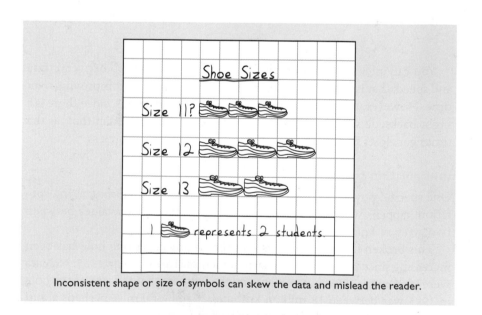

Inconsistent shape or size of symbols can skew the data and mislead the reader.

Misuse of Intervals

Interval bar graphs are supposed to use intervals of equal size. If unequal intervals are used, the graph can be misleading. For example, perhaps in an attempt to determine which interval to use to display his or her data, a student has created the two graphs on page 509. The graphs show the same data, but tell very different stories.

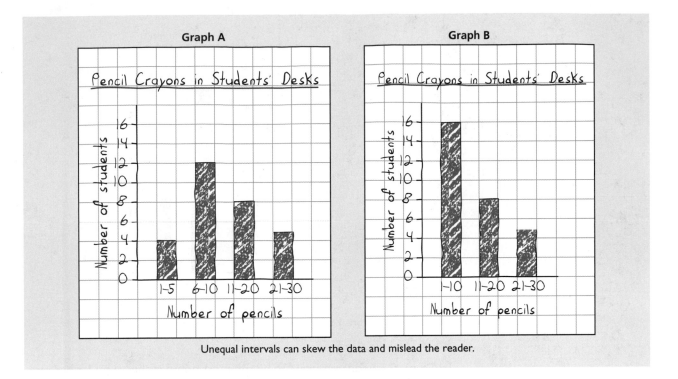

Unequal intervals can skew the data and mislead the reader.

Graph B is accurate, indicating that the group of students who have 1 to 10 pencil crayons is double the size of the group with 11 to 20, and more than triple the size of the group with 21 to 30. Graph A minimizes these differences because the data from the first interval on Graph B is graphed as two intervals on Graph A.

Misuse of Scale

Inappropriate Scale The importance of choosing an appropriate scale is exemplified by the two graphs below. In Graph A, a scale of 100 is used, necessitating the use of an axis break. In Graph B, the same data are shown using a scale of 1000. The impressions left by the graphs showing the same data are quite different.

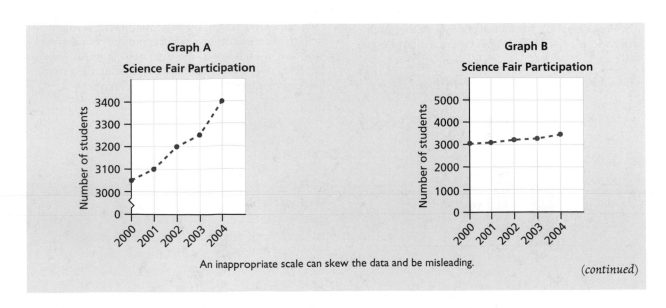

An inappropriate scale can skew the data and be misleading.

(continued)

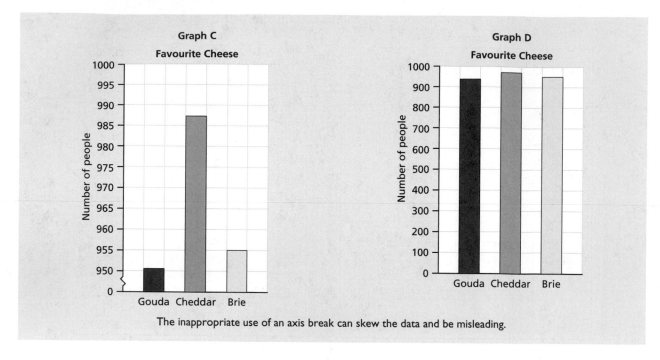

The inappropriate use of an axis break can skew the data and be misleading.

In Graph C, cheddar appears to be the most popular cheese by far because the height of the cheddar bar relative to the other two bars appears so much greater. In fact, this is only because of the axis break in the vertical scale between 0 and 950 people. As a result, the first square in each bar on Graph C actually represents 950 students, while the other squares only represent 5 people. In Graph D, every square represents 100 students. Graph D leaves a more accurate impression of students' cheese preferences, indicating that about the same number of people chose each type of cheese.

Common Errors and Misconceptions

Data Analysis: Strategies for Dealing with Common Errors and Misconceptions

COMMON ERRORS AND MISCONCEPTIONS	SUGGESTED STRATEGY
Misleading Graphs Students interpret graphs at face value and can be misled. For example, a student might look at this graph and conclude that Town A has twice as many people as Town C. 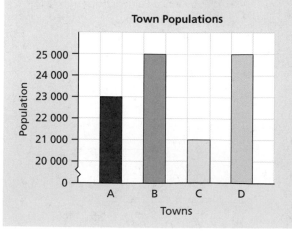	Alert students to aspects of graphs that can be potentially misleading, such as the axis break on this graph. (See *Misleading Graphs* on page 508.) Here, it might help to ask students to write the number of people who live in each town, and then make comparisons. Students might also benefit from creating their own misleading graphs using different techniques.

COMMON ERRORS AND MISCONCEPTIONS	SUGGESTED STRATEGY

Unrealistic Inferences

Students make unrealistic assumptions when drawing inferences. For example, a student might conclude from this graph that, since the temperature has risen 2° every hour, it will continue this pattern and reach 27° by 4 p.m.

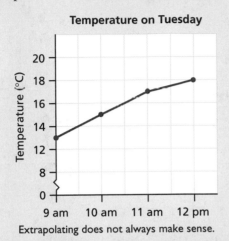

Extrapolating does not always make sense.

It is important for students to be able to justify any inferences they make. (See *Drawing Inferences from Graphs* on page 506.) In this case, you might ask students whether the temperature is likely to keep rising throughout the day, and what this would indicate about the temperature at midnight.

Inappropriate Interpolation

Students interpolate between discrete data points on broken-line graphs. For example, suppose the data were based on science fairs held in April. It would not make sense to say that, in October 2001, participation in the science fair was a little more than 3000, because the science fair is held only once a year.

Interpolating does not always make sense.

Make sure students know that when a line graph uses a solid line, it can indicate that the data values are discrete or continuous. (See *Line Graphs* on page 487.) Remind students to think about the meaning of the data and whether it would make sense to interpolate between the plotted points.

Assessing Student Understanding

- Make sure that you separately assess students' ability to read a graph, draw inferences or conclusions from it, and create it. These are separate skills and you probably want to know which skills are problematic for students and which are not.

- Ask questions that encourage students to consider which graph to use in a particular situation and to explain their reasoning. Often, teachers tell students what graph to use instead of leaving the choice to them.

- Provide students with the opportunity to translate data from one type of display to another. In this way, students will interpret one graph and create another. They will also have the chance to show you whether they recognize when the translation is inappropriate.
- For many students, it might be valuable to provide tools to make the drawing of graphs easier, whether it is grid paper or circle graph templates marked in percents.

Appropriate Children's Books

The Great Graph Contest (Leedy, 2005).
This book for primary students instructs them on how to create different types of graphs. The characters are a toad and a lizard who are competing to create the best graph. There are instructional suggestions provided at the end of the story.

Tiger Math: Learning to Graph from a Baby Tiger (Nagda and Bickel, 2002).
This book charts the growth of an orphaned tiger in a zoo using picture, circle, bar, and line graphs. The book is most appropriate for Grades 4 to 8.

Applying What You've Learned

1. What strategy did you use to solve the chapter problem? Why was that strategy appropriate?
2. For what purpose is each type of graph that you learned about in this chapter most appropriate? Least appropriate?
3. Why is it important that students be encouraged to use both horizontal and vertical pictographs, picture graphs, and bar graphs?
4. How could a teacher who is teaching students about stem-and-leaf plots or histograms use students' knowledge about bar graphs to support the instruction?
5. How might you respond to a student who creates the following graph as a bar graph to show the ages of Mai's aunts?

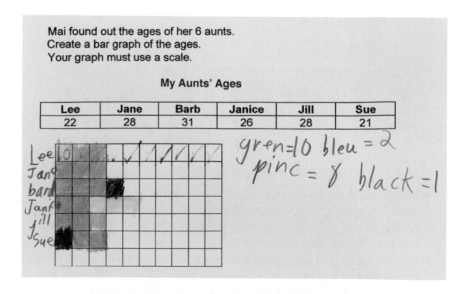

Mai found out the ages of her 6 aunts.
Create a bar graph of the ages.
Your graph must use a scale.

My Aunts' Ages

Lee	Jane	Barb	Janice	Jill	Sue
22	28	31	26	28	21

6. Create an activity you would use to introduce the notion of using a scale on a pictograph. Explain why the selected activity is appropriate.

7. Read an article about graphicacy (e.g., Friel and Bright, 1996). Explain what graphicacy actually is and make an argument for the importance of developing graphicacy at the K–8 level.

8. How can you use work with graphing and data display to support students' number sense development?

Interact with a K–8 Student:

9. Tell students that you want to create a graph to compare the number of cans of food brought in by different classes for a food drive for the needy. Ask for their advice on how they would do this.

Discuss with a K–8 Teacher:

10. Some teachers believe that students should create data displays about topics of personal interest to them, so students choose the topics to graph. Others are concerned that important ideas about graphs might not come out unless the teacher sets up the situation in advance. Ask a teacher how he or she feels about this topic, and why.

Selected References

Aldrich, F., and Sheppard, L. (2000). Graphicacy: The fourth 'r'? *Primary Science Review*, 64, 8–11.

Bamberger, H., and Hughes, P. (1999). *Super graphs, Venns & glyphs.* New York: Scholastic.

Bright, G.W., Brewer, W., McClain, K., and Mooney, E.S. (2003). *Navigating through data analysis in grades 6–8.* Reston, VA: National Council of Teachers of Mathematics.

Chapin, S., Koziol, A., MacPherson, J., and Rezba, C. (2003). *Navigating through data analysis and probability in grades 3–5.* Reston, VA: National Council of Teachers of Mathematics.

Copley, J.V. (2000). *The young child and mathematics.* Washington, DC: National Association for the Education of Young Children and National Council of Teachers of Mathematics.

Curcio, F. R. (2001). *Developing data-graph comprehension in grades K–8* (2nd ed.). Reston, VA: National Council of Teachers of Mathematics.

Friel, S.N., and Bright, G.W. (1996). Building a theory of graphicacy: How do students read graphs? *Paper presented at the Annual Meeting of the American Educational Research Association,* New York: American Educational Research Association. (ERIC Document Reproduction Service No. ED 395 277).

Friel, S.N., Curcio, F.R., and Bright, G.W. (2001). Making sense of graphs: Critical factors influencing comprehension and instructional implications. *Journal for Research in Mathematics Education*, 32, 124–158.

Grummer, D. (1995). Plotting Margo's party. *Teaching Children Mathematics*, 2, 176–179.

Harper, S.R. (2004). Students' interpretation of misleading graphs. *Mathematics Teaching in the Middle School*, 9, 340–343.

Jones, G.A., and Thornton, C.A. (1993). *Data, chance & probability, grades 4–6 activity book.* Lincolnshire, IL: Learning Resources Inc.

Lappan, G., Fey, J., Fitzgerald, W.M., Friel, S.N., and Phillips, E.D. (1998). *Data about us.* (Connected Mathematics). White Plains, NY: Dale Seymour Publications.

Leedy, L. (2005). *The great graph contest.* New York: Holiday House.

Lehrer, R., and Romberg, T. (1996). Exploring children's data modeling. *Cognition and Instruction*, 14, 69–108.

Nagda, A.W., and Bickel, C. (2002). *Tiger Math: Learning to graph from a baby tiger.* New York: Owlet Paperbacks.

Niezgoda, D.A., and Moyer-Packenham, S. (2005). Hickory dickory dock: Navigating through data analysis. *Teaching Children Mathematics*, 11, 292–300.

Sakshaug, L. (2000). Which graph is which? *Teaching Children Mathematics*, 6, 454–455.

Sheffield, L.J., Cavanagh, M., Dacey, L., Findell, C., Greenes, C., and Small, M. (2002). *Navigating through data analysis and probability, prekindergarten–grade 2.* Reston, VA: National Council of Teachers of Mathematics.

Small, M. (2006). *PRIME: Data management and probability: Background and strategies.* Toronto: Thomson Nelson.

Stewart, M. (2007). *Giraffe graphs.* New York: Scholastic Children's Press.

Torres-Velasquez, D., and Lobo, G. (2005). Culturally responsive mathematics teaching and English language learners. *Teaching Children Mathematics*, 11, 249–255.

Chapter 18

Collecting and Describing Data

IN A NUTSHELL

The main ideas in this chapter are listed below:

1. Most data collection activities are based on the prior sorting of information into categories.

2. To collect data, you must create appropriate questions and think about how best to gather the data.

3. It is often useful to "summarize" data by using a statistic that, in some way, reflects the whole data set.

CHAPTER PROBLEM

Create a set of 6 different numbers so that the mean is 42 and the median is 12.

Data Organization

Sorting and Classifying

Students' early work in data management includes sorting and classifying objects. *Sorting* is the physical act of grouping objects according to shared characteristics. *Classifying* is the process of differentiating among the groups by giving each group a category name.

Many of the basic concepts and skills involved in sorting and classifying objects are also fundamental to the organization of data. Students must be able to sort and classify, or organize and categorize data, in order to record the results of data collection in an effective way. For example, if students gather data about siblings, they can use different classifications or categories to sort or organize the results, whether the numbers of siblings, genders of siblings, ages of siblings, or some other set of categories, depending on the problem to be solved.

Students need frequent practice with sorting and classifying objects, especially, although not exclusively, in the early grades. Sorting and classifying activities can be done with everyday materials, or with materials created specifically for the purpose.

Recognizing Attributes

Before sorting and classifying objects, it is important that students understand that any object has many *attributes*. Usually, activities that build this understanding are exploratory in nature—an object is displayed and students are asked to describe it. For example, students are shown a T-shirt and asked to describe it.

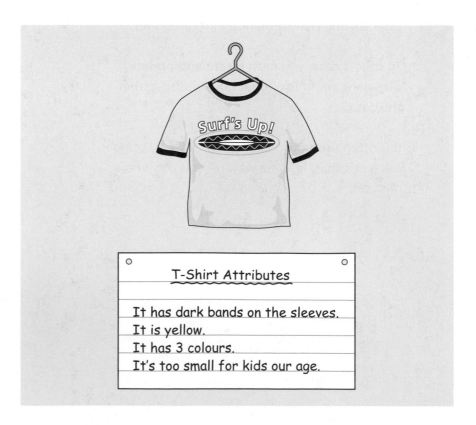

T-Shirt Attributes

It has dark bands on the sleeves.
It is yellow.
It has 3 colours.
It's too small for kids our age.

Some students respond with more ideas if they have two objects to compare and contrast. For example, show a pencil and a ruler and ask for ways in which the objects are the same and ways they are different.

ACTIVITY 18.1

Ask students to compare two items, like a pencil and a ruler.

Comparing a Pencil and a Ruler	
Same	Different
straight	You write with a pencil, but not a ruler.
in my desk	Rulers have numbers, but pencils don't.
useful in school	Pencils have more sides.

Attributes and Characteristics

It helps to have an understanding of some of the terminology associated with sorting. People often use the terms *attribute* and *characteristic* interchangeably.

An attribute is a way to compare objects (for example, by colour), while a characteristic describes how the attribute is reflected in a particular object (for example, red, blue, green). It helps for the teacher to understand what these words mean so that she or he can model appropriate language, but students should not be assessed on their ability to make the distinction.

Describing a Sorting Rule

Students also need practice in recognizing and verbalizing a *sorting rule* for a pre-sorted set of objects. This task is often appealing to students because it involves solving a "mystery." One possible activity is outlined in **Activity 18.2**.

You can re-sort using other characteristics.

Sorting by hair colour: blond and not blond

ACTIVITY 18.3

Where Does It Belong?

Show two containers with wooden shapes in one and plastic shapes in the other. Do not describe the contents of the containers. Hold up a shape, for example, a wooden one, and ask which pail it belongs in and why. Drop the shape in the appropriate container, but do not ask for or reveal the sorting rule yet. Continue with more objects until it appears that most students have figured out the rule.

You can also engage students in activities where they decide where an object belongs when there are pre-sorted sets (**Activity 18.3**), or what object does not belong (**Activity 18.4**).

ACTIVITY 18.4

Which One Does Not Belong?

Show a group of objects in which all the objects but one fit a sorting rule. Ask which object does not belong, and why. In the example shown here, students will likely say that the button with four holes does not belong because the sorting rule is "buttons with two holes." Be aware that students may sometimes surprise you by identifying unexpected sorting rules. For example, a student might indicate that the yellow button does not belong if the sorting rule is "colours with one syllable." For students who are very comfortable with this type of activity, you might want to provide a group of objects and challenge them to identify a series of sorting rules that would exclude each object, in turn, from the group.

Which button doesn't belong?

Sorting by One Attribute

When sorting by one attribute, students sometimes apply a sorting rule simply by moving items together or grouping them if they are alike. For example:

Sorting by One Attribute—Colour: Grouping by Colour

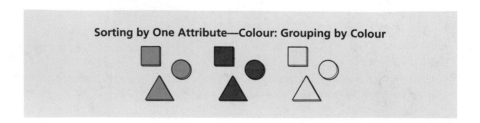

If they are asked simply to sort in order to find all the red shapes, objects that are not red are simply put outside of the sorting circle marked red.

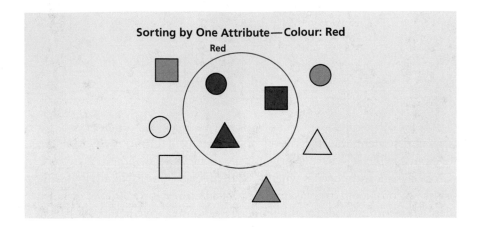

Sorting by One Attribute—Colour: Red

It is sometimes helpful to use concrete organizational tools to assist students in sorting. For example, the teacher might provide two (preferably transparent) containers labelled "Red" and "Not red" into which students can place shapes as they are sorted. Alternately, they could use sorting "mats," plates, or yarn or hula hoops to enclose items.

Some students have difficulty dealing with objects that do not have the characteristic that is the focus of the sort. In the example above, they find it easy to put the red objects together, but may be uncomfortable without a name for the other objects. Rather than using the phrase "not red," they may come up with another term, such as "blue or yellow."

In the sample shown below, this student has sorted a number of foods in terms of whether they are junk ("goke") food or healthy food. Notice that the student did not say "healthy" and "not healthy." Although the sorting may appear to involve two attributes, it really involves only one since, from the student's perspective, the groups are opposites: "junk" is just another way to say "not healthy."

Student Response

This student has chosen his own way of describing the sort.

Sorting by Multiple Attributes

In a number of situations, students may need to sort in terms of two attributes, for example, by colour and size. Organizational sorting tools such as those mentioned earlier can also be used to help students sort by two or more attributes as shown on page 520. A two-way sorting table is also helpful.

Sorting by Two Attributes—Colour and Size

	Red	Blue
Big	⬤ ⬤ ⬤	⬤ ⬤
Small	⬤ ⬤	⬤ ⬤ ⬤

Later, students can use more sophisticated sorting tools such as Venn diagrams, which are particularly useful when *cross-classification* is involved. Cross-classification occurs when a single item has multiple attributes that must be considered in the same sorting situation. For example, if the student who sorted foods for the Student Response above had used the categories "Hot Foods" and "Healthy Foods," then a food such as corn would cross-classify because it has both characteristics.

Venn Diagrams

Venn diagrams are a commonly used sorting tool. Each circle is used to contain all the objects with a particular characteristic. The name of the sorting rule is shown as a label for each circle. The number of circles depends on the number of characteristics being used to sort the items. In each case, the circle or circles are included in a large rectangle that represents the "universe," or the whole set of objects being sorted. Every object being sorted has to have a place in the diagram, even if it is outside the circles but inside the rectangle.

When introducing students to Venn diagrams, hula hoops or large rings of string or yarn can serve as concrete Venn diagram circles. Initially, students can sort actual objects into these hoops. Later, they can draw the circles and objects. Later still, students can sort words, that is, the names of the objects (e.g., Big and Blue, Small and Blue).

Venn Diagrams for One-Attribute Sorting

This one-circle Venn diagram shows a set of hexagon and rectangle attribute blocks being sorted according to whether they are hexagons. The rectangle blocks are outside the circle but still inside the rectangle, as they are not hexagons but they are still part of the universal set being sorted.

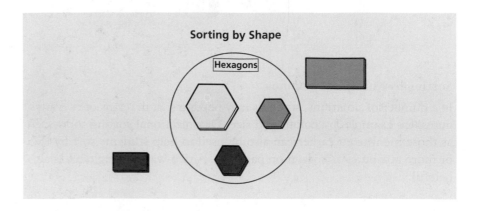

Sorting by Shape

Venn Diagrams for Two-Attribute Sorting

Venn diagrams are excellent tools for sorting by multiple attributes because they make it easy to see when there are items that cross-classify. For example, the buttons in this Venn diagram are being sorted according to two attributes—colour and number of holes. The buttons in the middle where the circles overlap have both characteristics (two holes and blue). The button outside the circles does not have either characteristic.

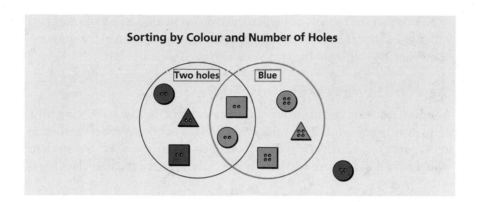

Sorting by Colour and Number of Holes

To introduce the notion of how cross-classification is shown in Venn diagrams, set out two hoops, side by side, and label each one with a sorting rule. Ensure the sorting rules and objects to be sorted lend themselves to cross-classification, for example, triangles and square corners (not triangles and quadrilaterals). Have students sort objects into the hoops until they come to an object that cross-classifies. Discuss where the object belongs and elicit the idea of crossing the hoops to form an overlap.

Note that the circles of a Venn diagram do not have to overlap. They can be two discrete circles if the attributes are exclusive, for example, if one were used to contain girls and one contained boys. They could also be separate circles if the items involved in the sort do not exhibit the same characteristics, even if they have the potential to do so. For example, if a group of shapes were sorted using the characteristics red and striped, the Venn diagram circles would remain as separate circles if there were no shapes that were both red and striped. As soon as a striped red shape was included in the set, the circles would have to overlap to accommodate that shape in the intersection of the two circles. Students can use Venn diagrams to solve problems like the one in **Activity 18.5**.

> ### ACTIVITY 18.5
>
> In a class of 22 students, 10 play hockey and 15 play basketball.
>
> a) Is it possible that there are some students who play neither sport? What is the greatest possible number of students who do not play either sport? Explain your answer. Show your work.
>
> b) Is it possible that all 22 students are involved in one sport or the other or both? Explain your answer. Show your work.

Carroll Diagrams

Carroll diagrams are tables that work much like Venn diagrams, for the purpose of cross-classification. Two attributes are being used for sorting, with one attribute of each characteristic being the focus. For example, shapes might be sorted by whether they are round or not, and whether they are blue or not.

A table is created with four cells to show the four possible combinations of these two attributes. Either the items themselves or the count of how many items of each type are put in the cells.

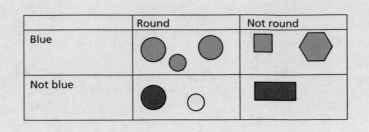

	Round	Not round
Blue		
Not blue		

Notice that the top left cell is like the overlap section of a Venn diagram with two circles, and the bottom right cell is like the section of the universe not included in either of the two Venn circles.

Student-Invented Sorting Tools

At times, students invent their own organizational tools for showing how items have been sorted. This student has created her own model for sorting items that cross-classify. It would be interesting to see what the student would have done if there had been more than one item to cross-classify.

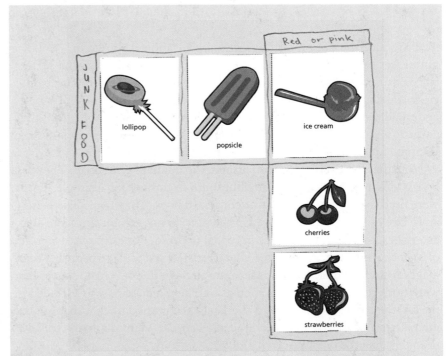

This student has classified in terms of whether they are red or pink and whether they are junk food. The ice cream, which fits both categories, is located at the intersection.

IMPORTANT POINTS ABOUT DATA ORGANIZATION

- Sorting and classifying objects will help students with organizing and categorizing data.
- Sorting is the action of grouping (or organizing) objects (or data); classification (or categorization) is the naming of the groups of objects (or data).

- Students need opportunities to explore attributes and characteristics of objects that can be used for sorting.
- When students sort by two or more attributes, there is potential for overlap or cross-classification.
- A Venn or Carroll diagram is not only an organizational tool for sorting, but is sometimes a form of data display that can be used to display an object or data when the categories overlap.

Common Errors and Misconceptions

Data Organization: Strategies for Dealing with Common Errors and Misconceptions

COMMON ERROR AND MISCONCEPTION	SUGGESTED STRATEGY
Using "and" and "or" When students engage in sorting activities, they often have trouble distinguishing between the words "and" and "or." The student that sorted the foods on page 522 has correctly labelled the red/pink category "Red or pink." Another student might have used the incorrect label "Red and pink." The word "and" indicates that each item in the group would have both red and pink on it.	Explicitly consider situations where the words "and" and "or" are used, and discuss with students what is meant in each case. For example, you might say, "Bring up your report if you are presenting it Monday or Tuesday." Emphasize that this means that you want both groups to bring up their reports. On the other hand, if you say, "Stand up if you have brown hair and blue eyes," then only students who have both brown hair and blue eyes should stand.
Using Venn Diagrams When students use Venn diagrams to show a sorting, they ignore the items that do not belong inside the circles.	Whenever students create a Venn diagram, ensure that they show the universe as a rectangle around the circle(s). Regularly ask them to think about what kind of items belong in the circles, and also what kind of items belong in the rectangle, but not inside a circle. For example, the blue square and green circle may not belong inside the sorting circle, but they do have a place outside the circle and inside the rectangle. 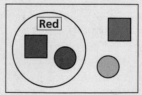 As often as possible, ensure there are objects that will not fit in either circle so students have many opportunities to place objects in the region outside the circles. Another strategy is to make a list of the places where objects can go. For example, in the case of a two-attribute sort, objects can go • inside the left circle • inside the right circle • in the intersecting or overlapping region • in the region outside the circles but inside the rectangle 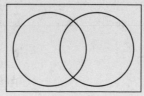

Appropriate Manipulatives

Data Organization: Examples of Manipulatives

ATTRIBUTE BLOCKS	EXAMPLE
Attribute, or logic, blocks are ideal for sorting because of their many attributes: size, colour, shape, and thickness.	Students can use attribute blocks to practise sorting with a Venn diagram. 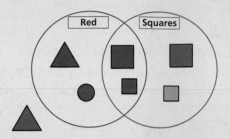

OTHER SORTING MATERIALS	EXAMPLE
Materials such as cards or tiles (commercial or teacher-made), as well as items found in the home and classroom (buttons, writing implements, footwear, etc.), can also be used to practice identifying attributes through sorting.	The sorting tiles have many attributes: size, colour, type of animal, and design (stripes or polka dots). The tiles shown here could be arranged in two discrete sorting circles, for example, "Large" and "Small," or they could be placed in a Venn diagram with overlapping circles for "Large" and "Stripes."

GEOMETRIC SHAPES	EXAMPLE
Shapes of different sizes are useful for sorting. Geometric shapes, both 2-D and 3-D, can be teacher-made or commercial. Attributes such as number of sides, concavity or convexity, and symmetry can be included.	The blocks below can be sorted according to a variety of attributes: • symmetry • equal sides • parallel sides • number of sides 

Appropriate Technology

Computers

There are several programs that students can use to practise sorting skills. Very young children might enjoy Disney's *Ready for Math with Pooh* (where they can sort bugs), the Learning Company's *Reader Rabbit Math Adventure*, or *Learning Buddies Little Bear Preschool Thinking Adventure*. Older students might use software to help them organize their CDs. An example is a program called *Album Tracker*.

Children at various developmental levels might enjoy using the *Buckets* software by Good to Think. *Buckets* presents a series of increasingly challenging puzzles in which players determine rules they can use to sort collections of objects. Students can also sort images downloaded from the Internet or clip art from a drawing program, using the software's cut-and-paste feature to arrange the images. For example, the pictures below could be classified into items that you can or cannot buy at a movie theatre, or items that you do or do not eat with butter.

Data Collection

Why People Collect Data

People collect data in order to solve problems. Children do this naturally even before they come to school. For example, suppose a child is given a new and unfamiliar toy. The child now has a problem to solve: how does the toy work? The child may conduct a variety of "experiments" to collect data—trying many different things and often repeating actions—in order to figure out what the toy can do. The child may also ask questions about the toy, with the intention of gathering further data from caregivers or other children.

School activities should support this idea that data collection is a tool that can help solve problems, rather than an end in itself. There should always be a purpose for collecting data, and the method of data collection should suit that purpose.

Asking Good Survey Questions

Young children constantly ask questions to gather data. They also watch their caregivers use questions to solve problems in everyday situations. For example, asking "Do you want chicken tonight?" involves collecting data in order to gather the data needed to solve the problem of what to have for dinner.

Students know intuitively that questions can help them gather data, but activities at school can help them learn to ask the right questions in the right way. For example, a student might conduct a survey to find out what books his or her classmates like to read. If the student asks a group of people an open-ended question such as "What is your favourite book?", there might be eight or more different answers—too much data to draw any useful conclusions about reading preferences. If, on the other hand, the child asks, "Do you like detective stories? Yes or no.", the data will be easier to use—the child will learn whether more students do or do not like these books and how the proportions compare.

If the student were to ask, "Which is your favourite type of book to read?", and then provide several categories of books to choose from, such as stories about the past, fantasy, detective stories, or nonfiction, they would get even more data that could be organized in a form that is useful to them.

What is your favourite book?
If You Give A Mouse a Cookie
Green Eggs and Ham
Franklin Plays the Game
I Spy Treasure Hunt
Mud Puddle
Dinosaur Day
Green Eggs and Ham
Angel and the Polar Bear

Open-Ended

Do you like detective stories?	
Yes	No
HHT HHT	HHT
HHT HHT	

Yes/No Answer Choices

Which is your favourite type of book to read?	
Type of Book	Number of Students
Stories about the past	HHT I
Fantasy	HHT HHT II
Detective stories	III
Non-fiction	III
Other	I

Multiple but Limited Answer Choices

Initially, students should be encouraged to ask yes/no questions because it is much easier to collect and organize data when only two responses are possible. Later, students can ask questions with more than two possible answers, but where choices are still limited. In the multiple-choice example, notice the category labelled "Other." This is a handy category for the odd, unexpected answer. However, if students get a lot of data in this category, it is an indication that their categories need to be revised.

Asking questions with multiple possible answers can sometimes lead students to the discovery that questions involving levels or ratings can produce useful information. For example, students might ask the yes/no question "Can you swim?" Students who respond to the question may have difficulty answering with a simple yes or no since some are able to swim short distances, and still others are strong swimmers. The student can then go back and refine the question by including levels of swimming ability.

Students' previous work with Venn diagrams can help them formulate good questions to use for collecting data. Consider the following set of answer choices for a survey about books:

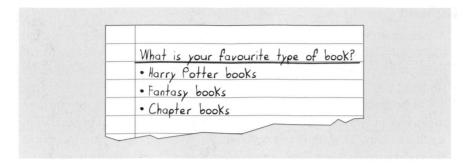

Students' understanding of cross-classification should help them realize why this set of choices will not work. A student who likes Harry Potter books will need to respond yes to all three categories. With an understanding of what it means to cross-classify, students will realize that these categories are not distinct or *discrete* because there is overlap, just as there would be if the students' responses were sorted in a Venn diagram with circles labelled to show these categories.

With support, an atmosphere that encourages risk-taking, good question models to follow, and opportunities for practice, students will be able to create good questions that include a limited number of appropriate and discrete choices. It is important to use a trial-and-error approach that will help students learn from their mistakes. Encourage them to try out their questions with their classmates or others, and then refine their questions to reflect what they learned from their trials.

Audience

To make sure a question is clear enough to elicit meaningful data, students have to think about who will be reading or using the data they plan to collect and put themselves in that person's shoes. For example, Grade 4 students might want to find out, through a survey, which night of the week should be homework-free for their class. They might develop a survey such as the following, and distribute it to each classmate:

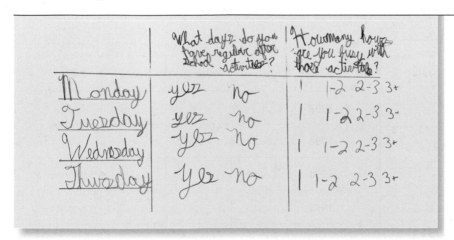

Student Response

By asking clear questions about their classmates' after-school activities, students are likely to get specific and useful data that they can present to their audience (the teacher) for consideration.

Note that once all these individual survey sheets are collected, the pieces of data will have to be combined and organized in such a way that they can be analyzed to determine which is the busiest night. Students could also display this combined data using, for example, a table or graph to provide their audience with supporting evidence for their recommendation.

Questionnaires

A *questionnaire* is really a collection of survey questions, usually all related to the same topic. It can be conducted by interview or on paper. Because of their complexity, questionnaires are generally more appropriate for older students.

Questionnaires can be complex, particularly if respondents are expected to answer in writing, because the data must be collated and organized in a suitable way. This step can sometimes be skipped when questionnaires are conducted by interview, if the interviewer records the data in a pre-organized structure, for example, by making tallies in different parts of a chart.

Interviews

Interviews have their own difficulties. Extraneous data may be offered by interviewees, and less-experienced interviewers might find it difficult to focus on the relevant data. For example, if one student asks another to name a favourite fast food, it is easy to imagine the interviewee digressing about who in his or her family likes that food. Again, providing the interviewer with a pre-organized structure can help him or her extract and keep track of important data. Sometimes, an interviewer might opt to include space for additional comments.

Choosing Data Collection Topics

Primary students are interested mostly in issues related directly to their own lives, such as activities they like to do, or their measurements, toys, hobbies, family's clothing, or pets.

Later on, students become increasingly interested in the broader world, whether it is geography, sports, politics, or other cultures, although, not surprisingly, they remain interested in topics related to their own lives.

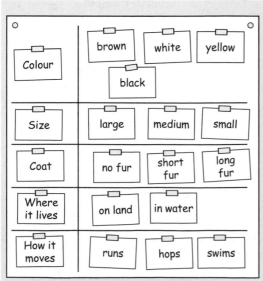

Collecting and organizing data on pets

Olympic Medals Won by Canadian Figure Skaters

	Men	Women	Dance	Pairs
2002				Gold
1998	Silver			
1994	Silver			Bronze
1992				Bronze
1988	Silver	Silver	Bronze	

Collecting and organizing data on figure skating results

Data Management Topics

TOPICS FOR YOUNGER STUDENTS	TOPICS FOR OLDER STUDENTS
Some interesting data management topics for younger students include • stories they like to hear • activities they would like to do in the gym • extracurricular activities in which they participate • their favourite authors • their favourite cartoons or movies	Some interesting data management topics for older students include • results of experiments • costs of items over time • temperatures in different places • popularity of computer games • populations in different cities, provinces, or countries • information about government, for example, the number of elected representatives for different geographic regions • sports statistics

Data Sources

Data sources are directly related to the topics under investigation.

Primary or Firsthand Data

Primary data is firsthand data that students collect themselves or with their classmates or teacher. Using primary data makes sense when students are looking for answers to questions about objects and people in their own environment. It also makes sense when students are just beginning to learn about data, or when the amount of data is limited, for example, a survey of only 10 or 20 people rather than hundreds.

Secondary or Secondhand Data

Later, students collect and analyze *secondary data* from secondary sources such as atlases, almanacs, other reference books, and the Internet. Browsers make it easier than ever for students to access secondhand data. The difficulty lies in deciding what data is really useful and what data is reliable or accurate.

Secondary Data Resources

These are some of the excellent resources that provide secondary data for students:

- *World Almanac for Kids*
- *Scholastic Book of Lists*
- *Time for Kids Almanac*
- *The World Almanac and Book of Facts*
- *The Canadian Global Almanac*
- *The Top 10 of Everything: Canadian Edition*
- *Guinness World Records*

Factors Influencing Data Collection

Older students are more likely than younger ones to begin to think about how the methods they use to collect data can affect their results. They will be ready to consider issues such as the potential for *bias* or how many people they should include in their survey.

Sometimes, students will be able to conduct a *census*, that is, survey everyone from a given population. For example, suppose students want to conduct a survey to find out where to go on a school trip. It would be easy to ask everyone in the class. With a larger population, it is impractical to survey everyone, so students need to use a *sample group*. Suppose they want to conduct a survey to find out whether people in their community support year-round schooling. In this case, they will have to carefully consider whom to ask (the make-up of the sample), how many people to ask (the sample size), and when to gather the data. For example:

- If they ask only students, the results will not reflect the concerns of other segments of the community, including parents, teachers, or people who operate summer businesses such as camps or resorts.
- If they ask mainly adults who do not have school-age children, the results will not reflect the views of those who are concerned— students and parents.
- If they conduct their survey at the end of the summer, they may get a different answer than if they do it in the middle of the winter.
- If they ask only a dozen people, they might get significantly different results than if they ask 100 people.

Students need to begin to think about ways to gather data so that the results will be both reliable and useful. This means that they should be able to use the results from the sample to make generalizations about the population. These considerations become even more important as students move on to secondary school and study statistical concepts at a more sophisticated level, for example, random sampling techniques, or ways to select samples to ensure they are appropriate.

IMPORTANT POINTS ABOUT DATA COLLECTION

- Data should be collected to solve relevant problems.
- A good survey question has a limited number of answer choices, yet enough to accommodate everyone (one of the answer choices may be "Other"). The choices or categories should be discrete, that is, they should not overlap.
- When designing a survey, students must consider the audience—who will use the information and how they will use it.
- Data collected using a questionnaire will require more sophisticated techniques for collating and organizing.
- Data can be primary (collected directly by students) or secondary (collected by others and used by students). Younger students work with primary data; older students work with both primary and secondary data.
- There are many data collection factors that have the potential to influence the results, such as bias and sample size.

Common Errors and Misconceptions

Data Collection: Strategies for Dealing with Common Errors and Misconceptions

COMMON ERRORS AND MISCONCEPTIONS	SUGGESTED STRATEGY
Unclear or Vague Survey Questions When students develop survey or questionnaire questions, they do not consider the clarity of the wording or the vagueness of the question. For example, if students want to know whether children are likely to be the ones who care for their pets or whether they leave it to their parents, they might simply ask, "How much do you look after your pet?" This can mean very different things to different respondents. Some might tell how many times they feed the pet, others might just say "a lot."	Have students try out their questions on a variety of different audiences to see the kind of responses they get. For example, by asking the pet question of an older sibling or parent who might respond with "What do you mean?", it becomes clearer that the question needs refinement. Encourage students to ask questions that will result in responses that are unambiguous because they ask for specific information. For example, asking "How many times a week do you feed your dog?" will usually prompt specific responses.
Non-Discrete Categories When students create survey questions, they include choices that are not exclusive or discrete. For example: What is your favourite type of game? • *Monopoly* • *Sorry* • Board games • Games of chance	It is important to remind students that, if they want to compare the sizes of the groups who chose each answer, or determine the total number of people who were surveyed, then they cannot ask questions where the same person chooses more than one answer. In the case of the survey question shown here, you might ask why someone who likes *Sorry* might have trouble deciding whether to choose *Sorry*, board games, or games of chance. Encourage students to review the list of categories to see how they can refine it so that categories do not overlap.

Appropriate Manipulatives

Data Collection: Examples of Manipulatives

CONCRETE GRAPHING MATERIALS	EXAMPLE
Younger students may prefer to use concrete materials to keep track of survey results. Note that, in many cases, the results of the data collection also serve as a data display.	Students can use concrete materials for surveying in a variety of ways, including • hanging clothespins on a string • linking cubes to make a "tower" for each possible response • making rows of stickers • stacking paper cups • using magnetic pictures or name tags (made from the lids of frozen juice cans) • placing craft sticks in labelled cups 

(continued)

CLIPBOARDS	EXAMPLE
Many students enjoy using clipboards when they are surveying others.	Clipboards make it easy for students to conduct surveys anywhere.

Appropriate Technology

Computers

Students can use word-processing programs to print out questionnaires or to create and print charts they can use to record responses. They can use e-mail to send out surveys and retrieve results. Spreadsheets can help them total the results of their surveys and make calculations with the data. For example, older students could determine the percentage of people who chose each response.

The Internet

The Internet provides older students with access to large quantities of secondary data about topics such as sports, world records, and Canadian statistics. Examples of sites to visit include the Guiness World Records site, the Statistics Canada site, and sites operated by sports organizations such as the National Basketball Association.

One particularly interesting site is the *Census at School* site, operated by Statistics Canada. This site is part of an international project designed to gather data about students from around the world. Students who visit the website can complete a brief online survey about themselves, and then examine a wide variety of data collected from others who have completed similar surveys.

Statistics

The study of data inevitably leads to the study of *statistics*. Statistics involves using numerical values to describe a set of data. For example, a number of 10-year-olds might be measured and their individual heights recorded. The average height is then calculated in order to describe the group of students with a single value that will give someone a good idea of how tall a typical student from the group might be. Most statistical study is undertaken at the secondary school level, but the calculation of averages is a topic that students learn about prior to that.

Measures of Central Tendency

There are three *measures of central tendency*, or *averages*, that students encounter: *mean*, *median*, and *mode*. Each one is a way to describe a set of data with a single meaningful number. In some situations, only one of these averages makes sense, but in other situations, two or three averages are meaningful, even if they are different.

The Mean

The *mean* is the number that people are usually referring to when they talk about "the average." A mean describes a set of data by indicating the value that would result from putting all the values together and distributing them evenly. It is calculated by adding up all the data values and dividing by the number of values.

For example, suppose there are the following numbers of students in six different groups. To calculate the mean group size, you add all six numbers for a total of 30, and then divide by 6 to get 5. The mean indicates that, if all students were redistributed into six equal groups, there would be 5 students in each group.

Group A	Group B	Group C	Group D	Group E	Group F
3	5	4	7	5	6

The mean is $\frac{3 + 5 + 4 + 7 + 5 + 6}{6} = \frac{30}{6} = 5$.

> **ACTIVITY 18.6**
>
> Ask students to create three data sets that they think are quite different, but still have the same mean.

> **ACTIVITY 18.7**
>
> Provide students with an incomplete list of data and the mean of the data, and ask them to identify the missing data. For example, tell them that the mean of 7, 9, 10, 15, and x is 11, and ask them to figure out the value of x.

When the Mean Is Meaningful A mean of 5 is an appropriate representation of the data above because there are a few groups that have slightly fewer than 5, a few that have slightly more than 5, and two groups that have exactly 5. However, when the group sizes are quite different (as shown below), but one size is more typical than any other, then the mean is not always the best indicator of the "average" group size. In such a case, it might be better to use the mode—the number that occurs most often.

Group A	Group B	Group C	Group D	Group E	Group F
1	1	7	7	7	7

The mean is $\frac{1 + 1 + 7 + 7 + 7 + 7}{6} = \frac{30}{6} = 5$.
However, this number does not appropriately represent this particular set of data.

Working Concretely to Establish the Notion of Mean

ACTING IT OUT

When students are first introduced to the concept of mean, they should have opportunities to act it out and explore it concretely.

To model the first grouping situation above, students could arrange themselves into one group of 3, one group of 4, two groups of 5, one group of 6, and one group of 7, and then redistribute themselves into six equal groups to find out how many students would be in each new group.

Students will likely use trial and error to form equal groups. Or, they might form one large group, and then break off into smaller groups by moving people one at a time to each of the six groups, always keeping them equal.

(continued)

> When we made the groups equal, we ended up with 5 in each group, so 5 is the mean.

USING LINKING CUBES

Another way to model the same grouping situation is to use linking cubes, with a different colour for each original group. The mean number of cubes could be found in two ways:

- combining all the cubes into one larger group, and then sharing them equally among 6 groups
- making a cube train for each group, as shown here, and redistributing the cubes until all of the trains are of equal length

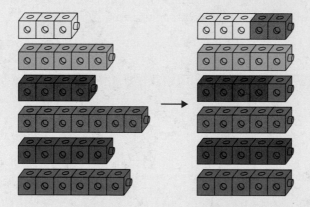

Redistributing cubes to find the mean

USING A STRAIGHT LINE

Another way to find the mean is to move a ruler or taut string along the cube trains representing the groups until the number of cubes above the mean (to the right of the string) exactly balances the number of empty spaces below the mean (to the left of the string). This can be seen in the visual on page 535. The vertical line represents the mean, which is 5. The total length of the arrows on the left of the vertical line, or mean, is $2 + 1 = 3$. The total on the right of the mean is $2 + 1 = 3$.

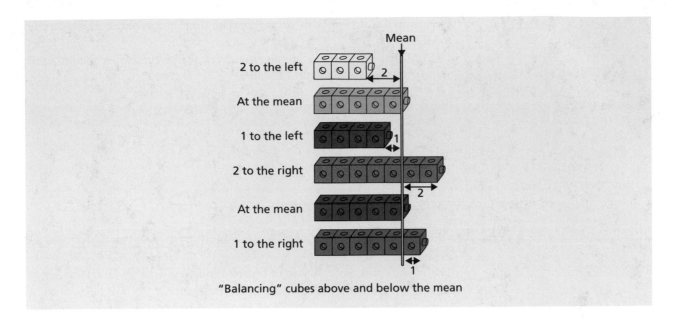

"Balancing" cubes above and below the mean

Exploring Properties of the Mean There are many properties of the mean that older students can explore, as described in **Activity 18.8**.

The Median

The *median* is another kind of average used to describe a set of data with a single value. It is the middle value when the data is in order. To find the median group size of the six groups of students below, the values are first put in order from least to greatest. The number in the middle is the median. In this case, there are two middle numbers, but they are the same, so the median is 5. (If the two middle values had been different, the median would have been the mean of the two values.) Notice that half of the numbers are above the median and half are below. Also, note that the median and mean of this set of data are equal. This is not always the case.

ACTIVITY 18.8
Ask students to record a set of 8 numbers and calculate the mean. Now have them do the following:
a) Add 10 to each value and recalculate the mean. Ask what they notice.
b) Multiply each value by 10 and recalculate the mean. Ask what they notice.

Group A	Group B	Group C	Group D	Group E	Group F
3	4	5	5	6	7

The median is 5.

When the Median Is Meaningful A median of 5 is an appropriate representation of the data above in the same way that the mean of 5 was appropriate. The median is particularly valuable if there are just one or two very extreme pieces of data. In this case, the mean is often influenced by the extreme data much more than is the median, so the mean may be less representative of the entire set of data.

There are occasions, though, when the median might be less representative than the mean in representing a set of data. With the data on page 536,

ACTIVITY 18.9
Ask students to consider whether it is possible for a set of data to have a mean that is exactly 1 greater than the median.

the mean (9) might be a more appropriate description of the data than the median (5).

Note that the number of values is even, so the median is the mean of 1 and 9.

Group A	Group B	Group C	Group D	Group E	Group F
1	1	1	9	19	23

The median is $\frac{1+9}{2} = \frac{10}{2} = 5$.
However, this number does not appropriately represent this particular set of data.

The Mode

The *mode* is another measure of central tendency used to describe a set of data. It is the most frequent value in the data set.

Group A	Group B	Group C	Group D	Group E	Group F
3	5	4	7	5	6

The median is 5.

A set of data can have one mode, multiple modes, or no mode at all. (If each number in a set of data values occurs as frequently as the rest, there is no mode, for example, the set 2, 3, 4, 5 has no mode; there are multiple modes for 2, 2, 3, 3, 4, 4, 5, 5.)

If there are many pieces of data, the best way to determine the mode might be to write all the values in order and look for the longest set of matching numbers.

It is easy to determine the mode from a bar graph, a line graph, or a stem-and-leaf plot. The mode is the value described by the highest bar, the highest point, or the longest set of leaves.

When the Mode Is Meaningful A mode of 5 is an appropriate representation of the data above in the same way that the mean and median of 5 were. However, if the other data values were all quite different from the mode, as in the situation below, using the mode to describe the average group size might be misleading. In this case, the mean might be a more appropriate description of the data.

Group A	Group B	Group C	Group D	Group E	Group F
12	12	1	2	3	4

The mode is 12. However, this number does not appropriately represent this particular set of data.

There are certain real-life situations where the mode is the only appropriate measure. For example, a shoe store might keep a record of the shoe sizes it sells most often (the mode) to help with making orders for new stock.

A mean or median shoe size of, for example, 4.2, is not useful information, nor does it make sense, because there is no such thing as a 4.2 shoe size.

Measures of Data Spread

Range

There are many sophisticated measures of the spread of data. Although mathematicians most frequently use a statistic called a standard deviation, its calculation is difficult. One statistic that is accessible to K–8 students is the *range*. The range is the difference between the least value and the greatest value, so it shows the spread of the data. For example, in the set of values below, the smallest group has 3 students and the largest group has 7. A student would subtract $7 - 3$ to determine a range of 4.

Group A	Group B	Group C	Group D	Group E	Group F
3	4	5	5	6	7

The range of this set of data is 4 ($7 - 3$). It appropriately represents the spread of data in this particular set of data.

What the range does not show is whether the values are distributed evenly or whether there are gaps or clusters. The set of data below has the same range as the set above, but the distribution of the data is very different. In this case, identifying the range as 4 gives the group of 7 more weight than is appropriate, since the other groups all contain 3 students.

Group A	Group B	Group C	Group D	Group E	Group F
3	3	3	3	3	7

The range of this set of data is 4, but the range does not appropriately represent the set of data. The mode (3) would be a better choice.

Combining Statistics

Sometimes using an average and a range together can describe a set of data better than using just one or the other. For example, the data below could be described as having a mean group size of 11 and a range of 9.

Group A	Group B	Group C	Group D	Group E	Group F
6	9	10	11	15	15

The median is $\frac{6 + 9 + 10 + 11 + 15 + 15}{6} = \frac{66}{6} = 11$. The range is 9 ($15 - 6$).

Using Graphs to Determine Statistics

One graph that is useful to use to read off statistics is a stem-and-leaf plot. A stem-and-leaf plot shows each individual piece of data, making it easy to determine the median, mean, mode, and range directly from the graphical display. (See page 486 for more information about stem-and-leaf plots.)

Ask students to create sets of data to meet various statistical criteria.

For example, they might be asked to create a set of data with a mean of 10, a median of 5, and a range of 33.

For the set of data displayed in the stem-and-leaf plot below,

- the median test score is 89. This is the middle data value in the set of 29 data values (counting to the halfway point, the 15th number, from either end). There are as many pieces of data below it as above it (14).
- the mean is 86.3. This is calculated by finding the sum of all 29 data values and dividing by 29.
- the mode is 90. It is the most frequently appearing data value.
- the range is 98 − 71 = 27.

Test Scores	
7	1 2 2 7 8 9
8	0 0 3 4 4 5 8 9 9
9	0 0 0 0 1 1 2 2 3 3 3 5 5 8

IMPORTANT POINTS ABOUT MEASURES OF CENTRAL TENDENCY AND DATA SPREAD

- The purpose of a measure of central tendency is to assign a value, usually a single value, to a set of data that is a good representation of the data.
- Three measures of central tendency are mean, median, and mode.
- The mean indicates the value that would result from putting all the values together and distributing them evenly.
- The median is the middle value when pieces of data are listed in order. If there are two middle values, the median is the mean of these values.
- The mode is the most frequent value(s) in a data set.
- Sometimes a combination of range and mean, median, or mode gives a better picture of the data than one measure alone.

Common Errors and Misconceptions

Statistics

INCORRECTLY CALCULATING THE MEDIAN

There are a number of difficulties students have in calculating the median:

- They sometimes forget to put the numbers in order and simply write down the middle number in the unordered list.

For example, they might write 8 if the data were: 7, 8, 1.

- When there is an even number of values, students often use one or the other of the middle values, rather than their mean, as the median.

Also, when there are many values, students might simply take half of the number of values and incorrectly identify the median.

For example, if the data were: 2, 3, 5, 9, they would say there are 4 pieces of data, half of 4 is 2, and use the second number (3), rather than the mean of 3 and 5.

Remind students often that once the median is located, there should be just as many numbers in the data set above that median as below it.

If this does not occur, the median was incorrectly identified.

This provides a check that will uncover a number of possible errors in the calculation of the median.

INCORRECTLY REPORTING RANGE

Students describe the range using the minimum and maximum data values rather than calculating the single-value difference. For example, a student might describe the range of these values as "from 4 to 9" rather than "5."

4, 4, 5, 7, 7, 7, 8, 9

Tell students that, like the mean or median, the range is a single value. While measures of central tendency are single values used to identify a typical data value, the range is a single value used to describe the spread of the data.

Appropriate Manipulatives

Data Analysis: Example of Manipulatives

LINKING CUBES

Linking cubes and grid paper are good tools to use when you first introduce the concepts of mean, mode, and median.

EXAMPLE

Students can create cube trains to represent values in a set of data. To determine the mean, they adjust the trains until they are all the same length, as was shown on page 534.

To determine the median, students line up the trains in order, from least to greatest, and identify the middle train. (If there are 2 middle trains of a different value, they might be able to move cubes from one of these trains to the other until the trains are equal.)

To determine the mode, students line up the trains in order and identify the most frequent length. In this example, the mode is the same as the median and the mean. (Usually, these are different.)

Appropriate Technology

Calculators

Calculators are useful to older students for calculating statistics such as the mean or the range.

Computers

Most word-processing programs have spreadsheets that can be used to support data analysis. Students can use spreadsheets to calculate means from entered data, or to explore how changing the data values can affect the mean. There is some specially developed spreadsheet software available for students. Two well-known programs are *Tabletop Jr.* and *The Cruncher*.

The Internet

There are applets available online that students can use to explore measures of central tendency. As well, students who have access to the Internet can find many statistics to analyze about a wide range of topics.

WebConnect

www.makingmathmeaningful.nelson.com

Visit the Making Math Meaningful website for links to Internet tools that can help students explore measures of central tendency.

Assessing Student Understanding

- As you assess students' ability to sort, it is important to recognize that the attributes they use to sort may not be what you anticipate. So, for example, if you ask "What doesn't belong?" and they give an unanticipated response, it is essential that you inquire about the sorting rule upon which they are basing their conclusion.
- As students classify objects, they often do not include objects in the universe that are not inside the sorting circles. You may have to

prompt further to see whether they can correctly use a Venn diagram.

- Link sorting activities to mathematics in other strands. For example, you might ask students to sort sets of numbers based on a variety of characteristics or they might even sort graphs or patterns.

- Be careful not to ask students to calculate an average without specifying what measure of central tendency you intend for them to use.

- It is important to assess not only students' ability to calculate statistics, but also their understanding of what those statistics really tell you about data. For example, instead of providing a set of data and asking students to calculate the mean and median, you might pose a question such as, "The mean of a set of data is much lower than the median. What do you know about the data?"

Appropriate Children's Books

Is It Red? Is It Yellow? Is It Blue? (Hoban, 1978).
This book of photographs focuses younger students on sorting by colour.

More or Less a Mess (Keenan, 1999).
A girl who is asked to clean her room organizes and reorganizes the mess in the room in different ways—an opportunity for students to see a real-life example of sorting and re-sorting. Some classroom sorting activities are suggested at the back of the book.

Applying What You've Learned

1. Why is the chapter problem a good one for discussion?

2. Do an Internet search to learn more about Carroll diagrams.
   a) How are Caroll diagrams like Venn diagrams? How are they different?
   b) Which would you introduce first? Why?

3. A student in your Grade 3 class is preparing to do a survey to find out how fellow students get to school. The student's question is: How do you get to school?
   a) What are some potential problems with this question?
   b) How might you get the student planning the survey to think of those possible problems?
   c) How might you ask how the student is choosing whom to survey?

4. Examine the Statistics Canada website. In particular, look at the Census in School section. Create a lesson plan where data from the website can form the basis for exploring data collection or statistics.

5. One topic that was not raised in this chapter is the topic of "outliers." Find out what they are if you are not already familiar with the term. Discuss whether and why you think a focus of outliers should be a topic prior to secondary school.

6. The chapter showed some physical models for calculating a mean. What physical models might you use for calculating a median or a mode? Explain.

7. Many teachers define the mean as the sum of a set of data values divided by the number of values in the set. What are the shortcomings of this definition?

Interact with a K–8 Student:

8. Develop a game that focuses on sorting skills at an appropriate level for students with whom you plan to talk. Have them play the game. Report on what was involved in the game and what you learned as you observed students playing it.

Discuss with a K–8 Teacher:

9. Many teachers spend time teaching students how to read, interpret, and create graphs, but less time on data collection. Talk to a teacher about how important he or she feels it is to teach data collection concepts, and why. Do you agree with the perspective you heard? Explain.

Selected References

Ash, R. (**Published yearly**). *The top 10 of everything: Canadian edition*. Toronto: Dorling Kindersley.

Ash, R. (**1996**). *Incredible comparisons*. Toronto: Dorling Kindersley.

Bamberger, H., and Hughes, P. (**1999**). *Super graphs, Venns & glyphs*. New York: Scholastic.

Bereska, C., Bolster, C., Bolster, L.C., and Schaeffer, R. (**1998**). *Exploring statistics in the elementary grades*. Book one (K–6). White Plains, NY: Dale Seymour Publications.

Bremigan, E.G. (**2003**). Developing a meaningful understanding of the mean. *Mathematics Teaching in the Middle School*, 9, 22–27.

Bright, G.W., Brewer, W., McClain, K., and Mooney, E.S. (**2003**). *Navigating through data analysis in grades 6–8*. Reston, VA: National Council of Teachers of Mathematics.

Chapin, S., Koziol, A., MacPherson, J., and Rezba, C. (**2003**). *Navigating through data analysis and probability in grades 3–5*. Reston, VA: National Council of Teachers of Mathematics.

Colombo, J.R. (**Published yearly**). *The Canadian global almanac*. Toronto: Macmillan Canada.

Copley, J.V. (**2000**). *The young child and mathematics*. Washington, DC: National Association for the Education of Young Children and National Council of Teachers of Mathematics.

Curcio, F.R. (**2001**). *Developing data-graph comprehension in grades K–8* (2nd ed.). Reston, VA: National Council of Teachers of Mathematics.

Folkard, C. (**Ed.**). (**Published yearly**). *Guiness world records*. New York: Random House.

Greenes, C., Schulman, L., and Spungin, R. (**1989**). *Thinkermath*. Sunnyvale, CA: Creative Publications.

Hoban, T. (**1978**). *Is it red? Is it yellow? Is it blue?* New York: Greenwillow.

Keenan, S. (**2002**). *More or less a mess*. New York: Scholastic.

Lajoie, S. (**Ed.**). (**1998**). *Reflections on statistics*. Mahwah, NJ: Lawrence Erlbaum Associates.

Lappan, G., Fey, J., Fitzgerald, W.M., Friel, S.N., and Phillips, E.D. (**1998**). *Data about us*. Connected Mathematics. White Plains, NY: Dale Seymour Publications.

Lehrer, R., and Romberg, T. (**1996**). Exploring children's data modeling. *Cognition and Instruction*, 14, 69–108.

Mokros, J., and Russell, S.J. (**1995**). Children's concepts of average and representativeness. *Journal for Research in Mathematics Education*, 26, 20–39.

Oleson, V.L. (**1998**). Incredible comparisons: Experiences with data collection. *Teaching Children Mathematics*, 5, 12–16.

Russell, S.J., and Corwin, R.B. (**1989**). *Used numbers: Real data in the classroom*. White Plains, NY: Dale Seymour Publications.

Sheffield, L.J., Cavanagh, M., Dacey, L., Findell, C., Greenes, C., and Small, M. (**2002**). *Navigating through data analysis and probability, pre-kindergarten–grade 2*. Reston, VA: National Council of Teachers of Mathematics.

Shulte, A.P., and Smart, J.R. (**Eds.**). (**1981**). *Teaching statistics and probability*. Reston, VA: National Council of Teachers of Mathematics.

Small, M. (**2006**). *PRIME: Data management and probability: Background and strategies*. Toronto: Thomson Nelson.

Speer, W.R. (**1997**). Exploring random numbers. *Teaching Children Mathematics*, 3, 242–245.

Stremme, R., and Buckley, J., Jr. (**2003**). *Scholastic book of lists*. New York: Scholastic Reference.

Time for kids almanac. (Published yearly). New York: Time Warner.

The world almanac and book of facts. (Published yearly). New York: World Almanac Books.

The world almanac for kids. (Published yearly). New York: World Almanac Books.

Zawojewski, J.S., and Shaughnessy, J.M. (**2000**). Mean and median: Are they really so easy? *Mathematics Teaching in the Middle School*, 5, 436–440.

Chapter 19
Probability

IN A NUTSHELL

The main ideas in this chapter are listed below:

1. Probability is a measure of likelihood. It can be expressed qualitatively or quantitatively as a fraction or decimal between 0 and 1 or an equivalent percent.

2. Unless an event is either impossible or certain, you can never be sure how often it will occur.

3. To determine an experimental probability, a large representative sample should be used.

4. To determine a theoretical probability, an analysis of possible equally likely outcomes is required.

CHAPTER PROBLEM

What is the probability that at least one person in your class was born on the 11th day of a month?

Fundamental Notions about Probability

Probability is the study of measures of likelihood for various events or situations. How likely it is to rain tomorrow, how likely it is that a contestant will spin a particular number on a game show, or how likely it is that a particular candidate will win an election are all examples of probability situations. Probabilities are sometimes calculated theoretically. For example, the probability of tossing a head on a coin is $\frac{1}{2}$ since there are two equally likely possible outcomes, and only one of the two is a head. Experimental probability is the probability you calculate by actually performing an experiment.

To determine a probability experimentally, you need many samples, or a very large sample, before you can confidently draw a conclusion about the probability of an event. The greater the sample size, the more confident you can be about the probability. For example, suppose students want to know the probability of a Grade 6 student being 11 years old when he or she starts school in September. They could survey their own classmates and find that 7 students in 28, or $\frac{1}{4}$, of the students, were 11 when they began school this year. They cannot conclude that this is the probability in the greater population from that small sample. They could expand their survey to include the other Grade 6 classes in the school, where they may or may not get similar results. As the sample size increases, so should their confidence in the probability.

You can never be sure what will happen on a particular occasion, unless the event is either impossible or certain. For example, many students will predict that, if they flip a coin, say, 10 times, it will land heads up 5 times. However, it is quite possible to flip the coin 10 times and have it land heads up anywhere from 0 to 10 times. This is because of the randomness of flipping a coin. If you repeat the 10-flip experiment many times, the average number of heads is likely to get closer and closer to 5.

Probability Misconceptions

Young students and even some adults often have naive ideas about probability. These ideas are often common misconceptions. For example, many students think that if a coin is flipped and lands heads up 5 times in a row, it is likely to land heads up again. Others think just the opposite—that it is unlikely to land heads up next time. It takes experience and/or logic to understand that the chance that the coin will land heads up each time is no different than it was the time before. Each time, the probability of landing heads up is $\frac{1}{2}$.

Early Work with Probability

Initially, students think about familiar everyday events in their lives and assign very rough probability measures to describe them. This is in keeping with the idea of working at a "concrete" level. "Concrete," in this sense, means familiar contexts that have relevance to students. Events might include the following:

- the sun will rise tomorrow
- a parent will be home when you get home from school
- you will have spaghetti for dinner
- an elephant will come to school on Friday

Young students are often asked to describe events such as these by using probability language. Teachers introduce the words *always* and *never* as well as *likely* and *unlikely*.

Using a Probability Line to Describe and Compare Probabilities

A *probability line* is a pictorial model that shows relative probabilities, making it a useful tool for helping students describe and compare the likelihoods of events. The arrows describing the parts of the lines sometimes say *less likely* and *more likely*, and sometimes *less probable* and *more probable*. The labels at the ends of the line sometimes say *impossible* and *certain*, and sometimes *never* and *always*. An event at the midpoint of the line is one that is *equally likely* to happen or not happen.

Event A below could be any event that is fairly probable, or likely.

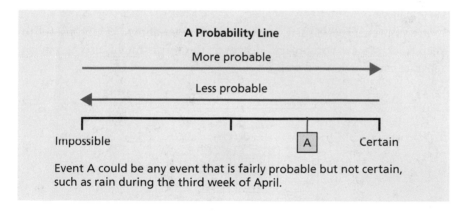

A Probability Line

More probable

Less probable

Impossible   A   Certain

Event A could be any event that is fairly probable but not certain, such as rain during the third week of April.

Students often find a probability line useful when they are working with multiple events since the line allows them to compare the events' probabilities. One event is more likely than another if its position is farther to the right on the line. An event is less likely than another if its position is farther to the left.

ACTIVITY 19.2

Students could be asked to suggest activities that might be represented by the boxes A, B, and C, below.

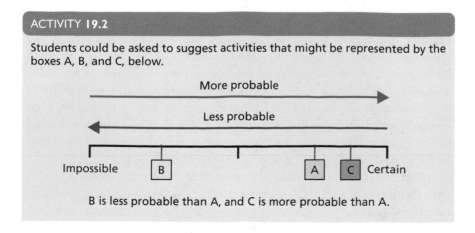

More probable

Less probable

Impossible   B   A   C   Certain

B is less probable than A, and C is more probable than A.

ACTIVITY 19.1

Students might sort themselves using probability concepts. For example, all students who are "likely to watch TV after school" could stand in one row on a concrete graph, and those who are "unlikely to watch TV after school" could stand in another row.

By examining the graph, students might begin to see how probability ideas can be useful for prediction. For example, you could ask, "If a new student comes to the class, do you think he will be likely or unlikely to watch TV after school?"

As students are ready, additional terms can be used to describe parts of the probability line.

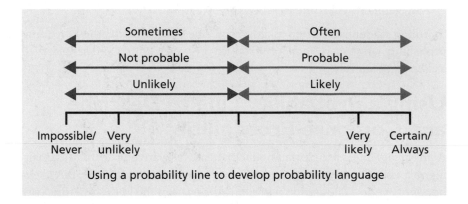

Using a probability line to develop probability language

One difficulty that students encounter is the incongruity between the way certain terms are used in everyday language and the way these same terms are used in mathematics. On a probability line like the third one above, an event might be defined as *likely* if it had any probability greater than $\frac{1}{2}$. Some students reserve the term *likely* for events that are very likely.

A comprehensive display, such as that shown above, can be useful to keep track of new vocabulary. However, the terms might also be put on separate cards on a word wall.

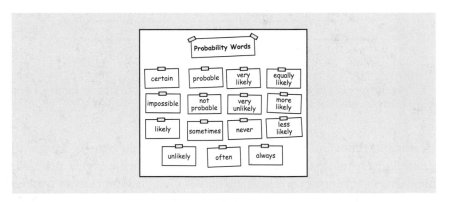

Outcomes, Events, and Sample Space

The possible results of a probability experiment are called *outcomes*. For example, the *possible outcomes* of flipping a coin are heads and tails. If you roll a standard die, the possible outcomes are 1, 2, 3, 4, 5, and 6. You could be interested in the probability of any one of those outcomes, such as the probability of rolling a 5, or you could be interested in the probability of a combination of outcomes, such as the probability of rolling an even number (which includes the outcomes 2, 4, and 6). The term *event* is used to describe the outcome or combination of outcomes that one is interested in, for example, rolling a 5 or rolling an even number.

In secondary school, students encounter the term *sample space* to describe the set of all possible outcomes. They also learn the term *favourable outcome* to describe the outcome or combination of outcomes that they are "looking for." For example, if students are conducting an experiment to calculate the probability of the event: rolling a number greater than 3, the sample space is any roll from 1 to 6, and any roll of 4, 5, or 6 is considered a favourable outcome.

Simple and Compound Events

SIMPLE EVENT	COMPOUND EVENT
A *simple event* is simply one event, such as the probability of drawing a heart from a deck of cards. To determine the experimental probability, a card can be drawn from a deck of cards numerous times (with the card returned to the deck each time and the deck shuffled), and the number of favourable outcomes can be compared to the total number of trials. Thus, if hearts are drawn 23 times in 100 draws, the experimental probability is $\frac{23}{100}$.	A *compound event* is an event that involves two or more simple events, such as the probability of drawing a heart and then another heart from a deck of cards. To determine the experimental probability, two cards can be drawn from a deck of cards (returning the first card and shuffling the deck before drawing the second card each time), and the number of favourable outcomes can be compared to the total number of trials. If two hearts are drawn in a row 9 times in 100 trials, the experimental probability is $\frac{9}{100}$.

Since the last draw is a heart, the probability of drawing a heart is $\frac{23}{100}$.	Since the last draw is not a heart, the probability of drawing 2 hearts is $\frac{9}{100}$.

Compound Events: Independent and Dependent Events

In the card-draw experiments described above, the first card you draw has no bearing on the second. When one event does not influence the other, the two events are said to be *independent events*. If, on the other hand, the first card had not been returned to the deck before the second draw, then the two events would be *dependent events*, meaning that the second event would be influenced in some way by the first. For example, if the first draw is a heart, then there is less chance of drawing a heart on the second draw because one heart has already been removed from the deck. Although at the elementary level it is certainly not necessary to use the language of independent and dependent events, the concept will come up and can be dealt with informally at the middle school or junior high level.

Probabilities as Fractions

As students get older, they begin to assign fractions to probabilities. The least possible value of a probability is 0, which indicates that the event could never occur; the greatest is 1, which indicates that the event must always occur.

The probability is defined as the fraction or ratio that relates all favourable outcomes to all possible outcomes. For example, an experimental probability of $\frac{3}{10}$ means that, out of 10 trials, a favourable outcome occurred 3 times.

Students can continue to use probability lines, but the labelling is now numerical. The label *equally likely*, in the middle of the line, is replaced with $\frac{1}{2}$; the label *certain*, at the far right of the line, is replaced with 1; and the label *impossible*, at the far left, is replaced with 0. Once students become comfortable with percents, they might use 0% and 100%, instead of 0 and 1, as the end points of the probability line.

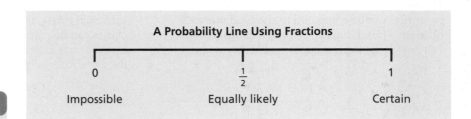

A Probability Line Using Fractions

0	$\frac{1}{2}$	1
Impossible	Equally likely	Certain

The benchmark fraction of $\frac{1}{2}$ is an important one in the study of probability. The words *equally likely* describe a situation where the probability of an event is $\frac{1}{2}$. It is important to mention that the words *equally likely* can also apply to other fractions. For example, the probability of rolling each of the numbers 1 to 6 on a standard die is $\frac{1}{6}$, and these six probabilities are all *equally likely*. You generally attach the word *likely* to events with probabilities greater than $\frac{1}{2}$, and *unlikely* to events with probabilities less than $\frac{1}{2}$.

As students learn to add fractions, they will notice that the probabilities of all the possible outcomes in a situation must add to 1. This makes it possible to calculate the probability that an event will *not* occur. For example, to calculate the probability that a standard die will not roll 3, they must determine the probability of rolling a 3 and subtract this number from 1.

Experimental Probability

Most of the probability studied at the elementary level involves experiments. This is in keeping with the notion that students should begin their work with concrete activities. The transition to theoretical probability will come later when students are better able to deal with more abstract notions.

In an experiment, students find out what happens when they try things. For example, when they roll a die, does each number come up equally often? When they roll two dice, does each sum come up equally often? When they spin the spinner, which colour is likely? Even at the earliest grades, students can conduct simple experiments. For young students, however, the teacher will need to carefully define exactly what must be done.

Typical experiments require random probability devices that produce two or more randomly occurring outcomes—those that cannot be predicted with any certainty. Random devices include tacks, paper cups, coins, two-sided tiles, dice, spinners, and draw bags containing small items. Typical experiments might involve the following:

ACTIVITY 19.3

Students might research what a weather forecaster means when she or he says, "The chance of rain today is 70%."

ACTIVITY 19.4

Students can flip two-coloured counters, red on one side and yellow on the other, repeatedly to see how many times each colour comes up.

If young students flip 10 counters, they practise the sums for 10 at the same time as they think about probability.

ACTIVITY 19.5

Prepare 3 opaque bags, one with 2 blue and 8 yellow cubes, one with 5 blue and 5 yellow cubes, and one with 8 blue and 2 yellow cubes.

Tell students the content of the 3 bags, but not which bag is which.

Pull a cube from one of the bags, allow students to see the colour, and then return the cube to the bag.

Repeat the draw 10 times.

Ask students how many yellow cubes they think are in the bag—2, 5, or 8.

- tossing 10 tacks repeatedly to see how often 5 or more land with the point up
- flipping a coin repeatedly and counting the number of times each face comes up
- drawing coloured cubes from an opaque bag repeatedly and keeping track of the colours drawn
- rolling a die repeatedly and observing the numbers rolled
- spinning spinners with coloured or numbered sectors repeatedly and keeping track of the results

Sample Size

Students need to make sure that an experiment has many trials and/or repeat an experiment a number of times to ensure that the sample size is large enough to allow them to generalize from their results. In an elementary classroom environment, however, it is important to keep in mind that the number of trials and/or repetitions of the experiment should be reasonable.

One way to increase sample size is to use technology (applets) to perform multiple simulations of flips, rolls, and spins very quickly. (See *Appropriate Technology* on page 561.)

Our Class Coin Flipping Results

Possible results	Number of students who got this result
0 heads and 10 tails	0
1 head and 9 tails	0
2 heads and 8 tails	0
3 heads and 7 tails	3
4 heads and 6 tails	5
5 heads and 5 tails	5
6 heads and 4 tails	3
7 heads and 3 tails	3
8 heads and 2 tails	1
9 heads and 1 tail	0
10 heads and 0 tails	0

Consolidating results to increase sample size

An alternative to multiple trials is to have each student conduct just a few trials, and then consolidate everyone's results. In a coin-flip experiment, one student may flip a coin 10 times and flip 8 heads and 2 tails. From just 10 trials, it is not reasonable to conclude that heads is more likely than tails. However, if everyone in the class did the same experiment and the teacher consolidated the results in a chart, then the class could make a reasonable conclusion about the probability of flipping heads or tails. From the chart above, you could reasonably conclude that it is very likely to get equal or nearly equal numbers of heads and tails, and very unlikely to get all heads or all tails.

Reporting Experimental Probability

Once they are familiar with fractions or percents, students can report the results of their experiments using quantitative values. For example, a student who rolls a die 10 times might get the results shown in the frequency table on page 550. The student could report that, for this experiment, the experimental probability of rolling a 6 is 2 out of 10, or $\frac{2}{10}$, or $\frac{1}{5}$. Some students will find it easier to use 2 out of 10 than $\frac{2}{10}$ initially.

ACTIVITY 19.6

Show students how they can use a spinner as a tool to help them make a decision. For example, present a scenario like this:

Mike cannot decide whether to build his science project around the topic of lions or tigers.

How could he use this spinner to help him decide?

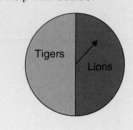

My Rolls	
I rolled	This many times
1	2
2	1
3	0
4	3
5	2
6	2
Total rolls	10

Probability of rolling a 6: $\frac{2}{10}$ or $\frac{1}{5}$

Making Predictions Based on Experimental Results

Making predictions is an important part of any experiment. You want students to use prior experiences to help them predict what will happen next. Students need to learn that it is all right if their predictions do not come true; in fact, it is critical to their understanding of the concept of probability that they recognize that they can never be certain of what will happen. Still, students should be able to explain or justify the predictions they make.

For example, after a die-rolling experiment like the one above, a teacher might ask the class to predict how many 6s they expect to see in another 10 rolls of the die. Many students will say 2, basing their prediction on the prior results, but other students may think that since 3 did not come up in the last set of rolls, there will be more 3s next time and, therefore, fewer 6s. As students develop their understanding of probability, they will begin to use theoretical probability to make their predictions. (See *Theoretical Probability* on page 551.) Once they understand that the theoretical probability of rolling a 6 is $\frac{1}{6}$, because there are 6 possible and equal outcomes, they might reason that there will be about two 6s in the next 10 rolls.

ACTIVITY 19.7

One way to find out what students know about making predictions is to ask them to create a situation that will reflect a given probability. For example, you might ask them to make a spinner where the experimental probability of spinning green might be 6 in 10 spins. Or you might give them three spinners and ask which one is most likely to result in green 6 times out of 10. For younger students, you might use qualitative descriptions, for example, asking them to make a spinner that is more likely to spin green than red.

Which spinner will result in green 6 times out of 10?

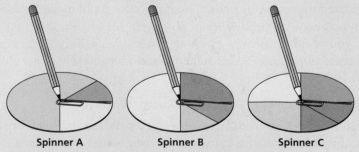

| Spinner A | Spinner B | Spinner C |

Spinner A is the most likely to spin 6 greens in 10 spins.

Try "reverse" prediction activities where you provide results and students predict what caused them.

Theoretical Probability

Students usually start to think about *theoretical* or *expected probability* more formally somewhere around Grade 5 or 6 after students have had ample opportunity to work with experimental probability. However, informal work with theoretical probability begins much earlier. For example, when students look at a spinner that is $\frac{1}{2}$ red and predict they will spin red half the time, or when they predict that about half of their coin flips will land heads up, they are using theoretical probability, albeit informally.

Making the Transition from Experimental to Theoretical

Coin-flipping experiments serve as an excellent lead-in to the notion of theoretical probability. For example, students are asked to predict what will happen if they flip two coins 100 times. In an initial discussion of the possible outcomes, they might decide that there are three possible outcomes: 2 heads, 2 tails, or 1 head and 1 tail. Since a coin is a fair device, it might appear as if each of the 3 possible outcomes will occur about the same number of times. When students conduct the experiment with a large enough sample size, they will discover the 3 outcomes are not equally likely, as shown below.

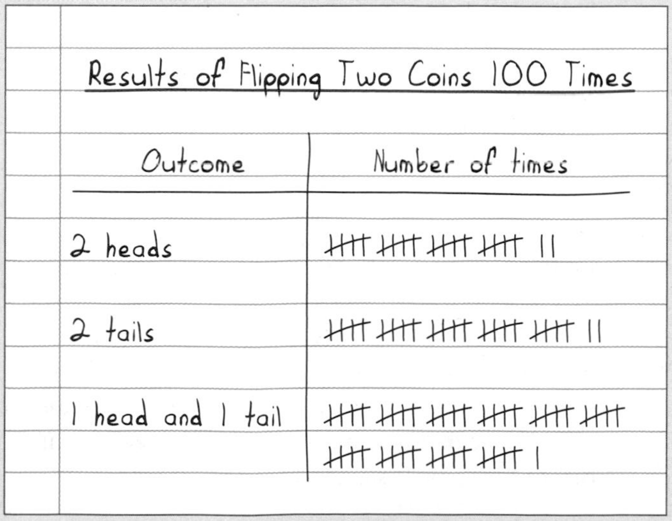

Results of Flipping Two Coins 100 Times	
Outcome	Number of times
2 heads	卌 卌 卌 卌 II
2 tails	卌 卌 卌 卌 卌 II
1 head and 1 tail	卌 卌 卌 卌 卌 卌 卌 卌 卌 卌 I

Flipping a head and a tail appears to be most likely.

Students can then be asked to explain why the "1 head and 1 tail" outcome occurred more often than predicted. They might conclude that the sample size was too small and, if they add more trials, the results for the 3 outcomes will even out. If they continue flipping, however, they will soon discover this is not the case. At this point, students need to begin looking at theoretical probability and how they can analyze the situation differently.

There are different models students can use to do this. A tree diagram, for example, can be used to systematically display the possible results for flipping two coins. (See *Models for Determining Theoretical Probability* on page 554.) They will discover that there are, in fact, 4 possible outcomes because there are 2 outcomes "hidden" in the 1 head and 1 tail outcome. A new experiment with all 4 outcomes listed might show a more equal distribution of results, as shown below.

Results of Flipping Two Coins 100 Times	
Outcome	Number of times
2 heads	ЖЖ ЖЖ ЖЖ ЖЖ I
2 tails	ЖЖ ЖЖ ЖЖ ЖЖ ЖЖ I
1 head and then 1 tail	ЖЖ ЖЖ ЖЖ ЖЖ ЖЖ ЖЖ II
1 tail and then 1 head	ЖЖ ЖЖ ЖЖ ЖЖ I

There are 4 possible outcomes when flipping two coins.

Using experimental results as a vehicle to inquire about theoretical probability.

Using Logic and Analysis to Make Predictions

Experimental probability is determined by the results of an experiment that has already occurred. In contrast, theoretical probability involves analyzing possible outcomes in advance, and using logic and reason to predict what is likely to happen. For example, when you roll a die, you expect that, if the die is random and fair, each outcome is just as likely as any other. Since there are 6 possible outcomes for rolling a die, the probability of rolling a particular number is $\frac{1}{6}$.

Like experimental probability, theoretical probability can also be used to determine the likelihood of an event that involves more than 1 outcome. For example, for the spinner shown below, a student could expect to spin a number less than 3 about half the time, since the sectors for numbers less than 3 cover $\frac{2}{4}$ or $\frac{1}{2}$ of the spinner's area.

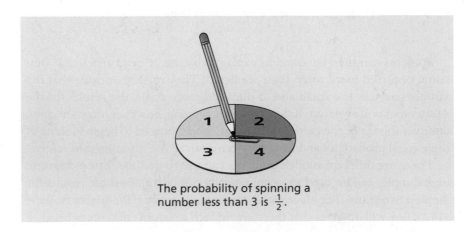

The probability of spinning a number less than 3 is $\frac{1}{2}$.

Reconciling Theoretical and Experimental Probability

It is important for students to understand that, while theoretical probabilities can tell them what is likely to happen, they cannot be used to predict what will certainly happen in a particular situation. Many students feel that something must be wrong if they know intuitively that the probability of flipping heads is $\frac{1}{2}$, but they have just flipped 10 times and ended up with 7 heads, or even more.

Some of the results that surprise students might not be those that teachers expect. For example, some students think that it is harder to roll a 6, or sometimes a 1 or 6, on a die than the "middle numbers." It is only through many experiences that they overcome these misconceptions.

This is where it is important to emphasize the importance of a reasonably large sample size. The results of a small number of trials or just one experiment can be misleading, but when multiple trials are used and/or an experiment is repeated many more times, the experimental probability will gradually approach the theoretical probability. This seeming incongruity between experimental and theoretical probability can sometimes be confusing for students.

Determining Theoretical Probability

When all the possible outcomes of an event are equally likely, the theoretical probability of the event can be expressed as a fraction as shown below:

$$\text{theoretical probability} = \frac{\text{number of favourable equally likely outcomes}}{\text{number of equally likely outcomes}}$$

For example, the probability of rolling an even number with a single roll of a fair die is $\frac{3}{6}$ because there are 3 equally likely favourable outcomes (2, 4, and 6), and 6 equally likely possible outcomes (1, 2, 3, 4, 5, and 6).

Determining theoretical probability becomes more challenging when the outcomes are not equally likely. For example, the spinner on the left below has 4 sectors, 3 of which are red, but the probability of spinning red on this spinner is not $\frac{3}{4}$. The sectors are different sizes, and so they are not equally likely to be spun. To determine the probability, the sectors need to be partitioned into equal parts as shown below on the right.

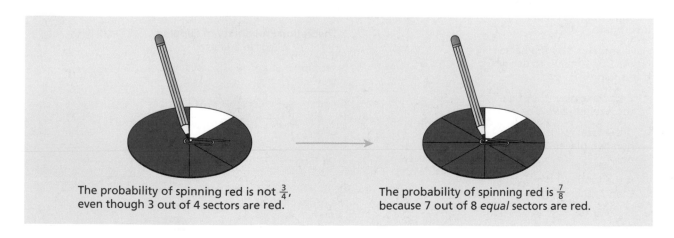

The probability of spinning red is not $\frac{3}{4}$, even though 3 out of 4 sectors are red.

The probability of spinning red is $\frac{7}{8}$ because 7 out of 8 *equal* sectors are red.

Models for Determining Theoretical Probability

There are several models that students can use to determine theoretical probability.

TREE DIAGRAMS

A tree diagram is a graphic organizer that can help students determine all the possible outcomes for a compound event. It is important for the student to make sure that any outcomes represented in the diagram are equally likely, or the results will be misleading.

This tree diagram shows the possible results of 2 coin flips. The outcomes for each coin (heads/tails) are equally likely.

By looking at the tree diagram, you can draw conclusions about the theoretical probability. For example, this diagram not only shows that there are 4 possible outcomes, but also that the probability of flipping 2 heads in a row (HH) is 1 out of 4, or $\frac{1}{4}$, and that the probability of flipping 1 head and 1 tail (HT or TH) is 2 out of 4 or $\frac{2}{4}$.

There are 2 outcomes, heads or tails, for Flip 1. For each of those, there are 2 outcomes for Flip 2. So there are 4 possible outcomes altogether.

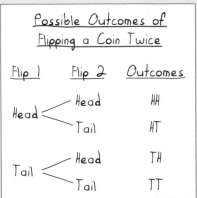

Possible Outcomes of Flipping a Coin Twice

Flip 1	Flip 2	Outcomes
Head	Head	HH
	Tail	HT
Tail	Head	TH
	Tail	TT

AREA MODELS

Another model for displaying and/or determining the theoretical probability of a compound event is an area model. Again, this pictorial model relies on students' abilities to represent the situation with equal parts.

Suppose you want to show the possible results of flipping a coin twice. The first diagram clearly shows that the coin will land on heads half the time, and tails the other half. The second diagram shows the possible combinations for 2 flips, making it very clear in a visual way that the probability of flipping 2 tails is $\frac{1}{4}$.

Theoretical Probability of Flipping 2 Tails in 2 Flips

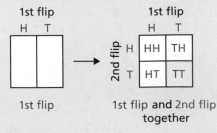

1st flip

1st flip and 2nd flip together

The probability of flipping 2 tails is $\frac{1}{4}$.

Simulation Experiments

A simulation is an experiment that is used to determine or estimate the experimental probability of a situation that is difficult or impossible to analyze so as to determine a theoretical probability. Simulations are designed to mimic the conditions of the problem situations.

Litter Simulation Experiment

Suppose students want to find out the probability that, in a litter of 3 Snow Leopard cubs, there will be at least 1 male and 1 female cub.

STEP 1 FIND A SUITABLE RANDOM DEVICE

Since male and female cubs are about equally likely to be born, students could use a two-sided counter (yellow and red) to model each birth. A yellow flip could represent the birth of a male cub, and a red flip the birth of a female. A coin, a two-part spinner, or a draw bag with 5 cubes of one colour and 5 cubes of another colour would also be suitable devices because each has 2 equally likely outcomes, each with a theoretical probability of $\frac{1}{2}$.

Until they are developmentally ready, students may struggle with how flipping counters can really provide information about the gender of baby Snow Leopards. It is critical to spend the time talking about the mathematical similarity of the situations, recognizing, of course, the very different contexts. In some ways, it is no different from recognizing that the expression $3 + 2$ is just as valid for determining a total number of elephants as a total number of counters.

STEP 2 CONDUCT THE EXPERIMENT AND RECORD THE RESULTS

A student flips 3 two-sided counters to simulate the birth of 3 cubs in a litter. If 3 reds or 3 yellows come up, the student records a check mark beside "No" to indicate that only male cubs or only female cubs were born. However, if a combination of reds and yellows comes up, the student records a check mark beside "Yes" to indicate that the cubs were of different genders. Trials are done repeatedly to create a sample large enough to use as a basis for drawing conclusions. The results of 20 trials might be as shown in the table below.

	\multicolumn{20}{c}{My Flips}																		
Trial	1	2	3	4	5	6	7	8	9	10	11	12	13	14	15	16	17	18	19	20
Yes	✓	✓		✓	✓	✓	✓	✓			✓	✓	✓	✓	✓	✓	✓	✓		✓
No			✓						✓	✓									✓	

STEP 3 DETERMINE THE PROBABILITY

The chart above shows that the experimental probability of having at least 1 male cub and 1 female cub in a litter of 3 was $\frac{16}{20}$ or $\frac{4}{5}$, which is very likely.

STEP 4 CONSIDER THE RESULTS

It is important for students to consider the results and realize that

- there could be different results in another experiment with 20 trials
- the more trials in an experiment, the more confident you can be about making generalizations that will apply to the greater population

Fishpond Simulation Experiment

Another common simulation is for students to determine the number of times they would need to go "fishing" in a fishpond to collect 3 different prizes that are equally represented.

STEP 1 FIND A SUITABLE RANDOM DEVICE

The fishpond contains equal numbers of fish labelled A, B, and C. Each letter represents a different prize. A spinner with 3 equal sections would make an appropriate device as each of the 3 prizes is equally likely. Each section of the spinner could correspond to a different prize. (Again, any random device with 3 equally likely outcomes would be a suitable device.)

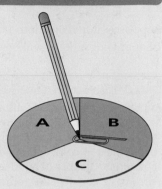

A random device with 3 equally likely outcomes

STEP 2 CONDUCT THE EXPERIMENT AND RECORD RESULTS

Students spin the spinner as many times as necessary until they have spun at least 1 of each letter. That would be one trial. Spinning simulates catching a fish and winning a certain prize.

Here are the results of one possible experiment with 15 trials. A circled letter indicates when all 3 prizes have been caught and the trial is over.

Spinning for Fish

Trial \ Spins	1	2	3	4	5	6	7	8
1	A	B	A	Ⓒ				
2	C	A	Ⓑ					
3	A	A	A	B	A	Ⓒ		
4	C	C	A	Ⓑ				
5	C	A	C	Ⓑ				
6	A	B	A	Ⓒ				
7	C	C	C	C	B	Ⓐ		
8	B	C	C	Ⓐ				
9	C	A	C	A	A	Ⓑ		
10	A	B	A	B	A	A	A	Ⓒ
11	C	B	C	C	Ⓐ			
12	A	C	A	Ⓑ				
13	B	A	A	A	Ⓒ			
14	A	B	A	A	Ⓒ			
15	B	B	A	B	B	Ⓒ		

The least number of spins it took to get all 3 letters was 3 and the greatest was 8.

STEP 3 DETERMINE THE PROBABILITY

From the chart, students might conclude any or all of the following about the probability of collecting all 3 prizes:

- You would need to catch between 3 and 8 fish (the minimum and maximum).
- Most people would need to catch about 4 fish (the mode).
- It would take an average of 5 fish (the mean).
- A good estimate of the number of fish would be 5 (the median).

STEP 4 CONSIDER THE RESULTS

It is valuable to have students consider data they have collected. For example, after the experiment, you might ask questions such as the following:

- In which trials did it take 6 spins to collect all 3 prizes?
- How can you tell that 3 was the least number of spins required?
- Which trial took the greatest number of spins? How many spins did it take?
- Why do you think you did not get results like the ones in Trial 10 very often?

Common Errors and Misconceptions

Probability: Strategies for Dealing with Common Errors and Misconceptions

COMMON ERROR OR MISCONCEPTION	SUGGESTED STRATEGY
Understanding Independent Events Students think that previous events affect future ones even though the events are independent. For example, they might think that, if you roll a die 5 times and the results are 1, 2, 3, 6, 4, the next result will likely be a 5 because it has not been rolled yet.	This is the kind of misconception that can be remedied through experience. By performing this experiment many times, students come to see that the next roll could be any number. (Note that, when compound events are dependent, previous events *do* influence future events. See *Compound Events: Independent and Dependent Events* on page 547.)
Influencing Experimental Results Students think that the purpose of a probability experiment is to get a desired outcome most often, rather than to see what will happen in a fair and random situation. For example, they might be tempted to peek inside a draw bag to make sure they will choose the counter that is their favourite colour.	Help students to understand that there is no purpose for doing an experiment if you already know for certain what the result will be. On the other hand, if the experiment is conducted fairly, students are likely to learn something interesting that can help them in other situations. Most students will outgrow this sort of behaviour as they mature.
Beliefs about Chance Students' own cultural or personal beliefs or intuition about chance can sometimes convince them that events will or will not happen. For example, a student might believe that, if he rolls a die, he will roll a 4 because 4 is his lucky number and he is lucky today.	Again, this kind of misconception can be remedied through experience. Students should also be encouraged to be objective and skeptical of their intuition when it comes to probability.
Looking for Patterns So much of students' mathematical education has been based on patterns that the topic of probability is jarring. Here events are random. Just because you get HHT in the first 3 tosses of a coin, it may not happen again. Some students keep expecting a pattern.	Students need many early experiences with experimental probability to fully appreciate randomness. They need to see that even the most reasonable prediction can be incorrect because of randomness. *(continued)*

COMMON ERROR OR MISCONCEPTION	SUGGESTED STRATEGY

Probability Language

Students believe that the word *likely* means *almost always*.

This is not a misconception so much as a vocabulary issue. Words such as *likely, unlikely,* etc. need to be discussed. Placing a variety of events along a probability line can also help.

"Hidden" Outcomes

Students do not identify all of the possible equally likely outcomes. For example, they identify only 3 possible outcomes for a double coin flip: 2 heads, 2 tails, or 1 head and 1 tail.

2 heads

2 tails

1 head and 1 tail

Encourage students to conduct an experiment with multiple trials. (See *Making the Transition from Experimental to Theoretical* on page 551.) As the results accumulate, students will begin to look for an error in their thinking. For example, in the double coin-flip experiment, they will come to realize that there are actually 4 possible outcomes:

- heads / heads
- tails / tails
- heads / tails
- tails / heads

A tree diagram or area model (see page 554) can also help students discover "hidden" outcomes.

Unequal Outcomes

Students fail to recognize when possible outcomes are not equally likely. For example, when spinning a spinner with 4 unequal outcomes, such as that shown below, students think the probability of spinning blue is $\frac{1}{4}$ because there are 4 outcomes.

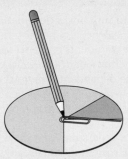

Provide several different four-sector spinners with the sectors labelled 1, 2, 3, and 4. On one spinner, the sectors should be equal. On the rest, they should be unequal. Ask students to spin each spinner 20 times to see how many times they spin a 4. This experiment should illustrate that the relative size of each sector labelled "4" affects the likelihood that 4 will be spun.

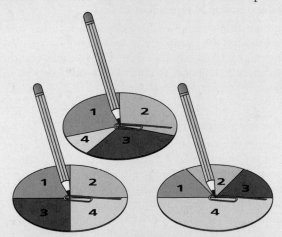

Even though there are 4 sectors on each spinner, the probabilities will differ.

Equivalent Probability Situations

Many students do not recognize the equivalence of different probability situations. For example, students do not realize that flipping 10 coins each once is equivalent to flipping one coin 10 times. Either could be used to determine the experimental probability of flipping heads or tails. Or they may not recognizes that drawing a red cube out of a bag of 5 red and 5 blue cubes is equivalent to flipping heads. Either could be used in a simulation that calls for a device with a probability of $\frac{1}{2}$.

Working with different probability models can be helpful in establishing this equivalence.

The probability of rolling an even number is $\frac{1}{2}$.

The probability of flipping a head is also $\frac{1}{2}$.

What is the probability of rolling a 3 when you roll a die?

The probability of rolling a 3 is $\frac{3}{6}$ it can be possible but it is unlikely.

This student has incorrectly described the probability of rolling 3 as $\frac{3}{6}$ instead of $\frac{1}{6}$. This is not surprising since the numbers he or she is thinking of are 3, the value of the roll, and 6, the number of outcomes.

Appropriate Manipulatives

Probability: Examples of Manipulatives

COINS

Real or play coins can be used to conduct coin-flip experiments. Coins can also be used as a random device for simulating any situation with 2 equally likely outcomes.

EXAMPLE

Students can flip 2 coins to conduct a simulation to answer this question:

In a family with 2 children, how likely is it that both children will be the same sex?

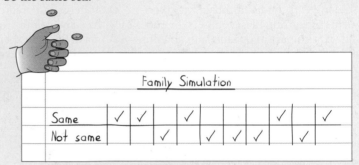

The experimental probability of 2 siblings being the same is $\frac{5}{10}$ or $\frac{1}{2}$.

SPINNERS

Students can use many types of spinners for probability experiments. Spinners can be adapted by changing the number of sectors, and/or by mixing equal and unequal sectors. Sectors can be numbered or named to represent categories of interest.

To create a spinner, use a fraction circle along with a pencil and a paper clip. The paper clip is spun as the pencil holds it in place.

EXAMPLE

Students can determine the probability of spinning a particular number, colour, season, or food item, as well as the probability of various combinations.

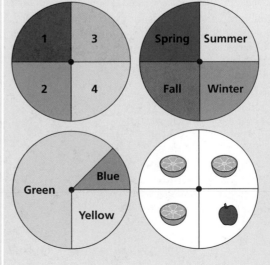

Spinners are versatile because they can be adapted to any context, or number of sectors, and the sectors can be equal or unequal.

(continued)

TWO-SIDED COUNTERS

Counters with a different colour on each side can be flipped or spilled. Students can use these to conduct various probability experiments.

EXAMPLE

Students can flip 2 counters repeatedly to estimate the probability that both flips will result in the same colour.

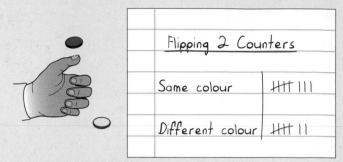

Flipping 2 Counters

Same colour	HHT III
Different colour	HHT II

The experimental probability of both counters landing the same colour up is $\frac{8}{15}$.

Counters provide an alternative to using coins.

DRAW BAGS

Students can conduct probability experiments by putting tiles, counters, or cubes of different colours in opaque bags and drawing them from the bag.

EXAMPLE

Students can predict the probability that they will draw 2 tiles of the same colour from a bag containing 5 red tiles and 5 blue tiles. In a draw-bag experiment, each draw should be returned to the bag after being recorded so that the events are independent.

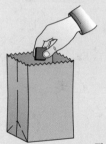

Drawing Coloured Tiles

Different colours	✓ ✓ ✓ ✓ ✓ ✓
Same colours	✓ ✓ ✓ ✓

The experimental probability of drawing 2 tiles of the same colour is $\frac{4}{10}$ or $\frac{2}{5}$.

Draw bags are versatile probability devices because the contents can be adapted to reflect any proportion.

DICE OR NUMBER CUBES

Dice or number cubes are versatile tools for probability experiments. They come with different numbers of faces, with different symbols on the faces (blank cubes are also available), and in different colours.

Using two different-coloured dice helps students uncover "hidden" outcomes. For example, it makes it easier for them to see that rolling a blue 5 and a red 6 is different from rolling a red 5 and a blue 6.

You can make dice even more versatile by labelling the faces with different words, numbers, or pictures. Because they are so easy to obtain and adapt, dice are useful random devices for simulations.

EXAMPLE

Students can roll 2 four-faced dice to determine the probability that the sum of the numbers rolled is 6 or more.

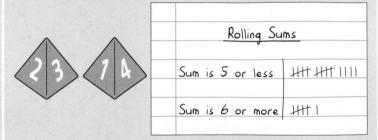

Rolling Sums

Sum is 5 or less	HHT HHT IIII
Sum is 6 or more	HHT I

The experimental probability of rolling a sum of 6 or more with these dice is $\frac{6}{20}$ or $\frac{3}{10}$.

Dice are available in a variety of shapes and colours.

TOSSING MATERIALS

Items such as thumbtacks and paper cups can land in different ways when you toss them. Have students conduct experiments to determine the experimental probability that an item will land in a certain way. For example, a paper cup could land right side up, upside down, or on its side.

These materials are excellent for working with experimental probabilities because the theoretical probabilities of events are less obvious than when coins, spinners, and dice are used.

EXAMPLE

Students can toss 10 thumbtacks many times to find the probability of half or more of them landing point up.

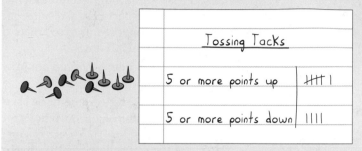

In this experiment, the probability of tossing 10 thumbtacks and having 5 land point up is $\frac{6}{10}$ or $\frac{3}{5}$.

Thumbtacks and paper cups are interesting probability manipulatives to experiment with because, unlike spinners, dice, and coins, the outcomes are less predictable.

PLAYING CARDS

Playing cards are useful in probability experiments because of their richness:

• 52 different cards
• 4 different suits
• 2 different colours
• 13 different card types

EXAMPLE

Students can use a shuffled deck of cards to investigate probabilities such as the following:

• the probability of drawing a red card $\left(\frac{1}{2}\right)$
• the probability of drawing a diamond $\left(\frac{1}{4}\right)$
• the probability of drawing a 3 $\left(\frac{1}{13}\right)$
• the probability of drawing a 3 of diamonds $\left(\frac{1}{52}\right)$

Students can also investigate compound independent events, such as the probability of drawing four 3s.

Appropriate Technology

Computers can play a powerful role in probability experimentation, particularly because it is possible to replicate an experiment so quickly on a computer. In addition, spreadsheets can be used to record the results of experiments and calculate totals quickly and easily.

There are a number of computer applets that are useful for conducting probability experiments with dice, coins, and spinners. The applets allow the experimenter to generate large amounts of data.

WebConnect

www.makingmathmeaningful
.nelson.com

Visit the Making Math Meaningful website for links to Internet sites with probability activities and applets.

Assessing Student Understanding

- Be clear with students as to whether you intend them to calculate a probability experimentally or theoretically.
- Although some students should be using a provided tool to record experimental results, once they are ready, students should have opportunities to create their own recording schemes for organizing their data.
- Students should not only perform experiments, but also interpret provided results.
- Questions might be asked where students interpret the reasonableness of a probability statement. For example, you might ask, *Which of these statements is most likely? Why?*
  – I rolled a die 10 times and I got 2 heads.
  – I rolled a die 100 times and I got 20 heads.
  – I rolled a die 1000 times and I got 200 heads.
- Make sure to ask students in Grades 6 to 8 questions that help them deal with the notion of randomness. For example, you might ask the following:

Student Response

This student recognizes the variability of experimental results, but assumes that they will be close to theoretical results.

Paul and Chris each flipped a coin **100** times.
Paul got heads **55** times.
Chris got heads **48** times.

a) How many heads would you have predicted?
_____53_____ heads

Explain your prediction.
I predicted this because most of the time you will not get half right on, but it is usualy extremely close.

b) Why did they get different results?
It was possible for them to get the same but with it being near so it could be over or under.

Appropriate Children's Books

No Fair! (Holtzman, 1997).
Two children play games trying to decide which ones are fair. This book is suitable for primary children. It is written to support the mathematics curriculum, rather than as a story on its own merits, so the plot is not as engaging as some of the other plots; however, it is an attractive way to raise the idea of fairness.

Pigs at Odds (Axelrod, 2003).
Pigs are playing games at a fair. Mr. Pig struggles to win; he believes that the odds are against him. This book is suitable for students in Kindergarten through Grade 4.

Probably Pistachio (Murphy, 2001).
A variety of probability words are introduced as the character in the story experiences a very bad day. This book is suitable for young elementary students.

Charlie and the Chocolate Factory (Dahl, 1998).
This Roald Dahl classic has as its main premise the winning of tickets in a draw. You can make a connection to probability by holding similar "mock" draws in the school. Many children will know the story from having seen the film.

Cloudy with a Chance of Meatballs (Barrett, 1978).
This funny story provides an excellent backdrop for probability simulations. It is a funny story for students of all ages, but it particularly suits the mathematical development of students in Grade 4 or later.

Do You Wanna Bet? Your Chance to Find Out about Probability (Cushman, 1991).
Two boys recognize the role probability plays in their everyday lives. This book is probably more suitable for students in Grade 4 or higher.

Socrates and the Three Pigs (Mori, 1986).
A wolf tries to figure out the likelihood of finding one of three little pigs in five possible houses. This book is suitable for students in Grades 6 to 8.

Applying What You've Learned

1. What was your solution to the chapter problem? How did you solve it? Is it reasonable for different students in different classes (or the same class) to get a different solution?

2. What do you see as the most important probability ideas for students to learn in each grade grouping: K–2, 3–5, 6–8?

3. Make sure you are comfortable with these vocabulary terms. How might you assure that students are comfortable with the terms they need at their grade level?

Probability Vocabulary

Experimental probability	Outcome	Dependent event
Theoretical probability	Event	Sample size
Random	Sample space	Equally likely
Sample	Simple event	Favourable outcome
Representative	Compound event	Tree diagram
Probability line	Independent event	Simulation

4. Use one of the children's literature suggestions listed above. Develop the outline of a lesson plan for probability that uses the book as a basis.

5. Find a journal article on the learning of probability ideas at the K–8 level. You might use the references listed on pages 364–365 to choose from, or you might find an article on the Internet. List three new things you learned reading that article.

6. There is plenty of literature on what are called "fair games." Some of this literature is posted on the Internet (http://www.nzmaths.co.nz/ Statistics/Probability/FairGames.aspx). How valuable do you think an introduction to the topic of fair games is for the learning of probability concepts? Why?

7. List three ways to use a TV game show or an Internet game to enrich a probability unit for students in Grades 6 to 8.

8. Use both a tree diagram and an area model to calculate the probability of spinning two 3s on the spinner shown below. What are the advantages of each model?

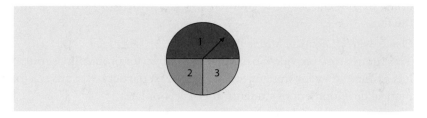

9. Some people argue that probability is too abstract for young students to deal with. In fact, it used to be a high school topic. Argue both sides of the debate. Where do you stand?

10. At some point, we introduce the notion of recording a probability as a fraction. How might a teacher integrate the exploration of fraction concepts with an exploration of probability concepts?

Interact with a K–8 Student:

11. Play the game below with a student in Grade 4 or higher. Adapt the game for a younger student using a single die and single-digit numbers for a total of 6.

   a) Ask them what they liked best about the game.

   Sixty-Six

   Take turns with the student.

   On each turn, the player rolls two dice to create a two-digit number.

   Predict whether the sum of this number and the next one will be greater than 66.

   Roll again to make the second number. Add to your first number.

   Win a point for a correct prediction.

   Win the game with 10 points.

   b) Once you have completed the game, analyze its value for practising number skills.

Discuss with a K–8 Teacher:

12. How much time do you usually spend teaching probability? Do you wish you had more time for it, or do you think that the amount of time is adequate? Could you elaborate?

Selected References

Amir, G.S., and Williams, J.S. (1999). Cultural influences on children's probabilistic thinking. *Journal of Mathematical Behavior,* 18, 85–107.

Axelrod, A. (2003). *Pigs at odds.* New York: Aladdin Picture Books.

Barrett, J. (1978). *Cloudy with a chance of meatballs.* New York: Macmillan.

Brahier, D.J. (1996). Truth or coincidence? *Teaching Children Mathematics,* 3, 180–182.

Bright, G.W., and Hoeffner, K. (1993). Measurement, probability, statistics, and graphing. In Owens, D.T.

(Ed.). *Research ideas for the classroom: Middle grades mathematics.* Reston, VA: National Council of Teachers of Mathematics, 78–98.

Burns, M. (1994). *Math by all means: Probability, grades 3–4.* Sausalito, CA: Math Solutions Publications.

Chapin, S., Koziol, A., MacPherson, J., and Rezba, C. (2003). *Navigating through data analysis and probability in grades 3–5.* Reston, VA: National Council of Teachers of Mathematics.

Dahl, R. (1998). *Charlie and the chocolate factory.* New York: Puffin USA.

Fischbein, E. (1975). *The intuitive sources of probabilistic thinking*. Hingham, MA: Kluwer Academic Publishers Group.

Fischbein, E., and Schnarch, D. (1997). The evolution with age of probabilistic, intuitively based misconceptions. *Journal for Research in Mathematics Education, 28*, 96–105.

Frykholm, J.A. (2001). Eenie, meenie, minie, moe . . . building on intuitive notions of chance. *Teaching Children Mathematics, 8*, 112–118.

Holtzman, C. (1997). *No fair!* New York: Cartwheel Books.

Jones, G.A., Langrall, C.W., Thornton, C.A., and Mogill, A.T. (1999). Students' probabilistic thinking in instruction. *Journal for Research in Mathematics Education, 30*, 487–519.

Jones, G.A., and Thornton, C.A. (1993). *Data, chance and probability: Grades 4–6 activity book*. Vernon Hills, IL: Learning Resources Inc.

Jones, G.A., Thornton, C.A., Langrall, C.W., and Tarr, J.E. (1999). Understanding students' probabilistic reasoning. In Stiff, L.V., and Curcio, F.R. (Eds.). *Developing mathematical reasoning in grades K–12*. Reston, VA: National Council of Teachers of Mathematics, 146–155.

Konold, C. (1987). *Informal conceptions of probability*. Washington, DC: National Science Foundation. (ERIC Document Reproduction Service No. ED 287 703).

Lamphere, P. (1995). Fair or unfair—that is the question! *Teaching Children Mathematics, 1*, 500–503.

McCoy, L., Buckner, S., and Munley, J. (2007). Probability games from diverse cultures. *Mathematics Teaching in the Middle School, 12*, 394–402.

Mori, T. (1986). *Socrates and the three pigs*. New York: Philomel.

Murphy, S. (2001). *Probably pistachio*. New York: Harper-Trophy.

Shaughnessy, J.M. (1981). Misconceptions of probability: From systematic errors to systematic experiments and decisions. In Shulte, A.P., and Smart, J.R. (Eds.). *Teaching statistics and probability*. Reston, VA: National Council of Teachers of Mathematics, 90–100.

Sheffield, L.J., Cavanagh, M., Dacey, L., Findell, C., Greenes, C., and Small, M. (2002). *Navigating through data analysis and probability, pre kindergarten grade 2*. Reston, VA: National Council of Teachers of Mathematics.

Shulte, A.P., and Smart, J.R. (Eds.). (1981). *Teaching statistics and probability*. Reston, VA: National Council of Teachers of Mathematics.

Small, M. (2006). *PRIME: Data management and probability: Background and strategies*. Toronto: Thomson Nelson.

Speer, W.R. (1997). Exploring random numbers. *Teaching Children Mathematics, 3*, 242–246.

Tank, B. (1995). *Math by all means: Probability, grades 1–2*. Sausalito, CA: Marilyn Burns Education Associates.

Usnick, V., McCarthy, J., and Alexander, S. (2001). Mrs. Whatsit "socks" it to probability. *Teaching Children Mathematics, 8*, 246–249.

Way, J. (2000). *The development of young children's notions of probability*. CERME 3: Third Conference of the European Society for Research in Mathematics Education.

Chapter 20
Patterning and Algebraic Thinking

IN A NUTSHELL

The main ideas in this chapter are listed below:

1. Patterns represent identified regularities. There is always an element of repetition, whether the same items repeat over and over, or whether a "transformation," for example, adding 1, is what repeats.

2. Patterns can be represented in a variety of ways.

3. Some ways of displaying data actually highlight patterns.

4. Much of the mathematics of the other strands is built on a pattern foundation.

5. Algebra is a way to represent and explain mathematical relationships and to describe and analyze change.

6. Relationships between quantities can be described using variables.

CHAPTER PROBLEM

There are 20 students in a class. On the first day, the teacher asks each student to shake hands with each other student. How many handshakes were there?

Patterns

Students begin working with patterns in early elementary school, and, unlike work with numbers, pattern work follows all the way through high school. Although a focus on algebra replaces a focus on patterns at the secondary level, some attention to patterns remains throughout the grades.

One of the most fundamental concepts in pattern work, but also one not clear to all students, is that, although the part of the pattern that they see is finite, when mathematicians talk about a pattern, they are talking about something that continues beyond what the student sees.

The notion of pattern is integrated into the number, geometry, measurement, and data strands in most of the curriculums across the country. In fact, there is an underlying aspect of data management, specifically classifying and sorting, inherent in any pattern. This is why, in some curriculums, the expectations/outcomes for sorting and classifying are found in the patterning strand of the curriculum rather than in the data strand.

Types of Patterns

Repeating Patterns

Students' first experiences with patterns generally involve repeating patterns. Initially, the repeating patterns are "intuitive." Students hear rhythmic patterns in sounds, songs, and stories, and recognize patterns in physical actions such as the "hokey-pokey" game patterns. They also observe patterns in their environment. They use these patterns to help them predict. Soon after, they are explicitly introduced to repeating colour, shape, size, and position patterns, and usually somewhat later to repeating number patterns.

Core of a Repeating Pattern The shortest part of the pattern that repeats is called the core. In a pattern like the one below, the core is the set of three shapes found at the start of the pattern since this is the shortest string that repeats.

The core

Sometimes determining the core can be difficult for students. For example, the following pattern has a five-element core. A student might see the small circle repeating in the 4th spot and guess that the core is 1 small circle and 2 large circles. When the student checks farther along in the pattern, however, he or she will realize that this is not correct and may look for the next small circle in the pattern to see if the core ends there.

The core

It is good practice to show at least three full repetitions of the core of a pattern to make it reasonable for a student to identify it. One of the reasons for this is to remove some of the inherent ambiguity. For example, a pattern beginning 5, 10, ... could be 5, 10, 15, 20, ... or 5, 10, 20, 40, ... The complexity of recognizing patterns is increased when patterns repeat in more than one direction. For example, students need to think about more than one aspect of these shapes to fully identify the 2-D pattern below.

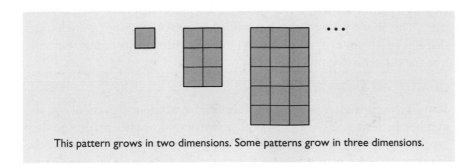

This pattern grows in two dimensions. Some patterns grow in three dimensions.

Representing a Repeating Pattern Repeating patterns are sometimes described using a letter code. An AB pattern has a core of two different elements that repeat over and over (for example, 1, 2, 1, 2, 1, 2, ...). An AABC pattern has a core of four elements, where the first two are the same and the others are different (for example, 3, 3, 4, 5, 3, 3, 4, 5, 3, 3, 4, 5, ...). This is, of course, much simpler for students than recording the repetitions and remembering to use the ... notation to show that the pattern continues. Mathematically, all AB patterns are the same, but to a student, the specific elements are the focus. Younger students view a pattern made up of a repeating circle and square as different from a repeating number pattern like 1, 2, 1, 2, 1, 2, ... because they are focused on the actual attributes rather than the underlying pattern. They may fail to see that the cores of all AB patterns are similar, that is, two different items.

An AB position pattern

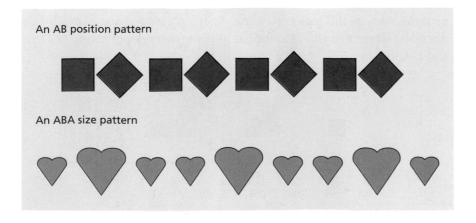

An ABA size pattern

Multi-Attribute Patterns In the early grades, the patterns students observe are built on a single attribute, such as colour, shape, or sound. Eventually, students deal with more complex patterns with two attributes. For example, the pattern on page 570 involves both shape and colour.

A multi-attribute pattern using shape and colour

It is possible for students to deal with patterns with even more than two attributes. When the attributes are highly visual, such as colour or size, the task is easier for students. It is often a challenge for students, however, to identify a pattern with multiple changing attributes that have different core sizes. The above pattern changes colour in an AAB pattern but changes shape in an AB pattern, thus causing difficulty for students unless they analyze the pattern attributes separately.

Growing and Shrinking Patterns

Some growing patterns are quite familiar to students, particularly the number pattern 1, 2, 3, 4, ... As children develop mathematically, they experience other growing (and shrinking) patterns. Growing means the numbers increase in size. Shrinking means they decrease in size. These patterns may be

- arithmetic sequences, where each number is a fixed amount greater or less than the preceding one
  – 3, 5, 7, 9, ... (fixed increase of 2)
  – 12, 10, 8, 6, ... (fixed decrease of 2)
- geometric sequences, where each number is a fixed multiple of the preceding one
  – 2, 4, 8, 16, ... (doubling pattern)
  – 100, 20, 4, ... (dividing by 5 or multiplying by $\frac{1}{5}$ pattern)
- other number sequences where the growth is not constant
  – 3, 4, 6, 9, 13, ... (increase by 1 more each time)
  – 20, 18, 14, 8, ... (decrease by 2 more each time)

Students are generally able to recognize and extend arithmetic sequences before they are comfortable with the other types of growing and shrinking sequences, because arithmetic sequences are based on simply adding or subtracting the same amount each time. There can also be growing shape patterns, such as the patterns below. These growing shape patterns can often be represented and described as growing number patterns: 1, 3, 5, ... and 1, 4, 9, ...

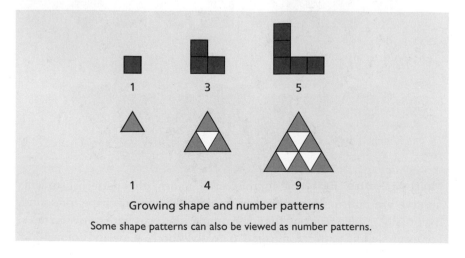

Growing shape and number patterns

Some shape patterns can also be viewed as number patterns.

Recursive Patterns

A recursive pattern is one where each element in the pattern is defined based on a previous element or elements. Some of the growing patterns described in the previous section can be defined recursively. For example, for the sequence 2, 4, 6, 8, ..., each term is defined as 2 greater than the preceding term. However, some recursive patterns are more complex. For example, for the pattern 2, 3, 6, 18, 108, ..., each term is defined as the product of the two preceding numbers.

Some particularly famous recursive sequences include:

- the triangular numbers—beginning at 1, each term is found by adding 1 greater than was added previously: 1, 3, 6, 10, 15, ... (Start at 1, add 2, then 3, then 4, then 5, ...)
- the Fibonacci sequence—beginning with 1 and 1, add two terms to get the next term: 1, 1, 2, 3, 5, 8, 13, 21, 34, ... (Start with 1 and 1; add the first two terms to get the 3rd term; then add the 2nd and 3rd terms to get the 4th term, then add the 3rd and 4th terms to get the 5th term, ...)

Describing and Extending Patterns

Extending Patterns

Once students have identified a pattern, you normally ask them to either extend it or describe it so that you can see that they "understood" the pattern. It is often easier for students to demonstrate their recognition of the pattern by extending it rather than describing it.

Sometimes when you ask students to extend a pattern, there is ambiguity in terms of what you expect and what students understand or perceive. For example:

- Students legitimately view the pattern in a different way than you expect because no pattern rule is provided or not enough elements have been included. For example, a teacher asks a student to extend the pattern 2, 3, 5, 8, ... The teacher is expecting the student to say 13, 21, ... (where each term of the pattern is the sum of the two preceding terms), but there are many other legitimate ways to extend the pattern, such as
  – 2, 3, 5, 8, 2, 3, 5, 8, ... (repeating a four-term core)
  – 2, 3, 5, 8, 12, 13, 15, 18, 22, 23, 25, 28, ... (adding 10 to each of a group of terms)
  – 2, 3, 5, 8, 8, 5, 3, 2, 2, 3, 5, 8, 8, 5, 3, 2, ... (repeating four terms forward and backward)
  – 2, 3, 5, 8, 12, 17, ... (adding 1 first, and then adding 1 more each time)
- Students seem to find it easier to extend a pattern at the end of a full repetition of the core, rather than starting in the middle of a repetition. For example, students might be asked to extend *clap, clap, snap, clap, clap, snap, clap, clap, snap,* ... Many students do not find this difficult, and they respond *clap, clap, snap.* However, if students are asked to extend *clap, clap, snap, clap, clap, snap, clap,* ..., they will often repeat the entire core of *clap, clap, snap,* ignoring the fact that there was already one clap of the core included.

ACTIVITY 20.3

Students can explore some of the properties of the Fibonacci sequence (1, 1, 2, 3, 5, 8, 13, 21, 34, ...) with these tasks:

a) Choose a number in the sequence. Multiply it by itself. Then multiply the next number in the sequence by itself. Add the two products (e.g., $3 \times 3 = 9$; $5 \times 5 = 25$; $9 + 25 = 34$). What do you notice?

b) Choose a number in the sequence. Divide it by the previous one. Repeat several times. What do you notice?

ACTIVITY 20.4

Ask students to continue a pattern in two dimensions:

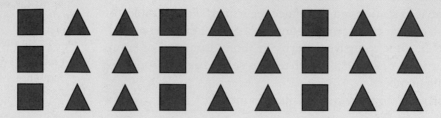

Student Response

This student is able to extend a pattern in more than one direction.

Draw out or explain the next three figures to continue the pattern.

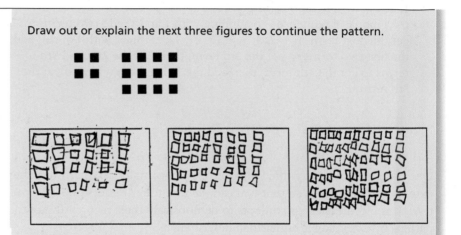

Describing Patterns

Teachers often ask students to describe a pattern to ensure that they understand it. Ideally, a pattern's description is a *pattern rule*, whether described verbally, pictorially, or symbolically. The rule is an unambiguous description of the pattern.

Student Response

This student used a verbal pattern rule.

Use words to describe this pattern:

3, 7, 11, 15, ...

Start at 3 and keep adding 4.

Frequently, students focus on one aspect of the description, but forget another important part of it. For example, if a student describes the pattern 4, 7, 10, 13, ... as "an add 3 pattern" without indicating that it starts at 4, the pattern rule is incomplete. Clearly, this is not a problem if the first part of the pattern is shown, so it may seem superfluous to say that it starts at 4. Formally, students should learn that a pattern rule must describe how each and every element of the pattern is described (including the first element).

Sometimes students find it easier to describe a pattern by comparing it to another one. For example, they describe the pattern 3, 6, 9, 12, 15, ... by suggesting that it is like 2, 4, 6, 8, ... but the numbers start at 3 and go up by 3 instead of by 2.

Translating Patterns

To determine whether a student is focused on the mathematical structure of a pattern, it is natural to ask her or him to translate a pattern into a different, but equivalent, form. For example, a student might be shown the pattern below using brown, blue, and white squares and triangles, and asked to show the same kind of pattern using red, yellow, and green circles and squares. The pattern is ABB for shape, and ABC for colour. There are many possibilities, as shown below.

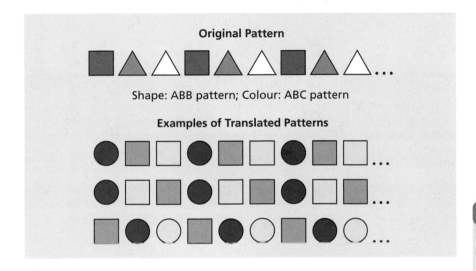

Original Pattern

Shape: ABB pattern; Colour: ABC pattern

Examples of Translated Patterns

Creating Patterns

Students should be encouraged to create patterns as soon as they have an understanding of what patterns are. By exposure to many types of pattern, and patterns of various structures based on many different attributes, students' patterns will be richer.

Most young students will need to create patterns with concrete materials, then pictorial representations, and then number patterns at a more abstract level.

Sample Criteria for Creating Patterns

There are many criteria that can be used to structure students' patterns creation. There can be less or more structure imposed on what is required.

Mathematical Situations Rich in Patterns

A number of charts and tables rich in patterns are regularly used in mathematics classrooms.

The Calendar

The calendar is one of the first places where young students are exposed to "ready-made" number patterns. Some of the many patterns that students might observe using the calendar are shown on page 574.

ACTIVITY 20.5

Ask students to choose a criterion from the list below for creating a pattern:

- Use three colours of counters to create a pattern.
- Create a repeating pattern that has a core of three elements.
- Create a repeating pattern where the 5th element is a large blue square.
- Create a growing pattern where the 10th term is 100.
- Create a pattern that grows but not by the same amount each time.
- Create a shrinking pattern where the 4th term is 16.

Sunday	Monday	Tuesday	Wednesday	Thursday	Friday	Saturday
	1	2	3	4	5	6
7	8	9	10	11	12	13
14	15	16	17	18	19	20
21	22	23	24	25	26	27
28	29	30				

Calendar Patterns

MONTHS-OF-THE-YEAR PROGRAM

There is a pattern in the months that repeat as you go through years; that is, January, February, March, April, May, June, July, August, September, October, November, December is the core of a 12-element repeating pattern of months, year after year.

DAYS-OF-THE-WEEK PATTERN

The days of the week form a 7-element repeating pattern with a core of Sunday, Monday, Tuesday, Wednesday, Thursday, Friday, Saturday.

ROW PATTERNS

You always add 1 when going across a row.

7	8	9	10	11	12	13

COLUMN PATTERNS

You always add 7 when going down a column.

6
13
20
27

DIAGONAL PATTERNS DOWN AND TO THE RIGHT

Each arrow like the red one (going diagonally down to the right) results in adding 8 to the top number. This is because you are going down a row, which adds 7, and over to the right 1, which adds 1 (and $7 + 1 = 8$)

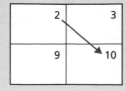

DIAGONAL PATTERNS DOWN AND TO THE LEFT

Each arrow like the blue one (going diagonally down to the left) results in adding 6 to the top number. This is because you are going down a row, which adds 7, and back to the left 1 (and $7 - 1 = 6$).

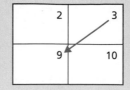

ADJACENT-SQUARE PATTERNS

With each box of four adjacent dates, the following are true:

- The sums of the diagonals are equal (in this case, $9 + 17 = 26$; $16 + 10 = 26$).
- The products of the diagonals are always 7 apart (in this case, $9 \times 17 = 153$; $16 \times 10 = 160$; $160 - 153 = 7$).
- The sum of the four numbers is always a multiple of 4 (in this case, $9 + 10 + 16 + 17 = 52$; $4 \times 13 = 52$).
- The sum of the four numbers is always 16 more than 4 times the least number (in this case, $9 + 10 + 16 + 17 = 52$; $4 \times 9 + 16 = 52$).

9	10
16	17

The 10-Frame

Early in their work with numbers, students meet the 10-frame. (This was modelled in Chapter 5.) In a 10-frame, students shade a square (or place a counter) to the right each time a number is increased by 1 until 5 squares are shaded; then they shade squares in the next row until the frame is full. Additional 10-frames are used depending on the required quantity to be displayed. The visual patterns emphasize the numerical patterns that they model.

Example 1

Pattern: 1, 2, 3, 4, 5, ...

These 10-frames show that the numbers are increasing by 1.

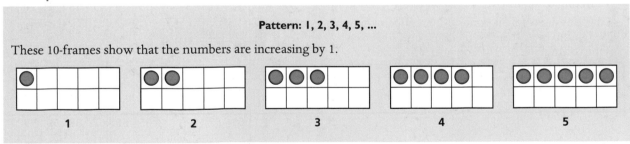

Example 2

Pattern: 5, 10, 15, 20, ...

These 10-frames show that the numbers increase by 5 because another full row of 5 is filled each time.

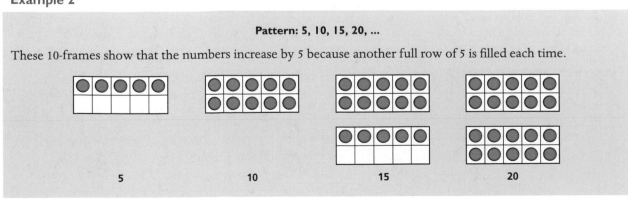

Example 3

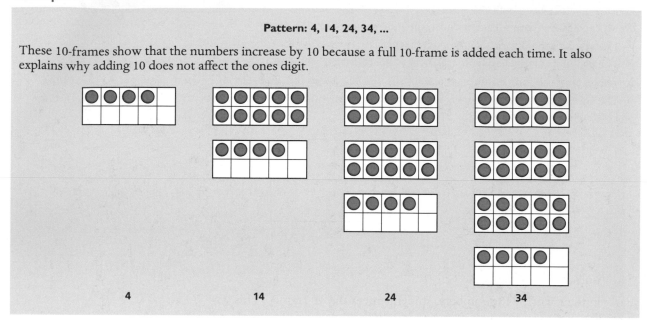

Pattern: 4, 14, 24, 34, …

These 10-frames show that the numbers increase by 10 because a full 10-frame is added each time. It also explains why adding 10 does not affect the ones digit.

4   14   24   34

The 100 Chart

The 100 chart is a tool students use through many elementary and middle school grades. Some of the patterns found in the 100 chart are shown below.

PATTERNS INHERENT IN THE PLACE VALUE SYSTEM

- Every 10th number ends in a 0.
- The pattern of ones digits is always 1, 2, 3, 4, 5, 6, 7, 8, 9, 0, repeating over and over.
- The tens digits form groups of 10 numbers that repeat and then jump by 1; then another 10 repeat followed by another jump of 1, etc.: 1, 1, 1, 1, 1, 1, 1, 1, 1, 1; 2, 2, 2, 2, 2, 2, 2, 2, 2, 2; 3, 3, 3, 3, 3, 3, 3, 3, 3, 3; 4, 4, 4, 4, 4, 4, 4, 4, 4, 4; ….
- If you go down a column, you keep adding 10.
- If you go across a row to the right, you keep adding 1.

1	2	3	4	5	6	7	8	9	10
11	12	13	14	15	16	17	18	19	20
21	22	23	24	25	26	27	28	29	30
31	32	33	34	35	36	37	38	39	40
41	42	43	44	45	46	47	48	49	50
51	52	53	54	55	56	57	58	59	60
61	62	63	64	65	66	67	68	69	70
71	72	73	74	75	76	77	78	79	80
81	82	83	84	85	86	87	88	89	90
91	92	93	94	95	96	97	98	99	100

PATTERNS IN 3-BY-3 GRIDS

If you take the mean (average) value of all the numbers in any 3-by-3 square, the result is in the middle of the square. For example, the mean average of 72, 73, 74, 82, 83, 84, 92, 93, and 94 is 83.

72	73	74
82	83	84
92	93	94

MULTIPLES-OF-9 PATTERNS

If students put counters on every multiple of 9, two diagonals going down to the left are formed. This makes sense since each multiple of 9 is 9 more than the preceding multiple, so you add 10 by going down 1, and then left 1 to subtract the extra 1 that was added.

1	2	3	4	5	6	7	8	9	10
11	12	13	14	15	16	17	18	19	20
21	22	23	24	25	26	27	28	29	30
31	32	33	34	35	36	37	38	39	40
41	42	43	44	45	46	47	48	49	50
51	52	53	54	55	56	57	58	59	60
61	62	63	64	65	66	67	68	69	70
71	72	73	74	75	76	77	78	79	80
81	82	83	84	85	86	87	88	89	90
91	92	93	94	95	96	97	98	99	100

Using Patterns to Develop Mathematical Concepts

A rich mathematics program at the K–8 level is full of opportunities for teachers to use patterns to develop and clarify mathematical concepts, as well as to provide insight into how the number system works. The examples below should provide some understanding of the important role that pattern plays in developing mathematical thinking.

ACTIVITY 20.6

Ask students to explore an addition or multiplication table to find as many patterns as they can in the table.

Computational Patterns

Sometimes you use patterns to help set up a computational relationship that you may want students to explore. Five examples are shown below.

Using Patterns to Explore Computational Relationships

EXAMPLE	COMPUTATIONAL RELATIONSHIP
31 + 5 = 36 41 + 5 = 46 51 + 5 = 56 61 + 5 = ▢	As students complete each answer, the patterns inherent in the place value system should become apparent. When adding the same amount to a number that is 10 greater, the sum is 10 greater; the tens digit changes, but the ones digit does not. Thus, the sum of 61 + 5 must be 66.
32 − 18 = 14 42 − 28 = 14 52 − 38 = 14 62 − 48 = ▢	As students complete the subtractions, they should notice that when both the minuend and the subtrahend increase by the same amount, the difference is the same. Thus, the difference for 62 − 48 must be 14.
4 × 3 = 12 4 × 30 = 120 4 × 300 = 1200 4 × 3000 = ▢	As students determine each answer, they should observe that each time an additional 0 appears at the end of the second factor, there is an additional 0 at the end of the product. Thus, the product of 4 × 3000 must be 12 000. Although this pattern does not explain why this is so, it is a good visual model to start off the conversation about multiplying by powers of 10.

(continued)

$3 \times 2 + 3 \times 3 = 3 \times 5$ $3 \times 2 + 3 \times 4 = 3 \times 6$ $3 \times 2 + 3 \times 5 = 3 \times 7$ $3 \times 2 + 3 \times 6 = 3 \times \blacksquare$	As students determine each answer, they should observe that the second factor on the right is the sum of the two red numbers on the left side of the equation. Thus, the answer to $3 \times 2 + 3 \times 6$ must be 3×8. Again, this is not an explanation, but it piques the curiosity of students so that the concept can be explored and reasoned through.
$4 \times 2 = 8$ $4 \times 1 = 4$ $4 \times 0 = 0$ $4 \times (-1) = \blacksquare$	At the middle school level, patterns are often used to explain operations with integers. Based on the mathematical pattern inherent in the first three products, students should see that $4 \times (-1)$ must be -4.

Patterns Relating Fractions to Decimals

There are an extraordinary number of patterns that can be uncovered in working with fractions. One very interesting pattern emerges when students explore the decimal expressions for what are called the unit fractions—the fractions with numerator 1.

A bar over digits in a decimal indicates that the digits repeat. For example, the 6 in $0.1\overline{6}$ repeats ($0.166\,66\ldots$), and the sequence 142 857 in $0.\overline{142\,857}$ repeats ($0.142\,857\,142\,857\,142\,857\ldots$).

Students might observe a number of patterns in unit fractions up to $\frac{1}{20}$ and their decimal expression (see list below):

PATTERNS IN UNIT FRACTIONS

$\frac{1}{3} = 0.\overline{3}$

$\frac{1}{4} = 0.25$

$\frac{1}{5} = 0.2$

$\frac{1}{6} = 0.1\overline{6}$

$\frac{1}{7} = 0.\overline{142\,857}$

$\frac{1}{8} = 0.125$

$\frac{1}{9} = 0.\overline{1}$

$\frac{1}{10} = 0.1$

$\frac{1}{11} = 0.\overline{09}$

$\frac{1}{12} = 0.08\overline{3}$

$\frac{1}{13} = 0.\overline{076\,923}$

$\frac{1}{14} = 0.0\overline{71\,4285}$

$\frac{1}{15} = 0.0\overline{6}$

$\frac{1}{16} = 0.0625$

$\frac{1}{17} = 0.\overline{058\,823\,529\,411\,7647}$

$\frac{1}{18} = 0.0\overline{5}$

$\frac{1}{19} = 0.\overline{052\,631\,578\,947\,368\,421}$

$\frac{1}{20} = 0.05$

- Reading down the list of fractions, the first digit after the decimal place either stays the same or decreases. (This is because the fraction equivalents are decreasing in value, so the decimals have to decrease as well.)
- For any unit fraction, the number of digits appearing in the repeating cycle of the decimal is the same as the number of digits appearing in

the repeating cycle for the unit fraction with a denominator twice as great. For example, there is 1 repeating digit in the decimal for $\frac{1}{6}$ (0.166 666 ...), 1 repeating digit in the decimal for $\frac{1}{12}$ (0.083 333 ...), 6 repeating digits in the decimal for $\frac{1}{7}$ (0.142 857 142 857 ...), and 6 repeating digits in the decimal for $\frac{1}{14}$ (0.071 428 571 428 5 ...).

- Students might observe that the number of digits that repeat for all the prime denominators except 2 or 5 is a factor of 1 less than the denominator. For example, there are 6 repeating digits for $\frac{1}{7}$ (6 is a factor of 7 − 1), and 6 repeating decimals for $\frac{1}{13}$ (6 is a factor of 13 − 1).

There are also interesting patterns in the equivalents for fractions with denominators of 9, 99, and 999 that students can explore.

$$\frac{1}{9} = 0.\overline{1}$$
$$\frac{2}{9} = 0.\overline{2}$$
$$\frac{3}{9} = 0.\overline{3}$$
...

$$\frac{1}{99} = 0.\overline{01}$$
$$\frac{2}{99} = 0.\overline{02}$$
$$\frac{3}{99} = 0.\overline{03}$$
...

$$\frac{1}{999} = 0.\overline{001}$$
$$\frac{2}{999} = 0.\overline{002}$$
$$\frac{3}{999} = 0.\overline{003}$$
...

ACTIVITY 20.7

Students might explore the decimal equivalents for

$\frac{1}{11}, \frac{2}{11}, \frac{3}{11}, ...$ and $\frac{1}{101}, \frac{2}{101}, \frac{3}{101}, ...$

Common Errors and Misconceptions

Patterns: Strategies for Dealing with Common Errors and Misconceptions

COMMON ERROR OR MISCONCEPTION	SUGGESTED STRATEGY
Students do not recognize that there are different ways to continue a pattern if a pattern rule is not described. For example, if given 5, 10, 15 ... as the beginning of the pattern, they may only see it as a repeating pattern and will not consider that it might be a growing pattern.	Students who only relate to repeating patterns need many opportunities to work with growing patterns using concrete materials and pictures before working with numbers. For example, provide blocks for students to make a growing pattern of 1 row of 5 blocks, then 2 rows of 5 blocks, and then 3 rows of 5 blocks. Discuss how there can be more than one correct pattern. For example: 5, 10, 15, 20, 25, 30, ... 5, 10, 15, 25, 35, 50, 65, ...
Students omit important information in describing a pattern rule. For example, for the pattern 4, 6, 9, 13, 18, ... , a student might state the rule as "Just keep adding 1 more."	Follow students' rules literally to show them the incomplete nature of their rules. For example, with the rule "Just keep adding 1 more," you might continue the pattern by writing down 4, 6, 9, 13, 18, 19, 20, 21, ..., literally adding 1 more. This should help the student see the need for a clearer and more complete rule such as, "Start with 4 and add 2, then add 3, then add 4, each time adding a number that is 1 greater than the time before."
Students have difficulty fully describing a pattern that changes by multiple attributes. For example, the pattern below changes by colour, size, and shape, but the description must account for the different core lengths for each attribute. 	Have students begin by listing the attributes that change: colour, size, and shape. Then, for each attribute, have them identify the pattern (ignoring the other attributes as they focus on one at a time). Colour: red, green, yellow, red (ABCA) Size: small, big (AB) Shape: star, diamond (AB)

Student Response

This student has incorrectly interpreted the pattern rule as a description of a repeating pattern. This may be because the student is still more comfortable with repeating patterns.

Make a pattern that follows this pattern rule:

Start at 4 and add 3 each time.

Write the numbers in the blanks.

4 3 4 3 4 3

Student Response

This student has applied the pattern rule incorrectly. This may be because the student is still more comfortable with arithmetic patterns that grow by a constant amount.

Make a pattern that follows this pattern rule:

Start at 4 and add 1, then 2, then 3, and so on.

Write the numbers in the blanks.

4 , 14 , 24, 24, 44, 54, 64

Appropriate Manipulatives

Patterns: Examples of Manipulatives

COUNTERS	EXAMPLE
Counters can be used for sorting work. For example, counters of the same type but different colours can be used for simple sorting by colour. Counters of different shapes, for example, square and circular, can be used for simple sorting by shape. Counters are also useful to model number patterns or repeating colour patterns.	Counters can be used to show that each successive odd number is "one pair" more than the preceding one.  1　　　　3　　　　5

ATTRIBUTE BLOCKS	EXAMPLE
Attribute, or logic, blocks are ideal for sorting because of their many attributes: size, colour, shape, and thickness. Because of the number of potential attributes, they can also be used to show a variety of simple patterns based on colour, size, thickness, and shape.	This repeating attribute block pattern is based on size (small, big; small, big; small, big; ...), shape (square, triangle; square, triangle; square, triangle; ...), and colour (blue, blue, red, blue; blue, blue, red, blue; blue, blue, red, blue; ...). 

SORTING MATERIALS	EXAMPLE
Items that are often used for sorting, such as the commercial set shown here, can also be used to create patterns because of the deliberate variety of attributes and characteristics. They can be used in the same way as attribute blocks, but are more fanciful and, therefore, more interesting to some students. Students can begin by sorting to focus on the attributes, and then create patterns based on those attributes.	The sorting tiles shown below have many attributes to use for sorting and patterning: size, colour, type of animal, and design (stripes or polka dot). This pattern shows what is called a one-difference train—each element differs from the preceding one in only one way.

GEOMETRIC SHAPES	**EXAMPLE**
Random shapes of different sizes are useful for sorting and creating patterns. Geometric shapes can be teacher-made or commercial. Attributes such as number of sides, concavity or convexity, and symmetry can be included.	This pattern is based on symmetry (symmetrical, asymmetrical; symmetrical, asymmetrical; symmetrical, asymmetrical; ...) and number of sides (3, 3, 4; 3, 3, 4; 3, 3, 4; ...). 

LINKING CUBES	**EXAMPLE**
Linking cubes can be used to show both shape and number patterns. They can also be used for simple colour sorting activities.	These linking cubes show the odd number pattern. 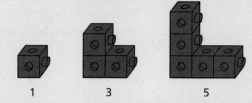

TOOTHPICKS	**EXAMPLE**
Toothpicks can be used to create shape patterns of various sorts, whether repeating patterns or growing ones.	Growing patterns (4, 7, 10, 13, ...) and repeating patterns (3, 6; 3, 6; 3, 6; ...) can be created with toothpicks. 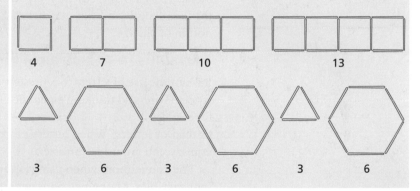

Appropriate Technology

Calculators

Calculators are useful for students to see growing patterns and other recursive patterns. For example, by using the repeated constant feature on certain calculators, students can

- show patterns of multiples. For example, to show the multiples of 5 pattern, press 5 $\boxed{+}$ 5 $\boxed{=}\boxed{=}\boxed{=}\boxed{=}$ to calculate the numbers in the pattern 5, 10, 15, 20, 25, ...
- show patterns of powers. For example, to show the powers of 5 pattern, press 5 $\boxed{\times}$ 5 $\boxed{=}\boxed{=}\boxed{=}\boxed{=}$ to calculate the numbers in the pattern 5, 25, 125, 625, 3125, ...
- show integer patterns. For example, the following sequence is an interesting introduction to negative numbers: 50 $\boxed{-}$ 10 $\boxed{=}\boxed{=}\boxed{=}\boxed{=}\boxed{=}\boxed{=}$.

Computers

There are a number of software packages that students can use to model and display patterns. Most simply, they can use the drawing programs of word processors to create shapes or other objects that can be resized or coloured to show patterns. They can also use a program like *KidPix* where

---

ACTIVITY 20.8

Use a calculator to determine the first 10 numbers in each pattern. Use what you learn from the first 10 numbers to predict the last two digits of the 40th number in each pattern.

a) 5 × 5 = = = = =

b) 15 × 15 = = = = =

c) 6 × 6 = = = = =

they can "stamp" patterns. Some software includes a problem component. An example is Tenth Planet's *Introduction to Patterns*.

In addition to this, there are some software packages that promote pattern thinking. One example is *Millie's Math House*. There is also an interesting service on the Internet that allows the user to input a sequence, and it will extend it for you.

Algebra

What Is Algebra?

Work on patterns leads naturally to algebraic thinking. Most people think that algebra is math with letters. However, mathematicians view algebra as a system that allows one to

- represent mathematical relationships
- explain relationships among quantities
- analyze change

For example, when you write the formula $P = 4s$ to describe how to determine the perimeter of a square, you are representing a mathematical relationship. By exploring the formula and noting that, for example, as s increases by 1, P increases by 4, you are exploring the relationship between the side length and the perimeter. You are simultaneously exploring the notion of change.

Variables in Algebraic Thinking

It is not the use of letters to represent quantities that defines algebra; in fact, students are also thinking algebraically when they solve open number sentences like $4 + 3 = \blacksquare$ or $7 - \blacksquare = 3$, which use boxes, or open frames, instead of letters. When letters or open frames are used in mathematics, you say you are using *variables*.

The convention, when using letters, is to use lowercase letters to represent variables. Mathematicians generally use the letter n when representing whole numbers; however, other popular letters are x, y, and z. The progression is usually from the use of the open frame ($\blacksquare$) to letters.

Variables, however, are used for different purposes, and this creates some confusion among students.

Using Variables to Represent Unknown Values

In the equation $x + 5 = 8$, or $\blacksquare + 5 = 8$, the variable represents a specific value yet to be determined. Sometimes there is only one possible value for the unknown, sometimes there are no possible values, and sometimes there are multiple values or an infinite number of values.

Values of an Unknown

NUMBER OF POSSIBLE VALUES	EXAMPLE	VALUES
One possible value	$2 \times \blacksquare + 8 = 16$	The only possible value is 4.
No possible values	$2 \times \blacksquare + 8 = 0$ $\blacksquare$ is a whole number.	$2 \times \blacksquare + 8 \geq 8$ so $2 \times \blacksquare + 8 \neq 0$; therefore, there is no possible value for $\blacksquare$.
An infinite number of possible values	$2 \times \blacksquare - 3 > 10$ $\blacksquare$ is a whole number.	Possible values: 7, 8, 9, 10, ...

Later on in this section, there is a discussion of how students learn to determine these values by solving equations or inequalities.

Using Variables to Generalize

Mathematicians are always looking for succinct, symbolic ways to describe multiple situations. For example, young students learn that "the order in which you add numbers doesn't matter" (the commutative property of addition). Although the words make it clear, mathematicians choose to describe this with symbols. A typical format would be $a \times b = b \times a$. This is a way of saying that no matter what numbers you use to replace a and b, if you multiply them in one order, you get the same result as multiplying in the other order. At some point, students learn that this format can be written in a shorter form as $ab = ba$ with the multiplication signs understood. Some other examples of using variables to generalize relationships are listed below.

Common Algebraic Generalizations

ALGEBRAIC EXPRESSION OR EQUATION	GENERALIZATION
$a + b = b + a$	You can add numbers in any order without changing the product (the commutative property of addition).
$2a + 2b = 2(a + b)$	The effect of doubling one number and adding it to double another number is the same as if you added the numbers first, and then doubled (the distributive property of multiplication over addition).
$(n + 1)(n - 1) = n^2 - 1$	To calculate the product of the two numbers on either side of a number, you can square the middle number and subtract 1. For example, $11 \times 9 = 10^2 - 1$. This is very handy for some calculations; for example, you can quickly calculate 301×299 as $300^2 - 1 = 90\,000 - 1 = 89\,999$.
$\dfrac{a}{b} + \dfrac{c}{b} = \dfrac{(a + c)}{b}$	To add two fractions with the same denominator (in this case, b), you can add the numerators to determine the new numerator, and then use the same denominator. This use of a variable to generalize also describes a general computation process.
$4n$	To symbolize an arbitrary multiple of 4, a mathematician uses the expression $4n$, since $4n$ is the result of multiplying a whole number n by 4.

Simplifying Expressions

Students working with expressions like $2n + 3n - 2$ might represent these using algebra tiles. If, for example, a rectangle is used to represent n, then students soon observe that $2n + 3n = 5n$. Usually, one colour is used to present positive amounts, for example, n or 1, and another colour to represent negative amounts, for example, $-2n$ or -4.

ACTIVITY 20.9

Students can create situations involving variables that are true some of the time, but not all of the time, and others that are always true.

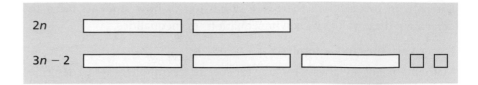

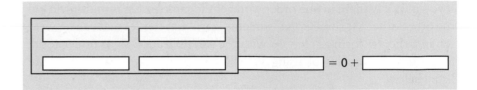

The zero principle that is used to help students work with positive and negative integers is also applied to these algebraic expressions. So, for example, $2n - 3n = -n$ is shown as:

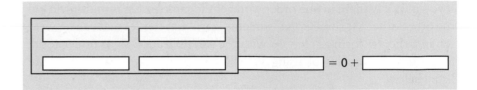

Describing Relationships and Functions

A formula is a special algebraic equation that shows a relationship between two or more different quantities. It might be a formula

- relating speed (or rate), time, and distance ($D = rt$)
- describing the volume of a rectangular prism ($V = l \times w \times h$)
- relating the value of a term in a pattern to its position in the pattern; for example, in the pattern 2, 4, 6, 8, 10, 12, ..., each term's value is double its position in the pattern: $t = 2p$

One of the earliest student introductions to this notion of relationship, or *function*, involves the concepts of input and output. A function is a relationship that leads to a particular output for a particular input. For example, if the function is "double the number," the input is the number to be doubled and the output is the double. Often these inputs and outputs are shown in a table to make it easier for students to infer relationships.

Using a Table

A table (sometimes informally referred to as a t-chart because of its internal "T" shape) is a graphic organizer that allows students to describe a relationship or function by listing the inputs in one column and the corresponding outputs in the other. The table below shows the relationship "subtract 1 and double," as you subtract 1 from the number in the Input column, and then double the result to get the number in the Output column. In high school, this would be described as $f(x) = 2(x - 1)$, with $f(x)$ being function notation.

T-Chart Showing a Relationship

Input	Output
3	4
4	6
5	8
6	10

A table is an appropriate way to show the numbers in a pattern, with the input being the position in the pattern and the output the value of the number in the pattern. For example, the pattern 4, 7, 10, 13, 16, ... could be modelled in a table as shown below. To get each output value, each input value is multiplied by 3, and then 1 is added. Algebraically, this could be described as $o = 3i + 1$.

T-Chart for the Pattern 4, 7, 10, 13, 16, ...

	Input		Output	
The position of the number in the pattern	1		4	The value of the number in the pattern
	2		7	
	3		10	
	4		13	

In the table above, many students will see the pattern in the output column (4, 7, 10, 13, ...), but may not be able to figure out the relationship between the Input and the Output columns. Determining this relationship can be difficult, but it is what will enable students to make predictions about the value of a number in a pattern based on its position.

Using a table to show how the value of the terms of a pattern relates to the position of the term highlights the difference between a recursive pattern and relationships. When students see the intervals of 3 in the Output column above, they are thinking recursively. When students recognize that you can take the input number, triple it, and add 1 to get the output number, then students are thinking about a relationship. The ability to determine these relationships typically comes later than an understanding of recursive patterns in students' mathematical development, although students should be encouraged to read across the table, and not just up and down. Just as was the case in extending patterns, students can only be sure of the relationship rule if they are provided with enough specific information to rule out other possibilities.

ACTIVITY 20.10

Determining the relationship in a table can be approached as a "guess my rule" game. You can dramatize this idea by building a box that, metaphorically, houses the rule. There is a hole in which inputs can be inserted on small pieces of paper, and a hole from which outputs emerge. The back of the box is open so that you can ensure the correct output number comes out.

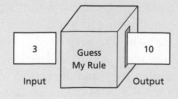

Solving Equations

Students begin early in their mathematical careers to solve open number sentences. Later, you refer to these as equations, but the idea is the same. An equation is a mathematical sentence with an equals sign. For some students, the equality sign poses a difficulty. Although they are comfortable with, for example, the sentence $4 + 5 = \blacksquare$, they interpret the equality sign to mean "find the answer." Therefore, when students see the sentence $\blacksquare - 4 = 5$, they may not be sure what to do as they think the answer is already there. Similarly, students might solve $4 + \blacksquare = 5$ by adding 4 and 5 to "get the answer." The notion of an equation as an expression of balance is not apparent to them. This long-standing problem is exacerbated by the fact that many calculators require the ⊟ key to be pressed to get an answer, so students are reinforced in interpreting the $=$ sign as synonymous with "get the answer."

It is important for students to recognize that the equality sign should be viewed as a way to say that the same number has two different names, one on either side of the equals sign.

Solving an Equation Using Manipulatives

When a number sentence is simple enough, students can either call on a fact they already know or model the situation using manipulatives, for example, counters, to determine the missing value. For example:

- To solve $4 \times 5 = \blacksquare$, students model 4 sets of 5 to calculate the 20.
- To solve $4 \times \blacksquare = 24$, students create 4 groups and keep putting out counters until 24 counters are placed in 4 equal-sized groups. Students then observe that each group includes 6 items.
- To solve $3 \times \blacksquare + 6 = 21$, students distribute 21 counters so that an equal number are in each of three circles and 6 are outside the circles. The solution is the number of counters in one circle, 5 counters, so $3 \times 5 + 6 = 21$, as shown below.

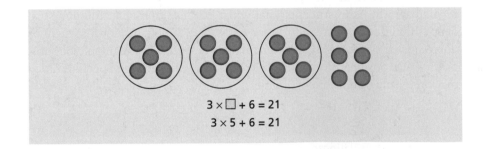

$$3 \times \square + 6 = 21$$
$$3 \times 5 + 6 = 21$$

Solving an Equation by Working Backward

ACTIVITY 20.11

Students can try this number trick, and then do it in reverse to see how the trick works.

a) Select any number. Double it. Subtract 3. Double again. Add 2. Divide by 4. What number did you end up with?

b) Now try the trick in reverse. Select a number and work backward. What did you do? What number did you end up with?

Students can think about working backward to solve an equation like $4 \times \blacksquare = 24$. What the equation says is that a number is multiplied by 4 to get 24. The "reverse" of multiplying by 4 is dividing by 4. So students can work backward and divide 24 by 4 to get 6.

Students might solve the more complex equation, $5 \times \blacksquare + 2 = 27$, by thinking "I multiply a number by 5, and then add 2 to get 27. So, if I work backward and subtract 2 $(27 - 2 = 25)$, and then divide by 5 $(25 \div 5 = 5)$, I will end up with the solution, 5."

A more involved example of this strategy is found in **Activity 20.11**, to the left. After students apply the steps in part (a), they can follow the steps in reverse to see how the trick works.

Some equations, such as $2n + 3 = n + 5$, do not lend themselves to working backward. Other strategies that students can use to solve equations like this are guessing and checking, or balancing.

Solving an Equation by Guessing and Checking

To solve the equation $2n + 3 = n + 5$, a student might think the following:

Solving $2n + 3 = n + 5$

GUESS	REASONING	CHECK BY SUBSTITUTION $2n + 3 = n + 5$
First guess: 10	I'll start with 10 because it's an easy number to work with mentally.	$2 \times 10 + 3 = 23$ $10 + 5 = 15$ 23 is not equal to 15.
Second guess: 5	I'll try a number less than 10 because, if n is too great, doubling it and adding 3 (the left side of the equation) will make it a lot more than just adding 5 to it (the right side of the equation). I'll try 5.	$2 \times 5 + 3 = 13$ $5 + 5 = 10$ 13 is not equal to 10.
Third guess: 4	I'll try 4 because I notice that 13 and 10, the numbers I got when I used 5, were closer together than the numbers I got when I used 10.	$2 \times 4 + 3 = 11$ $4 + 5 = 9$ 11 is not equal to 9.
Fourth guess: 3	I'll try 3 to get numbers that are even closer together.	$2 \times 3 + 3 = 9$ $3 + 5 = 8$ 9 is not equal to 8.
Fifth guess: 2	I'll try 2 to get numbers that are even closer together.	$2 \times 2 + 3 = 7$ $2 + 5 = 7$ 7 is equal to 7. n must be 2.

Solving an Equation by Maintaining a Balance

Students should start out using manipulatives such as a balance scale with small paper bags holding the unknown number of cubes. For example, to model $2n + 3 = n + 5$, students put 2 open empty paper bags ($2n$) and 3 cubes on one side of a balance, and 1 open empty paper bag (n) and 5 cubes on the other side (see the balance scale below). Students then put the same number of cubes in each bag, increasing the value until the sides of the scale balance. The number of cubes in each empty bag is the value of the unknown, n.

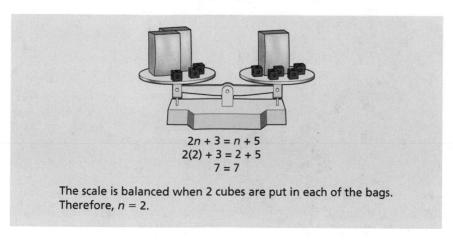

$$2n + 3 = n + 5$$
$$2(2) + 3 = 2 + 5$$
$$7 = 7$$

The scale is balanced when 2 cubes are put in each of the bags. Therefore, $n = 2$.

On a symbolic level, the equation $2n + 3 = n + 5$ can still be considered a balance. If either side of the equation is changed, the other side must be changed the same way to maintain a balance. Therefore, if 3 is subtracted from both sides of the equation, $2n + 3 - 3 = n + 5 - 3$, the balance is maintained. This also results in an equation that is easier to solve. For example:

$2n + 3 = n + 5$
$2n + 3 - 3 = n + 5 - 3$ (Subtract 3 from both sides.)
$2n = n + 2$
$n + n = n + 2$ (Substitute $n + n$ for $2n$ since $2n = n + n$.)
So, $n = 2$.

"Dividing" to Balance the Scale The equation representing the situation shown below on the balance scale on the left is $2b = 6$. Note that, in this model, the bags are closed and each contains the same number of cubes. To find out how many cubes are in each bag, each side could be separated into 2 equal amounts. This is equivalent to dividing both sides by 2, as shown by the balance scale on the right.

How many cubes are in each paper bag?

$2b = 6$

1 bag can be balanced by 3 cubes so there must be 3 cubes in each bag.

$b = 3$

"Subtracting" to Balance the Scale The equation representing the situation shown below on the balance scale on the left is $2b = 6 + b$. To find out how many cubes are in each bag, a bag could be taken off each side. This is equivalent to subtracting b from both sides, as shown by the balance scale on the right.

How many cubes are in each paper bag?

$2b = 6 + b$

1 bag can be balanced by 6 cubes so there must be 6 cubes in each bag.

$b = 6$

Solving an Inequality

Working with Inequalities

Students also should work informally with inequalities (for example, $3 + \blacksquare < 10$ or $4 + \blacksquare \neq 10$). At this level, students will likely guess and test to find values that satisfy the inequality. They will observe that there are often, but not always, many possible whole number solutions.

Solutions for Inequalities

INEQUALITY	NUMBER OF WHOLE NUMBER SOLUTIONS
$3 + \blacksquare < 10$	7 solutions: 0, 1, 2, 3, 4, 5, 6
$3 + \blacksquare \neq 10$	An infinite number of solutions: any number other than 7
$3 + \blacksquare < 3$	No whole number solutions

Using Graphs to Describe Relationships

Graphs are effective models for describing relationships between various variables or quantities. Some examples are shown below.

Graphs That Show Relationships

RELATING NUMBERS OF TRICYCLES AND WHEELS	RELATING SIDE LENGTH AND PERIMETER OF A SQUARE
This graph shows a way for students to display the relationship between the number of tricycles and the total number of wheels; that is, as the number of tricycles increases by 1, the number of wheels increases by 3. By using the graph, the pattern inherent in counting tricycle wheels is highlighted.	This graph shows that the perimeter of a square is related to its side length.

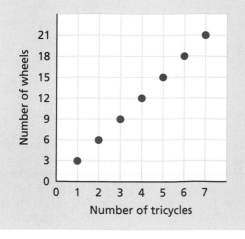

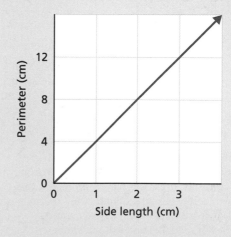

RELATING SIDE LENGTH AND AREA OF A SQUARE

This graph shows that the area of a square is related to its side length.

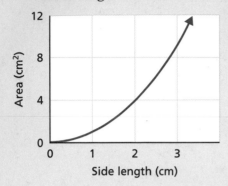

RELATING MONTHS OF THE YEAR TO HOURS OF DAYLIGHT

This graph shows that the length of daylight increases until June, and then decreases until the end of December.

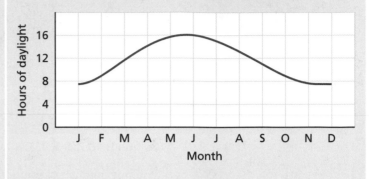

Common Errors and Misconceptions

Algebra: Strategies for Dealing with Common Errors and Misconceptions

COMMON ERROR OR MISCONCEPTION	SUGGESTED STRATEGY
When letters are used to represent variables, students are often confused between x as a variable and x as a multiplication sign. For example, if a student sees 3 x y, he might wonder if he should find the product of 3, x, and y, or the product of 3 and y.	One way around this problem is to avoid the use of the variable x in early stages of using literal variables. In early algebra work, n is often used to represent a whole number. As well, using variables that represent what they are modelling is also helpful. For example, if the variable represents the number of cubes in a bag (see page 587), perhaps b or c would be a more easily understandable variable. Another option is to clearly differentiate the symbols; for example, use a small italic x to represent a variable and a large non-italic capital X to represent multiplication. Once students become familiar with the notion that $ab = a \times b$, this will no longer be a problem. However, a new problem might be created if they think that ab means a 2-digit number (see next page).
Students often incorrectly interpret the equality sign. For example, to solve $3 \times 8 = \blacksquare \times 4$, they use 24 to replace the $\blacksquare$ since 24 is 3×8.	Students need to participate in conversations about what the equality sign means; that is, both sides of the equation represent different names for the same amount. It also helps if students see a variety of equation types. For example: $8 + 7 = 15 \qquad 15 = 7 + 8 \qquad 6 + 9 = 10 + 5$
Students may misrepresent a relationship in words when using symbols. For example, to represent the fact that each teacher has 30 students, they might write $t = 30c$ instead of $c = 30t$ (where t stands for the number of teachers and c the number of children).	Provide students with practice in moving from verbal descriptions of a relationship to symbolic ones using familiar relationships. Trial and error with a familiar context is a reasonable strategy in this circumstance. For example, students know that there are 10 pennies in a dime. They can write the equations $d = 10p$ and $p = 10d$ and use different values for p to find corresponding values for d. They soon realize that the appropriate equation is $p = 10d$.

COMMON ERROR OR MISCONCEPTION	SUGGESTED STRATEGY
When letters are used to represent variables, students are often confused, for example, between $4n$ as the product of the numbers 4 and n, and a number in the 40s with a ones-digit of n. (See the **Student Response** below.)	It is not obvious to students why you omit the operation sign when you multiply a variable by a number. This requires specific discussion with students and practise with reading these values. It is most likely because of the potential confusion of the multiplication sign with the variable x that mathematicians adopted this convention. A small dot is sometimes used between two values as another way to represent multiplication and avoid confusion, for example, $4 \cdot n$.

Can x be any number at all for this to be true? $2x - 6 = 18$

Circle (Yes) or No

Explain your answer. _24 minus 6 equals 18_

so you could change the X to a 4

Student Response

This student appears to have incorrectly interpreted the variable x as the digit 4 (part of the number 24) instead of as the number 12 ($2x = 2 \times 12$).

Appropriate Manipulatives

Algebra: Examples of Manipulatives

COUNTERS	EXAMPLE
Counters are useful to model the solution of whole number equations.	Counters can be used to solve $2 \times \blacksquare + 8 = 16$ by distributing 16 counters so that an equal number are in each circle, and 8 are outside of both circles. 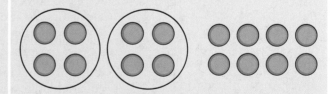 $2 \times \square + 8 = 16$ $2 \times 4 + 8 = 16$ *(continued)*

BALANCE SCALES AND PAPER BAGS	EXAMPLE
Balance scales and paper bags can be used to model solving equations.	To model $3n + 2 = 2n + 4$, put 3 empty paper bags and 2 cubes on one side of a balance scale, and 2 empty paper bags and 4 cubes on the other side. Then put the same number of cubes in each bag, increasing the number until the sides of the scale balance. 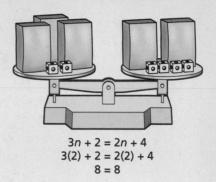 $3n + 2 = 2n + 4$ $3(2) + 2 = 2(2) + 4$ $8 = 8$

Appropriate Technology

Calculators

The constant key function of the calculator is a very useful one for studying the concept of a variable. For example, the relationship between the expression $8 \times \blacksquare$ or $8n$ and repeated addition is modelled using the constant key function by pressing $8 \boxed{+} 8 \boxed{=}\boxed{=}\boxed{=}\boxed{=}$ .... If students record the results in a t-chart (as shown below), they will see that $8n$ is the result of adding 8, n times.

Number of 8s added	Total
1	8
2	16 (2 × 8)
3	24 (3 × 8)
4	32 (4 × 8)

Calculators can also be used for guessing and testing

- the relationship between input and output values in a relationship table (see page 584)
- different values for a variable in an equation or inequality to make the equation or inequality true (see pages 586 and 589)

Computers

Spreadsheets are a very useful tool for exploring relationships between quantities. They can also be used for solving equations. For example, suppose you want students to explore the relationship between two quantities. Teachers can set up a spreadsheet with a formula. Students enter an input value and the computer automatically displays the output. Students can use this tool over and over until they are ready to guess the rule. For example, the second column of the spreadsheet on page 593 is programmed to show the relationship $b = 3a - 5$.

WebConnect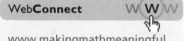

www.makingmathmeaningful
.nelson.com

Visit the Making Math Meaningful website for links to models for solving equations.

B2	▼	fx = A2*3-5	
	A	B	C
1	Input (a)	Output (b)	
2	10	25	
3	15	40	
4	20	55	
5	25	70	
6	30	85	
7	35	100	
8	40	115	
9	45	130	
10	50	145	

This spreadsheet uses the formula $b = 3a - 5$.

Assessing Student Understanding

- Create opportunities for students to look for patterns in their environment as well as in the mathematics they are doing, and point them out, even when pattern is not the mathematical topic currently under discussion.
- Make sure to remember that unless a pattern rule is provided, there is no single way to extend a pattern. Thus, if you ask a student to continue, for example, 1, 3, 5, 7, ... and the extension is not 9, 11, 13, ... as expected, make sure to ask the student to explain his or her reasoning. It might be correct.
- As students explore patterns in tables such as the addition table, make sure that they attempt to describe the patterns as unambiguously as possible (with a pattern rule for students who are ready to use them), and that they attempt to explain why they think the pattern works.
- As students respond to situations involving variables, make sure that the variables appear on the right side of the equals sign some of the time, and on the left side other times.

Appropriate Children's Books

Anno's Magic Seeds (Anno, 1995).
This book about how a magic seed produces 2 seeds for each 1 seed planted allows students to explore relationships between numbers.

Anno's Mysterious Multiplying Jar (Anno, 1983).
This classic, more appropriate for older elementary and middle school students, explores the pattern that results from multiplying 1, 1 × 2, 1 × 2 × 3, ... through wonderful illustrations that describe a very simple story.

The Rajah's Rice: A Mathematical Folktale from India (Barry, 1994), and The Token Gift (McKibbon, 1996).
The exponential pattern (1, 2, 4, 8, 16, 32, ...) that comes from repeatedly doubling is explored in both versions of a very famous story about the wisdom of someone who recognizes how quickly numbers can grow when you multiply. Older students can use t-tables to predict the exact amount at various points in time.

Pattern Fish (Harris, 2000), and *Pattern Bugs (Harris, 2001).*
Using these nicely illustrated books with few words, young students can explore a variety of types of repeating patterns, with each pattern being represented in a number of different ways.

Two of Everything (Hong, 1993).
In this ancient folk tale, a poor old man finds a pot that has the effect of doubling whatever is put into it. This situation would allow students to explore the algebraic relationship between numbers and their doubles.

Sea Squares (Hulme, 1999).
This attractive book allows students to explore the pattern of square numbers (1, 4, 9, 16, ...) in a visual way.

Nature's Paintbrush: The Patterns and Colours Around You (Stockdale,1999).
This book for young students shows how various patterns found on animals help those animals to survive.

Lots and Lots of Zebra Stripes: Patterns in Nature (Swinburne, 1998).
Many patterns in nature can be explored by young students in this book, not only zebra stripes, but also ridges on pumpkins and scales on snakes.

Applying What You've Learned

1. What problem-solving strategy did you use to solve the chapter problem? Did you make a model? Draw a diagram? Use a pattern? How could the problem enhance a student's understanding of pattern?

2. Consider the two multi-attribute repeating patterns below. Why do you think the first might be easier for a student to extend than the second?

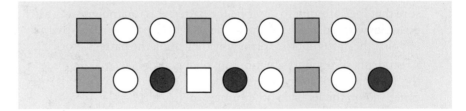

3. This chapter showed you some ways patterns come up in the number strand, for example, in computational patterns or in patterns in various tables and charts. What are some ways you think pattern might come up in the measurement strand?

4. Describe a variety of ways to use coloured multi-link cubes for students to work with both single-attribute and multi-attribute repeating patterns, as well as growing and shrinking patterns.

5. Develop an activity that will help students at about the Grade 4 level begin to recognize the relationship between where a number appears in a number pattern and its value.

6. Read several journal articles to get a sense of why the metaphor of a balance for an equation is important and powerful. List several of the important points that were raised.

7. Topics like solving equations of the form $[\ ] + b = c$ used to be listed in curriculum documents as number topics; now they are listed in many documents as patterning and algebra topics. How do you think that might affect the teaching of those topics?

Interact with a K–8 Student:

8. Ask a student to create three different patterns that include the numbers 10 and 12.

   a) Ask the student to compare the patterns. Does his or her description focus on the pattern structure, or does it simply list elements of the patterns?

   b) Ask what the 20th number in the pattern would be and how the student knows. What sorts of number concepts does the student use to determine his or her answers? What pattern concepts does the student use?

Discuss with a K–8 Teacher:

9. Choose one:

   Discuss with an elementary school teacher about how she or he integrates work with patterns into work with other mathematical strands.
   OR
   Discuss with a Grade 6 to 8 teacher about how she or he uses manipulative materials to support work in algebra.

Selected References

Anno, M. (1983). *Anno's mysterious multiplying jar.* New York: Philomel.

Anno, M. (1995). *Anno's magic seeds.* New York: Philomel.

Barry, D. (1994). *The rajah's rice: A mathematical folktale from India.* Gordonsville, VA: W.H. Freeman & Co.

Blanton, M.L., and Kaput, J.J. (2003). Developing elementary teachers' "algebra eyes and ears." *Teaching Children Mathematics, 10,* 70–77.

Cai, J. (1998). Developing algebraic reasoning in the elementary grades. *Teaching Children Mathematics, 5,* 225–229.

Carpenter, T., Franke, M.L., and Levi, L. (2003). *Thinking mathematically: Integrating arithmetic and algebra in elementary school.* Portsmouth, NH: Heinemann.

Clements, D.H., and Sarama, J. (1997). Computers support algebraic thinking. *Teaching Children Mathematics, 3,* 320–325.

Cuevas, G.J., and Yeatts, K. (2001). *Navigating through algebra, grades 3–5.* Reston, VA: National Council of Teachers of Mathematics.

Curcio, F.R., and Schwartz, S.L. (1997). What does algebraic thinking look like and sound like with preprimary children? *Teaching Children Mathematics, 3,* 296–300.

Falkner, K.P., Levi, L., and Carpenter, T.C. (1999). Children's understanding of equality: A foundation for algebra. *Teaching Children Mathematics, 6,* 232–236.

Femiano, R. (2003). Algebraic problem solving in the primary grades. *Teaching Children Mathematics, 9,* 444–449.

Ferrini-Mundy, J., Lappan, G., and Phillips, E. (1997). Experiences with patterning. *Teaching Children Mathematics, 3,* 282–289.

Friel, S., Rachlin, S., and Doyle, D. (2001). *Navigating through algebra, grades 6–8.* Reston, VA: National Council of Teachers of Mathematics.

Greenes, C., Cavanagh, M., Dacey, L., Findell, C., and Small, M. (2001). *Navigating through algebra in prekindergarten–grade 2.* Reston, VA: National Council of Teachers of Mathematics.

Greenes, C., Dacey, L., and Spungin, R. (1999). *Hot math topics: Patterns and reasoning (grade 3).* White Plains, NY: Dale Seymour–Addison Wesley Longman.

Greenes, C., and Findell, C. (1998). *Groundworks: Algebra puzzles and problems, grades 4–7.* Chicago: Creative Publications.

Greenes, C., and Findell, C. (1999a). Developing students' algebraic reasoning abilities. In Stiff, L., and

Curcio, F.R. (Eds.). *Mathematical reasoning, K–12: 1999 yearbook*. Reston, VA: National Council of Teachers of Mathematics, 127–137.

Greenes, C., and Findell, C. (1999b). *Groundworks: Algebraic thinking, grades 1–3*. Chicago: Creative Publications.

Harris, T. (2000). *Pattern fish*. Brookfield, CN: Millbrook Press.

Harris, T. (2001). *Pattern bugs*. Brookfield, CN: Millbrook Press.

Herbert, K., and Brown, R.H. (1997). Patterns as tools for algebraic reasoning. *Teaching Children Mathematics, 3*, 340–345.

Hong, L.T. (2003). *Two of everything*. Morton Grove, IL: Albert Whitman & Company.

Hulme, J. (1999). *Sea squares*. New York: Hyperion.

Kenny, P.A., and Silver, E.A. (1997). Probing the foundations of algebra: Grade 4 pattern items in NAEP. *Teaching Children Mathematics, 3*, 268–274.

Kieran, C. (1991). Helping to make the transition to algebra. *Arithmetic Teacher, 38*, 49–51.

Lubinski, C.A., and Otto, A.D. (1997). Literature and algebraic reasoning. *Teaching Children Mathematics, 3*, 290–295.

Lubinski, C.A., and Otto, A.D. (2002). Meaningful mathematical representations and early algebraic reasoning. *Teaching Children Mathematics, 9*, 76–80.

McKibbon, H.W. (1996). *The token gift*. Toronto: Annick Press.

Schifter, D. (1999). Reasoning about operations: Early algebraic thinking, grades K through 6. In Stiff, L., and Curcio, F.R. (Eds.). *Mathematical reasoning, K–12: 1999 yearbook*. Reston, VA: National Council of Teachers of Mathematics, 62–81.

Schliemann, A.D., Carraher, D.W., and Brizuela, B. (2007). *Bringing out the algebraic character of arithmetic: From children's ideas to classroom practice*. Studies in Mathematical Thinking and Learning Series. London: Taylor & Francis.

Small, M. (2005). *PRIME: Patterns and algebra: Background and strategies*. Toronto: Thomson Nelson.

Speer, W.R., Hayes, D.F., and Brahier, D.J. (1997). Becoming very-able with variables. *Teaching Children Mathematics, 3*, 305–308.

Stockdale, S. (1999). *Nature's paintbrush: The patterns and colors around you*. New York: Simon and Schuster Children's Publishing.

Sulzer, J.S. (1998). The function box and fourth graders: Squares, cubes, and circles. *Teaching Children Mathematics, 4*, 442–447.

Swinburne, S. (1998). *Lots and lots of zebra stripes*. Honesdale, PA: Boyds Mills Press.

Thompson, F.M. (1988). Algebraic instruction for the younger child. In Coxford, A.F., and Shulte, A.P. (Eds.). *The ideas of algebra, K–12: 1988 yearbook*. Reston, VA: National Council of Teachers of Mathematics, 69–77.

Usiskin, Z. (1997). Doing algebra in grades K–4. *Teaching Children Mathematics, 3*, 346–356.

Willoughby, S.S. (1997). Functions from kindergarten through sixth grade. *Teaching Children Mathematics, 3*, 314–318.

Yackel, E. (1997). A foundation for algebraic reasoning in the early grades. *Teaching Children Mathematics, 3*, 276–280.

Chapter 21

Assessment and Evaluation

Marble Mania

Tian will run a marble game at the school's fun fair. His game needs 300 marbles. He finds a store that sells marbles for the prices shown on the three bags.

a) How many marbles do you think are in the large bag? Show your work.

b) What do you think is the best way for Tian to buy the marbles? Give a reason for your answer.

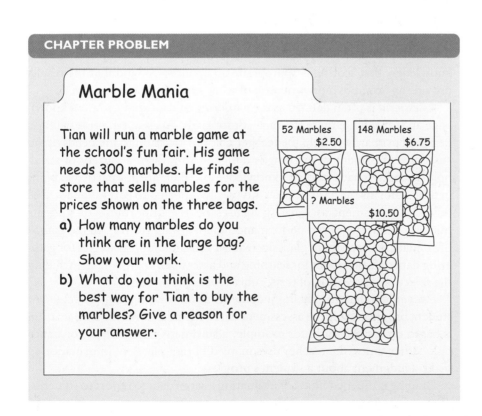

52 Marbles $2.50

148 Marbles $6.75

? Marbles $10.50

> **IN A NUTSHELL**
>
> The main ideas in this chapter are listed below:
>
> 1. There are important differences between assessment, evaluation, and grading.
>
> 2. Assessment for learning is a substantial part of the assessment a teacher should do.
>
> 3. Assessment data should be gathered in many ways and at different times to be reliable and valid.
>
> 4. There are many types of assessment a teacher can use. The type of assessment used should reflect the purpose for gathering the data.

Introduction

In the past two decades, attention to assessment practices has been heightened. A focus has been placed on ensuring that assessments are consistent with their purpose, that students have a fair opportunity to demonstrate their knowledge, that scoring is appropriate and consistent, and that the results provide an accurate representation of what students know and can do.

Assessment is often defined as the gathering of data about student knowledge and/or skills, either informally or formally. Assessment for learning is designed primarily to help the teacher tailor instruction to the needs of the student. Assessment of learning is designed to inform a variety of stakeholders about what a student's knowledge and skills are at a particular point in time. It forms the basis of what is typically reported to parents and school officials. Assessment as learning focuses on the importance of students thinking about their own performance and learning from it. In the course of building an assessment plan, the teacher must identify strategies for gathering data on assessment for learning and assessment of learning, including the selection or creation of tests, rubrics, interview tools, etc.

Evaluation refers to making judgments about or assigning a "value" to student progress using the assessment data collected. Sometimes evaluation is based on a single task, for example, a summative chapter performance task. Other times, the teacher uses many different pieces of information to make a judgment about a student's progress.

Grading is the specific act of evaluating a set of data to report to students, parents, or education authorities.

How Assessment Has Changed

With the push of professional organizations like the National Council of Teachers of Mathematics and ministry and board officials, many teachers have begun to look at what is important in mathematics in new ways.

Views on assessment have also changed. For many teachers, the focus is now on assessing each student's performance relative to the curriculum expectations/outcomes, rather than comparing students to each other. As well, many educators now want to gather information about a broader range of learning—the ability to solve problems, to communicate, to apply concepts, to reason, and to use procedures. Since the range of information needed is greater, a broader range of strategies and tools is required.

The most important change may be in the increased emphasis on assessment for learning. Teachers are interested not just in discovering what students have or have not learned, but also in using that information to alter their instructional approaches. For example, if a student's problem-solving performance shows that she or he has difficulty in the understand-the-problem stage of the problem-solving or inquiry process, the teacher will spend more instructional time on that aspect of problem solving.

Characteristics of Good Assessment

Information about a student's knowledge and abilities needs to be collected from a variety of sources on many occasions to ensure that the information is reliable and valid. These sources might include written work, oral performance in class or in an interview situation, performance tasks, student self-assessment, and tests or quizzes. By combining these sources of information, a teacher gets a good sense of what a student knows or can do.

A Good Assessment Plan

A good overall assessment plan

- **balances the measurement of both mathematics content and processes:** The mathematics education community has come to value both the content knowledge and the process abilities that students acquire. For example, a student may be an excellent communicator, but misunderstand a certain piece of content; the reverse can also be true. By finding this out, the teacher knows where to place her or his emphasis.
- **is appropriate for its purpose:** If the teacher's goal is, for example, to collect information about student communication, it is important that the communication task be rich enough to allow for a broad range of performance in communication.
- **includes a variety of assessment formats:** Many students reveal a more accurate picture of their understanding using some assessment formats rather than others. Some show their understanding better in written situations, some by talking, and some by manipulating materials. Some students respond very well to the pressure of formal assessment, but some do not. Using many formats allows each student has an opportunity to show her or his best.
- **is aligned with student needs and expectations:** To have reliable information, it is important that students not be surprised by the task proposed in an assessment situation. The task can and usually should be new to students, but it should be consistent with the way they have learned and the kinds of tasks met previously. Otherwise, performance may not really reflect the level of understanding.
- **is fair to all students:** This is more likely if the teacher collects information from many types of tasks and allows certain accommodations,

where appropriate. Some accommodations would be suggested in a student's individual educational plan. Other times, small adjustments are possible on the spot. For example, a teacher may allow a student who is asked to explain something in words to explain it using a diagram.

- **is useful in assisting students to assess their own learning:** It is important that students understand what is expected. When students complete an assessment task, they should have a sense of how well they have done. Whether it is through examples or descriptions, students need to know how to look at their own work and assess themselves. This allows them to self-monitor and improve on their performance the next time.

- **measures growth over time:** The educational system is built around helping students grow academically, socially, physically, and emotionally. You should always be focused on whether student understanding has improved, no matter what the level of the initial or final performance.

- **sets high, yet realistic, expectations for students:** Research has shown that students respond to teachers' expectations (Bamburg, 1994). Teachers who do not expect a lot do not get a lot, whether from their top students or from their weakest ones. Teachers who set higher, yet realistic, academic expectations are often gratified at how well all students perform.

Sample Assessment Plan

A complete assessment of a topic should involve all of the aspects discussed above. In considering a topic in the number strand, such as subtracting 3-digit numbers, a teacher might gather multiple data.

Initially, a teacher might gather diagnostic information about a student's readiness for the planned unit of instruction. If the student is not ready, the teacher will certainly want to provide bridging activities and might well need to differentiate instruction during the teaching of the unit. If the student is well beyond the topic of instruction, the teacher will want to provide more enrichment activities.

Over the course of the unit of instruction, teachers might gather formative assessment data and, at the end of the unit, summative assessment data about the student's

- performance of the skill, for example, several computations to perform
- interpretation of the symbols, by asking students to describe a situation or display a model for a particular computation
- solution to a straightforward word problem where subtraction is required
- solution to a rich problem that involves subtracting, for example, "The difference between two 3-digit numbers is 472 less than their sum. The difference is a palindrome (a number that reads the same forward as backward). What could the numbers be?"
- relevant communication and reasoning, for example, a question such as, "How can you use $346 - 125 = 221$ to calculate $345 - 126$?"
- use of estimation, for example, to determine whether a suggested answer is reasonable
- communication about the "big picture," for example, a question such as, "Some people say that subtraction is the reverse of addition. Explain what they mean and why this might be useful to know."

Sample Assessment Tasks

Sometimes this information can be collected through the assignment of one broadly based task; other times it can be gleaned using a series of separate questions or tasks.

A Performance Task The following performance task (**On the Move**) could be assigned at the end of a Grade 4 unit on addition and subtraction (assuming students have already completed a unit on data management). The task requires students to *subtract, relate subtraction to addition, estimate, use relationships,* and *calculate.* It also integrates previous learning about bar graphs.

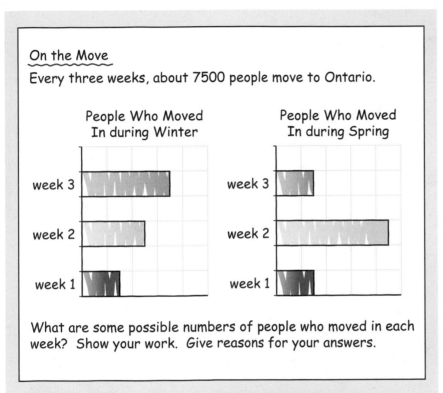

On the Move

Every three weeks, about 7500 people move to Ontario.

People Who Moved In during Winter

People Who Moved In during Spring

What are some possible numbers of people who moved in each week? Show your work. Give reasons for your answers.

Discrete Tasks For the topic of subtraction discussed above, a teacher might also choose to use a number of separate small tasks, such as those given below:

1. a) 569   b) 312   c) 400   d) 621
   −245   −106   −223   −374

    ← Several skills

2. Create a new set of four subtraction questions with the same four answers as above.

    ← A question requiring the use of addition and subtraction principles

3. Create two word problems, using different meanings of subtraction, where each is solved by one of the computations in Question 1.

    ← A question relating to the meaning of the operation

4. Explain why the result when you subtract can be greater or less than the number you are subtracting. Tell how you can predict which it will be.

    ← A higher-level question involving synthesis or problem solving

Framing Assessment Tasks for Specific Purposes

Once a teacher decides on what is to be assessed and in what format, the nature of the task or questions asked can still vary considerably. In each case, the teacher may learn something different about her or his students, and students may get a different impression about what mathematics is all about and what aspects of mathematics the teacher values.

Suppose, for example, that the teacher is interested in assessing students' ability to extend patterns. The following is a brief list of choices the teacher might make and what information she or he could gather.

Assessment Tasks for Pattern Work

ASSESSMENT TASK	WHY WOULD THE TEACHER USE THIS APPROACH?
The pattern rule is: Start at 3. Then, add 4 more each time. What is the 10th number in the pattern?	To determine students' ability to apply a simple pattern rule.
The pattern is 3, 7, 11, 15, ... What is the pattern rule? Explain how you know.	To determine students' understanding of what a pattern rule is.
The pattern is: 3, 7, 11, 15, ... How much greater is the 20th number in the pattern than the 10th number?	To determine students' insight into pattern behaviour. For example, some students will extend the pattern to calculate each term, and then find the difference. Others, however, will recognize that the difference has to be $10 \times 4 = 40$ because the numbers are 10 terms apart and the difference is always 4.
The pattern rule is: Start at 3. Then, add 4 more each time. In which position would you find the number 399?	To determine students' ability to use the pattern rule in reverse. This can give some insight into students' algebraic thinking. For example: A student might recognize that each number in 3, 7, 11, 15, ... is 1 less than the corresponding number in 4, 8, 12, 16, ..., and then relate 399 to 400. This student examines the pattern 4, 8, 12, 16, ... to determine the position of the term 400. He realizes that the pattern rule is to multiply the position number by 4. Therefore, to find the position of the term 400, he uses the inverse operation and divides 400 by 4 to determine that 400 is the 100th term in the pattern 4, 8, 12, 16, ..., and 399 is the 100th term of the pattern 3, 7, 11, 15, ... Or a student might think about how many 4s must have been added to the first term 3 to get to 399 by subtracting 3 from 399 and dividing 396 by 4 to get 99. If 99 fours were added to the first term to get to 399, then 399 must be the 100th term.
Create three different patterns where 15 is the fourth term. Calculate the 10th term in each pattern.	To determine students' ability to solve problems related to pattern.
The pattern is 3, 7, ... Why can't you be sure of what comes next?	To see if students realize that a pattern rule or many more terms in the sequence are required before one can be certain of how to extend it.

Sources of Assessment Data

Some sources for classroom-based assessment data include the following:

- portfolios (which could include many of the following)
- performance tasks
- projects
- journals
- observations
- interviews
- homework
- tests and quizzes

In each case, the data might be gathered in a group setting or in an individual situation. Students might also assess themselves.

Evaluation Tools

Scoring of gathered data can be accomplished using a variety of tools—perhaps a scoring guide, a rubric, or anecdotal comments, depending on what is appropriate for the task.

A **scoring guide** is a document that suggests the assignment of points or marks for various aspects of a piece of work. For example, a question might ask a student to list three factors of 12, and then three multiples. The guide would indicate what performance is required for different numbers of marks.

A **rubric** is a continuum for assigning a score to a level of performance on a student task that allows for a wide range of performance. Often, the guide is descriptive. A rubric may be used to evaluate work on a rich problem, a portfolio, or a performance task.

If it is possible, rubrics should be shared, if not negotiated, with a class prior to their use. Sometimes, the sharing of a rubric for a particular task may actually "give away" the strategies to be assessed; in that case, rubrics for a similar task might be shared. By knowing what is valued, students have the best opportunity to achieve those goals. Students can practise using the rubric to evaluate their own or a peer's work to really understand it.

It is useful if teachers within a school collaborate in the development and interpretation of rubrics. This consistency helps students make better sense of what is important. Examples of generic rubrics for assessing the use of math processes are found in Appendices 5, 6, and 7.

Anecdotal comments, that is, comments without any "score," are another way to evaluate student work. They provide useful feedback for a student, but can also be kept by the teacher to include in her or his bank of assessment information. Other times, the teacher will simply note that work has been done, and provide verbal feedback without keeping a permanent record.

Portfolios

The purpose of an assessment portfolio is to serve as a record of growth related to a student's mathematical thinking. It can serve as the centrepiece of a student-led parent–teacher conference.

Portfolio Product Rubric

Name: _____

Date: _____

- *Use this rubric to assess the contents of individual students' portfolios.*
- *Ideally, assess the portfolio with the student present.*
- *Do not attempt to assess everything in the portfolio. Remember, you are looking for evidence of the student's learning and growth.*
- *Each portfolio should be individualized by the student. Avoid looking for sameness or consistency.*

CATEGORIES/CRITERIA	LEVEL 1	LEVEL 2	LEVEL 3	LEVEL 4
Contents	• **few** required pieces are included	• **most** required pieces are included	• **all** required pieces are included	
	• **few** student-selected pieces are included	• **some** student-selected pieces are included	• **required number** of student-selected pieces are included	
Thinking/Reflecting	• reflection sheets are **incomplete** and/or attached to **few** selections	• reflection sheets are partially complete and/or attached to **some** selections	• reflection sheets are complete and attached to **all** selections	• reflection sheets are detailed and attached to **all** selections
	• reflection sheets show **limited** evidence of thoughtfulness or insight	• reflections sheets show **some** evidence of thoughtfulness and/or insight	• reflection sheets show **clear** evidence of thoughtfulness and insight	• reflection sheets show **rich** evidence of thoughtfulness and insight
	• selections reflect a **limited** understanding of the portfolio process (i.e., purposeful collecting, selecting, and reflecting on pieces to improve learning	• selections demonstrate **some** understanding of the portfolio process (i.e., purposeful collecting, selecting, and reflecting on pieces to improve learning	• selections demonstrate a **solid** understanding of the portfolio process (i.e., purposeful collecting, selecting, and reflecting on pieces to improve learning	• selections demonstrate a **thorough** understanding of the portfolio process (i.e., purposeful collecting, selecting, and reflecting on pieces to improve learning)
	• selections demonstrate **little** originality or creativity	• selections demonstrate **some** originality and/or creativity (e.g., a creative mind map)	• selections **demonstrate** originality and/or creativity (e.g., a creative mind map)	• selections demonstrate a **high degree** of originality and/or creativity (e.g., a creative mind map)
	• selections demonstrate **little** evidence of growth and learning over time (e.g., initial and revised responses to questions; first and revised written drafts)	• some selections demonstrate growth and learning over time (e.g., initial and revised responses to questions; first and revised written drafts)	• several selections demonstrate growth and learning over time (e.g., initial and revised responses to questions; first and revised written drafts)	• many selections clearly demonstrate growth and learning over time (e.g., initial and revised responses to questions; first and revised written drafts)
Organization	• portfolio contents lack organization into the required sections and sections are not labelled clearly (e.g., first drafts, personal reflections)	• portfolio contents are partially organized into the required sections and sections are labelled to some degree (e.g., first drafts, personal reflections)	• portfolio contents are appropriately organized into the required sections and sections are labelled appropriately (e.g., first drafts, personal reflections)	• portfolio contents are highly organized into the required sections and sections are clearly labelled for ease of use (e.g., first drafts, personal reflections)

Sample Portfolio Items

Suppose the topic is multiplication of whole numbers. Any of these items might be included in a portfolio:

- a video or photo showing a student modelling a computation with manipulatives, or of a skit that models a certain computation
- a set of word problems showing that students understand different meanings of multiplication
- a piece of writing in which students talk about how multiplication and addition are alike and how they are different
- a drawing that incorporates a number of different multiplications
- a solved problem involving multiplication, with the solution described
- a discussion of some mental math strategies involving multiplication

Evaluating Portfolios

The portfolio can be evaluated over time—each time with the teacher examining a small range of criteria. The teacher would likely use a rubric to guide this evaluation. The sample rubric from Cooper (2007), shown on page 604, could be used to evaluate a student-created portfolio.

In addition to this overall evaluation, the teacher should also provide feedback about both strengths and areas for growth. The categories used to describe the strengths and areas for growth will likely depend on jurisdictional focus. Individual items could be evaluated with other tools.

Performance Tasks

Performance tasks, as noted earlier, are rich tasks that allow students to show what they know about a topic. Ideally, a performance task elicits elements of the mathematical processes: problem solving, communication, representation, connections, and reasoning.

A performance task is designed so that process can be examined as well as product. It should be consistent with curricular goals, ideally representing the "big ideas" of the content being explored. It should be authentic, rich, and engaging, requiring active participation by students, and open ended enough to allow exceptional students to show how far they can go with it. It is, of course, also important that a performance task be achievable in a reasonable amount of time and that it be accessible to all students at some level.

Sample Performance Task

Notice that the task shown on page 607 (**Name Patterns**) has a student-friendly context and is open ended. It could be assigned after a Grade 4 or 5 unit on patterns. In this task, the student must

- solve a problem
- communicate
- apply a pattern rule
- relate patterns to number

Chapter 3 Task Rubric

CURRICULUM OUTCOME	EXCELLENT	PROFICIENT	ADEQUATE	LIMITED
N9. Demonstrate an understanding of addition of numbers with answers to 20 and their corresponding subtraction facts, concretely, pictorially, and symbolically, by	Easily distinguishes between an addition scenario and a subtraction scenario; recognizes that sometimes either operation is appropriate	Accurately distinguishes between an addition scenario and a subtraction scenario	Sometimes distinguishes between an addition scenario and a subtraction scenario	Cannot distinguish between an addition scenario and a subtraction scenario
• using familiar and mathematical language to describe additive and subtractive actions from their experience • creating and solving problems in context that involve addition and subtraction	Easily creates and solves simple but appropriate addition and subtraction number stories; sometimes proposes or solves two-step stories	Accurately creates and solves simple addition and subtraction number stories	Creates and solves simple addition and subtraction number stories, with some support	Inconsistently creates and solves simple addition and subtraction number stories, and usually requires support
• modeling addition and subtraction using a variety of concrete and visual representations, and	Effectively represents simple addition and subtraction number stories connecting appropriate models, pictures, and number sentences	Clearly represents simple addition and subtraction number stories, connecting appropriate models, pictures, and number sentences	Partially represents simple addition and subtraction number stories, connecting appropriate models, pictures, and/or number sentences	Represents simple addition and subtraction number stories, but only partially connects appropriate models, pictures, and/or number sentences
recording the process symbolically.	Clearly and accurately communicates number sentences that represent both number stories	Accurately communicates number sentences that represent both number stories	Partially communicates number sentences that represent both number stories	Partially communicates a number sentence that represents one number story

Name Patterns

Nisha uses different-sized square grids to write her name over and over. The grids have fewer than 50 squares.

a) What size grid can she use that will have full copies of her name? Explain your thinking.

b) Use names with different numbers of letters to fill a 6 by 6 grid with full copies of the names. What names did you use? Choose one. Explain why it works.

c) How do the numbers of letters in the name relate to the size of the grid?

Possible Solution

a) NISHA has 5 letters so the grid has to have a number of squares that can be divided by 5 with no remainder: 5, 10, 15, 20, 25, 30, 35, 40, 45
The grid also has to be a square so the grid must have 25 squares (5 by 5).

b) I used names with 2 letters, AL, 3 letters, IAN, and 4 letters, LISA. Here's what I did for LISA:

L	I	S	A	L	I
S	A	L	I	S	A
L	I	S	A	L	I
S	A	L	I	S	A
L	I	S	A	L	I
S	A	L	I	S	A

A 6 by 6 grid has 36 squares. LISA has 4 letters. 4 divides evenly into 36 so LISA can be written 9 times in the grid.

c) The number of squares in the grid can be divided by the number of letters with no remainder.

Evaluating Performance Tasks

A performance task would generally be assessed using a rubric. Sometimes, the rubric is a combination of various relevant generic process rubrics. Some teachers use a more general performance task rubric, while others create task-specific rubrics.

A specific rubric for a task requiring early Grade 1 students to write and illustrate an addition and subtraction story is shown on page 606.

Observation

Observational data is collected on an ongoing basis. This is not just a matter of getting a sense of a student's overall progress; it is a deliberate process to provide insight into a particular aspect of a student's performance.

Observing Mathematical Performance

For example, the teacher might be observing any of the following aspects of performance:

- regularity of use of mental math strategies and estimation
- regularity of computational or careless errors
- appropriate, or inappropriate, use of calculators
- a student's understanding of a particular concept
- clarity of a student's oral mathematical communication, and the use of correct math language and terminology
- a student's ability to use manipulative materials to model a concept
- insightfulness of a student's approach
- whether a student relates new ideas to previously learned concepts by making important connections
- originality of a student's response
- a student's comfort with predicting and the reasonableness of the student's predictions
- regularity with which a student considers the reasonableness of his or her responses
- how likely a student is to consider all possibilities

Teachers might create a chart with a short checklist listing some of the behaviours or performances they are looking for along the top of a sheet of paper, and the students' names along the left side. They could carry a clipboard and check off instances of observing the desired behaviours for various students. An example is shown below, followed by a set of probing questions that a teacher might use to elicit some of the behaviors to be observed.

Checklist

Student	Names 3-D Shapes	Describes Properties of 3-D Shapes	Sorts 3-D Shapes According to Geometric Attributes	Constructs Models and Skeletons of 3-D Shapes	Estimates, Measures, Records, Compares, and Orders Objects by Capacity	Estimates, Measures, Records, Compares, and Orders Objects by Mass

PROBING QUESTIONS

- How are these shapes alike? How are they different?
- What parts of a shape do we see with a skeleton? What parts do we not see?
- What has a greater capacity than a juice box?
- What has less mass than your backpack?
- How can you order these 3 things by mass?

Interviews

With younger students, interviews are essential for gathering reliable information. An interview differs from observation in that the starting question is more formally planned.

In an interview situation, the teacher can ensure that a student understands the question or task being posed, and can add scaffolding questions where appropriate. Teachers of older elementary students tend not to use interviews as often, but they remain an effective way to gather information as well.

To create an interview, a teacher would focus on the important curricular goals of a unit of work and develop a few critical questions around those goals. An example of a summary sheet to guide an interview with a young student during a measurement unit is shown below.

Sample Interview Summary Sheet

MATERIALS	WATCH AND LISTEN FOR CHECKLIST
Provide a metre stick, a 30-cm ruler, and some ribbons or strands of yarn in the following lengths and colours: red (10 cm)　　　　blue (25 cm) green (50 cm)　　　orange (1 m) brown (4 m)	❑ Uses measurement terms such as "longer" and "shorter" to describe relative lengths ❑ Orders items by length ❑ Chooses an appropriate measuring tool and unit, and justifies the choice ❑ Uses a measuring tool correctly to measure length ❑ Estimates lengths

QUESTIONS/PROMPTS

- Which ribbon is the shortest? the longest?
- How can you put the ribbons in order from shortest to longest?
- Which measuring tool, the ruler or the metre stick, would you use to measure the longest ribbon? Why?
- How long is the shortest ribbon?
- About how many times do you think the blue ribbon would fit along the length of the metre stick?

Managing Interviews

Below are some pointers about interviewing students:

- Use interviews when your intention is to be interactive, and use a student's responses to probe further.
- Forewarn students that when you ask why, it does not mean they are wrong, but that you want to understand their thinking.
- Take notes to be sure that what is said can be recalled. You might use a tape recorder or video as well, which can be reviewed later. Videos

are an excellent medium for showing parents some responses and how they can be interpreted to show understanding.

- Try not to be judgmental during the interview. Absence of criticism should encourage a student to respond comfortably.
- You can often interview two or three students at one time, but sometimes individual attention is needed to ensure independent thinking. It is critical to plan for what each student will be doing during the interviews. For example, one student might answer a question, and then you ask the other student if she or he agrees, and why.
- Pay attention to the kinds of questions a student asks of you during the interview. This can provide great insight into a student's level of understanding.
- Ask questions and assign tasks that involve performing or interacting. For example, if the topic were the measurement of mass for a young student, the following interview questions might be asked:

APPROPRIATE INTERVIEW QUESTIONS ABOUT MEASURING MASS

- Show me how you will use this pan balance and these masses to measure the mass of this apple.
- Pick the item that you estimate has a mass of about 50 g. Test your estimate.
- Find two potatoes that are about the same size. Check to see if you are correct. About how many potatoes this size would be in a 1-kg bag?
- Fill a backpack with items so that the mass of the items is between 2 kg and 3 kg.
- Select two items whose masses you think differ by about 500 g. Test your prediction.

Criteria for Evaluating Performance in an Interview

A teacher might want to use a standard form to record interview results, such as that shown on page 609 (Sample Interview Summary Sheet). Normally, the results of an interview would then be described as anecdotal comments. Alternatively, a teacher might be prepared to check off a performance level on a rubric describing a student's ability to communicate or a student's problem-solving ability.

Homework

Teachers can discover a great deal about a student's mathematical learning by examining a student's homework. It has potential value as assessment for learning. However, using homework as assessment of learning is problematic for two reasons. The first is that homework is meant to be a learning opportunity, so mistakes should not be penalized. The second is that a teacher cannot really know how much support a student received in completing the homework. Completion of homework can, of course, be measured, as it is part of assessing a student's disposition and learning skills, but making judgments about level of performance is more problematic.

Tests and Quizzes

Tests and quizzes are generally time-constrained situations where students' answers show their understanding and knowledge. Quizzes can often be completed fairly quickly. They are particularly useful for very straightforward skill assessment, and the assessment of some conceptual understanding and simple application of knowledge. They are also useful for providing immediate feedback.

Tests can also be used to test skills, application, and simple concepts, but because of their length, it is sometimes also possible to assess some process skills, whether problem solving, communication, reasoning, etc. In addition to this, tests act as preparation for large-scale assessments.

Sample Items for Tests and Quizzes

Suppose the topic is the representation of numbers up to 1000. Some sample items are shown below.

Sample Quiz Items for Representing Numbers to 1000

SKILLS	CONCEPTS	PROBLEM SOLVING

• Write each number:
  a) nine hundred eight
  b) 3 hundreds + 4 tens
  c) 200 + 40 + 3
• What number is 200 less than 436?
What number is 20 less?
What number is 2 less?
• Which is greater: 387 or 378?
	• What is the least number of base ten blocks you can use to represent 348? Explain how you know.
	• How could you use 33 base ten blocks to represent 348?
	• Find three ways to make this true and explain your thinking: ▪ 28 > 3 ▪ 4
		• How many 3-digit numbers can you create with the digits 2, 3, and 0? Which is greatest? How do you know?
		• There are three odd numbers with three digits each. The second is 244 greater than the first. The third is 202 greater than the second. The sum of the digits of the first number is 5. What could the three numbers be?

Creating Tests and Quizzes

Many teachers encourage students to contribute items for tests or quizzes. Once students have seen prototypes for the level and types of items that the teacher is seeking, they enjoy becoming question writers. They need to realize that not every question they write will be used, but including a student's question on a quiz is very affirming to that student.

It may be appropriate to allow for some choice when students write a test. For example, if there are several items that would allow a student to show understanding of the concept of prime numbers, it may be appropriate to allow a student to choose one of the two or three items.

Depending on a student's reading comprehension level, it may be necessary to revise test questions for some students by

- allowing students some choice in the way they represent their understanding
- simplifying language by using shorter sentences, defining words, and paraphrasing to exclude extraneous words
- including graphics (such as charts, graphs, pictures, and maps)

Whatever instruments are used to gather data—a test or quiz, an interview, observations, or a task of some sort—it is essential that a teacher attend to what aspects of the curriculum are important so that the instruments reflect this.

Keeping Track

With the large amount of data that teachers might collect, it is important that they develop tracking tools that are useful.

A summary sheet for a unit of work for each student might include references to the curricular goals being assessed, both content and process; a summary of anecdotal records from observations or homework; and a summary of interview, quiz, test, and task data.

Assessing Processes

Because of the attention to the mathematical processes, it is important that teachers become comfortable assessing them, particularly problem solving and communication.

Assessing Problem Solving

Performance on a rich problem can be evaluated using a rubric. Some teachers teach in jurisdictions where there are common generic rubrics. For example, in Ontario, there is a general problem-solving rubric that can be applied to any problem-solving task. Alberta teachers are supported by rubrics that are part of the Classroom Assessment Materials Project (CAMP) materials. Some rubrics are designed according to the stages of the problem-solving or inquiry process: Understand the Problem, Make a Plan, Carry Out the Plan and Look Back, and Communicate, whereas others are more holistic.

Sample Assessment Task: Problem Solving

PROBLEM

Every year the school fair has the same two problems. They run out of some balloon colours and have lots of other colours left over. Also, they run out of hot dogs, but have lots of popcorn left over.

Do a survey to help the school-fair planners solve these problems.

Present your results and recommendations.

SAMPLE SOLUTION

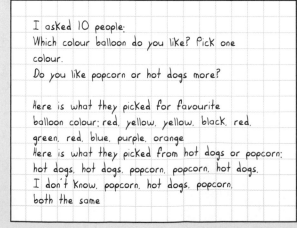

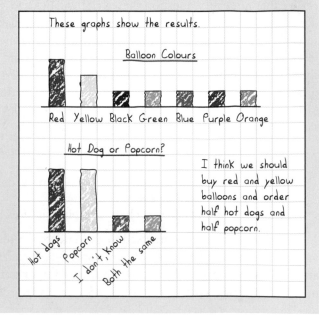

ASSESSMENT

This is Level 3 problem solving because the student

- only partially restated the problem by implying that he or she knew it had something to do with balloon colours and food
- modelled the problem correctly by realizing that he or she had to ask questions related to both balloon colours and food and present the results and recommendations
- solved the problem to a reasonable extent by creating somewhat appropriate questions, but the solution has some minor flaws because the first question did not sufficiently limit responses, and neither question included any reference to the school-fair context
- communicated his or her results by creating appropriate and correct graphs to present the data, and making recommendations that reflected the results

Sample Problem-Solving Rubric

CRITERIA	LEVEL 1	LEVEL 2	LEVEL 3	LEVEL 4
Understand the Problem	Is unable to restate the problem	Has difficulty restating the problem	Restates the problem	Rephrases the problem in own words
Make a Plan	Struggles to model the problem	Models part of the problem	Models the problem correctly	Models the problem in an efficient or creative way
Carry Out the Plan/Look Back	Solution is seriously flawed due to major errors in procedures; student gives up if plan does not work	Solution is faulty due to several errors in procedures; student is hesitant to change plan	Solution is correct, though there may be minor procedural errors; student revises the plan as necessary	Solution is correct and there are few, if any, errors in procedures; student is flexible about the plan and revises it as necessary
Communicate	Provides an incomplete explanation of the results that is unclear and/or imprecise	Provides a partial explanation of the results that is somewhat clear and precise	Provides a complete, clear, and precise explanation of the results	Provides a thorough, clear, and insightful explanation of the results

Another source for problem-solving rubrics is Cooper (2007), and many others are available on the Internet. You will find that some rubrics go from 1 to 4, with 1 being poorer performance; others go from 4 to 1, starting with exemplary performance on the left; and still others use descriptors like "Excellent, Proficient, Adequate, and Limited."

Assessing Communication

Student communication is an important component of mathematics performance. Teachers may set a task that includes a communication component or a task focused primarily on communication. Teachers may evaluate a piece of writing using a generic communication rubric or create a task-specific rubric. As with problem solving, some jurisdictions provide generic communication rubrics that could be applied to any communication task.

It is important to note that an accurate assessment of communication requires that a student be willing to share his or her knowledge and understanding. This can only happen in a climate where risk taking is encouraged and supported.

A good piece of writing should be mathematically correct and can be assessed with respect to any of the following criteria:

- explanation and justification of mathematical concepts, procedures, and problem solving
- organization of material (written, spoken, or drawn)
- use of mathematical vocabulary
- use of mathematical representations (graphs, charts, and diagrams)
- use of mathematical conventions (units, symbols, and labels)

Student Response

This student's communication is clear, organized, precise, and concise.

Can you estimate to decide which grade has more students or do you need to find an exact total? Explain.

	Number of students in each class			
Grade 3	27	32	31	28
Grade 4	30	22	25	26

you don't need anax d number because grade 3 had a higher number except for one e and that was only by 3.

Sample Assessment Task

The following task was used to assess communication with respect to understanding of fractions concepts for a student in the middle elementary grades.

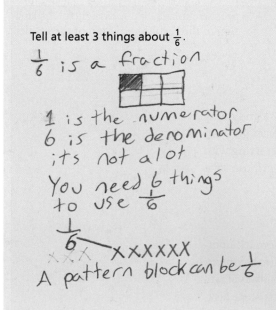

Tell at least 3 things about $\frac{1}{6}$.

$\frac{1}{6}$ is a fraction

1 is the numerator
6 is the denominator
its not a lot
You need 6 things
to use $\frac{1}{6}$

$\frac{1}{6}$
XXX XXXXXX
A pattern block can be $\frac{1}{6}$

This is Level 3 communication because

- some explanations are partial but with some clarity and logic
- organization is sufficient but not effective
- there is clear and precise use of some (but not a broad range of) mathematics vocabulary
- there are representations of two meanings of a fraction. There is a vague reference to another meaning (pattern block), but it is not followed through.
- the diagrams are labelled; the convention for showing a fraction is used correctly

Sample Communication Rubric

CRITERIA	LEVEL 1	LEVEL 2	LEVEL 3	LEVEL 4
Explanation and Justification of Mathematical Concepts, Procedures, and Problem Solving	Provides incomplete or inaccurate explanations/justifications that lack clarity or logical thought, using minimal words, pictures, symbols, and/or numbers	Provides partial explanations/justifications that exhibit some clarity and logical thought, using simple words, pictures, symbols, and/or numbers	Provides complete, clear, and logical explanations/justifications, using appropriate words, pictures, symbols, and/or numbers	Provides thorough, clear, and insightful explanations/justifications, using a range of words, pictures, symbols, and/or numbers
Organization of Material (written, spoken, or drawn)	Organization is minimal and seriously impedes communication	Organization is limited but does not seriously impede communication	Organization is sufficient to support communication	Organization is effective and aids communication
Use of Mathematical Vocabulary	Uses very little mathematical vocabulary, and vocabulary used lacks clarity and precision	Uses a limited range of mathematical vocabulary with some degree of clarity and precision	Uses mathematical vocabulary with sufficient clarity and precision to communicate ideas	Uses a broad range of mathematical vocabulary to communicate clearly and precisely
Use of Mathematical Representations (graphs, charts, or diagrams)	Uses representations that exhibit minimal clarity and accuracy, and are ineffective in communicating	Uses representations that lack clarity and accuracy, though not sufficient to impede communication	Uses representations that are sufficiently clear and accurate to communicate	Uses representations that are clear, precise, and effective in communicating
Use of Mathematical Conventions (units, symbols, or labels)	Few conventions are used correctly	Some conventions are used correctly	Most conventions are used correctly	Almost all conventions are used correctly

Another source for communication rubrics is Cooper (2007), and others are available on the Internet.

Self-Assessment

Many teachers recognize the value of having students assess their own work; it is with self-assessment that students become independent learners. Many of the rubrics described previously for communication and problem solving can be used by students to self-evaluate. Another option is to use a guide like the one on page 616 for self-assessment after a unit on graphing. It is important to cultivate students' objectivity in looking at their own work. Some students find it either too easy or too difficult to criticize themselves. Students need to be helped to attend to details.

Sample Self-Assessment Guide

I CAN ...	HOW OFTEN?		
Draw a bar graph where each square is worth 1.	Not often	Sometimes	Usually
Draw a bar graph with a simple scale where each square is worth 2 or 5.	Not often	Sometimes	Usually
Read a pictograph with a scale.	Not often	Sometimes	Usually
Decide which symbol to use for a pictograph with a scale.	Not often	Sometimes	Usually
Solve simple problems that use information from graphs.	Not often	Sometimes	Usually
Read a circle graph.	Not often	Sometimes	Usually

Some self-assessment may be more "affective." A list of unfinished statements to which students might respond and which would provide valuable information for the teacher could include the following:

- When I got stuck, I ...
- I explained my work best when I ...
- I checked to see if I was right when I ...
- I explained my work in a mathematical way when I ...
- What I understood best was ...
- I need to find out more about ...

Group Assessment

One of the difficulties a teacher in today's classroom faces is dealing with individual evaluations when many activities are performed in a group setting. Many educators believe that group work is critical, not only because it mirrors real-life situations where adults work on teams to accomplish projects, but also because of the belief that the interaction within a group facilitates learning. The issues are varied. One concern is how to or whether to assign individual scores to different members of the group. Another is how to or whether to evaluate performance as a group member. The issue is, of course, ensuring that any evaluation is perceived as—and actually is—fair and equitable.

Sometimes it is perfectly reasonable to treat the group as a whole and use any of the rubrics or schemes previously discussed to describe the group's performance. The difficulty some teachers have is deciding whether to use that same evaluation to describe the work of each group member. (See *Including Group Evaluations* on page 618.)

Grading and Reporting

One of a teacher's important tasks is communicating assessment information to students and their parents. There are many opportunities to communicate about particular items of work, and these have been discussed earlier. At some point, though, these assessments must be integrated into an overall grade or mark. The following discussion details some of the issues surrounding this aspect of a teacher's work.

Anecdotal versus Letter Grades or Percents

Some teachers are not required to report a single or small set of measures about a student, but can describe student work in anecdotal ways. These teachers may use a student's portfolio as the centrepiece of a student-led conference with parents. A student is an active participant in talking to his or her parents about his or her mathematical knowledge. Sample items from the portfolio will clarify the comments the parents may have received from the teacher.

Other teachers are expected to find a way to summarize anecdotal data, rubric measures, and numerical scores into a single set of measures to describe student achievement. Circumstances will vary, so how this summary can be accomplished is affected by local practice, but some principles are fairly universal. These teachers must make some decision about weighting the various pieces of data collected.

The percentages in each case should depend on the amount of data from each source and the reliability of the data from that source. If, for example, in an upper grade class, there had been only one test on a topic, but many pieces of work were submitted for a portfolio and a number of interviews were held, it might make more sense to weight tests and quizzes less.

Other times, a teacher sorts the assessment information in other ways. A teacher may determine an overall performance level for each of the achievement categories, for example, understanding concepts, applying procedures, communication, and problem solving. Then the performance in the categories is weighted according to one of jurisdiction-based, school-based, or personal weightings.

Using Discretion

Even once the percentages or weightings are decided, teachers should feel free to take some latitude. Suppose a teacher administers a test and a student's performance is significantly lower than all of the other evidence that the teacher has collected for performance on that topic. A teacher should feel free to take this information under advisement, rather than simply feel obligated to factor it in as planned. Alternatively, some teachers reasonably choose to give a lower weight to scores on work collected early in a reporting period since the work at the end of that period is more likely to be a more accurate demonstration of students' understanding of the relevant material.

Pitfalls of Percent Grades

It should be noted that using letter grades or rubric descriptors is generally preferable, where the choice exists, to using percent grades. There are several reasons for this.

Categorical data is more reliable. A student who earns a B or a score of excellent is likely to earn the same score even if the teacher were to select slightly different tasks to assess this student. It is much less certain that a score of 92% would remain that exact score with slightly different questions. Thus, the categorical score is more reliable.

The use of percent scores seems to focus students on what they get wrong instead of what they get right. This is not as affirming to students as it should be.

The use of percent scores seems to set up some unhealthy competitions. For example, a student who scores 92% cannot realistically be seen as one who knows more than a student who scores 91% on a particular test or quiz.

Including Group Evaluations

Two reasonable positions can be taken on this matter. One is that the purpose of the group work is to learn, but the ultimate goal is individual accountability; for this reason, only scores on individual assessments are used in computing a mark. The other position is that performance within the group should be evaluated. Some teachers assign all members of the group the same mark, with the understanding that it is the group's responsibility to ensure that all participants have earned that evaluation. Many teachers provide the opportunity for students in the group to report on how the work was shared and to compare, usually in advance of the teacher's evaluation, the relative performance of group members.

Weighting Schemes

Teachers of Grades 4 to 8 might use this weighting scheme:

> Observations 30%
> Portfolio 30%
> Interviews and journal 10%
> Tests and quizzes 30%

A primary teacher might use a scheme like this:

> Observations 45%
> Portfolio 40%
> Interviews and journal 10%
> Tests and quizzes 5%

Evaluations Based on Observation Assessment Data

Some teachers are still reluctant to use observation data in a formal way when weighting performance measures. They worry that this information is too subjective, but this concern is probably unwarranted. Assuming that the information was collected systematically and that it focused on academic performance and not on other aspects of student behaviour, it is as meaningful as written work.

Ultimately, a teacher's role is to use the information collected in the most meaningful way to communicate to students and their parents what they need to know to maximize a student's mathematical potential.

Large-Scale Assessment

Canada, along with most other developed countries, has embraced a significant amount of testing in mathematics. Some districts, boards, or provinces test in every grade, and others test in selected grades. Some tests are administered to every student, whereas others are administered only to a sampling of students. There are also pan-Canadian and international tests in which many Canadian students participate, including the Pan-Canadian Assessment Program (PCAP, formerly SAIP), sponsored by the Council of Ministers of Education across the country, and international tests like Third International Math and Science Study (TIMSS).

Most provincial and local tests are built around curriculum expectations/outcomes for the jurisdiction, whereas national and international tests, by their very nature, cannot be as specific.

The form of these assessments varies a great deal. Below are samples of the types of items that appear on some Canadian provincial tests. Some items are multiple choice, some require explanations, and some require work to be shown, but not explanations.

Grade 3 Ontario

1. Which of the following is another way to show 4×6?
   - ❏ $4 + 4 + 4 + 4$
   - ❏ $6 + 6 + 6 + 6$
   - ❏ $4 \times 4 \times 4 \times 4$
   - ❏ $6 \times 6 \times 6 \times 6$

2. The picture shows Tarah next to her front door.

Tarah's older brother, Rhaj, is 50 cm taller than Tarah.

How tall is Rhaj?

Explain your thinking.

Rhaj is about _____ tall.

Grade 6 Ontario

1. Examine the input-output shown below.

Input	Output
2	5
3	8
4	11
6	17

Which of these rules describes the data?
a. Multiply by 2 and add 1.
b. Multiply by 4 and subtract 3.
c. Multiply by 2 and add 5.
d. Multiply by 3 and subtract 1.

2. Draw the three-dimensional figure that will be created when the following net is folded. Show all vertices and edges.

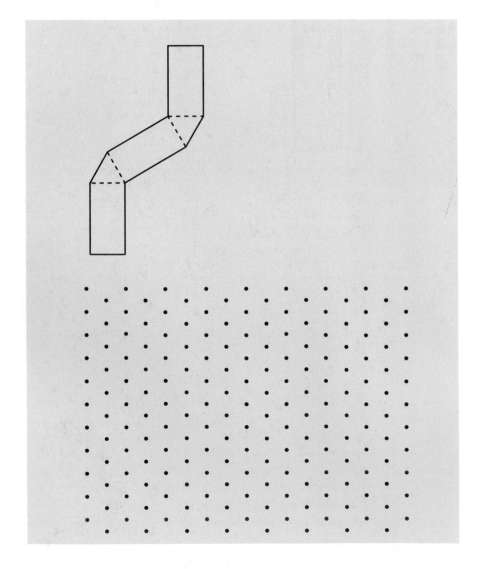

Grade 4 BC

1. A store at the Nature Park sold the following items:

Milk	$1.25	Whistle	$0.85
Granola Bar	$0.90	Postcard	$0.70
Candy	$0.55	Pencil	$0.65

Jenna bought a granola bar and a postcard with a two-dollar coin. Show **ALL** the ways she could get her change if she received no pennies.

2. The class wants to feed birds and squirrels.

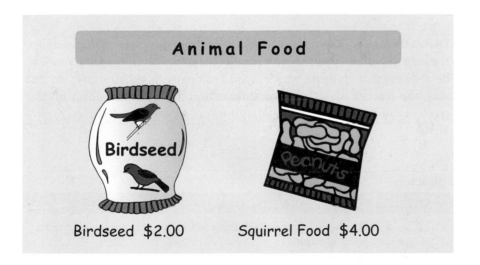

Show **ALL** the ways students can spend **exactly $24.00** on animal food if they buy at least 1 bag of each type.
Show **ALL** your work.

Preparing Students for Large-Scale Assessment

Since these large-scale assessments have likely become permanent, it is important to do your best to ensure both that the data collected is reliable and that students are as comfortable as possible when taking these tests.

Most importantly, teachers must encourage students to do their best, but not to be overly concerned if there are unfamiliar questions or material on the tests. Students should be made aware that many students take the test, so the items reflect many possible topics, not all of which may be familiar to each and every student. In some jurisdictions, teachers include the score on these tests as a small factor in their evaluation of student progress. This ensures that students take the assessment seriously, but reflects the fact that the situation may not be a completely fair assessment of what a particular student has had the opportunity to learn.

It is important that students are familiar with the formats of the types of questions they might meet on these large-scale assessments, whether it is a question that requires them to explain their thinking or a multiple-choice question. Many of the earlier parts of this chapter have addressed more open-ended questions, but below you will find some material to consider about acquainting students with the multiple-choice format.

Multiple-Choice Question Formats

Multiple-choice questions are one of the formats used frequently on large-scale assessments. However, many young students are unfamiliar with them. First of all, students may need practice in using "bubble" or optical scanning papers. They may also need some suggestions for pacing themselves, for example, going through and responding to the questions they are sure of first, and then returning to other items. Students also need practical suggestions for ways to respond to these types of questions, as well as some experience with them. The teacher might create some practice multiple-choice questions or use released samples from various ministries of education or testing agencies.

Distracters Good distracters (the wrong answers on a multiple-choice test) are important. They are not meant to trick students; they are meant to be answers that students with misconceptions will find attractive. In this way, the teacher is able to revise instruction appropriately. Ideas for distracters can be gathered by looking through student work to find typical errors.

Understanding Multiple Choice Distracters

EXAMPLE	DISCUSSION
Which shape is a triangle-based pyramid? 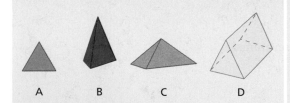 A B C D	**A.** might "distract" students who are only comfortable with 2-D names **B.** is the correct response **C.** might "distract" students whose interpretation of pyramid is only the traditional square pyramid **D.** might "distract" students who do not distinguish between prisms and pyramids
Sam described how you can cut a parallelogram into other shapes. Which description is not true? a) You can make two congruent triangles. b) You can make two congruent parallelograms. c) You can make two non-congruent parallelograms. d) You can make two non-congruent triangles. 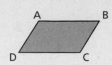	a) might "distract" students who believe that, when you cut a shape, you have to end up with the same shape that you started with b) might "distract" students who think only about vertical cuts c) might "distract" students who think only in terms of cutting into halves d) is the correct response

Using Logical Reasoning to Eliminate Answers Students should be encouraged to use logical reasoning to eliminate unreasonable answers. For example, consider the question below:

What number below is the 45th term in the pattern 4, 10, 16, 22, ...?

a) 55   b) 268   c) 49   d) 190

Speech bubble: All the numbers in the pattern so far are even, and they have to stay even because you're adding an even number. So it can't be a) 55 or c) 49.

Students can use logical reasoning to eliminate possibilities.

By recognizing that all the numbers in the pattern have to be even (because evens are added to evens), students can immediately eliminate a) and c). As well as realizing that the answer must be even, they also may realize that if you add 6 more than 40 times, the result must be in the 200s, so d) can also be eliminated.

Applying What You've Learned

1. How did you solve the chapter problem? Why might it be a suitable performance task for Grade 3 students?

2. Some teachers count homework and/or participation toward a student's math mark. Why might this be problematic?

3. Sometimes a student who is doing fairly well in math in school performs relatively poorly on a provincial examination.

   a) Why might this happen?

   b) How would you determine which mark best reflects the student's level of performance relative to the provincial expectations/outcomes?

4. Create a rubric that could be used to evaluate students' performance in solving this problem:

   > You are buying 100 animals for $100; a horse costs $10, a cow costs $1, and a sheep costs 50¢. How many of each can you buy?

   Keep in mind the curricular expectations/outcomes for your region when creating your rubric.

WebConnect

www.makingmathmeaningful.nelson.com

Visit the Making Math Meaningful website for links to a variety of assessment tools.

5. Imagine planning a multiple choice quiz on the topic of multiplication of 2-digit numbers by 1-digit numbers. Create three items that you think are suitable. For each item, explain how you chose the distracters that you chose.

6. Find an article in a mathematics education journal that focuses on assessment.

    a) What is the important message?

    b) How well was the case made for the message? Explain.

7. Choose a mathematical topic and grade level of interest. Prepare a potential assessment plan that you could use for that topic and level.

Interact with a K–8 Student:

8. Talk to a student about how his or her teacher finds out what he or she knows. Ask the student to elaborate on which form of teacher assessment he or she is most comfortable with, and why.

Interact with a K–8 Teacher:

9. Ask the teacher what large-scale assessment his or her students have taken. Ask the teacher how he or she has prepared students for that assessment, or if not, why not.

Selected References

Bamburg, J. (**1994**). *Raising expectations to improve student learning.* Oak Brook, IL: North Central Regional Educational Laboratory.

Bright, G.W., and Joyner, J.M. (**1998**). *Classroom assessment in mathematics.* Blue Ridge Summit, PA: University Press of America, Inc.

Britton, K.L., and Johannes, J.I. (**2003**). Portfolios and a backward approach to assessment. *Mathematics Teaching in the Middle School, 9,* 70–76.

Burrill, J. (**Ed.**). (**2005**). *Grades 6–8 mathematics assessment sampler.* Reston, VA: National Council of Teachers of Mathematics.

Bush, W.S. (**Ed.**). (**2001**). *Mathematics assessment: Cases and discussion questions for grades K–5.* Reston, VA: National Council of Teachers of Mathematics.

Bush, W.S., and Leinwand, S. (**Eds.**). (**2000**). *Mathematics assessment: A practical handbook for grades 6 to 8.* Reston, VA: National Council of Teachers of Mathematics.

Cooper, D. (**2007**). *Talk about assessment.* Toronto: Thomson Nelson.

Gawronski, J.D. (**2005**). *Grades 3–5 mathematics assessment sampler.* Reston, VA: National Council of Teachers of Mathematics.

Ginsburg, H.P., Jacobs, S.F., and Lopez, L.S. (**1998**). *The teacher's guide to flexible interviewing in the classroom: Learning what children know about math.* Boston: Allyn and Bacon.

Glanfield, F., Bush, W.S., and Stenmark, J.K. (**Eds.**). (**2003**). *Mathematics assessment: A practical handbook for grades K to 2.* Reston, VA: National Council of Teachers of Mathematics.

Kulm, G. (**Ed.**). (**1990**). *Assessing higher order thinking in mathematics.* Washington, DC: American Association for the Advancement of Science.

Liedtke, W. (**1988**). Diagnosis in mathematics: The advantages of an interview. *The Arithmetic Teacher, 36,* 26–29.

Marzano, R.J., Pickering, D., and McTighe, J. (**1993**). *Assessing student outcomes: Performance assessment using the dimensions of learning model.* Alexandria, VA: Association for Supervision and Curriculum Development.

National Academy of Sciences. (**1993**). *Measuring up: Prototypes for mathematics assessment.* Washington, DC: National Academy Press.

Small, M. (**2005a**). *PRIME: Number and operations: Background and strategies.* Toronto: Thomson Nelson.

Small, M. (**2005b**). *PRIME: Patterns and algebra: Background and strategies.* Toronto: Thomson Nelson.

Small, M. (**2006**). *PRIME: Data management and probability: Background and strategies.* Toronto: Thomson Nelson.

Stenmark, J.K. (**Ed.**). (**1991**). *Mathematics assessment: Myths, models, good questions, and practical suggestions.* Reston, VA: National Council of Teachers of Mathematics.

Stenmark, J.K., and Bush, W.S. (Eds.). (2001). *Mathematics assessment: A practical handbook for grades 3 to 5.* Reston, VA: National Council of Teachers of Mathematics.

University of Alberta. (1993). *Principles for fair student assessment practices for education in Canada.* Edmonton: University of Alberta.

Westley, J. (1994). *Puddle questions: Assessing mathematical thinking, grade 3.* Mountain View, CA: Creative Publications.

Yeatts, K.L., Battista, M.T., Mayberry, S., Thompson, D.R., and Zawojewski, J.S. (2004). *Navigating through problem solving and reasoning in grade 3.* Reston, VA: National Council of Teachers of Mathematics.

Chapter 22

Planning Instruction

IN A NUTSHELL

The main ideas in this chapter are listed below:

1. Planning is key to effective instruction in mathematics. Planning means taking the time to get to know and understand the content to be taught and how it can most effectively be communicated, and also thinking about how to tailor instructional goals to the children who are being taught.

2. Planning should be done at both the micro and macro levels.

3. Many resources, including texts, can be useful to the teacher in her or his planning.

4. Strategies for teaching mathematics may need to be massaged if students have too high a level of math anxiety; usually, anxiety can be dissipated with effective instruction and teaching strategies that are open and inclusive.

CHAPTER PROBLEM

Each letter of the alphabet is assigned a value based on its position. For example, A = 1, B = 2, C = 3, ... , Z = 26. Create three different words that are each worth 43.

Special Challenges in Teaching Mathematics

The teaching of mathematics presents some unique challenges for teachers. One of the issues is, of course, its abstractness. Mathematics is the study of concepts like number and shape, which are abstractions of objects that you see in the world. Yet that, in itself, is not the problem. Many of the concepts studied in science, social studies, health, etc., are also abstractions.

One of the main challenges in teaching math is the level of anxiety it seems to have historically evoked in many adults and, consequently, in some teachers and some children. Children hear adults saying from early on that math is hard or that they did not like math; this is a big obstacle for some children to overcome.

Causes of Math Anxiety

People who feel math anxious are unable to prevent their stress and worry about doing math from interfering with their ability to perform. Their worry about math so occupies their thoughts, it is hard for them to actually think about the math. What contributes to the creation of math anxiety? and why is it more prevalent in math than in other subject areas?

The emphasis on "black and white" or "right and wrong" answers—no middle ground—is something that has contributed to math anxiety. A teacher asks a student, "What is $23 + 38$?" There is no evading; the student either knows or does not know that the answer is 61. If the student does not know the correct answer, he or she is embarrassed and nervous. Contrast this with a question that might be asked in language arts, for example, a child is asked to retell a story in his or her own words. There are many possible directions in which to go; the chance of success is much greater, and the opinion of the child is relevant.

The emphasis on speed, and the fact that the speed has to be demonstrated in a very public way, has also contributed to math anxiety. Students used to, and sometimes are still asked to, compete against one another, with the winner being the one who could recall most quickly. Those who knew the math but perhaps needed a little thinking time became more anxious.

Another contributing factor is a view of math as a set of rules. Many students lack confidence that they can figure out a math problem without recalling the relevant memorized rule. When confronted with a real problem, where a rule is not immediately obvious, they do not know how to begin and become even more anxious.

Even in computational situations, math is different from other subjects in that, despite the fact that a rule may have been learned, it must be applied to a new situation each time. For example, you might, for a social studies class, memorize the capitals of the provinces, and all you need to do is repeat them. However, even if you have learned the rules for adding, you must always adapt what you learn to a new set of numbers. This adds to the stress.

There is a belief among many that you are either born being able to do math or not. Students experiencing difficulty could easily attribute their lack of success to their lack of innate ability. Then, rather than working on improving their performance, they simply assume that they cannot do math —it is not their fault. This perceived inability simply adds to the anxiety.

Diminishing Anxiety

The new approaches to math discussed in previous chapters should decrease the level of mathematics anxiety in our schools.

- We now focus on math as making sense, not as an arbitrary set of rules that have to be memorized.
- The use of manipulatives helps ensure that the math makes sense and also provides a starting point for students who may not be sure how to begin. Students who may be less certain of themselves with written work or even oral work feel more comfortable if they can explain themselves using concrete materials.
- We now ask many more questions that have alternative responses. Students have many more opportunities to be right.

Diminishing Teacher Anxiety

There are many ways that teachers can diminish their own anxiety and, indirectly, help students do the same:

- Teachers must give themselves the same "breaks" that they give students. They, too, should feel comfortable taking their time to find an answer, not being sure right away, or asking another teacher a question.
- Using manipulatives can often help a teacher who is math anxious.
- For many teachers, the active classroom, where they are not at centre stage but just another important player, can diminish anxiety. Working with a small group is often less intimidating than standing up front with 30 pairs of eyes intently watching.
- Preparation is an effective way to diminish anxiety in any situation. If teachers are uncomfortable with a new topic they are teaching, seeking teaching support in a variety of professional resources can make a significant difference in both the teacher's confidence and the effectiveness of the lesson.

Unit Planning and Lesson Planning

Year Planning

It is critical that teachers plan for both the long term and the short term. To ensure that the curriculum is appropriately covered, most teachers develop a long-range plan that maps out the year—what strands, or what topics, will be covered when. Some teachers like to cover all of a strand together, although most teachers like to revisit a strand several times over the course of a year. In some districts or boards, teachers have collaborated to offer a suggested, although rarely required, sequence that teachers might follow.

Unit Planning

It is equally important that each unit of instruction within that year have some coherence. Thus, most teachers create what they call unit plans. They think about their teaching goals for the unit, they consider what aspects of the curriculum might need to be adapted or modified for a particular group of students, and they organize the materials that they will need to support instruction during that unit.

Like any good story, a unit of instruction needs a beginning, a middle, and an end. The beginning is normally some sort of activity to set the stage for the unit and to provide teachers with important diagnostic information about their students. For example, if teachers are teaching a unit on multiplication, they might want to find out what students already know about the subject, what kinds of problems they can solve, what manipulatives they are comfortable with, any missing prerequisites, etc. Teachers also might want to think about integrating other strands into the delivery of the unit.

There are many ways to introduce a unit. Many teachers use mind maps, concept webs, or organizers like the Frayer model, shown below, that let students show what they know about a topic—in this case, ratio.

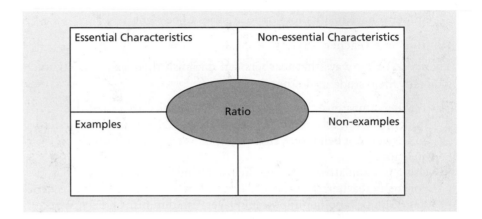

Some teachers use an anticipation guide—an activity where students are asked to agree or disagree with statements the teacher proposes about the content that will be addressed. Later, at the end of the unit, these ideas are readdressed and students have an opportunity to reflect on their learning. An anticipation guide about measurement might include a statement such as: *The best way to measure length is to use metres.* Students get to agree (or strongly agree) or disagree (or strongly disagree). They discuss with others why they made that choice. Then, after a unit of instruction on, in this case, length measurement, they revisit their belief.

The middle of the story is the instruction and formative assessment that are an essential part of good instruction. Teachers base their instruction on the curriculum outcomes/expectations for their jurisdiction, but instruction also needs to be tailored to the particular groups of students they are teaching. This is further discussed in the section on differentiated instruction (see page 639). One valuable strategy that some teachers use to plan their instruction is to consider the assessment tasks they would want students to be successful with at the end of the unit, and then work backwards, thinking carefully about what students would need to experience in the unit to be able to be successful.

The end of the unit needs to include opportunities for students to consolidate their understanding and connect the new ideas they have learned to mathematical knowledge that they already had. It will often include assessment of learning activities as well.

There are many unit plan templates that teachers can use. One is provided in the Appendix.

Lesson Planning

Each individual lesson also needs a plan. By planning, teachers can ensure that they have the appropriate materials ready. More importantly, however, planning makes it more likely that teachers will make good choices about how students spend their instructional time. Classrooms are complex environments. If the teacher has not streamlined the teaching to make sure that the most important ideas are front and centre, it is easy to lose valuable instructional time and make it more difficult for students to attend to the more important ideas.

A lesson would normally have three parts. In Ontario, materials for teachers at Grades 7 and 8, called Targeted Implementation and Planning Supports (TIPS), identify the three parts as

Minds On …

Action!

Consolidate/Debrief

Whether these or other names are used, the lesson still needs these parts. The intent of the first part of the lesson is to allow students to connect with the topic. It may involve a warm-up activity, a provocative question for students to consider, or some other device to get students "hooked."

A significant portion of the lesson should involve the solving of a problem that helps students make sense of the new ideas being learned. This portion of the lesson should normally conclude with some sort of reflection on what has been learned to make sure that students are ready for more independent work.

The last part of the lesson involves consolidation, where students apply what has been learned, and have an opportunity to reflect back, once again, on their learning. By closing the lesson with an explicit reflection on the ideas presented in the lesson, whether through oral or written activities, it is much more likely that the lesson goals will be achieved; the communication about the mathematics allows students to "hear" what needs to stay in their heads.

It is helpful to have notes to teach from. A good lesson plan template reminds teachers of

- what materials they will be using
- what groupings they will use and when
- the amount of time to spend on each activity
- some short notes about each component of the lesson
- what important questions they want to make sure they ask students in the various parts of the lesson

Just as important as planning what to do is planning what to say. (See *Suggested Template* in the Appendix.)

The power of planning with others cannot be overstated. One of the most rewarding forms of professional development is the opportunity for teachers to work with other teachers to discuss their plans for lesson delivery. A professional development approach called Lesson Study, borrowed from the Japanese, is specifically built around teachers jointly planning a lesson, watching its delivery, debriefing, and re-planning.

Planning Support

When planning a unit of instruction, teachers use a variety of resources. Some of these sources have been discussed in earlier chapters and others are discussed in Chapter 23. Here, the focus will be on the support offered by texts since many teachers still use textbooks all or some of the time. The advantage of a textbook is that it has been through a rigorous review and editing process that helps to ensure the mathematics is correct. In addition, the authors, usually experts in the field, have very likely used an appropriate pedagogical sequencing, appropriate contexts for instruction, and appropriate assessment strategies. Most often, these textbooks have been designed around provincial/territorial curricula and include material to help teachers and students prepare for large-scale tests. This leaves teachers free to concentrate on adapting developed lessons to meet the needs of their own students.

Current textbooks are more likely to ask for explanations, expect reasoning, emphasize problem solving and communication, and provide rich contexts in which to learn math. Although there continue to be skill exercises to consolidate learning, they rarely dominate textbooks anymore.

Examples of the types of things you might see in today's textbooks are shown on pages 633–635.

How to Use a Textbook

Textbooks can be used for introducing topics, extending them, or practising them. Although some teachers use their own teaching/learning activities and only use the textbook for additional practice, the textbook also can provide the rich introductions that teachers can follow up in their own way.

Teachers should use the teacher's resource that comes with a textbook. Many of the problems that teachers will face have been considered and planned for. The teacher resource often provides

- sample responses for the open-ended questions in the textbook
- additional questions to pose that are not found in the textbook
- insight into how students might handle some of the questions posed in the textbook
- information about situations to avoid
- assessment strategies
- organizational tips
- suggestions for helping struggling students
- suggestions for enriching the instruction for more advanced students

Following the Order of the Textbook

Because authors of textbooks often spend considerable time thinking through an appropriate sequence, it is recommended that the chapters of a textbook be followed in the order they appear. However, it is often possible to follow an alternative order as long as the teacher is prepared for the odd question in the text that has been designed with the original chapter sequence in mind.

Act It Out

To Solve the Problem

Here is Ben's pattern.

Make Ben's pattern.

Keep Ben's pattern going.
Use more beads.

Can you make a different pattern?
Try it!

NEL

This Grade 1 student spread focuses the student on problem-solving strategies.

Reading a Textbook

In an attempt to base teaching on real-world situations, and to explain ideas rather than simply demonstrate them, more and more of the presentation of mathematics in texts involves words rather than just symbols. Part of instructional planning should include acquainting students with how to read a math text since the required skills are somewhat unique. Examples of peculiarities of math textbooks include the following:

- rhetorical questions (such as those used as introductions to stimulate discussion)
- some pictures that contain critical information, yet others that are contextual or decorative

Creating Multiplication Problems

Chapter 9
Lesson 10

You will need
• pencil crayons

GOAL

Create and solve multiplication problems.

Alec loved the book *Amanda Bean's Amazing Dream* by Cindy Neuschwander. In that book, Amanda used multiplication to count large numbers of things, from sheep on bicycles to balls of yarn.

Alec wrote his own book.
Each page had a multiplication question on it.
The words on the page went with the multiplication question and included the product.
All together, the pages told a story.
He read the book to his classmates and explained how he calculated.

7 x 45
Kelly practised piano 45 minutes
a day every day of the week.
That makes 315 minutes.

? **How can you create a story about multiplication?**

341

This Grade 4 student page presents a very open-ended problem linked to children's literature.

• worked examples, which are to be read and then referred to and not acted on
• question stems that apply to multiple parts, for example:

Question Stems

USING QUESTION PARTS	CONTINUING THE QUESTION
How many cartons will Peter need for **a)** 50 eggs? **b)** 100 eggs?	How are addition and multiplication the same? different?

6.5 Subtracting Integers Using Counters

YOU WILL NEED
- red and blue counters

GOAL

Develop a counter model for subtracting integers.

LEARN ABOUT the Math

Ashley, Nick, and Gail have electronic gift cards to buy items online. They can add money to their cards when the balance is low or negative. Money is subtracted from their cards when they buy an item.

? **How can you subtract integers using counters?**

Example 1	Subtracting a positive integer

Ashley's card had a balance of −$10. Then she spent $5. What is the balance now?

Ashley's Solution

−10
○○○○○○○○○○

I had to calculate $(-10) - (+5)$.
I used blue counters to represent −10.

−10　　　　　−5　　+5
○○○○○○○○○○　○○○○○ ●●●●●
−10　　　+　　　　0　　= −10

I know that −10 + 0 is still −10.
I wanted to subtract +5, so I needed five red counters. I used the zero principle to get more blue and red counters.

−10　　　　　−5
○○○○○○○○○○　○○○○○ (●●●●→)

I subtracted 5 red counters, or +5.

○○○○○○○○○○　○○○○○
　　　　　−15
(−10) − (+5) = (−15)

The balance on my card is now −$15. It makes sense that the balance is less than −$10, because now I should owe more.

Addition and Subtraction of Integers　**261**

This Grade 7 student page provides models of communicating mathematically that students can emulate.

- question parts that read in different directions. For example:

Reading Question Parts

READING FROM LEFT TO RIGHT	READING FROM TOP TO BOTTOM
Use 20 + 20 = 40 to calculate each sum. **a)** 19 + 21　**b)** 19 + 19　**c)** 22 + 21	Use mental math to calculate each total cost. **a)** $17.99 + $14.99 **b)** $12.98 + $3.50 **c)** $2.50 + $6.75

READING FROM TOP TO BOTTOM *AND* FROM LEFT TO RIGHT

Use mental math to calculate.

a) 73 + 21   **c)** 71 + 29   **e)** 54 + 19
b) 32 + 28   **d)** 49 + 33   **f)** 39 + 49

Some specific strategies for helping students learn to read math textbooks include alerting students to the need for

- recognizing what the title and subheads tell you about what you will do or what will happen in the lesson or section
- deciding if a question is meant to be answered right away, if it is simply an introduction, or if it will be answered later
- recognizing that an illustration to support the text may be positioned above, below, to the right, or to the left of the text
- deciding whether the illustration is "decorative" or essential to the question
- deciding whether the expectation is to write or to say an answer
- looking for math terms and making sure that the terms are familiar; using a glossary to find unfamiliar terms
- understanding how questions are numbered, particularly questions divided up into parts, and whether to look down or right to find the next thing to do (see *Reading Question Parts* on page 635)
- deciding what the various icons mean, for example, a calculator icon denoting that a calculator can be used for a particular question

Planning Opportunities for Practice

Part of the planning process involves thinking about how to ensure that students receive sufficient practice opportunities. One of the struggles educators have had in convincing the public to accept the changes that have been made to the mathematics curriculum is around the issue of practice. The experience of many parents of school-aged students, and certainly of their grandparents, has been that mathematics is about learning rules and then practising them. It is assumed, and it makes sense to many people, that the more a skill is practised, the better the student will be at that skill.

Lately, though, the nature of the work that students bring home in math has changed. To an untrained observer, there does not appear to be much practice.

Is Practice Important?

Of course, skills need to be practised. Ask any athlete or musician whether he or she believes that practice makes him or her a better player, and the universal answer will be "yes." By practising, students "automate" certain aspects of their mathematical work so that they can concentrate on the aspects that require more thought.

As well, many mathematical concepts build on one another. Unless prerequisites are firmly entrenched, learning new ideas becomes more difficult than it needs to be.

What Should Be Practised?

Initially, you might think that practice may help most in developing specific skills, for example, batting practice for a baseball player, practising scales for a pianist, and practising computation in mathematics. But there also needs to be practice of the following:

- problem solving
- visualization
- communication
- metacognition

How Much Practice Is Needed?

The amount of practice will vary with the complexity of what is being practised. For example, time will be needed to commit basic facts to memory because there are so many of them.

As well, a great deal of practice is needed to become proficient at visualization, problem solving, communication, and metacognition. In each of these cases, not only is there a range of strategies to learn, but there are also nuances, which are not skill-based, in selecting what strategy to call on in a particular set of circumstances.

What Should Practice Look Like?

Ideally, practice should be planned to be engaging and varied, as well as useful. Practice can also be multi-purpose. Take, for example, the possibility of practicing 2-digit addition. Rather than preparing a worksheet with 20 addition questions, a practice task such as the one shown in **Activity 22.1** could be given to practise both computation and problem solving.

Practising Metacognition, Visualization, and Communication

Metacognition is practised by ensuring that students are regularly asked to explain how they decided to start a problem, what to do next, why they drew a picture, etc.

Visualization is practised by encouraging students to imagine visual configurations of numbers. For example, you could use activities like the ones in **Activity 22.2**.

ACTIVITY 22.1

Place the digits 0 to 9, each once, in one of the boxes to make each true.

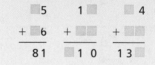

ACTIVITY 22.2

a) Imagine 9 counters in a 10-frame and another, empty 10-frame. Add 6 counters, filling the first 10-frame before going on to the second. What do the frames look like now?

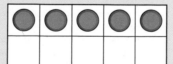

b) Imagine a pile of base ten blocks. There are more ten blocks than one blocks. What number are you seeing?

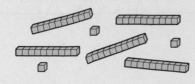

Communication is practised by focusing students on the clarity, accuracy, and vocabulary of the language they hear and its use in the context of doing mathematics. For example, you might ask students to record their own explanation for why it is really easy to multiply by 0, and then to look critically at what they wrote. They would ask themselves, for example, if someone else would be able to follow their thinking, if they were clear, and if they showed their knowledge of words such as "multiply" or "product."

Some texts even provide communication lessons for students to practise these skills. An example is shown below.

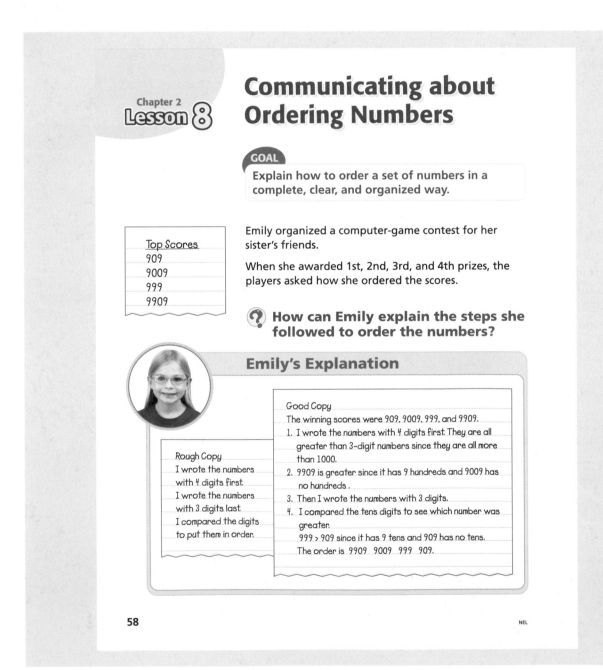

Chapter 2
Lesson 8

Communicating about Ordering Numbers

GOAL

Explain how to order a set of numbers in a complete, clear, and organized way.

Top Scores
909
9009
999
9909

Emily organized a computer-game contest for her sister's friends.

When she awarded 1st, 2nd, 3rd, and 4th prizes, the players asked how she ordered the scores.

How can Emily explain the steps she followed to order the numbers?

Emily's Explanation

Rough Copy
I wrote the numbers with 4 digits first.
I wrote the numbers with 3 digits last.
I compared the digits to put them in order.

Good Copy
The winning scores were 909, 9009, 999, and 9909.
1. I wrote the numbers with 4 digits first. They are all greater than 3-digit numbers since they are all more than 1000.
2. 9909 is greater since it has 9 hundreds and 9009 has no hundreds.
3. Then I wrote the numbers with 3 digits.
4. I compared the tens digits to see which number was greater.
   999 > 909 since it has 9 tens and 909 has no tens.
   The order is 9909 9009 999 909.

58

NEL

Differentiating Instruction: Supporting Individual Differences

Although students in front of a teacher may all be the same age or even have come from the same class last year, they are different. The most critical, and most difficult, part of a teacher's job may be to figure out how to tailor curriculum delivery to the needs of those individual students.

Moving from the Concrete to the Symbolic

Part of instructional planning involves making informed decisions about where students are on the continuum of concrete to symbolic thinking and adapting practice to the needs of those particular students.

The literature has been clear, as has conventional practice, that you move students from the concrete to the symbolic. Teachers know that students learn through all of their senses, so the use of concrete materials, or manipulatives, makes sense from that perspective alone. However, what makes the use of manipulatives even more critical in mathematics is that most mathematical ideas are abstractions, not tangibles.

Earlier chapters in this book provided guidance on which concrete materials are most helpful in teaching various topics.

What follows are some examples of concrete, pictorial, and symbolic models for a few concepts, to let you see how the same idea can look different at different stages. Teachers could decide where different groups of students are on this continuum for a particular topic and appropriately tailor instruction.

Modelling Subtraction Problems

Modelling the Problem: There were 15 ducks and 3 flew away. How many are left?

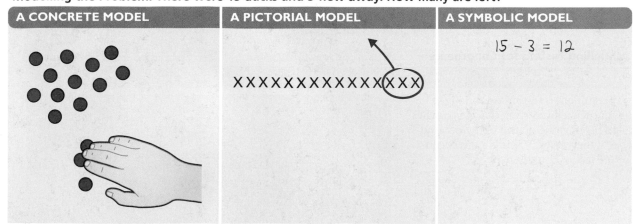

A CONCRETE MODEL	A PICTORIAL MODEL	A SYMBOLIC MODEL
	XXXXXXXXXXXX(XXX)	$15 - 3 = 12$

Modelling Integers

Modelling the Integer Equation $-2 + 3 = 1$

A CONCRETE MODEL

Two-sided tiles or counters can be used to represent integers. Each red tile is -1 and each white tile is $+1$.

Each pair of red and white tiles has a value of 0, so that leaves $+1$.

(continued)

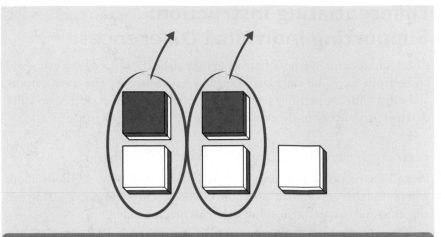

A PICTORIAL MODEL

A number line is a common and very useful pictorial model for integers. Movement right and left on the number line represents adding and subtracting.

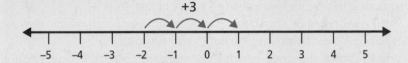

A SYMBOLIC MODEL

$-2 + 3 = 1$ is a symbolic model.

Modelling Congruence

The following example shows how students move through the three stages—concrete, pictorial, and symbolic—to determine whether two shapes are congruent.

Modelling Testing for Congruence

A CONCRETE MODEL

This student is testing two triangles for congruence by cutting out the triangles and placing one on top of the other to see if they match. This is a direct concrete test of congruence.

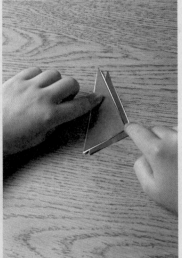

Using a concrete test to see if two shapes are congruent

A PICTORIAL MODEL

This student is testing two triangles for congruence by tracing one of the triangles, and then placing the tracing on top of the other triangle. This takes the representation to a more abstract level and is less direct because the student is using a picture to represent one of the triangles.

This method takes the test to a more abstract level.

Using a pictorial test to see if two shapes are congruent

A SYMBOLIC MODEL

This student is testing two triangles for congruence by measuring the angles and side lengths in each triangle to see if they match. This is more abstract than the pictorial method because the student is determining congruence by comparing the properties of the triangles rather than by comparing the triangles directly. At the elementary level, students need to measure all three angles and all three sides in each triangle to determine congruence. Later, less measuring will be needed because students will know that the triangles are congruent if all three pairs of corresponding sides match, or if two pairs of corresponding sides and the enclosed angles match, or if two pairs of corresponding angles and the connecting sides match.

Comparing angle and side length measures is more abstract because it is an indirect comparison.

Using a symbolic test to see if two shapes are congruent

Modelling the Concept of an Unknown

The same algebra concept can be modelled in a variety of ways. In the following examples, finding an unknown in an equation is shown using three models.

Modelling 2 + ■ = 5 to Find an Unknown

A CONCRETE MODEL

There are 2 cubes and a bag of cubes on the left side of the scale, and 5 cubes on the right side. The sides are balanced. Therefore, there must be 3 cubes in the bag on the left side to balance the 5 cubes on the other side.

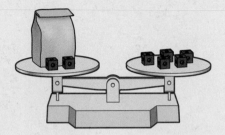

There must be 3 cubes in the bag.

A PICTORIAL MODEL

You have 2 squares and need 5 squares. If you add 3 squares to the 2 you started with, you will have a total of 5 squares.

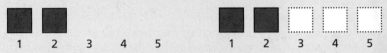

A SYMBOLIC MODEL

If you add a number to 2, it is equal to 5. Add 3 to 2 to make the sum of 5.

$$2 + \Box = 5$$
$$2 + 3 = 5$$

One common misconception made by teachers of mathematics is assuming that, once students reach a certain age, they no longer need the concrete stage. Even with older students, if new concepts and skills are being introduced, a concrete model is always a desirable beginning. How quickly students move to pictorial and then symbolic models will vary.

Managing Differentiation

Because there are usually 20 to 30 different students in a class and only one teacher, it is essential that the teacher use a variety of manageable strategies to meet those students' needs. Some possible strategies are addressed here.

Open-Ended Tasks

An open task is a task that can be approached very differently, but meaningfully, by students at different development levels. A key feature of such a task is that there are many possible answers, and many ways to get to the answers.

To create such a task, you might choose one that is centred around a key concept you want students to deal with at any level of development. For example, the key concept for the task shown below is "Shapes of different dimensions and their properties can be described mathematically," with a focus on distinguishing and relating shapes.

Open Multi-Phase Tasks

OPEN MULTI-PHASE TASK	FOLLOW-UP QUESTIONS
A certain 2-D or 3-D shape makes me think of a rectangle, but it's not a rectangle. a) What might the shape be? Name or sketch the shape. b) How is the shape like a rectangle? How is it not like a rectangle? c) Repeat parts a) and b) for a different shape.	• Which shapes did you suggest? • Why did you choose each shape? • In what ways is each shape like a rectangle? • In what ways is each shape different from a rectangle? • What are some other shapes you could have suggested?

Students are provided with the appropriate concrete and/or pictorial models to work with. Students not as mathematically sophisticated are likely to relate a rectangle to another polygon, and to relate and distinguish the two shapes based on global properties, for example, whether one has more vertices than the other. More mathematically sophisticated students may relate a rectangle to another quadrilateral or to a 3-D shape with at least one rectangular face. They will distinguish the shapes based on specific properties, such as the number of sides, vertices, and faces, and the relationships among sides and vertices, such as the number of equal sides or the sizes of the angles.

Although some teachers may worry about covering the curriculum if they use open-ended tasks, they can be constructed in such a way as to minimize that concern.

Parallel Tasks

Teachers can offer students a choice of two or three tasks that focus on the same key idea(s), but that reflect different developmental levels. The tasks are related closely enough that the same follow-up questions can be used to frame a follow-up discussion in which all students look back and communicate about what they did and what they learned.

Parallel tasks allow all students to experience success and learn from peers by seeing responses not only to their own task, but also to a related task completed by others. This ensures that students see the same underlying mathematical concept in different contexts.

For example, both tasks on page 644 ask students to describe a situation to match a probability description. Choice A suits students who can match situations to qualitative probability descriptions; choice B suits students who are able to match situations to numerical descriptions of probability.

CHOICE TASKS

You can put 10 square tiles in a draw bag. The tiles can be any combination of red, blue, and yellow. Then, you will draw one tile from the bag.

Choice A

What tiles will you put in the bag so that it is possible, but not likely, to draw a red tile? Explain your thinking.

Choice B

What tiles will you put in the bag so that the probability of drawing a red tile is $\frac{2}{5}$? Explain your thinking.

FOLLOW-UP QUESTIONS

- How did you decide how many red tiles to put in the bag?
- How do you know the tiles in your bag match the situation you chose?
- Did you think carefully about how many blue or yellow tiles you needed? Why or why not?
- Talk to someone who did the other task. What was the same about what you both did? What was different?

Centres

Teachers can set up activities at different centres to suit students at different levels. The teacher can direct the appropriate students to the appropriate centres, and then circulate to interact with the various groups.

Adapting Existing Lessons

Small adjustments to a previously prepared lesson can make it more inclusive. For example, suppose a Grade 4 class includes some students significantly behind.

The teacher examines an upcoming textbook lesson about creating a bar graph with a given scale. The teacher can scan the lesson to look for questions that could be adapted to facilitate and strengthen struggling students' knowledge about bar graphs. For example, any questions that focus on scale could be adapted to allow those students to create simple bar graphs that use a single square to represent a single piece of data.

WebConnect

www.makingmathmeaningful.nelson.com

Visit the Making Math Meaningful website for links to sources related to teaching math to students with learning disabilities.

Students with Learning Disabilities

Many forms of learning disability affect math learning, many of them resulting in difficulties with calculations, with problem solving, and/or with memorizing multi-step procedures. In addition to this, mathematics texts that require a high level of reading ability can create additional challenges for students with learning disabilities.

Many students with learning disabilities have difficulty keeping one piece of information in their minds while processing other information. Thus, it is not a question of not being able to do A or B, but having difficulty doing them together. Many mathematical situations are complex and require multiple subtasks, thereby creating problems for these learners. An example might be dealing with patterns with multiple attributes where students find it difficult to deal with two or three attributes simultaneously. Information processing difficulties may limit what you can expect these students to handle within one question.

Teaching that focuses on a small number of big ideas or key concepts to make connections is helpful for students with learning disabilities because it provides a natural structure to new learning. This is where a big picture of mathematics can be of great assistance to a teacher.

General Instructional Adaptations Regardless of the specific problem, many general strategies or adaptations can ensure the success of students with learning disabilities. These adaptations may include

- breaking the material into manageable sequential chunks
- providing very explicit instructions
- providing more structure, even to open-ended activities
- providing more structure for problem solving
- providing instruction in the problem-solving strategies, with lots of opportunity to practise those strategies
- using visuals to support learning as much as possible
- revisiting related material to allow students to make connections
- revisiting vocabulary and concepts with appropriate practice over time
- welcoming unusual approaches
- assigning problems that are related to what is currently of interest or under discussion
- modifying the content to be learned to take into account the developmental level of the student

Organizational Tools and Strategies A number of useful organizational tools and strategies can help students who require more structure. Teachers can

- outline the lesson or activity and post the outline, making sure the goal of the activity is clear
- encourage students to create their own graphic organizers to summarize concepts learned
- prepare study guides or graphic organizers, such as concept maps, to help students before and after the lesson or unit of study; for example:

Concept Map before Studying Growing Patterns

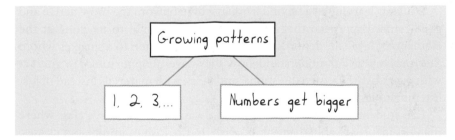

Concept Map after Studying Growing Patterns

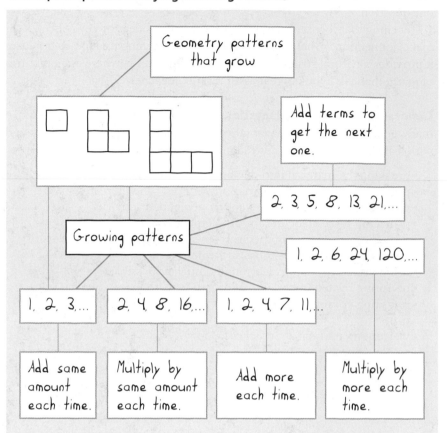

ESL and Immersion

A number of students learn math in their second or third language. It may be because they are immigrants for whom English is a second language (ESL). They may be francophone students learning in English, anglophone students learning in French, or students who have taken "immersion" classes in Ukrainian. The fact that children are learning a fairly abstract subject in an unfamiliar language means that some accommodations probably will be required. This is even more the case now than it used to be in mathematics as a result of the increased focus on problem solving in context and communication.

Students learning in a second language benefit from the more active and child-centred approach that has become fundamental to teaching at the elementary level. Students do not simply have to listen to a speaker whom they may or may not understand; now they have an opportunity to interact with peers, ask their own questions, and work with materials instead of just listening to unfamiliar words.

ESL students are often, although not always, a minority in a class where many students are able to speak English. In the case of immersion classes, most students are functioning at approximately the same level of language "disadvantage."

Considerations for ESL Students

Some important considerations are listed on page 647 for teaching in ELL classrooms in particular:

- There may be value in initially grouping ESL students with others who share their first language. This strategy allows these students to discuss concepts in a familiar and comfortable way while they acquire the English language, which they will need in order to proceed.
- Cooperative work with English-speaking students can also be helpful in that ESL students hear more models of English. They can also develop vocabulary for using English to clarify, justify, explain, compare, etc.
- Working in groups may be more consistent with the cultural practices of some of these students, since many cultures value this kind of interdependence.
- It is particularly important to be sensitive to the use of contexts. Many children who have had different home or cultural experiences are mystified by contexts that their teachers assume are familiar to all students. Teachers need to be sensitive to these potential difficulties and anticipate them as much as possible. An example might be a problem related to shaking hands after a tournament. Furthermore, contexts designed to be whimsical or humorous could cause particular problems for students coming from cultures in which make-believe is not part of their experience, or perceived "silliness" is frowned upon. In fact, humorous contexts can be problematic even within a specific culture because senses of humour vary greatly.
- Not only is sensitivity to these differences necessary, but there must be attempts to bridge these differences through a combination of explaining the contexts and finding alternative contexts that are more familiar to the various cultural groups represented in the class.
- Although we normally think of a natural mathematics progression from the concrete to the pictorial and then symbolic, some slightly older ESL students, who have been schooled in other countries, may be more familiar with a symbolic presentation of mathematical ideas than with their concrete representations. Their experience with manipulatives would be minimal or non-existent, and they may need additional instruction on their use.
- Make sure that communication about homework or other math requirements is straightforward enough for an older sibling to deal with. In many families, where the parents do not speak English, older siblings serve as the go-between with the school and often help their younger siblings at home with their homework.

Strategies for ESL and Immersion

The following strategies are important to consider in order to make mathematics instruction comprehensible to ESL students. Some of the strategies are equally applicable to immersion and ESL classrooms.

- Provide visual support, such as graphs, pictures, diagrams, charts, posters, and word cards.

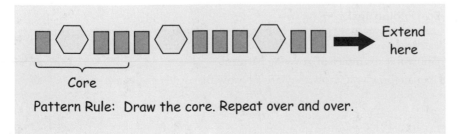

Pattern Rule: Draw the core. Repeat over and over.

- Provide concrete support such as models, manipulatives, and real objects.
- Simplify the language used in teaching rather than the ideas being taught.
- Use as few extra words as possible, and introduce them with manipulative or contextual support.
- Use nonverbal cues such as gestures, facial expressions, and body language to clarify meaning.
- Avoid slang and idioms.
- Allow and encourage students to touch and feel to learn.
- Speak directly to students, emphasizing important words.
- Provide sufficient wait time after asking a question to give these students time to interpret the question, and then think about a possible response.
- Ascertain prior knowledge and vocabulary and build on this.
- Clarify the goals of the activity in advance.
- Write legibly, perhaps using prepared, typed overheads or chart paper notes, rather than board writing.
- Ensure that audio materials are clear and free from unfamiliar accents.
- Be sensitive to alternative symbols used in other cultures, such as a comma instead of a decimal point.
- Encourage students to ask themselves, "What help do I need?" "Who can I ask?" "How should I ask?"
- Repeat, rephrase, or paraphrase key concepts and directions.
- Identify, pre-teach, and expand on key vocabulary required for the development of the concept.
- Encourage students to express themselves orally, focusing on meaning rather than form.
- Spend additional time on the understand-the-problem stage of the inquiry process.
- Have students rewrite problems in their own words.

Assessment As in the case of students with learning disabilities, teachers need to be flexible when assessing second-language students in mathematics. Performance tasks are most likely to provide a venue where these students can experience success. When assessing, the following strategies can be helpful:

- Delay the assignment of marks until the student has sufficient English to be assessed fairly.
- Allow for oral or pictorial, rather than just written, responses.
- Provide scaffolding, such as that shown below, for written tasks. Scaffolding assists students in understanding what it is you are asking for and how much they need to do. For example:

Scaffolding Tasks

ORIGINAL TASK

Show five examples of growing patterns.

Explain how you know they are all growing patterns.

SCAFFOLDED TASK

Here are 5 examples of growing patterns:

1. _____

2. _____

3. _____

4. _____

5. _____

I know they are all growing patterns because

_____

_____

_____

Modifying Tasks

ORIGINAL TASK	MODIFIED TASK
Sketch a pattern with two changing attributes. Make your pattern repeat three times. Tell how the attributes change.	Use **all** of these shapes:  Make a **pattern**. **Repeat** 3 times. **Tell** about your pattern.

- Include graphics (such as charts, graphs, pictures, and maps).
- Look at a number of ways for students to represent their understanding (for example, diagrams, charts, frame sentences, cloze sentences, and graphic organizers).
- Provide examples as part of the structure of the question; for example, "5, 10, 15, … and 4, 8, 12, … are both skip counting patterns. What are some other skip counting patterns?"

Enrichment for the Mathematically Gifted

Some students are mathematically gifted; others are average in mathematical ability but are interested and keen to do more. Although society has shown great concern for the needs of students with disadvantages, gifted students have received much less attention. Yet, each of these students, too, deserves enrichment opportunities.

Mathematically gifted students need some special treatment; they need to proceed more quickly than their peers. They usually have deeper levels of understanding, and are prone to losing interest in mathematics if the pace is too slow and if existing interests are not cultivated to a sufficient depth. Some of these students balk at being required to show their work or provide written explanations, especially if they arrive at an answer fairly quickly. Some students who are gifted in understanding concepts and solving problems are less adept at communicating mathematically. Hence, these students benefit from being asked to explain their work.

Gifted mathematics students thrive in a problem-centred classroom culture. Here, the teacher teaches through problem solving, using a problem to motivate and provide a context for the learning. For example, a teacher can focus young students on skip counting by 5s by displaying 6 nickels and asking students to figure out the total value of the nickels. In the course of this activity, the skip counting emerges as the individual nickels are counted. Or, in a classroom with older elementary students, the teacher might ask students to determine the total number of squares in a 10-by-10 square array. Many students will realize that starting with smaller squares, using a chart or organized list, and looking for a pattern will help to solve the problem. Thus, in the course of solving a problem, they have worked with patterns, square numbers, and graphic organizers.

Problem-Centred Learning

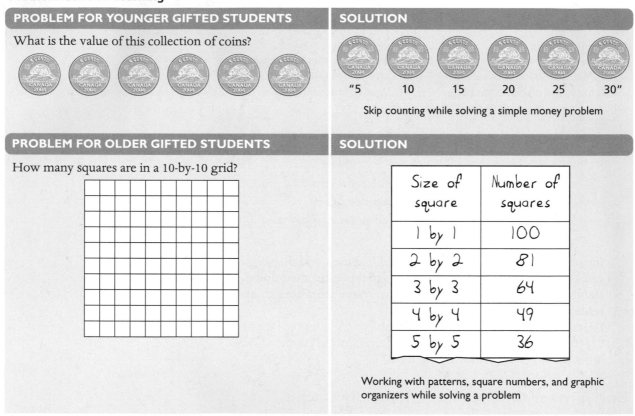

PROBLEM FOR YOUNGER GIFTED STUDENTS

What is the value of this collection of coins?

SOLUTION

"5   10   15   20   25   30"

Skip counting while solving a simple money problem

PROBLEM FOR OLDER GIFTED STUDENTS

How many squares are in a 10-by-10 grid?

SOLUTION

Size of square	Number of squares
1 by 1	100
2 by 2	81
3 by 3	64
4 by 4	49
5 by 5	36

Working with patterns, square numbers, and graphic organizers while solving a problem

Gifted students also thrive in classrooms where extensions are regularly proposed, for example, by the teacher frequently asking, "What if ...?" questions. For instance, in exploring a pattern involving circles and squares, the teacher might ask, "What if we included triangles in our pattern?"

Strategies for Motivated and Gifted Learners

Some of the ways to meet the needs of both highly motivated learners and gifted students include

- finding a variety of problem, puzzle, and activity sources with mathematics content that suits their interests (Logic problems are often of interest to these students.)
- letting students create math puzzles for other students to solve
- establishing math clubs for interested students

- providing opportunities for these students to respond frequently to higher-level questions
- encouraging the use of manipulatives in creative ways
- providing alternative but related assignments or tasks. For example, while working on a unit about patterns, if it becomes clear that a particular student has already mastered the ideas to be presented, she or he can learn about more complex patterns, such as the Fibonacci sequence.
- offering alternative projects, problems, or assignments, if the students already know the concepts and skills that are to be taught
- providing access to Internet resources
- encouraging their creativity both in assignments and on formal assessments
- differentiating assignments, so that the most able students do not simply do more of the same problems
- allowing students to extend their work beyond the mandated curriculum
- finding ways to ensure public recognition of their talents (Unlike artistically, musically, or physically talented students, these students are unlikely to receive external validation for their accomplishments.)
- using a teacher-librarian or other external helper like a parent volunteer to work with these students
- providing opportunities for these students to participate in contests or competitions, which can be motivating and which can provide a way to externally validate their abilities. Many math competitions provide rich and challenging questions, which can also be used with students who are not gifted but who enjoy working competitively.

Applying What You've Learned

1. The chapter problem at the start of this chapter is a "standard" problem in mathematics. How could it be adapted to meet the needs of other groups of students to focus on operations other than addition, or on other types of numbers rather than whole numbers?

2. Search the Internet to find an article about math anxiety. Read and summarize it. What strategies does it provide that might help you, as a teacher, either overcome your own anxiety or help a student with math anxiety?

3. Choose a mathematical topic of interest to you. Show how you would move from the concrete to the pictorial to the symbolic with that topic. Research to see at what grade levels those stages are expected for that topic.

4. Imagine you are building a unit plan to teach 3-D geometry to a group of students at a level of your choice. Describe how you would divide up the material into lessons for that unit, and justify your approach to the unit. Remember to include activities to start and conclude the unit.

5. Develop a lesson plan for a mathematical topic of your choice at a level of your choice. Make sure to put it in a format that would make it easy for you to navigate during a teaching period. Include at least three questions that you would pre-plan to ask students.

6. Find an article about lesson study. Why might you find it useful to participate in a lesson study situation? Do you see any "downsides"?

7. Investigate a Canadian math text with a copyright date after 1990. List 5 to 10 examples of features or approaches in the text that reflect more current views about the teaching of mathematics.

8. Using the text from Question 7, choose a lesson. Describe how you would adapt the delivery of that lesson if it were appropriate for some students, but needed adaptation for some struggling students.

9. This chapter discusses the special care that might be taken to consider how to adapt instruction to meet the needs of learning-disabled, second-language, or gifted learners. Are there other groups of students you think a teacher should be knowledgeable about in terms of delivering math instruction? Explain.

Interact with a K–8 Student:

10. Ask a student to describe to you how he or she likes a math class to start, and why he or she likes it to start that way. How might you use this information to plan your own math lessons?

Discuss with a K–8 Teacher:

11. Ask a teacher to share with you her or his approaches to yearlong unit and lesson planning in mathematics. Discuss with that teacher what aspects of planning have changed as she or he has gained more teaching experience.

Selected References

Buxton, L. (1991). *Math panic.* Portsmouth, NH: Heinemann.

Cocking, R.R., and Chipman, S. (1988). Conceptual issues related to mathematics achievement of language minority children. In Cocking, R.R., and Mestre, J.P. *Linguistic and cultural influences on learning mathematics.* Hillsdale, NJ: Lawrence Erlbaum Associates, 17–46.

Fernandez, C., and Yoshida, M. (2004). *Lesson study: A Japanese approach to improving mathematics teaching and learning.* (Studies in Mathematical Thinking and Learning). Hillsdale, NJ: Lawrence Erlbaum Associates.

Ministry of Education, Ontario. *Leading Math Success* [Online]. Available: http://www.edu.gov.on.ca/eng/studentsuccess/lms.

Sheffield, L.J. (1999). *Developing mathematically promising students.* Reston, VA: National Council of Teachers of Mathematics.

Small, M. (2005a). *PRIME: Number and operations: Background and strategies.* Toronto: Thomson Nelson.

Small, M. (2005b). *PRIME: Patterns and algebra: Background and strategies.* Toronto: Thomson Nelson.

Small, M. (2006). *PRIME: Data management and probability strand kit.* Toronto: Thomson Nelson.

Small, M. (2007). *PRIME: Geometry: Background and strategies.* Toronto: Thomson Nelson.

Sowell, E.J. (1989). Effects of manipulative materials in mathematics instruction. *Journal for Research in Mathematics Education,* 20, 498–505.

Targeted Implementation and Planning Supports (TIPS). http://www.edu.gov.on.ca/eng/studentsuccess/lms/files/ELLMath4All.pdf.

Thornton, C.A., Langrall, C.W., and Jones, G.A. (1997). Mathematics instruction for elementary students with learning disabilities. *Journal of Learning Disabilities,* 30, 142–150.

Tobias, S. (1995). *Overcoming math anxiety: Revised and expanded.* New York: W.W. Norton and Co.

Chapter 23

Developing a Teaching Style

IN A NUTSHELL

The main ideas in this chapter are listed below:

1. A teaching style has many elements. Some of those elements reflect the teacher's personality and predispositions, but others are ones that a teacher can choose.

2. Aspects of teachers' teaching styles become evident in their choice of lesson designs, the types of tasks they set for students, the types of questions they ask, and their approach to their own professional growth.

CHAPTER PROBLEM

How many rectangles are in the picture?

A Teaching Style

Each teacher develops a teaching style. It manifests itself in the structure of lessons used, the types of questions asked, the types of tasks set, interactions with students and their parents, and the teacher's approach to his or her own professional development.

Rather than letting a teaching style develop without thinking about it, teachers who make conscious decisions about the classroom environment that they create will likely have greater control over the effects of their teaching choices and, as a result, greater teaching satisfaction.

Lesson Style

The Importance of Varied Lesson Styles

One decision that teachers can make is about the lesson structures they will use. Although teachers all acknowledge the value of keeping learning interesting, it is easy to get into the pattern of teaching all mathematics lessons in the same way. Sometimes this makes the teacher's life easier— following a familiar straightforward model makes planning quicker. Sometimes this is done for predictability—some teachers feel that students prefer and need predictability in how a lesson will flow. But there is value in developing a teaching style that allows for some variety.

Different lesson styles appeal to students with different learning styles or work habits. As well, different lesson styles better suit the nature of the different types of mathematics to be learned. For example, getting a sense of the size of larger numbers is better suited to an exploration-style lesson than is the learning of the traditional division algorithm. Teachers can take the time to think about the balance of types of lessons, described below, that they will use.

Different Lesson Styles

Exploration

Exploration lessons provide students with an opportunity to have more input into the direction of a lesson. Sometimes it makes sense to set up an exploration at the start of a unit of study. Sometimes an exploration makes a suitable concluding activity, where students explore a reasonably complex situation using what they have learned in the unit. There also may be specific expectations/outcomes within a unit of study for which an exploration would be effective.

In an exploration lesson, students may be using different approaches and may end up with different conclusions. They may not even be working on the same topic. Teachers provide some guidance to get students started, but students have significant latitude in how to proceed.

Explorations can be done individually or in small groups. Examples of tasks suitable for exploration include a lesson to create as many models and expressions as possible for the number 10, or a lesson to explore the number of possible results using any of the four operations with a set of four numbers (for example, what the greatest and least possible result is using addition, subtraction, multiplication, or division, and the numbers 10, 11, 12, and 13). Another example is one where students make as many different composite shapes as they can using the same five congruent squares.

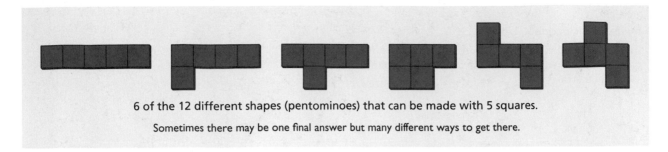

6 of the 12 different shapes (pentominoes) that can be made with 5 squares.

Sometimes there may be one final answer but many different ways to get there.

Guided Activity

In a guided activity lesson, students move toward a common goal or set of understandings. However, under the guidance of a teacher, they have a significant participatory role in the development of those understandings.

Examples of topics that might suit this style of instruction are a lesson on different ways to represent a number with base ten blocks, on exploring how multiplication and division are related, or on examining a set of data to choose an appropriate scale for a pictograph.

Direct Instruction

In a direct instruction lesson, students are led through a mathematical concept or skill under the direction of a teacher. This makes the most sense when students are introduced to rules or approaches that have been externally selected as standards, or conventions. Examples of topics that might suit this style of instruction are a lesson demonstrating or modelling an addition algorithm, a lesson showing how to use a number line to determine the multiples of a number, or a lesson on reading a clock.

Using Different Lesson Styles

There is a tendency among many teachers to use more direct instruction lessons in teaching number and operations, as compared to, say, geometry, but this need not be the case. For example, one possible outline for a guided activity lesson on fact families, often taught through direction instruction, is shown below:

Fact-Family Guided Activity Lesson

POSE A PROBLEM	BRING IT TOGETHER
I have 13 notebooks altogether. Some are on my desk and 5 are in my backpack. How many are on my desk? **Make Sure Students Understand** Ask a student to restate the problem in his or her own words.	Ask questions that ensure students look back at their work and communicate about the relationship between subtraction and addition. Ensure that they understand that to solve $5 + \blacksquare = 13$, you can solve $13 - 5 = \blacksquare$ because $5 + 8 = 13$ and $13 - 5 = 8$ are in the same **fact family**. (Introduce the vocabulary.) **Consolidate the Learning** Provide opportunities for students to practise and extend the ideas encountered.

(continued)

Suggest a Strategy

Encourage students to act it out or use counters to model the problem.

Invite Participation

Encourage students to work on the problem in small groups. Ensure students have the opportunity to share their strategies.

Close the Lesson

Ask a question to bring it all together: How can an addition and subtraction sentence describe the same story?

Grouping for Instruction

Just as there is value in a balance of lesson styles to support different learning styles, different ways of grouping for instruction also makes sense to meet various students' needs. Teachers can develop their own approach to grouping.

Sometimes teachers might group students because they want students to communicate with one another. Sometimes there are practical reasons; for example, it may be easier or necessary to share manipulative materials. Mostly, teachers recognize that students are more comfortable taking the risk of asking or answering questions in a small group of peers than in a teacher-whole class interaction.

Grouping makes sense in situations where a task is open enough that input from a variety of students with a variety of perspectives is valuable. In situations where students have an opportunity to work on a problem or to develop their own algorithms, group discussion can be very useful.

Heterogeneous and Homogenous Grouping

Sometimes teachers use heterogeneous groups. In a situation where students of different ability levels could all contribute toward the solution of a problem or completion of a task, this type of grouping makes sense.

Teachers use different techniques to form such groups. Sometimes, they count off students: 1, 2, 3, 4, 1, 2, 3, 4, ..., grouping all the 1s together, all the 2s together, etc., to form four groups. Other times, they provide short computational tasks directing students with the same question to work together, or they allow students to decide with whom they want to work. Still other times, they simply assign groups based on proximity of seating.

A suitable task for a heterogeneous group of varied abilities is shown below. What makes this task suitable for a heterogeneous group is that students can select different items from the flyers, depending on their confidence with particular number values.

ACTIVITY **23.1**

Provide supermarket flyers to each group. Ask them to create a "shopping" list with a total cost of close to, but not more than, $10.00.

On the other hand, there may be times when homogeneous groupings are more appropriate. A teacher may want to pull aside a group of students struggling with a particular topic to work together to deal with the difficulties they are having. Or the teacher may want to provide an enrichment activity for students who are already comfortable with a topic she or he is planning to teach. Homogeneous grouping is useful in differentiating instruction.

The activity below would be enrichment for students who can already read and represent 2-digit and 3-digit numbers.

ACTIVITY 23.2

Ask the group to determine the number of palindromes (numbers that read the same forward and backward, like 99 or 121) that there are between 10 and 1000.

Group Size

There is no ideal group size. Sometimes the size depends on the task, and other times it depends on the interpersonal dynamics in the class or the amount of available material. It is important not to make groups so large that some students end up being left out. Sometimes there is a danger with groups of three that two students might work so well together that the third group member feels left out.

Cooperative Grouping

When students are grouped to work together on a problem or to discuss a concept, it is often referred to as cooperative grouping. Students who are grouped simply to share manipulatives or who are sitting together and helping each other as they work individually are not cooperative groups.

Cooperative groups work together on a task, contributing equitably (not necessarily equally) to a single task. For a cooperative group to work effectively, there needs to be individual accountability for the learning. Each student must be held responsible, on an individual basis, for what is learned. Without that individual accountability, too many students simply opt out, leaving it to other students to complete the work.

Suitable Tasks for Group Work

As mentioned earlier, grouping makes sense in situations where a task is open enough that input from a variety of people with a variety of perspectives is valuable. Here are some sample tasks that are suitable for groups:

- Create a set of math stories to show that subtraction is used to solve more than one type of problem.
- Come up with a way to use base ten blocks to show that when you multiply a 2-digit number by a 2-digit number, the answer could be a 3- or a 4-digit number.
- Create a pattern using a set of animal counters.

Limitations of Grouping

It is important to recognize that not all students function best in a group, and some allowances for this should be considered at least some of the time.

Although it may be appropriate to place stronger academic students in groups with weaker students for the purposes of helping those weaker students, it is not appropriate to do this too frequently. The stronger student, too, needs appropriate learning challenges.

Balancing Whole Class, Small Group, and Individual Instruction

It is important for teachers to provide opportunities for students to work as a large learning community (as a whole class), in small groups, and also sometimes on their own. Often there will be a mix of these approaches within one lesson, and certainly over the course of several lessons. Teachers' choices about the appropriate balance reflect not only their own individual styles, but perhaps also the content being explored and the personalities of students.

Effective Questioning

Questioning is an important part of instruction. Some sources suggest that teacher questions typically take up as much as 30 to 50 percent of instructional time (Black, 2001).

Sahin, Bullock, and Stables (2002) suggest that teachers use questions primarily to check understanding, mostly convergent and low-level questions not designed to initiate discussion, invite curiosity, begin inquiry, or stimulate critical thinking. Harrop and Swinson (2003) report that only 10 percent of questions asked are of the open solution type; all others are either questions of fact, closed solution, task supervision, or routine questions; in other words, there are few opportunities for discussions initiated by a teacher question. In fact, Stigler and Hiebert (1999) posit that the videos of classrooms created as part of the Third International Mathematics and Science Study show that teachers in the United States use "rapid-fire" questions that require one-word responses and, even then, use voice tone and questioning to almost give away the answers. It is not likely that the situation is much different in Canada.

It is up to individual teachers to consider carefully the kinds of questions they ask. One valuable strategy is to pre-plan at least some of the questions to be asked. Teachers can spend time thinking about what sorts of questions are best to ask to start the lesson, which are best to ask to keep the lesson going in rich directions, and which questions might be best to bring closure to the lesson. Teachers can also think about how inclusive their questions are, that is, whether they are accessible to all students in the class.

Nature of Tasks Posed

In other chapters, there has been discussion of teaching through problem solving and using rich tasks to engage students in mathematical thinking. But teachers might also consider how much they want to make sure that at least some tasks integrate mathematical strands so that students can see the connections between different mathematical topics. As well, teachers might consider whether or how much they want to use cross-curricular tasks, so students can see the relationship of mathematics to other subjects, too.

Examples of tasks that integrate strands include

- creating patterns that highlight geometric properties of shapes
- measuring to create scale models based on ratios
- exploring the probability that numbers in a certain range have certain properties, for example, the probability that an integer between 1 and 100 is a prime

Examples of cross-curricular tasks include

- creating artistic tessellations that involve interesting designs
- exploring the effect of mass and string length on the period of a pendulum
- writing math stories
- creating musical compositions based on geometric transformations

You might become a teacher who chooses to teach with themes, with cross-curricular activities becoming a real focus.

Using Technology

Teachers can also choose how much to make technology an integral part of their teaching. For example, some teachers teach with interactive white boards as a regular part of their teaching. In this way, students can more actively explore complex situations in a milieu that allows for a permanent record of what transpired, and that also allows for the integration of tools like dynamic geometry software.

You might choose to become a teacher who encourages students to take advantage of tools like calculators, virtual manipulatives, and spreadsheet programs, as much as non-technological tools in the classroom. This takes planning, but most teachers find that the more they use technology, the more adept they become and the more valuable uses they find for it.

Classroom Interaction

It goes without saying that teachers need to be supportive of and positive with their students. But some teachers develop teaching styles where their interactions with students also accomplish the following:

- cultivating student self-confidence: This often comes from giving students the time to come up with their own answers to questions and problems. It also comes from accepting and inviting all students' responses.
- cultivating an environment where students are happy to help each other: This often comes from encouraging just the right balance of competitiveness and cooperation.
- cultivating perseverance: This often comes from modelling perseverance to your students and also from giving enough time and encouragement that students are willing to go on.
- cultivating a positive attitude toward mathematics: This often comes from modelling a positive attitude yourself.

Supporting the Student at Home

Part of developing a teaching style involves a decision about how you will interact with students' families. Teachers vary in how they approach this.

For example, some teachers choose to interact with parents only at formal, prescribed times, like parent–teacher interviews. Other teachers decide to interact more regularly by

- holding games nights and inviting parents and students to play math games together
- sending regular e-mails to update parents about what is happening in the math classroom
- inviting parents in both as observers and as helpers to experience, first-hand, what students are learning
- providing interesting investigations that students can do with their parents. One source for this is the Figure This! Math Challenges for Families website at www.figurethis.org.

By having parents "on side," students are better supported and teaching becomes more rewarding.

WebConnect

www.makingmathmeaningful
.nelson.com

Visit the Making Math Meaningful website for links to Internet sites that provide interesting investigations for students to do with their parents.

Professional Growth

Teachers vary in how much time they devote to keeping up with their profession by attending workshops, reading journals and other professional resources, participating in research projects with local researchers, and interacting with colleagues to discuss educational issues.

Professional development opportunities have been increasing over the past 10 years. More and more of them focus on teachers taking the time to work with colleagues to re-think in fundamental ways how they teach, as opposed to attending workshops where they might learn about an activity or two that they might use.

One powerful movement is the movement toward professional learning communities (PLCs), where teachers, often in the same school, interact with each other to discuss professional issues. Sometimes PLCs are attached to "book studies," where teachers agree on a professional book they will all read and discuss.

Another movement that has become popular is the lesson study movement borrowed from the Japanese, where a group of teachers plan a lesson thoughtfully together, one of them delivers it with the others observing, and then, together, they consider the results, often re-planning the same lesson.

A third movement that has become important to professional development in mathematics is the linking of research to practice. This takes many forms, but in all cases, it relates to a link between what researchers are learning and how teachers can use those ideas, often with teachers as part of the research team.

An important part of being a professional is keeping up with new knowledge in the profession. Part of the decision teachers make about their own teaching style involves their level of commitment to their own professional growth. Those who participate in professional growth experiences usually find that their careers are more rewarding.

Applying What You've Learned

1. The chapter problem at the start of this chapter is an example of a figure–ground perception problem that requires you to use what you know about properties of rectangles. It was selected for this chapter because it is a reminder that the whole figure (or your whole teaching style) is made up of parts. How many rectangles did you find?

2. Look in a textbook and select a lesson that you might deliver using a different lesson style from the one the authors have selected. Explain why you would select the other style and show how the lesson would flow.

3. Read about the pros and cons of teaching using cooperative grouping strategies. How much grouping of students do you think would suit your teaching style? Why?

4. Using the lesson you developed for Question 2, list three or four questions that you might pre-plan to use in the delivery of that lesson. Explain why each is a good question for that lesson.

5. Talk about how important you think it is for a K–8 math teacher to infuse technology into his or her instruction. Use several sources to support your opinions.

6. Given the many demands on teacher time, including spending time planning and working with individual students, how important do you think is time for professional development? Use resources that you have read to support your position.

Interact with a K–8 Student:

7. Ask a student what sorts of math tasks she or he would and would not want to do at home with a parent, and why.

Discuss with a K–8 Teacher:

8. Ask teachers if they ever use themes to organize instruction. Have them talk to you about why they do or do not take this approach.

9. Ask teachers how much they are involved in professional development opportunities, which of those opportunities they value most, and why.

Selected References

Black, S. (2001). Ask me a question: How teachers use inquiry in a classroom. *American School Board Journal,* 188, 43–45.

Eaker, R., DuFour, R., and Burnette, R. (2002). *Getting started: Reculturing schools to become professional learning communities.* Bloomington, IN: National Educational Service.

Fernandez, C. (2002). Learning from Japanese approaches to professional development: The case of lesson study. *Journal of Teacher Education,* 53, 393–405.

Fogarty, R. (1991). *The mindful school: How to integrate the curricula.* Palatine, IL: Skylight Publishing, Inc.

Harrop, A., and Swinson, J. (2003). Teachers' questions in the infant, junior and secondary school. *Educational Studies,* 29, 49–57.

Sahin, C., Bullock, K., and Stables, A. (2002). Teachers' beliefs and practices in relation to their beliefs about questioning at key stage 2. *Educational Studies,* 28, 371–384.

Small, M. (2005). *PRIME: Number and operations: Background and strategies.* Toronto: Thomson Nelson.

Small, M. (2007). *PRIME: Geometry: Background and strategies.* Toronto: Thomson Nelson.

Stenmark, J.K. (1986). *Family math.* Berkeley: University of California.

Stigler, J.W., and Hiebert, J. (1999). *The teaching gap.* New York: The Free Press.

My name is _____.

one

Draw 1.

My name is _____ .

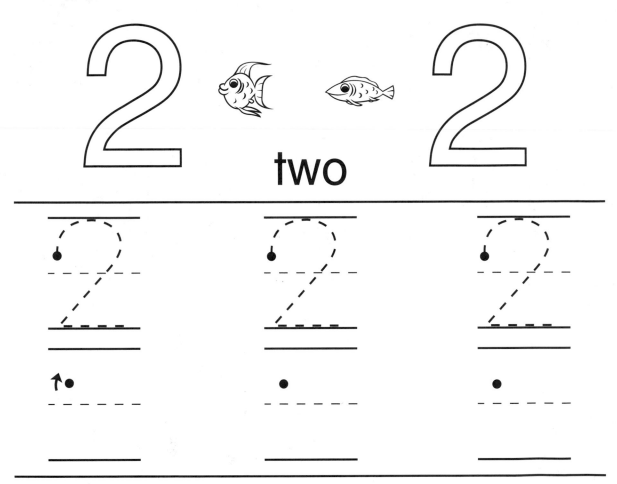

two

Draw 2.

My name is _____.

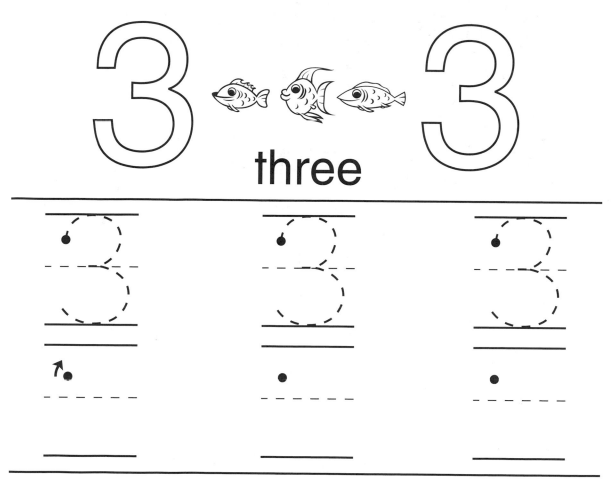

three

Draw 3.

My name is _____.

4   four   4

Draw 4.

My name is _____.

five

Draw 5.

My name is _____.

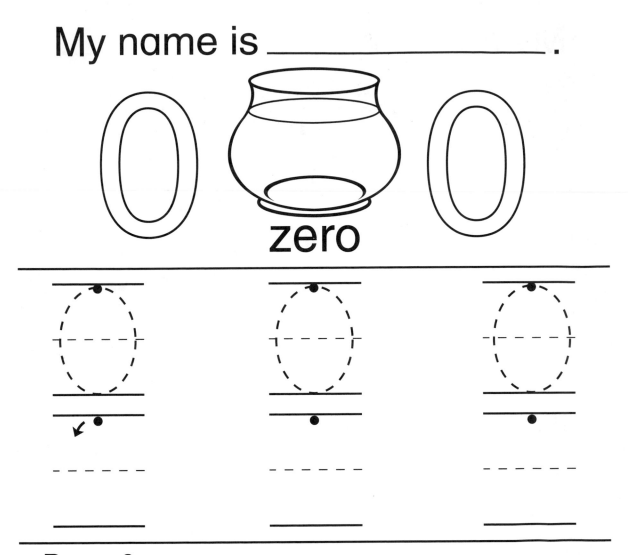

zero

Draw 0.

My name is _____.

six

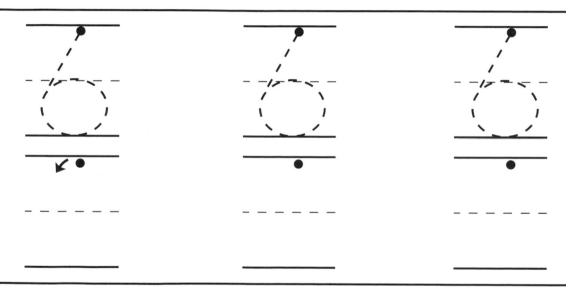

Draw 6.

My name is _____.

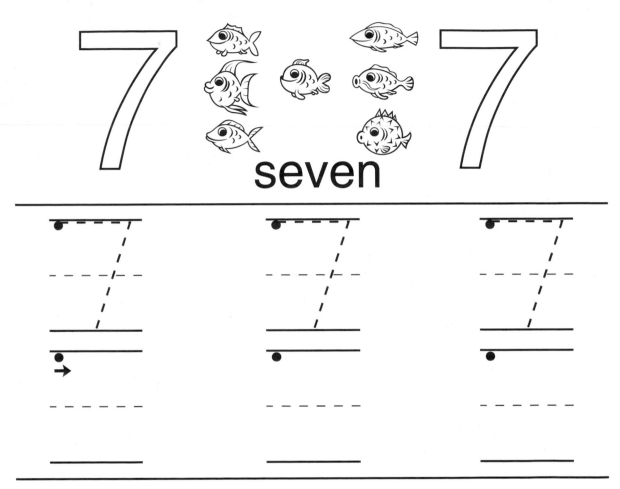

seven

Draw 7.

My name is _____.

eight

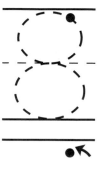 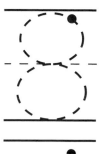 

Draw 8.

My name is _____.

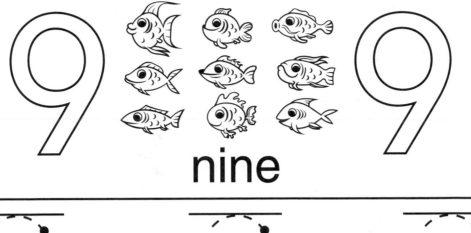

nine

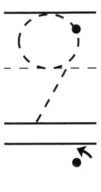 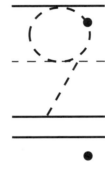 

Draw 9.

My name is _____.

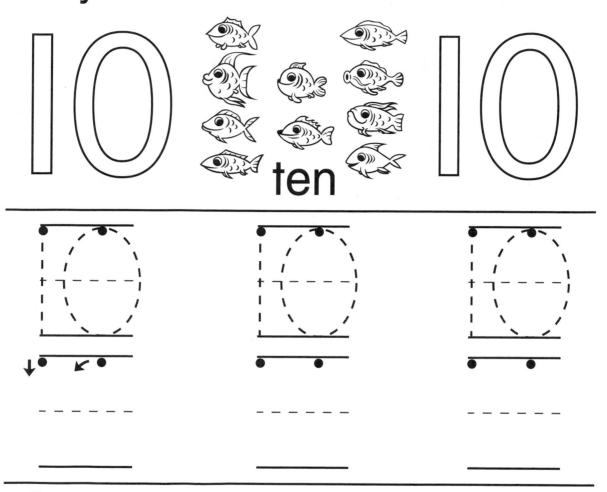

Draw 10.

Unit Planning Template

Topic:

Allocated Days of Instruction:

Curriculum Outcomes / Expectations to Cover (including from other strands):

Diagnostic Assessment for the Unit Start

Planned Final Assessment Strategy

Organization of the Lessons

Day 1	Day 2	Day 3	Day 4	Day 5
Day 6	Day 7	Day 8	Day 9	Day 10
Day 11	Day 12	Day 13	Day 14	Day 15

Lesson Planning Template

Lesson Goal:

Relevant Outcomes:

Manipulatives I Need:

Grouping Strategies:

Minds-On (Warmup) (_____ minutes)

    Important Questions to Ask:

Action–Main Activity (_____ minutes)

    Important Questions to Ask:

    Any Necessary Adaptations:

Debrief/Consolidation (_____ minutes)

    Important Questions to Ask:

    Any Necessary Adaptations:

Final Tie-up Question/Activity:

Teaching Notes

Sample Problem-Solving Rubric

General Rubric for Determining Achievement Levels in Problem-Solving

Thread	Level 1	Level 2	Level 3	Level 4	Level 5
Persistence	• You need help, even for very simple tasks. • You give up quickly, often just wanting someone to give you the answer.	• You can do simple parts of the problem with little help. • You start working on the harder parts but unless you have much help, you give up.	• You work by yourself to complete simple parts of the problem. • For hard problems, you proceed by yourself after you get help, but may return for help often.	• You try very hard on your own and only get help once you have tried many strategies and thought hard.	• You like working hard on challenging questions and don't need much help. • You may extend your thinking beyond the problem and make new ones.
Strategies used	• It is hard to identify any strategy used. • You may only re-copy the given data and show no under-standing.	• There is some evidence of a strategy although its use is unclear or flawed. • You may have tried one approach that did not work and then gave up.	• The strategy used is clear and appropriate but it was not carried out far enough to reach a solution or was incorrectly used.	• An appropriate strategy was successfully carried out for a relatively complex task. • There is no evidence that you tried to think about a possible better strategy.	• You use a variety of strategies and often select ones that are most appropriate to complex tasks.
Conceptual understanding	• You show very little understanding, even for simpler tasks. • You may only re-copy the given data and show no under-standing.	• You understand and apply basic concepts in isolation for simple problems.	• You understand and can apply combina-tions of a couple of basic concepts as problems get a little more complex.	• You understand and apply complex concepts and/or combinations of several concepts when working with different problems.	• Your work on the problems may allow you to develop an understanding of related concepts that you have not yet studied.
Accuracy of work	• You make a lot of calculation and copying mistakes.	• You only make occasional mistakes with basic number concepts, but make several mistakes with more-advanced number concepts.	• You make a few calculation and copying mistakes. You usually need someone to point them out to you before you correct them.	• You make occasional calculation and copying mistakes. Once you know the answer is wrong, you tend to find and correct most of these mistakes yourself.	• You make few careless errors, thoroughly checking your work and correcting your own mistakes before handing in your work.
Communication	• You do not give explanations or show your work.	• Your explanations are not complete and they are very hard for the reader to follow. • You do not accurately use math terminology.	• Your explanations are not precise, but the reader has a general idea of what you mean. • You use some basic math terminology, where appropriate.	• Your work is organized in a clear, systematic way and your explanations are clear and complete. • You use math terminology effectively to add to your precision.	• Your work and explanations are clear, concise, and complete. • You use a variety of ways to communicate your answer (words, terminology, pictures, graphs, symbols, etc.)

NCTM Standard Rubric

	LEVEL 1	LEVEL 2	LEVEL 3	LEVEL 4
PROBLEM SOLVING	• uses one strategy and attempts to solve the problem but does not arrive at an answer	• carries out a plan to solve the problem using one strategy, and develops a partial or incorrect solution	• solves the problem by carrying out a plan effectively, using an appropriate strategy and having an accurate solution	• solves the problem accurately while showing flexibility and insight when carrying out a plan
UNDERSTANDING OF CONCEPTS	• demonstrates a limited or inaccurate understanding of how to tell time and work with coins	• demonstrates a growing understanding of how to tell time and work with coins	• demonstrates a grade-appropriate understanding of how to tell time and work with coins	• demonstrates an in-depth understanding of how to tell time and work with coins
APPLICATION OF MATHEMATICAL PROCEDURES	• records times and the values of coins or sets of coins inaccurately, or recordings are incomplete	• records some times and the values of coins or sets of coins accurately	• records most times and the values of coins or sets of coins accurately	• makes almost no errors when recording times and the values of coins or sets of coins
COMMUNICATION OF REQUIRED KNOWLEDGE RELATED TO PROCEDURES AND PROBLEM SOLVING	• uses very little measurement terminology when working with and discussing telling time and using money	• uses a limited range of measurement terminology when working with and discussing telling time and using money	• uses appropriate measurement terminology when working with and discussing telling time and using money	• uses a broad range of measurement terminology when working with and discussing telling time and using money

Selected References

Ministry of Education in Saskatchewan. *General Rubric for Determining Achievement Levels in Problem-Solving.* [Online.] Available: http://www.sasked.gov.sk.ca/docs/rubrics/math/gr5crit.html

Small, M., Kestell, M.L., Kelleher, H., et. al. (2005). *Nelson Mathematics K.* Toronto: Nelson.

Small, M., Kestell, M.L., Kelleher, H., et. al. (2006). *Nelson Mathematics 2.* Toronto: Nelson.

Index

Credits

This page constitutes an extension of the copyright page. We have made every effort to trace the ownership of all copyrighted material and to secure permission from copyright holders. In the event of any question arising as to the use of any material, we will be pleased to make the necessary corrections in future printings. Thanks are due to the authors, publishers, and agents for permission to use the material indicated.

Text

From Small/Simmons et al. *Math Focus 1* TR Chapter 10. © 2007 Nelson Education Ltd. Reproduced by permission. www.cengage.com/permissions

From Small/Hope et al. *Math Focus Grade 4* Student Book. © 2008 Nelson Education Ltd. Reproduced by permission. www.cengage.com/permissions

From Small/Hope et al. *Math Focus Grade 7* Student Book. © 2008 Nelson Education Ltd. Reproduced by permission. www.cengage.com/permissions

From Small et al. *Nelson Mathematics Professional Learning Program K–6 Numbers/Operations* TR. © 2004 Nelson Education Ltd. Reproduced by permission. www.cengage.com/permissions

From Small et al. *Nelson Mathematics Professional Learning Program K–6 Geometry* TR. © 2007 Nelson Education Ltd. Reproduced by permission. www.cengage.com/permissions

From Small et al. *Nelson Mathematics Professional Learning Program K–6 Patterns/Algebra* TR. © 2005 Nelson Education Ltd. Reproduced by permission. www.cengage.com/permissions

From Small et al. *Nelson Mathematics Professional Learning Program K–6 Data Management/Probability* TR. © 2005 Nelson Education Ltd. Reproduced by permission. www.cengage.com/permissions

From Zimmer/Small et al. *Nelson Mathematics 8* Student Text. © 2006 Nelson Education Ltd. Reproduced by permission. www.cengage.com/permissions

From Small et al. *Nelson Mathematics Grade 2* TR Chapter 11. © 2004 Nelson Education Ltd. Reproduced by permission. www.cengage.com/permissions

From Kelleher et al. *Nelson Mathematics (Kindergarten).* TR © 2004 Nelson Education Ltd. Reproduced by permission. www.cengage.com/permissions

Chapter 5

p. 84: Gelman, R. and Gallistel, C.R. (1978). *The child's understanding of number.* Cambridge, MA: Harvard University Press. **p. 86:** *The Geometer's Sketch Pad,* Key Curriculum Press, 1150 65th St., Emeryville, CA 94608, 1-800-995-MATH, www.keypress.com/sketchpad.

Appendix

p. 677: General Rubric for Determining Achievement Levels in Problem-Solving. Saskatchewan Ministry of Education. Found at: www.sasked.gov.sk.ca/docs/rubrics/math/gr5crit.html.

Photos

Chapter 3: p. 40 (both): Photodisc Blue/Getty Images. **Chapter 4: p. 63:** Jim Cummins/Taxi/Getty Images; **p. 67:** Chip Henderson/Index Stock; **p. 69:** Shelly Harrison/Index Stock; **p. 76:** Courtesy Manuel Silva. **Chapter 5: p. 90:** Photodisc/Getty Images. **Chapter 11: p. 259:** Shutterstock/Edwin Verin. **Chapter 13: p. 286:** PhotoEdit/David Young-Wolff. **Chapter 14: p. 339:** Getty Images/Photodisc Blue/Kevin Patterson; **p. 341:** Alamy/VStock. **Chapter 15: p. 374:** Photos.com; **p. 396:** Getty Images/Leland Bobbe. **Chapter 16: p. 421:** Getty Images/Purestock; **p. 431:** © Dennis MacDonald/PhotoEdit; **p. 442:** Getty Images/Jayme Thornton; **p. 451:** Getty Images/Mel Yates; **p. 453:** Shutterstock/Josep M. Peñalver Rufas; **p. 454 (top):** Photos.com; **p. 454 (bottom):** PhotoEdit Inc./David Young-Wolff. **Chapter 17: p. 475:** PhotoEdit/Lon C. Diehl; **p. 504:** Getty Images/The Image Bank/Stephen Marks. **Chapter 18: p. 518:** Getty Images/Stone/William Howard. **Chapter 19: p. 554:** PhotoEdit/David Young-Wolff.